MARLOWE UP CLOSE

MARLOWE UP CLOSE

AN UNCONVENTIONAL BIOGRAPHY

WITH A SCRAPBOOK OF HIS CIPHERS

ROBERTA BALLANTINE

Library of Congress Control Number: 2006909434
ISBN: Hardcover 978-1-4257-4381-9
Softcover 978-1-4257-4380-2

This book was printed in the United States of America.

To order additional copies of this book, contact:
Xlibris Corporation
1-888-795-4274
www.Xlibris.com
Orders@Xlibris.com

36806

Acknowledgements:

To Evadne Mela, my editor, critic and tireless helper for seventeen years, to Marlovian David More as well as critical thinker Professor Mike Malioutov, and Professor Alfred Barkov who created my website—to J.R. Ulatowski, and friend from the English Marlowe Society Isabel Gortázar, loyal aide Bill Hutchinson, and my gifted ongoing partners in the field, Alex and Robert Ayres, to my patient family, readers Karen Copeland and Linda Kast and the kind staff at Xlibris, I offer heartfelt thanks.

Contents

MARLOWE UP CLOSE
An Unconventional Biography

Introduction 1
Deciphering Marlowe's Anagrams 5
Marlowe's Life, Part I 7
Part II 33
Part III 49
Part IV 65
Afterward 85
Notes 91
Illustrations 163
Marlowe's Ciphers 177
A Timeline 551
A Bibliography 643
Index 665

DEDICATED

to my teachers:

DR. DOROTHY DOOLITTLE

VIRGINIA PRINCEHOUSE ALLEN

MARIA OUSPENSKAYA

HERMAN HYDE

JOHN MURRAY ANDERSON

EDITH HENRY

BILL BALLANTINE

MARLOWE UP CLOSE

An Unconventional Biography

by Roberta Ballantine

Introduction

Biographies of Marlowe have been censored and colored by the secret service for which he worked. Published accounts of his life are inaccurate, laced with legend, full of holes—writers admit he was a mysterious man. About his story, vehement discussions arise. This brief sketch is offered in hope it may furnish a frame of reference for his steganographic messages and that within the outline a view of avenues for research will become visible.

Reading Marlowe years ago I came across his way of ciphering and began setting down some of his hidden writings. Communications inside his texts changed biographic scraps I'd garnered—they became detailed pictures, some of them surprising. I pasted a sheet on my desk: "His ciphers authenticate, confirm, validate, extend my research." To those who believe these messages must be misleading I can say that given the scope and style of the ciphered lines, the weight of combined interlocking stories so relentlessly produced over the decades of Marlowe's life, I gratefully accept them as honest, often inspired, work. A measure of drama is here—he was a playwright—but these intimate communications are demonstrable parts of the most respected, earliest texts attributed to Shakespeare. People have created short anagrams from another author's text, but only the author, and one who is a genius, could have invented these long (three hundred, five hundred lines long) perfectly connected anagrammatic messages which make narrative *sense,* creating thoughtful essays and tales of adventure and love, at the same time maintaining a plaintext of excellent quality. Starting with his first two lines of dialogue, and continuing usually two lines by two lines of flexible pentameter, Marlowe offers reports, revelations and admissions, recollections of journeys, deaths, condemnations of evil deeds in high places, tongue-in-cheek short stories, thoughts of civic improvement—and once in a while a critique of the play into which his cipher is woven.

In Marlowe's day, evening entertainments included music, books, dice, play-parties, backgammon, cards or scrabble—no video games or movie channels. For Marlowe's friends, especially Henry Wriothesley while he was confined in the Tower, working out messages could be an amusing, enlightening pastime.

The first anagram I ever found is not linked, but long, maybe the longest ever created. About Marlowe and signed "H," it could have been made by his longtime employer Henry Wotton, who's credited with creating Bacon's anagrammatic epitaph.

Marlowe Up Close

During WWII my husband worked overseas for the Office of War Information, a forerunner of the CIA; after the war he left government work. He never revealed to me any secret about his service except a special handshake. But in 1995, when I was looking at a transcript of the six-line poem carved long ago into the Shakespeare monument in Stratford-on-Avon, Bill leaned over my shoulder and I wondered out loud, "Why, when the first lines are so good, does the rest of this thing sort of fall apart? You can make out what it means, but it's peculiar—and look at the punctuation!"

"It's probably an anagram," he told me, "and better on the inside. See these letters carved so they touch each other? They'd go over into the inside message together to make it easier for the decipherer. And sometimes there's a handle, a hint to clue you in."

Bill went back to work, and I sat there and puzzled. The outside poem reads, in caps,

Stay, passenger, why goest thov by so fast?
Read if thov canst, whom envious death hath plast,
Within this monvment Shakspeare: with whome,
Quick natvre dide: whose name doth deck Y^{s} tombe
Far more then cost: sieh all, Y^{t} he hath writt,
Leaves living art, but page, to serve his witt.

The word Dide seemed odd—could it be part of Dido on the inside? There was a Q—maybe for Queen Dido? That was the name of a play Marlowe wrote when he was very young—and letters to spell the name King Lear were there, too. Was the anagram saying something about plays?

It took me two weeks to fit all the letters into place, making the inside message visible—a neat pentameter poem rhyming ababcc. One M was turned upside down to make a W, and every punctuation mark had found a better place. It reads:

Was Marloves star entombd by thieves,
Within this crypt? The epitaph Y^{t} decks this close,
Fragment that: see throvgh, knit vp, the woolsey weaves
Of Qveen Dido, King Lear: in both, one avthor shows,
Whose art his name with love hath writ:
That fact mvst save Y^{s} damned, savage wit. H.

The Y's with tiny letters (they should be on top) are called thorns, old-fashioned shorthand for that and this.

That translation introduced me to anagrams. Later I read Secret Diplomacy, by history professor James Westfall Thompson and historian Saul K. Padover, dean of the School of Politics at the New School of Social Research in New York, a man who'd held various wartime "secret diplomacy" posts. On page 253 I found these astonishing lines:

> "The use of cryptic symbols for communication is perhaps as old as diplomacy . . . Anagrams were part of the Attic tragedies. Authors of Greek tragedies constructed their first eight iambic lines so they not only made sense but also provided letters to make eight other iambic lines, the first two giving the writer's name, the next two the Olympiad, the third a homage to Athena, and the last couplet a warning that the show was about to begin. This Greek anagram may, possibly, be the earliest systematic cryptography which, by a natural process of transference, came to be applied to statecraft."

Marlowe, university educated and a serious dramatist, could have used an adaptation of the Greek playwrights' formula. After banishment he was supposed to be dead and could never again put his name out front on his works, so for him to hide it in a cipher wasn't just possible, it was highly probable.

I started looking for his anagrams in facsimiles of early editions of writings credited to Shakespeare—quartos, "apocryphal works" and the Norton facsimile of the First Folio.

Marlowe's ciphers are not found in stage directions; the analyst must begin with the first two lines of dialogue. Now and then the author would make one cipher from four lines together, and in works he thought would be printed only once, he'd sometimes use single, scattered interior lines identified by otherwise meaningless quotation marks in the left margin.

Kit (all his life, Christopher Marlowe's friends called him Kit) possibly learned this technique in his youth, for even his earliest plays (The Lord Cromwell, Selimus, Sir John Oldcastle) are furnished with ciphers. Or did he return to these early works later, rewriting their beginnings with interior messages? Did his natural father Roger Manwood teach him? Roger was learned; internal evidence in his own writings shows him familiar with medieval texts.

Kit may have practiced interior writing in 1579 and 1580 as a student at the King's School in Canterbury. Headmaster John Gresshop was a scholar hired for his knowledge of ancient Greek drama; he may have shown the students how anagrams were a traditional part of those tragedies.

Marlowe kept the ancient custom of identifying himself in his first two interior lines, sometimes casually saying, "Chr. M. wrote this," or "Kit M. penn'd this." He'd call himself Christopher, Christofer or Chr. Marlowe, Kit Marlowe, Marley or Marloe, and once in a while Gregorio de' Monti, a name he used for many years in Italy. In the Sonnets he often calls himself the Moth, an early nickname, or the Yat. His girl friend, angry with him, called him a yat (a yataghan, a mean Turkish knife).

Kit's rambling style in the ciphers that follow his byline was noticed by his friend John Marston, who wrote: "H'ath made a commonplace booke [a scrapbook] out of plaies, and speakes in print." And he does speak—nothing is held back.

Deciphering Marlowe's Anagrams

Linked anagrams are steganographic. Literary steganography is a special kind of communication hidden in an innocent-seeming outside message, different from codes which display non-sequitur words or numbers to be decoded by means of a code-book. Steganographic messages are called dead-drops; they just hang in there, waiting to be found.

Marlowe, a genius in many fields, was a spy and the best steganographer of his time. Characteristic of his ciphers is the use of carefully crafted stammering in stressful parts to show dramatic fear and trembling. He puts exclamations in the exciting places and often uses descriptive sounds, such as 13 E's together when a typhoon hits his ship on the Black Sea.

Early editions must be used by analysts of Marlowe's ciphers, and early printing conventions must be dealt with: On the inside, U and V may be interchanged—on the outside (the plaintext), V is always used at the beginning of a word starting with *V or U;* J is I; sometimes Y and I can be interchanged; two U's or V's together can become a W, and inside, once in a great while, a W or M may be used upside down. Though one message-unit is usually derived from letter-rearrangement of two plaintext lines, five accents to a line, occasionally more stresses creep in, and extra care must be taken when counting accents of prose passages. In early printing jobs, compositors sometimes ran out of "e"s on their trays—"e"s which may be needed to correctly complete ciphers—and though replacement of these missing vowels is considered acceptable emendation, in the following works any such replacements are marked in the plaintexts with parentheses.

I work in caps (marking M, W, C, U, Z on the bottom to show which way is up), cut out each letter, count how many of each letter I have and make a list of the result, which I call the signature of that particular cipher. Then comes the process of finding and arranging the words, with a place for every letter in the completed message. The finished anagram is taped on notepaper and later typed on the computer in a boldface column right beside its outside words—reproducing exact spelling and offering the reader an opportunity to determine the validity of the inner message. Inside and outside messages are checked and rechecked for typos, using an anagram-checker on the internet.

Although anagrams may have been the first sort of secret writing used in government communiqués, they're not the most suitable for that purpose, because to a limited extent their syntax is determined by the analyst. This would bother any official: "Smith shot Becker" could be "Becker shot Smith!" Nevertheless, meaning can be made clear in the context of narrative, and Marlowe achieves countless riveting passages in stories he tells using this medium.

One important thing: his writings—outside and in, early and late, English, Greek, Spanish, Italian—all are meant to be heard. The play may look dead on the page, and the anagram crude, but read it out loud and it'll come alive.

f

Below is a rough biography of Marlowe. Not merely speculative, the sequence of events derives from conventional research bolstered by Kit's own ciphered letters.

Marlowe's Life, Part I

In the 1500's the best secret government agents in England, Europe, North Africa and the near East were the Marranos (the "pigs"), men and women of Jewish blood whose families had been forced to accept Christian ways but who secretly kept parts of their old faith. Some suspected of backsliding had been evicted from their native states,[1] others survived by moving a few miles and assuming new identities.[2] Those agents knew how to travel, had friends in many countries, understood disguises ("Where's that beard I had yesterday?" Cervantes writes), how to send and receive messages and figure every angle to be good stewards for their rulers. Those enmeshed in spying were called spirits by their peers—shadows, and honest men.

Kit's natural father, Roger Manwood, was born to such a family. Roger's grandfather served Anne Boleyn—he was one of the men who carried her canopy when she was crowned[3]—and young Roger helped put Anne's daughter Elizabeth Tudor on the throne of England. In gratitude she rewarded him with a handsome manor near the west gate of Canterbury.[4]

He advised her as a friend, she admired him, knighted him[5], gave him a unique gold chain of office,[6] and he became Lord Chief Baron of Exchequer.[7]

In 1563 Manwood was the judge of Dover admiralty court when he met a young matron, Kate Arthur Marley, daughter of William Arthur, a seafaring yeoman out of Dover. On board ship the yeoman was the clerk, customarily responsible for reporting cargo.[8] Kate, by going to bed with the judge, may have persuaded him to drop charges against her father in a smuggling case—and Kate and Roger, unlikely lovers, began an amorous liaison which lasted till Manwood's death.[9]

On 6 February 1564 Kate bore a swarthy son, handsome but with a club foot like her own.[10] Judge Manwood seems to have cared for the baby from birth, for Kate's legal husband John Marley at once became a full-fledged shoemaker in Canterbury, three years before his apprenticeship was to have ended, and he soon remodeled the front of his house to hold a shop filled with supplies. In later years the judge helped John start a business in bailbonds.[11]

Kate's new baby, baptized Christopher and called Chris or Kit,[12] was precocious: At age four he became mascot for a federation of tough Canterbury youths and started a career of street-crime, hoping to augment his folks' income.[13] Kate was worried; to give her boy a different occupation she took him to his grandfather at Dover, and the child must have shipped out with his grandad, for Kit became a skilled sailor.[14] In his ciphers he speaks of Dover as home port and tells of voyages, some in ships he captained, and a ship he owned in later life.

After about four years at sea, an injury may have brought Kit ashore for repair at Roger Manwood's house outside Canterbury.

Just as Kit's later life has been kept from public view, much of his childhood is hidden, too, but we can see that after coming to land he was influenced by the lifestyle of inhabitants of great houses; evidence shows him to have been present—perhaps as a page—in the several homes of Roger's wealthy patron Sir Thomas Gresham,[15] the queen's merchant and munitions manager.[16] Gresham employed a soldier-poet named Thomas Churchyard—his writings and Kit's show that they knew and liked each other.[17] Gresham rented a house (in the neighborhood of his own big Bishopsgate house) to the queen's eldest secret son, young Ned de Vere, Earl of Oxford, [18] and for years Churchyard worked for Ned, too.[19] Ned loved the theater and created plays for the court and Revels productions for Queen Elizabeth's Progresses.[20] (In summer, Elizabeth visited private homes "on Progress," each year traveling a different route, and at every great house she was entertained by plays and masques.)

Flashes in Kit's shadowy childhood suggest his first appearance onstage as an Italian sailor-boy in an entertainment produced by Ned de Vere for a double wedding at the Viscount Montague's Bankside home.[21] Later, the child seems to have gone with Thomas Gresham to the famous party at Kenilworth; Gresham attended to talk to the queen about his expense account.[22] In the following year, Kit sailed to Turkish Constantinople as sailor and factor for Gresham, supervised by master's mate Christopher (Kester) Carleill, step-son of Francis Walsingham,[23] friend of Roger Manwood and Gresham.[24] On the way, Carleill, Kit and the crew captured a ship called el Tigre (the Tiger); Carleill became her captain and sailed her to the Golden Horn and back to England. He and Kit had a love-affair on the voyage (cipher, Sonnet 126) and were friends for the rest of Carleill's life.[25]

Ned de Vere produced the entertainments for the next summer's Progress, 1578,[26] and in Churchyard's "Greeting for Her Majesty at Norwich," Kit could have played the "Turkish Boy," dressed in a costume bought for him on his fourteenth birthday in Constantinople.[27] Besides clothes, he'd brought home memories to be used in his youthful play Selimus,[28] and details for his later hits, Tamburlaine I and II. Ned de Vere employed Kit intermittently for years; in spite of a vast difference in social status, they shared a serious interest in theater. That they were both bastards was always in their thoughts. Then, too, Ned made a habit of using the youngest players in his companies as sexual servants,[29] and Kit, adept, willing, was encouraged by Manwood to become Ned's lover; Roger reasoned that if Ned became king, Kit could be the favorite.[30] One of Kit's earliest nicknames was the Moth; he was attracted to Ned.

After Progress was over, Roger Manwood stepped in: it was time for schooling. Kate agreed, Manwood managed a scholarship, and Kit attended the King's School in Canterbury for the only period of uninterrupted study he'd ever be allowed.[31]

His headmaster, a scholarly teacher of ancient drama, encouraged the boys to write playlets in Latin and Greek. The King's School was known for production of student plays performed on the raised dais of the Almonry Chapel,[32] but the plays produced there during Kit's months of attendance have never been publicly mentioned. Kit may have created a short dramatic version of his later work, the Erotokritos, a poem in sailors' Greek which he completed in Crete early in 1594; he never threw anything away and often recycled early works. The Erotokritos, a touching romantic ballad, was popular in and around Athens for 350 years.[33]

Marlowe left the King's School for Cambridge at the end of 1580, after Roger Manwood, who'd been a friend of Archbishop Parker, [34] arranged for the youth to receive a Parker Scholarship in Divinity at Corpus Christi College, and right away Kit was thrown into boiling religious discussions. The steward at Corpus Christi College, a fellow there and probably Kit's first tutor, ended his life less than a decade later, burned at the stake as a heretic.[35] Friends from Corpus Christi and other Cambridge colleges were to suffer trying times in later years, including hanging and death in jail.[36] One man escaped to America on the Mayflower.[37]

The first two years of Kit's residence at Corpus Christi were the last two of relatively open philosophical discussion there, for in 1583 a new Archbishop of Canterbury began to suppress theological discussion of any religion not purely Anglican. In later years, John Whitgift's mainmost inquisitorial purpose was to eliminate puritanism,[38] but in 1581 English religious unrest focused on various efforts to re-establish Romish Catholicism in Britain. Dr. William Allen, an Englishman ordained a Catholic priest at Mechlin about 1565, was a proselytizer who founded English Catholic seminaries in France, Spain and Rome, soliciting English youth. Allen offered his students instruction in the faith, ordained them and sent them, each with five pounds, to be secret missioners in England. His manner was kind, calm and gentle, though only a few years passed before he knew perfectly well that the English hedge-priests he was sending back across the Channel were being executed, and in his college refectory at Reims he'd stand up and read aloud lists of new martyrs with descriptions of how they died.[39] From his seminary he declared his purpose: to see the Romish Church preeminent in England. He expected to be a cardinal there and said he lived for the day when Elizabeth would be dragged through Rome naked in chains before being burned at the stake. He frightened her.

So in the early 1580's Elizabeth's childhood companion Francis Walsingham[40] now her Secretary and chief of State Secret Service, sent undercover workers to report on current events at Allen's college in France.[41]

Gabriel Harvey, probably an SSS recruiter at Cambridge, was a Fellow of Trinity Hall who introduced young Marlowe to Spenser's poems[42] and some tricks of rhetoric, as well as entry-level undercover government jobs which soon carried the youth away from campus for odd periods of time. His absences can be roughly figured from entries in the buttery-book at Corpus Christi. Sometimes, though, while he was away a friend must have signed Marlowe's name on the book, and for his longest periods of absence accounts are simply missing.[43]

After successfully completing intelligence work at Allen's seminary in Reims, Kit, who'd taken a B. A. degree, was due for SSS training in military art. He went to serve with Walsingham's step-son Carleill at Colerain in northern Ireland, and from there on a campaign against Sorley Boy Mac Donnell.[44] Reporting to Lord Deputy Perrot at Dublin, Kit and Carleill may have stayed with Edmund Spenser and met pentagon-designer Paul Ive,[45] who might have been in town consulting with Perrot about English fortification.

Walsingham planned to give a fatal jollop to Catholic William Allen; evidence suggests Marlowe was the chosen instrument.[46] Soon after he left school under cover to attend Allen's college at Reims, Allen became ill, but didn't die: Kit had given the man a small dose, thinking a scare might reform him: Allen burned his papers, went to Spa and then to the English seminary at Rome. He never looked back, never changed his harsh opinion of Queen Elizabeth.

That job at Reims gave Marlowe a shock—showed him a moral dichotomy in his activities. When his coming-of-age-portrait was painted, and the artist asked what message to put in the corner, Kit said, "Quod me nutrit, me destruit," paraphrasing a message in les Devises heroiques de Claude Paradin. Paradin's version shows a burning torch turned upside down, with words: "Qui me alit, me extinguit." (What sets me alight extinguishes me.) Kit used the idea in his play Pericles and again in Sonnet 73: "Consum'd with that which it was nourish'd by," and in an Italian play Kit made in 1610, Ippolito says to Ortensia, "Se m' era di benefizio al corpo, m' era danoso al anima," harking back to the motto. An upside-down torch is held by a cherub on the Shakespeare cenotaph in Trinity Church at Stratford-on Avon.

Freckled Tom Nashe, a dazzling prose writer, a funny young man, had come to St. John's in the fall of 1582.[47] He and Kit became pals, going swimming against the rules, attending the local fair with their friend Robin Greene,[48] spending time at the Golden Dolphin, even going to out-of-town inns where the girls were. They showed each other their writing—Kit had just finished Locrine for Roger, to be played at home.[49]

When twelve-year-old Henry Wriothesley (already Earl of Southampton) came to St. John's in 1585, the chancellor of the university, who had a special interest in Wriothesley as the queen's youngest child, seems to have chosen Nashe to serve the young nobleman and act as secret guard. Marlowe remembered Wriothesley as the baby Elizabeth had borne while staying at the Greshams' Mayfield home in summer 1573.[50]

Nashe and Kit were soon showing Lord Harry around town. Kit called him Hen, and in the next months a friendship bloomed which would last as long as Kit lived. Many of the cipher-stories in Marlowe's plays and poems were written for Hen.

In spring 1585 Walsingham, feeling that Marlowe was ready for heavy duty, involved him in a plan to reveal Mary Queen of Scots' organized effort to gain the English throne. Mary had been offered aid by French followers and a naïve young English Catholic named Anthony Babington, and Sir Francis wanted to give the conspirators a chance to lay complete plans, every step observed by undercover agents.[51]

The brightest and most daring of those agents—the one who devised the plan which led Mary to trust new secret messages—was Marlowe. He operated as a ringer for a Catholic man named Gilbert Gifford who'd just committed suicide in Paris, unbeknownst to his family. Mary knew the Catholic Gifford family home was near her prison, Chartley, and that fact gave Kit, as Gifford, an entrée when he swam across an icy moat to be smuggled into Mary's chamber by her laundresses.[52] Kit also devised the method of opening and resealing her mail, leaving no trace of intrusion: a shoemaker's knife, sharp all the way around, heated carefully, was used to lift off the sealing wax and later to replace it undamaged.[53]

The plan worked famously, but when it was over, Kit was not quite free; Walsingham asked him to convince Gilbert's angry family that the young man had not been killed by secret service after being used. Kit said he'd offer evidence that Gilbert was alive and well in Europe, and this he managed concurrently with his 1587 mission to scout Spanish naval preparations for attack on England. Kit continued to impersonate Gifford just long enough to get his name registered as a newly-ordained priest at Reims. (Kit filed in last, out first in a line of deacons ordained presbiters at Reims, 14 March, 1587, shielded by agent John Fixer, a deacon honestly ordained.)[54] After leaving his official Gilbert Gifford code to be used by another agent staying at a Paris safe-house, Kit darted off to Lisbon, where he met Miguel Cervantes, formed a warm alliance that would prove lifelong, and gained information which made possible Drake's successful June raid on Cádiz.[55]

At Ságres, after telling Drake where to find the grand ship San Felipe[56] (grateful, Drake must have praised Kit to the English council),[57] Marlowe rowed ashore from Drake's hospital ship off the north coast of Spain, turned up wet and bedraggled in a silk suit of Drake's (the two were the same size), and told local authorities he was Arthur Dudley, illegitimate son of Queen Elizabeth and Robert Dudley, that he'd been shipwrecked and wanted to talk to Don Felipe of Spain. After a difficult trip to Madrid Arthur Dudley fooled King Philip's English secretary Engelfield[58] but not the king, who suffered him for only a short time[59] (long enough for Kit to gather news of the Armada, aided by Walsingham's agent, Italian artist Zuccaro[60]). Philip soon ordered the young imposter kicked out of Spain.

Kit shipped home by way of Bordeaux and Utrecht, thinking he'd never get his degree because he'd been in Madrid at commencement-time. But a letter from the council had spoken for him, and he was graced with MA.[61]

He had a month to see his family, pack out of Cambridge, settle in with Ned de Vere and the theater-writers at Ned's place, Fisher's Folly.[62] During those weeks Kit hastily finished a rough play of Edward III. Thinking of the shocking fate of the Mary Queen of Scots conspirators, Kit put in a scene in which someone tries to persuade the ruler that mercy is a good thing.[63]

He delivered the play unpolished—and then he was in Paris, using the name Gilbert Gifford, trying to find out what was happening in the English embassy there. The first secretary of the embassy, Lylly, who like the ambassador was a secret member of the Catholic League,[64] grew suspicious of Kit, invited him to a Christmas party at a brothel managed by the secretary's mistress.[65] There Kit would have been murdered if he hadn't proclaimed himself a priest, shouting he regretted his sins and demanding to be taken at once to the bishop's jail.[66]

It was done. He'd avoided the would-be assassins but he couldn't get out of jail; to escape to the street would have meant death anyway. He tells the whole story in ciphers for three plays he drafted during the eight months he was locked up—Doctor Faustus, Measure for Measure and All's Well.[67] Thinking of scenes in his recent Massacre at Paris, he undoubtedly added to that passionate scramble of writing during his months locked up in the Four de l'Evèque.

At last he escaped by drinking a potion that made him look dead. (Did SSS chemist Petruccio Ubaldini send a vial to Kit's friends in Paris?) Loyal friends carried him, unconscious, to a boat on the Seine, and when it reached the Channel it was swept to Dover on the same winds which were wrecking the Spanish Armada in the North Sea. He tells of his landing and much more in ciphers in his rewrite of The Jew of Malta.[68]

Home again, sick, pale and thin, Kit spent time first with his Canterbury folks, then with Roger. It may have been at this time that Kit sat for a portrait which shows him worn and weary.[69] At the top is written, *"AE' SVAE 24—1588."*

Late in the year, Kit went to work on a play-writing project with Ned de Vere in London. Ned, conscious of his Never-Neverland nearness to the throne, suffered serious mood-swings and schizoid spells, and quite possibly the queen had asked Roger Manwood to keep an eye on her son.[70]

Ever since Kit became a divinity student at Cambridge, Manwood had hoped his boy would become a minister with a difference, and in 1583 Roger had bought the vicarage of Chalk Church, on the Dover Road at the foot of Gad's Hill,[71] thinking it might serve as a place for Kit after graduation, but Kit never did become a parish priest. The little church is still there; over its front door is an ancient pagan basrelief of a laughing man holding a jug and looking up at a strange acrobat. In the neighborhood the laughing figure is known as Puck.[72]

Roger may have chosen the Chalk Church vicarage because it was near Gad's Hill, Shorne, where Roger owned a house. Also, about a hundred and seventy years before, Chalk Church and neighboring churches had been used by a lay preacher whose philosophy Roger admired—Sir John Oldcastle, who'd lived nearby at river edge. Oldcastle used to speak out on Sundays, disagreeing with the prelates of the day, preaching that a parishioner could go on pilgrimage and be damned, or refuse to go to church and be saved, and spreading other nonconformist ideas which ultimately got the poor man horribly executed in the time of Henry V.[73]

Roger's house at Shorne served him as a halfway house when he had to travel between Canterbury and London at term-times. The location is handsome, with a wide view and cedar trees at the bottom of the drive. Charles Dickens' last home now stands on the site of Roger's old house[74], and a local legend says Dickens used to walk down the Dover Road at sunset, stand before the front porch of Chalk Church and take off his hat to gaze at Puck.

In Kit's later comedy, Merry Wives (1597), his ciphers show he knew the neighborhood well: William Brooke, Lord Cobham, the leading character in the Merry Wives cipher-story, was Roger's neighbor at Shorne, and Kit's very early play The Lord Cromwell was partly inspired by the view of the Cromwell estate available from Roger's rooftop. As a boy, Kit must have roamed around Shorne.

Since he didn't want to be a minister, when time came for him to choose a career Kit was offered a chance to learn law; Roger found the youth a place at an Inn of Chancery. (My guess is Clement's Inn—all its records after 1583 appear to be lost.)[75] Roger opened files of his own early law cases to him; was it at this time or much earlier that Kit wrote Arden of Feversham? Study of jurisprudence was hard for Marlowe and soon became impossible—there were too many distractions. Ned needed him to write and rewrite plays, Kit's first big hit, Tamburlaine, was on the boards, and Manwood, up to his ears in a risky project, needed Kit's help:

Back in 1563 the queen had approved Thirty-nine Articles to be obeyed by English clerics if they didn't want to be called heretics and schismatics, and later she entrusted all exercise of church matters to a Commission for Ecclesiastical Causes, which the new Archbishop John Whitgift, enthroned in 1583, quickly twisted into a weapon he turned against everyone he disliked, particularly puritan ministers. Although Whitgift's set-up for Ecclesiastical Causes was a big commission, and several judges, Roger among them, had been appointed to keep it lawful, soon only the archbishop's voice could be heard. Roger believed in the Magna Carta and trial by common law; Whitgift believed God had given him the job of stifling puritans any way he could. (He seemed to smell hated Marrano precepts behind puritan procedures.) Four days before his enthronement in Oct. 1583 Whitgift sent Eleven Articles to the bishops, ordering strict enforcement. No one had any trouble with the article about pledging allegiance to the queen, but ministers were expected to agree to the whole package and swear an oath, termed the oath ex officio, declaring they'd not broken any church rules; often, therefore, they had to bring evidence against themselves or else perjure themselves. Whitgift cut the old thirty-nine rules down to twenty-four, but they were tougher, and the one which made many ministers bridle was the article requiring them to swear that the entire Book of Common Prayer was the Word of God.[76] Well, anyone might have a doubt or two, and because puritans were so scrupulous that one article got them into all sorts of trouble. No divine called before the Commission was ever reprieved, and after a while Roger just stayed away from the meetings. His wife was a puritan.

Together, the ministers of Kent suspended from their ministries sent a strong remonstrance to the privy council, and soon afterward the ministers of Suffolk sent one, too, and the House of Commons attacked Whitgift's use of the oath ex officio. When the privy council urged Whitgift to be more moderate he refused, saying there were only ten nonconformists of any account in his Kent diocese, and that everyone else agreed with him.

Alarmed at the control Whitgift was gaining over jurisdiction which the lawyers felt belonged rightly to the courts of English law (the archbishop now had power to impose sentences not only of deprivation but of imprisonment and even death), judges and lawyers increasingly opposed the man.[77]

A month later Whitgift became a member of privy council. He attended all its meetings and all meetings of Star Chamber and went on working for his tiresome, dangerous Cause of Uniformity.[78] Biographer Sidney Lee wrote: "In his examinations of prisoners he showed a brutal insolence which is alien to all modern conceptions of justice or religion. He invariably argued for the severest penalties."[79]

Elizabeth kept strangely silent.

In late summer 1588, frustrated, wanting to give a voice to people who were being jailed incommunicado and even hanged in gags, Roger Manwood started making serious fun of the clergy in privately printed, anonymous pamphlets. Though he said he was no puritan, he invited some puritan divines to share space in his printed satires. Each pamphlet, no matter who'd written it, was signed Martin Marprelate. Roger asked Kit for aid in writing and distribution, and Kit helped. Using an idea of his, the finished booklets were distributed at court by Humphrey Newman, a "cobbler" (really a bookman) who hid the printed pamphlets among leather "stacks of ten" packed in his handcart.

In ciphers for an epitaph he made for Roger, Kit admits he collaborated in the writing: "Anger against 'im for our satiric vvritings led to a cruel end."

Authorship of the pamphlets has never been made public. There were seven; Roger made the Epistle, the Epitome; he and Kit cooperated on Hay Any Work for Cooper; Schoolpoints was written by someone else; Theses Martinianae is the only one which seems to have been written by Kit alone; The repellant Reproof was slipped in at the printery by a provocateur, and the touching last booklet, the Protestation, was Roger's.[80] The satires were much laughed at,[81] and Whitgift, insulted and convinced the writings were linked to sinister activism, furiously vowed death to all concerned.

Some printers were caught; Roger saw he'd done harm, visited the men in jail, instructed them about their legal rights—a lot of good it did. Whitgift sent out pursuivants—detectives—and the persecution escalated.[82]

Ned de Vere became chief of the Theater Wing,[83] a branch of SSS which had been suggested to the queen by William Pickering, a friend of Elizabeth who'd stayed away from England during the years of Mary Tudor's reign. Pickering visited Elizabeth when she first came to the throne,[84] and it seems revealed to her that in France and Italy he'd met privileged companies of players subsidized by their rulers. Those players performed propagandistic dramas for the public and also played in the great houses, reporting all they'd seen and heard there to their rulers. In simple terms, these players, spirits and honest men, were spies.

The idea intrigued Elizabeth, and she told her confidant Robert Dudley, who immediately created a carefully-selected playing company. He wrote to a friend: "and they are all honest men."[85] Very soon other companies appeared, all sponsored by relatives and friends of the queen, companies ostensibly competing with one another but in truth cooperating, together forming a valuable intelligence wing of SSS.

While the companies soon proved useful, it was clear that to stay that way they needed a steady stream of good plays. For a long time Ned tried unsuccessfully to write good plays himself. At last the queen hired ten university-trained dramatists to aid him (in ciphers for Henry IV Part I Kit writes about his part in this arrangement), and the writers lived, or came to work, at Fisher's Folly, Ned's big house just outside Bishopsgate in Norton Folgate. Ned sold the house at the end of 1588, but Kit's friend Tom Watson stayed on there, tutoring the children of the new owner.

One day in September 1589 a young man named Bradley was walking by, looking for an extension on a loan from the man who lived next door to Fisher's Folly. Bradley was a son of the vintner at the Bishop's Head Tavern, where a meeting of Whitgift's anti-Marprelate poursuivants had been held, and Bradley may have overheard the latest bulletin on Marprelate: he was "halt, and club foot,"[86] and named Jaques—Jakes or Jack.[87] (Kit, with that cover name, had taken Marprelate scripts to the printers.)

Kit came out of the house (where he'd been visiting Watson?), limped down the street, and when Bradley, testing, called, "Jakes!" Kit turned around. Bradley accused him, challenged him; they drew and were fighting when Watson came out and intervened. Bradley turned to attack Watson, and Kit, withdrawing, tried to strike down Bradley's sword till Watson could draw. By that act Watson was badly cut, but he defended himself and at last killed Bradley. (Kit used the strike-down move as the fatal hit for Mercutio in his fight with Tybalt, in Romeo and Juliet.) That day showed Kit he was in danger, but he didn't abandon Manwood.

Archbishop Whitgift declared that lawyers and judges who objected to his despotic methods were stupid men whose education was too limited to warrant attention, but Roger was a learned Serjeant-at-Law, and as such, bound to serve "the king's people."[88] He tried to uphold the law of praemunere and opposed rule by expediency—Whitgift's unbridled habit of setting forth any sort of edict that seemed best to him. Among Roger's friends who stood by him through what he considered a crisis of law were Walter Mildmay, Manwood's chief at Exchequer and founder of Emmanuel College at Cambridge; Francis Walsingham, Elizabeth's Secretary and chief of Secret Service; and Thomas Randolph, who'd been ambassador in Scotland and Russia and was Postmaster of England as well as Chancellor of Exchequer after Mildmay's death, and Tom Walsingham's brother-in-law.[89] They were Marranos, bound by family ties and long service to the queen, and the archbishop was convinced they constituted a dangerous subversive cell.

The historian Macaulay wrote of Whitgift: "a narrow-minded, mean, and tyrannical priest, who gained power by servility and adulation, and employed it in persecution." Macaulay was right about everything but the servility and adulation. Whitgift was not flattering the queen; he was *blackmailing* her:

Elizabeth's secrets were her children. In Marlowe's ciphers, he says they were just "little hedge-heresies," but to her it was imperative that she not be called a mother in public. She felt sure that would ruin her image, destroy her credibility.

Whitgift must have threatened to leak the story of her secret offspring if she took any step toward saving her Marrano servitors. Why abandon them: an admired administrator, an old lover, friends who'd helped her to the throne—who'd seen her through her roughest times? But no, to Whitgift the men were simply insufferable nonconformists.

Since her early teens Elizabeth had fostered a virginal image that became primary to her royal being. Born under the sign of Virgo in the Chamber of Virgins at Greenwich on the eve of the birthday of the Virgin Mary, as she grew up she became averse to husbands. Her father had ordered the deaths of two wives, including Elizabeth's own mother, and later Elizabeth watched as the husband of her half-sister Mary tried to manage England. But her rejection of matrimony wasn't one-dimensional; over and over she cleverly manipulated the possibility of a political marriage, always backing away at the end. In ciphers for The Merry Wives, Kit tells about the last of those diplomatic encounters (one never publicized), with a German duke.[90] And for Elizabeth and her lovers, circumstances truly made recorded marriage impossible—marriage, but not babies.

No one has to break into secret files to find traces of Elizabeth's babies and their fathers. Reading contemporary comment and historical records can bring a small crowd of them into view, and they're not pale wraiths, but vigorous famous characters of their day. To light up shadowed parts of this queen's still-mysterious life, parts essential to Marlowe's biography, here are facts and opinions, indications of courtships, conceptions, pregnancies, parturitions, adoptions, and the fatal sibling tensions that followed:

After her father's death, Elizabeth lived with her stepmother, Catherine Parr, and Catherine's husband Tom Seymour (an uncle of little King Edward). Tom was Admiral of England, a rough pirate who'd proposed marriage to thirteen-year old Elizabeth before he married Catherine.[91] Bess had refused him,[92] but they all lived together till Catherine found the admiral and the youngster in a serious embrace.[93] Elizabeth was sent away to Walsingham's mother's childhood home at Cheshunt, where the girl was surrounded by Marrano protestants—Anne Boleyn's friends. Ill that summer, Elizabeth may have miscarried there. Under suspicion of collaborating with Seymour to bring about insurrection, she was moved into house arrest at Hatfield, interrogated by Robert Tyrwhit and his wife, and at Christmas time Tom wrote he was coming to see her.[94]

He must have impregnated her then. From Hatfield came rumors the girl was enceinte. Tom was arrested in January, executed without trial in March, and by that time, as Elizabeth was beginning to show a full form, she was dressing in the flowing robes of a nun.[95] She admitted nothing to her inquisitors, retired to her chamber: "By midsummer she was a helpless invalid."[96] Discreet doctors came to see her; she asked them for return of her nurse Cate, and it seems that with Cate's help Elizabeth bore twin baby boys in October. If the first arrived while Tyrwhits listened at the door, and the baby's birth cries were stifled as he was whisked out a back way, the child may have suffered minor brain damage that caused lifelong problems. The second baby was not traumatized. She named them both Edward and gave the first to the Veres, the second to the Manners family. In later years the boys were cared for in William Cecil's home and became known as the "wolfish earls of England."

In Marlowe's Dido, Queen of Carthage, he writes: "Till that a princess priest, conceived by Mars/Shall yield to dignity a double birth."[97] Here Marlowe speaks of Rhea Silvia, vestal virgin, and the god Mars. The two Edwards were born of virgin Elizabeth and her warrior god Seymour, and like Romulus and Remus, were adopted. This play of Dido written by Kit was said to have been produced at Ipswich by Ned de Vere in the spring of 1587.[98] (Kit was away; his friend Tom Nashe may have been on the spot for rehearsal and rewrite. Nashe's name is printed with Kit's on the title page of the quarto.)[99]

It looks as if Prince Philip of Spain fathered Elizabeth's next babies. In February 1554, Elizabeth, suspected of plotting against Queen Mary Tudor, was locked up in the palace.[100] On the second of March Prince Philip arrived incognito with lawyers who came to make a marriage contract between Philip and Mary Tudor—adventuring incognito was something the prince liked to do.[101] The lawyers stayed till the 13th, and quite possibly during those days Philip heard of a beautiful young princess locked up over Lady Lennox's kitchen and paid a guard to let him have a look. If so, Elizabeth must have begged the prince to save her life; that they made love and started a baby is highly probable.

Philip did soften Mary's heart toward her half-sister, and Elizabeth was sent to the Tower alive. Walking on the leads with another young inmate, Robert Dudley, she may have told him she was carrying Prince Philip's child and had no money to bribe her keeper. Dudley sent his steward to sell land and fetch money for the princess, and offered a great favor: his sister Mary Dudley Sidney would take the baby! Elizabeth was transferred to a miserable private jail, and her warder let her go to the Norris family at Ryecote for the birth, on 7 November, of her baby who became Philip Sidney—his godfather, Prince Philip of Spain.

Spanish Philip and Elizabeth may have been in love even though each had ulterior motives for maintaining their liaison. (For the rest of her life she kept his picture near her.) Just before Philip left England in 1555 it seems they conceived fraternal twins Philip and Mary—Mary adopted by John Vere, 16th Earl of Oxford, and Philip installed next year in the home of Elizabeth's cousin, ('bad') Thomas Howard. Philip of Spain became the little boy's godfather.

The youngest child of Elizabeth and Philip seems to have been conceived in June 1557, when Philip, now king of Spain, said goodbye to England for the last time. Ferdinando, born some time around March 1558, remained nameless till he was adopted early in 1559 by Henry Stanley and Margaret Clifford.[102] Years later Ferdinando was chosen by Catholic activists as their candidate to be Elizabeth's successor. (Kit wrote the proto-Grand Guignol play, Titus Andronicus, on contract for Ferdinando's players.)

Near the end of 1558 Elizabeth became queen, and in January 1559 Philip sent her a marriage proposal, which she refused. He never got over it.

Her next baby she considered a product of indiscretion. On the night of the Moorish and Queen dance, 10 April, 1560, Elizabeth danced in a parade with her childhood friend, her "Moor," Francis Walsingham.[103] The parade ended at the palace, and apparently that very night Elizabeth and Francis started a baby who nine months later turned out to be a dark, damaged little boy, Francis, born at York House and adopted by Walsingham's family friend Nicholas Bacon. Nicholas himself had been born "probably in a house belonging to the parents of Sir Francis Walsingham at Chiselhurst, Kent."[104] The child Francis grew up, became a chief of Secret Service after his natural father's death, and for twenty-three years largely controlled Kit's secret service activities.

At the time of baby Francis's birth Elizabeth was already deeply engaged in an affair with Robert Dudley. Dudley apparently impregnated her very soon after baby Francis arrived. Elizabeth Jenkins writes that in 1560 Ann Dowe of Brentwood appeared before justices, charged with saying that if the queen had no child yet, Dudley had "put one to the making."[105] Jenkins says there were perennial rumors about the queen's children by Dudley, who became earl of Leicester. Henry Hawkins wrote, "That my lord Robert hath had fyve children by the Queene, and she never goeth in progress but to be delivered."[106] The queen might have married Robert after his wife's death—that lady fell down a steep flight of steps—if her death hadn't been so suspicious it made public marriage politically impossible. The queen and Dudley were secretly wed at Christmas, 1560, at a house owned by Dudley's friend Henry Herbert, Earl of Pembroke.[107] The first-born child of the queen and Dudley appears to have been Mary, adopted by Dudley's sister Mary Dudley Sidney, who was already rearing little Philip. Baby Mary Sidney grew up to be a beautiful red-haired lady in love with theater—she managed her pirate husband's playing-company. She and Kit were off-and-on lovers for years, friends forever.

During a pregnancy in October 1562 Elizabeth suffered smallpox and measles at Hampton Court. The baby born later was so crippled by measles she thought he'd die, but he survived, and she gave him to William Cecil, who proudly reared him as his own son Robert. From 1590 till his death in 1612, this Robert was official chief of State Secret Service. Another Robert (all Elizabeth's boys by Dudley were Roberts) was born in November 1563, and he, too, was adopted by Dudley's obliging sister and her husband, Henry Sidney.

Elizabeth seems to have borne two more girls, another Mary and an Elizabeth. Then in November 1566 the last Robert arrived—a baby she gave to her cousin Lettice Knollys Devereux. He became the tragic second earl of Essex. Kit served him as secretary in France in 1591, worked for him and Bacon while they operated a foreign news-diplomatic service. Kit helped Essex with his Cádiz raid in June 1596, went with him to Ireland in 1599, and tried unsuccessfully to advise him in 1600.

Elizabeth's last baby was born at Thomas Gresham's Mayfield house in the first week of August, 1573,[108] and it was Roger Manwood who found a home for the boy with Mary Browne and her husband the Second Earl of Southampton. The child's natural father was Elizabeth's first son, Ned de Vere, Seventeenth Earl of Oxford.[109] A sad story; Kit put echoes of the affair into Hamlet. (The baby was Hen Wriothesley, who saved Kit's life and remained his friend as long as Kit lived.) So, this tale of procreation was not for publication. To keep her place, the queen must keep the myth of her virginity.

And now, reminding her she'd relinquished to him all responsibility for punishment of heretics and schismatics, Archbishop Whitgift told Elizabeth he was forced to arrange secret deaths for her four most important Marrano servitors. Elizabeth succumbed but insisted the deaths be painless; she'd read that Seneca had bled to death without pain; let her own Doctor Lopes do the jobs, with gentle blood-letting. And let the families be no way deprived, and each man choose his date of death, and—God's lids—give each man at least three months to change his mind!

It didn't work out that way. The deaths were secret, all right. For Mildmay, the three months were whittled down because the date he chose was 31 May, 1589, the mildest day of May, to suggest his death was somehow contrived.[110] Lopes did the job.

Walsingham did not go easily, but submitted for the sake of his family, on 6 April, 1590. Earl of Essex Robin Devereux had just married Sir Francis Walsingham's daughter Franke (Philip Sidney's beautiful widow), and on the night his father-in-law was executed, Essex was in the room, horrified by Lopes's cruelty—no gentle bloodletting, but repeated brutal thrusts of a sharp rod deep into the victim's intestines. Essex could only guess the doctor had been paid by the archbishop to make the death as painful and degrading as possible. Essex told what he'd seen to Walsingham's natural son, Francis Bacon, and they planned revenge: they couldn't touch Whitgift but determined to do away with Lopes.[111]

Two months later, in Thomas Randolph's ancient house on Peter's Hill, Lopes killed Ambassador-Postmaster Randolph in the same grisly way. (In Charles Dickens' Little Dorrit, that was the house where something unspeakable had happened—the house which ultimately collapsed from its weight of guilt.)

Of course the sudden loss of three key advisers caused administrative turmoil. The bulk of Walsingham's operation was to be transferred to William Cecil, now Lord Burghley, and his adopted son Robert, but Essex and Bacon had already moved Sir Francis's files to Essex House. Using the wealth of Walsingham's letters and agents' names, the two young men started a foreign service which they hoped would soon be recognized and funded by the queen as part of SSS,[112] though Burghley and Robert Cecil frowned on the idea. Bacon worked to develop an airpost with homing pigeons,[113] later installed his foster-brother Anthony as Essex's correspondence secretary,[114] and dreamed of becoming invisible chief of a secret Secret Service.

Meanwhile Kit was becoming famous. Tamburlaine I had made a truly enormous hit on the London stage, and forgetting law-study, Marlowe quickly finished Tamburlaine II, another smash success.[115] His mother Kate and Roger disapproved of his sudden celebrity—Kit loved it and speaks of it in ciphers.

That summer it seems Tom Watson and Sam Daniel took Kit to Cardiff Castle to meet Elizabeth's daughter Mary Sidney Herbert, twenty-nine years old, educated, devoted to theater and the art of writing. Permanently estranged from her pirate husband, she still mourned the death in 1586 of her half-brother Philip Sidney.[116] Mary and Kit had a lot to talk about; she invited him to her library, then to her bedroom, and at her request Kit extended his stay in Wales.

Back at his Inn of Chancery, Marlowe drafted scenes for King Leir, a story that interested Lady Mary. He tried to study law, sat in at trials at the Old Bailey and often ate supper at the nearby St. George Inn, where the host and hostess were agents who relayed news of the lawyers' world to Bacon and news of import-exporters to Roger. Kit liked hostess Jane Davenant[117] and would have seduced her; she told him she'd rather be friends.

At this time Ned was arranging a marriage—his daughter Elizabeth to Henry Wriothesley.[118] Ned mentioned his plan to Kit, saying that Hen was a bit reluctant; he was young, of course. Ned said he'd pay Kit well if he'd write some sonnets about—oh, the joy of married life and the importance of having a family. Kit agreed and promised to set to work.[119]

Ned had sold Fisher's Folly and moved his writers to the Randolph house on Peter's Hill: After Randolph's death, his widow had leased half their enormous antique home to Julie Arthur Penn Hickes, a Bristol widow who wanted to run a boarding house. Ned sent his theater writers into Julie Arthur's half of this house and even moved in himself.[120]

Kit moved in, too. He and Ned, who'd worked (together with Roger) on The Famous Victories, now worked hard polishing Henry V,[121] and Kit tossed off other plays, not very good ones, for the Theater Wing. Walsingham's death in April and Randolph's in June cast a shadow for Kit, and he worried about his dad Roger.

Near the end of December 1590, Kit and Tom Nashe left London for Titchfield, where they read Italian with Hen Wriothesley's tutor John Florio, and on 10 January '91 new style, the three young men started a tour of the south coast in Hen's pinnace,[122] with Kit as sailing instructor. When they reached Dover, Tom and Kit rode to Canterbury to see Kit's family,[123] but Hen stayed aboard, too shy to mix with the lower classes at home. He'd have liked to sail across the Channel to aid Navarre, but Kit and Tom said he should go later.[124]

In that spring, '91, rehearsing in a new production at Shoreditch, Kit fell and broke his bad leg.[125] Laid up at Julie Arthur's place, he started writing reams of not-too-real historical drama, a trilogy showing conflict between the houses of York and Lancaster and their final union. The inspiration came from his dad Roger Manwood's gold chain of office, adorned with symbols of this bit of history.[126]

A writer friend of Kit's named Tom Kyd needed a place to stay, so Kit heeled him into his chamber and they talked about plays: Tom Kyd's specialty was revenge; a sort of proto-Hamlet crossed their minds.

In July Essex sailed for France with soldiers to help Navarre, and Kit, his leg still not completely healed, went as a staffer. Hen stowed away on the flagship—the queen had forbidden him to go. Discovered, he begged not to be sent home.

While the main force set up camp, Essex, Hen, Kit and a few friends sneaked through enemy territory to rendezvous at Noyon with Navarre, Longueville and Biron.

After three days of discussions, sport and entertainment with irresistible ladies, the little embassy worked its way back to camp at Pont de l'Arche, where the French general Lord Chartres, once governor of Malta, surely told stories which Marlowe would have put away for later use.[127]

In the nick of time Kit sailed Hen across the Channel in a pinnace, to change into something decent at Titchfield just as the queen drove up to the house on Progress.[128]

When Marlowe got back to Peters Hill everyone was packing; they were going to entertain the queen at Elvetham with a water show—poems, music, mermaids, artificial islands. A super swimmer who could dive was needed to retrieve a jewel from lake-bottom for her majesty, and Kit was drafted.[129] In spite of a dank afternoon, Elizabeth came out to the lake, and the show was a success. Most of the performers stayed overnight in tents, but Kit slept upstairs with very drunk Ned, who asked him if he'd finished those sonnets for Hen about being married.

Not yet, said Kit, but he'd work on them right away.

Autumn came, and Kit feared for Manwood. His wife's cousin, a puritan, was imprisoned by Whitgift and soon died in jail in spite of Roger's efforts to aid him, and the archbishop then put a sharp watch on the whole family. Roger was also in deep controversy with Burghley over the upcoming trial of powerful Sir John Perrot, ex-Deputy of Ireland:[130] Hatton, Ralegh and Manwood were gathering evidence against the pirate Perrot, long protected by Burghley.

Kit spent time on the sonnet cycle he'd promised to make—about how wonderful it would be for Hen to marry and have children. Ned had already paid for the work, and Kit was obliged to finish it. But now he was shocked to learn from Roger, over supper at Roger's town house, that Hen's real father was Ned de Vere, the prince himself, who'd engaged in a short affair with his own mother Queen Elizabeth at Windsor in 1572. This revelation threw the poems Kit was creating into a swirl of menippean satire, plaintexts backed by ciphers telling Hen, *No!* Don't do it—each interior message touching a different aspect of the worrisome situation. The cycle became a marathon—there were to be 17 poems—to be given to Hen on his seventeenth birthday. Kit decided he ought to talk to Hen up close—instruct him about the dangers of such a marriage.

Instead, Kit threw himself into theater work (polished up a play of King John?), didn't see much of his friends or even his dad—visited him sometimes at West Smithfield, sometimes at the Old Bailey.

One day Tom Watson and Kit were surprised by a message from Lady Mary Herbert at her town house, Baynard's Castle. Would they come to visit tomorrow, and bring some of their charming new writings? Kit was touched.

When they arrived, Mary presented them to Walter Ralegh, and soon Kit was attending evening seminars in Ralegh's apartments—avant-garde instructions in math and geography for navigation and lectures on chemistry, philosophy, religion and literature—sponsored by Ralegh and Henry Percy, the Catholic Earl of Northumberland.[131] All this in the face of Whitgift's disapproval. (Percy's father, locked in the Tower, had died of a gunshot wound which many believed was inflicted by the Ecclesiastical Commission.)[132]

By working late nights, Kit finished and delivered the seventeen-sonnet cycle to Ned. Then he found Hen and told him the truth—that his real dad was Oxford. As soon as Hen realized the genetic possibilities of the union being forced on him, he went to his guardian, Master of Wards Lord Burghley, and refused the match. Burghley, who stood to gain financially from the marriage (the girl was his granddaughter), demanded to know who'd told such a lie, and why Southampton had believed it. He grilled the youth till Hen admitted Kit had told him, and he trusted Kit—*he* got it from someone who knew!

From that moment, Burghley hated Marlowe. Hen was angrily told that if he persisted in refusing the match, on the day he turned twenty-one he must pay Burghley a £5000 fine all at once, no "estallment."[133]

Hen dismissed, Kit was sent for, verbally abused, told he was not to speak to or see the earl of Southampton. Kit packed up and sailed a week later on a shipboard job with Captain Carleill, intercepting Spanish bottoms on the Channel.

On the day after Kit's interview with Burghley, Ned showed up roaring drunk at the writers' boarding house, staggered into the room where a script was spread on the floor for editing, stamped on it, kicked over the ink, declared there was a Judas in the chamber and left forever (climbing out the window and down the trellis to avoid the landlady), saying the hostess could whistle for her rent. He never paid.[134] (In ciphers, Marlowe says Queen Elizabeth finally paid the bill.)

In January, Marlowe debarked from Captain Carleill's ship Tyger[135] at Flushing, and there he was met by Rick (Bull) Baines, an agent of questionable loyalty whom Kit hadn't seen since old times when Baines had been jailed in Reims for trying to kill Dr. Allen, president of the English College, by poisoning the soup of the whole faculty.[136] Kit had tried to aid him in jail; the two had parted bad friends. Now Rick told Kit he'd been sent by Burghley to be a partner. (He'd really been sent by Ned?) They were to listen for news of Parma's progress towards Rouen, news of aid to Catholic Leaguers from English expatriates, and to find out how counterfeit coins were being received and spent by officers of William Stanley's company, which had defected to the Spanish side. Rick seemed friendly, and the two worked together for about a week. Suddenly Baines turned up with police, exposed Kit's real name, accused him of counterfeit-coining and having once used the name Gilbert Gifford as an alias. Governor Sir Robert Sidney sent both men back to Burghley under guard.[137] Humiliated, Kit was rescued by Roger, who warned him he must settle down and study. This may be his last chance.

But Kit had deadlines for Henry VI and The Jew of Malta, and he'd started a play called Edward II. He didn't see much of his father in the next weeks, till one day Manwood took him along to a Jewish service held with diplomatic immunity by an envoy, a man sent to Elizabeth by Alvaro Mendes, a Kentish neighbor of Roger's who owned diamond mines in India and was now a power in Constantinople. Mendes was protesting a plan (set in place by Bacon) to confiscate all Mendes' assets, giving half to the sultan and the rest to Mendes' half-brother Antonio, Pretender to the throne of Portugal, a man known as the Prior of Ocrato, who'd taken refuge in England and was hating Mendes for not giving him more and more diamonds with which to win Portugal.[138]

Bacon may have told Kit to write The Jew of Malta to show an impossible Jew who was mean to his own people, but Kit made *everyone* in the play awful. It was on the boards at the time of Mendes' embassy,[139] and the envoy must have enjoyed it. Elizabeth wrote him a letter assuring no ruin would befall her friend Alvaro Mendes, and the envoy went home.[140] (In Venetian slang, the envoy's name was Cor'mano, cormorant. Did he or Roger tell Kit that in Hebrew the name was Shalach? Kit may have used it when he wrote The Merchant of Venice.)

There was a little club out in Shoreditch where on many nights the 'university-wits' (hired by the queen to help Ned write plays for the Theater Wing) gathered at the gaming tables.[141] The year before, Elizabeth had made gambling illegal, encouraging men to practice archery instead,[142] but Kit liked cards and dicing—Roger had taught him to play barcabudi—and besides, the hostess at the club was a gorgeous woman, Emilia Bassano. She was mistress of the lord chamberlain, who'd set her up in this Italianate villa and was probably responsible for the gaming operation, managed on the spot by Fonsie Ferrobosco, one of her Majesty's musicians, and Fonsie Lanier, who'd soon be one. Emilia made a perfect hostess—twenty-two years old, bright, intellectual without being overbearing, sociable, slim, graceful, fashionable and possessed of dark, smoldering, almost incredible beauty.[143] Taking advantage of the lord chamberlain's absence, Kit had been making love to this paragon.[144] She liked him a lot but made him promise never, never to impregnate her. If she were to become enceinte, her magic existence would fly away, leaving her homeless and helpless. When he proposed marriage, she laughed.

Kit was living the life of a famous dramatist—forgetting his family, moving around town beyond his means.[145] Emilia pawned her diamond ring for him and feared he'd let the time go by and lose it.[146]

Kit often thought about Hen's impending £5000 fine. He, Kit, knew he was responsible for turning the youth away from marriage with Elizabeth Vere.

At the end of March, Roger called. He had to leave town for a few days; would Kit go by the goldsmith's and pick up his chain which had been left for repair? The goldsmith was closing for vacation.

Hen came to see Kit, and in spite of Burghley's warning they rode across town together, and after picking up the chain, went out to the club. Kit introduced Emilia to the earl—she was impressed—and they spent the evening dicing. Kit said all his winnings would go toward Hen's fine. The gold chain was in Kit's pocket; why not wager it at gold-play and give the proceeds to Hen? Barcabudi was the game Kit couldn't lose.

At midnight bets were placed, and Emilia joined the game. Kit didn't know she was worried about her diamond ring and planned to recoup. In barcabudi, each player uses his own cup to hold his dice,[147] and Emilia's was furnished with a gaff. Kit lost.

At one o'clock on the morning of April first, 1592, Kit saw his life fade to nothing. The Fonsies whisked the gold chain away and doused the lights.

When Manwood found out he sent word to the fence, Roger Underwood,[148] saying he should come to chambers and bring the chain. When the man arrived he was told he'd bought stolen property, that gambling had been made illegal by his queen, and to avoid prosecution he'd better hand over the chain.[149] Underwood did, but then he went to the club with his story, and Emilia declared the lord chamberlain would have something to say about *that!*

With Henry Carey, Lord Hunsdon, chamberlain of the queen's household, as unlikely patron, the fence appeared before the privy council the following week, telling his story of Manwood's confiscation of a collar which Underwood asserted he'd lawfully bought from long-time clients, two of her Majesty's court musicians, who worked under the special protection of the lord chamberlain. Underwood stood trembling, but the archbishop at the head of the table and the Lord Treasurer Burghley seemed pleased, clucking in sympathy when Underwood described his poverty and sacrifices he'd made to pay for the great chain. No mention of dicing, no indication the chain might have been received by the musicians as payment of an illegal debt.

The goldsmith dismissed, Roger was sent for by writ, citing Underwood's suit and requiring Roger to produce the chain. What came back to the council on 13 April was a testy letter from Manwood refusing to accept the council's jurisdiction in the case. He wrote of the treasurer's overt bitterness against him in a recent interview, and referring to other persecutions, "I do with David hold myself contented accounting the same to be God's visitation upon me, which such bad folks in their bad causes have heretofore prevailed against me." He asked that his goods, meaning his chain, be not drawn from him upon private complaint, "without due course of justice in some of her Majesty's public courts."

He included an educational jingle. A thrill of disbelief ran around the council table as it was read aloud:

Malas causas habéntes	Those whose case is wrong
Fugiunt semper ad poténtes.	Run ever to the strong.
Ubi non verítas	Where there are lying tales,
Praevalent auctorítas!	Authority prevails.
Curret lex,	Let law-givers give
Vivat rex!	And may the prince live![150]

Some of the council members were mystified and some thought the lord chief baron had gone mad, but Burghley and Whitgift felt progress was being made. Manwood, like a bull in the ring after the exit of the picadores, was cracking up.

He was committed to house arrest and cooled there all through Easter Term, feeling abandoned, as Perrot's trial approached and passed. He kept still till that drama was over; on that score his hands were clean. Then he sent the council a humble submission and was told to appear before them at Greenwich on 14 May and bring the chain. He did.[151] Forced to sign an apology, he was instructed not only to pay Underwood the sum the man had given for the chain but to deliver the chain immediately to William Brooke, Lord Cobham, a council-member seated at the table, to do with as he saw fit.[152] That rankled. Lord Cobham, a neighbor at Shorne, had been an adversary in Manwood's Kent career. Why should Brooke take the chain? The council also decided that after Trinity Term Roger was to ride circuit as a justice of assize—a chore he'd performed years ago at the start of his career. His circuit would include the little market towns of Berkshire. As he left the room he was sourly advised that since he was so great for the Law, he'd better stick to it.

Kit still didn't understand that Emilia had cheated in the dice game. In love with her, he frequented the club, taking Hen along; Hen was charmed by her, too. One night, upstairs with Emilia, Kit declared his love once more and once more asked her to marry him. He said Bacon might send him on a job to Italy and she could come with him and wait for him at her family's home in Bassano. Nothing was farther from Emilia's plans, but for some inexplicable reason, she let him enfold her, and she enfolded him.

When she realized she was pregnant, Emilia was furious. Kit could never pay for this child! Filled with hate and a wish to destroy the man, she may have taken some philosophical essays from Kit's room (she had a key) and sold them to Burghley. But the baby? How in the world could she afford to rear it? She'd lose Hunsdon—lose the club!

She thought of Hen: he was naïve, and he had money. If she could make him think the baby was his, he'd help!

Emilia seduced Hen that August. Terribly pleased, he took her to Whitely, his rustic lodge, for a weekend.[153] Hen's bodyguard John Florio had been looking the other way, but when Kit told him Emilia was dangerous and not to be allowed near his charge, Florio told Hen's foster mother Mary Browne, and Hen was packed off to Oxford.[154]

Hen did help pay for Emilia's child, in secret at first, and when the boy was eleven Hen arranged for Emilia's husband Fonsie Lanier to profit from all the hay and straw brought into London and Westminster: sixpence on every hay load, threepence on every straw load, for twenty years.[155] Young Henry Lanier became a court musician; Emilia never admitted he was Kit's baby. Henry Lanier's son Adrian disappeared in America—could Sidney Lanier or Tennessee Lanier Williams be descended from Kit?

On 19 August 1592 Roger, riding circuit, came to Windsor, spent the night at the Garter Inn and on Sunday prepared for Monday morning court. Also on the 19th, Count Mömpelgard, a corpulent German nobleman touring England with a small band of followers, said farewell to the queen at Reading, rode fifteen miles to Windsor and stopped at the Garter Inn. Roger heard on the grapevine that the count had asked the queen to marry him!

After inspecting the castle on Sunday, the count and his men tried to hire fresh horses, but because the count's friends were as heavy as he was, they were disappointed; the Garter host said he had no mounts sturdy enough. But early on Monday morning the stablemaster came to tell the host that the count's party was heading toward Uxbridge—on Garter Inn horses!

Mömpelgard and his companions were rounded up by the constable's men and led back, complaining, to Windsor, where they waited their turn in Roger's court. Roger knew who the men were, but the words at the council table came back, "stick to the law."

Far as I may, he thought, and greeted the new parties at the bar with a hint of a smile. To the astonished defendents he explained the body of English law on horse-stealing, the development of that law from ancient times—amendments which expressly stated that none who feloniously stole horses should have benefit of clergy—meaning of course that stealing horses was a hanging offense. However, an accessory to horse-stealing, if he were literate, might get off with a brand. Everyone was shaking until Roger decided the travelers could get out of town as soon as the right number of dray horses could be found for them.[156]

In early September '92 Marlowe followed Ferdinando Stanley's Lord Strange's Players to Canterbury, where they probably showed The Jew of Malta, and there Kit stayed with his mother Kate, his legal father John, half-sisters Dorthy and Anne and his half-brother Tom, in the big house on High Street. He may have been in front of the house after a performance of the show when he met an old friend, chorister Will Corkine. Will had disliked the play. Kit made some quip, Will challenged him, and they squared off and started to fight apprentice-style, with knives and staves.[157] Kate flew out of the house and stopped them.

It was not quite over. Will's friends, seeing Kit had lopped buttons off Will's jacket, decided Will must sue, and a civil case claiming assault by Kit was entered in the plea book of the Canterbury Town Serjeant on 26 September.

Kit countered with a criminal charge against Corkine in autumn quarter-sessions before the Grand Jury on the same day, but Kit dropped his charge and the indictment was thrown out. Corkine left his suit on the book; John Marley acted as surety for Kit to appear in court, which he did on 2 October. He asked for a week to prepare rebuttal, but on Monday 9 October accuser and defendant returned, told the court they were friends and the case was dropped.

A year later, in late September *1593*, when he heard rumors of Kit's death, Will Corkine must have thought of a memorial, but the Deptford grave said to be Kit's was unmarked, so Will left a rosebud in a *new* plea book into which the Canterbury Town Serjeant had just finished *copying* the cases from September and October *1592.* The pressed flower still exists.

Marlowe came back from Canterbury in October '92 to his rented chamber in Bishopsgate to hear sad news. Emilia—how could she? At that minute she was at St. Botolph's Aldgate, marrying Fonsie Lanier![158] Kit ran to the church—too late—they were coming down the steps—white lilies—flower girls . . . .

Tom Nashe came by to say that their friend and mentor Tom Watson had died, leaving his last book ready for the printer. Would Kit see it through? Watson had wanted Kit to put a dedication up front for Lady Mary Herbert, and he did.

Depressed, lonely, full of guilt about the chain, Kit thought of Roger. They were alienated, maybe forever. Manwood had gone to work through Michaelmas Term at Hertford because of plague in London. Some young ex-Oxfordians, John Donne and Barnaby Barnes, came around to see Kit—they seemed like alien innocents—and Hen was probably still at Oxford. Nashe, needing cash, had sold out to the archbishop and was writing against Marprelate. And Ned hated Kit.

To go in front of Watson's new book Kit wrote an elegant baroque Latin paragraph addressed "to the most illustrious noble lady, adorned with all gifts both of mind and body, Mary Countess of Pembroke," and when the book was finished he took her the first bound copy.

She and her husband the pirate earl were in London at Baynard's Castle, their ancient pile at river's edge—in the same house, but not together. Kit saw her eyes shine with the old flame; she seemed more lovely, more self-confident, than he remembered her. They talked a long time by the fire in the library. Her own new Pembroke Players were scheduled to present two plays at Hampton Court during Christmas holidays, and she wanted them to be Kit's. The first, they decided, would be Edward II, about a king who made Mary think of Ned, and for the second, maybe some parts of Henry VI, edited up together; Mary was excited by the prospect. Ferdinando Stanley's company was going to play there, too, during the holidays and would help with production details. Mary's dates had already been set: 26 December and Twelfth Night, the sixth of January.[159]

Before leaving for Hertford, Roger had privately printed a last essay, unsigned but hardly anonymous, and not a satire. Whimsically but clearly it explained several points of law. He called the work, "A Petition Directed to her most excellent Maiestie." (sic) After fifty-two pages he incorporated the words of puritans who'd been incommunicado, then came back himself for a strong ending paragraph.

As soon as Whitgift read the piece[160] he fashioned a letter which the privy council sent to the Lord Keeper, a directive boldly putting words in the queen's mouth: "Her Majesty upon very good reason is moved to think it requisite that all the officers and under-officers belonging to any of the Courts of Records should take the oath of Supremacy . . . and commandeth that forthwith your Lordship do make the Judges of both benches and the Lord Chief Baron of the Exchequer acquainted herewith . . . and . . . at some convenient time you do . . . cause . . . to be ministered the said oath to all officers and under-officers of the said courts. And if . . . any shall refuse to take the oath *as is prescribed* [in new Whitgift form], to sequester them from execution of their offices till her Majesty's pleasure be further known."

The archbishop proudly, publicly said he was the second most powerful person in England; I believe that letter made him the first. It was sent on 16 November, and when it was Roger's turn to swear, not only to Elizabeth's supremacy in the state (no trouble with that), but to her primacy as Promulgator of God's Perfect Prayer Book, in his mood of reform he must have found he could neither sign nor open his mouth.

What happened next can be reconstructed from time-line, after-events and Marlowe's detailed ciphers. Manwood was told to report in private to the archbishop, from whom he learned that authorship of his anti-episcopal writings had been uncovered: documentary evidence as well as reliable oral testimony had been received. He was not told the name of his accuser. (He must have wondered; could it have been Kit?) No use for Roger to assert he'd struck a blow for freedom, that he deserved a trial in court, that his accuser should come forth. He'd been convicted already.

Whitgift must have said something like this: "Go home to Canterbury. Archdeacon William Redman will help you make the arrangements, help you remake your will.[161] Your family will feel no worldly deprivation so long as public discussion of your death is avoided; there need be no disgrace if those concerned remain discreet. The queen has granted leave for you to appoint the hour of your death, to be effected within thirty days. Be ready, directly you reach home, to inform the archdeacon of your decision. You'll be allowed to determine the place of death by means of conference with Dr. Lopes, who is charged with execution of her Majesty's order. That's all."

Overcome at first by confusion, fear and horror, Roger soon gathered his thoughts, rode out past Shoreditch to Ned's house at Hackney. Lord Ned would aid him, for old time's sake. But there was no help there.

Roger started for Canterbury, got as far as Shorne, stayed overnight to catch his breath. An idea came to him. Forget Lord Ned. What day was this? Saturday, December second. As his day of death, he'd choose 14 December, the hundred seventy-fifth anniversary of the death of the lollard Sir John Oldcastle, who'd lived at Cooling Castle in the marsh just north of Gad's Hill here. Oldcastle had been executed by ecclesiastical court on 14 December in 1417, for the same politico-religious pseudo-crimes of which Roger himself now stood accused—speaking and writing for reform.[162] A man after Roger's own heart. Sir John had been a lay-preacher right down the road at Chalk Church.

He hiked down to the church. Did Father Lawrence Dakin agree to let him speak from the pulpit to combined congregations of Chalk and neighboring churches on Sunday the tenth? Subject, Sir John Oldcastle? Maybe Roger got a little of his own back.

Perhaps he didn't tell his wife at Canterbury; saying only that he had to talk to Archdeacon Redman, then go back to London on business, to be home again soon. But he told Kate, for she was with him at the end: we see her as Hostess in Henry V Act II, describing Falstaff's death, and in Kit's ciphers for Taming of The Shrew, where Kate as herself washes Roger's body for burial. Roger's legitimate son Peter was there with his dad when he died,[163] and I think the end came at Shorne. Shorne would be inconvenient for Redman, easier for Lopes.

Churchyard may have come to Mary's Baynard's Castle to tell Kit that Roger was dead, but it was from Peter Manwood and Kate that Kit learned details of his dad's murder. The brutality of the killer, the rodding, the pain, the mess, Roger's bravery—all are set down in ciphers, and from the ones in "Epitaph for Sir Roger Manwood" it seems Kit saw the body.

Manwood was not simply the victim of an execution; he was victimized by a far-flung, ongoing character-assassination started by the archbishop and Burghley—falsification, sliding down the years. And physical evidence shows that Roger's burial vault has been violently robbed of its male occupants.[164]

Marlowe, angry, heartbroken, knew he'd let his dad down, made him vulnerable. He could never talk to him again—no chance to make things right about the gold chain. But Kit and Mary planned to make a statement using the Pembroke Plays at the Hampton Court Christmas festival: they rewrote some scenes to show and tell everyone what had happened to Roger.

Edward II died from the same treatment Roger had suffered, but in the play Edward died offstage, and on 26 December that play was heard to the end, even though a good part of the audience was uncomfortably aware of what the dramatist was thinking. But on 6 January, the day of Epiphany, the specially-edited Henry VI was a show-stopper.[165] In one scene Duke Humphrey had just been murdered by secret order of a prelate on the pretext that the duke might be planning to commit a crime. A vivid simulacrum of the duke's mutilated body was brought onstage in a death-bed covered with blood and feces, and the odor was sickening. People—bishops—rose and left the hall. Elizabeth stood up, and the party was over. Furious, she told her daughter Mary she'd never visit her again, and she never did, and the Pembroke playing company soon shriveled and disappeared. But Mary, loyal to Kit, felt they'd done the right thing.

Kit tells the story of that performance in ciphers in Henry VI, Part III. From the stage that night he delivered lines which "sealed my doom." There's a cogent passage in the first scene plaintext: "May that ground gape, and swallow me alive,/Where I shall kneel to him that slew my father."

The archbishop decided then and there that Kit must die. He'd be examined by council and remanded to the ecclesiastical commission for trial and condemnation. But as weeks passed, Kit wondered why he wasn't arrested. Whitgift's detectives came to the Revels Office to confiscate Kit's writings "and art" (did Kit make stage designs? costume sketches?), but his friend George Buck, already working there, hid them and saved them.[166]

Bacon and Essex wanted to send Kit abroad on a mission, but they seem to have been waiting for money. As spring came, London was wrapped in deadly plague, and Bacon managed to move most of his SSS operatives out of town to stay with honest man Tom Walsingham. Tom lived in a roomy country place called Scadbury near Chislehurst in Kent, and Kit, a friend of Tom's, was glad to go there and wait for whatever.[167] They all figured Whitgift's people were looking for hard evidence against Kit so they could prosecute him, because hauling him in for the tasteless play would only incriminate Whitgift himself.

Kit was working on Hero and Leander, a long poem he'd started for Emilia. Inside is an echo of the mission Bacon had chosen for Kit—a job beyond the Hellespont. There are shadows of Emilia herself: Hero is a votary of Venus (a nice way of saying it) who plays with the swans and sparrows all the day (in SSS jargon, male and female whores).

Young Audrey Shelton (she called herself Udrey), a distant relative of the queen, was staying at Tom's to avoid the plague, and she and Kit may have roamed the woods together. Carved on a nearby ancient beech tree letters can still be seen; upsilon sigma in mixed cases: UΣ; they could stand for "us," or "Udrey Shelton" in Greek-letter English, or "Christopher Marlowe" in plain English looked at sideways.[168]

It was May; agents had come and gone, but Kit stayed on at Scadbury. (Why *didn't* Bacon send him oversea?) Meanwhile in London, his would-be prosecutors found evidence, a somewhat skewed report about Marlowe's ideas furnished by Rick Baines, the very agent who'd betrayed Kit in Flushing in 1591/2. Also unearthed, from a different source, was an excerpt from The Fall of the Late Arrian, a document Kit had read at one of Northumberland's seminars in Ralegh's apartment. It could have been copied from a book that was once in the headmaster's library at the King's School.[169]

On Saturday 19 May a messenger from the Queen's Chamber came to arrest Kit and take him to Nonsuch. The man stayed overnight at Scadbury, and next day the two rode into town and talked to Clerk of Star Chamber, Master William Mill, working overtime at Westminster Hall. When Mill mentioned the MS page of the Arrian Heresy (found among Tom Kyd's papers) to be presented as evidence, Kit said yes, he owned that copy (thinking, Emilia, how could you! She could have taken it from Kit's room, sold it to Burghley, and Ned could have paid police to "find" it in Tom Kyd's room). Since Kit admitted the page belonged to him, it was possible to avoid the rigamarol of answer to the bill, interrogatories, replication, rejoinder and exams. He could just go on Wednesday, offer excuses and receive the judges' decisions aurally. Kit posted bail and headed for Hen, who must have been at Nonsuch with the queen.

Hen had wanted Kit to write a poem for Elizabeth, asking to be spared burning. Kit had finished it at Scadbury and now gave it to Hen to take, right away, to his mother. It starts "Shall I Die? Shall I Fly?" and contains ciphers—one a plea for exile instead of death. Another, a compound anagrammatic acrostic, yields a bitter tiny story of his and his dad's predicament.[170] The ciphers make the poem stiff, but it's a shy love poem, meant to touch her heart. It worked! Intrigued, she invited him to a private interview and promised to send a letter of exile to the council on Wednesday. The queen may have been using French law—justice retenue: though she'd formally delegated to Whitgift her right to deal with heretical or schismatic problems, by writing in her own hand and sealing it with her own seal, she could still write lettres de grace and lettres de cachet, and for Kit it was a lettre de cachet addressed to SSS,[171] sending him into exile right away without a trial: *No more fooling around! Get the kid out!*

Marlowe's ciphers tell a good deal about that 23 May meeting of the council, which may have been convened at Nonsuch to avoid plague in London, and what happened afterward. He was banished. Wanting to thank Elizabeth, he went back to see her, and they spent an amazing night of love together, documented in ciphers of Love's Labours Lost, where he calls her Hoo-Hoo, and he's Citt-Citt.

But the next day SSS agent Robin Poley came to say that Whitgift had hired him to eliminate Kit before he could leave England. The archbishop had determined that every person connected with Marprelate should die, and he was close to his goal—Poley felt sure that if he didn't do this hit Whitgift would kill *him.* Roger's lawyer-friend Henry Barrowe (shadows suggest he was related to Dickens' maternal grandfather's family) had been hanged in April with John Greenwood, a friend of Kit's from Corpus Christi.[172] John Penry (Ap Henry), another Cambridge friend of Kit's, a minister who'd managed the Marprelate printeries, had gone on his trial a week ago.[173] Possibly, Poley thought, the man leaked under torture and incriminated Kit.

Kit's employers and friends were consulted, and the only answer anybody could think of was to have Kit seem to die and disappear across the Channel. Only then would Whitgift stop searching for him. How to do it?

The queen took charge. She arranged for a safe-house on the Strand at Deptford, the port on the Thames from which Essex had already arranged for Kit to sail across the Channel as soon as he could leave on the mission Essex and Bacon had been planning. The Deptford house was owned by a widow, Elinor Whitney Bull, member of an old pirate family and relative of Elizabeth's nurse Blanche Parry (Ap-Harry). Since her husband's death Elinor had offered room and board to a few respectable travelers and sea captains, and she was willing to take in government men on a secret mission as a favor to her queen.[174]

Elizabeth also provided the corpse of a recently-hanged criminal to be presented as Kit's body at the time of inquest.[175] In England in those days there were hangings every week. It was agreed that Kit would have to seem to attack, and then be killed, by a comrade; the killing must be in self-defense so the comrade could get out of the Deptford jail. Elizabeth's own coroner could take care of the inquest: she'd temporarily moved her court to Greenwich[176] and use of her coroner would be legal. The jury would be straight; the coroner would display a fresh wound over the dead man's eyeball, below the bone, and the telltale bruise from his hanging would be concealed by a bandana or a winding-sheet tied close around the dead man's neck.

My own scenario: Poley, with Essex's man Nick Skeres and Tom Walsingham's man Ingram Frizer supporting the upright corpse (dressed in Kit's good-looking leather clothes and seemingly dead drunk), went up to a big chamber in the widow's house before lunch on Wednesday, 30 May. Kit, disguised as a white-haired old man, was already upstairs in a smaller room. He came into the men's chamber, took off his wig and changed into his own clothes, which had been on the corpse, (the dead body had been hidden under the bed.) Lunch was served in the room, and the servants saw the drunk man had recovered: he was Kit.

Poley, Skeres, Frizer and Kit then went walking for a long time in the widow's garden, *in plain sight,* so any observer could see that Kit was there alive and well, talking with his friends. At dusk they went upstairs together to eat supper in their big private chamber: Kit took off his own clothes, laid them on the bed and put on his old-man disguise again. He went back to his old-man's room and later quietly left the house to board the little ship at the dock, and wait. Upstairs, Skeres and Frizer carefully re-dressed the corpse in Kit's clothes and placed it lying on the bed facing the wall, so when the servants brought the supper they thought it was the Kit character, gone to sleep. After supper, Poley, Skeres and Frizer locked their room door, started a noisy phony fight. (The drinks were in dispute, Kit says in a cipher). Frizer struck his knife on his own scalp to make it bleed, then thrust the blade as deep as he could *over the ball of the dead man's eye,* into the brain. The constable came to the door, and Frizer, Skeres and Poley were taken to jail to await the inquest.

All SSS had to do was wait for the outcome of the inquiry; Coroner Danby fixed everything.[177] Afterwards, Poley, the queen's special agent, was duty-bound to take Kit across the Channel and return to tell her that her poet-spy was safely gone. But sailing was delayed: Kate showed up weeping, and there were long good-byes.[178] Essex, who wanted Kit to meet Navarre outside Paris just about now, sent a nervous little note,[179] but soon Kit and Poley were sailing downriver into a rough sea.

On 8 June, Poley reported to Elizabeth that Christopher Marlowe had left England.[180] Marlowe, under cover, was riding hard across France on multiple secret missions for Bacon, Essex, and the queen.

f

Marlowe's Life, Part II

Once upon a time the life of a young spy-poet was saved by his queen, who ordered him banished instead of burned at the stake for crimes of heresy. Before he left the realm he was approached by his spymaster, one of the queen's secret sons,[181] and induced by him to participate in a strange charade. The chief declared that as long as the poet lived he'd be pursued and harassed by the archbishop who hated him, until sooner or later the prelate would successfully end the poet's life. The only way out, said the chief, was for the poet to seem to die, and for the death to be documented by an incontrovertible authority such as the queen's coroner.

Convinced, the young poet cooperated: the corpse of an already-hanged convict was exhibited as the poet's body, and the queen's coroner officially declared the poet dead.

What murky motives prompted the creation of that legend? The archbishop was indeed intransigent, and the queen truly wanted to save her agent's life, but the spymaster may have been trying to gain ascendency over the banished man—to be able to say, I saved your life; now it belongs to me. A great admirer of the poet's dramas, the spymaster had already offered to preserve the best of them someday in a tome in which he intended to place his own secret code-story, telling the miserable circumstances of his life as an unrecognized son of the queen. He said he could do this in any book he'd see through the press, using patterns he'd create from differently-angled type-fonts, but he felt the poet's work was going to last longer than any other author's and so would be the most suitable matrix.

Before leaving to live in exile, the poet was informed that his every move would be noticed by secret agents, that he was to continue to provide plays, lots of good ones, for Secret Service, and that on his way across Europe he was to deliver messages and later complete three important missions for his chief and his chief's partner. Yes, the poet could freelance, but he must save time to do jobs for his English chief, who would still be his employer.

These instructions seemed reasonable to the young man and were in a way welcome; after all, since college days, government work had been his career. Separation from beloved family and friends, from sights and sounds of his dear homeland—he knew that was what exile was about. But there was something else: the ugly realization of the loss of his professional name was a blow that came close to killing him. He'd been born a momzer, a special kind of bastard; his parents were married but not to each other, and since childhood, making a name for himself had been his primary goal. For the last few years, until the signing of the coroner's report, he'd been the most famous playwright in his country; now it seemed he'd be doomed to write for hire or write using bylines borrowed from kind friends. He asked to be allowed to put his new Italian name on future plays he'd send home.

No, he was told: people would look for him abroad, find him, expose the legend of his death, and his enemies would pounce on him. A suitable secret agent had already been tapped to serve as front-man for the desired flow of literary works from abroad. And by the way, a new piece of writing was wanted, to be published at once with the front-man's name, to seal the deal. The poet said he had a work already at the press; he'd remove his by-line and write a dedication signed with the front man's name: William Shakespeare.[182]

This may sound like a dream, a fairy-tale, but for Kit Marlowe it was here and now real. The work at the printer's was Venus and Adonis,[183] and from its cipher-story we see he must have redone the first lines and dashed off the dedication at the last minute while he waited at Deptford aboard the little boat which would carry him across the Channel. The first copy of Venus and Adonis known to be sold was purchased on 12 June 1593 by Richard Stonely, who'd worked with Kit's dad Roger Manwood at Exchequer[184] and may have known the author to be Roger's son.

Bacon's code-man Phelippes, waiting dockside to see Kit's boat sail, would have carried the rewrite of the poem back to London, perhaps along with a play Kit had just finished polishing, Richard III.[185]

In France at last, Kit, using temporary name Jaques (Jakes) Colerdin, rode to St. Denis, where he delivered to Henry of Navarre a letter from Essex offering to aid Henry's struggle for the throne. Kit reminded Henry about the week in autumn 1591 when Essex, with a small party including Kit, went to Navarre's headquarters at Noyon, and then Henry, remembering Kit as the clown, asked him to stay the night.[186]

The next morning Marlowe set off to cross France. He must have ridden around the closed city of Paris, taken the coche de l'eau to Bassau; his ciphers say he tried a public wagon, probably to Saulieu. Too slow! He rode post to Mâcon, crossed the border into unfriendly Savoy (thanks to Phelippes' papers) and on—Bourg, Nantua, an inn in the woods, then uphill. He walked beside his horse past Pert du Rhone, past the Savoy Arsenal, remounted to ride through the great double gates of Geneva.[187]

He'd been told to wait at the home of Professor Isaac Casaubon, where he was to meet English agent Harry Wotton,[188] a Kentishman who'd studied at Oxford and knew Kit's friends the Donnes, Barnzy Barnes and Lord Northumberland. Harry knew Italy; he'd go with Kit over the Alps to Mantua, where they were to deliver Essex's offer of aid to Gonzaga in his effort to resist aggression by the Pope.[189]

Packing out with Kit, Wotton told Casaubon that since this was a secret mission he'd probably be gone for months: if anyone asked, Isaac should just say Wotton had rented the room for the whole summer and would be back.

Wotton and Kit crossed the Alps, going part of the way on skiis.[190] The Simplon Pass was not often used in those days, but Harry had traveled that trail. On a steep downhill slope they both slid into an icy little crevasse off the track and were stuck, cold and scared, for hours. In ciphers for 3 Henry VI and Lucrece, Kit tells how they were saved. After dark they reached the Milanese border, where every paper was examined—and approved, thanks to Phelippes. Hours more along a dark path brought them to the inn at Duvedro, and next day they rode to Domodóssola and along a green valley to the lake, then took a boat south, rested at Sesto. At dawn there was another boat trip down the Ticino; two hours, twenty miles, eleven rapids! Afterwards they transferred to a scow. Leonardo da Vinci's locks and the horses on the tow-path made the thirty-mile trip to Milan a peaceful journey of seven hours. Kit mentions the scow in ciphers for Sonnet 116.

From Milan he and Harry rode out the north-east gate, past St. Gregory's Well. Kit mentioned that St. Gregory had lived in a town in Cappadocia where different religions, pagan, Christian, Muslim, mixed together peacefully—baked their bread in the same ovens, and St. Gregory was all for that. Kit was thinking about choosing a permanent Italian name for himself; Gregorio might not be bad. Harry, a fierce Protestant, said he couldn't agree.

Harry spoke of the thrust of the Bacon-Essex foreign service—anti-Spanish and resistant to expansion of papal power. That was why English aid had been offered to Navarre and would be offered to Vincenzo Gonzaga. Though Gonzaga and other north Italian princes would of course remain Roman Catholic, they didn't like the Spanish occupation of south Italy and Milan or having the Pope tell them how to manage their own states.[191] Using an underground coalition of Resistance workers once fostered by Francis Walsingham, many princes were cooperating with England's policies. There were undercover chiefs behind the lines, in parts of Italy held by Spain: At Naples, Gianbattista Manso[192] kept a clearing house, and famous Giambattista Della Porta,[193] in guise of scientist and writer, entertained foreign protestant diplomats at his home. Inside Parma, a state with close ties to the Vatican, the beautiful Barbara Sanseverino, Countess of Sala, operated as a freedom fighter from her home at Colorno[194]—unsuspected. Wotton knew them all.

The two men rode out toward Mantua along the foot of the mountain to rest at Bergamo. Kit wondered why they couldn't go straighter, maybe to Palazzuo. Harry explained the woods were crawling with highwaymen, and Kit put that bit, and the whole landscape, away in his head for The Two Gentlemen of Verona, which he was starting to plot.

At Mantua in the Castello Kit saw impressive murals showing the Trojan War,[195] which he thought he'd describe in a second poem he was making for Hen. It would be called Lucrece, a companion for Venus and Adonis. He wanted to give his friend Hen an elegant gift as thanks for saving Kit's life by taking the Shall I Die cipher-appeal to Elizabeth. A pair of poems might do it, reflecting the subjects of Titian's famous pair of paintings which Kit had seen in Madrid, thanks to Zuccaro.[196]

Though it was hot and mosquitoey, the court hadn't yet moved to the Summer Palace because the duke's mistress was there, and his wife didn't want to go. But after Harry and Kit delivered Essex's letter to Gonzaga, he invited them both to stay over and attend a party there,[197] and there Kit was surprised to meet his old friend Tom Lodge and learn they'd be going on to Verona and Venice together: Harry Wotton had to head for Genoa alone. At the party were people who'd become Kit's long-time friends: the elegant, privileged Andreini Players and young musician Claudio Monteverdi, not long since evicted from his cottage because a newly contracted, protected (spy) play-producer came to town and needed a place to stay.[198] Monteverdi introduced Kit to a fine lutenist, Salomon Rossi[199]—a real Jew, not a Marrano. There was dancing and singing, and Kit met a famous musical comedian, Flaminio (Flavio) Scala. Outside, a gamelan of frogs made its own music.

Next morning Harry left on his mission and Tom slept late, but Kit got up early (saw a mongoose running along the upstairs corridor—put it into his poem). He went back to the Sala de Troia with his notebook and studied the painted Trojans and Grecians. Then he and Tom left, heading for Venice.

They stopped in Verona, saw the crumbling five-story house where Juliet was said to have lived, saw shields of Flaminio Scala's family on several buildings. The shields showed a hawk sitting on a ladder, and Kit laughed and said, "that's a picture of me, waiting for the prisoner to come down." Tom looked blank, and Kit explained that after they reached Venice he hoped he'd be hired to sail to Constantinople on a mission to rescue a man from a Turkish jail. His friend Hen, in London, had given him a silk-gut ladder, very light and concealable, to help make the break—and Kit's college nickname was Merlin, the littlest hawk, right?

It didn't seem funny to Tom—the man was going off to get killed for sure.

At the duomo in Verona they saw the statues of Charlemagne's bravos, Roland and Oliver, standing at the big front door. "Two gentlemen like us," said Kit, and Tom said, "yeah, two bravi like us." They rode on, and at Padua boarded an old traggetto which took them into Venice.

Tom Lodge had often worked for England in Italy. He'd even been caught by the Inquisition trying to deliver gold to Resistance workers, coins he'd loaded into little pockets all over the inside of a specially-tailored suit.[200] The Inquisitors discovered the gold, and he was jailed but escaped to England. To account for his long absence from London he told everyone he'd been on a voyage to America.[201] After that, his SSS nickname was Golde, an anagram for Lodge.

In Venice Tom introduced Kit to Battista Guarini, who'd be Kit's Italian spymaster and friend for many years. Battista was spare, about fifty-five years old, with fair, graying, short-cropped hair and large sunken eyes of startling pale blue. He'd been professor of literature at the University of Ferrara[202] and worked undercover for Duke Alfonso and the Resistance. He'd just moved back to Venice from Mantua.[203]

Guarini approved Kit's mission to Turkey—the sooner the better—but secretly he felt the youth would not be coming back. He told Kit one of the prisoners in the tower—there were several—was an important Venetian, and that two ships, Silvestra and Liona, had left several weeks ago for Stambool[204] with instructions from the Secretary of the Council to deal for the gentleman's release, offering ransom money. Tough for Kit: it meant Turkish interest would be aroused and a heavier guard placed on the prison. Battista arranged immediate passage for Kit on a ship waiting for clearance at Malamocco. Kit saw his banker, bought some things for the job and soon embarked on a stop-and-go voyage to the Golden Horn.

Who were those prisoners? Some seem to belong to the continued story of Antonio, Prior of Ocrato, Pretender of Portugal. After fleeing to England, he repeatedly sent out expensive expeditions trying to win back Portugal and repeatedly failed. He'd recently sent his son to Constantinople to ask Sultan Murad, *again*, to confiscate the great fortune of Antonio's half-brother Alvaro Mendes (now servant of the sultan and governor of Mytilene),[205] and give half the proceeds to Turkey, half to Antonio.

Hearing of the plan, Mendes sent pirates who'd captured the legate's ship and transferred Antonio's son to a prison at Fez;[206] members of his train and some other passengers were sent on to Constantinople and presented as slaves to the sultan. Sort of a brotherly squabble.

At Stambool Kit learned that the slaves were not in small Leander's Tower, as he'd believed, but were kept together on the seventh floor of a big tower in an enormous fortress on the Bosphorus north of the city, Rumeli Hisar.[207]

Pretending to be the English ambassador's barber, Kit visited the slaves on several days, taking along a barber-surgeon's toolbag and providing the prisoners with means to cut a hole in their floor. Fifteen of them wanted to make the break.[208] The men worked with knives and bone-saw whenever they could. The floor was wood. (with tiles over it?) They cut a deep square in the floorboards almost but not quite through to the room below, and set tiles (or a bed?) back on top.

The prisoners made their move on a Friday, while the Janissaries were in their little mosque in the inner courtyard; all but the lookout at the front door of the tower were gathered in the mosque to pray. The barber debarked from his little boat, moored at the east entrance to the fortress, and before climbing the stairs to the prisoners' cell, drank with the guard, slipping him a sleeping potion. At a signal the men in the locked room jumped hard on the square, landed on the floor below, ran downstairs to the first floor through the rooms recently vacated by the Janissaries—and climbed out a window into the central courtyard. The hapless guard slept, out of sight. Fifteen prisoners sneaked through rough brush in the courtyard, past the soldier-filled mosque, to the east wall. Kit the sailor clambered up the rough surface (Rumeli Hisar had been hastily built by the Ottomani the year before they captured Constantinople—the wall was made of rough concrete with great chunks of ancient buildings stuck in as filler; pieces of columns and architraves stuck out.[209]) Kit fastened his silk-gut ladder to a projection so the other men could climb up, and soon all stood on the crenellated top. But on the water side—the water came right to the rampart[210]—it was a long way down, about 40 feet. Kit refastened the ladder, climbed down the fragile stretch, which wasn't quite long enough; they'd have to jump. Give thanks for the water. One by one, all fifteen came down, swam to the little boat, and one by one Kit helped them climb in under a sail he'd stretched across the deck. The boatman cast off—sounds of gunfire from the watch-station on the wall above—and the little craft shot away toward the city on the swift current. The freed men were quickly stowed aboard the two Venetian ships, Silvestre and Liona, which headed for home, slipping past Gallipoli in dark night.[211]

Sultan Murad, filled with fury when he heard the slaves were gone, ordered the grand vizier to detain English Ambassador Barton till the barber was produced.[212] Kit was questioned, thrown into prison and tortured[213] until time for the feast of Bairam. His knees were badly beaten.

He'd sent a note to Elizabeth—a visitor to the jail must have slipped it into the dispatch bag—but before it could have arrived the queen must have known and sent help. Like magic, an elegant English ship bedecked with flags sailed in, shooting salvos, laden with strange English novelties for the sultan and a big cargo of tin at a bargain price.[214]

And the sultan set Kit free.[215]

The Henry VI ciphers continue the story; a note from SSS chief Robert Cecil directed Kit to take a separate package of tin which Cecil had stolen from the cargo and sell it somewhere along the Black Sea coast. Ciphers tell of a clash with pirates and a typhoon that swept Kit's cargo overboard, broke up the ship and left the mariners beached, rebuilding for weeks. When they finally moved the ship into the road they found the tin, all slimy, on a sandbank, and sold it for Cecil in a city. (Shadows from another source suggest Trebizond.)

Back in Venice early in December, Marlowe sent home Lucrece, The Two Gentlemen, and Taming of The Shrew. (*A* Shrew, by Oxford, was an older play Kit had brought along for rewrite—Ned's concoction had perhaps been a malicious attack on Kit's mother, made to hurt Kit.[216])

Kit quickly prepared for his next chore, to go to Crete and buy all the sweet wine for sale there. The queen had given Essex lease of the farm of sweet wine in England[217] and he wanted to sell a lot and plow profit into his and Bacon's foreign service.

Kit talked shipping with Venetian merchants Francesco Rizzardi and Prospero Colombo. Crete had suffered dry years and a famine, and though pestilence was now in the air,[218] this would be the first year there'd be wine to sell, and the ship that got there first would get it. An old Venetian law forbade sailing in December—too dangerous—but Prospero and Francesco bent the rule and supplied Kit with one of their marciliane. He was to take a cargo of soap and sardines[219] to sell in Crete and bring back Essex's sweet wine. (All cargo destined for England from colonies of Venice had to transfer at the city before going out to the Atlantic.)

Using cover-name Giacomo (Jake) Coderin, Kit captained the ship, setting off on 15 December in the Rizzarda et Colombo. At first there were halcyon days, then a storm hit the ship off Cattaro, where they were glimpsed in trouble by a ship working up to Zara. Rain came down in great waterfalls; the cabin broke loose, slid forward and broke the mast. The hatch washed off; the pumps were manned. Kit looked down and saw his chest, with his clean suit in it—his legate's clothes—slip into the hold to float in the bilge.[220]

Jury-rigged, the Rizzarda et Colombo reached the forbidden Illyrian (Albanian) port of Durres, where Kit made friends and replaced the ship's mast before sailing on to Candia.

At the island's capital town, Duke Giandomenico (Zuan) Cicogna[221] eagerly accepted Essex's written proposals about wine. The duke came to the dock himself to supervise lading the casks.

Behind the row of date palms along the malecon, Kit could see a miniature ducal palace with graceful Venetian façade, and from a window on the top floor a beautiful dark-eyed girl was looking out at the dock. Kit fell in love with her. He asked the duke who she was—could he meet her? Cicogna said she was his daughter, contracted to be married to the Count Paris Avogadro, a man who'd be one of the treasurers of the colony in the coming year.[222] It was already arranged. But the duke didn't seem very happy about it. In fact, he was weeping.[223]

That evening, standing under her window, Kit spoke to the very young lady, introduced himself as the son of one of the great English queen's most favored advisers,[224] offered love and marriage if she'd come away with him in his little ship. He learned her name—Marina.[225] He sang a lovely song, sent up a bracelet made of his own hair. She was enchanted, and so was her nurse.

Years later, in a book Kit wrote for his and Marina's daughter, he looked back at himself as a wicked old kidnapper,[226] but then the girl and the captain were caught in a magic frame, where they remained till Marina's death.

When Essex's wine was loaded, and Kit sailed away, racing to reach Venice in twenty-two days, the girl and her nurse were on board below decks. (He tells how it was done in ciphers for Henry VI, Part 3.) Marina-Rita wore her pearl-embroidered wedding dress.[227]

When they reached the Venice lagoon Kit stopped, and they were married in a church of Santa Maria. (On the Lido? A church perhaps recommended by the nurse, Rita's aunt, who lived there.) A note of the wedding and the song of the sailors can be found in ciphers, Henry V and 3 Henry VI. Then their boat crossed the lagoon in fog and docked in the dead of night, surprising the ship-owners in the morning. Prospero and Francesco had just applied for their insurance, giving salvage rights to a firm in Cattaro,[228] but their ship was back, and in fairly good shape.

With the dowry Rita brought along in a package, the couple bought a little home in Padua. In Henry VI Part 3 ciphers, Kit protests (too much?) that he hadn't known about the money. Kit attended the university, sending back news of student activity to England. Rita, pregnant, kept house and sewed—they ran on the beach, and their summer was a dream of happiness.

Word came from London: Kit was expected to do the third chore he'd promised to undertake when he left England, a secret job in Rome he'd refused years ago. Duty bound, at the end of September, promising to be back before the baby was born, he rode to Rome, where he joined the household of Cardinal Allen, Queen Elizabeth's relentless enemy. Other SSS agents were already there, masquerading as the cardinal's servants.

On 16 October, 1594, Cardinal Allen died in the 16th day of an illness resulting from the presence of mercury sublimate in the honey butter, and on that day blind old Frank Engelfield was visiting. Though he couldn't see Kit, he may have recognized the voice of Arthur Dudley, the spy he'd met years ago in Madrid.

Kit barely escaped, pursued by Inquisition riders. He lost them at Siena[229] and reached Marina just before their baby girl was born.

Rita named the baby Isabel, for the great English queen. But the young mother hemorrhaged, and quite suddenly died.[230]

Kit asked members of Marina's family living in Venice for permission to bring her pale corpse to the Cicogna family vault, but the request was refused,[231] so he built her a lonely tomb on the beach by the lagoon, and on Hallowe'en laid her remains on a shelf inside, staying with her.[232]

Bereft, with no real SSS assignment and a baby girl and a dry-nurse (Marina's aunty-nurse and midwife at the birth) to care for, he bought a friendly milk cow and learned to milk so the baby could eat.

An SSS messenger (Bacon's Cousin Cooke?) arrived from England with pay. He wanted to take home two plays—one for Gray's Inn Christmas and one for Ned's daughter's wedding to the earl of Derby—a richer man than Hen. (So, did Ned forgive Kit?) The messenger could stay only a couple of weeks; it would take 25 days to get back to England.

Kit's Comedy of Errors was ready, and he slaved over changes to Midsummer Night's Dream, something he'd made for Rita. The messenger left on time with both scripts and a book, Scipio's Dream, which Kit had bought for Bacon.

Clouded months followed: Kit finished, polished Romeo and Juliet and tried to invent Pericles; he reached to the bottom of his trunk for The Troublesome Reign of John, rewrote it.

From his friend Miguel Cervantes in Spain came a letter inviting Kit and his family to stay with him at Seville, a kind, generous offer. In his ciphers, Kit calls Cervantes by his nickname, Manco—Crippled. Cervantes' left hand had been ruined years before when his gun exploded at the battle of Lepanto. Manco had been a loyal worker, friend and fellow agent of Kit since 1587, when Kit met him while scouting for Drake.

Having a place in Seville would give Kit advantage; from the great port of Seville he could gather Spanish news to send to England. So in spring he bought horses and set off from Padua with baby Isabel, her milk cow and her nurse. They crossed the mountains to Genoa and took ship for Valencia. The cow, though, refused to go aboard, and Kit was afraid the baby would starve without food on the voyage, but the trip turned out to be too rough even to think of eating. Kit details the story of the voyage and the long journey south from Valencia as a ciphered reminiscence in As You Like It.

On a rough, lonely mountain trail they found a young nobleman lying collapsed, heat-stricken, nearly unconscious, insisting he was dying for love. His name was

Cardenio. Kit and the nurse revived him, tied him on Isabel's horse with her and took him home to his castle, where his parents gratefully harbored the tired travelers and their animals (Kit had bought a new cow in Valencia), and gave them a fresh start on the road.[233]

At Seville Kit's cover was theological study at the church, and Cervantes loved the baby, who loved everything about being there. But Manco suffered terminal trouble with the Spanish government: he was falsely, egregiously, accused by Treasury accountants in Madrid who refused to pay him money due him for tax-collecting and instead figured he owed the crown. (Did they suspect he was a double agent?) Manco might go to prison. But after Kit made a fast trip to Naples and back, to move funds offered by the secret service chief there, things settled down toward year's end, and all members of the odd little family wintered happily together in Seville. During those months Kit may have written Richard II.

Early in 1596 Essex started planning a naval raid on Cádiz and sent word that he wanted Kit and Cervantes to scout the town; English ships would be sailing in, maybe in May. When the amah heard the news she was fearful, wanted to go home to Venice right away and take Isabel with her, out of harm's way. But Kit wanted Isabel to stay in Seville and go with him to Cádiz; he hoped that after the raid she might sail to England to be reared there. He took the nurse all the way home to Venice, managing some covert mission (with financier Manso?) at the same time, while Isabel stayed with Cervantes. When Kit got back to Seville, she'd grown a lot and was cheerfully speaking Spanish.

Time for the raid was approaching. Disguised as a new commissioner of ordnance, Cervantes, with Kit impersonating his clerk, visited the forts of Cádiz, tampering with lists of different sizes of ammunition to be provided for the various great guns which were trained on the harbor. Ersatz commissioner and clerk went themselves to shift the piles of cannonballs beside the big guns, moving bigger balls to stations by smaller guns and vice versa, mixing things up so the Spanish soldiers would have a hard time firing the cannons.

The scheme worked: History records that "artillery fire from the forts fell short of the marauders; many of the land guns were assigned ammunition that did not fit them; a number simply blew up."[234] In ciphers for Henry IV and Henry V, Kit tells about how they went in the rain from Seville to Cádiz to set things up.

Near the end of June the English ships appeared, and the raid was a great success for Essex. But though the English became masters of the harbor, soldiers drowned because Ralegh, wanting to go in ahead of everyone else, swept his ship past troops of English trying to wade to shore, heavily laden, at the edge of the town. Ralegh's wake knocked them galley west. Cervantes transmutes this happening to fiction in his Viaje del Parnaso, and Kit mentions it in ciphers for Henry IV Part I.

When the English left Cádiz, Kit and his little girl said goodbye to Cervantes and sailed aboard the flagship of Good Tom Howard, Admiral of the Third Squadron. On his knees, Kit begged Howard to find Isabel a home with "kind rich people," and the admiral said he himself would take care of her.[235]

Back in England under cover, Kit saw his family at Canterbury, then went to the palace for a reunion with the queen. They were making love when Lord Chamberlain William Brooke, Baron Cobham, walked in on them. Not recognizing Elizabeth without her wig, Brooke said hurtful things that made the distressed lady weep and gave Kit a hard time. After the air cleared and Kit thought everything was restored, the chamberlain surreptitiously returned as a voyeur. He was fired, and Kit made a special comedy for Elizabeth as a sort of apology, The Merry Wives of Windsor, in which a snoopy man using the name Brooke makes it his business to ferret out evidence of possible sexual misdemeanors. The play premiered on the night of the Garter Feast at which the new lord chamberlain-to-be, George Carey, was honored, and in its ciphers Kit tells of the unfortunate episode in the palace.

Elizabeth had read or seen parts of Kit's new Henry IV Part I and wanted to see Falstaff in love, so Kit put Falstaff in Merry Wives, too, but made him oddly fat, resembling Elizabeth's current suitor, corpulent Frederick, Duke of Württemberg—a man who years before, when he was Count Mömpelgard, had been called into Roger's circuit court at Windsor for horse-stealing. The play is filled with allusions to real people, both of Windsor and far-away Shorne, where Brooke lived next to Roger's old house on Gad's Hill, and attorney George Page and his wife were parishioners of Shorne Church. Kit slips inside jokes into Merry Wives, making fun of Dr. Caius of Cambridge, the physician who thought breast milk was the best food. (In the play, Dame Quickly is his "dry nurse."[236]) The comedy was expressly created to make the queen laugh.

For several months Kit stayed in England with his daughter and the Howards at Audley End and wrote The Merchant of Venice—its ciphers a critique of the play. Meanwhile, Essex sailed for the Azores with warships, while Bacon and Wotton and Essex's secretary Henry Cuffe attended a secret meeting in the Grisons about a protestant league, and then went to Padua U. law school before hurrying back to England—Bacon in the nick of time to attend Parliament, which the queen had postponed till he came home.[237]

Bacon had very quietly decided his partnership with Essex was to end; Robert Cecil had offered terms Bacon found more attractive, and the two of them apparently set out, now, to destroy their brother-half-brother Essex.

Essex, too, returned in autumn from his expedition, which is called a failure by historians, a success by Harry Wotton.[238]

As factor for Essex, Kit took two ships and precious cochineal captured in Cádiz to sell in Italy. Leaving the cochineal with the Leghorn agent of a Venetian merchant friend, Kit then sailed around to Venice, sold the two "hulls"[239] and went to winter at Battista Guarini's home, la Guarina, near San Bellino.

Guarini's old patron in Ferrara, Duke Alfonso, was dead, and it looked like the new duke, Cesare, was about to lose the whole state to the Pope. Essex had asked Kit to help Guarini save at least part of Ferrara for Cesare, and this Kit discusses in ciphers in Henry IV, Part I. Earlier in 1597 Guarini had been in Rome trying to deal with the Pope without success, but near the end of the year (the time was short) he and Kit went back with gold money for Clement VIII, and Modena and Reggio were ceded to Cesare, who was allowed to keep the title of duke.[240] Some success at last!

At the start of May 1598 everything was looking good at la Guarina when something awful happened: Guarini's daughter Anna was murdered by her own husband, Ercole Trotti, who'd been fooled into believing she was unfaithful.[241] Kit tried to dissuade Trotti, but the stupid man, incensed by a trick, killed the innocent lady. (It's not impossible that the murder was slyly provoked by Guarini's political enemies.) Kit tells the story in a strange, super-difficult, triple-ciphered treatment at the start of Much Ado About Nothing and treats it also in the plaintext, trying to show the blindness of the murderous man, who in the play is engaged but not yet married to the lady. Kit managed a happy end for Much Ado—Othello would be different.

Essex now sent Kit a message: he'd be wanted as staffer on Essex's Irish campaign in spring 1599. Kit, Tom Lodge, Harry Wotton and Tom Nashe were to go as aides, and Hen would be going in charge of cavalry.

In England at the end of 1598, the Chamberlain's Players took down the timbers of their old Theater at Holywell and barged them across the river to create what was to become the famous Globe Theater. Was Kit in England in time to help? He'd suggested the move in ciphers he wrote early in 1597, in Henry IV: "Bear Garden property available . . ." He'd outlined the process of carefully moving the building, to which he said they had a deed, as a way of getting a "dead drop on them." Ownership of the Holywell lot on which the building had stood was being disputed, and the man currently on top wanted much money for a new, unfavorable lease. The old lease had expired back in March 1597, and the Theater stood in danger of being destroyed by one or the other of its quarrelsome landlords.

The barge-move was made at night, and the Chamberlain's Men were helped by a stranger (a sailor?) calling himself William Smith, who was angrily mentioned in a complaint made by one of the former landlords.[242]

The first show played in the new Globe on the Bankside, on 12 and 13 June, 1599—was it Kit's earliest draft of Julius Caesar?

With much fanfare Essex left England for Ireland in March 1599, taking an army, and Kit was with him. Something of what happened to Essex and Hen there can be read in Essex's published letters to the queen and hers to him. What happened to Kit, Tom Lodge, Tom Nashe and Harry Wotton while they were there is ciphered into the beginning of Marlowe's play Troilus and Cressida. And in other ciphers, Kit speaks of his "Irish streak." He was sympathetic to the Irish.

It was a difficult campaign. Essex, boyish and gullible, seems to have followed wrong-headed confidential instructions from "friends" in England who wished him no good. After a rout in which two hundred fifty of his men fled, Essex, like a Roman general, further depleted his troops by decimating them, "for discipline."[243]

Hugh O'Neal, Earl of Tyrone, the man Essex had been sent to defeat, asked to parley, and Essex met him on 6 and 7 September at a river, Essex on the bank, Tyrone on his horse in the water. Essex had already told Kit and Tom Nashe to prepare a treaty that would let Essex go home (he'd tired of the conflict), so on those two days in September the "toy treaty," as Kit called it,[244] was agreed upon, and Essex sent home news of the pact to the queen. She wrote back that she hated it. Essex thought he should go talk to her, so he hurried to England, saw the queen at Nonsuch. Though it was early morning and she was deshabille when he rushed into her chamber, she was glad to see him. He went back later and she was fine, but the third time he talked to her she was changed, cold and distrustful, and said he didn't have permission to come home.

She appointed others to hear him. He was in house arrest at York House till March 1600 n.s. Then, still captive, he was moved to Essex House. A lot has been written about this situation,[245] but bare facts, and Kit's ciphers, make it obvious that Robert Cecil and Bacon were trying to move a brother out of the game. As they worked on Elizabeth, maybe telling her lies about things Essex was supposed to have said about her, his own attitude didn't help him: his excessive pride in his honor and his susceptibility to provocateurs (and to army-issue hash?) worked on his mind. He and Elizabeth became more and more alienated. Bacon smoothly claimed he'd tried and tried to help poor Essex.

Disgusted, Kit went to stay at Mary Herbert's Wilton House, wrote Troilus and Cressida (a bitter metamorphosis of Irish campaign memories), wrote a first draft of As You Like It for Mary to play at home, and they made desperate love before he went down to see the Walsinghams in Kent, then returned to London. In town he may have stayed in a room over Marco Lucchese's Italian restaurant, where downstairs Kit seems to have earned his meals telling stories to the diners.[246] He started a new play for Mary, Antony and Cleopatra, and did his best, without success, to make Essex capable of calmly discussing matters with Elizabeth.

He went to Canterbury, then to see Isabel at Audley End, and there Good Tom told him news: Judith and William Basset, friends of the Howard family and of Hen's foster mother, Mary Browne, had just lost a baby girl. Their physician may have warned Judith another pregnancy could be fatal, so the Bassets were talking of adopting Isabel as their own child; she'd become Elizabeth Basset, be reared a good Catholic, as her real mother would have wished, and as an only child she'd have not only a dowry but an inheritance.[247] Yes, said Kit, and it was done.

Essex, pent up, had become openly resentful of his mother the queen, saying rude things about her, recalling unkind words his dragon of a foster mother had spoken, and no doubt the queen was hurt. Kit advised the earl to write loving letters to Elizabeth. Essex said he'd tried that, and he didn't want to talk to Kit any more. Plainly, Bacon, Cecil and their provocative sidekicks were still managing the young man as well as the queen. Kit hid in town for months, listening. He was incensed by Ben Jonson's Cynthia's Revels, with its suggestion that the queen should kill Essex. The earl was in mortal danger; Kit could see that. He re-thought Much Ado about Nothing, and with the aid of an old story by Cinthio, a Ferrarese author who'd been a friend of Guarini's family long ago, Kit began to write a tragedy—the story of a big-hearted leader, a man instead of a queen, led to destroy someone beloved—Desdemona, not Essex—fooled by sly machinations of an envious villain—roll Bacon and Cecil into Iago. Not that simple—keep working. The play would become Othello.

Essex finally broke. He set off with a few foolish real friends and some false ones, intending to enter the palace at Whitehall and remove, probably kill, the hated people he'd find whispering lies in his mother's ears.

He didn't get anywhere near the palace. The bishop of London and Roger Manwood's son-in law Sir John Leveson stopped him,[248] and after a dangerous scuffle Essex went down to the river, and he and his men took boats back to Essex House.

Before he'd left for the palace that day Essex had locked in his library the Lord Keeper and other very important people whom the queen had sent that morning as emissaries. They were released when Essex returned, and he went up, lost, onto the roof. His secret brother Robert Sidney came and stood in the yard, trying to talk him down. They called each other brother, brother, and Essex asked how would Sidney feel about being penned up so long?[249] Essex finally came down. The trial was quick and shocking: Bacon and Cecil had it their way.

Hen had gone along with Essex on the aborted trip toward the palace, and both were sent to the Tower under sentence of death. Essex was beheaded on 25 February 1601 new style, and according to Kit's ciphers in As You Like It, Hen was left in the Tower in a cramped dark cell.

Some Essex followers were put in house arrest; others were hanged or beheaded; there were suicides. Loyal men who could manage to go left town: Harry Wotton crossed the Channel, Tom Lodge disappeared. Kit badly wanted to get out, but he stayed trying to save Hen's life and get him a room in the Tower with a window and a desk. Frightened, he went into the palace to talk to the queen. (Another of Essex's men had gone to talk to her and had been dragged away and executed.[250]) She was kind to Kit, and during a last assignation he persuaded her not to kill Hen: "best not t' behead al the goy-lad youth in th' family."[251]

The Essex affair reverberated through Europe. Crowned heads who'd known the young man as Elizabeth's son could hardly forgive her. Easy to see she'd been fooled. The spate of hangings finished, some of Cecil-and-Bacon's double agents melted away with fat rewards, and Kit's second dream of possessing political influence was gone.

His first hope, of course, had been that he might aid Ned de Vere if Ned inherited the throne. Now Kit looked back on those days, and starting with the sketch he and Tom Kyd once worked on, created a serious study of Ned that became an early version of Hamlet.

The queen, always good to Kit, gave him a year's work in Venice. He was to take along a band of young actors and playwrights to be trained in Catholicism so they could come home and work as chaplains (really as secret intelligencers) in the houses of Catholic noblemen. Ben Jonson went along as SSS agent "Mr. Fox."[252]

When he reached Venice, Kit went to the primitive tomb he'd made for Rita on the beach, then begged her father once more to let her body be moved to the Cicogna family vault on the tomb isle. The duke said yes and carried her corpse to his boat, and Rita was laid to rest beside her mother. Cicogna was kind to Marlowe at last, and invited him and the young students with him to a ball at his palace.[253]

At start of summer 1602, as soon as Kit returned to England with his educated honest men, he and Ben Jonson wrote new dialogue for Tom Kyd's old Spanish Tragedy. Ben fronted as author of the additions, and they split the fee.[254]

On a visit to Audley End Kit learned that Isabel's adopted father William had died in December, and the little girl, still living at Audley End, was now an heiress in the hands of the Court of Wards.[255] Her first guardian, Lord Henry Cobham, kept her wardship for two days in May, then sold it to Ralegh, with Robert Cecil signing as witness. On the day Ralegh bought the wardship he made a private written agreement with Robert Cecil stating that Ralegh's purchase from Cobham was truly meant to be in trust "to the only use and behoof of the said Robert Cecil." Cecil coveted the wardship—it was lucrative—but since he was Master of Wards he didn't want it recorded in the book that he'd given it to himself.

Broken-hearted about Essex, Queen Elizabeth tried to be cheerful, sociable, attend to business. She set off on Progress. On 31 July 1602, she was welcomed at Harefield by Thomas Egerton, who entertained her (did he know what he was doing?) with a tryout of the new tragedy called Othello.[256] Eyes opened, she realized what Bacon and Cecil had done to their brother—too rough to contemplate. Too late, too late. She must die.

She thought of the succession: Wriothesley would live but never be king. Ned was dying of an incurable disease. Bacon? Never! Cecil? She could barely speak to him. Robert Sidney? Long ago, he'd said no. James Stuart would have to do.

On 14 January the royal court moved upriver to Richmond, where Elizabeth, deeply depressed, planned to retire till death came. But on 17 January she made a last trip back to London, to the Charterhouse, where she visited Good Tom Howard.[257] I believe she came to meet one of her royal wards and talk to Howard about the child, Kit's daughter.

There's a story in Cervantes' Novelas Ejemplares, "La Española Inglesa," about a little orphan girl brought to England after the Cádiz raid by an admiral of the English fleet, and the child's later interview with Queen Elizabeth, an interview which Cervantes may have described just as Kit told it to him: In Cervantes' story the child was "about seven years old, more or less," and her name was Isabela. She was dressed in a pearl-embroidered gown.

The child knelt and greeted her sovereign. Self-possessed, darkly beautiful, Isabel was really 9 years old but was supposed to be younger. In the story she spoke freely in Spanish and English, and the queen was charmed. Someone said, "but the girl's Catholic!" and the queen replied that Isabela was loyal to her mother's faith, and loyalty was an admirable trait. Did Elizabeth go to the Charterhouse that day to do a good turn for Kit? She may have signed a directive conveying Isabel-Elizabeth out of Cecil's wardship, freeing her of taxation and loss of her rents to Cecil, freeing her of duty to marry the man Cecil would have chosen for her. The queen could have done this; after all, though Cecil was Master of Wards, Isabela was Hoo-Hoo's Royal Ward and Citt-Citt's daughter, and as years passed, it became obvious that her estate was not plundered and she was able to marry a man she knew and liked. In Cervantes' story the admiral who'd been taking care of Isabela brought her to London to ask the Queen's permission for the girl to marry the admiral's son, and in 1613 the real Isabel did marry young Henry Howard, the admiral's third son. In the story it was made clear that the queen's permission was necessary, and after the queen said she esteemed Isabela as her own daughter, the child got down on her knees again and said, "now that you've given me the name of daughter, no matter what happens, what evil can I fear, or what good fortune can I not hope for?"

Elizabeth returned to Richmond. Retired, silent, she suffered a throat infection near the end of February, sat on pillows on the floor, refused food and liquid. Did she think of Tantalus, deprived of food and drink forever because he'd killed his own son? Finally she was lifted into bed, given broth—too late. As she lay dying, she called the wicked Archbishop Whitgift to kneel beside her and pray, for hours. When he'd try to leave, she'd move her arm and hand, and he'd have to go on praying. She got a little of her own back.

f

Marlowe's Life, Part III

His queen gone, Marlowe was nowhere. There were no jobs in Italy; he hid out in London undercover. No longer a friend of Francis Bacon, he wrote some letters for the man, who was still Marlowe's government chief.

King James and his family came from Scotland, and after his coronation he made Bacon a knight, and Hen was freed from the Tower and granted governorship of the Isle of Wight. Hen suggested to James that if Marlowe could be pardoned he'd be a good on-the-spot administrator. That gave Kit hope, and he wrote the news to Cervantes.[258]

Widowed, Mary Sidney Herbert was living at Wilton House, and late in August 1603 the king went there to see a performance of As You Like It. Mary wrote to her son, "we have the man Shakespeare with us."[259] After the show, Mary may have asked the king to pardon Marlowe; if she did, her request was refused.

But a change was coming for Kit. Some weeks later the earl of Northumberland's secretary, Dudley Carleton, to whom Kit had written about hard times,[260] may have had an idea that would change Kit's life and give him a legitimate job with a salary. King James, planning to open an embassy at Venice, chose Henry Wotton to be ambassador there. Kit applied to be part of the embassy, and it was decided that using his name Gregorio, he'd serve as Harry's Italian social secretary, his "secretary of compliments," and be mediator with the Venice Collegio.

So in February 1604 new style, Kit was at Mary's Wilton House, saying goodbye, polishing As You Like It and her special play Twelfth Night. Inside Twelfth Night he put two ciphered love-letters for her, with a farewell, "Watch the post!"

Early in March Kit may have left England, perhaps with a group of English players bound for the Frankfurt Easter Fair. If so, he left them there and headed for Venice to set things up for Harry's arrival. As soon as he, as Gregorio, reached the city, he leased the Palazzo da Silva, a handsome old house in Cannaregio near the Ponte degli Ormesani and the entrance to the Ghetto.[261] Singing nuns in a nearby convent made him think of his early play Measure for Measure, which he would now reshape. The palace wouldn't be vacant till December, so he rented temporary quarters too, and a villa with a garden at Noventa, on the River Brenta, as a retreat for Harry.[262]

Kit-Gregorio settled down to write. Ned de Vere had died in June, and when Kit heard about it he fiercely revamped Hamlet, rearranging scenes, deleting and adding lines. He inserted "goodnight, sweet Prince,/And flights of Angels sing thee to thy rest." He also made a new sonnet containing uncomplimentary ciphers about Ned. Gregorio wrote to Cervantes, giving news about Isabel and about his own job as secretary of compliments, and Manco replied: an approaching thaw of Spanish-English relations would be sending Spanish envoys to London, and if a treaty were signed, a great party would be held in Valladolid next spring. Funded by Gianbattista Manso in Naples, Manco was setting up a Valladolid observatory from which he'd report the pulse of peace, if it came to pass, to the underground community. Cervantes' honest-men reporters would include his family and actors from the new Vallejo Company. Kit made a note: Harry should subscribe to Cervantes' newsletters.

Don Quixote I was finished now, and sold to Francisco de Robles, and at the last minute, thinking of Kit, Manco had put in a bit about how Sancho Panza might become governor of an island.[263]

On Friday, 13 July 1604, Sir Henry Wotton quit London for Venice.

Guarini, who'd been working in Urbino, came to discuss the peace party with Gregorio in Venice, and together they read Othello, the play so close to Anna Guarini's murder. Kit would soon send the revised tragedy to England along with newly polished versions of Measure for Measure and Hamlet.

September brought Harry and his "family" of attachés to Venice. At the end of the month, Wotton, his train and all English subjects in Venice and Padua, were taken in gondolas to Isla San Spiritu, where they entered the monastery gardens to meet sixty splendid Venetian senators.[264]

On the first of December the embassy moved into the Palazzo da Silva, already furnished with elegant green leather chairs rented from merchants in the Ghetto. Venetian law prohibited Wotton from socializing with any Venetian nobles, so the embassy was an island; they spent evenings reading, writing, playing cards and making music—Harry played the cello. (Years later Kit sent a viola home to his friend Mike Hickes.[265])

Harry's chaplain Nathaniel Fletcher was a brother of a playwright who'd studied at Kit's college, and it wasn't long before Nathaniel knew about Kit's secret identity.

Harry Wotton must have felt he was on probation. He was only thirty-six and had never before held a diplomatic post, so when Doge Marino Grimani secretly asked an irregular favor, Harry panicked and decided he must comply. Through a dark glass we see an evil kinsman of the Doge, Mauritzio Cavagion, who lived with two sons in Vicenza. These ruffians were extorting protection money from the licensed prostitutes of Venice—bleeding a source of city revenue—but since the men were Grimani's relatives (in-laws?) he didn't want public accusations and a court case. Did Wotton possess a bravo? It would be good if all three Cavagioni were to die, but the Doge must not be implicated. Harry may have begged Kit to do the job so the English Embassy wouldn't be in mal odeur before it even started to function. Anyway, Kit agreed.

The Cavagioni lived in a well-guarded villa and were not seen walking on the street. At Easter and Christmas, however, all citizens of the Republic were required to attend church, so on 9 April, waiting for Easter, Kit hired two "broken men" to help him, and next day when Cavagion and his boys appeared at the Vicenza duomo for Easter mass, Kit knifed and killed the father. The sons eluded the broken men, but Kit got his accomplices out and away down Carpan Street, and they disappeared over the bridge.[266]

Grimani was irked because the sons were still alive, so Kit suggested a stakeout at a high class bordel, the only one where the Cavagion boys themselves were ever seen. Kit said he'd work things out when he returned in July after doing another job.

Shocked more than Harry understood, Kit left for the Peace Party at Valladolid, where Cervantes joyfully greeted him. Don Quixote was in print and had made Manco famous, though not rich. Man-of-the-hour Cervantes, his friend Juana Gaitan and his sister Magdalena toured the crowded town, probably with under-cover-Kit. Kit in disguise may even have stayed in Cervantes' apartments. Last autumn Manco, family and friends had moved into three floors of a still-unfinished building in a new slum, the Rastro quarter of Valladolid, and lots of colorful people were jammed in there. Manco's biographer infers he was patriarch of a seamstress-shop bordello. No, he was presiding over a nest of Peace-Party observers—among the friends staying there till next June were young actors who in later years would be famous members of the Vallejo Company, probably paid now, in 1605, to mingle under cover with the guests at functions during the Party and to report to their government chiefs.[267]

About four hundred English dignitaries were in the city, and with them came their own secret service guards.[268] With the English SSS were Kit's old friends from the St. George Tavern, intelligencers John and Jane Davenant (they'd moved to Oxford, changing their operation to student-watching).[269] They told him that Bacon, who'd hoped for advancement from Cecil after prosecuting Essex, was instead being left behind his legal confrères.

Everyone was drinking too much, and Kit asked Jane just once more, after all these years, to go to bed with him. Yes, she said—she loved him. She sensed his desperation—he confessed his crime at Vicenza—she comforted him.[270]

Too soon Kit was called back to Venice, where he found Harry upset. The Collegio, incited by the irritable Doge, had been hostile. If only the Cavagion affair hadn't been left at loose ends!

At once Kit, using name Augustine Carpan, hired two bravi and arranged room and board at the stakeout spot, the house of a licensed madame on the island of Murano, in a neighborhood of gardens and rich merchants' homes. Kit's friend the exporter Carlo Helman, recently dead, had lived here, and Kit visited the family, knew their gatekeeper.

Kit and his bravi spent a lot of time playing cards with the madame at the bordel, waiting for a shakedown visit from the young Ca'gioni. But the extortionists saw Kit on the street, recognized him and planned his ruin. They bribed a young prostitute of the house, who told the madame some new clothes would be delivered to the girl's room upstairs, in a big basket. Really the basket held her eight-year old sister Antonia, drugged to sleep and deflowered by their impoverished father on the promise of a rich dowry for the child if the trick worked.

Upstairs, Kit woke in the night; there was blood all over the bed. A child—it looked dead—lay naked beside him, apparently bleeding. (The tricksters had poured pig-blood over Antonia.) Hearing steps in the corridor, Kit jumped naked from the balcony into the garden below and ran out onto the street. He turned the corner, banged on Helman's gate—it was a long time before the gatekeeper answered.

Kit returned to the embassy, but the police, no doubt sent by the angry Doge, had been in his room; his clothes and money were gone. Part of the money would be set aside for the child's dowry, and the surprised madame, imprisoned, was also fined for Antonia's benefit. Convicted in absentia in his cover name, Augustine Carpan,[271] Kit slipped out of town with borrowed money and fled to England. He'd tried to do Grimani a favor, and now the man was an enemy.

At Canterbury, sad news; Kit's legal father John Marley had died in January, and Kate—Kate was gone, too! The ship was sinking.[272]

Near the end of August, Kit's friend Sam Daniel left London for Oxford to see one of his plays performed before the king. Kit went along, and there at Oxford he saw Jane Davenant, who confided she might be pregnant with his child.

At the Oxford parties for James there was "provision made for a magician." Kit was good at sleight of hand—in ciphers for King Lear he says, "I can juggle, too." Prestidigitation may have helped pay his way at the gala. He always thought of himself as a clown.

The King, out walking on the day he arrived, had been greeted by Mathew Gwynne's sketch of "tres Sibyllae." James was intrigued, and his interest may have inspired Kit's idea for the three witches in Macbeth, [273] which was swiftly appearing on paper, laced with startling scraps of memories from Kit's day at Vicenza and the night at the island bordello.

His two efforts to eliminate the Cavagion gang had left Kit with serious emotional problems, but he was writing in every spare hour; his old play King Leir would soon become King Lear.

A lot is known about the multiple sources used in his plays; Lear and Macbeth are well-seeded with historic as well as contemporary incidents, including the Gunpowder Plot and some recent fluttering pages of Archpriest Controversy. But at bottom these two deep tragedies of Kit's are motivated by experiences: The blood-spattered, blood-soaked dialogue in both works returns double entendre, over and over, to the awful killing in Vicenza, the awful night of the frame-up in Murano. Emily Dickenson wrote:

> The Outer—from the Inner
> Derives its magnitude—
> 'Tis Duke, or Dwarf, according
> As is the Central Mood—
>
> The fine—unwavering Axis—
> That regulates the Wheel—

Though spokes—spin—more conspicuous
And fling a dust—the while.

The Inner—paints the Outer—
The Brush without the Hand—
Its Picture publishes—precise—
As is the inner Brand—

On fine—Arterial Canvas—
A Cheek—perhaps a Brow—
The Star's whole Secret—in the Lake—
Eyes were not meant to know.

Kit returned to Valladolid in September. Harry may have told him not to go back to the Venice embassy—the angry Doge could be looking for him. Manco tried to help him write in Spanish, and Kit made a stab with Milon y Berta, using the name of a friend, Antonio de Eslava, as out-front byline. In Valladolid Kit met Manco's patron, Pedro de Castro, Count of Lemos,[274] a friendly young man who said someday he'd be viceroy in Naples, and he meant to take with him many good poets and dramatists, including Cervantes. Kit said he'd like to go, too.

At year's end, Doge Marino Grimani died, Harry presented his condolences, and Kit went back to Venice.

Harry's chaplain Nathaniel Fletcher, called home to England, was soon replaced by William Bedell,[275] a humane man who admired Kit. Bedell was helping Harry meet and deal with the learned friar Paolo Sarpi, a hardboiled chief intent on politically distancing Venice from the Vatican, and that was what Harry wanted; he secretly dreamed the Republic might someday forget the Pope altogether.

The genial new Doge, Leonardo Donato, was a friend of the Resistance, and his stance gave Harry hope.

Back in England, James, who at first leaned toward Catholic toleration, had been prodded towards a harsher view. Suddenly the king was made an adversary of the Pope by a Catholic plot (Cecil and Bacon SSS incited), a scheme to kill king and council at Westminster by exploding gunpowder in the cellar of the house of Parliament. As a provocateur, Ben Jonson had used his bricklaying skill to cut out and modify cellar walls. At the last minute he faded and the plot was revealed in time, leaving James shaken and anti-Catholic.[276]

So James encouraged Venice to stand up against offensive dicta of Paul V, and Harry, translating James' remarks, embroidered them, letting the Doge believe a great naval alliance had been promised. Donato refused to deliver to Rome two priests on trial in Venice, and the angry Pope excommunicated the Republic! Donato ordered Venetian church-people to go on working; the Jesuits refused and were ejected.[277]

Battista Guarini was sent to Rome as secret correspondent for Venice and stayed there till a settlement was made.[278]

Kit was dispatched toward Milan to rob the posts of Jesuit packets. With unique skill he removed seals (using that heated shoemaker's knife sharp all the way around), copied the contents of Jesuit messages, replaced the undamaged wax and sent the packets on their way, turning over the copies to Harry for Doge Donato. (King Lear. Act 4. 6. "Leaue, gentle waxe, and manners: blame vs not / To know our enemies mindes, we rip their hearts; /Their papers is more lawfull.")

On this tour of duty Kit's path led to a country place at Colorno belonging to Barbara Sanseverino, Countess of Sala, related to a fiercely anti-Inquisition nobleman of Salerno. Salerno was an ancient seat of freedom of religion, even of cooperative religions, but Barbara was not tolerant: she was a steely singleminded undercover worker against Spain and the Holy Office. Not young, but still a slim, glittering beauty, Barbara had been in line of duty the mistress of a super-Catholic duke of Parma. Using a flock of elegantly dressed little dwarves traveling by coach, she sent overt gifts and secret messages to courtier-agents in the capitals of Italy and received their replies carried by her tiny helpers. Barbara enjoyed presiding over meetings of the literary club of the Amorevoli,[279] and Kit may have paused there to polish plays. Also he seems to have visited Mantua, for the next play produced there by his friend Giambattista Andreini was set in a Scottish forest and a Scottish castle.[280]

Back in Venice there was a letter from Jane Davenant about her new baby boy, born in February. His name was William; his eyes were like Kit's.

In that year Harry asked Gregorio to oversee printing of anti-papal pamphlets on a press owned by G. B. Ciotti, Guarini's publisher. Harry's partner in this enterprise was the famous friar Paolo Sarpi, now the Republic's ecclesiastical counsellor,[281] who said they should fix it so Gregorio would be blamed if the printed pieces were discovered by the Nuncio. Unfazed, Kit wrote and sent home Antony and Cleopatra.

Donato, Harry and Paolo Sarpi secretly cooperated to frame demands for concessions from Rome, and though to Harry's embarrassment James backed away, Navarre, now Henri IV, stepped in to arrange with the Pope terms favorable to Venice. The dispute ended in spring 1607, resentment smoldering in the Vatican.

Meanwhile in England Bacon looked in vain for favor from James, who'd been good to Elizabeth's other surviving children. James felt he could do no more than suffer this presumptuous man whose natural father, Walsingham, brought James's mother to her death, and Bacon had brutally prosecuted James's friend Essex at his trial.

Though James wouldn't help Bacon, Cecil might; he wanted to deal with a lawyer who had some not-very-well-dowered stepdaughters to marry off, and Cecil suggested to Bacon that if he'd marry one of them, good things would happen. Early in May 1606 Bacon married[282] and was left in the cold the next time promotions were given. A burning fury possessed him—he was Queen Elizabeth's eldest living son, and just before he was born she'd secretly married her lover Dudley. Though that man wasn't his biological father, Bacon was convinced the ceremony legitimized the baby she was carrying. *He* should be king!

In Venice, Harry took advantage of the Pope's retreat by pushing religious reform, and the Pope complained that the ambassador was promulgating heretical printed materials, entertaining Venetian theologians. Not so, said Donato. Idealistic publisher Ciotti said he believed in a publisher's right to print all opinions, but though Kit spent lots of time at the printery, it was nothing he enjoyed. He had a full-time job at the embassy, letters to write and necessary visits to the Collegio and the Council of Ten.

In March and April Harry went to Cabinet and Collegio asking that Girolamo Monte of Vicenza be pardoned for causing the death of Cavagion, and declaring that Augustine Carpan was innocent of all charges. In April Girolomo Monte was pardoned, but there was no word about Carpan.

Life at the Palazzo da Silva continued to be familial. Harry kept messenger pigeons on the roof; Kit brought home an ape given him by a sailor. Musical evenings and play-parties were enjoyed and the billiard-room was popular. A copy of a new edition of Don Quixote I came in the post, but though Wotton was familiar with Italian he couldn't easily read Spanish. Kit wrote an off-hand translation of the whole book, later published with byline Thomas Shelton, but Harry never seemed to have time to read it.

In September 1607 Guarini came to Venice for the winter. Kit introduced him to friends—some married ones—and the cronies spent evenings at one anothers' houses and apartments roasting pears and chestnuts, telling stories that provoked different critiques. Kit tried to put that into a book in Spanish for Isabel, who was old enough for grown-up instruction, as he says in his ciphered introduction for her ("various severe appraisals of love, decency and reason"). The book is Noches de Invierno—Winter Nights[283]—not severe at all, but rambling and romantic. The language tripped him up, but he kept trying. He signed his work Antonio de Eslava at the suggestion of a clerical friend in Valladolid, Ivan Eslava. The frontispiece coat of arms may be that of the book's patron Mauleon, or Kit could have made it up; across the top, a chain loops back and forth; below it, Kit's real father's coat of arms, a lion rampant facing left, appears near a phalanx of nine little men with bodies like trees. (A Manwood? Birnam Wood starting to move?) There's a cross on two foundations, a checkerboard, some bands, and a boar under a cloud. (The badge of Kit's SSS employer Bacon was a boar, and so was Ned's.)

In January 1608 young Englishman Juley Caesar died at Padua, impaled *en brochette* by his fencing instructor Brochetta, and the embassy necessarily investigated the deed. Kit might have sat down then to rewrite his early Julius Caesar, creating the sophisticated play he left us.

One day two big boxes marked Books came from England to Harry's chaplain Bedell, and at once the Nuncio suspected they were boxes crammed with heresies.[284] No one has ever revealed what was in them. Could they have held the script, or galleys, for the Bible James had ordered? For almost three years fifty-four learned men had labored to revise the Bishop's Bible, and though their work was nearly done, few

Doctors of Divinity were poets. James may have asked Kit to improve the phrasing of awkward passages, which he'd have done gladly.

There was a great wedding festival in Mantua that May and June—an astonishingly convoluted comedy by Battista Guarini premiered, along with an entr'acte sent by Cervantes[285] and the bloody tragedy by Andreini set in the Scottish castle. Claudio Monteverdi was there, and Battista and Gregorio wrote lyrics for some of Claudio's madrigals, Gregorio's wryly ciphered in English.[286]

When Kit went back to Venice he wrote Coriolanus, thinking about Essex, and then revised Antony and Cleopatra. In ciphers for the revision he says he's angry with Shakespeare, who'd cut the first run short—perhaps because he didn't like all the brief proto-cinematic scenes, set in many different places. Kit rewrote but left them in.[287]

Young Tom Coryate came from London with news from Kit's friends at the Mitre and Mermaid, and Kit showed him the city, making up funny stories about various attractions, which Tom put in his travel book. When he got home he had trouble finding a publisher; the work was finally published in 1611, partly by W.S., partly by Thomas Thorpe.[288]

September 1608: Kit left for Spain as intelligencer, taking along a script of Noches de Invierno and his translation of Don Quixote to show Cervantes. Manco suggested that someone he knew named Mauleon might be a patron for Noches, might give Kit some money, but though the book's plaintext was dedicated to him, Mauleon hated the thing, and Manco, offended, put a few unkind remarks about the man in The Dogs' Colloquy. Manco took Kit to visit the Count of Lemos, who was indeed going to Naples, and Lemos repeated his offer to take the friends as court-poets.

As soon as he came back to Venice and went to Ciotti's printery, Kit heard news from the Bookmen's Guild: any copies received of a book by King James on religious reform were to be handed over to the Inquisition.[289] When Harry learned this he tore his hair, said he was through, told the Collegio he was going home—and then cooled off. But he was tired. Making Venetians into protestants wasn't easy after all.

Bacon was in trouble; he'd wanted SSS to fund a band of young investigative natural scientists, roaming students who'd go from university to university across Europe, collecting information on natural phenomena (and on current political climates), sending home data (and coded intelligence reports). He'd even phase out the Theater Wing to pay for this upgrade of the Service. Cecil, convinced Bacon had lost touch with reality, fired him, saying he could run SSS by himself. And forget the Theater Wing. Bacon could take his homing pigeons, his actors and legends and science-magic—he was through!

Bitter, Bacon withdrew. He knew Cecil had been manipulating Parliament, trying to strip James of power in exchange for a steady allowance of funds. Because the king maintained lavish separate households for himself, his wife and Prince Henry, royal debts were growing fast. Bacon would quietly shift his loyalty from Cecil to James, finding a little money for him so he could weather the parliamentary squall.

Bacon was writing a book on ancient stories "available for the instruction of modern man,"[290] and leafing through legends he came to one about Trophonius, a needy prince who fixed a removable stone into the wall of a treasury forbidden to him, so he could take out all the money he wanted. How simple! Bacon took private banker Mike Hickes into his confidence, and old Julius Caesar, and Lord Knevet, Treasurer of the Household, and soon Ben Jonson found a place to make a hole in the cellar of the Mint, and many bars of silver and chests of silver coin were carried off at night from this modern Trophonean Den. The accounts were tampered with so it looked like very little silver had been taken in.[291]

Without Bacon, unbalanced though he was, Cecil didn't do well. James had made Bacon Solicitor, his reversion to the clerkship of Star Chamber had come through, his bride's few row-house rents helped out. Let Cecil swing or fade away.

Harry's salary was sent to Venice irregularly, sometimes not at all. Kit washed dishes, brought home firewood, and they began to depend on the orchard at the villa for more than landscape. The roof-cote messenger-pigeons that used to come from Bacon's man Toby Mathew in Florence were cooked for stew. Kit dug into his trunk for old plays that might be revamped for sale in England, worked them over and sent off pot-boilers. He spent extra time refashioning a play Ned had given him for revision many years ago—Kit thought it might be a present for Isabel. He called it Cymbeline.[292]

In 1609 a sheaf of sonnets was published in London by Marlowe's old publisher Thomas Thorpe. Did Kit send them north along with Cymbeline and other redone things? Surmises about provenance have been published, but nobody knows. A facsimile of the quarto Shake-speares Sonnets shows that the poems have been slightly arranged by subject, and they're as good inside as outside, which is saying a lot, for there's some beautiful writing in the plaintexts of these largely ignored little works. The ones I've analysed are ciphered all the way through. The book deserves careful study, for decipherment of all hundred fifty-four poems would add much to Marlowe's biography.

In the same year, Kit's long-ago lover and betrayer Emilia Bassano Lanier (excoriated in the sonnets), was polishing a book of her own, serious, stiff but well done and holier than thou or anyone, to be ready for publication in 1611.[293]

In Venice, news came to Guarini from agent G.B. Marino in Turin: Savoy and Henri IV were preparing an attack on Milan that would knock the Spaniards out of north Italy! Wotton was not elated; he disapproved of Henri IV because he'd turned Catholic. Since Harry was in a bad mood, Kit, Guarini and Resistance people rode down to San Bellino to celebrate, and when they came back they heard a shocking report: Henri IV had been murdered! A terrible blow to the Resistance! Guarini went to Rome to listen, and Kit stayed to help Harry, who'd gone to bed sick, wanting to go home.[294]

Early in June 1610 Kit rode to Naples hoping to see the count of Lemos arrive as viceroy. Just in time! Kit, as Antonio de Laredo, got a job at the palace; he was to bring news from Venice and do intramural investigation as well as being generally useful, writing letters and acting as play-party director for naïve Lemos. (The news from Venice would be nothing startling, and all the time Kit would be listening for Spanish plans.)

Manco was not part of the viceroy's court—a sad surprise for Kit. The man in charge of poets said Cervantes was, well, too ill to make the trip.

The Sanchez Playing Company, part of Lemos' cultural retinue, was getting off the boat in Naples,[295] and when Kit met their leading lady he was lost. For years he'd been making out with sailors, a poet or two, and now here was this magnificent creature! Micaela Lujan[296] was a gifted singing, dancing actress. She's in encyclopedias of music, and actors' rosters list her among top performers of Spain, 1604-1616. She liked Kit, and right away they found a rough, private little shack at the beach where they made a home. She cooked for him, and they went swimming and hiking when she wasn't on stage—astonishing! She wanted to give him babies; she thought they'd surely turn out to be good writers. He said as a couple they were too theatrical, too old to have children. Even if they could, he didn't want to be mixed up with Catholic-Church family rules. But she was hurt and insistent, so he said they'd try.[297]

At the end of August he had to ride to Venice to take news to Harry and get some, and some money to bring back. Good luck—a job moonlighting on the waterfront—100 ducats from a Scots captain to recover a bill of sale for freight the captain brought from Trapani.[298]

Sir Dudley Carleton would arrive at year's end to be the new ambassador,[299] and Kit should be there, but not till then. Back to Naples he went, to stay till late November. He may have sailed around the south coast; he now had a little ship.

Cervantes wrote to Kit and Micaela, sorry he couldn't be part of Lemos' train. He didn't know why. No, he wasn't sick. For news: the duke of Osuna was on his way to be viceroy in Sicily, and he and his wife would stop to visit Lemos and his wife at Naples. That reminded Kit of an old story, and he wrote The Winter Nights Tale, with a long newsy ciphered letter to Hen inside. He also made a comedy in Italian for Micaela, L'Ippolito, using byline Gregorio de' Monti. She starred as sort of a Blue Fairy who saved her young protégé from serious scrapes by appearing in disguise in the nick of time. The show was a hit—the Folger has a copy of the third edition.[300]

Micaela confessed to Kit that she'd come to Naples on assignment from Lope de Vega, a member of the spy family.[301] Lope was a dramatist who worked for the Duke of Sessa. She'd been told to watch Viceroy Lemos for signs of detachment from Spain, because Lemos and the Duke of Osuna were suspected of planning to take Naples and all of south Italy for their own.

For more than twelve years Micaela had been working for Lope in Madrid; she'd loved him, loaned him money, borne him children. He'd been married when she met him, and he'd always figured to keep Micaela only as mistress and agent. When she boarded the boat for Naples she decided not to go back—and now she belonged to Kit.

Kit told her about his work, how dangerous it was and how careful they must be. Yes, Osuna[302] was a real worry; he and his brainy side-kick Quevedo[303] were thinking about a plan to subdue Venice and use the city as a stepping stone so the Spanish army in Italy could climb over Austrian Alps to Holland (where there was a truce), and then move across the Channel to England, a country they'd coveted ever since Philip II had to leave it long ago.

Why did Micaela and Kit, two middle-aged sophisticates from rival countries, trust each other? Tell me.

Returning to the English embassy in Venice in November, Kit found Harry packing, the new ambassador Dudley Carleton unpacking, and a visitor staying as a guest—Mary Herbert's new lover, Dr. Mathew Lister.[304] He'd brought Kit a special packet of news from Mary.

Dr. Lister was shepherding two young men, Robert Cecil's son[305] and Good Tom Howard's third son Henry, who was anxious to talk to Kit in private. It turned out that Henry had come to Venice especially to ask for Isabel's hand in marriage. Kit wept and said yes, if she wanted the match, but he had no say in the matter. He thought Queen Elizabeth had decided for them. Henry said her dispensation left things so they could choose for themselves.

That night Kit wrote the news to Manco and opened the package from Mary, which held a strange, long, descriptive letter sent by a man who'd been shipwrecked on Bermuda.[306]

After the company left and Harry started his wintry trip to England, Kit went home to Naples and began to write The Tempest, thinking of youthful Isabel and Henry Howard, thinking of Bacon, the possible end of the Theater Wing and of Kit's own roles as good and bad SSS spirits. And he hoped the play might reconcile Bacon and Cecil.

When he wrote to Hen Wriothesley Kit mentioned the letter about Bermuda and the prospect of the New World as a place where people might start over and do better, and Hen wrote back about his investments across the Atlantic, and how he was trying to acquire Bermuda for the Virginia Company.[308]

Someone in London had noticed there was only a smidgen of silver in the Mint. James appointed Bacon, Julius Caesar and Knevet to "investigate," and Bacon made a three-card-monti-style report which seemed to deflect further inquiry.[308]

Bacon wasn't being taken seriously as an advisor. He needed leverage. Some time ago he'd suggested to Cecil that since James was always complaining about Prince Henry's extravagance, Bacon could casually suggest that some SSS spirits do away with the prince, and if James didn't actually say no and it was done, Bacon could say to the king, "we've done your will, Sire; the wastrel is dead." Then James might be glad, but he'd be scared, too: an accessory before and after the fact, he'd agree to anything to keep the affair quiet.

Cecil had refused to consider the idea, but now Cecil was ill and dying. Bacon conferred with a sinister uncle of Good Tom's, old Henry Howard, famous for machination. He enthusiastically backed Bacon's plan, sure that the Catholic cause and Spain would be interested if Bacon had real power over James.

In Naples, the count of Lemos served as viceroy from June 1610 to June 1616, and those were the only years in the history of the viceroyalty in which public works were achieved.[309] Lemos was supercilious but impressionable, and he liked his cultural aide. (Was Kit responsible for the improvements? At the King's School he'd studied Thomas Eliot's Book of the Governor; later he'd dreamed of managing Hen's Isle of Wight. I think Kit set wheels turning.) The plight of Naples' many poor people was serious; there was not enough work, or water, or grain. Any wealth was siphoned off by Spanish masters—Kit speaks of a tax in his ciphers for The Winter's Tale—and an insidious trade in opium and hashish from the Levant debilitated all but the dealers.

Astonishingly, someone encouraged the viceroy to provide work-programs for building and repair in the city and to create grain-mills outside the city walls near Nolana Gate, where water would be led by new canals from Preziosa.[310] Kit, an Aquarian, remembered the canal Drake made to Plymouth, with mills along the way,[311] and thinking of reclamation and preservation of fertile land in the Romney Marsh at home—between Romney and Appledore, the old Rhee Wall which held back water from 40,000 acres of the finest cornland—Kit may have prodded Lemos to start work on swamp drainage to improve health and make productive fields crossed by useful roads.[312] (Roger Manwood had owned the Old Court Lodge near Dymchurch—Romney Marsh was like home to Kit.)

One day at a meeting of the literary society, Lemos confided to Kit that Cervantes hadn't been invited to Naples because Lemos had read Francisco Quevedo's novel, El Buscon,[313] and Quevedo told him its sordid stories were inspired by Cervantes' own life. After that, the sheltered Lemos and his countess found Cervantes repellent.

Gregorio knew Manco was without money in Madrid, so he sent him part of his own salary, and when Gregorio sailed to England (I think to deliver packets from Carleton) in mid-1611, he took along his translation of Don Quixote I to be published for Manco's benefit. He also took his play of Cardenio to the Chamberlain's Players. He was soon home again at Naples with Micaela and their baby—but for an unknown reason he had to sail back to England at the end of the year.

As soon as he came ashore in England in January 1612, n.s., he was sent by Bacon to a secret job at Exeter which turned out to be so brutally mismanaged by the local SSS chief that Kit decided to leave the Service. A suspect had been cruelly tortured, and Kit dispatched the man to end his pain. The whole revolting day had been observed by a new member of SSS, a local youth just home from Oxford. Shocked, he thought of telling the truth to everyone and said so, but the depraved local chief hired a groom to kill the intern as he rode home that night.

At once Bacon sent Kit a note telling him he must write an elegy for the dead novice, a poem clearly stating that the youth was an innocent country gentleman (no way connected with SSS), who'd been struck down by a highwayman. Kit wrote a remarkable piece of work furnished with out-front innuendo and one set of ciphers for SSS and a more hidden set telling rock-bottom truth: A Funeral Elegy for Thomas Peter, signed W.S. and registered by Kit's publisher Thomas Thorpe only nineteen days after the young man's murder.[314] Kit sailed home, figuring he was finished forever with Bacon and Cecil. He'd stay in Italy, work for Guarini. At Naples, news: Mantuan Duke Vincenzo Gonzaga was dead, and the cell at Colorno was being raided. The Inquisition was secret, but Barbara Sanseverino was publicly beheaded, her friends and family executed, and no one knew which names of other workers had been revealed by prisoners on the rack. Every worker was in danger.[315] At la Guarina they said Battista had gone to Rome, so Kit rode on to Venice, where he learned that Doge Donato, too, was dead! The Resistance was crumbling.

Lemos was preparing a magnificent fiesta in Naples to celebrate the engagement of the Infanta Ana and Louis XIII, and Kit, as Antonio de Laredo, was writing, casting and directing a big pageant. In that summer of 1612 he rehearsed everyone but the elephants, who wouldn't come till dress rehearsal. He went back and forth, Venice-Naples. The baby and Micaela were in Naples—she'd be acting in the pageant. Peter Manwood's eldest son Roger, in Venice on tour, made friends with Kit and in August may have ridden back to Naples with him and Toby Mathew to be part of the fiesta, which turned out a success for Lemos.[316]

Battista Guarini, on assignment in Rome, was deathly ill. He slowly made his way home to San Bellino, then traveled on—to Ferrara, to Venice. On 7 October he was in town at Kit's apartment in San Moisé. It was just seven o'clock—19 hours—when Battista closed his eyes and died in Kit's arms.[317]

Next day Guarini's son came to entomb the tortured body; Kit burned papers, left some with Carleton, carted things to la Guarina, came back to check with the embassy—and found a message from Harry in London. Trouble! Come right away! Impossible. Not now! He went to Naples to stay with Micaela and the baby.

February in London, and Kit had just docked his "pp boat." Kit's daughter was about to wed Good Tom Howard's son Henry, and in a much more public ceremony, King James' daughter was marrying Frederick V, the Elector Palatinate.[318] The town was boiling with expensive celebrations. George Chapman had made a theatrical entertainment about Virginia, and Kit in clown disguise was drafted to play Capriccio, master of ceremonies for the antimasque of this best of many masques.[319] There were also plays, extravagant parties—no end of a jolly good time.

But Prince Henry Stuart had died last November under clouds that could not be dispersed, and Bacon held King James by the nose at last. In tense conference with his lover Robert Carr and Carr's secretary, Thomas Overbury, the frightened king realized a cover-up was necessary.

At Wotton's apartment in Westminster Harry briefed Kit on Bacon's doings. Now Cecil was gone, Francis Bacon, suddenly a more important person, was allied with old Henry Howard, who was slyly using as agents members of his nephew Good Tom's family.[320] Kit feared for his own daughter, living at Audley End with the Howards. Wotton told Kit that Prince Henry's death was a job done by Bacon and old Henry Howard. For the king, or for Spain? The prince had been actively anti-Catholic. Wotton suspected that Bacon, with his yearning for royal power, felt he'd get the backing he needed only from Spain's ruling favorites, and he was setting a new course. An excellent Spanish ambassador would be coming to London in April, to stay.

But first, work was required of SSS: on 14 March, Bacon, using Will Shakespeare as a front, bought the Blackfriars Gatehouse.[321] It looked like an innocent shift of ownership; Shakespeare as buyer, but with an entail ensuring transfer of title to three co-signers chosen by Bacon in case of Shakespeare's death. The Gatehouse, an ancient building where Francis's father Walsingham had lived as a young lawyer, had fascinated Bacon since childhood: many secret passageways led out from it in different directions—one of them to the Great Wardrobe, one down to the river. The place was perfect for his secret Secret Service, and now, at last free of Cecil, Francis could work on a plan he'd had in mind for several years. He wanted to edit history, get rid of embarrassing records, but there were no shredders in those days, and he couldn't burn rolls of parchment in his fireplace. Using the Gatehouse he had a chance: there he'd pile up all the state papers that frightened or offended him: he'd ferry them across the river at night, stash them in the Globe Theater—and burn the theater! The building was round, tall—made like a chimney, put together with wood and straw—how simple!

Many of the hated records were in a depository at the Whitehall Banquet House.[322] Bacon's agents were instructed to wrap the records in cloth to look like bolts of fabric (Tom and Audrey Walsingham were working there in the Hall as costumers for plays and pageants being produced for the royal wedding),[323] and so disguised, the unwanted records were to be carted over into the Great Wardrobe, later carried through the underground passageway to the Gatehouse and through another secret tunnel to Puddlewharf, where they'd be loaded into boats and rowed across the river to the Globe. Obeying their chief, SSS would do it.

Harry talked to Kit about this criminal plan. What could they do? Harry'd been set against the idea, and after he told Francis he'd refuse to help, Francis had done his best to defame Harry, quickly spoiling his good chance of being chosen secretary of state. (Cecil had left a sealed letter recommending Harry for the job.) Now Bacon intended to further blacken Harry's name by planning to tell everyone after the fire that Henry Wotton had started it because he was angry at some of the players.

Kit said no, nobody will say that! He got out a never-performed play of his (where did he stash these things?) and put in a scene about Henry VIII going to visit the cardinal and Anne Boleyn, with guns fired off in greeting. He said they'd shoot a burning wad of something onto the thatched roof of the theater, and they could say it was an accident—if it had to be done.

And no, they would not leave the historic state papers to be burnt: Kit promised he'd get them out of the cellar of the Globe after Bacon went home, just before the burning day. Kit and Hen could row them up to Queen Anne's landing and put them ashore there, using her crane. Harry was immensely relieved and grateful.

To aid their own plans, Harry accepted responsibility for logistics of the burning. The Burbages, who held the Globe's title, were warned and paid; owners of the concessions building next door would be compensated after the fact. On the day of the fire the house would be papered with honest men, and the records—Aha!—would be safe in Queen Anne's basement.[324]

Kit rode to Oxford town to meet his son Will Davenant and received an ambivalent welcome from John and Jane Davenant, hosts of the Crown Tavern.[325] Jane was still beautiful; the boy looked more like Kit. Right away young Will loved Gregorio, introduced as his godfather. Together the two went to London, where they toured the Exchange with Harry Wotton and the visiting marchese from Savoy, who'd come to tell James the Resistance was not dead, and to ask for aid: Savoy needed ships to guard its tiny coast, money to outfit an army.

Harry and the envoy, Kit and his son went across to the Globe to see Much Ado. At seven years, young Will was already fascinated with plays and poems, which would serve as the foundation for his life's work. When the boy was returned to the Crown Tavern, godfather and son promised to write to each other.

The night before the appointed firing Bacon watched as SSS water-coachmen transported piles of fabric-wrapped records across the river to be stashed in the Globe. Then, satisfied that all were properly disposed, he went home. Kit and Hen got the bulky papers and rolls into an open boat, and early the next day, as the tide started in, they rowed upstream to Denmark House, where they unloaded at Queen Anne's lobby. After that, the two men nearly drowned; the whole adventure is detailed in ciphers for the re-written Tempest in the Folio.

The day of the fire dawned: a gray day, 29 June. The play began, Henry VIII, or All is True. Offstage, the gunner landed a fiery wad on the roof, but nothing happened; the thatch was damp. The Tempest ciphers explain how this crisis was resolved, and by evening the whole theater had been consumed, and everyone but Bacon was crying.

Queen Anne wanted to see Kit, so he cleaned up and went to Denmark House. He recalls the meeting in The Tempest ciphers: they talked about the rescued papers, Kit arguing for immediate release of news about the whole affair, Anne sadly declaring that future generations should judge her husband. Reluctantly, at her request, he returned the orphaned state records to an official repository—in the Banquet House?

Sometime in the last night of June Kit sailed away in his ship. Hen embarked then, too, to be gone for about a month. Did he go with Kit?[326] What would they have talked about? Kit was changing his career. Never again would he work for Bacon, and never again would he see England: Dover, Canterbury, Cambridge, Shorne, London—all would be memories, and his future was foggy. He and Micaela had two babies to care for now, and no real prospects. He'd work for Carleton and Harry as a newsman; he'd work for England, not for the traitor Francis.

Hen, a principal investor in the company colonizing Bermuda as part of the Virginia Company,[327] knew the colonists were hungry. The people on the island needed ships so they could go to Virginia or sail home to England if they needed to. Hen thought of buying some new ships at Venice and lading them with supplies so Kit could take them across, look around, report on things. Hen had had no luck at all years ago when he asked James to pardon Kit so he could govern the Isle of Wight. Things might be different now; a good governor was needed on Bermuda, and as it was so far away, out of the public eye, James might at last grant Kit a pardon, and the job. When he heard this, optimistic Kit dreamed of taking his family to live in an island paradise.

f

Marlowe's Life, Part IV

Gregorio was back at the beach with Micaela and the babies, and he worked at his post in the palace in Naples, reporting to Carleton. A letter came from Manco, ill and poor but happily writing. His Novelas Ejemplares were ready for print, and he was finishing Viaje del Parnaso, a long poem honoring the poets of Spain. There was a cameo of Gregorio in Naples guiding Cervantes in a dream to a place where he could see a great pageant.[328]

Kit was touched. Manco warned him not to take drugs in Naples, where they were easily found, and described what opio did to poets. He wrote that Quevedo would soon leave Spain to go to Sicily as advisor to the Duke of Osuna.[329] No, Cervantes hadn't seen Quevedo for a long time.

From his own salary Kit sent money to Manco, saying it came from the Viceroy Lemos. Cervantes returned warm thanks to Castro, who, when he learned the truth, may have relented and sent Manco a small stipend.

Kit found Lemos toying with the idea of sending galleys against Savoy, and dissuaded him.

Bacon's leverage was working: he was now Attorney General, and Thomas Overbury, who might have revealed Prince Henry's murder, was conveniently dead in the Tower.[330] The coast looked clear.

The new friendly Spanish ambassador had arrived—Don Diego Sarmiento de Acuña, Conde de Gondomar. Aware of English pirates in the Mediterranean, Sarmiento was suggesting that Spain and England cooperate to fight pirates around Tunisia, and Hen had been made a commissioner to send ships of reprisal.[331] Hen's greater concern was the safety of Bermuda; Spain, who considered Bermuda her own property, was planning a naval operation to kill or carry off the few Bermuda settlers.

Hen sent commission-papers plus money to Gregorio, authorizing him to buy in Venice two good marciliane and arm them as pirate-chasers, and after catching some pirate ships, to sail them and the marciliane with arms and food to Bermuda; Gregorio to be in charge. (Big deal! Just like that? Was this Kit's idea, or Hen's?[332])

Early in July 1614 Gregorio set forth with two new, well-armed little ships. (Shadows suggest his half-nephew Roger Manwood may have been aboard, with a relative from Kent, adventurous young John Boyes.)[333]

In Turk-troubled waters off Tunisia they sighted the Tiger, a familiar English ship that often stopped at Venice on her way to and from the Levant: long ago her former owner-captain, Kester Carleill, had been a friend of Kit's. It seemed the vessel had recently been captured by pirates; her poop, cut-down for speed, was crowded with Turks. Gregorio's little ships converged on this target, and after a bloody boarding—Roger received a serious leg-wound—Gregorio claimed the Tiger and its contents for his commissioner, and the pirate captain surrendered. Surprise! He was Kit's friend Captain Sampson Denball, alias Ali Reis, turned Turk, and his cargo consisted of aquavit and many chests of Spanish reales.[334] Gregorio knew Captain Sampson had sailed with Drake and Carleill to the New World[335] and promised him freedom if he'd help navigate to Bermuda. The man couldn't refuse. After capturing another good pirate ship and putting its crew into a captured petache[336] to sail to the coast, the little armada put in at Malta to add cannon, smaller artillery, other munition and food supplies for Bermuda. Gregorio may have decided to carry the reales along to the colony; they belonged to Hen now.

At Malta, Gregorio left letters for Carleton, Micaela, Manco and Hen, and intended to set Roger ashore for treatment of his wound, but the youth, determined to make the voyage, seems to have stayed aboard. The tiny fleet headed for the Atlantic and found Bermuda after a six (?) week crossing, during which Roger's leg may have been amputated.[337]

Bermuda's Governor Moore was afraid of the gun-bristling vessels and kept them at the far end of the bay, but Gregorio rowed ashore in the skiff to present credentials, and Governor Moore learned that the exotic little marciliane were sent by the earl of Southampton for the colonists. Moore then grudgingly allowed unlading and directed the private burial of several chests (company property) on a vacant island (Hen Island, or an outlying one?). Moore now impounded the marciliane, afraid they'd attack Spanish ports, bringing reprisals to Bermuda. Captain Sampson and Roger's companion John Boyes had already sailed off in the Tiger to forage in Virginia.[338]

Gregorio came ashore at desolate St. George's Town to stay in a hut by the water.[339] Moore lived in the only frame house on the island and extended no invitation to a man he considered dangerous. Moore wanted to go back to England. Nothing here had ever gone right. Obsessed with fear of Spanish invasion, he'd pressed the settlers into day-and-night work on fortification, keeping them from tending their food-gardens until everyone was famished and some had starved to death. With Roger's aid, Gregorio offered to help organize foraging parties to outlying places, bringing back fish and birds and even pond mussels to make stew for everyone. Moore was encouraged to relax martial rule and let people go home. An agricultural conference was called, and for ten days Gregorio worked writing suggestions for setting up a representative assembly of surviving settlers. Moore, truculent, scorned these ideas, ordered the intruders out and even challenged Gregorio to a sword fight. But Moore did keep the two marciliane, sending one of them, despite bad weather, to England for more supplies. A shadow suggests Roger went with her, vowing to come back.

Gregorio must make for Italy. What could he take Micaela? A coral necklace and some bladders the children might use for water wings, Cervantes says in Don Quixote

II, where he describes Sancho's suffering on the island. Kit sailed for home in the last-captured pirate ship, and storm-tossed and ragged, he reached Villafranca late in November. He paid his crew and headed home to Micaela at Naples, where he held their new tiny baby as it was dying.[340]

A message from Carleton in Venice: soon he'd have to leave for Turin, and he wanted Kit to be chargé d'affaires of the embassy till Harry Wotton could come back from the Hague.[341] Kit might be in charge for several months. Micaela didn't want to be left alone, so the whole family packed up and headed for Venice, but then Carleton's leave-taking was deferred to February, so Kit took an interim job as a reader in medicine at Padua University.[342]

Without enough money to rent an apartment in Padua, Kit pitched a tent—but cold winds forced the family onto a boat on the river, and one day the unthinkable happened: both children fell or jumped overboard and drowned! Kit tried to commit suicide and spent time in a hospital. These tragic happenings and his voyage to Bermuda are remembered in ciphers inside a constitution which Kit had started for Bermuda and revised for a friend who wanted to set up a colony in Virginia, Bargraves Polisie by Ignotus. The original papers are kept by Lord Sackville at Knole Park in Kent.[343]

Marlowe, with Micaela, did hold down the fort at Carleton's embassy house in Venice, all through 1615. Early in 1616 a letter came from Hen with bad news: The Bermuda Company, which had been eaten up by the Crown near the end of 1614, would soon be granted a new royal charter, but there was no hope for Kit to be governor, or even a sharer.[344] (James feared the Spanish ambassador in London, who hated what Kit had done to strengthen Southampton's holdings in Bermuda. Hen himself stayed in only by the skin of his teeth, criticized by James as guilty of "pernicious government.")

Kit, as chargé d'affaires of the English embassy in Venice, was paid irregularly at first, then not at all. Feeling sad, on 21 March he gave the Ciotti Press a collection of poems praising Guarini. And not long before Wotton returned in mid-May 1616, the primitive steam-heater in the house blew up (no safety valve), ruined every room and killed their pet dog, Signorina Scala, who'd been sleeping on the furnace. Harry didn't blame Kit—just got a new house.[345]

Lemos and his train, including the Sanchez Players, were scheduled to leave Naples late in June 1616, to return to Spain. Micaela said she wasn't going with them, but Kit suggested (did Harry suggest it to him?) it would be a good idea for her to go back to Madrid, keeping her distance from Lope, and collect news to bring to Venice.[346]

She was incensed. They quarreled; she said he was using her—he didn't even love her enough to make their marriage correct in the eyes of the Church—they weren't really married! She was tired of being a tool. Yes, she'd go to Spain, and she wouldn't come back! She shot off to Naples.

Kit followed her; she evaded him. He went to work with the literary and dramatic clubs at the Naples court, and for the Oziosos directed a farcical playlet about Persephone going to the underworld. He was at the top of the stage playing Pluto and getting laughs when suddenly he twisted his bad foot and fell down on the other actors, breaking his ankle and stopping the show.[347] Micaela, still in town, couldn't be reached. He didn't have a good doctor.

Lemos and his court, Micaela and the Sanchez Company sailed away, leaving Kit abandoned, hurt, unloved and feeling sorry for himself.

In pain, he rode back to Venice to work at the Ciotti Press and stay in Guarini's old apartment. There he made a bitter rewrite of an old college play of his, Timon,[348] calling it Timon of Athens (1616). Bitter outside and in: inside, about Micaela. They *were too* really married! (Had she gone back to Spain to sell the information she'd gathered about England in her years with him? Damn!) But he wrote to her at her theater in Madrid, told her if she'd come home over the Brenner Pass he'd meet her up there, and yes, he'd marry her.[349]

Details of Micaela's adventures in summer and fall 1616 have been preserved in two accounts which fit together, making a clear story. Both her lovers were writers, and each tells his view of what happened, Kit in remarkable ciphers for Bargraves Polisie, and Lope in eleven letters he wrote to his patron, the duke of Sessa, fortunately preserved in Lope's published biography.[350]

On 6 August, Lope wrote from Valencia that he met la Loca—Micaela—as she got off the ship. He'd been waiting for her for weeks—had a cold from waiting for her—he felt awful—he was a wreck. The Sanchez Company had been playing comedies on shipboard and in Barcelona for the last month. She came to see Lope in Valencia and told him he should write to Sessa that in her the duke had a slave.

From Valencia she went to Madrid with the company, and near the end of August Lope went to see her in a show there. La Loca looked neat, he wrote, and was good when the guitars came in. (He called her la Loca because she was so standoffish.) He took her and the children to the bullfight, and he couldn't help wishing she was the bull.

Every night for twenty nights he stood and argued with her in the shadow of her door[351]—the great doorway of the crumbling Lujan Tower? She must have told him that Gregorio was the best playwright in the world, for Lope wrote: "I'd very much like to see some writing made by that angel of the Palace, for after I saw the ignorance of Don Gregorio, any entanglement seems possible to me."[352]

About 20 September Micaela disappeared, and Lope found a new girl, "intelligent, clean, amorous, grateful and compliant." Lope wrote that la Loca told Lemos's nephew that he, Lope, "made love like a nun, and spoke more impossibilities than prayers in a parlor," and the nephew circulated these statements in a paper, "but already the caballero is repentant and knows that he was not well informed."

Meanwhile, disguised as men, Micaela and her maid set off with their page, riding toward the Pyrenees and France on their way to the Brenner Pass, as Kit had suggested. A punishing trip; Micaela was very pregnant with a baby she and Kit had started early in February just before they split. (Kit didn't know.) From Madrid the riders would have gone through Siguenza, Zaragoza, over the Pyrenees at Bagnares de Luchon, to Toulouse, Lyon, on to Basel, Zurich—ever onward to the Brenner Pass. Kit wasn't there. Micaela and her aides started down and got as far as an inn (at Bolzano?), where they had to stop—the baby came.

The rest of the story, except for two notes in Lope's letters to Sessa, is told in Kit's Bargraves Polisie ciphers: Kit, still thinking Micaela had abandoned and perhaps betrayed him, started for the pass but was met on the track by her page, who told him his wife, with a new baby, was up at the inn. The ciphers describe the awful climb to the inn, how later he did officially marry Micaela, how the party got down through snow to Venice and his cold old bachelor quarters—no food.[353]

On 7 October he sent a famous letter crosstown to Harry, with a bit of Catholic news, confessing he and Micaela had been joined in wedlock by the Church and begging not to be abandoned. "I have married a wife who is poor and homely, so she will never be proud, and I'll never be jealous."[354] If Micaela had looked worn at that moment, it would be understandable. Harry answered (he'd promised this) by giving Kit's family a handsome apartment in the embassy house.

Soon Lope wrote Sessa, "there came a maidservant of that person and told me her life and miracles since she left here, and they are such that till today I have not returned to my senses." And in another letter, "Neither when I'm alone or with someone do I remember that base woman, especially since I learned her low tricks. They write to me that they regret."[355]

1616 had been a rough year for Gregorio, and though Carleton had written Chamberlain several letters about how Harry was doing nothing to help, Harry was doing a lot: besides giving Kit and his family a big apartment in the embassy house (Kit describes it appreciatively in ciphers), on 11 October Harry wrote Secretary of State Ralph Winwood, *privata*, an important letter[356] (with private separate inclusions, not for our eyes or those of Winwood's office help)—a crisp communication saying his expense account will be presented by his attorney, and that it includes an allowance for Gregorio—30 ducats a month, "which amounteth to less by some forty pound yearly than is allowed Signor Maggio, who hath an entertainment from the French King for the same service here under his ambassadors. And I am bound to say in truth that he hath merited it, and more, from his Majesty, not only for ten years' service under Sir Dudley and me, and for those months when he supplied the place alone during Sir Dudley Carleton's absence in Savoy, but likewise for some hazards that he hath run here, besides the spoiling of his fortune for ever in all other places of Italie by this dependence. In which considerations I have thought fit to beseech his Majesty to sign a few lines for his better protection to the effect of the enclosed, which will give him security and courage in his service. (In a private part of this letter Harry puts his idea of what those lines should say?) Harry's discreet; he puts in a paragraph about how his solicitor will be coming to see Winwood and will show him a new invention for draining fens. But that's not all; Harry writes, "With my solicitor, the merchant, Mr Blunt, will likewise repair unto you, with all the information for the business." What business? Fen-draining or publishing? John Chamberlain's letters contain frequent references to "Ned Blunt, Stationer of Paul's"—a friend of Kit's who published his

Hero and Leander and other things. Does Harry speak of that Edward Blunt (Blount), who's working on the business of putting together a folio of Gregorio's best plays? I bet Harry himself is helping the project, for the last paragraph of the letter starts, "I have written to my solicitor to send me one hither whose hand I shall use in copying of some things; whom, if it shall please you to dispatch with a packet in answer of those points that I have now handled . . ." (in the "privata" part) your Honour shall do me a special favor." Will Kit's old friend Ralph Crane be coming to copy some plays? "And now, having worn out my pens and my matter, both public and private, I commit your Honour again to God's dear love . . ."

Scrivener Ralph Crane (a Carleton in-law?), a skilled scribe known to Kit from Marprelate days, may have come down to Venice to copy things. The Riverside Shakespeare states that scholars believe Ralph Crane copied at least eight of the Folio versions of "Shakespeare" scripts: The Tempest (last ciphered rewrite c. 1615. RB), Two Gentlemen of Verona, Merry Wives, The Winters Tale, Measure for Measure, Cymbeline, Henry IV Part II, Timon of Athens. (written and ciphered 1616, redoing the old college play. R. B.).

1616 was a rough year, truly. Kit didn't learn till May that Cervantes was dead of diabetes in Madrid. Will Shakespeare died at Stratford from a fever said to have been contracted after a meal with Ben Jonson and Mike Drayton. Kit's almost-promised pardon was shelved, and though James had been asked by Kit's most powerful friends to send Gregorio something to make up for his lack of pay while he'd been in charge of the embassy, perhaps the king figured it was cheaper just to send a nice letter, which he did, on the next-to-last day of the year.[357] Kit copied it and sent the original to his son Will Davenant.

In England things were almost indescribably bad. The youth who'd killed Overbury in the Tower had voluntarily, publicly, confessed he'd been hired to do it! Something Bacon never counted on. (Overbury was the man who threatened to leak about Prince Henry's murder.)

Attorney General Bacon was striking out right and left in spasms of damage control, sacrificing his own operatives to death. (Kit's accusations in The Tempest rewrite ciphers are explicit.) Bacon used Good Tom Howard's daughter Frances as a goat: she'd been divorced—Bacon may have thought that made her a fallen woman already—easy to pin a crime on her. The girl was told she would not die, and James pardoned her, but of course her life was ruined; she was pardoned but never exonorated. I suppose Bacon told his agents all this ugly stuff would protect the king's good name, and truth was never told.

Kit feared for Isabel, living in Good Tom's house. Isabel's husband, young Henry Howard, tried to visit his sister Frances in jail, and perhaps declared to all that he was going to speak out, because one evening in late September or early October he died, speechless, at supper, leaving Isabel a shocked and very youthful pregnant widow.[358]

In this year the Venetian ambassador in London, Barbarigo, also suffered death; on 16 January he'd written home that Bacon's ally Robert Cotton had been arrested, charged with giving state documents to the Spanish ambassador in London. Barbarigo's letter was too revelatory; he was in danger. In a later dispatch, reporting the Overbury murder trial, he hinted at Prince Henry's poisoning—and on 28 May Barbarigo died, attended by Theodore Mayerne, the physician who'd been Prince Henry's doctor.[359] The ambassador left two little orphaned sons in London. The children went home to Venice, and at the end of October the Council of Ten in Venice granted leave for them to go to Harry's house for Hallowe'en with Harry's "family."[360]

There was an old English saying, "May my death come from Spain," because it would be so long coming. Francisco Quevedo's biggest plan was not new, nor was it a secret, but at long last it looked as if it was ripening. Years before, though, Marlowe had made his own secret counterplan—a sting that could defuse the Spaniard's plot. He described it in a ciphered letter to Hen Wriothesley inside The Winter's Tale.

Francisco Quevedo y Villegas, the man who wrote the mean novel about Cervantes' life, was advisor to the duke of Osuna, the new viceroy of Naples who moved in as Lemos sailed back to Spain. Naples was the home of Spain's navy, and Quevedo wanted Spanish ships, laden with arms and soldiers, to sail up the Adriatic while the city of Venice was being infiltrated by undercover mercenaries, ready to fire the Arsenal at a signal from their leader. As the city burned, soldiers from the Spanish galleys would come in across the lagoon in lighters to take control, while soldiers would be marching east across the Veneto, claiming that land for Spain. Once Venice had been defeated the soldiers would move north with artillery across the Hapsburg Alps to the Netherlands, where Spain had a truce, and from there—one tiny hop to England, where Spain had been promised aid by a rising politician, a privy councillor.

Marlowe's counterplot was a play, a secret pageant to fool Osuna and Quevedo. Early in 1617 he went into the palace at Venice and laid his idea before the old pirate Doge Bembo. Amused, Bembo said, "go ahead, but first get permission from King James. We'll pay you if you succeed." "Spain will pay us first," said Gregorio.

He waited for word from James, and it came in March 1617 in the form of a patent (re)confirming Gregorio in the service. This Harry handed over to the Collegio on March twenty-second.[361]

As a crippled old Normandy pirate and his weary wife (some of her teeth blacked out?) Kit and Micaela sailed his boat to Naples and talked to the duke of Osuna.[362] Kit said he was Captain Jaques-Pierre (pronounced Jakes-Peer),[363] that he'd served the Spanish crown in Sicily and Naples, and recommended by the Duke of Savoy he now worked for the Venetian Republic at the Arsenal, where he had a companion who knew all about artillery. The Captain said he'd heard something about a proposed attack on Venice from Naples and wanted to offer his services with a plan: he knew many brave corsairs up north who'd gladly come as soldiers of fortune to infiltrate Venice for Spain.[364]

At a signal they'd take possession of the city from within, burning the Arsenal for a start, while Spanish soldiers, debarked from galleys anchored out beyond the Lido, were being floated across the lagoon on lighters. Landing, the soldiers would mop up and take charge of the city for Spain. A simple plan, but one that would work, if the right sort of mercenaries were engaged.

Osuna asked how long it would take to find such men, and the Captain said probably about a year, and he'd need money up front, so the pirates he'd approach could see he was in earnest about the job. When Osuna hesitated, the Captain pushed Micaela forward and said if collateral was needed, he'd leave his wife as hostage till he could get back. Osuna laughed and said it was a deal, all except the hostage.[365] Kit and Micaela sailed home with Spanish reales and went to work.

Kit wanted a cast of hundreds. He told all his friends they'd fool the Spaniards, letting them think Spain could destroy the Republic, when the mercenary infiltrators would truly be Venetian citizens plus all the actor-friends Kit could get to come down from England.

Henry Mainwaring, an ex-pirate and the best sailor in England now that Drake was gone, was coming to Venice to work undercover and chase off any Spanish ships that came up the Adriatic thinking to attack Venice.

Kit's first Venice friend, Prospero Colombo, the shipping magnate, wanted to be an infiltrator; so did old Dr. Asselinau, secret secretary of the French embassy; and poet G. B. Marino was coming from Turin.

Micaela would be a beautiful Greek coffee-shop-owner—her little restaurant serving as the clearing-house, the nerve center of the "mercenary" operation, keeping track of who stayed where, how close were the Spanish, and inside news in general. Operations would begin when the main body of "soldiers of fortune" arrived from the English theater, probably early in 1618.

Meanwhile in England Bacon was feeling good. He'd just been made Keeper of the Great Seal a week before the death of the previous keeper, who had relinquished his job, knowing his end was near.[366]

James went to Scotland on a sentimental journey in March, leaving his Lord Keeper more or less in control. Those were Bacon's finest months. He forgot to publish James' proclamation telling the gentry not to hang around London but to go home.[367] Queen Anne so distrusted Bacon she refused to attend meetings of the privy council. He conferred often with the Spanish ambassador Sarmiento de Acuña, Count Gondomar;[368] in fact, Bacon disappeared for ten days in May, and it was whispered that he'd been with Gondomar all that time.[369]

In June Wotton went to see Spanish ambassador Bedmar in Venice, and they talked an hour and a half. What Harry said there no one knows, but in August a nasty letter came to the Doge and Council in Venice from the Secretary of the Spanish Embassy in London, trying to defame Harry: Nobody liked that Henry Wotton; Henry Wotton was a rat.[370] Harry was getting the treatment, not for the first time.

In late August, the pirate Jaques-Pierre submitted a ten-page report to the Council of Ten with full details of a Spanish plot to take over Venice, to be sent to the Savii of the Cabinet after enjoining secrecy.[371]

September: King James returned to England, and in Naples Osuna sent an English merchant to England with money to buy six good ships to sail to Naples with cover of salt fish—ships to send against Venice.[372] Queen Anne knew which way the wind was blowing and turned against the whole Spanish party.[373]

Early November: Harry introduced Ned's son Henry Vere at the Collegio; he'd like to aid Venice and promised to provide 20 men to be French-sailor-infiltrators, but that was off the record. And in England, Bacon's closest agent, Toby Mathew, who'd been exiled, was back in London, visiting the Spanish embassy almost every night.[374]

November: in the Cabinet, Venetian Senators asked Harry to ask James for help. Pedro de Toledo was threatening the Republic from the west, and word had come that Osuna would soon sail 22 ships against Venice from Naples. Harry said he'd already sent off a courier.

On 7 November an English ship was detained and armed at Naples against the wishes of the owner. Six "saltfish" galleons were on their way from England to Naples, and Malta was sending a galleon.

Things were getting really tough in December: "a very leading member of the privy council" in London had reported awful things about Wotton to the Venetian Ambassador, Piero Contarini. Wotton was said to talk nightly with the Spanish ambassador in Venice. Contarini forwarded this news to the Doge.[375]

At year's end at the Collegio, Harry was again asked for English aid. Osuna was readying a galleon for himself at Naples. Harry cheerfully wished everone a good New Year and went back to his house.[376]

But in London on that very night, Ambassador Piero Contarini and his chaplain climbed the secret stairway of Queen Anne's Denmark House to confer with her, and they arranged aid that James was afraid to give: her Queen's Players, with their director John Holland, and Sam Daniel's Bristol company, and other groups of players, would soon leave England to pretend to be soldiers of fortune infiltrating Venice according to Jakes-Pierre's plan. She said not to worry about the Spanish ships; Henry Mainwaring would have Dutch ships rented by Contarini and English ships ready to scare Osuna; the Spanish soldiers would not be able to disembark. Anne offered to pay for the actors' travel, board and room; Contarini assured her all "mercenaries" who'd go to Venice to help the sting would be paid in Spanish gold before the trap was sprung. They shook hands, wished each other Happy New Year and goodbye.[377]

On the first day of the new year in Venice, an hour before dawn, Harry's house caught fire. It started under the kitchen in a basement room where the landlord stored extra beams, planks and boxes, and it soon roared into the room above. The key on the kitchen table was unreachable, so the front door had to be broken down, but everyone got out.[378] How it started, no one knows.

The scene was being set for Kit's charade: as the actors landed[379] they signed in at the Spanish embassy and were billeted in unlicensed boarding houses, most of them belonging to the Jews of Venice. (Quevedo was not the Jews' favorite person: though he was of Jewish blood, he'd written a famous anti-Semitic book.) And he didn't like actors, either.

Tall old Dr. Asselinau, aka Nicolo Reynault, spent most of his days bent over a table at Micaela's Greek coffee-house, teaching basic French to any soldiers of fortune who needed it, for all the "mercenaries" were obliged to seem basically French when they registered with Spanish Ambassador Bedmar. Everyone had a cover name; even Mainwaring served secretly, because the Spanish ambassadors in England and Venice would have objected to his presence in the Adriatic.

Bedmar passed out some allowance money to the "French" adventurers, but Kit was determined not to pull the plug on the party till every one of his helpers received full pay from Naples. So together, Captain Jakes-Pierre and "the Petardier Langlad" (Prospero Colombo) posted from Naples—Quevedo came along with them[380]—across south Italy to Brindisi, to sail up the coast with a load of money. Quevedo wanted to see for himself how things were going. On that trip they conversed, and Quevedo wrote in his diary that Jaques-Pierre confided his nickname was Bornío—the littlest hawk, a merlin (a college nickname of Kit's).[381] Quevedo knew some Shakespeare works; his own writings show he knew Lucrece, and he wrote a Venus and Adonis and something that sounded very like the voice of melancholy Jaques. Anyway, they arrived in Venice, the mercenaries were all paid, and the big day was at hand.

On 12 May the Doge received a letter from the Venetian ambassador at Rome saying that by now four galleons and fourteen galleys from Naples would have entered the Adriatic.[382] Things in the city were tense: Jaques Pierre and two confrères were said to be out at sea with the Venetian navy. As Spanish vessels came in sight, tangling with the Venetian navy and Dutch and English ships, Quevedo saw the hired bravos stirring, ready for arson. Then—surprise!—two well-dressed Frenchmen stepped out of a little boat at the Piazzetta, hurried across it and went inside to talk to the Council. They were Kit, as Gabriele Montecasino, and a friend. They said they'd been conspirators but couldn't bear to see the city destroyed—and they revealed the plot![383]

Immediately word went out that the police were rounding up suspicious characters. A message was sent to the Captain General at sea: quietly execute Jaques-Pierre, his secretary and aide and throw their bodies overboard. (They weren't there, of course.) The next day police illegally entered the house of Spanish ambassador Bedmar and found it a Santa Barbara—a powder keg—filled with munitions. Quevedo, who'd taken refuge there, stayed only long enough to see himself burned in effigy on the street before he was hustled out of the city and set on the road south towards Ferrara. Quevedo never learned the truth; later he seriously wrote of the experience as genuine history.[384]

The French ambassador's house was searched—nothing bad—and the Greek coffeehouse. Its beautiful hostess was gone. On the seventeenth of May Gregorio as himself went to the Council, then to the Inquisitors, and on the eighteenth the real bodies of two Uscock pirates who'd been executed in the jail were dressed as "French soldiers of fortune" and exhibited upside down between the two fatal pillars on the Piazzetta. Venice politely asked Spain to remove her ambassador, and Bedmar left for Flanders.[385]

By that time the foreign adventurers who had crowded the city streets had disappeared from Venice. The popular belief was that they'd all been executed, their bodies thrown into the deep Canale degli Orfani, or that some had been taken to Friuli for hanging. While this was going on the Spanish warships were indeed chased away, and although over the next years Osuna persistently tried to make a landing at Venice, he never could get close.

For the first time in many months Harry received pay from England.[386] About the sting, he wrote home, "No public minister resident upon this lake doth know more of it than myself," and in October he sent to England his own report[387]—sent in secret to Secretaries Naunton and Lake, but seen by Bacon? Destroyed by Bacon?

In June and again in July, Bacon's home account-book shows a payment to "an Italian." (A messenger bringing information of events in Venice? re the Plot?)[388]

In August Kit gave his patent to Harry to send back to James—job done.[389] As Gabriele Montecasino, Kit received £100 from the Council of Ten,[390] and in October the city ordered a solemn public Thanksgiving. Looking back, it was remarkable: with no blood, just sleight of hand, Kit had managed to

— create and direct the biggest production of his career,
— foil an English traitor,
— save Venice, and possibly England, from Spanish aggression,
— give English actors, some very poor and out of work, a terrific Italian vacation with pay,
— give the Venice Jews a role in foiling an anti-Semitic crusader,
— humble that destructive man and curb the power of a greedy one,
— and make money doing it.

I know this sketch should be compact, but here, from the Calender of State Papers Venetian, vol. 15, is an eyewitness report from a boardinghouse keeper who spoke to the Inquisitors: Diana Palermitana, a tobacconiste (widow of English John Bartlett), living at Ca' Moro at San Giovanni in Bragora, told the Inquisitori that some English lodged, without license, at a very large house kept by one John Holland and belonging to Sig. Giovanni Baptista Bragadino at S. Giovanni in Bragora del Piovano, at la Crosera (the house called Tedesca).

She says a Parvis procured a wife Lucretia for John Holland—that Parvis had given his own wife, la Gritti, to young Henry Vere, who took la Gritti to England with him. Henry Vere lodged with Parvis and had 20 men with him. All left town soon after the conspiracy was revealed. They were of various nationalities. When the troubles happened, all the foreigners at John Holland's house left, too—20 at least. John Holland was protected by the English ambassador, so he could lodge foreigners without bulletins. Her husband (now dead), had lodged foreigners without bulletins, and none was ever jailed; if an official came and the English ambassador heard of it, he sent his secretary to the place where her husband was cited, to fix things. Other nationalities beside English came, and she'd seen many very poor, who later had money and were well-dressed—doesn't know who supplied them. All have gone—left after the Troubles.

Before the conspiracy these English went about seeing the city, taking notes and drawings and said, "this is the fortress of the Venetians," but they did not speak of taking it. There were young students among them and in their conversations they said that their bertons (?) could do this and that. They had great disputes about Palma and talked of going to see it and who would get there the quickest. When they returned they praised the fortress and the country, calling it fine . . . . She didn't think they meant harm. They said would to God our king had such fine fortresses in England and such a country. The Captain now lodging with her says to her he's done a good service to the Republic. John Holland is still here and three or four days ago asked her to take four or five English, but she said no.[391]

After most of the actors sailed for home, Harry planned a play-party afternoon at his house for friends who stayed: Hen Wriothesley was still there, also Henry Vere, Nathaniel Fletcher (Harry's first chaplain at Venice),[392] and Nathaniel's brother John, a playwright who'd studied at Kit's Cambridge college. Harry wanted Kit to make the entertainment, but he said he was too tired; would John help out? John was glad to collaborate, and together (at the start of their opus Kit ciphered, "John 'n' Monti pen this playe") they made a short farce which they called The Two Noble Kinsmen. (The long quarto is a rewrite.) Henry Vere and Henry Wriothesley, secret half-brothers, performed the title roles, and Kit and Micaela played the jailer and the jailer's daughter—she danced and sang. The Kinsmen played proto-Tweedledum-and-Tweedledee, arming each other for a battle to the death. They fought, each wearing a basket-horse, for the hand of the noble Lady Emilia. Tweedledee won the joust, galloped off, and his kinsman was about to be executed for losing, when suddenly, with loud noises, Tweedledee was squashed to death offstage by his horse, so Tweedledum won Emilia after all.[393]

Hen and Kit dreamed about Bermuda. Hen still hoped—who knew how?—to reorganize Bermuda along progressive lines. Kit mentioned the possibility of starting a local government something like the one here—the Republic—a select council of elders plus an elected assembly with meaningful votes, a body representative of all neighborhoods in the settlement.

One night they sat on the beach and talked of a daring but decent way to break Bacon's insane grip on James' policies, Bacon's insistence on the submissive rapprochement with Spain which threatened Hen's hope for the future of the Bermuda colony. James alone could never ignore Bacon. Gregorio and Hen conceived a plan in which Hen, who'd always been a private person, must act in a bold way if another Parliament were ever called. Bacon had become Lord Chancellor in January 1618, so he'd be sitting in the House of Lords,[394] if and when there'd be a Parliament.

Gregorio told Hen there was a precedent for making the House of Lords a court of impeachment—the members were able to sit in judgement on one of their own. Hen was incredulous, but Gregorio was sure. He said when he was at Cambridge he'd seen in his college library old manuscript chronicles donated by Mathew Parker, and one of them, the Chronicon Angliae, clearly showed the House of Lords impeaching a fellow member. It hadn't been done since the late 1300's, but there it was, a precedent for making the House of Lords a court of law.[395] The members could prosecute Bacon. If he were investigated there and condemned, he'd have no recourse: James could honestly say his hands were tied—James could not be blamed.

What could be the charge? Would Bacon be called murderer? arsonist? traitor? No, the purpose was not to kill the man, but to draw his teeth so he'd no longer be a threat to king or country. The charge could be—well—taking bribes. And the punishment? Exile would be best, at least from the court. And when the process was complete, if Bacon made any statement about royal involvement in murder, he'd simply be laughed at. James' favorite, Buckingham, must help by playing a role; he must disagree with the investigating committee and be overridden. It just might work.

And now the last of the visiting English were embarking. Hen and Henry Vere had heard some of Kit's memories of their father Ned—good memories, so both men felt better about their dad. Hard for Kit to say goodbye to these friends. It would be forever; already he was on crutches, in a fog of pain.

We don't need a signed document to know Bacon was furious about the escapade in Venice. When the Queen's Players and Sam Daniel's Boys of Bristol and other actors came home through Customs,[396] no doubt Bacon, even if he hadn't read Harry's report to James, figured they'd been fooling around in Venice spoiling things for Osuna. Queen Anne's Players! That feather-brain was behind it! Queen Anne, who'd been suffering from gout and thought she was getting well, now began to sink into inexplicable illness.

One day in January when Bacon sent a clerk to the repository in the Banquet House for a paper from the archives, the youth returned to say there was a great bundle of unsorted documents there; what were they? Investigation revealed them to be the very state papers Bacon thought he'd burned in the Globe, years ago!

On 12 January, in spite of determined fire-fighting by a duke and some earls, the Banquet House burned. The fire consumed Signet, Privy Seal and Council Chamber archives in the basement.[397] Did Bacon learn that records he'd discarded had been saved, taken first to Queen Anne's lobby? Anne took a sudden turn for the worse in February.

Early in March, Anne died, but her funeral was postponed, week after week after week. Harry in Venice spent his own money for mourning weeds for his "family" to wear. They all knew how much Anne had helped Venice and England.

March ended, April passed, still no funeral. One historian wrote, "The players in the theaters grew clamorous at losing their livelihood while their theaters remained closed through this unconscionably long period of public mourning."[398] Mourning? Anne's body was just lying over there; James was not mourning. James did what Bacon wanted, and Bacon wanted to punish the players for what they'd done in Venice. At last, ten weeks after her death, and just a year after the Venice Sting, Anne's body was laid to rest, on 13 May Julian.

Good Tom Howard, Earl of Suffolk, had been made lord treasurer of England. When Harry Wotton learned (how did he find out?) that Bacon was about to make Tom the goat for those withdrawals of silver and money from the Trophonean Den, for the use of King James—from the treasury as well as the mint—Harry sent a hasty ciphered warning which arrived just in time for Tom to recheck amounts on hand and put in some money of his own before being "investigated" by Bacon.[399]

Letters and mementos came to Gregorio in Venice, telling of his daughter Isabel's remarriage. Her new husband was a young man who'd ridden with Harry on an embassy to Savoy in 1612, William Cavendish, a person almost incredibly kind, handsome and wealthy.[400] The newlyweds sent gifts, and plans for a house they were remodeling—it would look like a miniature St. Mark's.[401]

At last—good news for the Resistance: Savoy and Venice had formed an overt defensive league, and in England the Savoy ambassador asked James to join, with the protestant princes of Germany and the United States of the Netherlands. That was what Harry, Gregorio, Guarini, Sanseverino, Navarre, Manso, Della Porta and Marino had worked for! Thinking of Bacon's disapproval, James just shifted in his chair and started talking about something else.

The Spanish ambassador in London opposed any union of protestant princes, of course, and Bacon, with his tight hold on James, clung to a policy of Spanish appeasement. Bacon's attitude was becoming increasingly clear to others who dealt with English affairs. Hen Wriothesley had become Bacon's opponent when the earl, overtly aided by Gregorio, tried to further English presence in Bermuda while Gondomar was pushing to have the colonists removed. And Gregorio had gone ahead to mastermind the blow-up of the Spanish plot to subdue Venice. He was on Bacon's short list.

In Venice, Gregorio was revising his best plays, still hoping a folio would be published in England by Edward Blount. A quiet winter passed. In the spring, Harry determined to help the Protestant league, and in May 1619, he and a nobleman, Queen Anne's cousin, left Venice together to visit protestant German princes.[402] Harry told the Doge that Gregorio would take charge of the embassy.[403] Gregorio then began a series of more than sixty dispatches to Secretary of State Robert Naunton.[404] Kit and Naunton were friends from Cambridge days—Naunton was aware of Bacon's resentment—call it hatred—of Kit-Gregorio's support of Hen Wriothesley's efforts to develop Bermuda. Knowing Bacon was preventing James from sending any pay to the embassy in Venice, Naunton sent money of his own to help Kit's family.

Beside his official letters, Gregorio had started sending gossipy, entertaining, anonymous news-notes to a man named Marcantonio de Dominis, ex-Archbishop of Spalato, who'd defected from the Roman Catholic Church to live in England—a man who was great friends with Archbishop of Canterbury George Abbott. The Venetian ambassador in London was in trouble because of various irregularities, and Gregorio had sent an official dispatch confirming the deeds of this ambassador, who then asked Archbishop Abbott how Gregorio knew so much. The archbishop displayed one of the informal, private letters to de Dominis and said that England had an anonymous informant in Venice who knew all secrets.[405] That arrogant statement caused consternation when it reached the Venetian Council—all secrets? Who could this person be? (Kit, frightened, writes about this situation in ciphers in his Bargraves Polisie.)

Not much was going on at Venice, but news from other places trickled in: Trouble was boiling up for King James' daughter and her husband the Elector Palatinate, who wanted to rule Bohemia.

And a report came from England: ex-Treasurer Good Tom Howard was in the Tower, framed for embezzlement of treasury funds. At first, angry, he'd threatened to tell the truth about the Trophonean Den; then he quietly submitted. James would soon reduce his fine and release him; the permanent damage, of course, was to his reputation.[406]

By the beginning of 1620 Gregorio had received no pay for months. Robert Naunton sent more of his own. Gregorio and Micaela had a new baby.[407]

The Venetian ambassador in London wrote home again about the amazing news that had been coming out of Venice to de Dominis. (De Dominis was letting everybody read Kit's funny letters! Scary!) The ambassador was trying to discover the author's name.

Behind-the-scenes gossip was easier for Kit to collect than news suitable to put into official dispatches. Kit had to struggle; he wrote to Secretary Naunton about Paul Pindar, the English ambassador retiring from Constantinople and arriving in Venice. Pindar stayed in Venice for a month before heading for England. During those same weeks, news came from the Valtelline of a Spanish massacre of protestants, a deed intended to make that valley safe for Spanish troops marching north.[408]

Letters authorizing knighthood for Pindar arrived in Venice. The commander of the English ships here helping the Republic was supposed to do the honors but didn't come ashore, so Gregorio himself presented the documents.[409]

One day a young employe of the Spanish embassy in Venice recognized old Prospero Colombo as one of the "mercenary petardiers" who'd come to the Spanish embassy at the time of the Troubles. The youth told his friends the man must be a traitor, and while Prospero was walking on the street with his wife and friends, three boys from the Spanish embassy accosted him with a pistol. A shot was fired and a shout went up: "Kill, kill the Spaniards!" Though the young man dropped the pistol in fear, stone-throwing bystanders killed him and wounded the others. Gregorio wrote of this in his dispatch.[410]

The post brought Gregorio news from Isabel; her husband William had been created viscount. They wanted to come to Venice, maybe next fall, because at the first of the year William must attend a Parliament. Aha, thought Kit—a Parliament!

The Venice State Inquisitors heard from their ambassador in England: a man had been found, Don Celso Galarato, who said he knew the author of the odd news coming from Italy. Don Celso had worked for the ex-archbishop but had quarreled with him and was going home. When he reached Brussels he'd tell the author's name, and things truly extraordinary.[411]

Why did Gregorio write those indiscreet letters? He was penniless, trying to rear children, and as he was paid for the news-bits, he may have reached too far to make them entertaining. They've never been made public; they were sent in confidence, and Archbishop Abbott blew it when he told the Venetian ambassador. Did Abbott realize what he was doing? Was he being malicious?

It was late November before reports reached Venice of the defeat of the protestant Prince Frederick and his queen, James' daughter Elizabeth. Bohemia was lost to them; Prague had been taken and Frederick was shown to have been dishonest.

At New Years, 1620/'21, Gregorio was in bed with a cold; it persisted, but he kept on sending dispatches with aid from Micaela, and on 29 January he wrote to Robert Naunton, surprised and grateful: he'd just received a letter from the Secretary saying that he, Gregorio, would soon receive a great honor. Kit wrote he hoped he'd be "permitted to come to England for the ceremony." A knighthood, after all these years?[412] Yes—the papers must have been sent to Venice, and Micaela, Kit and friends would have gone out to dinner to toast the first banished man ever knighted. Here's his letter, translated:

"Illustrious Lord, my most Reverend Lord.

"With the mail of this week I have received a letter from your Most Illustrious Lordship of the 28th of last month [Dec. 1620] which has given me the greatest contentment, for it testifies that my humble services are viewed with favor by His Majesty. For this I render thanks first to God, then to His Majesty who has deigned to bestow on me such great honor; and I shall remain eternally obliged to Your Illustrious Lordship for what you have done on my behalf in securing the great favor of which I am the recipient. Thus, I pray God that I may be allowed to come and attend in person this ceremony, and humbly kiss His Majesty's feet. Meanwhile, I beg to remain in your good graces and to commend now my humble family to the benevolence of our Gracious Patron.

"The two Gentlemen whom your Most Illustrious Lordship has commended to me are today in Padua, where they wait. I shall serve them well and do everything in my power to implement their orders in all circumstances; the results you will see will be evidence of my zeal.

"Otherwise, there is nothing to report but that the projects of those gentlemen seem to advance rather slowly: they are waiting (as everyone seems to think) to see what the Most Christian King will do with regard to the answer that the Catholic King will give him. On the morning of the 20th of this month the Pope was victim of a most serious accident, so that now he is with fever; and according to the observations of the physicians, in general, in men of that advanced age, such accidents are messengers of death. I end here in kissing with reverence the hands of your Most Illustrious Lordship, praying God to grant you a long and happy life.

"Of your Most Illustrious lordship
I am your most humble and obedient Gregorio."

In whimsical ciphers for his Bargraves Polisie, ll 465-466, Marlowe wrote: "Ye late Sir Kit, mean and shameless . . ."

The only printed encomium I've found for Kit as a knight was written by John Taylor the Water Poet—a backhanded memorial pamphlet printed in 1622, crammed with cryptic biographic notes and titled, "Sir Gregory Nonsence His Newes from no place."(sic)[413] Five cryptic names on the title page make an anagram:

Marlowe's Life, Part IV

"Queer Kyt M; he has gone up to spy on Pluto.

Coachman."

John Taylor, an honest man, was a watercoachman on the Thames.

The first Parliament to sit in seven years opened on 30 January, 1621, and Lord Chancellor Bacon, now also Baron Verulam and Viscount St. Albans, swept into the House of Lords without the customary bow. Hen was there, mindful of his talk with Gregorio on the Venice beach. Bacon's behavior in Chancery was to be examined, and if the right of the Lords to impeach was questioned, the precedent in the Chronicon Angliae would be cited.

To this day Bacon is defended by adherents who don't see he was tried on secret charges. To those people it seems Bacon was gunned down only for taking bribes, a crime all too common at the time. But the charges were well founded, and bad enough.

A commission was formed to investigate; Henry Wriothesley, Third Earl of Southampton (Hen), and Mary Herbert's son William and Good Tom's nephew Arundel were members. On 17 April, after a message from the King, Hen was first to speak: he brought up the Lord Chancellor's case and directed the appointed committees to proceed. On 19 April, Hen said he'd examined many persons and had given the records to Mr. Attorney. "We heard publicly that the Lord Chancellor, having ordered matters in court, did afterwards alter them upon petition."[414]

Bacon had gone home sick, and Hen wanted him to come and answer charges. He didn't, but sent messages and a confession that wasn't a confession. When the House started to deal with other matters, Hen, polite but persistent, brought it back to the Chancellor's case. There was talk of bail. Hen said, "imprisonment may be easier than bail." Bacon offered to be good, said he'd give up the Great Seal; let that be his punishment.

The commission was gentle but firm: Bacon would keep his titles, be fined and imprisoned during the king's pleasure, and—the bottom line—be unable to hold any office, place or employment in State or Commonwealth, never sit in Parliament or come within twelve miles of the court. This meant he'd no longer be Chancellor, Keeper of the Great Seal, or chief of SSS.[415]

James dragged his feet about sending Bacon to the Tower, but Hen insisted, and Bacon was imprisoned. Some historians write that he sent "desperate pleas" to James, asking for release, but no, he sent a crisp directive: "Procure the warrant for my discharge this day."[416]

Soon he was out, filled with fury, and Hen was jailed. William Parkhurst, ex-secretary at Wotton's Venice embassy, was chosen by James to be Hen's jailer. They had a lot to talk about, and though the detention, intended to soothe Bacon's wrath, was soon over, James was forced to continue giving Hen a bad time about Bermuda, because of Gondomar's persistent influence.

Continuing to visit the Spanish ambassador in London, Bacon, officially out of SSS, put his decipherer Thomas Phellippes to work trying to crack the Venetian Republic's cipher. Bacon thought of Wotton and de' Monti as false servants. (A man doesn't *retire* from SSS! Did stupid Harry and Gregorio put Southampton up to that mess in the House of Lords?) When Phelippes came with an intercepted note about the Venetian Inquisitors' quest for the author of the rash news from Venice and the imminent revelations of Don Celso, Bacon moved. There must be no foreign public investigation of anyone who'd served English State Secret Service abroad for so many years!

Now we must deal with shadows: Did Bacon send an urgent coded letter to his favorite agent Toby Mathew? Toby was at Rubens' house in Antwerp, ostensibly dealing for a painting Carleton wanted to sell Prince Charles, secretly dealing with Catholic agent Rubens about a faintly possible (fictitious) future marriage contract between Prince Charles and the Infanta. Toby suddenly left, heading for Italy, riding fast.

The summer of 1621 had been oddly cold and rain-soaked in Venice. Harry Wotton was back as ambassador again, disillusioned by the war in Europe, gloomy about the picayune nature of his job here and lack of pay from the English government.

Gregorio and Micaela's children were growing. There were three boys—each with a more or less twisted foot like his dad's (but there was nothing wrong with their brains, Kit says in Bargraves Polisie), and a little girl, Cleo, with two good feet, who wanted to be an actress.[417] One of the boys was named Iseppo;[418] the others' names I don't know. Gregorio had finished writing the constitution he made for Captain John Bargrave. In those ciphers we learn details of Kit's worsening sickness, which more and more often slipped him into coma, so Micaela had to finish the government dispatches he was supposed to send to England. He was still revising plays and starting to teach his children reading and arithmetic.

Micaela took her husband to hear Claudio Monteverdi direct a great requiem at the Church of Zuan e Paulo, and they came home through rain, Gregorio depressed. Sooner or later the Venice Inquisitori would send for him, and right now he and Harry were Bacon's targets. Micaela and the children should go south to la Guarina at San Bellino, to stay with Guarini's son's family. But she said no, she wouldn't go without Gregorio, and he couldn't leave Harry unprotected.

In the second week of October Harry took his "family" to his villa at Noventa for Octoberfest, and the celebrants carried along wine decanted into flagons from the butt in the cellar. Gregorio and his family stayed in town to deal with any business.

Gregorio decanted some wine; he and Micaela drank several glasses during the next day—felt sick. Gregorio went to bed. Micaela called a doctor. Fever and pain persisted. Word came that six people, including Harry, were sick in bed at Noventa; some went to the hospital. Harry's ex-steward Will Leete, who'd come over from Padua University for supper, was dying.

Feeling better, Micaela brought the mail from the Hotel Rossi: there was a letter saying that Gregorio's friend Mary Herbert was dead.[419] The ship was sinking. Vomiting and fever stuck with Kit.

On 21 November Wotton, very weak, came back to Venice. Will Leete was dead, a secretary had been left in bed at Padua, and now Harry's steward Edward Deering had to be carried to bed upstairs at the embassy house, where Gregorio lay sick in his separate apartment.

About midnight he let go: Micaela held him, the chaplain prayed, and Kit Marlowe, Sir Gregorio, died. The next day the embassy chaplain held a service, and at Harry's request the Council allowed art-collector Andrea Vendramin(?) to send a sculptor, who made a plaster deathmask.[420]

Alone at his desk, Harry wept and wrote to the Secretary in England, saying he was working on a separate dispatch about Gregorio plus a ciphered report on some strange things. He blamed "the crudity of the wine."[421]

Was Kit's body buried at sea? His skull may have been preserved. His papers were carefully kept. In shock, Micaela paid for a mass, took Gregorio's portrait, their personal belongings and their children and carted them into the shadows. I believe she took them south to San Bellino and accepted a job as housekeeper for Guarini's son's family, because later generations of Montis worked as stewards of the neighboring Ferrarese Calcagnini estate. A Calcagnini had been professor of Belles Lettres at Ferrara U, a Guarini his teacher,[422] and Battista himself later filled that post.[423] (Several generations later, a famous poet, Vincenzo Monti, was born of the line of Montis who worked for the Calcagnini. Micaela would have liked that; she told Kit once that babies make you immortal, and she was partial to poets.)[424]

Near the end of January 1622 the last victim of the strange wine, Harry's cousin and steward Edward Deering, died at the English embassy house in Venice.[425] If it had been revenge, it was over.

f

Afterward

Back in England on 28 December 1621, Toby Mathew had landed at Dover, hurried to James and then to Bacon,[426] who right away looked for an agent of his named John Borough, soon located by Bacon's secretary.[427] Before long Borough was on his way to Venice, ostensibly to buy Italian manuscripts for Bacon's pal Robin Cotton, really to bring back Gregorio's play-scripts from the English embassy house.[428]

Through the dark glass, do we see Bacon planning to use a published folio collection of those plays as a worthy matrix for his own ciphered messages, his last big scheme? Using his already published version of a respected cipher,[429] he may have intended to record, in Latin, his frustrated longing for royal power, the secret of his birth, excuses for his miserable treatment of his half-siblings. He hoped that though his life may end in ignominy, readers in a distant future may find, decipher and believe messages telling of the suppression of his spirit by usurpers, messages showing Francis Bacon to be a worthy prince. Such an effort would be akin to sad phrases carved by a prisoner on a dungeon wall, or notes bottled up and thrown in the sea by a castaway, except for the fact that in his bitterly contrived remarks Bacon might not resist lying, and his ciphers could claim authorship of "Shakespeare" plays. (Kit, in ciphers for Sonnet 135, very angrily mentions that not only Shakespeare, but *Bacon* was claiming to have written Kit's work.[430])

Harry still wondered who poisoned the wine: the Venetian Inquisition, the Spanish Embassy—Francis Bacon? When Borough showed up so promptly with a note from Bacon demanding release of Kit's playscripts and corrected quartos, Harry was dubious; he knew Kit had been preparing a folio for London publisher Edward Blount. Harry told Borough it would take a while to find the works.

But as soon as Wotton left in his gondola, Borough must have re-entered the house with an assistant and told a secretary what he'd come for. He must have been provided at once with a stack of scripts, fair copies and edited rough-copies as well as quartos pasted up with corrections and additions—more than thirty plays, enough to fill the big cases brought by Borough and his aides.

When Harry came back he was dismayed to learn what had happened and sent a letter off to Blount.

In the same post to England there'd have been a letter for Bacon from Borough listing titles of the plays he had lifted, and with this information Bacon went to the

Master of Revels, telling him to issue the required certificates and submit to Stationers' Register the titles and the name of the publisher Bacon had selected.

But the Master of Revels was Sir George Buck, Kit's friend from days when they were poor poets at Fisher's Folly. Kit and George had been together at the Cádiz raid of 1596,[431] and George had followed Kit's hidden career through his plays and the players, and by talking with Blount, publisher of Kit's Hero and Leander, his translations of Don Quixote I and II and other things. George knew Blount had been buying from the players rights to publish the many plays Kit had been revising. Bacon was no longer SSS chief, no longer controlled a theater wing. Buck advised him to talk to Blount about registry.

Francis Bacon coldly denounced Kit as a worthless dead slave whose work had been produced at Bacon's order, practically at his dictation. He said he'd see to it that if Buck didn't cooperate he'd not hold his position much longer.

A week later the Revels Office burned: George Buck's office-books, his script of The Baron, his long history of The Art of Revels—all his unpublished works—were lost. He suffered an emotional breakdown, then a stroke.[432]

Edward Blount was no fool. When Harry's letter reached him he suspected Bacon's purpose; the man had already stuffed some ciphers into the works of Ben Jonson. Blount wanted to protect his rights in Marlowe's works and also preserve the validity of the edited texts.

He went to Bacon and made an offer. Of the plays Borough was bringing to London, fifteen unpublished ones had been bought by Blount—he could prove payment. He didn't want to be unfriendly; a mutual adventure would be fine with him. He'd share expenses and profit with Bacon's chosen publisher; he'd insist on sharing printing labor, too, and if amicable terms were reached, Blount in addition could provide presentation copies of three other unpublished plays of Kit's—copies more accurate than any prompt-books Bacon might find. If agreement was not possible, Bacon must be satisfied with only those plays of Kit's which Blount did not possess.[433]

A decent proposal, but Bacon hesitated, not wanting to reveal to Blount the typesetting problems to be created by implantation of the Bacon cipher. Why should the man insist on helping with printing?

When Blount said he knew Bacon's intent, Bacon was almost relieved and accepted him as a partner, swearing him to secrecy.

Bacon's secret operation seems to have consisted of setting into certain printed italics (In blocks or separate words) two typeface fonts leaning at different angles, used in combinations and at intervals suitable to create his messages. Blount helped set type himself to make sure no distortion touched the text. Composition and printing were done at the Jaggard shop with men selected by Bacon, and he joined in the labor. The crew, seen as shadows, may have been Bacon as watcher, young Isaac Jaggard, printer, and compositors Ben Jonson, Edward Blount, Robert Cotton, Bacon's old friend George Carew, (Baron Carew of Clopton) and a Master Herbert who'd been translating Bacon's works into Latin. (At some point in the printing process Herbert seems to have to bowed out sick. Who'd have succeeded him?)

The door was kept locked, the shades drawn, and the work seemed endless. Bacon and Herbert re-checked only the blocks of Bacon's own cipher-copy; Ben Jonson and Edward Blount proofed most of Kit's text. They knew Kit had inserted thousands of linked anagrams in his finished copy. His idiosyncratic spelling, creating his messages, had to be preserved. That Jonson and Blount managed to do this so well is truly astonishing: in the parts Kit ciphered, at least, proofing is meticulous—evidenced by the two-column work in the pages of ciphers presented in this book. Only in Othello are ciphered lines badly mangled—so badly it looks as if Kit was trying for minimalism.

Inserting Bacon's noodley cipher was time-consuming. The eyestraining printing and proofing process dragged on for about twenty months—to the end of December 1623.[434]

Prince Charles was to receive the first copy at a party, so Ben Jonson made a masque, Time Vindicated, or the Prince's Masque.[435] The first version of the anti-masque of this work is filled with allusions to the dreary months of labor at the printery. The audience for the masque was a small courtly group of initiates. Bacon was of course absent.

In the playlet Bacon's behavior is satirized (he's called Chronomastix, the timewaster) along with that of his secret compositors, called the Mutes, who come at the bidding of Chronomastix in order to snub Fame for having insulted him. Ben Jonson says one of the Mutes is the printer in disguise, who conceals himself and "his presse in a hollow tree, and workes by glow-worm light, the moon's too open." The Mutes crowd into a dark place to work their eyes out "*on an angle*"—measuring the different angles of the italic letters? "What a confederacy of folly!" Fame cries.

But Ben shows the audience that in spite of all that, the time spent on the folio has been vindicated, for here come the leading characters of the plays in costume, bringing the big book itself to Prince Charles. The show ends with a sober remonstrance:

"Man should not hunt mankind to death!"

After the Folio was printed, Bacon wanted to destroy the manuscripts containing Kit's handwriting, scripts which had been used as copy, especially those that were foul-papers revised—evidence of Kit's authorship of the plays. All the folio source-material had been piled up in Ben Jonson's library, so it was easy for Bacon to set the room afire while Jonson was out for the day. Not only Kit's authorial scripts (including Pericles and Cardenio? not printed in the Folio), but Ben's own unpublished works and his lifelong collection of books and manuscripts, were burned to ashes in a few hours.[436] Ben wrote an accusatory poem about Bacon's love of arson, "Execration of Vulcan," and kept it hidden till his own death.

Before the Shakespeare folio appeared, a monument to Shakespeare had been erected inside Trinity Church, Stratford-on-Avon, and how it got there is a mystery. Bacon probably chose the spot, but why so long after Will Shakespeare's death? Could it have been an advertisement for the soon-to-be-published First Folio?

It can be shown that Kit's friends, after his real death, managed to control the monument's design. Except for the idea thrust forth out-front in the six-line poem's text, and the spear on the coat of arms, it's a memorial to Kit. Even the nobody-in-the-niche, in some lights, at some angles, resembles the Droeshout engraving, a not very good portrait of Kit. How could Marlowe's friends have accomplished so much? Which friends were they? Bacon surely didn't realize he'd allowed sly characters to do the work.

The architecture of the monument resembles Kit's real father's monument at St. Stephens outside Canterbury, though Sir Roger's, designed by famous Maximilian Coult, is more elegant and costly. (Roger gave Maximilian his first big job.[437]) Manwood's cenotaph features white Bethesden marble from Kent and black marble. So does Kit's. The half-statue in the niche at Stratford has a high bald crown like Kit's and a pose like Roger's. The Stratford man's mouth is open; he's trying to tell us something. On his doublet are twenty-nine buttons, for Kit's twenty-nine years an English subject? And count 'em again for his nearly twenty-nine years of exile?

Two putti sit on cornices above the Stratford statue. The one on the right touches a sculptured skull with his right hand while his left holds a torch upside down, extinguished by its own burning. The other cherub holds a shovel signifying all the dirty work Kit did for SSS over years. Between the two children is a large box (an ossuary?) decorated in front with a small shield diagonally crossed with a spear that looks to be a pen, and above it a plumed black helmet especially suitable for Kit, since he lived so long under cover of Pluto's helmet, death, which had made him invisible. The box has a low pyramidal roof topped by a mysterious real skull with high cranium, septum in the nose and two missing teeth. The lower jaw seems to be sunk in cement.

Chiseled into the top of the stone panel below the niche are two Latin lines describing Kit's own character and achievements—in both plaintext and interior message, which is in English. The ciphers are signed by Kit's half-brother Peter, and are included in this book. Underneath is carved an important poem of six pentameter lines praising "Shakspeare" on the outside. Its cogent inside message, also in pentameter, rhyming ababcc, is a tribute to Kit signed with the letter H—standing for Harry, or Hen? Kit's bitter cipher on Will Shakespeare's tombstone, on the floor of the chancel, is also included in these pages.

A postscript may help finish the story: When his natural father, Kit, died, William Davenant was sixteen years old. Orphaned within the next months but befriended by Isabel-Elizabeth and William Cavendish, the boy was working for the duchess of Richmond as a page.[438] He wrote a memorial poem for his ghost-writer father and showed it to Prince Charles, who objected to the word "captive." Will changed it to "captain," and Charles kept the verses.[439]

Will Davenant grew up to become an energetic theatrical producer, the first in England to present real actresses onstage, the first to use music which brought some of his productions close to opera.[440] He became poet laureate of England, not because he was a good poet, but because of Kit? Knighted, Davenant served as lieutenant general of ordnance: he was in charge of the ammunition Queen Henrietta-Maria brought north for Newcastle in February 1643.[441] As the queen came ashore at Bridlington, she was attacked by enemy guns,[442] and shadows suggest that Isabel-Elizabeth, who'd come from Welbeck to meet her, was wounded trying to shield her and died of the wound on 17 April 1643.

After Kit died, Harry made mistakes in Venice, wanted to go home. When long-time worker Paolo Sarpi was laid to rest in January 1623, Harry gave up hope for religious reform in Italy and left Venice that October, crossing the Alps for the last time, reaching England in December.[443] James owed him a lot of money and couldn't pay, but the Provostship of Eton was vacant. Both Wotton and Bacon applied for the place, and in July 1624 it was Wotton who won out and became part of academe.[444] It may have been in that month that Bacon became unhinged.

Now the real live two Noble Kinsmen, Henry Vere and Hen Wriothesley, sailed for Holland as soldiers—Hen as leader of an army, taking along his son James. England was at last allied with Holland, France, and Venice,[445] and Bacon's dream of Spanish glory was dead. In Holland that November 1624, Hen and his son died of fever, and their bodies were brought back to Southampton.[446]

In March 1625 James died a painful three-day death. His faithful Scots physician, Dr. George Eglisham, came to the new King Charles with a warning: King James and Henry Wriothesley, Earl of Southampton, had been intentially poisoned (Hen's son's death was a mistake, the doctor thought), and Charles must beware.[447] Charles vowed revenge. Dr. Eglisham believed that James' favorite, Buckingham, had planned the murders, but Charles thought otherwise. Harry was called from Eton to be a detective, and after a trace-job Buckingham was cleared and other leads were followed.

A week before Easter 1626, King Charles conferred with royal physician Dr. Witherborne, and Bacon was informed that his last hour was near. Medicated, he and the doctor set off for an outing in a closed carriage, driving into the snowy hills behind London. Thinking of escape, Bacon stopped the coach. Then, deciding he must create a death worthy of his image, his instauration, he climbed out—they'd drawn up before a farmstead—asked for a dead plucked chicken and stuffed it with snow, discoursing before the goodwife on the possibilities of refrigeration before vomiting and re-entering the carriage. He was driven to an Arundel house where the steward showed doctor and patient to a bedchamber in an unused wing, and there Bacon vomited again, sent for old Julius Caesar to come and stay with him, dictated a graceful note of thanks to his absent host, and died of medication, on Easter day.[448]

Harry grew old at Eton, his burglar tools wrapped up and willed to his lawyer.[449] Feeling he'd "arrived near those years which lie in the suburbs of oblivion," he received students, masters and guests in his smoky study, inducted young John Milton into the Resistance and Izaak Walton into SSS. Milton he sent to Naples to talk to undercover genius Gianbattista Manso,[450] and later Milton spent a month in Ferrara and Venice.[451] (Did he stop at San Bellino, meet Micaela and her children by Gregorio?).

Izaak Walton and Harry fished from a skiff at a bend of the Thames near Eton, at a place called the Black Pots. Baiting their hooks with frogs, they spent peaceful hours talking of SSS skills and projects. Izaak was editing a book about Harry's life[452] and decided to include in his own book (about fishing) Kit's poem, Come Live with Me. Izaak knew Harry'd been commissioned by the king to write a history of the Service. They spoke of what the different honest men were really like, about old times. The boat slid through the water. No words, only the murmur of their voices reached the shore.

f

Notes

1 Lucien Wolf. "Jews in Elizabethan England." Transactions of the Jewish Historical Society of England. vol XI, 1927. Page 9 tells of the secret Synagogue in Antwerp in 1593 to which English Marranos sent donations.

Leo Rosten. The Joys of Yiddish. NY: Washington Square Press, 1968, p 224. "Marrano Jews founded the modern Jewish communities in Amsterdam and London." Rosten cites Cecil Roth. History of the Marranos, 3rd edition. Oxford, 1959, and Proceedings of the American Academy for Jewish Research. vol xxxi, 1933. B. Netanyahu. "The Marranos of Spain."

2 A.D. Wraight and Virginia Stern. In Search of Christopher Marlowe. NY: Vanguard, 1965, p 280: Pedigree of Walsingham, second family of that name in England, begins with a Sir Richard who died during the reign of Edward I, the Edward who outlawed Jewish families in England.

Conyers Read. Mr. Secretary Walsingham and the Policy of Queen Elizabeth. Cambridge, MA: Harvard U. Press, 1925, vol 1, p 3. The far-back Valsung Walsingham "ancestors" are mythical.

Robert Tittler. Nicholas Bacon, the Making of a Tudor Statesman. London: Jonathan Cape, 1976, p 15. Sir Nicholas Bacon's family, too, was the second family of that name in England, unrelated to the 13th-century family of Roger Bacon. Earliest known relatives of Sir Nicholas appeared around Hesset and Drinkstone in Suffolk at start of the 16th century.

3 Edward Foss. The Judges of England. NY: AMS Press, 1966. vol 5, p 516.

4 Sir Roger Manwood. DNB. The gift was made in 1563: the royal manor of St. Stephen's or Hackington, Kent.

5 Ibid. Knighted mid-Nov. 1578 while Elizabeth was at Richmond.

E.K. Chambers. The Elizabethan Stage. Oxford: Clarendon Press, 1923, Appendix A, "A Court Calendar," p 95.

6 Robert J. Blackham. The Story of the Temple, Gray's and Lincoln's Inn. London: Sampson, Low, Marston & Co, n.d. Chain described on pp 180, 181. (note 127 here)

7 Ibid. Manwood became Chief Baron on 17 Nov. 1578.

8 Willam Urry. Christopher Marlowe and Canterbury. London: Faber and Faber, 1988, notes, and A. D. Wraight and Virginia Stern. op. cit. Both identify this William

Arthur as of Dover, and yeoman, and Urry says an older William Arthur, perhaps Kate's grandfather, had kept a pied-a-terre creekside in Dover. A yeoman of Dover would be a petty officer, a clerk, aboard ship; yeomen aboard often declared cargo at customs. Public Record Office. Sandwich and Dover Port-Books. E 190/638, 4, 5, 13, and E 190/640,1, 7 show yeomen declaring cargo for their captains.

9 Kate Arthur, seen as Hostess in Henry V, Act II, 3, tells of Falstaff's (Roger Manwood's) death: "Nay, sure, he's not in hell; he's in *Arthur's bosom,* if ever man went to Arthur's bosom"—and ll. 10 through 26 tell correct details of Manwood's dying. In the last part of Marlowe's cipher for The Taming of The Shrew, Kate as herself speaks loving words as she washes Sir Roger for burial.

10 William Pierce. An Historical Introduction to the Marprelate Tracts. London: Archibald Constable, 1908, p 283. Anti-Martinist writers called the author of the tracts, "halt and club-footed." [Marlowe had been delivering scripts of the satires to the printer. RB.] Marlowe wrote two youthful plays about famous characters known to be lame, though he omitted mention of their deformities.

Bakeless, John. The Tragicall History of Christopher Marlowe. Westport, CT: Greenwood, 1970 (1942), vol 1 pp 218, 219. Tamburlaine was lame—and club-footed, according to Bakeless' footnote quoting Perondinus' 1556 ed. And in the Tragedie of Dr. Faustus there's Lucifer, portrayed in other dramas as lamed by his fall from heaven.

11 Bakeless. Ibid. vol 1, pp 21 and 27. A shortened apprenticeship, and later a business in bailbonds.

12 John H. Ingram. Christopher Marlowe and his Associates. Cooper Square Pub. NY: 1970 (1904), p 17. A photo of the baptismal font (now gone) opposite this page. Marlowe was christened 26 Feb. 1564 at the Church of St. George the Martyr.

13 Antonio de Eslava. Noches de Invierno. Pamplona: Carlos de Labayen, 1609. copy preserved in N.Y.C. in the Library of the Hispanic Society of America. Mascot for a street-gang; the story of Kit as mascot, in a jacket bearing the colors of the boys' federation, is fictionalized in this strange book Marlowe wrote years later in Spanish. It contains a dedicatory anagrammatic cipher in English for Kit's daughter Isabel-Elizabeth Basset, whose first language was Spanish. On pp 160, 161, Orlando, child of Milon and Berta, brings his mother bread and other alms; the street boys in town (a federation of four parishes), seeing him poor and almost naked, take him as mascot, make him a jacket of cloth of the colors of the four parishes.

Thomas Frederick Crane. Italian Social Customs of the Sixteenth Century. NY: Russell & Russell, 1971 (1920), pp 630, '31, '32. With quotations from several observant scholars, Crane makes an excellent case for the author of Noches de Invierno as author of The Tempest. [Many stories in Noches contain Marlowe-like references.] The author, says Crane, appears to be a foreigner writing in Venice, but not a Spaniard. As Crane notices, the theme of the book [written for Kit's daughter Isabel] is a case for the cultural and political importance of women.

14 Alexander Frederick Falconer, Lieutenant Commander, Royal Naval Reserve. Shakespeare and the Sea. London: Constable, 1964. Kit as sailor-boy. 155 pp of examples demonstrating that author Shakespeare "turns to the sea and ships for illustrations, even when there is nothing in the theme itself that is connected with them . . . the wording and working out of likenesses rest on *professional knowledge.*" On p 67 Falconer says, "Alone of its kind in all literature, and beyond the range of painter or any but the supreme artist in words, is the picture of the boy sailor 'on the high and giddy mast, wet, overwatched and overcome by slumber.'" (Henry IV, Part 2. 3. 1. ll.18 ff.) Many of Marlowe's cipher-narratives also deal with sea and ships.

15 Manwood DNB. Also Edward Foss. The Judges of England. op. cit., vol 5, p 517, and Sir Thomas Gresham's biography, noted below.

16 John William Burgon. Life and Times of Sir Thomas Gresham. 2 vols. NY: Burt Franklin, 1965 (1839). A perceptive work.

17 Ibid. vol 1, p 204. "Churchyard . . . found a patron as well as an admirer in Sir Thomas Gresham." In his poem,"Shore's Wife," Churchyard wrote "They brake the bowes and shakte the tree by sleight,/And bent the wand that mought have growne full streight." In Doctor Faustus, Kit paraphrased, "Cut is the branch that might have grown full straight/ And burned is Apollo's laurel-bough . . ."

Gresham first hired Churchyard in the 1560's as intelligencer; in later years, working for Oxford, Churchyard would have known Marlowe and perhaps taught the boy first steps of drama-writing.

18 Ibid. vol 2, p 461. Ned rented from Gresham in the parish of St. Peter the Poor.

19 Dorothy and Charlton Ogburn. This Star of England. Westport CT: Greenwood, 1952, p 122. "Oxford's faithful steward, Thomas Curchyard . . . When Oxford was only seventeen years old he sent Churchyard . . . to Dillenburg, near Cologne . . . to raise troops to combat the Duke of Alva . . . Churchyard was still serving the earl loyally in 1590."

20 J. Thomas Looney. Shakespeare Identified. 2 vols. ed. Ruth L. Miller. Port Washington, NY: Kennikat Press, Minos Publishing, 1975, passim, and Ogburns. This Star of England. op. cit., passim. Evidence of Ned's interest in the Theater Wing of English State Secret Service is displayed in confused but valuable perspective in these works. The SSS Theater Wing became the love of Oxford's life; at first, interest in theater itself predominated; later he concentrated on SS pursuivance of persons he considered traitors-to-the-state. Some titles of his own efforts at dramatic writing can be obliquely viewed in A. Feuillerat. Documents Relating to the Office of the Revels in the Time of Queen Elizabeth. 1908, Materialien xxi. Kit completely rewrote several of Ned's plays. Kit's ciphers in Henry V and Henry IV Part I show Ned trying to write and produce things at court and on Progress in the 1570's and early '80's, with faint help from Churchyard, John Lyly, Anthony Munday, George Gascoigne. Oxford produced

using The Children of the Chapel, Paul's Boys, Oxford's Boys and other boys' companies.

E. K. Chambers. The Elizabethan Stage. Oxford: Clarendon, 1923: In his section on Boy's Companies, vol 2, Chambers mentions "Oxford's Boys" only as a full-line title on p 76 (no text), referring the reader to Oxford's adult companies, vol 2 p 99.

Ogburns. This Star of England. op. cit., p 14. When Ned managed the entertainment for Elizabeth's Progress in 1578, she granted him £250 annually.

Alan H. Nelson. Monstrous Adversary. The Life of Edward de Vere, 17th Earl of Oxford. Liverpool: Liverpool U., 2003, p 310. On 26 June 1586, the queen granted Ned an additional £1000 annually under a Privy Seal Warrant, to be paid quarterly—probably for theater.

21 For this entertainment, with its Italianate sailor boy and mention of Montagues and Capulets, see George Gascoigne's "An Hundreth Sundrie Flowers." copy in Folger Shakespeare Library, 1907 ed.

22 Gresham at Kenilworth party. Anti-semitic monograph: Gresham DNB. A negative view of his expense-accounts. A different opinion:

Richard Ehrenberg. Capital and Finance in the Age of the Renaissance. NY: Harcourt, Brace & Co., n.d., pp 252-255. Ehrenberg praises Gresham. "In his capacity of 'royal merchant' . . . he is one of the most important figures of the sixteenth century and the history of England." That Kit was with him as page is suggested by the fact that elements of the shows performed at the Kenilworth party are identifiable in Shakespeare plays: Halpin. "Oberon's Vision Illustrated," Shakespeare Society, 1843, quotes A Midsummer Night's Dream 2. 1. ll. 148-168 as example of what Shakespeare saw at the party. See also Twelfth Night, 1. 2. l.15, and John Nichols. The Progresses & Public Processions of Queen Elizabeth. London: for and by J. Nichols & Son. vol 1. reprint 1966, pp 422—523. Also Nichols vol 1 p 458, re Arion on the dolphin.

E. K. Chambers. Eliz. Stage. op. cit., and E.K. Chambers. William Shakespeare, A Study of Facts and Problems. Oxford: Clarendon, 1930.

23 Christopher Carleill DNB. Also Francis Walsingham's bios. as well as James A. Williams, The Age of Drake, London: Adam and Charles Black, n.d., S.A.S. Skilliter. William Harborne and the Trade with Turkey. London: Oxford U Press, 1977, chap. one, pp 19, 20. (taken from PRO, SP12/114, ff. 84-5).

A voyage in 1577, '78 ostensibly to trade at Alexandria, really to trade with Constantinople: Contraband tin figures in the cargo estimated for the Swallow and Pelican "for a voyage to the Levant, June 1577." This voyage began with more than one secret: Drake's Pelican split away to sail around the world as the Golden Hind, and the Swallow was accompanied to the Levant by another ship, the Judith, sent by Walsingham, Gresham, Hatton, George Barnes, the queen and others. Aboard the Judith, Carleill was master's mate, but on the way the Tigre was captured; her Spanish sailors sent ashore, Carleill became her captain. Kit and his Gresham cargo must have transferred to her: ciphers, Sonnet 126. The Tiger became Carleill's favorite ship; he sailed several times to Russia in her. T.S. Willen. Early History of the Russia Co. 1553-1603. NY: Augustus M. Kelley, 1968. On p 181 is a thumbnail genealogy of this soldier-seaman, Carleill. In George Malcolm Thomson. Sir Francis Drake. NY: Wm Morrow Co. 1972, Carleill's portrait is reproduced opposite p 223. Carleill sailed to America in the Tiger with Drake in 1585, served ashore there as a soldier with Captain Sampson, another friend of Kit's.

24 Manwood DNB and Burgon. op. cit. and Edward Foss. The Judges of England. op. cit., vol 5, document the friendship of Manwood and Gresham, and Manwood was one of the executors of Gresham's will. (Burgon. op. cit., vol 2, pp 491, 492.) Gresham was friends with Sir Francis Walsingham's closest circle of relatives and in-laws. Although Manwood's bio is fragmentary, evidence shows many of Sir Roger's friends and in-laws were Walsingham's, too, and it was Walsingham, *not Burghley*, who employed Sir Roger's son Kit in secret service work as long as Sir Francis lived. Kit is known to have been friends with Francis Walsingham's young cousin Tom Walsingham IV, of Scadbury (grandson of Sir Francis's uncle Edmund), and Tom's son, Thomas Walsingham V, married Roger Manwood's granddaughter Elizabeth. Wraight and Stern. In Search of Chr. M. op. cit., p 280, offer a Walsingham genealogical table, erring only in reporting early death for Walsingham's younger daughter Mary, who became Carleill's wife and lived at least till 1609. (Christopher Carleill DNB.)

25 Kit's cipher in Sonnet 126, addressed to Captain Kester (Christopher Carleill), reveals not only that they were lovers on the 1577-'78 voyage to the Levant, but substantiates the fact that they were together in the action against Sorley Boy Mac Donnell at Dunanany in the Glinns, Ireland, late in Dec. 1584. Sorley Boy's problems are made apparent in CSP Eliz, Sept. 1584 into May, 1585. (CSP is incorrect in dating the English attack at Dunanany 2 December: the combined forces of Carleill, Bagenall and Stanley arrived 30 Dec. CSP Ireland Eliz p 547 offers Bagenall's letter of 5 January.) Carleill's DNB suggests that on coming ashore from a privateering job, he was not informed (Bacon, his step-brother, should have told him) that Kit's 1593 death was a charade. The monograph quotes an early anonymous reporter: "Carleill died in London on 11 Nov. 1593, 'and, as is supposed, for grief of his frends death.'"

26 Ogburns. This Star of England. op. cit., p 141.

27 John Nichols. Progresses of Queen Elizabeth. op. cit., vol 1, prints out Churchyard's verses for the Turkish Boy, and details of other entertainments presented during the Progress of 1578.

28 John Burgon. Life and Times of . . . op. cit., vol 2, p 478, mentions a work dedicated to Sir Thos. Gresham c. 1570 by a friend, Henry Goughe. (NB his name: *Henry* Goughe, not Thos. Goffe, another writer on Turkish subjects, who may have been Henry's son.) Henry's book, titled Offspring of the House

of Ottomano, served as a source for Selimus, an early play of Kit's inspired by his 1577-'78 voyage to Constantinople and bolstered by geographical works of Ortelius, another friend of Gresham and Roger. Offspring such as those of the Ottomans appear in Selimus. Kit's byline is ciphered into the play.

29 Millia Davenport Harkavy, author of The Book of Costume. NY: Crown, 1948, and a costumer for Orson Welles' Mercury Theater, told me everyone in the company knew Ned de Vere buggered the children in his playing companies. This is backstage history passed from generation to generation of showbiz folk. Shadowy evidence of Ned's proclivity is found throughout Ned's bios: Alan H. Nelson. Monstrous Adversary, the Life of Edward de Vere, 17th Earl of Oxford. op. cit., pp 213-218, devotes all of Chap 41 Part VI to Ned as "Sodomite," but here Nelson does not include Oxford's decades-long (often sub-rosa) control of the boy-players. Let's make things clear: when Rosencrantz mentions the child players to Hamlet (Hamlet. 2. 2. ll. 339-341) as "little eyeasses," and follows by saying they're "tyrannically clapp'd for it," he's not thinking of them as baby birds but as youthful victims ruthlessly infected with syphilis. Here in the play, Hamlet apparently has only a detached interest in the young players; in living truth, the secret prince discreetly managed those boys for court entertainments.

30 Henry IV Part I ciphers. ll. 95, 96, 97, 98, " . . . Yet it's true their plans were immoderately ambitious—th' syc hopes f-fuckin' high . . ." But he cooperated.

31 Dr. William Urry. Christopher Marlowe and Canterbury. London, Boston: Faber and Faber, 1988. His chapter 3 offers excellent coverage of Marlowe's months of schooling.

32 Wraight and Stern. In Search of Christopher Marlowe. op. cit., pp 41, 42.

33 The Erotokritos. A ballad with happy end, attributed to Vincenzo Kornaros of Crete. Surely Kit had already read Arthur Brooke's Romeus and Juliet, published 1562. Kit was in Crete during the first two months of 1594—see text ahead. In the ballad there's a scene showing knights from various Greek states jousting, well-suited to a Greek-language King's School play crammed with youngsters not fluent in Greek—lots of action and few words. Kit would have played Erotokritos—his banner a Moth. In his later Pericles, too, there's a parade of Greekish knights ready to joust, and in the first, farcical, version of The Two Noble Kinsmen, written and produced in Venice May 1618 by John Fletcher and Kit, there's a jousting scene, a fight between the two kinsmen. When acted out, as at King's School or in burlesque, the actors would have worn "basket horses"—popular features of clownish acts at fairs in those old days and today still seen in circus walkarounds.

John Mavrogordato. The Erotokritos. London: Humphrey Milford for Oxford U Press, 1929, offers a close paraphrase of this work, aware of the ballad's mysteriously resonant relation to Shakespeare plays. The Erotokritos seems to have been first printed at Venice, 1713. The only known MS of the poem, dated 1710, was bought in Corfu for five guineas in 1725 for Edward Harley (d. 1741), husband of Kit's great-great-granddaughter Henrietta Cavendish Holles. The script is in the Harleian Collection in the British Museum.

34 James Mc Mullen Rigg's monograph on Manwood, DNB, mentioned the friendship. Rigg also wrote that Manwood's letters to Parker were held in Parker Corresp., Parker Society Papers, pp 187-192, 338, 405. They may have been removed; Rigg wrote of other of Sir Roger's letters preserved with "Manwood Papers" in Inner Temple Library, and I was informed on the phone by the librarian there that no such collection exists.

35 Francis Kett. DNB. Also William Urry. Chr. M. and Canterbury. op. cit., p 55. Burned alive for heretical opinion, in the castle ditch at Norwich, 14 Jan. 1589. In Marprelate writings, scathing remarks for the bishops who ordered this death.

36 John Greenwood, at Corpus Christi, Cambridge, became an "independent divine," suffered and was hanged—along with Roger Manwood's outspoken lawyer-friend Henry Barrowe—6 April, 1593. Both died at order Archbishop Whitgift. John Penry of Peterhouse College, Cambridge, independent minister, was hanged 29 May, 1593, at order Archbishop Whitgift. John Udall, puritan of Trinity College, Cambridge, was imprisoned under sentence of death as a heretic. In early June 1592 the queen signed his pardon, which was ignored, and on 15 June 1592 Udall died in jail. DNB for each of the above.

37 George Walker. Haste, Post Haste. London: Geo. Harrap & Co. 1938, pp 86-93. Puritan Will Brewster of Peterhouse left Cambridge 1583 to work for the Post—travelled to Holland and back, served Postmaster Thomas Randolph 18 years as postmaster and pastor at Scrooby, fled to the Netherlands and returned to sail in the Mayflower to Plymouth Plantation, where he lived the rest of his life a pilgrim in America. A sideline: a letter to me from Dr. Wm. Urry 25 Sept. 1978 says the Mayflower was hired by Canterbury grocer Robert Cushman, who'd lived in the house once occupied by Goodwife Roose, midwife for Kate when she bore Kit.

38 Dr. Powel Mills Dawley. John Whitgift and the English Reformation. NY: Charles Scribner's Sons, 1954, presents a bio of this archbishop, a work perhaps intended to be sympathetic. Close-reading of that text, along with study of Whitgift's DNB by Sidney Lee and many items in G.B. Harrison. An Elizabethan Journal, Being a Record of Those Things Most Talked About During the Years 1591-1594. NY: Cosmopolitan Books, 1929, present a clear picture of a power-mad zealot. Sidney Lee wrote, "In his examination of prisoners he showed a brutal insolence which is alien to all modern conceptions of justice or religion."

39 Martin Haile. An Elizabethan Cardinal, William Allen. NY and London: Sir Isaac Pitman and Sons, 1914. Valuable. Crammed with true facts.

40 Francis Walsingham. Elizabeth Tudor called Walsingham her Moor. That he was her childhood friend can be deduced from the fact that his stepfather, Sir John Carey, when appointed bailiff of the royal manor of Hunsdon in 1538, took his wife and presumably his family to live there. Elizabeth was a

child at Hunsdon during a period in which her tutors brought children of the household to study with her, so in all probability she and Francis were classmates.

Conyers Read. Mr. Secretary Walsingham and the Policy of Queen Elizabeth. NY: AMS Reprint 1978. (Cambridge, MA: Harvard U Press, 1925), vol 1, p 13. Conyers Read says, "through his stepfather . . . whose brother had married Queen Elizabeth's maternal aunt, Walsingham had something of a special claim on the consideration of the Queen herself." Walsingham's mother, Joyce, was daughter of Sir Edmund Denny of Cheshunt, and both Elizabeth and Francis spent time at Joyce's brother Anthony's place there in childhood. Ibid. vol i, (p 11?)

41 Ibid., and Douay Diaries: The First and Second Diaries of the English College, Douay, with Appendix of Unpublished Documents. (Intro by Thomas Francis Knox, D.D.). London: David Nutt, 1878.

42 Virginia F. Stern. Gabriel Harvey, His Life, Marginalia and Library. Oxford: Clarendon Press, 1979, pp 15-16, 39n, 49, and more. Edmund Spenser was Gabriel Harvey's admired friend, whom Harvey regarded as a genius protégé and pupil.

43 Wraight and Stern, In Search of Chr. M., op. cit., pp 69 and 70.

44 Sonnet 126, ciphers: On campaign with Carleill we follow Marlowe as he joins Carleill's actions in the Glinns; see their sympathy for Sorley Boy Mac Donnell and some altercation with Lord Deputy Perrot.

45 John Bakeless. Trag. Hist. op. cit., vol 1, pp 205-208, specifies Kit's debt to Spenser in Tamburlaine. Spenser DNB. Spenser lived in Ireland: secretary to the lord deputy and clerk of the Irish court of chancery, he had a place in the country and a house in Dublin. (Probably Gabe Harvey at Cambridge showed those verses to Kit, but he could have read them at Spenser's house in Dublin.)

John Bakeless. Trag. Hist. op. cit., vol 1, pp 210, 211, and Ive DNB mention Paul Ive, fortress architect, as an influence on Kit's writing. Bakeless says Marlowe must have seen Paul Ive's The Practice of Fortification before publication. That book was dedicated to Francis Walsingham, and a letter to me 6 Jan. 1991 from Robert Hunter, a teacher of history at Coleraine, tells that early in the 1580's Lord Deputy Perrot wanted Ive to design forts in Ireland, but the crown wouldn't pay for them. Ive finally built two, but only after the turn of the century. No doubt Walsingham's stepson Captain Carleill, Kit's friend (on the spot with him in 1584-'85), was interested in the designs.

46 Martin Haile. An Elizabethan Cardinal, op. cit., details events in the summer of 1585, revealing an attack by poison on Dr. Allen late in July. Timing of Kit's absence from college: Bakeless. Trag. Hist. op. cit., vol 1, pp 71, 75 as well as E. K. Chambers. Eliz Stage. op. cit., Appendix A, p 101, about the Queen's visit to Walsingham's Barn Elms on 11 July, suggest Kit was selected to deliver the jollop at Reims. Haile states that on 3 August Allen was carried to his coach and taken away to Spa. He recovered and moved to Rome.

47 Thomas Nashe DNB. Also, Works of Thomas Nashe, edited from the original texts by Ronald B. Mc Kerrow. Reprint edited by F.P. Wilson. 5 vols. Oxford: Basil Blackwell, 1958. Nashe's writings well presented with useful notes.

48 Robert Green. Greene's Groatsworth of Wit. Number 4 in Elizabethan & Jacobean Pamphlets. ed. George Saintsbury. Books for Libraries Press. Freeport, NY: 1970 (1892). Robin Green was one of 10 University Wits (perhaps John Lyly, Tom Nashe, Robin Greene, Samuel Daniel, George Chapman, Tom Lodge, Tom Watson, George Peele, Kit and Matt Roydon?) hired by the queen to aid her eldest secret son, Prince Ned de Vere, with his work in the Theater Wing of State Secret Service. Kit, in ciphers for Henry IV Part I, lines of dialogue 121-132, writes of the "shaggie, raw, stagey aggregations o' tales U showed your mother, who saw ye goin' on 'n' on alone, pitiable, laughable, 'n' suggested a concert of ten authors t' write 'em? We tvtors taught our leader t' shine for th' queen, 'n' while traces of my long-gone style adher'd t' his MT work, he began on (hum . . .) not-honest liftin' of some o' my best dialogue. E-e-e! VVe all resented that breech, see, 'n' feared h-he'd been one fat-ass miserable sad waste of time, but SSS hired us, and euen tho' Ned left, good nabob Regina's money came in, 'n' meals 'n' candy too. We ten vote to write some howls on Ned 'n' that love-mess he cal'd Hell . . . ." Ned's Hell was a love-affair he'd had with his mother the queen; Tom Lodge and Robin Green did write a play touching incest, A Looking Glass for London and England, performed in March, April and June 1592 at the Rose Theater (Henslowe's Diary). Greene alienated himself from Theater Wing and all other SSS undercover work and started writing pamphlets exposing the tricks of con men very like secret-service spies. His last printed pamphlet (Greene DNB) before onset of his fatal illness in summer 1592, was an essay against dirty tricks, with villain Ned Browne. Greene said this was an introduction to his next work—a major exposé of undercover machination, to be entitled The Black Book.

At the Steelyard one night Greene ate supper with Tom Nashe and someone Tom identifies (Works of Thomas Nashe. op. cit., vol 1, p 287) as "Will. Monox—hast thou never heard of him and his great dagger?" Nashe broaches the subject of Greene's fate, p 286: "The secrets of God—must not be searcht into. Kings are Gods on earth, their actions must not be sounded by their subiects," and follows this statement with examples of writers who overstepped and were brought low by their rulers. (Oxford was a secret prince.) Walking alone after leaving the party that night, Greene was overcome by stomach pain and collapsed in the street; he'd have died there if a kind old couple hadn't taken him home and nursed him. Greene realized what had happened and in the month of life he had left wrote a sharp essay, accusatory, about how he'd been recruited by a very gay actor-agent to write plays for a privileged master, and how he'd suffered since then. Greene's editor Chettle admitted he'd censored the piece before it went to the printer. Some computer experts maintain Chettle wrote the whole story, but it seems he just messed it up and managed to exacerbate an accusation of Kit as heretic. Greene himself was trying to tell his fellow dramatists to *get away* from their lordly, condescending, insane patron and his crew of actor-spies—to get away before it was too late—never again to write for those creeps and their egoistic, plagiaristic maister who thought he could do anything he pleased and be "the only Shake-scene in a country." For several centuries academicians have taken Greene's use of the word "Shake-scene" to mean "Shakespeare." "Shake-scene" is still offered as evidence that Will Shakespeare in 1582 was already a powerful presence in London's theatrical world. Will Shakespeare, who abandoned his wife and tried to enclose his local Common, was no exemplary moral force, but neither was he a cruel psychopath; Greene *died* of that jollop.

49 With sources from freshman Cambridge studies, Kit created this pseudo-historic melodrama. In the play's first two lines of ciphers, he writes, "Youthful Marlowe wrote th' gross nothing for 's dad. Prai don't go 'n' report on e-each gag slob-Kit lets loose in th' mist! Wait! He'l learn, C, 'n' give ye higher matter, shril 'n' shrewd 'n' y' answer ta hard studie—but Dad saves this ol' green thing, seen home-acted 'n' dear to his heart. G-gr! Dad's honest lawyer friends uuere al suited for th' job of actin' shabby Velshmen . . ." (Here Kit speaks of his father Judge Manwood and lawyers who visited his house.)

50 Gresham's home at Mayfield. On 21 Nov. 1986 Sister Winifred Wickins, SHCJ, of the Convent of the Holy Child, which owned Mayfield Place in 1986, sent me a booklet showing plan of the rooms, the "new" stair tower built by Sir Thomas Gresham for the queen's visit, and photo-views of the "Old Palace."

E. K. Chambers. The Eliz. Stage. op. cit., Appendix A: A Court Calendar: On progress in 1573, Queen Elizabeth's train stayed at Eridge with Lord Abergavenny from 1 to 7 August, but during that week we are told she made a quiet visit to the Greshams at Mayfield.

51 Conyers Read. Mr. Secretary Walsingham. op. cit., vol 3, pp 1-70. An account of Mary Stuart's last effort to free herself from Elizabeth's supervision.

Antonia Fraser. Mary, Queen of Scots. NY: Delacorte Press, 1969, pp 470-493, details the progress of the two last intertwined plots to achieve Mary's escape and Elizabeth's death, generally thought of together as the Babington Plot. Fraser notes re 'Gilbert Gifford,' p. 482: "no one in Staffordshire was likely to recognize him, not even his father or his sister, since he had been abroad so long; as he still looked strangely young, his real identity would remain unsuspected. This story hardly matched with his early offer to make a . . . visit to Staffordshire on the excuse of seeing his father . . . the French embassy themselves never totally trusted Gifford, especially when he turned out to be lodging in London with Thomas Phelippes, one of Walsingham's chief agents."

52 No historian has ever told how Mary came to learn of the plan for transport of her private mail. Both Read and Fraser fudge this essential part of the sting. Read says Phelippes was sent "to Chartley to arrange a means"—but how? Fraser says

Gilbert told the plan to the French embassy—which he did, later. But how Mary, incommunicado, came to be informed is nowhere revealed. It had to be Gilbert who created the scenario, probably gaining access to her apartment by swimming the moat, and Gilbert is revealed to be Marlowe in his own ciphers—in Doctor Faustus, Measure for Measure and All's Well.

53 This method of opening and reclosing sealing-waxed mail by means of the shoemaker's hot knife has been successfully tested for me by Wayne and Marty Scott of Howey-in-the-Hills, FL, professional makers of handmade shoes for the clowns of the Ringling Bros Circus.

54 The First and Second Diaries of the English College, Douay, and appendix of Unpublished Documents. Intro by Thos. Francis Knox, D.D. London: David Nutt, 1878. John Fixer's promotion to deacon is noted in the second of The Diaries, 19 Dec. 1586, p 214. The ordination of "Gilbert Gifford" the following March, next to John Fixer, presbyter, is recorded below on the same p, on 4/14 March 1587. Fixer and Gilbert Gifford are also mentioned in Haile. op. cit.

55 William Byron. Cervantes, A Biography. Garden City, NY: Doubleday, 1978, p 310. Cervantes' presence in Lisbon at this time is probable; "Nothing is heard of Cervantes from early August 1586 until the following spring [On 28 April 1587 he was seen in Toledo] except for an appearance in October as godfather." Cervantes could have been working on spec for Antonio de Guevara in Lisbon, lading supplies on five galleons for the Armada, hoping for a contract for requisition of more naval provisions out of Seville. Cervantes did get that contract later in 1587: Byron, ibid., p 311.

56 George Malcolm Thomson. Sir Francis Drake. NY: William Morrow, 1972. p 212. The mystery of Drake's sudden take-off toward the San Felipe: "he picked up the information, probably somewhere on the Portuguese coast . . ." [Kit must have uncovered the news dockside at Lisbon and sailed down to Drake at Ságres in a petache with special protective flags.]

57 Drake's honest praise of Kit as intelligencer may have been the reason behind a letter of commendation sent by the council to Cambridge U authorities—a famous letter which made possible Kit's MA in absentia. Drake did credit his intelligencer about Cádiz: Encyc. Brit. 1955 ed. Drake, Sir Francis: "In 1587 he went to Lisbon with a fleet of thirty sail; and having received intelligence of a great fleet being assembled in the bay of Cádiz, and destined to form part of the Armada . . ."

58 Ogburns.This Star of England. op. cit., p 351. Sir Francis Englefield received and transmitted to Felipe II the legend of Arthur Dudley. Preserved in a document among the Simancas Papers, this recital is translated and printed in full by the Ogburns. Appendix, pp 1252-56.

59 Robert Dudley DNB. p 115. "Philip II received him (Arthur Dudley) hospitably, and granted him a pension of six crowns a day, but he was clearly a pretender."

60 Zuccaro's stay in Madrid is discussed in Spanish Cities of the Golden Age, The Views of Anton van den Wyngaerde. ed. Richard L. Kegan. Berkeley: UC Press,

1989, pp 32-37. For Zuccaro's life and his brother's: Mary Cable. El Escorial. NY: Newsweek Book Division, 1971, p 52. Also Encyc. Brit. 1955 ed., vol 23, and best, James Denniston. Memoirs of the Dukes of Urbino. London: John Lane, The Bodley Head, 1919, pp 355-372. Zuccaro was in Madrid that summer of 1587, and there he may have made an oil portrait of Kit (wearing an earring). A photo of a miniature copy of this picture labelled "the Cosway Zuccaro," is shown in Encyc. Brit. 1955 ed., vol 20, opp. p. 448, with an article, "The Portraits of Shakespeare," by Marion Harry Spielmann. The subject of the portrait is c. 23 years old. Spielmann writes p. 450: "Zuccaro came to England in 1574, and as his biographers state, 'did not stay long.' The conclusion appears to be definite." Farther down the page he says the Cosway Zuccaro is in America, but the reproduction of it exists in England in the miniature by Cosway's *pupil.* From the National Portrait Gallery in London I received this letter: "We have an old photograph of the miniature [sic] in question on file, dating from 1933, when the portrait was apparently in the collection of a dealer, Hermann Rothchild of Berlin-Wilmersdorf, presumably in Germany. Sadly we have no record of its medium and dimensions . . . or of its current location."

61 This letter is printed and the original is photographically reproduced in Wraight and Stern. In Search of Chr. M. op. cit., p 88.

62 John Stow. The Survey of London. NY: Dutton, 1980, pp 149, 150, 378. For c. 5+ years Fisher's Folly, a big house in Norton Folgate outside Bishopsgate, was owned by Ned, Lord Oxford, and used as a rooming house for his Theater Wing writers. He sold to William Cornwallis near the end of 1588, but Tom Watson stayed to tutor Corwallis' son. Alan H. Nelson. Monstrous Adversary. op. cit., pp 231, 319 & index, and J. Thomas Looney. Shakespeare Identified. op. cit., ed. Ruth Miller. op. cit., vol 2.

63 Edw. III. Act 5. sc 1. ll. 40-59.

64 The ambassador's and Lylly's wish to kill the queen. CSP Dom. Add. Eliz. vol. xxx, Dec. 1587, item 55, enclosure VII. "Thereupon the Ambassador by Lilly exhorted*** to kill the queen of England, with great promises; Gifford answered that he would never offend her, but durst not venture further; yet he has sent divers times to speak with Gifford, which he has always excused."

65 CSP Dom. Add. Eliz. vol. xxxi, p 279. Paris. Florence Bacot. In 1589 this woman wrote to Walsingham: "I am still living with Mr. Lilly."

66 The bishop's jail was the "Four de l' Évêque." A letter to me from Jean Favier, Director of the Archives of France, 9 June, 1983, tells the address of this now-gone prison: "située à l'emplacement de l'actuel no. 19 de la rue Saint-Germain-l'Auxerrois (1 er arrondissement). Les batiments de la prison s'étendaient entre la rue et l'actuel quai de la Mégisserie." And Gerard Ermisse, also of the Archives, sent me, 27 May 1992, useful pp from J. Hillairet, Dictionaire historique des rues de Paris (illus.). Paris: Editions de Jineut, 1961. The view from the prison's riverside windows was made clearer for me by John Russell's Paris. NY: Harry

N. Abrams, 1983. The meaning of the name of the prison is much discussed. To me it means the hell-oven where the bishop put those he damned. It was a long narrow building with two interior courts—built in 1222, not torn down till 1783.

67 Kit's friend, honest man Edward Grimston, second secretary of the Paris English Embassy and a skilled translator, provided Kit with pens, paper (Kit's ciphers thank Grimston) and a copy of the brand-new Faustbuch just published in German in Paris, from which Edward must have translated the hard parts so Kit could create his Doctor Faustus. The drama was was finished ready for the stage by the time Kit came home in Sept. 1588.

A suggestive note in Geoffrey Bullough. Narrative and Dramatic Sources of Shakespeare. 8 vols. NY: Columbia U Press, 1959-'75. vol 2, pp 405-406, introduction to Measure for Measure (discussing "monstrous ransoms"): "In S. Goulart's Histoires admirables de nostre temps (1606) which Edward Grimeston translated in 1607, the story is told of a Provost La Vouste. Goulart probably drew on L'Introduction au Traite de la conformite des merveilles anciennes avec les modernes. (1566)." Anyway, we can smell Grimston around here somewhere.

At the time of Kit's escape, Measure for Measure was not finished; he kept it for years before polishing it, probably in 1604 when he arrived in Venice to work for the English embassy there. For surprising cirumstances relating to first draft of Measure for Measure, see Professor J. Lambin. "Sur la Trace d'un Shakespeare Inconnu." in Les Langues Modernes 1951-1953. Lambin's notes are paraphrased in Alfred J. Evans. Sh's Magic Circle. Freeport, NY: Books for Libraries Press, 1970 (1956), pp 116-121. In the play, Isabella is about to enter a Clare nunnery; "Isabella of France founded the Clare nunnery in Longchamp." [It was next-door to the bawdy-house where Kit was invited for Christmas Eve, 1587.] "The severe rules of the order at Longchamp had . . . been greatly relaxed . . . a village had grown around the nunnery where the attractions were far from innocent; all resulting from a papal 'bull' of 'Mitigation' [in 1263] which ameliorated the strict rules of the order. In the play Lucio says, 'Behold, behold, where Madame Mitigation comes!' when speaking of the prostitute Mrs. Overdone. In 1583, near Longchamp, Henry III installed the monastic order of Hieronimites, whose principal founders were Thomas of Siena and Pierre de Pise—names of the two monks in Measure for Measure . . . It was the habit of Henri III to go frequently into 'retreat' at Vincennes, presumably for prayer and meditation . . . It was also [his] habit from time to time to disguise himself . . . as a monk. Lucio is a clever skit on a courtier of Henri III called Saint-Luc." And the name Ragozine in the play could have been inspired by Ragasoni, the papal legate.

Professor Lambin is convinced that whoever wrote Measure for Measure must have been in Paris at about the time of Claude Tonart's troubles, for the first written record of his story was published in 1621, the second not till 1733. Claude Tonart was a young Parisien condemned to death in 1582 for going to bed with his fiancée. Although the young couple was betrothed, the girl's father, Jean Bailly, a powerful politician, managed to get Claude convicted and sentenced to death. On the way to the gallows he was saved by public opinion and sent back to jail, and a few weeks later the King, returning from a retreat, heard of the problem and pardoned Claude. According to the Journal of Pierre de l'Estoile p 50 (ed. Nancy Lyman Roelker), the furious father was the third president of the chambres des comptes. While Kit was in the Four de l'Eveque this strange story, five years old, was still current: he could have heard it from his jailer or from Edward Grimston.

Looks as if Kit completed All's Well in the prison. His intent was to make Ned understand he should be kinder to his wife, but by the time Kit returned to London, Anne was dead—a suicide—so All's Well joined Measure for Measure for years at the bottom of Kit's trunk.

68 These ciphers begin with a reminiscence of Kit's homecoming to Dover and Canterbury, very sick, after his escape from the Paris jail. (At that time he wrote Sonnet 107, its inner messages a sympathetic memorial for the Spanish soldiers and sailors trapped in their storm-tossed vessels to crash on northern rocky shores.) The ciphers inside The Jew of Malta we have today contain a comic short story about an experience the Marlowes suffered with Shakespeare—so the version we have must be a rewrite.

69 The portrait is reproduced in Wraight and Stern, op. cit., p 217 and described, ibid. pp 219-222, together with thoughts regarding its provenance. Announcement by Thomas Kay of the discovery of this 'Grafton' portrait appeared in the Manchester Guardian, 18 February, 1907. The picture was said to be of Shakespeare and is believed to have been kept in the manor house of Grafton till the place was threatened (it was later destroyed) during the English civil war, when the portrait appears to have been moved to the manor farm house and saved there for c 300 years. Is it Kit?

70 Now Ned and Kit work together, probably at Fisher's Folly, on a first draft of Henry V. Kit's ciphers inside the first part of this show describe in detail the sad story of Ned's instability. Ned's mental problems are also displayed throughout Alan H. Nelson. Monstrous Adversary. op. cit.—with meticulous, merciless documentation.

71 Chalk Church. Reached by a walk down Gad's Hill and west along the Dover Road. Extensive passages of Roger's will are quoted by Lewis J. M. Grant. Christopher Marlowe, Ghost Writer of all the Plays, Poems of Shakespeare. Orillia, Ontario: Stubley Press, 1970, vol 2, pp 211-216—valuable copy. Roger willed this parsonage of Chalk Church to his second wife's nephew, Ralph Coppinger, but neither Roger's purchase nor his bequest is mentioned in the booklet of the history of Chalk Church, kindly sent me by Vicar Jim Fry. My source for Roger's purchase of the rectory in 1583 is Edward Hasted. History and Topographical Survey of the County of Kent. Canterbury: Simmons and Kirkby, 1790-1799. vol 3, pp 469-70.

My efforts to own a copy of Roger's will have failed: A letter from E.G.W. Bill, librarian at Lambeth Palace Library, told me the will was proved in the Prerogative Court of Canterbury, records of which are kept in the Public Record Office, London. Kent County Librarian H.V. Ralph wrote me that though Sir Roger Manwood's name appears on p 275 of Index of Wills proved in the Prerogative Court of Canterbury 1584-1604, (British Record Society 1901:Kraus Reprint 1968), the entry reads, "no will registered." Mr. Ralph continued: "I have contacted the Public Record Office and have been informed that it is possible that the original will still exists even though there is no registered copy among the Prerogative Court records. The original will may be in the care of the Public Record Office, but there would be a few days' delay in finding it because original wills are preserved in a store outside London." A few days? Requests to Mr. G. H. Martin, Keeper of Public Records, brought repeated letters saying the will was not in the box where it ought to be. I paid two searchers; they sent me a copy of Roger's nephew's will. I gave up. Can it be among papers of Lewis J. M. Grant of Orillia, Ontario, deceased?

72 On 15 Dec. 1982 Mrs. R.A. Purle, Reference Assistant at the Kent County Library, Rochester, Kent, sent me photocopies of this "gothic" carving of Puck above the door-lintel of "St. Mary's Church, Chalk."

73 Oldcastle DNB.

74 Lewis J. M. Grant. Christopher Marlowe, Ghost Writer. Part 2 op. cit., p 213. In Roger's will: " . . . my house at Shorne, Kente." My copy of a map showing Shorne, taken from Edward Hasted. Kent. op. cit., shows a house alone on the hill identified as Gad's Hill by the Kent librarian—N of Cobham Hall, SW of Oldcastle's Cooling Castle on the marsh. I sent her a Xerox of the 18th century map, asked her please to mark Dickens's 19th century house, and that lone house on the hill was marked, so Dickens seems to have chosen the site, at least, of Roger's halfway house—a place where Dickens had wanted to live since childhood. Lewis Grant quotes Baedeker's Great Britain, 1910, p 22: "About two and a half miles to the NW of Stroud on the road to Gravesend is Gad's Hill, (Falstaff's Inn), the scene of Falstaff's encounter with the men in buckram (Henry IV, 1, 1, 4) and also mentioned by Chaucer. It commands an extensive view; Gad's Hill Place, the residence of Charles Dickens (who died here in 1870) is an old-fashioned red-brick house near the inn. In the wilderness reached by a tunnel below the road are some magnificent cedars. About four miles to the N are the ruins of Cooling Castle, the home of Sir John Oldcastle . . . ."

75 Clement's Inn. (Clement is patron saint of sailors.) Kit may have studied here.

Robert J. Blackham. The Story of the Temple. op. cit., p 130.

Bruce Williamson. The History of the Temple. London: John Murray, Albemarle St.W., 1924. Pages 95 and 170 offer suggestive evidence: Kit's dad Roger may have stayed there before becoming a member of the Inner Temple, for Clement's Inn was an Inner Temple dependency.

Clement's Inn is mentioned in Henry IV Part II, 2. ll.14, 209, 280 (Justice Shallow reminiscing), and ll. 308 fol.: Shallow goes out, Falstaff enters and comments on Shallow in old days at Clement's Inn. This Inn no longer exists.

Mark Eccles. Christopher Marlowe in London. NY: Octagon Books, 1967, p 112, mentions a Christopher Morley of Clement's Inn—but that man died in Reading in 1610, and Eccles learned of his connection with the Inn only from the man's will—he was not Kit.

76 Powel Mills Dawley. John Whitgift and the English Reformation. op. cit., pp 162, 163, re the Prayer Book, and 167, 168, re the oath ex officio.

77 Ibid. p 168: "An ominous oposition to the bishops appeared at Court, compounded partly out of sympathy for the Puritans, partly out of a fear that the archbishop's severity would alienate the loyalty of many of the Queen's subjects at a time when Romanist activity and the menace of Spain imperiled the national security, and partly out of a new anti-clericalism spreading among the common-lawyers. Jealous of the Church's independent jurisdiction and alarmed at the growth of the prerogative courts, an alliance began between the Puritans and the lawyers."

78 Whitgift DNB.

Powel Mills Dawley op. cit. Though he quotes other people's cogent objections to the man's methods, Dawley seems sympathetic to Whitgift; on p 169 the author mentions Whitgift's "steadfast courage," which "preserved the integrity of the Elizabethan settlement." (Preserved how long? Whitgift created storm clouds which decades later burst into English Civil War.) On the same page we read that a number of Elizabeth's helpers—Leicester, Walsingham, Clerk of the Council Robert Beale, Francis Knollys and others—were speaking against Whitgift's despotic methods.

79 Whitgift DNB.

80 All the Martin Marprelate Tracts. The Scolar Press Ltd. 93 Hunslet Road, Leeds 10, England, n. d. The tracts in facsimile.

81 They also contained educational material: William Pierce. An Historical Introduction to the Marprelate Tracts, A Chapter in the Evolution of Religious and Civil Liberty in England. London: Archibald Constable & Co. 1908, p 165.

82 Ibid. p 177: Informers were promised pardons.

83 Activities of The Theater Wing, an adjunct of State Secret Service, were and are government secrets, and that fact gives an aura of mystery to De Vere's occupations reflected in his biographies.

84 Sir William Pickering DNB.

William Neville. Elizabeth the First. Neville states on p 27 that Sir James Croftes, Sir Thomas Wyatt, Sir William Pickering, Sir Nicholas Throgmorton and William Thomas plotted for Elizabeth in Mary Tudor's day. Pickering, away from England during several years of Mary's reign, returned in 1559.

85 Elizabeth Jenkins. Elizabeth and Leicester. NY: Coward McCann, 1962, p 52. Pickering and the queen had several long private talks in May, 1559. In June,

Robert Dudley formed his company of players (the first of its kind) and wrote to the earl of Shrewsbury guaranteeing that the actors were all "honest men."

86 William Pierce. An Historical Intro. op. cit., p 283, last paragraph: Antimartinist writers called Martin "halt and club-footed."

87 Ibid. p 197. 'The youth, Jack, as he is several times called' (that is, the author of Theses Martinianae). Pierce here assumes Jack is Penry—not so. Pierce also believes the provocateur Throgmorton to be Marprelate. (for a more practical theory: R.Ballantine. Mori Mihi Lucrum, Chap. 2.)

88 Alexander Pulling.The Order of the Coif. Boston, Mass: The Boston Book Co., Chas. C. Soule, Pres., Freeman Place Chapel, reprint 1897. Serjeants-at-Law, a small group of learned English lawmen who from earliest times were chosen Brothers of the Ancient Order of the Coif. Manwood was created Serjeant 1567. Reading the history of this intellectual society, it's clear that Roger would find abhorrent participation of the ecclesiastical commission in cases involving imprisonment and capital punishment, which he felt were better tried by English common law.

89 Walter Mildmay DNB. Francis Walsingham DNB. Also Conyers Read. Mr. Secretary Walsingham and the Policy . . . op. cit. Thomas Randolph DNB.

90 When he first visited England, this man was Count Mömpelgard; he became Duke of Württemberg.

91 Elizabeth Jenkins. Elizabeth the Great. NY: G.P. Putnam's Sons, 1967, p 25. In February 1547, when Elizabeth was almost thirteen and a half, Thomas Seymour sent her a proposal of marriage, which she refused. He proposed this union to the privy council before he married Catherine Parr.

92 Ibid. She kept the letter he'd written her . . .

93 Ibid. p 27. Catherine Parr realized the two were too often together, and "then one day in May [1548], she went into a room unexpectedly and found Elizabeth in his arms."

94 Mary M. Luke. A Crown for Elizabeth. N.Y.: Coward, McCann, 1970, p 212.

95 Donald Barr Chidsey. Elizabeth I. op. cit., pp 13-14.

96 Jenkins. op. cit., p 33.

97 Dido, Queen of Carthage. Act 1. 1. ll.106-108

98 Charles Norman. Christopher Marlowe, the Muse's Darling. NY: Bobs-Merrill Co., 1971 (1946), p 32. "the title page of Dido states that it was 'Played by the Children of Her Maiesties Chappell,' who, in May, 1587, when Marlowe's degree hung in balance, were performing at Norwich and Ipswich." That company was Ned's.

99 Bakeless. Trag. Hist. op. cit., vol 2, p 43: An elegy for Kit, written by Nashe and printed (tipped in?) in a copy of the 1594 quarto of Dido, was seen by Bishop Thomas Tanner (1674-1735) and by Thomas Warton the younger (1728-1790) but does not appear in any of the three known copies of the play. (some copies suppressed?)

100 Locked up. Luke. op. cit., p 419. Jenkins. op. cit., pp 46-47, and Martin Hume. Two English Queens and Philip. NY: G.P. Putnam's Sons, 1908, pp 49-51.

101 Martin Hume, ibid., pp 20 and 133, clearly suggests that Philip arrived incognito in London when the lawyers came to make a marriage contract between him and Mary. Disguise was fashionable—Philip was known to have gone incognito to Brussels, looking for adventure.

102 Whether or not Elizabeth became the godmother of this Ferdinando can't be shown, for the surviving list of christenings at which Elizabeth officiated begins November 1561. However at the College of Arms, London, there is a drawing of a christening procession in which the train of godmother Elizabeth is borne by Margaret Clifford. (College of Arms. London. MS6, f. 77 v.) J. Thomas Looney. Shakespeare Identified. op. cit.

103 E.K. Chambers. Eliz. Stage. op. cit. Appendix A, A Court Calendar, p 78.

104 Sir Nicholas Bacon DNB.

105 Elizabeth Jenkins. Elizabeth and Leicester. NY: Coward, McCann, 1962, pp 62-3 (from CSP Dom. Eliz. 1547-1580 vol xiii.)

106 E.K.Chambers. Eliz. Stage. op. cit., vol 1, p 107, sic. (from CSP Dom. Eliz. cxlviii 34)

107 Robert Dudley DNB.

108 E.K.Chambers. op. cit. Appendix A, p 89. (and see note 50 above.)

109 J. Thomas Looney. Shakespeare Identified. Ruth Loyd Miller, ed. op. cit., vol 1, p 476: That the public was not blind to the affair of Elizabeth and Oxford is shown in a comic caricature engraved by Hollar after Marcus Gheeraedt's larger etching, and reproduced by Ruth Loyd Miller. Oxford is seen holding the naked sword of state pointing to the zenith, and with his left hand he directs the scabbard toward a distinctly scrotum-like decoration at the end of long cords on the front of the queen's Garter costume. The pantomime; I've got my phallus, she has my balls. Gheeraedt's work is dated 1576, but Ruth Loyd Miller writes that the Hollar caricature represents the Garter procession of 18 June 1572.

110 Mildmay's monument in greater St. Bartholomew's. Ann Saunders. The Art and Architecture of London. Oxford: Phaidon Pub., 1984, p 46: "Sir Walter Mildmay (d. 1589), founder of Emmanuel College, Cambridge, who served Henry VIII, Edward VI, Queen Mary, and Queen Elizabeth, becoming at last Chancellor of the Exchequer and a Privy Councillor, has a large wall monument with the stoical inscription: 'Death is Gain to Us.'" (Roger, in his will quoted by Lewis J. M. Grant, op. cit., vol 2 p 211, 212, leaves "for some remembrance" gold rings to his wife, his son Harte and [his] wife "my daughter Anne, my sons-in-law Sir John Leveson and Robert Honnywood, my cousins John Boys, Edward Peake and Stephen Teobald, one ring of gold worth four marks with mine armes and this inscription or circumscription of words and letters: Mori Mihi Lucrum. R.M." [Death is a light to me.] This motto is also found on the gateway of the Church of St. Olave, at the junction of Hart St., Seething Lane and Crutched Friars in Old

Jewry: Ann Saunders. op. cit., p 81, writes: "a gateway surmounded with sculls, crossbones, and spikes with the motto 'Mors mihi lucrum'—'Death is a light to me.' Dickens described it in The Uncommercial Traveller, speaking of it as 'his best beloved Churchyard, The Churchyard of St. Ghastly Grim.'"

111 This they did, but apparently not till 1594. The revenge is detailed in 'Lopez' (sic) DNB and Lucien Wolf. "Jews in Eliz. Eng." op. cit., pp 30-32, with ample notes.

Jas. Spedding, with Ellis and Heath. Works of Francis Bacon. NY: Garrett reprint, 1968 (London: Longmans, 1857-1874). "Life and Letters," vol 1: pp 271-285 describe the incredible convoluted legend invented by Bacon to frame Lopes. Also see Lambeth MSS 649.40, Francis to Ann Bacon, 14 Feb., 1594: "I have sent your Ladyship the key of your jewel-casket . . ." On p 279, Bacon has given the queen a "very good jewel," (Ann Bacon's?) which he claims was sent by Philip II to Lopes to incite him to assassinate Elizabeth. Bacon uses torture to elicit false confessions and entangles innocent foreign agents to create the semblance of a "conspiracy." Lopes hanged, and others die, too. Kit touches the repellent caper as if he were involved, in L's L's Lost ciphers, lines of dialog 85-86 to 115-116.

112 Industrious, they were successful though never officially recognized: G.B.Harrison. The Life and Death of Robert Devereux Earl of Essex. NY: Henry Holt and Co. 1937, p 338: "The Hatfield Papers include many original letters written to Essex from abroad. At this time, and until his departure for Ireland in 1599, Essex was receiving fuller and more accurate information of foreign affairs than the Cecils. In the four years 1595-9 the letters to Essex average about 150 a year, to the Cecils about twenty-five. In addition there was the voluminous correspondence of Anthony Bacon."

113 Lambeth MSS 653.165. Original, quoted in Spedding, op. cit. In several letters to Anthony and Francis, Ann Bacon mentions she's sending them pigeons: "I send the first flight of my doves to you both." Sir Edward Durning-Lawrence. Bacon is Shakespeare. NY: John Mc Bride Co., 1910, reproduces several illustrations from a book on steganography which Bacon had published in 1624; Bacon appears in the pictures, doing different things. On p 115, he's receiving a letter from a humble messenger disguised as a shepherd while high above them a determined pigeon flies, about to be shot down, another letter held in its beak.

114 Daphne du Maurier. Golden Lads. Francis Bacon, Anthony Bacon and their Friends. Garden City, NY: Doubleday, 1975, p 63: "on February 4th 1592 . . . Anthony Bacon set foot on English soil for the first time in over twelve years . . . a room had been prepared for him at Gray's Inn by his brother Francis." The Index to the Papers of Anthony Bacon (1558-1601) in Lambeth Palace Library (MSS. 647-662) is evidence of this man's diligent occupation.

115 Many facts about the creation of the play Tamburlaine are unknown. My guess: Kit, inspired by his 1577-'78 voyage to Constantinople, quietly developed the

scenario over years. This way of working, slowly turning over ideas and scenes, incorporating all available material and then polishing, he always used for the big plays; he intended Tamburlaine to be a tragedy, but as he says in cipher in a reprint of Part 2, he rushed the conclusion, neglecting to clarify that the old man who'd spent his life triumphantly creating thousands of deaths was himself defeated by the death of his wife and his disappointment in his sons. When Kit returned from his near-eastern voyage he wrote Selimus, a boyish melodrama—his name is ciphered into its first two lines: "Chris M. made ye vvooly old drama for school. All of it! E-e-e! In it, an evil sultan . . ." [vvooly meant woolly—rough.] Scholars scorn to attribute this play to Marlowe—not good enough. But he was barely 15 then. Selimus contains shades of future King Lear and Titus Andronicus, and some characters related to those in Tamburlaine.

(Selimus is discussed in John Bakeless.The Tragicall History of Christopher Marlowe. Westport, CT: Greenwood 1970 (1942) vol 2, pp 278, 279). Before his voyage to Constantinople Kit almost surely worked as a page for Roger's patron Sir Thomas Gresham, and Gresham had in his library a book dedicated to him c.1570 by a friend, Hugh Goughe: The Offspring of the House of Ottomano, mentioned by Burgon. Life and Times of Sir Thomas Gresham. op. cit., vol 2, p 478. That copy of that book may have served as primary source for Selimus and also resonates with Tamburlaine. [Note the name of the author, Hugh Goughe, not Thomas Goffe, another writer on Turkish life who may have been Hugh's son.] Both parts of Tamburlaine were played at the Rose. When? Most scholars think 1587 or '8. Both parts stood London on its ear. Bakeless. Trag. Hist. op. cit., vol 1, Chap. 7, says Tamburlaine has a certain source in Ortelius. Theatrum Orbis Terrarum; a copy was in the library of Corpus Christi, Cambridge. A copy of Ortelius was in Gresham's library, too. Kit could have been developing Tamburlaine for years. Bakeless. op. cit., vol I p 205, says that beside numerous published sources for the work, "*Marlowe seems to have had access, in some unexplained way, to a group of facts about the historical Timur contained in Oriental works, none of which were translated during his lifetime.*" These could have been facts Kit learned from Turkish sailors or local suppliers while the ship sailed along the shores of Anatolia in January 1578. No one can tell how he learned Zenocrate's name, or Zabina's. My guess, hearsay.

116 Frances Berkeley Young. Mary Sidney, Countess of Pembroke. London: David Nutt, 1912. Still a good bio of Mary: Young's conclusions can be tempered by observations of John Chamberlain. Letters. ed. Norman Egbert McClure. Westport, CT: Greenwood, 2 vols. 1979 (1939).

117 Sir William Davenant DNB. Jane Davenant, William's mother: Jane Davenant and Kit started this baby Wm. at the Peace Party in Valladolid, 1605. A letter from William's legal father John is kept in Papers of Anthony Bacon. Lambeth Palace Library, 1593: MS 649, f. 319, for John was an honest man. A useful essay about John and Jane and their family after their move to Oxford is found in prefatory

material for The Dramatic Works of William Davenant. ed. William Paterson. Edinburgh, London: Sotheran & Co., 1872. 5 vols. William Davenant's portrait is reproduced in Richard Barber. Samuel Pepys Esquire. London: National Portrait Gallery. G. Bell and Sons, 1970, p 32, plate 61. Davenant was not a good playwright but a great theatrical producer.

118 C.C. Stopes. The Life of Henry, Third Earl of Southampton. NY: AMS Press, 1969 (Cambridge U Press, 1922.) Hen Wriothesley's proposed marriage to Elizabeth Vere is discussed, pp 33-37.

G.P.V. Akrigg. Shakespeare and the Earl of Southampton. Cambridge, MA: Harvard U. Press, 1968, pp 31-2, 39. Akrigg supports as factual what some other writers have called incredible. On p 39 he writes, "Father Garnet, in a manuscript preserved in the archives of the English Jesuits at Stonyhurst, noted, 'the young Erle of Southampton refusing the Lady Veere payeth 5000 li of present payment,'" and in the following paragraph Akrigg defends Father Garnet's credibility. Joel Hurstfield. The Queen's Wards. Cambridge, MA: Harvard U Press, 1958, is on the fence: p 142. Kit makes all explicit in ciphers, L's L's Lost.

119 Shake-speare's Sonnets. London: Printed by G. Eld for T.T., 1609. Proquest reprint, 2001. The outsides of the first seventeen of these poems represent a cycle of marriage-related messages that Ned paid Kit to write for Hen. Kit's menippean messages inside these sonnets make it clear he doesn't agree.

120 It seems this arrangement lasted from some date in 1590 to late December 1591, and all that time Ned didn't pay his quarterly rent. Maybe because Julie knew he was a secret prince she let things ride, thinking he'd surely pay all at once. But something awful happened that November.

121 Henry V. The first ciphers in The Famous Victories tell us that together, Kit and Ned and Roger made this rough farcical predecessor of Henry V. (Roger, misguided, was trying to cement a love-affair between Ned and Kit, thinking Kit would be preferred as favorite if Ned succeeded to the throne of England.) Later, Kit, bunking with Ned, tries a more serious dramatic approach to the story of slimy Henry V and his weird coup in France—a story Ned, lost in Never-Neverland, finds personally appealing as well as grist for a great propaganda piece. Early ciphers inside this play tell of harrowing conflict—Kit deletes melodrama Ned wants to include.

122 C.C. Stopes.The Life of Henry . . . op. cit., p 39. The three were probably in Southampton on 9 January, when the Corporation granted Hen the "freedom of the city." They sailed off after the ceremony or on the next day.

123 Adam Fouleweather (Thomas Nashe). A Wonderfull . . . Prognostication for this yeer of our Lord God. 1591. Imprinted at London by Thomas Scarlet, 1591. (In Elizabethan and Jacobean Pamphlets. ed. George Saintsbury. Freeport, NY: Books for Libraries Press, 1970 reprint.) It begins: "Sitting Gentlemen vpon Douer Cliffes, to quaint my selfe with the art of Navigation, and knowe the course of the Tides, as the Danske crowes gather on the Sandes against a storme . . ." In

the body of this piece, Nashe could be writing not just to make fun of Gabriel Harvey's brother Richard but to amuse John and Kate Marley in Canterbury.

124 My guess: Kit and Tom were supposedly looking after Hen, but he may have slipped away to cross the Channel when they left him at Dover: C.C. Stopes. The Life of Henry . . . op. cit., pp 39, 40, a letter from Hen to Essex from Dieppe, 2 March 1590-1 (Salisbury Papers, IV. 96).

125 Calvin Hoffman. The Murder of the Man who was Shakespeare. NY: Julian Messner, 1955, pp 44, 45, prints the fifth and sixth stanzas of an Elizabethan ballad about a man named Wormall (Marllow), a poem unearthed in 1836 by John Payne Collier: "A poet was he of repute/And wrote many a play/Now strutting in a silken suit/Then begging by the way.//He had also a player been/Upon the Curtain stage/But broke his leg in one lewd scene/When in his early age." The value of this rhyme is discounted because Collier was "proved" a forger; I believe he was ruined by secret service dirty tricks because he made other discoveries too close to truth.

E.K. Chambers. Eliz. Stage. op. cit., vol 2, p 302: "Beeston, Christopher, has been conjectured to be the "Kitt" who played a Lord and a Captain in 2 Seven Deadly Sins for Strange's or the Admiral's about 1590/1." This is not a reasonable guess, for Beeston was too young—an apprentice with the Chamberlain's Men in 15*98*.

In the theater, who else was known as Kit? Frederick Boas. Thomas Heywood. NY: Phaeton Press, 1975, p 129: in Book IV of Hierarchy of the Blessed Angels, published 1635, Heywood tells nicknames of his writer-friends:

> "Greene, who had in both Academies ta'ne
> Degree of Master, yet could never gaine
> To be call'd more than Robin . . .
> Marlo, renown'd for his rare art and wit
> Could ne'er attain beyond the name of Kit."

126 Roger is shown wearing it in his portrait in the National Portrait Gallery and on his monument in St. Stephens' Church outside Canterbury.

Colonel Robert J. Blackham. The Story of the Temple, Gray's and Lincoln's Inn. op. cit., pp 180, 181: "The significance of the letters S.S. has been hotly disputed . . . . The portcullis in the . . . collar refers to John of Gaunt, the loops to the union of the Houses of York and Lancaster, and the rose is, of course, the Tudor rose, as the Collar of S.S. was first given . . . by Queen Elizabeth. It was given in her reign to a judge of Common Pleas," [why not say his name? Sir Roger Manwood] "but since then has only been worn by the Lord Chief Justices . . . ."

127 Essex in France, July-Sept. 1591: slightly varying accounts of his experiences are found in G.B. Harrison. Life and Death of Robert Devereux . . . op. cit., pp. 47 fol., and in G.B Harrison. An Elizabethan Journal, Being a Record of Those Things Most Talked of During the Years 1591-1594. NY: Cosmopolitan Book

Corporation, 1929: pp 52,'3,'4—and on p 33 Lord Chartres is mentioned; he'd been governor of Malta.

128 In the nick of time. Elizabeth reached Titchfield as planned, on 2 Sept. E.K. Chambers. Eliz. Stage. op. cit. Appendix A, "A Court Calendar" p 106.

129 The Elvetham date was 20-23 September (ibid., p 106), and the water show took place on the 21st. Ida Sedgwick Proper. Our Elusive Willy. Manchester, Maine: Dirigo Editions, 1953, opp. p 168, reproduces a drawing of Kit at the Elvetham party, as Nereus in mortarboard, picdevant and nude torso; he stands in the water before the queen. Made twice as big as any other figure in the picture, his is the only real portrait in this contemporary illustration.

130 Sir John Perrot DNB. 1527-1592.

David Mathew. "The Cornish and Welsh Pirates in the Reign of Elizabeth." English Historical Review. vol 39, 1924, pp 337—348. Perrot is featured on pp 339, 341, '42, '47, '48—he was the Godfather.

131 This society, often called the "School of Night," is well-described in Wraight and Stern. In Search of . . . op. cit., pp 132-175, and William Urry. Chr. M. and Canterbury. op. cit., p 71.

132 Kit's friend was the 9th earl. His dad the 8th earl had been found dead in his bed in the Tower 21 June 1585, shot through the heart. DNB.

133 See note 119 for details.

134 Nov.? early Dec? 1591. Ned, furious that Hen Wriothesley has learned the truth about his parentage, slams out of Julie Arthur's boarding house on Peter's Hill without paying the rent: Dorothy and Charlton Ogburn. This Star of England. Westport CT: Greenwood, 1972, pp 930-31 (confused by interpolations); Mark Eccles' monograph on Sir George Buck, in Thomas Lodge and Other Elizabethans. ed. Sisson. Cambridge, MA: Harvard, 1933, pp 464-5, gives a clearer picture; and Alan H. Nelson. Monstrous Adversary. op. cit., pp 328, 329.

Through with Theater Wing, hating Kit, Ned goes away and marries Lady Elizabeth Trentham. Julie Arthur writes and writes to Ned and the queen, asking for what's owed; the queen finally pays (Kit's ciphers, Henry IV Part I), but Julie fades away, perhaps because of stress. Her half of the big old duplex house is taken over by her son Mike Hickes. (Mrs. William Hicks Beach. A Cotswold Family, Hicks and Hicks Beach. London: Wm. Heineman, 1909, p 71.)

135 Yes, Kit was probably sailing with pals Carleill in the Tiger and Sampson in the Sampson, pursuing Spanish ships in the Channel: Those two privateer-ships were still out hunting together in March '92 (Acts of the Privy Council, new series, vol 22, p 381: A ship called Tygure was out of Middleburgh or Flushing together with a ship called the Sampson.)

136 The Baines story: The First and Second Diaries of the English College, Douay, with Appendix of Unpublished Documents (Intro. by Thomas Francis Knox, D.D.). London: David Nutt, 1878: entry at 29 May, 1582, and Martin Haile. An

Elizabethan Cardinal, William Allen. NY and London: Sir Isaac Pitman and Sons, 1914, p 166.

137 Mark Eccles, "Brief Lives." Studies in Philology. Chapel Hill, NC: U of NC, 1982, pp 89-90. Also a letter printed in English Historical Review, April 1976, pp 344-'45. In this letter signed by Sidney, the amanuensis writes, "Gifford Gilbert." Baines may have repeatedly shouted the name, and the rattled secretary wrote it backward. Sidney sends both men home. I believe A.D. Wraight was correct, suggesting that Kit was investigating use of counterfeit coins by William Stanley, who had defected to the Spanish side but was stuck at Flushing without funds.

138 The envoy was Solomon Cormano, a diplomat representing the sultan and Mendes. A full account of his successful embassy is found in Lucien Wolf. "Jews in Elizabethan Eng." Trans. of the Jewish Hist. op. cit., pp 24-8. Cormano and his embassy came to London in March 1592.

139 Bakeless. Trag. Hist. op. cit., vol 1, p 329, quotes Henslowe's Diary: " . . . the Jewe of malteuse the 26 of febrearye 1591." (1592, n.s.) The Jew of Malta on the boards. Bakeless and others who can't see this play as a crazy black farce label it a failed tragedy. That Bacon told Kit to make the play an antisemitic attack on Mendes is indicated by the presence of lines suggesting the disagreement between Antonio Prior of Ocrato and Alvaro Mendes—III. 3. 43, 44: "Because the Prior dispossest thee once,/And [thou] couldst not venge it, but upon his sonne . . ." These verses refer to an episode in which the Prior dispatched his son on a voyage to the sultan to demand Mendes be deprived of his wealth; Mendes found out, pirates captured the son's ship and took him to a prison in Fez.

140 Lucien Wolf, p 27, prints an extract from Elizabeth's friendly letter to the sultan in favor of Alvaro Mendes. (Here she calls him by his eastern name, Solomon Abenjaish.)

141 The club stood on the west side of Shoreditch High Street, back a little from the road—near the Theater and next door to old St. Botolph's church. The place belonged to Henry Carey, the queens's lord chamberlain (and half-brother?).

142 G.B. Harrison. An Elizabethan Journal . . . 1591-1594. op. cit., p 38. "6th June 1591. Unlawful games are again to be put down, since the Queen is informed that archery . . . is now greatly decayed . . . she requires those games and pastimes prohibited by law . . . bowls, dicing, cards and such like, to be forthwith forbidden . . ."

143 Emilia Lanier. The Poems of Shakespeare's Dark Lady: Salve Deus Rex Judaeorum. Introduction by by A.L. Rowse. NY: Clarkson N. Potter, 1979. The introduction is exceedingly valuable. Rowse knew more than he was telling; his arrogant wrong pronouncements and fudging are a 39-page annoyance, but facts he offers are worth assimilating. Read "Kit" for "Shakespeare."

144 This was an intense affair he couldn't abandon even when it was over. Many interior messages are written to her in the Sonnets—invisible on the outside. He says he loves their baby, wants to take care of him. They ought to "forget their hot hate." But to her he was a worse-than-worthless fool.

145 He describes his state of mind in ciphers for Tamburlaine Part II.

146 Reflected in The Comedy of Errors. IV.3, lines 69, 70, 83, 84, and 94, 95, 96. The Courtezan: "Give me the ring of mine you had at dinner,/Or, for my diamond, the chain you promis'd . . ." "A ring he hath of mine worth forty ducats/ and for the same he promised me a chain . . . . He rushed into my house and took perforce/ My ring away. This course I fittest choose./For forty ducats is too much to lose."

147 Barcabudi. John Scarne. Scarne on Dice. NY: Crown Pulishers, 1974, pp 351, 352. "Barbooth or Barbudi. A favorite among Greek and Jewish players . . ." In Barbudi, the shooter retains the dice and continues to shoot as long as he wins. The same dice are used by all shooters, but each player uses his own dice-cup. Sounds like the way "passage" is played in Sir John Oldcastle, 4. 11.43 fol (an early play of Kit's, with his name, Marlovve, as ciphered byline), *not* as the The Compleat Gamester describes the game of passage.

C.F. Tucker Brooke. The Shakespeare Apocrypha. Oxford: Clarendon, 1971 (1908). Sir John Oldcastle dialogue on pp 148, 149. In L's L's Lost ciphers, Kit says that after he lost the chain, Roger went to the club and played at dice with Emilia to see her style. In a 4-line anagram (lines of dialogue 33-34, 35-36) Kit writes: " . . . [it] was Roger: Oye! Euer an artist uuith dice, at Emilia's he opened lo on *Barcabudee.* She, very hot, casts hi t' win, reset t' cast another try, but he sees her error: a *die-tylter*! E-e!"

148 Registers of the Acts of Privy Council, vol 22, 1591-92, new series, p 451. The fence was named Roger Underwood.

149 A third-hand version of this episode was recalled a decade later in The Diary of John Manningham. ed. J. Bruce. Camden Society, 1868. folio 70, November 1602, p 91: "Lord Cheife Baron Manwood understanding that his soone had sold his chayne to a goldsmith, sent for the goldsmith, willed him to bring the chayne, enquired where he bought it. He told, in his house. The Baron desired to see it, and put it in his pocket, telling him it was not lawfully bought. The goldsmith sued the Lord, and fearing the issue would prove against him, obtained the councel's letters to the Lord . . ."

150 J.M. Rigg, in his DNB monograph on Roger, quotes Roger's rhyme from the letter. Lewis J. M. Grant made the translation.

151 The text of Manwood's submission to the council on 14 May is printed in Registers of the Acts of Privy Council. op. cit., pp 449-450. (The gold chain haunted Kit. Besides his ambitious trilogy of Henry VI, inspired by symbols on the chain, in Comedy of Errors a gold chain writhes through the play, and a doomed father is reprieved at the end. In the play L'Ippolito, which Kit wrote in 1610, the wild young protagonist loses a gold chain in a gambling game.)

152 The chain was "delivered into the hands of the Lord Cobham . . . to be ordered as in equity and conscience his Lordship shall think meet and reasonable." Registers of the Acts of Privy Council. op. cit., p 451.

153 Whitely: the place is mentioned in C.C. Stopes. The Life of Henry . . . op. cit., p 27, and also in G.P.V. Akrigg. Shakespeare and the Earl of Southampton. op. cit., p 43: "Whitley [sic] Lodge, owned by the Earl of Southampton and a little less than two miles from his mansion at Titchfield." Kit refers to this adventure in Love's Labor's Lost. III, 1. ll.196 fol. "A whitely wanton with a velvet brow . . ."

154 Hen to Oxford U. C.C. Stopes. The Life of Henry . . . op. cit. p 50. Hen was incorporated of Oxford in August 1592.

155 A.L. Rowse. The Poems of Shakespeare's Dark Lady. op. cit., last three lines p 19.

156 G.B. Harrison. An Eliz. Journal for Years 1591-'94. op. cit., p 160: Mömpelgard arrived in London with friends on 11 Aug. 1592, intending to tour England; reached the queen at Reading on the 17th and came to Windsor on the 20th. "the count, who is corpulent and heavy," and p 164.

E.K. Chambers, Wm. Sh., A Study of Facts and . . . op. cit., vol i, pp 427-428. Mömpelgard took four days to get from Windsor to Uxbridge: 21-25 August, a distance of c. 11 miles. Almost certainly his party had been called into Manwood's court of assize at Windsor for having appropriated the host's horses. See Merry Wives of Windsor, IV, 5. Falstaff present. Also, the whimsical discourse on horse-thievery which Manwood put into his Petition Directed to her most excellent Maiestie (sic), pp 29 fol. It must have been a last-minute insertion. This last work of Roger's is available in microfilm from the Huntington Library in San Marino, CA, library ref. #85582, STC#1525 (Reel 376, English Books), where it's mistakenly attributed to a "Henry Barlow, 1590"). Printed in easy-to-read roman type.

Wm. Pierce. An Hist. Intro. to the Marprelate Tracts. op. cit., pp 244-47. Pierce writes of this Petition: "the ablest contribution to the controversy . . . Its erudition, legal and ecclesiastical, is immense, its forensic acuteness unfailing. And with all its strength, it is perfectly urbane; its admirable temper, amid the dust and heat and irritability of the ecclesiastical warfare of the time, is not the least of its distinctions."

157 Wm. Urry. Christopher Marlowe and Canterbury. op. cit., p 65-67. Kit was known to have been in Canterbury on 15 Sept. '92, and thereafter until 9 Oct. On the 15th, "somewhere close to the corner of Mercery Lane, and possibly in the great inn known as the Chequers where the city aldermen would often sit in the galleries watching dramatic entertainments in the yard below . . ." Kit got into a fight. That he was there with Strange's Players, and that they were playing The Jew is probable; because of plague in London all the companies were working out of town. Strange's was "afoot by 13 July and still on 19 December," and in their repertoire was the popular Jew of Malta. (E.K. Chambers. Eliz. Stage. vol 2, pp 122-23.)

158 The Poems of Aemilia Lanier, ed. Susanne Woods. NY: Oxford U Press, 1993, p xviii. On 18 Oct.1592 Emilia married Fonsie Lanier at St. Botolph's Church

Aldgate (not the St. Botolph next to the club). Kit's sorrow and chagrin are made clear in his ciphers for Sonnet 99. He'd believed they were married.

159 Kit and Mary Herbert: Mary's Pembroke Players were to make their first court appearances at these galas, her dates 26 Dec. and 6 Jan., Hampton Court. (E.K. Chambers. Eliz. Stage. op. cit. Appendix A, "A Court Calendar.")

160 BM., English Books, 1475-1640, microfilm reel 376. Copy at the Huntington Library, San Marino, CA, wrongly attributed to "Henry Barlow, 1590" (perhaps with thought of Henry Barrowe, a loyal lawyer friend of Roger's who may have contributed text to the middle part of the work). Interior evidence clearly shows the first 52 pp. of the essay to be Roger's, finished no earlier than August, 1592. When Whitgift read the part about horse-thieves, he must have been sure the petition was Roger's.

161 Dr. William Redman DNB. Archdeacon of Canterbury.

Lewis J.M. Grant. Christopher Marlowe, Ghost-Writer. part 2, p 212 fol. Grant explains that Dr. Redman was assigned to oversee revision of Manwood's will.

162 Sir John Oldcastle DNB.

163 Kit's half-brother Peter. Kit's ciphers for The Taming of The Shrew. ll. 17-18, 19-20: " . . . tu Dad's house to ope a vein, etc., 'n' emit red shyt. C—*Peter* told! 'e witness'd th' kill, C? Th' corse reek't o' filth. My mother Cate, euer braue, washt it al off to de feet. Gee, O, G—" Peter is also mentioned as present at the death of his father in ciphers for 2 Henry VI, ll. 15-16: "The crude queer" [Dr. Lopes] "hasn't quit; kuts a gut again tu get his fee. I' fear, *Peter* hears him: 'Tee Hee!'" [Lopes laughs.]

164 Manwood's tomb desecrated. Mr. John Ulatowski of Shelton CT sent me a Xeroxed typed report fom the archivist of St. Stephen's Church, Hackington, with pictures made by the Kent Messenger News organization. Ulatowski included an excellent photoprint in a sleeve—the same shot shown in the Xeroxes—clearly displaying the ripped-open coffins, their lids carelessly tossed aside. The coffins, which seem to have been originally placed on platforms running along either side of the vault, had been dragged to the brick-floored central space and left in confusion, "with clear evidence of the use of tools such as a pick-axe to open them." The report states that the vault was inspected in 1962, "to see if there were any documents therein of interest." Mr. Ulatowski also sent me clips from the Kentish Gazette (no dateline—ads suggest it was December) showing "the Rev'd Desch . . . and two assistants, working [upstairs] on the flooring to the Manwood Chapel in 1962 when the vault beneath was opened." Mr. Ulatowski wrote that every male body in the vault had been removed. No one seems to know how long ago the vandalism occurred or where the bodies had been taken.

165 E.K. Chambers. Eliz. Stage. op. cit. Appendix A, "A Court Calendar," p 107: "1592, December 26, Pembroke's. 1593, Jan. 6 [new style], Pembroke's."

166 3 Henry VI. Marlowe's ciphers, lines 5-6, 7-8: " . . . We wait a month for deadly raid, ere Buck re-reckons Reuels records, leauing Dido and other drama in a far corner . . ." This could be the earliest mention of Buck at the Revels Office.

167 Wraight and Stern. In Search of . . . . op. cit., pp 241-282. Excellent descriptions and illustrations of remains of Tom Walsingham's Scadbury place near Chislehurst.

168 Ibid., pp 262, 263. The tree and carving shown in photos.

169 William Urry. op. cit. Appendix II, p 116. Inventory of John Gresshop . . ."In the upper study by the schoole doore: fo 172 v. The fall of the late Arrian—2 d." [How did it happen that Kit's headmaster could have the whole thing, and no charges leveled? Before Whitgift.]

170 "Shall I Die? Shall I Fly?" A copy made c. 40 years after the work was composed is held in the Bodleian Library MSS. Rawlinson Poetry 160. fols. 108, 109. Restoration is possible, guided by its ciphers. The copy at the Beineke is too corrupt for decipherment. An astonishing attempt to seduce the queen, the verses were delivered to her by Hen Wriothesley.

171 The whole charade of his escape was created by Elizabeth, with secret service aid. Kit's ciphers make it clear that the idea of his death by attorney was Elizabeth's (probably inspired by the first lines of Kit's poem).

172 DNB monographs for both men.

173 DNB. Also, William Pierce. An Historical Introduction . . . op. cit. Activities of Barrowe, Greenwood and especially Penry are followed, passim.

174 J.Leslie Hotson. The Death of Christopher Marlowe. NY: Russell & Russell, 1967 (1925). Essential study for any student of Marlowe's escape: especially valuable is the description of the men's activities during the day of death at Deptford. Hotson found three important documents: the coroner's report, the writ of certiori summoning the case of Marlowe's murder into Chancery and the queen's pardon granted to Ingram Frizer.

175 Kit's cipher, ll. 17-18 in 3 Henry VI, is explicit: " . . . th' borro*w*'d body of a dirty hang'd shyster-man serues as me, U C."

176 E K. Chambers. Eliz. Stage op. cit,. Appendix A, shows Elizabeth at Nonsuch May 14-22, then a gap, but on the day of the "murder" she was probably at Greenwich, just downriver from Deptford. See Frizer's pardon; the action took place "within the verge in the room aforesaid within the verge" (within 12 miles of the queen).

177 J.Leslie Hotson. The Death . . . op. cit., p 33.The coroner's report states that the victim had suffered "a mortal wound over his right eye" (therefore the jury must have been told it was unnecessary to examine the whole body—and the awful bruise or wound from the hangman's rope was never uncovered.)

178 Kate came to Deptford; ciphers in Venus and Adonis, ll. 15-16, 17-18: " . . . sweet thin hickory rod, hath no wai to saue th' author 'n' end shame! So set off, diluting beer with *mother's tears.* (Drinks in dispute.) See, See, Se-e-e where the Channel tosses him!"

179 CSP Dom. Eliz. 1591-94, vol. ccxlv, p 358. In [early] June, 1593, Essex sent a note to Phelippes, who was waiting (probably at the Marley naval stores warehouse) as observer of Kit's leavetaking from Deptford. State Papers' calendared paraphrase

of Essex's note reads: "Earl of Essex to Thos. Phellippes. Hears Walton is not gone; the day for the appointed meeting is near, and the matter not to be played with. Asks him to wake up, as besides the duty they all owe, his own reputation is engaged in it; will not endure that the negligence of such a fellow should turn to Her Majesty's unquietness and his disgrace." Back in 1591 a William Walton, owner-captain of the Salamander, and Edward Marley, captain of the Mayflower, together took prize a Danish ship, the Whale (CSP Dom. Eliz. 1591-94, pp 138-139, Dec. 1591). So William Walton and Edward Marley had been working together, and since Edward was son of Anthony Marley, naval stores chandler at Deptford, quite possibly the Walton that Essex was writing about in the note above was William Walton, Captain of the Salamander, his boat tied up at the Marley Deptford naval stores dock, waiting to carry Kit across the Channel to deliver an important Essex-Bacon message to Navarre at San Denis.

180 8 June. Review of English Studies. Jan. 1933, pp 13-18. Eugénie De Kalb. "Robert Poley's Movements as a Messenger of the Court." Item 16. "To Robert Poolye upon a Warrant signed by Mr. Vicechamberlain dated at the Court xij^{mo} die Junij 1593 for carryinge of lettres in poste for her Majesties speciall and secrete affaires of great importaunce from the Courte at Croydon the viij of Maye 1593 into the Lowe Countryes to the towne of the Hage in Hollande, and for retourninge back againe with lettres of aunswere to the Court at Nonesuche the viij of June 1593 being in her Majesties service all the aforsaid tyme—xxx li."

Some of Poley's more secret affairs in her Majesty's service came between 8 May and 8 June. The Vicechamberlain says nothing about Poley's being at Deptford on 30 May, though his presence there is documented in Coroner Danby's report: J. Leslie Hotson. op. cit., p 31: " . . . when a certain Ingram ffryzar, late of London, Gentleman, and the aforesaid Christopher Morley and one Nicholas Skeres, late of London, Gentleman, and Robert Poley of London aforesaid, Gentleman, on the thirtieth day of May in the thirty-fifth year above named, at Detford Strand aforesaid in the said County of Kent within the verge, about the tenth hour before noon of the same day, met together in a room . . ."

181 Francis Bacon. Like his natural father Francis Walsingham, Bacon worked long years for State Secret Service, but unlike his dad, Bacon wanted to be a secret chief. Spedding. Works of Francis Bacon. op. cit., vol 14 p 313. Francis to Buckingham, 1621: " . . . that for which I was fittest, which was to carry things suavibus modus, and not to bristle or undertake or give venturous counsels, is out of fashion and request."

182 William Shakespeare, early on an honest man? George Walker. Haste, Post Haste! London: George G. Harrap, 1938, pp 130, '31. Walker cites an example of how Postmaster Sir Thomas Randolph prepared for a general muster of the nation when the state was in danger. [Date? Randolph died 8 June, 1590] "Mr. Gascoigne, the post of the Court, received the letters and immediately dispatched them by special messengers, making use of the posts. He sent his own men to

Northampton . . . . and . . . dispatched one *Shakespeare* to Yorkshire, Lincolnshire, and Durham, . . . *Dutton* to the eastern counties . . . *Browne* to Hertford." This Sir Thomas Randolph [one of Elizabeth's aides executed at Whitgift's order], had served SSS for many years—as ambassador in Russia, ambassador in Scotland. As Postmaster, always close to Walsingham's circle, Randolph made the English post into an effcient, smooth-working SSS organization. E.K. Chambers. Eliz. Stage. op. cit., vol 2, Chapter XV, Actors. p 304, tells of two *Brownes* who were well-known actors; Edward documented at Worcester's 1581, at Admiral's 1602; in 1599 he was a witness for Henslowe. Robert was at Worcester's 1583.

Ibid. p 314: the *Duttons* were quite famous: John worked for Warwick's, then in 1580 for Oxford's, and for Queen's in 1583 and 1588-'91. [Queen's players all handpicked by Walsingham.] Laurence Dutton worked for Warwick's, then Oxford's 1580, and Queen's, 1589-'91. Compare Walker's information with Chambers', and the probability of Will Shakepeare's presence in SSS as a riding messenger as early as 1588 is inescapable. Looks as if Randolph used trusty Theater Wing men as riders.

183 Entered in the Stationers' Register 18 April 1593, with no mention of William Shakespeare.

184 Recorded in the diary of Richard Stonely. Folger Library, MS V.a 460 f.9. On 12 June 1593 he bought a copy of "Venus and Adonay pr Shakspere xii d."

185 In the play, Richard was a conflation of hunchback Robert Cecil (now, as official chief of SS, a thorn in Bacon's side) and an extra-wicked Richard III.

186 ciphers, 3 Henry VI.

187 Wilfed Blunt. Sebastiano, the Advenures of Sebstiano Locatelli during his Journey from Bologna to Paris and Back, 1664-5. (Maps.) London: James Barrie, 1956. My version of Kit's journey from San Denis to Geneva is tentative but probable, deduced from these chapters of Blunt's: Paris to Saulieu, Saulieu to Lyons, Lyons to Geneva. (Simplon to Venice, maps and Kit's explicit ciphers.)

188 Logan Pearsall Smith. Life and Letters of Sir Henry Wotton. 2 vols Oxford: Clarendon Press, 1907, vol 1, pp 22-23 show Harry Wotton in Geneva late in June '93 with Professor Isaac Casaubon. Wotton tells the world he was with Casaubon for 14 months—a cover for several distant assignments during this period. Kit had to wait for him in Geneva: Sonnet 27: "Marloe wrote this. I'm delayed; I wait with th' professor every day . . ."

189 Sonnet 116—much information compressed.

190 Ibid.

191 Adele J. Haft, Jane G. White, Robert J, White, The Key to the Name of the Rose. Harrington Park, NJ: Ampersand Associates, 1987, pp 73, 74. Like Roger Manwood, Marcilius of Padua, who finished his Defensor Pacis in 1324, set forth the idea that "the source of all political power is the people and the . . . power of the church must be limited to preserve and protect the unity of the state . . .

Marcilius . . . has been called the precursor of the Protestant reformation and a prophet . . . of democracy."

192 Michele Manfredi. Gio. Battista Manso, nella vita e nelle opera. Napoli: Casa Tipografico Editrice, Nicola Jovene, 1919. For more than 50 years Manso was the leader of the movement to curtail the Pope's influence—the nerve center of the Resistance movement. He was a poet and philosopher and a rich man who put his money on the line for religious freedom—usually discreet but sometimes going out on a limb for fellow-workers. He became Marchese di Villa.

193 Louise George Clubb. Giambattista Della Porta, Dramatist. Princeton, NJ: Princeton U. Press, 1965. Close-read. Della Porta wrote on cryptography, made plays, was a friend to Manso, Tasso, Sarpi, Marino (an honest man who'd worked in England and was close to Kit), Guarini (Kit's Italian spymaster), and Kit.

194 Maria Ballonci. A Prince of Mantua. Stuart Hood transl. NY: Harcourt, Brace, 1956. Chap 2. Barbara Sanseverino, 30 in 1580, had married old Count Sanvitale, who gave her the beautiful fief of Colorno. She became lover of her husband's son Alessandro Farnese, governor of Flanders. (As she was later obviously on the side of the Resistance, shadows suggest she may have taken part in his wasting.) Cool, she dispatched her spies—midgets and dwarves—traveling by coach to deliver and receive secret messages.

195 by Giulio Romano. Kit mentions him appreciatively ("Jiulio Romano") in The Winter's Tale.V. 2. l. 97.

196 Spanish Cities of the Golden Age, the Views of Anton van den Wyngaerde. ed. Richard L. Kagen. Berkeley, L.A., London: U C Press, 1989, pp 18, 19 and 22. King Philip's secular collection, kept in a modern addition to the old alcázar, contained Titian's Venus and Adonis and his Tarquin and Lucretia. Viewing the collection in the summer of 1587, probably with Zuccaro, Kit (aka Arthur Dudley) may have decided then to make a pair of elegant poems, which he wrote for Hen and published in 1593 and '4, as if by William Shakespeare.

197 Sonnet 116 cipher: "his voice is shie,'n' I, being a fool, said, 'Bet U feel better nouu we SSS've made it here!' U thot hee shook wi' horror; 'e bowed deep, man, 'n' referr'd us to a privee nonni reuel!"

198 Winifred Smith. Italian Actors of the Renaissance. NY: Benjmin Blom, 1968 reprint, pp 70, 71. For months Vincenzo had wanted "Claudio" out, so the house could go to producer Drusiano Martinelli. The author concludes that the Duke made a contract with Martinelli binding his acting company to the (secret) service of Mantua. She quotes a letter from Drusiano to the Duke: "Once in your employ, I can easily find some legitimate excuses to continue serving Your Highness honorably without losing the favor of the Grand Duke entirely . . . I hope too to be able to show Your Highness some secrets which will be pleasing to you and at the same time useful in great measure."

199 Ricardo Calimani. The Ghetto of Venice. Transl. Katherine S.Wolftal. NY: M. Evans, 1987, p 143. Salamon Rossi had modern ideas; he believed that to join singing with music in the synagogue did no damage to the integrity of the Jewish faith.

200 Many pockets sewn inside, each to hold a goldpiece for secret transport. Caught by the Inquisition at Padua, 1587, he spent months in jail. (Cardinal Sega's Report, Appendix, Diaries of the English College at Reims. op. cit.) The tailor, Topping, billed and billed Lodge for the suit. Henslowe finally provided the money, and afterwards Henslowe billed Tom for a long time. Thomas Lodge DNB. Tom may have resisted paying for something he felt was a government expense.

201 Tom was seldom where biographers thought he was; he told the world he'd been on a voyage, and used the alibi again later, saying he'd sailed to America with Cavendish. Mark Eccles dissolved the "voyage" myth, showing that Tom was not among listed survivors of the Cavendish voyage. Mark Eccles. Thomas Lodge and Other Elizabethans. Ed. Chas. J. Sisson. Cambridge: Harvard U. 1933, Part One, pp 1-164. Tom was a kind man who became a physician, died in London 1625 caring for plague victims after most doctors had fled.

202 Vittorio Rossi. Battista Guarini ed il Pastor Fido, studio biographico critico. Turin: Ermanno Loescher, 1886, passim. Bio of another honest man who was often busy somewhere else.

203 Ibid. Guarini worked the Resistance angle for most of the North Italian dukes. We see him in Venice, Ferrara, Mantua and Urbino, and he often goes to Rome, apparently to listen.

204 CSP Venetian, vol 9. In a dispatch from Matheo Zane, Venetian Ambassador at Constantinople. 6 Sept. 1593: "The ships Liona and Silvestra." (The prisoners Kit rescued were safely carried back to Venice in these ships.)

205 Lucien Wolf. "Jews in Elizabethan England." op. cit., passim. Alvaro was Manwood's neighbor in Kent (at Higham, near Shorne), and an in-law, through the Boyes family. Alvaro, a shipping magnate, dealt with George Barnes and the Harts (SP 12/ 119. Dec. 1577; The Flying Hart, owned by Mendes, suffers piracy) and other in-laws of Francis Walsingham. See Abraham Galanté. Don Salomon Aben Yaèche, Duc de Mételin. Istanbul: Societé Anonyme de Papeterie et d' Imprimerie (Fratelli Haim), 1936: a bio of Alvaro using his Jewish name. His sister Catherine, aka Esther, married Ruy Lopes' brother Diego. Ibid. p 21.

206 Ibid., p 23. confirmed by a 1593 letter to Morocco, (from the sultan?) kept with Turkish State Papers, demanding that the son of Antonio, Prior of Ocrato, be sent from that prison to Constantinople.

207 Cengiz Taner, Regional Director of Culture at Istanbul, wrote me in Nov. 1989, saying that political prisoners were kept on the 7th floor of the North Tower of the Fortress of Rumeli Hisar. He also informed me that in the 16th-17th centuries the crenelated east wall against the Bosphorus came right to the water; the esplanade was not added till 1954.

Istanbul. 30 Color Plates. Munich:Wilhelm Andermann Verlag, 1961. Pictures of the fort. Hatchette World Guide. Istanbul and Environs. Imprimé en France par Brodard-Taupin Impremeur. pp 131, 132: picture and descrip. with history. All facts corroborate Kit's ciphers.

208 CSP Venetian. vol 9. Orig. Dispatch, Matheo Zane, Venetian Ambassador in Constantinople. Aug. 29 (sometime after the fact). "About 18 prisoners, who were in the fortress of the Black Sea, have broken the floors and escaped, all but a certain Alexander, cousin of Simon, Prince of Georgia, and two Poles who were nearly impotent. About *fifteen are off,* and as yet no one knows where they are." (deciphered in the Calendar.)

209 Hatchette Guide. Istanbul. op. cit., p 131.

210 Note 209 above—no sidewalk till 1954. Lucky.

211 CSP Venetian. vol 9, op. cit. Dispatch from Matheo Zane, Sept. 6. " . . . an officer has been sent to the Dardanelles to detain the ships 'Liona' and 'Silvestra' and to search them." (Though the ships evaded the searcher, the owner, still in town, was questioned.)

212 Ibid. Matheo Zane dispatch. Sept 6. "The Sultan is in a furious rage on account of the escape of the prisoners . . . . The Grand Vizir . . . caused the ambassador to be arrested by a cavass and told him to surrender the barber or he himself would be imprisoned . . . the Ambassador was forced to send for the barber . . . who would have been cruelly tortured by this time had not the feast of Bairam been so near." (deciphered.)

213 Kit's description of his imprisonment; ciphers, 3 Henry VI.

214 CSP Venetian. vol 9, op. cit. Matheo Zane dispatch, Sept 19. "The Barber . . . would have fared badly had not the ship bringing the Queen's presents to the Sultan and the Porte reached Gallipoli at this juncture." (deciphered.)

215 Ibid. Matheo Zane dispatch, Oct. 2. "The Sultan from his kiosk enjoyed the spectacle of the ship's arrival. It was dressed with scarlet cloth around the quarter deck and bulwarks, and with flags and pennants it came on with fanfares of trumpets and salvoes of harquebusses and artillery . . . . One result of the arrival of these presents is that the Ambassador is released from a difficulty by the liberation of his barber . . ." (deciphered.) A narrow squeak.

216 Bakeless. Tragicall History . . . op. cit., vol 2, pp 248-253. Perspicacious comment on A Shrew: "It is quite impossible to suppose that either Marlowe or Shakespeare wrote [this] earlier play. Indeed it is not quite accurate to speak of Marlowe's 'influence' at all. A Shrew shows no trace of his thought, his dramatic structure, his characterization, nor—except in purple patches very clumsily sewn in from Marlowe's known plays—of his mighty line." Bakeless calls the plagiarism "ruthless rifling." Sixteen quotations from both parts of Tamburlaine and Dr. Faustus are noted—and on p 249: "The author leaves Marlowe's other plays alone, perhaps because they had not yet been written." I can add the plagiarist's name with some confidence and suggest he wrote with malicious intent.

217 G.B. Harrison. Life and Death of Robert Devereux. op. cit, p 45. "1590: Essex's prospects at Court were brightening. The Queen was very generous to him, and amongst other gifts she had granted a lease of the farm of sweet wines, which would give him a princely income, so long as he held it."

218 A letter to me 23 Oct. 1982 from Maria Tiepolo, Director of the Frary Library in Venice, confirms the fact. Also: Alfredo Tenenti. Naufrages Corsaires et Assurances Maritimes à Venice, 1592-1609. 13 rue du Four, Paris: SEVPEN publishers, 1959, p 105: Capt. Cornelius Jansen, in the Fenice, had been dispatched in April on a voyage with cargo of wheat from England and Middleburgh to Venice, for relief. Arrived Venice 23 June. (2. Catti 3364, fol. 303, 23 Juin 1593).

219 soap and sardines: Alberto Tenente. Naufrages, Corsaires et Assurances Maritimes à Venise. op. cit. graphs on pp 124, 125, 126. Tenente shows notaries' info gathered 7, 8 March 1594, when Prospero Colombo figured his ship must have been wrecked because it wasn't back yet, and put in for insurance. On these pp we find the name of the ship, Rizzarda et Colombo; her captain, Giacomo Coderino [Jaques Coderin—Kit]; her merchandise, 17 big cases of soap, total weight 10727 pounds, sent by Francesco Fassiana, freightage 1 ducat per miaro. (notary Spinelli 11915, fol. 103 vo, 7 mars 1594). Also aboard were 14 barrels et moiazzi of sardines and anchovies, sent by Mondin Cossali, freightage 6 ducats. (notary Spinelli 11915, fol. 108, 8 mars, 1594.) In French.

A kind note to me April 1981 from Frederick Chapin Lane directed me to: Wilfred Brulez. Marchands Flamands à Venice. vol 1. Brussells-Rome: l' Institut Historique Belge de Rome, 1965. Professor Lane wrote, "this contains so much it might (?) mention Essex's factor." It does: p 162: "item 474, 8 March, 1594. (Notary Tenenti, n0. 94). Francesco Rizzardi is giving up to 12 insurers, headed by Cesare de Cordes, the marciliana Rizzarda et Colombo, Captain Giacomo [Jaques] Coderin, who has met with shipwreck going to Candia [Crete]. The policy was taken out on the 15th of the previous Dec." [Jaques Coderin was a cover name previously used by Kit in France.] A footnote below reads: "On 23 March, in light of the liberty accorded on 9 March to 22 insurers, headed by Cesare de Cordes, of the ship and its merchandise, Francesco Rizzardo et Prospero Colombo give appointment to Domenigo di Sandri, agent for salvage at Cattaro, and Girardo di Astori, for recovering all that they have or will recover. Ibidem, f. 128." In French. But of course they recovered nothing, for the ship was not wrecked but was back safe in Venice with her captain, his bride, her nurse and the cargo of wine, probably the next day.

220 Kit describes a similar storm in a book he wrote for his daughter using cover-name Antonio Eslava. Noches de Invierno. op. cit. (Note 13 above.).

221 A letter to me from Dr. Maria Tiepolo, Superior Director of the Archivio di Stato in Venice, 11 March 1985, mentions Zuan Domenico Cicogna, duke of Candia. (In an earlier letter, 23 December 1982, she'd enclosed a Xerox copy of all civil servants in Candia in 1594.)

222 He was on the list of civil servants, Candia (Crete), 1594, but refused the post: "Paris Avogadro q. Pompeo (el. 1592. 01. 26, entr.==, usc. 1595. 02.20, rifiuta la carica)."

223 Kit's ciphers, 3 Henry VI.

224 Erotokritos. op. cit. See Note 33 here.

225 In most ciphers, Kit refers to the lady, his first wife, as Rita. She was Marina Cicogna, and in ciphers for The Comedy of Errors, he tells her name: ll. 17, 18: "'In Canaan, in Canaan,' Marina says, 'Sir Roger's free, fit, best in Yauue's eyes.'" Soon after Rita died, Kit tried to make the play Pericles, in which Pericles' daughter was named Marina. And several years later, in Jonson's play Every Man in His Humour, Stephano (Kit) fears he's lost his purse; Lorenzo Junior says, "Nay, do not weep, a pox on it, hang it, let it go." Stephano: "Oh, it's here; nay, an it had been lost, I had not cared, but for a jet ring Marina sent me."

226 Antonio Eslava. Noches de Invierno, op. cit. Chapter One. Wry and touching.

227 Ibid., Chapter One. This dress is mentioned also in Kit's ciphers for 3 Henry VI—and in Cervantes's story of the "Spanish English Girl" in his Novelas Ejemplares, the protagonist (Marina's daughter), wears a pearl-embroidered gown when she meets the queen—probably her mother's wedding dress cut down.

228 Note 221 here.

229 L.P. Smith. Life and Letters of Sir Henry . . . op. cit., vol 1, p 17. "Fynes Moryson recounts how, three years later [1594], another young Englishman who visited Rome, apparently with a purpose similar to Wotton's [spying], was pursued as far as Siena by the Inquisition and took to his heels towards Padua, in such haste 'as he seemed to fly over the Appeninne without wings.' (Fynes Moryson's Itinerary, p 159.)" Ciphers, 3 Henry VI, describe the haste.

230 Ciphers, First lines of MN's D.

231 He speaks of this in ciphers made years later in Troilus and Cressida. (He has returned to Venice, goes to find his father-in-law: ll 233, 234 fol. "bitter, he'd not take her in his vault. Fy! Perhaps now he's free o' queer sh-shit, so I can sho him her sail-wrapped squalid shack, 'n' he can go lade a shelf in the closet h-hive tomb uuith th' lost daughter, 'n' uue gain, subito, an end to all the worrie about th' ghastlee plight."

232 In ciphers, As You Like It, Kit reminisced: "Dim memories stir'd. I weep so much the quill shakes, for my Rita became all white, C? Entombed at Hallowe'en."

233 Cardenio. In As You Like It ciphers for ll 207-208, 253-25, Kit talks about planning to make a play about the young man and his troubles. E.K. Chambers. Wm. Sh., A Study of Facts and Problems. op. cit., vol 1, pp 538-541, mentions Cardenio on p 539: "A play of Cardenno or Cardenna was given by the King's Men at court in the winter of 1612-13, and again on 8 June of 1613. The source was probably the story of Cardenio and Lucinda, as written in Thomas Shelton's translation of I Don Quixote (1612: S.R. 19 January 1611); and this, though with altered

names, was in fact the source of Double Falsehood, produced at Drury Lane on 13 December 1727 by Lewis Theobald as an adaptation from Shakespeare. Double Falsehood was printed the next year with a preface containing the following statement: 'There is a tradition (which I have from the Noble Person, who supply'd me with one of my copies) that it was given by our Author, as a Present of Value, to a natural Daughter of his, for whose sake he wrote it, in the Time of his Retirement from the Stage.'" Chambers writes on his p 541: "It is odd that nobody else appears to have seen the three . . . manuscripts which Theobald claimed to possess, and that they should all have disappeared at or before his death . . . It is oddest of all that Theobald, as a Shakespearean scholar, although he still asserted the poet's authorship in the edition of 1734 . . . made no attempt to publish the unadapted text." Not so odd if the original scripts belonged to Isabel. Not so odd if SSS decided the story was too close to the Sonnets—and Cervantes—to be made public. [Intriguing that Roger Manwood's first wife was a Theobald.]

The Manuscript Society News. vol xiv no. 4, Fall 1993, printed an article about a book dealer in NYC, Chas. Hamilton, who claimed he'd discovered a copy of Cardenio in the British Library. The librarian told me the script is a play called the Second Maiden's Tragedy.

234 William Byron. Cervantes. op. cit., p 382. Also G. B. Harrison. Life and Death of Robert Devereux . . . op. cit. p 114: "The two guns in the Puntal fort were fired off, but the effort was too much for them; one burst, the other collapsed." Not only did Kit and Manco move cannon balls around to the wrong guns; they arranged to have one Spanish ship crammed with guns and ammunition, and when the English left for home she was sailed off to England: "An 'argosy . . . whose ballast was great ordnance' was also secured."

235 As good as his word, Tom Howard, soon to become the first earl of Suffolk, took Isabel to live with his family at Audley End, where she was reared and where she lived with her first husband, the earl's third son Henry.

236 The Merry Wives. I, 2. ll. 4. "—or his dry nurse—"

237 L. P. Smith. Life and Letters of . . . op. cit., vol 1, p 31 writes that Henry Wotton was with Essex on the Azores expedition in summer 1597. Contraindication suggests that instead he'd gone with Henry Cuffe and Bacon on a secret trip to Switzerland to meet with "an Italian resident at Berne among the Switzers." L.P. Smith, inadvertantly setting the stage, ibid. p 33, says Wotton wrote Essex from Plymouth a few days after the return from the Azores. Harry's letter, printed in Smith's vol 1, p 304, includes a long paragraph in Italian about attempts of Philip II to win the Swiss from their allegiance to Henri IV. Here we learn Harry's "correspondent" at Berne was "one Paulo Lentulo." The information was probably derived from Lentulo at first-hand—not from a letter, but at a meeting—for there's an entry in the Padua University Register (not noticed by biographers?) on 23 August 1597:

"Ottavio B." (Ottavio Baldi is Henry Wotton's Italian undercover name, known to historians); "Henricus Cuffe" (Henry Cuffe was a well-known secretary of Essex's); and "Franc Bocons" (a not-so-pseudo pseudonym for Francis Bacon, all registered (to audit a law lecture ?) on 23 August, probably after attending Resistance meetings in the Grisons. Bacon returned to England late for the scheduled opening of Parliament. The queen postponed the opening, I think for him, but no one I asked knew why she did it; one authority said it was just a mistake.

238 L.P. Smith. op. cit., vol 1, p 31. Wotton described the Azores Expedition, "contrary to the verdict of history, as the best of the voyages of Essex: 'for the discovery of the Spanish weakness, and otherwise almost a saving voyage.'" Reliquiae Wottoniana, ed. Isaak Walton. 4th ed., 1672. p 178.

239 ciphers, Henry V, ll. 323 '4, '5, '6, " . . . til I'm sent t'sel th' erl's loot (from R humane, w-wilee foray), at Venice. UUe seek t' sel R take at a huge gross profit—R share o'lousee hulls."

240 Maria Bellonci. A Prince of Mantua. op. cit., p 177: "to [Cesare], Clement VIII conceded Modena and Reggio with their surrounding territory, together with the title of Duke." And ciphers, 1 Henry IV and Henry V.

241 Kit tells the sordid story in a tour de force, triple-play set of ciphers for Much Ado About Nothing—a play in which he manages to save the girl. Later he transmutes the situation in the complex tragedy Othello, using as a source a letter which the steward at Trotti's hunting lodge wrote to Cesare, describing the murder. Vittorio Rossi. Battista Guarini . . . op. cit. Documento XXI. p 290. Like Desdemona, Anna did not scream or struggle, and the line in Othello, "I kissed thee ere I killed thee," is also factual: Trotti committed a crime of passion. But he used a knife for the death, not a pillow, as onstage. The whole true affair is hashed out in Rossi's text, pp 116-119. Trotti, a courtier favored by Cesare, was not punished. Guarini put a Latin epitaph for Anna in the church of Santa Caterina, published by Lorenzo Barrotti (Mem. Storica. 11, 208, Cfr. Petrucci p 108.n.b.). Cesare ordered it torn down. Kit put one into Much Ado. V, 3.

242 A discussion of the problem of the lease, the dismantlement and transport of timbers, and aid from mysterious stranger W.S. is found in C.C. Stopes. Burbage and Shakespeare's Stage. NY: Haskell House Reprint, 1970, pp 73-76.

243 In Troylus and Cressida, both prologue and play, Kit's ciphers describe the summer in Ireland with matchless perception and detail. In ciphered lines 75-92 of the first act we relive Essex's heartless execution of one tenth of the troop that ran away. Kit served on burial-detail.

244 In Troylus and Cressida, ciphers ll.155-158, Kit thinks of how Hugh O'Neal " . . . may meet that MT toy treaty with laughter—home free—as he, Robin, twists, totally lost . . ."

245 G.B. Harrison. The Life and Death . . . op. cit., and C.C. Stopes. The Life of Henry, Third Earl . . . op. cit., and James Spedding. Works of Francis Bacon. op. cit., all offer detailed coverage.

246 S. Schoenbaum. A Documentary Life of Sh. NY: Oxford U Press, 1975, p 127: "Paolo Marco Lucchese . . . ran a restaurant in the parish of St. Olave . . . and

lodged Italian visitors . . . . In Othello . . . the Duke asks, 'Marcus Lucchese, is he not in town?'" In Ben Jonson's Cynthia's Revels, Amorphous, who likes Italian food, is hired by the hostess: "The wife of the ordinary gives him his diet to maintain her table in discourse; which, indeed, is a mere tyranny over her other guests, for he will usurp all the talk . . ."

247 Kit may have met William Basset of Blore at the home of Hen's foster grandfather, Anthony Brown, Viscount Montague. A friend of the Browns and the Howards, Basset was Catholic, which may have been why he was interested in adopting Isabel, whose mother had been Catholic; and Isabel had spent early formative months in Cervantes' Catholic home in Seville. CSP Dom.Eliz. 1593. item 98, 19 Sept., about pursuivant Topcliffe's suspicions of Basset's loyalty—how a priest employed by Montagues had fled to Wm. Basset; also, CSP Dom. Eliz. 1593 October, a long item, 138—confession of Robert Gray, priest, before Richard Topcliffe (infamous pursuivant), and three others, about accusations of priest-protection brought against William Basset of Blore and the Browns (Hen Wriothesley's foster-mom Mary was one of those Browns—Montagues)—at Cowdray. Hard to find information about this man. He was wealthy and of Plantagenet descent.

248 C.C. Stopes. The Life of Henry, Third Earl . . . op. cit., p 191. The two men put up the chain at Ludgate.

249 Ibid. pp 193, 194. A long dialogue.

250 Ibid. p 206. Captain Thomas Lea, who wanted the queen to grant Essex a private interview.

251 As You Like It. ciphers, ll. 67, 68.

252 CSP Domestic Eliz. 1601-1603. Vol. clxxxii, p 140, item 72: "Account of intelligencers employed abroad this year and sums they have received . . . . Mr. Fox, in Venice, 20 l." Tempting to think of Ben as Mr. Fox, especially since he later wrote the play Volpone (The Fox, set in Venice), and another good one called The Alchemist. David W. Davies. Elizabethans Errant. Ithaca, NY: Cornell U Press. 1967, p 145, writes that in Venice, "summer, 1602," (*early* summer 1602?) English secret service agent Simon Fox was keeping an eye on a certain Anthony Sherley, adventurer—and Anthony was working with an *alchemist* (pp 147, 148). Sherley had rented a big house, where he was living with "a numerous following." Sherley borrowed money from English secret agent Aurelian Townsend, who was also keeping an eye on Sherley, "although Townsend was not an efficient spy. He was Cecil's steward and a young poet who enjoyed the friendship of both Ben Jonson [aha!] and Edward Herbert." (After Ben Jonson came home to England, he lived for a year with Aurelian Townsend. Jonson DNB.)

253 The sequence of events described in some detail in ciphers, Troylus and Cressida.

254 DNB. Ben Jonson " . . . in June 1602, . . . the additions to Kyd's "Jeronimo," which Jonson executed for . . . Henslowe, . . . receiving the unusually high sum

of 10 l." Kit's ciphers praise Jonson's generous split of the payment for their collaboration.

255 Joel Hurstfield. The Queen's Wards (Wardship and Marriage under Elizabeth I). Cambridge, MA: 1958, p 300 re Robert Cecil's management-style as Master of Wards: various bribes displayed. On p 301 the author says: "More significant, perhaps, is the case of Elizabeth Bassett's wardship, which has a lot to tell us about Cecil's methods at this time. (H.M.C. Salis., xiv, 108: B.M. Lans. 88, f. 1051.) The story begins with a petition to Cecil during 1602 from a certain John Baxter claiming that he had given legal and other services to the late William Bassett, (sic) in Derbyshire, and subsequently to the queen in revealing that Bassett had held his lands by knight-service from the crown. As a result, a wardship had been discovered. Then, with a request for some reward for his efforts, Baxter drops out of the narrative, to make way for more eminent men. The wardship was in fact sold on 18 May 1602 to Henry Lord Cobham . . . brother-in-law of Cecil . . . Cobham kept the wardship for only two days and then sold it to Sir Walter Raleigh, (sic) 'for and in consideration of a certain sum of money'—not stated—and Cecil himself acted as witness to the agreement. But Cecil's role was by no means simply the passive one of witness. On the very day that Raleigh bought the Bassett wardship at second-hand, he entered into an agreement with Cecil himself, making provision, amongst other things, that in the event of Cecil's death within the ensuing two years, Raleigh would transfer the wardship to the executors of Cecil. The executors of Cecil? The explanation of this curious arrangement is to be found in the early part of the agreement. After reciting that Raleigh had bought the wardship from Cobham it states: 'the passing of which grant was truly meant and intended by the said Sir Robert Cecil and Henry Lord Cobham to be in trust, and to the only use and behoof of him, the said Robert Cecil and his assigns.' No transfer of wardship could take place without the authority of the Master of Wards. Cecil clearly wanted the wardship, but, for one reason or another, did not dare openly to grant it to himself. So Lord Cobham was brought in . . . and then Sir Walter Raleigh, whose agreement with Cobham would have to be entered on the official records of the Court of Wards. Finally Cecil executed a private trust with Raleigh—which, as a trust and not a re-sale, would not have to be recorded amongst the Court of Wards records. So Sir Robert Cecil, as Master, made it possible for Sir Robert Cecil, as a private individual, to reap the profits of a wardship. How many times he did this we cannot tell for we are dependent upon the chance survival of these private papers. (H.M.C. Salis., xii, 580-1: Hatfield deeds 192.6 and 10.) Elizabeth Bassett was heir to a substantial fortune . . . She is reported to have brought [her second husband—RB] an income of £2,400 a year and six or seven thousand pounds in cash."

256 John Payne Collier. New Particulars. p 57. On 1 or 2 Aug 1602, the queen, a guest of Sir Thomas Egerton at Harefield, sees a trial performance of Kit's Othello, performed by Burbage's men. This Othello is the first draft, made while Kit

was in Venice. Plot shows Elizabeth that someone can be fooled into thinking a beloved person is bad. Is Kit present at the show?

257 E.K.Chambers. Eliz. Stage. op. cit., "A Court Calendar." Monday 17 January 1603. Elizabeth keeps her last appointment in town: she visits Good Tom at the Charter House.

258 Cervantes inserted a mention near the end of Don Quixote Part One about how Sancho Panza wanted to be governor of an island.

259 Gilbert Slater. Seven Shakespeares. London: Cecil Palmer 1931, p 75. "Sir Sidney Lee threw doubt upon the authenticity of that letter, on the ground that Lady Pembroke would not have referred to the poet as 'the man Shakespeare.' . . . Captain Sidney Olivier commented, . . . 'the Letter was certainly at Wilton House up to 1874, in which year Lord Pembroke married, and his mother, the late Lady Herbert of Lea, left the house. The letter was inadvertently carried away from Wilton then.' Any further doubt about the existence of the letter is cleared up by the fact that when William Cory visited Wilton House in 1865, he made the following entry in his diary: 'the house (Lady Herbert said) is full of interest: above us is Wolsey's room; we have a letter, never printed, from Lady Pembroke to her son, telling him to bring James I from Salisbury to see As You Like It; 'we have the man Shakespeare with us.'"

260 CSP Elizabeth Domestic Addenda. vol. xxxvi, Feb. 1604. A note from J[aques] Cardén to Dudley Carlton, a sec'y to the earl of Northumberland, about how penniless is Cardén: the landlord took my cloak—can you please lend me one? The date is not solid; it could date back as far as Oct. 1603, when Carlton first went to work for Northumbeland.

261 Peter Lauritzen and Alex Zielke. Palaces of Venice. NY: Viking, 1978. Peter Lauritzen kindly sent me a reproduction of a watercolor of the Palazzo da Silva with a note, rec'd 20 July 1986: . . ."I don't know of any photographs of Pal. Da Silva (whose name Mr. Smith mis-spelled), but since I have owned an apartment of its piano nobile since 1980 I am sending this drawing we had made of it . . . ."

262 Wotton kept a villa on the Brenta till his last departure for home. It looks as if Kit was reworking Measure for Measure at the time he rented the villa for Harry in 1604, so I like to imagine he put a realistic picture of its garden into the play: V.1. ll.28-33.

263 Miguel Cervantes. The First Part of the Historie of Don Quixote. Thos. Shelton transl. 1612. Intro. James Fitzmaurice-Kelly: NY: AMS Press, 1967. (London: David Nutt, 1896.) Chapter XXV (the last). Sancho, returned to his wife, says he has brought her and the children gifts, and "therefore rest satisfied for this time; for and it please God, that we travaile once again to seeke adventures, thou shalt see me shortly after an Earle, or Governour of an Iland, and that not every ordinarie one either, but of one of the best in the World."

264 L.P. Smith. op. cit., vol 1, p 51.

265 Lansdowne MS 891 f. 129 r. About 1611, Arthur Gregory sent Mike Hickes a viol. "Arthur Gregory" was a cover name Kit used in 1586 while staying at Thomas

Phelippes' apartment in London during the Mary Queen of Scots case. That the viol-giver was the same Arthur Gregory is not improbable: Arthur, for Kit's mother's name, Gregory, for the name Kit chose to use so many years in Italy. A new avenue of study—Kit's mother's dad William Arthur was a seaman, and Mike Hickes's mother, Julie Arthur, was from Clapton, a village of seafarers near Bristol, her father a William Arthur [her last husband a Captain Robert Hickes]. Susan Hicks Beach. A Cotswold Family: Hicks and Hicks-Beach. London: William Heineman, 1909. Kit and Mike may have been kin. Find info about Mike's dad Robert Hicks ? (David Mathew. "The Cornish and Welsh Pirates in the Reign of Elizabeth." English Historical Review. vol 39, 1924, p 313, top of page and footnote. These tiny mentions about a Robert Hicks, a Saltash captain, one of the very few elite pirates who were hanged at Wapping, may explain a lot about Mike and his brother Baptist's mysterious banking careers: was their dad hanged because he refused to put a hidden haul of his on the Account?)

266 Venice. Consiglio X, Processi Criminali reg. 22, 9* April 1605. Girolamo da Monte kills Mauritio Cavagion in front of the Episcopal throne, in the Cathedral of Vicenza. (The Venice Recorder has put down the wrong date;* Harry says Easter Sunday, the 10th.) This delayed report is printed in CSP Venetian. vol 10, 27 March 1607, p 483. Also see street map, Vicenza. The Blue Guide: Muirhead's Northern Italy. London: Macmillan, 1924.

267 William Byron. Cervantes. op. cit., p 415. Byron names occupants: in Manco's own apartment: his wife and sisters. "Perhaps a servant as well; he is known to have hired a serving-girl named María de Ceballos early in 1605." Twenty-seven years later, working for the Vallejo Co., María de Ceballos was to play Cyntia in a great tragedy by Lope de Vega. Hugo Albert Rennert. The Life of Lope de Vega. NY: Benjamin Blom, 1968 (1904), p 340 note. Byron continues: "Opposite them on the same floor lived Cervantes' cousin Luisa de Montoya with her two sons . . ." In 1622, Juan de Montoya was an actor in the Vallejo Co. Rennert. op. cit., p 295 note. Over Cervantes' apt. lived a friend, Mariana Ramirez,with daughters. Rennert. ibid. p 298 note: original Vallejo cast included a Ramirez. Among intelligencers living with Cervantes in 1605, do we see startup for the Vallejo Company?

268 Byron. op. cit., p 443. Lord Howard of Effingham, Earl of Nottingham, was in Valladolid in May and June, "with a retinue of some five hundred persons to ratify the peace with England concluded in London in the previous year." (Many of the English were intelligencers and SSS bodyguards.)

269 The Dramatic Works of William Davenant. op. cit. Introductory pp offer information about Jane and her husband John.

270 A baby. DNB Sir William Davenant. " . . . born in Oxford at the latter end of February 1605 [1606, new style], was baptised at St. Martin's Church in that city 3 March in the same year." Conceived, then, while Jane and Kit were on duty in Valladolid, at the end of May or first of June, 1605. That William was Kit's child is made clear by the attitude of his legal father, meetings with his real dad, Will's

own assertions, evidence of exchange of letters, at least one gift, and poems to the end of Kit's life. Will wrote an extant epitaph for his real dad, kept by King Charles I.

271 CSP Venetian, vol 10, item 708. On March 27 1607, Harry is speaking to the Cabinet asking for pardons for Girolamo Monte of Vicenza, who he said killed Cavagion in the duomo in self-defense, and Augustin Carpan [Note that Carpan's name reflects the name of the street down which Girolamo Monte and the broken men escaped from the duomo that Easter.]—Augustin Carpan, who had affirmed all his trouble had come upon him from the machinations of a certain courtesan. Printed reports of these occurrances are in the archives of the Council of Ten: Ven. Consiglio X. Processi Criminali, reg. 22. April 9 [sic], 1605. Girolamo da Monte and a band of bravos attacked Mauritio Cavagion and two of his sons in the Cathedral of Vicenza, slew the father and wounded the sons. The cause of the quarrel was a dispute about a seat in the church. Mauritio was chased up to the Episcopal Throne and there fell. Girolomo avoided arrest, but was tried and condemned to perpetual banishment by the Ten. CSP Ventian says Augustin Carpan's crimes are to be left in the decent obscurity of a foreign tongue. Ven. Consiglio X. ut. sup. July 20, 1605. In Murano in casa de Anzola Mazina, Augustin Carpan had carnal commerce with Antonia, daughter of Hieronimo Verglierzin & Iseppa Furlana, just 9 years old & not only deflowered but sodomized and damaged. Anzola Mazina [the madame] jailed. Antonia given 500 ducats for dowry [all Kit's money]. (CSP Venetian, vol 10, March 27, *1607*, in Italian.) *Kit has been FRAMED by the bad guys*! Antonia was deflowered by her own father Hieronimo in hope of promised dowry.

272 William Urry, Christopher Marlowe and Canterbury. op. cit., Appendix VI. The wills of John and Katherine Marlowe [Marley] 1605, pp 133-136. In his will and in inventory of his goods taken after his death there's no mention of shoemaking tools or supplies. He just left everything to Kate; maybe she sold or gave away his tools before her own death about seven weeks later. Her inventory of tablecloths suggests she maintained a restaurant, which she did. (ciphers, The Jew of Malta), and her three dozen sheets suggest the rooming house she did operate. In her will, Kate asked to be buried "in the churchyarde of St. George's neare where as my husbande John Marlowe was buryed." David Riggs. The World of Christopher Marlowe. New York: Henry Holt, 2005, p 349, tells us she was not granted her wish but was buried "in the nearby parish church of All Saints." [Note the word "in," which gives her special status.] That church stood in the center of town across the street from Kingsbridge Hospital and no longer exists. Who knows where her body rests today? Dr. Riggs offers no source for his statement.

273 Riverside Shakespeare. Boston: Houghton Mifflin, 1974, p 1308.

Geoffrey Bullough. Narrative and Dramatic Sources of Sh. op. cit., vol 7. Macbeth. pp 429-30.

274 Marqués de Rafel, Alfonso Pardo Manuel de Villena. Un Maecenas Español del siglo XVII. Madrid: imprenta de Jaime Ratés Martin, 1911. A biography of this Castro, 7th Count of Lemos. Word-pictures of the young count and his wife appear in Don Quixote, and a play mentioned in Rafel's work, La Confusa, reflects Twelfth Night, together with shadows of Kit's play Henry VIII.

275 DNB. William Bedell.

L. P. Smith. op. cit., vol ii: multiple entries in index and a monograph on Bedell's life, pp 462, 463.

A Catalogue of Paintings in the Folger Shakespeare Library. New Haven: Yale U Press, 1993, pp 268, 269, offers shadowy suggestions. The Flower Portrait 'of Sh.', now at Stratford on Avon, some parts of which are shown to have been painted (not just overpainted) with modern pigments, may have been a gift to William Bedell (Harry's chaplain at the embassy) in Venice—and after the family sold or gave away the fine painting, a poor copy was kept, much later *bought from the Bedells* by the Folger Library. (just a thought.)

276 Paul Durst, Intended Treason. What Really Happened in the Gunpowder Plot. South Brunswick and NY: A.S. Barnes, 1970, p 85. Ben Jonson gets a mention, very low-key, but Durst does think Jonson might have been a spy.

277 L.P. Smith. op. cit., vol 1, pp 78-85. A coherent, objective report on this difficult period of Interdict, with focus on the role of the English embassy.

278 Vittorio Rossi. Battista Guarini . . . op. cit., Chapter XVII, pp 142, fol. Guarini's mission to Paulo V. During the Interdict, Guarini's journeys between Rome and Venice were secret.

279 Maria Ballonci. A Prince of Mantua. op. cit., p 18.

280 Winifred Smith. Actors of the Renaissance. op. cit., p 95.

281 L. P. Smith. op. cit., vol 1 p 79.

282 James Spedding. op. cit., vol 10, pp 290-1. Bacon married, 10 May 1606. His three chief wedding guests were Cecil's confidential secretaries. Bacon's marriage was unsuccessful, perhaps unconsummated, and apparently utterly without affection. A cryptic remark—vulgar—which Kit ciphered into the first four lines of the Folio version of Hamlet suggests that Ned Vere attacked Francis and emasculated him: "Here Kit Marlowe wrote of Ned de Vere's heh-nonny-nonnys. Alban is glad th' drug's flaua permits general use. Vere so cooly beckon'd Francis out to the roof to low-cut hym. You'v wet."

(OED. nonny-nonny. Formerly used to cover indelicate allusions. Indelicate? Yes, it looks as if what Ned did was unspeakable.)

283 See note 13 above.

284 CSP Venetian. vol 11, item 230, 11 April 1608. The Nuncio spoke in the Cabinet: "The English ambassador has caused to be sent to Venice two cases of books which must refer to his Sect, and they can easily be passed through many hands to the danger of our Faith." The Nuncio was jumping to conclusions, and the Doge told him so, saying the ambassador lived most retired and was modest and

circumspect in all his doings and that ambassadors must be respected, otherwise there would be a violation of the jus gentinum. It was not for them to pry into boxes. The Nuncio believes the English are up to no good: he will return when he knows more.

285 Leo Schrade. Monteverdi, Creator of Modern Music. Yale U Press, 1957, p 239. Monteverdi's opera was Arianna, now lost; Guarini's crazy comedy was L'Idropica. Leo Schrade read Cervantes's signature as "Monco," when surely it was "Manco;" he was known for his entre'acts. (The Interludes of Cervantes. S. Griswold Morley transl. Princeton, NJ: Princeton U Press, 1948.)

286 Claudio Monteverdi. Madrigali Amorosi. The Eighth Book of Madrigals, 1638. From Historical Anthology of Music. The Bach Guild. #4: Ninfa che Scalza il Piede: #8: Perche t'en Fuggi, and more, are Kit's lyrics. Kit ciphered them in English: see the Scrapbook.

287 The Riverside Shakespeare, 1974 op. cit. Frank Kermode, in his introduction to Antony and Cleopatra, mentions that on 20 May 1608 Edward Blount entered in the Stationer's Register "A booke Called Anthony and Cleopatra." Kermode says this was probably a blocking entry, and Blount had no real intent to publish at that time. Kit's cipher inside his rewrite tells the story: he says Shakepeare hated the play, sold it too early to "frugal Blount" and sent Kit a message declaring the piece was so bad Kit should stop writing. (Will Shakespeare must have influenced the company's productions and finances.)

288 Thomas Coryate. Coryat's Crudities. London: vol 1 finally printed by W.S., 1611 quarto, illus. The first part of vol 2 also printed by W.S., 1611 quarto; second part of vol 2 printed by Thomas Thorpe, 1611 quarto. A lot of valuable funny stuff.

289 L.P. Smith. op. cit., vol 1, pp 100-104, writes of James' book: James I of England. Premonition to all most Mighty Monarchs, Kings, Free Princes, and States of Christendom. This was James's own work, satirical and objectionable, with overt insults for the Pope as Anti-Christ. In 1609 it was sent to crowned heads of Europe who didn't want it. On 25 July 1609 (ibid. p 103) Wotton gave a copy to the Doge, who received it kindly, and as soon as Harry left, gave it to the Magnificent Grand Chancellor, who locked it in the secret Chancery, "from which it has never emerged." Harry soon heard that the book's circulation had been forbidden in Venice.

290 Bacon. De Sapientia Veterum. [Concerning the Wisdom of the Ancients]. 1609.

291 The Great Assizes Holden in Parnassus by Appollo and his Assessors. London: Richard Cotes for Edward Husbands, and are to be sold at his Shop in the Middle Temple, 1645. Several pp. of this anonymous work are reprinted in Sir Edward Durning Lawrence. Bacon is Sh. NY: John Mc Bride, 1910, pp 57-61, and in Gilbert Slater. Seven Shakespeares. op. cit., pp 116, 117.) In The Great Assizes, Bacon, "The Lord Verulan" (sic), is "Chancellor of Parnassus," and below there's a list of workers in the field (SSS bros) with their occupations. Interesting that

William Davenant, Kit's son, became a spy. And William "Shakespeere" is "the writer of weekly accounts" (Kit, when he was chargé d'affaires of the Embassy in Venice)—and "*Ben Johnson*"[sic*] is "Keeper of the Trophonian Denne.*" Being a bricklayer and Bacon's slave, Ben must have been used to make an inconspicuous reclosable opening in the side of the treasury (or the mint?), so treasure could be removed without walking in the door. Of course the scheme has awful repercussions, but Bacon himself will not be charged with these thefts.

William Hepworth Dixon. Personal History of Lord Bacon. Boston: Ticknor & Fields. 1861, pp 405-406: On Thurs. 10 August, 1609 Bacon writes Cecil (Letter in State Papers) re Mr. Chancellor, Mr. Att'y and "transportation of gold and silver." "The Frenchman never came or called about it. Henry Neville sent up a solicitor about it. Mr. Calvert says you want a copy of his answer."

292 Ciphers in Cymbeline identify the play as a complete reworking of something very early: "Chr. Marlowe uurote this too-broad nonny before he uuas sent to be ye monster-demon. O, U oversee th' remake o' this mouldie SSS thing Ned wrote. (I'd gag.)" Also in this year, 1609, Kit's book of stories, Noches de Invierno, was published in Pamplona with out-front byline Antonio de Eslava (a borrowed name), and cipher-dedicated to his daughter. See note 13, above.

293 Aemilia Lanyer. Salve Deus Rex Judaeorum. London: Valentine Simmes for Richard Bonian, to be sold at his Shop in Paules Churchyard, . . . 1611. Published in USA as The Poems of Shakespeare's Dark Lady. Salve Deus Rex Judaeorum by Emilia Lanier. Introduction (37 pp) by A. L. Rowse. NY: Clarkson N. Potter, 1979. Rowse, a notorious fudger who offers hints of the truth, gives valuable facts in his introduction to this work. Emilia was Kit's lover, not Shakespeare's.

294 L. P. Smith. op. cit., vol 1, p 490. News of the death of Henri IV reached Venice in May. A letter from Harry to Cecil, 28 May, 1610.

295 Hugo Albert Rennert. The Life of Lope de Vega. NY: Benjamin Blom, 1968 (1904). The Sanchez Co. was one of the best; Rennert's work includes many indexed references to its manager, Fernan Sanchez de Vargas.

296 Micaela Lujan. A famous actress, singer and dancer. None of her biographies can tell when she retired or died. She disappeared in 1616. Rennert. ibid. indexes her as Loca (La), as well as Luxan, Marcela; Luxan, Micaela de; Luzinda (Camila Luzinda, Lope's poetic nickname for her). And see p 1: she may have been Lope's childhood friend. Rennert makes some guesses about her, pp 113-fol. She bore Lope at least two children, Marcela and Lope Felix. On p 113 Rennert writes: "Every doubt has been cleared away by the publication of the baptismal certificate of the younger Lope. It reads: 'In the parochial Church of St. Sebastian of the City of Madrid, on the seventh of February, sixteen hundred and seven, I, Alonso del Arco, baptised a child [born] on January 28 of the said year, the son of Lope de Vega Carpio and of Micaela de Lujan, and gave him the name of Lope; his sponsors were D. Hurtado de Mendoza and Hieronimo de Burgos.' The name of the mother of Lope's son is then Micaela de Lujan or Luxan—for

both spellings occur . . ." Rennert's source: Pérez Pastor. Datos desconocidos (Homenage á Menéndez y Pelayo. vol 1, p 595. 2nd ed. p 262.)

297 Records of the Virginia Company of London. Susan Myra Kingsbury, ed. Washington, D.C.: Government Printing Office, 1905-1936, vol 4, pp 408, fol.: Bargraves Polisie. Here, as Ignotus (see ibid. vol 3 p 607), Kit offers his ciphered opinions re the constricting effects of Catholic dogma on families.

298 Greta Devos et Wilfred Brulez. Marchands Flamands À Venise. op. cit., vol 2 p 302, item 2643. "Giovanni Alli, Ecossais," John Allen, Scotsman . . . gives power of attorney to Gregorio de' Monti, secretary of the ambassador of Great Britain . . . . The secretary to receive 100 ducats for his trouble (and because, of course, he can't speak English, there's a translator: Jiulio di Franceschi).

299 Dudley Carleton to John Chamberlain, 1603-1624. ed. Maurice Lee, Jr. New Brunswick, NJ: Rutgers U Press, 1972. Intro., pp 10, 11. Carleton arrived in Venice near the end of November 1610; with him were his wife, his sister, and his friend John Chamberlain, who stayed till February. Interesting that editor Maurice Lee envisions Venice as a sort of nowhere, and characterizes Carleton's predecessor Harry as "an elegant and incompetent dilettante." (p 13.)

300 Italian Plays, 1500-1700, in the Folger Library. A Bibliography with Introduction by Louise George Clubb. Firenze: Leo Olschki Editore, 1968, p 97: De' Monti, Gregorio. L'Ippolito, commedia . . . terza impressione. Venetia, Pietro Baba, 1620. First edition 1611. Five acts, prose. Ded. to Alessandro and Guarino Guarini; Venezia, 2 Mar. 1620. The first edition was dedicated to their father, Battista.

301 Close-read Hugo Rennert's Life of Lope de Vega; Lope was an honest man.

Lucian Wolf. "Jews in Elizabethan England." op. cit., p 11: An English Marrano arrested in Spain in 1588 managed to extricate imself and was released "with the assistance of Antonio de Vega, the head of the Spanish espionage service in England at the time."

302 Luis Astrana Marin. La Vida Turbulenta de Quevedo. Madrid: Gran Capitan, 1945. On p 145 Marin introduces the Duke of Osuna, Don Pedro Tellez Girón, and for the next 207 pp the book is just as much about Osuna as it is about Quevedo. Osuna was an incorrigible child whose father and grandfather despaired of reforming him. He became a violent mobster; did as he pleased, maimed, murdered without compunction. Marin avoids details, only repeating that the duke's behavior was "off the map." Osuna's private secretary Francisco Quevedo seemed the one person able to guide him.

Giuseppe Coniglio. Collana di Cultura Napolitana, I Vicerè Spagnoli di Napoli. Naples: 1967: Osuna died in jail, Sept 25, 1624.

D. A. Parrino. Teatro eroico e politico de governi de Viceré del Regno di Napoli: 1730, vol 3, pp 95-134. Parrino offers a monograph on this amoral Duke of Osuna.

303 Don Francisco De Quevedo y Villegas. Obras Completas. Madrid: Aguilar. vol 1, 1958, vol 2, Luis Astrana Marin, editor, 1952 (sic). Both volumes contain valuable personal observations of political doings in Italy—pp mentioned in later notes.

304 L.P. Smith. op. cit., vol 1, p 501.

305 Ibid., vol 1, p 501.

306 Narrative and Dramatic Sources . . . Geoffrey Bullough, ed. op. cit., vol 8, pp 239-240. Bullough mentions three pamphlets of 1610 which have a bearing on the play, The Tempest, and then, "we must add a fourth work which Shakespeare must have read although it was not printed until 1625 . . . . This was the long letter to an 'excellent Lady' sent from Virginia on 15 July by William Strachey, secretary to Gates at James Town and to the council there." That the Lady was Mary Herbert is highly probable; Kit must have started The Tempest as soon as he read the letter—at the end of 1610, just after Mary's lover Michael Lister (chaperoning the two boys) arrived at the Venice Embassy house. Bullough gets close, p 240: "To Strachey the dramatist owed specific details, . . . roaring and darkness . . . fear, amazement and prayers . . . utter weariness . . . common toil . . . St. Elmo's fire on mast and rigging . . . safe harbour . . . recurrent storms . . . birds caught . . . a drink made of berries . . . a gentleman carrying wood . . . a plot against the governor's life." Knowing or unknowing, Bullough cites themes close to Kit's life: p 242: " . . . laid down in . . . Pericles, Cymbeline, and The Winter's Tale . . . love between parents and children . . . children separated from their parents . . . plots against the innocent . . . exile . . . wandering . . . contrast between high-born persons and true or apparent plebeians . . . good out of evil . . . visions . . . music." Oddly, Bullough even touches Kit's own Chapter 4 in Noches de Invierno, recognizing its close resemblance to the plot of The Tempest, though he says, p 248, "it is very unlikely that Shakespeare could have read Eslava's story, first published in 1609, and never put into English." (Well, Kit wrote it.) Then Bullough says, p 249: "If there was an English comedy behind this, it must have been a straggling piece like Mucedorus." Kit made that play, too. Not exactly straggling, it was played at court and was very suitable for home-play-party production: "Eight persons may easily play it." Mucedorus was Kit's most popular work ever: 17-count'em-17 quartos. The play is printed, in early spelling, in C.F. Tucker Brooke. The Shakespeare Apocrypha. Oxford: Clarendon Press, 1971 (1908), pp 104 fol. Its ciphers begin: "C. Marlowe cries theme o' death 'n' desert danger—later assists shy mates tu end wi' bed ioy. G . . ."

307 Hen was one of the earliest investors in the Bermuda islands—part of the Virginia Co. in 1607. (Southampton Parish is still on the map of Bermuda.) G.P.V. Akrigg. Shakespeare and the Earl . . . , op. cit., p 160.

308 A CERTIFICATE TO THE LORDS OF THE COUNCIL, UPON INFORMATION GIVEN TOUCHING THE SCARCITY OF SILVER AT THE MINT, AND REFERENCE TO THE TWO CHANCELLORS, AND THE KING'S SOLICITOR. Quoted by Spedding, Works of Francis Bacon. op. cit., vol 11, 1611, pp 255-259. (from Harl. MSS. 7020, fo.164. The heading is inserted in Bacon's hand.)

On p. 256: "Another point of the fact which we thought fit to examine was, whether the scarcity of silver appeared generally in the realm, or only at the Mint;

wherein it was confessed by the merchants, that silver is continually imported into the realm and is found stirring amongst the goldsmiths and otherwise, much like as in former times, although in respect of the greater price which it hath with the goldsmith it cannot find the way to the Mint. And thus much for the fact." Ye-es?

309 D.A. Parrino. Teatro eroico e politico . . . op. cit., vol 3, p 60 and fol: a monograph on "Don Pietro Fernandez de Castro, [7th] Count of Lemos, Marquis of Sarria, count of Andrada and of Villalva, of the Order of Alcantará—Viceroy, Deputy and Commander General in the Kingdom of Naples in the year 1610." Starting with some scummy scandals, progressing to viceregal inscriptions placed at various points in the city and countryside, these pp go to a story of hitherto unheard-of community and legal improvements decreed in Naples, extending over Lemos's years in power. We learn of Lemos's love of theater and membership in the Academy of the Oziosos (started by G. B. Manso), and the fact that Lemos was author of a play (Kit could have given it to him; it's lost; its shadows and scraps reflect Twelfth Night.) But it's the decrees that would interest students of Kit-Gregorio; the leaning toward humane judgement that shines through the Shakespeare plays glimmers here, too. p 91 fol.: I and II: "Children of the Moors of Valencia are not to be enslaved, but shall be reared and instructed by the persons having them until the age of twelve years, after which they shall serve the same persons for an equal number of years, to repay the work of education." VI, VII, VIII, and IX re gun control. XII: Ordinances for maintenance of the aqueducts, to the end that not only would water be not lacking, but that it be kept clear and pure. XVI: that sales taxes be kept at seven %, annuities at 10 %. XIX: that surgeons at the hospitals report to the governor all wounded who come there, and the nature of their wounds. XX: that the judge who permits payoffs to the Royal Exchequer shall not impede the progress of investigative action, and that regardless of that judge, the offenders could be summoned and sentenced. Death for any who commit crime with firearms; accessories' terms shortened from term of current law. XXIII: a decree of many ordinances adopted for the good conduct of the courts. XXX: re drug import: that no person take or use any kind of merchandise from vessels that come from the Levant as well as the Orient before having them inspected by the Deputies for Health. XXXI: That no Guardian may contract matrimony with persons under his guardianship without permission of a Judge. XXXII: In order to reform various abuses of the Courts, Lemos published a 'most excellent Decree, consisting of 83 items.' XXXIV: That litigants may not choose as their attorney relatives of Ministers of a rank forbidden by Royal Decrees.

310 Marqués de Rafal, Alfonso Pardo Manuel de Villena. Un Maecenas Español del Siglo XVII. [a bio of Pedro Fernando de Castro y Osorio, Seventh Count of Lemos.] op. cit., pp 140, '41 offer more of Lemos's good works. How many of these ambitious decrees were implemented—how many were merely idealistic

dreams of Lemos's sometime secretary, Antonio de Laredo y Coronel (Kit), whose real father had been a judge? We know that Lemos did transform former Viceroy Benavente's ludicrous luxurious stables into a university for Naples.

Hispanic Review. October, 1933. Otis H. Green. "The Literary Court of the Conde de Lemos at Naples, 1610-1616." The intriguing presence of the mysterious Antonio de Laredo y Coronel, a secretary chosen by the count of Lemos himself and not by the poets delegated to gather a literary group to accompany Lemos to Naples, is discussed by Otis H. Green.

311 As a south coast seaman, Kit would have known about Drake's Leat, finished in 1591, a famous canal that provided water to Plymouth. Its completion is still celebrated annually. Besides bringing fresh water to the town, its flow powered several mills. Information is available from the Devon County Library at Plymouth.

312 Richard Church. Kent. London: Robert Hale, 1979 (1948), pp 164-'65.

313 Francisco de Quevedo. La Vida del Buscón. Buenos Aires: Ediciones Troquel, S.A. 1971. These editors think the book was written between 1606 and 1611, but Cervantes and Quevedo were together in "gran amistad" at Valladolid in autumn of 1604 (Luis Astrana Marin. *La Vida Turbulenta . . .* op. cit., c. pp 90, 91 and ?) I believe Quevedo researched the novel there that fall—just before he came down with bronchitis. Much of the work was fashioned from Cervantes's life-story, probably told over drinks in friendly confidence but written down by Quevedo to be viewed in the worst light. The part about starving at school, though, is surely autobiographic.

314 A Fvnerall Elegye In memory of the late Vertuous Maister VVilliam Peeter of Whipton neere Excester. By W.S. Imprinted at London by G. Eld, 1612. Donald W. Foster made an excellent dissertation on this work and offered the results in a book of 318 pp, revealing the author of the elegy to be the same person as the author of the Shakespeare plays. Donald W. Foster. Elegy by W. S., A Study in Attribution. Newark: U of Delaware Press, 1989. Foster, who originally presented his work to the U. of California as his Ph.D. thesis, attributed the elegy to Shakespeare and seemed unconscious of the fact that the whole poem is riddled with sly digs and ciphers. On 14 Jan. 1996 The NY Times printed an appreciative article about this honest scholar and his work. Several years later, having volunteered to help the US government learn identities of persons sending anthrax powder through the mail, Foster studied handwriting on the offending envelopes, cooperating with the FBI. On 20 June 2002, The NY Times printed a surprising article about Foster: Foster Recants—unconditionally withdraws his thesis attributing the Elegye to the playwright. Could censorship cross the sea to silence Kit's long-ago effort at free speech?

315 Maria Bellonci. op. cit., p 300. In May, shortly after Vincenzo Gonzaga's death, Barbara Sanseverino was beheaded on a high platform in the main square at Parma.

316 Naples Fiesta, August 22 and fol., new style. A festival honoring the marriage of Louis XIII and the Infanta Ana of Austria. Hispanic Society microfilm roll #53 describes this pageant. I find no byline for Kit as author under any cover-name I know, but Cervantes says a lot in his Viaje del Parnasso about having a dream in Madrid and waking up in Naples to meet an old friend, young soldier Promontorio who has written the great Fiesta. And all through his Viaje del Parnaso Cervantes gives special treatment to Gregorio. The numerous "montes" taken together would be "monti" in Italian. Chap. 1, l. 229 fol. "The paths and roads are full of this useless rabble against the monte, not worthy even to be in its shade." Chap. 2, l. 351. Sancho Panza gets a mention along with the other poets (Sancho is Kit). Chap. 4, l. 319 fol. "El otro" is a man with a victorious theater. He's called "the swan." Like Shakespeare, his song is not funereal, and he's always first, as the most famous. So though he's masked (like Kit), his work is renowned. Could Kit be called "persona religiosa?" He studied divinity at Cambridge preparing to be a clergyman, and all his life kept an interest in religious controversy and a deeper one in moral concepts. He was a friend to ministers and rabbis and sometimes used the Cloth as a cover in SS work. Chap. 8, l. 245 fol: Here we are in Naples: Cervantes' friend arrives in disguise, and in l. 277 there's a touching reunion that puzzles editors. Who is Promontorio? Cervantes hears music, turns toward the sound and sees greater spectacles than Rome saw in best days. His friend speaks to him about the show's story—he you see appearing on that artificial mountain, he whose iron strength can oppress and subdue, is a high subject who has contempt for envy and rage, for they trample the virtue of the better path of gravity and smooth conditional agreement . . . Promontorio tells Cervantes that Don Juan de Tasis is the star of the show, because by his good delivery, "*my words*" ("mis palabras" Aha!) "are brought to my intent." (Don Juan can say the author's words the way they ought to be said.) Promontorio tells names of the producers—was all this in a letter Kit sent to Manco in Madrid? ll. 355 fol. Cervantes asks his friend to find a place where Cervantes can see without obstruction, because he wants to write it all up in verse—and Promontorio does so. After a few more tercets, though, Cervantes is back home resting, and the book is finished. His friend has been given the best spot, next-to-closing. Dudley Carleton to John Chamberlain. op. cit., p 132. Venice, Aug 14, 1612. (no indication of old or new style): "We have at this present a great confluence of English from all parts: my lord Roos and one Mr. Cansfield in his company . . . . Tobie Mathew (who is so broken with travail that Gregorio, 'not knowing his name,' terms him il vècchio) and one Gage, a sworn brother of the same profession. They are going to Naples, there to winter . . ." [RB. Maybe the others will stay for the winter; Kit will be back in October. Calling Tobie il vècchio was a joke; all of them must have been in disguise.]

317 Vittorio Rossi. op. cit., pp 157-158. Mortally ill, Guarini returned from Rome (where he'd been clergy-watching?), came home to la Guarina by June. Illness

worsened. In Sept. he sent his last letter—condolence about the death of a friend's son—in Rome?—then pressed on, to Venice. In footnote pp 157, '58, Rossi quotes publisher Ciotti's introduction to a book of poems gathered in Guarini's honor: "he wished to come to Venice, and, as if he had an intimation of his death, to close his eyes, as he has done, in his [Gregorio's] arms."

318 Frederick V, the Elector Palatinate. Josephine Ross. The Winter Queen, The Story of Elizabeth Stuart. NY: St. Martin's Press, 1979. Sixteen-year-old Princess Elizabeth was days younger than her husband the Elector. Harry was fond of Elizabeth Stuart, and years later, in time of sorrow, sent her an aolean harp with a ciphered poem. Kit helped; see Harry's poem among the ciphers below.

319 My assertion. Masque of the Middle Temple and Lincoln's Inn, Mon. 15 Feb., 1613. E.K. Chambers. Eliz. Stage. op. cit., vol 1, p 173, and vol 1, p 74 v. A George Chapman entertainment: In the the antimasque Kit would have played "Caprizzio, a Man of Wit." The play includes Virginians, a mountain, a gold mine, antimasque with monkeys, Caprizzio and fire-juggling. (in a cipher for King Lear, Kit had written, "Kit Marlowe made al these mad scenes. *Ay, he can iuggle, too*!") James, intrigued, asked the cast to a meal afterwards.

320 These machinations will prove disastrous; Bacon's cruel damage control, created to save James' "honor" includes using Good Tom's daughter as a goat as well as bringing other innocent people to a worse fate—the gallows.

321 An exhaustive study of the problem of the Blackfriars Gatehouse is offered by E.K. Chambers. William Sh., A Study of Facts and . . . op. cit., vol 2, pp 154-169. Chambers' report is carefully put together and rewarding; a long winter's evening could be spent looking it over. The personae and labyrinthine legal scrambles involved in the transfer of the gatehouse make a perfect example of a Baconian mental concoction—arcane, convoluted.

322 At the Banquet Hall. E.K. Chambers. The Eliz. Stage. op. cit., vol 1, p 16, footnote: "A record office was constructed below the banqueting house in 1597."

323 Tom Walsingham worked for SSS all his life, in hungry early years as agent for his cousin Sir Francis. On the Mary Queen of Scots job, among other chores he was "Barnaby's brother." Later his wife Audrey apparently worked with him on English jobs: Bakeless. Tragicall History . . . op. cit., vol 1, p 164. " . . . September 1599, a Lady Walsingham—who may be Lady Audrey—was so deeply involved in a political intrigue of some kind that Rowland Whyte, steward of Sir Robert Sidney, asked his master to assign a cipher symbol to her." (Bakeless cites Arthur Collins, Letters and Memorials of State., II, 126.) Bakeless. op. cit., vol 1, p 165, writes: "On July 26, 1603, when she [Audrey] was formally admitted to the Privy Chamber, the Queen made her guardian and keeper of the robes, at forty marks a year, an office which she shared with her husband after 1607. (CSP Dom. Add. 1580-1625, p 427; CSP Dom. 1603-1610, p 113.) "In this capacity, Lady Walsingham controlled the Queen's purchases of gold, silver, tinsel, and silk stuffs from tailors, embroiderers and haberdashers, and directed the cutting."

That she and her partner Tom were in the Banquet House cutting costumes (plus doing SSS work) for those spring festivals in 1613 is quite credible.

324 Queen Anne's basement. E.K. Chambers, Eliz. Stage. op. cit., vol 4, p 136: Peter Cunningham found some original Chamber Accounts for 1604-1605 and 1611-1612 under the vaults of Somerset House—far under the quadrangle in a dry and lofty cellar known by the name of the "Charcoal Repository." Kit and Hen had put here all the papers and rolls Bacon would have burned (Ciphers, First Folio rewrite for The Tempest), but Queen Anne asked Kit to return them to an official repository, which he did. Those Chamber Accounts Cunningham found must have been left by mistake. (Queen Anne lived in Somerset House, then called Denmark House.)

325 The Dramatic Works of Wm. Davenant. W. Paterson, ed. op. cit. Prefatory Memoir, pp xx & xxi. Though Paterson calls them "altogether unwarranted," he retells legends displaying William Davenant as a son of the Bard. And in Aubrey's Brief Lives. ed. Oliver Lawson Dick. Ann Arbor: U. of MI, 1962, p 85, a monograph on Sir Wm. Davenant: "Now Sir William would sometimes, when he was pleasant over a glass of wine with his most intimate friends . . . say, that it seemed to him that he writt with the very spirit that did Shakespeare, and seemed contented enough to be thought his Son."

326 Hen Wriothesley sails. C.C. Stopes. The Life of Henry . . . op. cit., p 362. "it is rather strange to find Southampton also was on the continent that summer." No one seems to know where he'd gone, and in August he was returning from the States to debark at some port on the North Sea coast.

327 Hen and the Virginia Co. Though Hen seems to have invested in Virginia as early as 1602 (C.C. Stopes. ibid., p 319—for rescue of colonists abandoned there), Stopes, pp 319-325 is dubious about evidence in William Strachey's Travailes in Virginia, bk 2, chapter v. She can't figure how Hen, in the Tower, could get money to invest. So? Strachey's vol 2, chap vi states that Hen invested again, in 1603, again in 1605 and 1608. Stopes says on 23 May 1609, Hen is a bona fide member of a new London Virginia Co. chartered by James.

328 Cervantes. Viaje del Parnaso. Capítulo 8, ll. 355-359.

329 Luis Astrana Marin. La Vida Turbulenta . . . op. cit., pp 208, '09. Quevedo probably arrived in Sicily near end Oct. 1613. More than adviser, says Marin, Quevedo is Osuna's alter ego, intimate, comrade, counsellor, agent—employed in delicate missions. And Quevedo sees Venice and Savoy as enemies.

330 A death much written about. Try G.V.P. Akrigg, Jacobean Pageant. NY: Atheneum, 1974. The sickening tangle re Overbury's murder is Bacon's created legend, leading straight to the gallows for several trapped SSS agents. Isabel-Elizabeth's sister-in-law Frances Howard was falsely accused, then 'pardoned.' Try State Trials. 13 Jas 1615, 14 Jas 1616, vol 11. T. Howell 1816, Longman, Hurst, Rees, Orme & Browne et al 1816, and make your own notes. Pages 914-1107 cover trials 103-09, editors' comments and Frances Howard's pardon. E Edward Le Comte. The

Notorious Lady Essex. NY: The Dial Press, 1969. A melodramatic reconfabulation with isolated flashes of truth: p 157: "That clan still did some sticking together: Although her parents lapsed into embarrassed silence, her brother Henry [Kit's daughter's husband] persisted in attempts to see her." ["her"—his sister Frances] No reference offered. In 1724 the Theater Royal in Drury Lane performed a play, "The Tragedy of Sir Thomas Overbury, written by Richard Savage, Son of the Late Earl Rivers." Its heroine, Isabella the Orphan, is in love with Overbury. (The British Library wd send microfilm.) Another Earl Rivers, Lord Darcy, was father of the wife of Peter Manwood's son Roger. So, was playwright Savage Kit's distant in-law? Genealogical info? The Savage family bought land from Kit's dad Roger Manwood. Somehow that Richard Savage heard about the baby Isabel that Kit left as an orphan to be reared by Thomas Howard at Audley End, home of the "notorious" Lady Essex, Frances Howard.

331 C.M. Senior, David & Charles Newton Abbot. A Nation of Pirates. London, Vancouver, NYC: Crane, Russak, 1976, pp 140, 141, about English efforts to suppress English piracy. Between 1610 and 1614, commissions to capture pirates were granted to several port cities, "besides a joint commission for the Earl of Southampton [Hen] and the Mayor of Portsmouth." This project was fostered by Spanish Ambassador Gondomar, hoping to keep British ships engaged in the Mediterranean, far from guarding home ports—and not busying themselves with Caribbean islands or Bermuda, which Spain thought of as its own turf.

332 Trying to find facts about the next year of Kit's life has been difficult. He did sail successfully to the Somers Isles (Bermuda) for Hen: evidence, in scraps, does exist, but no official record of the journey is visible. See Susan Myra Kingsbury. Records of the Virginia Company of London. Washington, D.C. Government Print Office. 1906-1935. Kingsbury, a devoted researcher, writes of her frustration in her introduction to vol 1, p 22: "*A Virginia-Bermuda court book* of the period from the 28th of January 1606, to the 14th of February, 1615 [1614 is the year I need. R.B.] was in the possession of the company as late as 1623, but unfortunately *no trace of the book has yet been discovered and even its existence has heretofore been unknown.*" Her footnote explains: "When the Privy Council demanded the records of the company, a receipt bearing the date April 21, 1623 was given to the secretary of the company for the 'several court books.' This document was discovered by the Editor among the Ferrar Papers, Magdalene College, Cambridge, in Dec. 1903. See List of Records, p 171, no. 470." [Has the Virginia-Bermuda court-book been destroyed?]

333 Dudley Carleton to John Chamberlain. Maurice Lee, ed. op. cit., p 138. Peter Manwood's son Roger(Kit's half-nephew) is at Carleton's embassy house in Venice, with a "Mr. Boys"—16 April, 1613. (in 1618 this Roger is a captain of soldiers on one of several ships sent to aid Venice. A John Boys is Roger's cousin.)

334 Dr. Maria Tiepolo, Director of the Archivio di Stato, Venezia, mailed me film of a letter from Domenico Domenici: Senato, Dispacci Firenze, filza xxix, cc. 132 r.-134 v. Venezia: "23 July, 1614. (Italian): Monsu de' Monti's marsigliane have captured at Tunis an English [pirate] ship which was coming from Algiers with a great quantity of reales. He has also taken another good ship [a "buonavia"] and a petache." [Captured cargo to go to the Bermuda Company.] "He is at Malta, and is said to be arming all the vessels which he takes, and he thinks it to be to his advantage, as in the case of the English ship, that they should have 22 pieces of artillery; and that he intends to procure the abandonment of the affairs of Barbary." A copy is held in English State Papers, calendared SP Venetian, 1614, and a footnote to that item is part of a letter from Carleton to Chamberlain 15 July (Eng. style), 1614: "We hear of an English ship, the Tiger, taken at Tunis by two marciliane sent out against pirates." (Copy of the complete letter in my file.)

335 George Malcolm Thomson. Sir Francis Drake. op. cit., pp 176, 185-'87, 192, 215, 185: fierce fights in Cartegena and St. Augustine, Sampson under command of Carleill, who fought beside him.

336 Captured petache, note 334 above.

337 Could the First Officer's lines in rewrite of Twelfth Night, when he introduces Captain Antonio, be poetically related to the author's memory? V.1. ll.62, 63: "And this is he that did the Tiger board, when your young nephew Titus lost his leg."

338 Conway Whittle Sams. The Conquest of Virginia, the Third Attempt, 1610-1624. Spartansburg, So. Carolina: Reprint Co., 1973 (1939), p 445. A John Boys was selected burgess for Martin's Hundred in Va., July 1619. Also became justice of the peace. Later killed by Indians. (See excerpt from Roger Manwood's will—a John Boys was a cousin.)

Records of the Virginia Company, ed. Susan Myra Kingsbury, op. cit., vol 3, pp 695-'96. 18 Oct. 1622: Sampson and the Tiger in Virginia: Sampson bet Thos. Hamour £200 that Sampson's ship the Tiger would not be sold at order of Nicholas Elford. Elford has since produced the order. [Shadows suggest Sampson then disappeared in the ship and in 1624, captured by Spain, was sent to the galleys. Curses—I've lost that note.]

339 John Smith. The General History of Virginia, New England, and the Summer Isles. The Historye of the Bermudaes or Summer Islands. Reprint 1982. (Reprint Birmingham: Edward Arber, 1884) (1624). Smith's information about the Summer Isles came to him from a distance, in dubious form: He was told the two little gift-ships arrived at St. George harbour about March or April of 1614—impossible, as we know from the Domenici document in Venetian Archives, and CSP Carlton's letter (note 337 above)—as well as from Sancho's letter to Don Quixote—that Kit didn't leave the Mediterranean till *July*. Smith's informants told him the ships were brought by someone who'd been there before and was bringing more colonists—a clear falsehood. Smith reports that Governor Moore hated the gift-ships, thinking they were offered to incite him to go pirating

in the West Indies. This is understandable: we know each marciliana had been armed for its protection by Kit, and had many pieces of good artillery, and since the escort ships Tiger and Buonavia had so recently been taken from real pirates at Tunis, the governor might easily have been suspicious of their appearance. (Smith's informants also wrongly call the escort ship the Margaret of England.) Smith sensibly writes, "For mine owne part, I should rather think that the true entention of their fittinge of them up, and sendinge them to the plantation, was for the secureinge of it against all casuall incidents of famine; that by them vpon all occasions, might be carryed a lawfull traide in corne with the natiues of the sauuage ilands . . . from whence they might be conueniently supplied with hogges, goats, together with many kindes of plantes and fruicts . . ." Good for you, John Smith. All other Bermuda "history" for 1614 has been incredibly twisted or censored.

Kit's voyage is believably fictionalized in Miguel Cervantes. Don Quixote II. Shelton Translation. London: Edward Blount, 1620. James Fitzmaurice Kelly intros. NY: AMS Reprint 1967 (1896). Eleven chapters tell Cervantes' view of Sancho's experience on the island. And Marlowe himself, in valuable ciphers for his Bargraves Polisie, makes things clear. Cervantes starts, in Part 2, Chap. 5 of the Shelton translation, p 45, "'Ile tell you wife (said Sancho) if I thought not ere long to be Governour of an Iland, I should die suddenly." His wife Teresa (really she's Micaela) says, " . . . Devill take all the Governments in the world, without Government were you borne, without Government have you lived hitherto, and without Government must you goe, or be carried to your grave, when it shall please God." (Kit, born illegitimate, was banished forever from England in 1593.) Most of this chapter is about how his daughter will make a "good" marriage, but in Chapter 36, at the very end, Sancho is writing his wife from "this Castle." (at that moment, the sterncastle of his ship?) He's on the way to his Government. "One way or other thou shalt be rich and happy; God make thee so, and keepe me to serve thee. From this Castle, the twentieth of July, 1614." [Note the correct date.]

In Chap. 42 Cervantes, who sees governing the island as a joke, nevertheless gives Sancho good advice and ends with "death shall take thee in a mature old age, and nephewes shall close thy eyes . . ." Is he thinking of Kit's nephew Roger Manwood,on board? In Chap. 44, Don Quixote misses Sancho—there's a diversion, then "the Grand Sancho Panza calls upon us, who meanes to begin his famous Government."

In Chap. 45 "Sancho and all his troope came to a Towne . . . the iland was called Barataria, eyther because the town was called Baratario, or else because he had obtained his Government so cheap." Sancho starts to govern: stories of Sancho as judge. (Kit tried to write rules for the colony—rules which years later he refashioned, with marginalia by John Bargrave?) as Bargraves Polisie.)

In Chap. 47 Sancho gets very hungry. The island is about to be attacked, and someone wants to kill Sancho. We don't see him again till Chap. 49, when he's walking the round on his Iland. Night-time stories, and: "The Round was ended for that night: and some two dayes after, his Government too, with all his designes were lopped off, and blotted out, as hereafter shall be said."

Chap. 50, and we're back at Sancho's wife's house—a page brings her a letter from Sancho. She's described: "she was not very old, for she lookt as if shee had beene about forty: but she was strong, tough, sinowie, and raw-boned." Manco thinks of Micaela—in those days actresses had to be strong, and bigger than life, so their features could carry to the last rows. [Two years later, 9 Sept., 1616, about the time Kit was starting up the hill to meet Micaela at the Brenner Pass—Harry may have thought of her, when he wrote in a letter about someone else, " . . . and doth herself (to use the phrase in Don Quixote) border upon forty years." L.P. Smith. op. cit., vol 2, p 104].

Chap. 51. Sancho's so hungry he can hardly do his job; he solves one tricky case by recalling advice: "I should apply myself to pitty." A letter comes from Quixote praising Sancho for discretion, encouraging him to dress neatly, be courteous to all and "see that there be plenty of sustenance, *for there is nothing that doth more weary the hearts of the poore, then hunger and dearth.*" Quixote writes, "I think to leave this idle life ere long, for I was not borne to it." Always kidding. Sancho answers the Don's letter, mentioning stale rotten hazelnuts that were being sold on the island and how he sent them to the Hospital boyes, who could sort the good from bad, and how he gave sentence on the seller, not to come into the market-place for 15 days. After the letter comes a veiled indictment of greedy London Adventurers and corruption in the Company Store. Sancho makes rules—"In conclusion," says Cervantes, "he ordered things so well that to this day they are fam'd and kept in that place, and are called, the Ordinances of the Grand Governour, Sancho Panza." (Though constrained by thoughts of what King James would allow, Kit did sketch a proto-constitution for Bermuda with plans for an assembly. Bargraves Polisie contains germs of democracy—things reviled as pernicious by the King and powers in London.) "Sancho's Tormentors joyning together, gave order how they might dispatch him from the Government."

Chap. 52 is a newsy letter to Sancho from his wife; in it she asks for a string of pearls. [In that year of 1614 a youth named Richard Norwood came to Bermuda to survey and search for pearls. He made a crude diving bell but found nothing of value. Jean Kennedy. Isle of Devils. Hamilton, Bermuda: Collins (Baxter's) 1971, p 81.]

Chap. 53 is the "end and up-shot that Sancho Panza's Government had." Manco thinks of his own death and of the brevity of Sancho's Government. Sancho's in bed after a week of work, "not cloyed with bread or wine, but with judging and giving sentences, making Proclamations and Statutes, when sleepe . . . shut his eyelids, hee heard such a noyse of bells and out-cries . . ." he had to get up and prepare to fight. He was in a hut by the water [at St. George's Town?], with a mud floor that got his slippers wet, and he's told to arm himself.

[Governor Moore so disliked Kit he challenged him to a duel, which Kit avoided. Moore was an irascible guy.] Sancho picked up and sailed: "No man can make any account of me but he whom my Ld the Duke will appoint: to him I goe, from hence so bare as I doe, there can be no greater signe that I have governed like an angell."

340 Bargraves Polisie ciphers, ll. 33-44.

341 Dudley Carleton to John Chamberlain. op. cit., Intro. p 16. Before long Carleton would be called to leave Venice for Savoy; he was to help with the Treaty of Asti in 1615.

342 Carleton's letter to Collegio. CSP Ven. vol 13, 20 Nov. 1614, pp 260-'61: "There is a Venetian subject of foreign nation at U of Padua. He asks for an increase, not in salary, but of dignity. As he is of high character and a dear friend of mine, I recommend him . . ." and also this note, Carleton to Collegio, "Dr. Gio. Prévotio asks for the readership in medicine rendered vacant by the death of Sig. Tarquinio Carpaneto." [NB] Also Dudley Carleton to John Chamberlain. op. cit., Intro. p 16—and Bargraves's Polisie ciphers, ll. 46-56. [Wouldn't you think Carleton could have rented an apartment for Kit and his family?]

343 Susan Myra Kingsbury. Records of the Virginia Co. of London. op. cit., vol 4, pp 408 foll. An excellent transcript: [marginalia written by Bargrave himself?] Ibid. vol 3, p 607: a note saying Bargrave's treatise was made by "a gentleman called Ignotus . . ." Ciphers clarify.

344 Ibid. Records, vol 1, p 125: On 6 March 1615-1616, a meeting of the Virginia Co. was held, and a new list of shareholders issued. Was the Bermuda Co. discussed, and was it then decided that Kit would have no role in administration of the colony? He puts cogent thoughts about it into Bargraves Polisie ciphers. Kit would have heard about it c. three weeks later; allow another two weeks for a letter from Kit to reach Carleton: On 8 April Carleton wrote Chamberlain (Dudley Carl. To John Chamb. op. cit., p 195), "If you can give Gregorio any comfort I shall be very glad, for the poor man doth much languish after it." Kit was depressed. In March, at low ebb, thinking of death, Kit had sent a compilation of encomia for Guarini to the Ciotti Press: Varie poesie di molti excellenti autori in morte del M. Illustre Sig. Cavalier Battista Guarini. ed. Gregorio de' Monti. Venice: Ciotti Pub., 21 March, 1616. Gregorio wrote sonnets for the work.

345 Dudley Carleton to John Chamberlain. op. cit., p 201. A newsy paragraph in a letter to Chamberlain, 24 May, 1616, about Signorina la Scala's death, as if it were a joke. Kit describes the accident in a more serious vein, in Bargaves Polisie ciphers, ll. 275-296.

346 Bargraves Polisie ciphers, ll. 297-308.

347 Marqués de Rafal (Alfonso Pardo Manuel de Villena). Un Maecenas Español del Siglo XVII. op. cit., 1911. pp 168-171 offer valuable information: the Duke of Estrada reviews the playlet Kit produced for the Oziosos, June 1616 (at the time he was hunting for Micaela at Naples). Estrada says: "the Secretary

Antonio de Laredo was a very well-made man, in face and figure very quick and daring to speak extemporé—so much so that in other comedies he had leading roles—performing in different voices and passing himself in different places where they spoke very much—and so graceful was he in all the very different parts that spoke, that he was the fiesta of the comedy—but beyond this natural grace, a very good subject in all media." Estrada describes the action of the play, telling how this Laredo turned his foot wrong in getting down from his pedestal at the end of the scene—falling on those below and almost hurting them. So now, because of a cross-reference, we can see Kit's cover name in Naples was Antonio de Laredo; we have Marlowe's own detailed description of his accident in Bargraves Polisie ciphers.

348 Geoffrey Bullough. Narrative and Dramatic Sources . . . op. cit., vol 6, pp 297 fol. prints Kit's well-made early play, Timon. Text from Dyce MSS 52, Victoria and Albert Museum, London. Modern spelling, but the first two lines still read, in cipher: "Kit Marlouue vvrit this tale re a sh-shy generous man—abandon'd, C, uuhen his last gelt had fled, C? C, test—"

349 Bargraves Polisie ciphers, ll.79 fol.

350 D. Cayetano Alberto Barrera. Nueva Biografia de Lope de Vega. The Spanish Academy, 1890. Lope's letters about la Loca are printed here in full, pp 173-177! (This book was completed in MS 1864. Was publication deferred 26 years because Lope had been a spy?)

351 Ibid. bottom of p 174.

352 Ibid. This quotation and others by Lope below are found on p 175.

353 Bargraves Polisie ciphers, ll. 119-134.

354 Copies in Public Record Office, State Papers, reference SP99-21-X/L09704, and in my file. (ciphers, Bargraves Polisie, ll.134-142.) Harry kept the original.

355 Lope's letters, Barrera, op. cit., p 175.

356 L.P. Smith, op. cit., vol 2, pp 105,106.

357 30 Dec. From Jas., Gregorio gets a cheery letter which he copies, sending the original to his son Wm. Davenant. Preface, The Dramatic Works of Wm. Davenant. 5 vols. ed. Wm. Paterson. op. cit.) Wm. Davenant once said he had a letter written to his father by the king. A *copy* of this letter, in Kit's Italian hand, is kept in the Public Record Office. SP99-21-X/L09704.

358 12 Oct. 1616. Letters of John Chamberlain. ed. Mc Clure. op. cit., vol 2, p 24: Chamberlain to Carleton: "Since I wrote last . . . Master Henry Howard died sodainly at the table without speaking one word as most say. His wife is thought to be with child, beeing a fresh, younge and rich widow." Isabel-Elizabeth's husband is dead! (Their baby was a girl, Elizabeth.)

359 CSP Venetian. vol 14, 28 May 1616.

360 CSP Venetian. vol 14, 31 Oct. 1616, p 339. Council of X grants permission for the orphans of recently-dead Ambassador Barbarigo to visit Harry's house on Hallowe'en.

361 CSP Venetian. vol 14, c. 15 March, Ven.1617. Gregorio has received from James a patent confirming him in the Service (of Venice-protection?) Quevedo's aggressive intent is now public: Don Francisco de Quevedo y Villegas. Obras Completas, op. cit., vol 2, p 871. Quevedo declares that Venice is to be punished. The patent means James (without telling Bacon?) quietly approves Gregorio's plan to foil Quevedo and Osuna. On 22 March 1617, Harry hands over Gregorio's patent at the Collegio (CSP Ven. vol 14, item 701, p 473), and tells the Doge of a remedy. "The secretary Gregorio is a subject of your Serenity and is high in the king's favour, owing to the accounts sent of him by me and my predecessors, who have employed him. Thus his Majesty last week sent him a patent confirming him in the service, and he may be believed in all matters which I commit to him, as if he were myself." And the Doge replied that the secretary and all who came on the ambassador's behalf would be readily admitted and heard. Backstage, Doge Bembo gives Gregorio permission to create his sting against would-be invaders.

362 A. Parrino. Teatro eroico è politico . . . etc. op. cit., vol 3, p 115 touches the Spanish Plot in Venice, mentioning Capitan Giacomo Piere and companions, and how at the very last moment all was revealed to the Council of Ten in Venice by two conspirators who weaseled out and confessed.

363 Charles E. Phelps. Falstaff and Equity. NY: Houghton Mifflin, The Riverside Press, 1901, p 62: "The line of investigation now being developed was entered upon with entire indifference as to whether the real author was named Bacon, or Shakespeare, or Jaques-Pierre, or Jack-Peter." In a letter to me 17 August 1983 Elizabeth Wrigley, Director of the Francis Bacon Library, Claremont, California, says: "I checked our little volume FALSTAFF AND EQUITY and read the line about Jaques-Pierre, or Jack Peter. I cannot anywhere else in the controversy literature find this term . . . . I think Charles Phelps was making a rather good pun. Jacques in England was pronounced JAKES and the French Pierre was pronounced PEER, so you have a rather close approximation to Shakespeare."

364 D.A. Parrino. Teatro eroico è politico . . . etc. op. cit., vol 3, p 115.

365 Ibid., p 116: "Osuna forever denied having taken part in such wickedness; and if the external and legitimate parts of the affair [legitimate??] give a guide to the inside of its heart, it's incredible that the Viceroy should suffer just on account of some meeting [with Captain Jacques Pierre and his wife], when in disgust he received from Piere, facetiously, the careful custody of his wife." [Italian.]

366 Spedding. Works. op. cit., vol 13. Life and Letters of Francis Bacon, 1616-18, p 151. Ellsmere gives up the Great Seal 6 March 1617, p 152. On 7 March it is given, in title of Lord Keeper, to Francis Bacon, who writes a touching letter of thanks to Buckingham: "It is both in cares and kindness, that small ones float up to the tongue, and great ones sink down into the heart with silence."

367 Ibid. Chap. 4 (1617) pp 159-161: Account of Council business, docketed in Bacon's hand: "For the proclamation that lieutenants . . . justices of the peace and gentlemen of quality should depart the city, and reside in their countries. We find the city so dead of company of that kind for the present, as we account it out of season to command that which is already done." [We don't need to do what the king says . . .] James no doubt made that proclamation so there'd be no meetings of potential conspirators while he was in Scotland; Bacon's cavalier waving of it away was suspect behavior.

368 Ibid. p 159. Bacon writes to Digby, proposing a Spanish-English Conjunction of the two kings—to impede popular estates and leagues that hinder monarchies. Bacon favored the movement, which Gondomar was encouraging at the time, to suppress the leagues of the Protestant Princes.

369 Ibid. p 200. After 9 May, Bacon disappears for 10 days, returns with ideas no doubt put forth by Gondomar about deploying English ships to fight pirates far from English shores. He writes James he's sorry he didn't do what James wanted, but a lot has been happening.

370 CSP Venetian. vol 14, pp 574—'75. 11 August from England—a nasty letter to Doge and Council from Giovanni Lionello, Venetian Secretary in England—hateful things about Harry. Who is masterminding this character-assasssination? Bacon has run the country for 5 months now and has had a chance to devil his enemies. On 26 June, Harry had visited Bedmar, the Spanish ambassador in Venice. CSP Venetian, vol 14, p 536; did Bacon approach Harry through Bedmar, asking for or ordering cooperation with Spain, only to be rebuffed?] Lionello, in England, went on collecting and sending much unfavorable gossip about Harry. Letter of Lionello, Ven. Arch. Communicate, 29 Dec., 1617. [Bacon stuff.]

371 CSP Venetian. vol 14, item 902, p 590, Aug. 30, 1617. Capt. Jacques Pierre to the Council: a report on designs (for an attack on Venice) projected at Naples—10 pp submitted with an "autograph signature." Vol. 15, p 2, Sept 2. This report is sent, after enjoining secrecy, to the Savii of the Cabinet. (Venetian Archives.)

372 CSP Venetian. vol 15, item 38, p18. The viceroy at Naples [Osuna] has sent one Alexander Rose, an English merchant, with 12,000 crowns . . . to England and Amsterdam to obtain four or six ships, under the pretext of trade, to use against Venice at an early opportunity. Also item 33, p 15. Cover of salt fish.

373 CSP Venetian. vol 15, p 6, 8 Sept.

374 The Letters of John Chamberlain. op. cit., vol 2, p 104, 18 Oct. 1617. " . . . one (3) [Sir Francis Bacon] that is attended by a sort of loose companions (4). I inquired of him after Master Mathew(5) [Tobie Matthew], who continues still very intimate with that Lord. I heare he is growne very gay . . . but that which is worse (and which I must tell you under the rose), he is noted for certain night walks to the Spanish ambassador . . . (6)" [Don Diego Sarmiento de Acuña, Count of Gondomar].

Ibid. p 123. Dec. 20, 1617. "Your frend Tobie Mathew shall remain here as it is bruited, and be dispensed withall for taking the oath of allegeance, which were it not in him I should think it might prove a case of strange consequence. His grand frend and protector [Bacon]" . . . and on.

Also, Arnold Harris Mathew. *The Life of Sir Tobie Mathew.* op. cit., p 152 re Tobie's "nightly visits to the Spanish Ambassador Gondomar."

375 CSP Venetian. vol 15, item 108, p 65, 1 Dec. 1617.

376 CSP Venetian. vol 15, item 141, pp 83,'4, 28 Dec. 1617. Harry's response.

377 CSP Venetian. vol 15, item 142, p 84, 28 Dec. 1617. Contarini's chaplain, Horatio Busoni, in a letter home, tells how he and the Venetian ambassador climbed the secret stairs and Contarini spoke with her in private: "After an hour and more his Excellency returned preceded by the lady, who for his safe guidance held a lighted candle in her hand. She raised the door curtain and appeared before us like an angel of radiant beauty . . ."

378 L. P. Smith. op. cit., vol 2, p 125. The fire. Harry's letter. 1 Jan. 1618, Venice.

379 Who were they? E. K. Chambers. Eliz. Stage. op. cit., vol 1 p 303, tells us Samuel Daniel worked for Queen Anne. And ibid., p 386: in 1618 the mayor of Exeter, a southern port city in Devon, complained that Daniel was traveling with a patent for a theatrical company called The Children of Bristol, but had with him men—only five youths among them. ["Mercenaries" going to work under cover in Venice.]

Whereabouts of Queen Anne's named playing company is documented by John Tucker Murray. English Dramatic Companies, 1558-1642. London: Constable and Co., 1910. On p 204: The Queen's Players' last date in 1617 was at Nottingham, 16 Dec. (It was near the end of that month that she secretly talked to Venetian Ambassador Contarini and offered her company to act as players in Kit's sting in Venice.) On Murray's p 204 a big gap appears; Queen Anne's Players didn't perform again in England till sometime around Oct.-Nov. 1618 (no town mentioned), and on 6 Dec. 1618 they were playing Ludlow—back in business. Almost a year.

Hen Wriothesley seems to have brought 20 actors to Venice. Thomas Heywood, a Queen Anne's player, is cited in his DNB monograph as having mentioned (in his elegy on Jas. I, the Introduction to Apology, p 5), that he, Heywood, had worked with *Southampton's Players*—there in Venice? Southampton never had an historically documented company of players. Henry Vere, Earl of Oxford, Ned's son, in a meeting with the Doge, offered to bring men, and though he was politely refused in public, he was there and did provide help under the rose: CSP Venetian. vol 15, 31 Dec. 1618, p 411: " . . . husband of la Gritti who went with an earl to England, the same earl who brought so much gold and came to bring troops; does not know the name" (The editor of the Calendar notes: "The Earl of Oxford.") John Holland was in charge of all the actors from England. Mentioned in CSP Venetian. vol 15, 31 Dec. 1618, pp 411, 412.

380 Luis Astrana Marin. op. cit., pp 262, 263 fol. Confused, Marin contradicts himself, offers odd dates for the attempted attack on Venice, but these pp seem reasonable.

381 Bornío. Quevedo himself, in his Obras Completas, op. cit., writes of "Jaques Pierres," Tomo 1 p 792, and in Tomo 2 p. 876 tells of the trip to Venice with "Xaquepierre and another janissery" and how after the plot was foiled he had to escape dressed in rags and barely evaded two bad men who pursued him. He discusses the plot in various scattered documents in Tomo 2, pp 934-955, and on p 943 mentions that Jaques-Pierre's nickname was "el Bornío." (Kit's Cambridge nickname)

382 CSP Venetian. vol 15, 1618, item 357, 12 May.

383 Progress and particulars of the sting can be followed by selecting the many cogent items in CSP Venetian. vol 15 May through Dec. 1618. The most valuable selections are those marked Senato, Secreto, Communicazioni or Diliberati. It should be noted that on 24 April 1618 Kit and the secret secretary of the French Embassy in Venice, Dr. Asselinau, under the name of Nicolo Rinaldi, wrote to the French King [His Most Christian Majesty], telling him in secret about the designs of Spain [and how Dr. Asselinau was going to be part of the sting as Nicolo Rinaldi—or Reynault—because all the 'mercenaries' had to seem to be French pirates, and the good doctor was going to help them sound French]. Read between the lines, items 336, 337, p 201. A copy held by the Senato, Secreto. Communicazioni of the Council of X. An interesting, not totally credible fictionalization of the caper was made by Le pauvre abbé de Saint Real. La Conjuration des Espagnols contre la Republique de Venise (published as a book together with another tale, Don Carlos.) Facsimile with notes by Andrée Mansau. Genève: Librarie Droz, S.A. 11 rue Massot, 1977 (1780), worth study with a grain of salt. People truly did *not* beseige the Spanish embassy when Bedmar went to the Senate; it was Osuna and *Quevedo* who were burned in effigy; Bedmar did *not* leave the Senate under escort (Venice never pushed). Note on p 642: "The receipt for 100 pounds given to [Gabriel] Montcassin [Kit] for his information, kept with his signature, can be found in the dossier of the Council of X." Kit needed the money. Interesting it was in pounds.

384 Quevedo. Obras Completas. op. cit., vol 2, p 876.

385 CSP Venetian. vol 15, June 2, item 383, p 226. Senato, Secreta. Diliberazioni. Venetian Archives. The ambassador of Venice at Rome is notified, for his information only, that a conspiracy against the city has been discovered. "It clearly appears that the Catholic ambassador resident here has taken a considerable part . . . This is for information only, and you will say nothing of our request to Spain to remove the ambassador or charge him with treachery . . . you will simply say that we are very dissatisfied with the Spanish ambassador and we have made representations at the Catholic [Spanish] court touching his person."

Ibid. same date. Item 384. Senato, Secreta. Diliberazioni. Venetian Archives. "to the ambassador in Spain. We send you for information what the Council of X communicated to us about a conspiracy and the offices of the Catholic ambassador. If questioned you will . . . simply declare that . . . powerful reasons have influenced the Council . . . the Spanish ambassador is abhorred by us and detested in the city. You will strongly urge his Majesty to remove the ambassador."

386 CSP Venetian. vol 15, item 362, p 217. Apparently it was on 18 May 1618 (English?) when a decision was made to pay Harry. Contarini writes, "After no little difficulty, Wotton, the ambassador at Venice, has at length obtained 4,000 crowns on account of his arrears. He remains creditor for 8,000 . . ."

387 Harry's report: L. P. Smith. op. cit., vol 2, p 151 note, and ibid. p 158: "His [Harry's] account was finally sent off [in the secret bag] in Oct. to Sir Robert Naunton . . . and although he sent a duplicate to Sir Thomas Lake (owing to the jealousy of these two secretaries he had to send copies of his dispatches to each), both these reports seem to be lost."

See Letters and Dispatches of Sir Henry Wotton in the Years 1617-1620. London: The Roxeburghe Club. print by William Nichol, The Shakspeare [sic] Press, 1855, p 84.]

388 Spedding. Works. op. cit., vol 13 pp 327-328 show excerpts from Bacon's personal account book. Under "Gifts and Rewards," written in the hand of his sec'y Edward Sherburn. p 327. "29 June, 1618. To an Italian, by your Lp order: 5£ 10*s* 0*d*." And p 328. "4 July. 1618. To an Italian, by your Lp order: 5£ 10*s* 0*d*."

389 Letters and Dispatches of Sir Henry Wotton. op. cit., p 47. Will Leete, Harry's steward, to Mr. Bargrave: "Gregorio is very thankfull to you for your good newes, hee hath delivered his pattent vnto my Lo. to sende, hee is ready to serve you in all occasions, or else hee dissembles."

390 Thanksgiving, Oct. 1618. L. P. Smith. op. cit., vol 1, p 157. "the Government of the Republic never made any expanation . . . only ordering, five months afterwards, a solemn thanksgiving for the preservation of the Republic."

391 CSP Venetian. vol 15, from pp 411, 412.

392 L. P. Smith. op. cit., vol 1, p 48. "Wotton's company when he went on his first journey to Venice, included . . . his chaplain Nathaniel Fletcher (a brother of the dramatist, John Fletcher), and several young men of Kentish families . . . ."

393 The gist of the plot of this impromptu play-party-farce is described by Kit in ciphers for Bargraves Polisie, ll. 155-165, and in the 1634 quarto, The Two Noble Kinsmen, and those ciphers also show the rattled, exhausted, Alzheimers'-like state of mind he was suffering.

394 DNB. Francis Bacon became Chancellor on 7 January 1618.

395 Colin G.C. Tite. Impeachment and Parliamentary Judicature in Early Stuart England. London: The Athlone Press, U of London, 1974, p 26. re Bacon's trial: "Two chronicles are of considerable value to the trials of the reigns of

Edward III and Richard II, to which the men of 1621 repeatedly turned." Kit had researched these reigns for his plays about their rulers. Manuscripts of parts of one, Chronicon Angliae, cover The Good Parliament and years up to 1388, and in late 16th century those scripts were in the library of Corpus Christi College, donated by Matthew Parker. [Kit was there.] Much later, one part "found its way into the Harleian library . . ." [RB. That collection, greatly enlarged by Edward Harley, husband of Kit's great-great-granddaughter Henrietta Cavendish Holles, contains a good many items close to Kit's life.]

396 Samuel Daniel's Boys. See Note 382 above.

397 Chamberlain to Carleton, ed. Mc Clure op. cit., vol 2, pp 201-202. letter 313, Jan. 16, 1619. "Fire at White-hall, which beginning in the banketting house hath quite consumed yt . . . One of the greatest losses spoken of, is the burning of all or most of the writings and papers belonging to the offices of the signet, privy seal and council chamber, which were under yt." [—and how about Star Chamber records?] Bacon has found out that someone—Queen Anne?—saved the papers that he wanted to burn in the Globe fire!

Ida Sedgwick Proper. Our Elusive Willy. op. cit., p 515: Privy council records burning this day included years 1608 to 1613.

398 G. P. V. Akrigg. Jacobean Pageant. op. cit., pp 268-270.

399 L. P. Smith. op. cit., vol 2, appendix 1, p 441, lists a letter sent by Harry from Venice to the Earl of Suffolk, 25 May 1618 NS, and kept as a Longleat MS. When asked about it, the custodians said it wasn't there.

400 Widowed Isabel-Elizabeth Basset Howard marries Wm. Cavendish. Nowhere in print can I find their wedding day, but as her first husband Henry died early in Oct. 1616, (note 361 above) early 1618 is a fair guess. Facts about Isabel-Elizabeth are ludicrously under-reported in every bio of Wm. Cavendish. After bearing him *ten children*, (five lived) as a loyal Catholic subject she aided her soldier-husband's projects in the civil war. After going to meet the queen at her unfortunate landing at Bridlington, 22 Feb., 1643 (Henrietta Maria came ashore in a hail of bullets and she and her ladies took refuge in a ditch), Isabel went home to Welbeck (wounded by gunshot?) to die 17 April 1643. In an extant play, Love's Adventures, written by William's second wife Margaret Lucas, Isabel seems to be remembered at last, as the Orphan Lady Soldier, "honoured by the Republic of Venice." Isabel's mother, who died at her birth, was a Venetian princess, Marina Cicogna, daughter of Zuan Domenico Cicogna, Duke of Candia (mentioned in note 223 above).

Alison Plowden. Henrietta Maria, Charles I's Indomitable Queen. Gloucestershire: Sutton Publishing, 2001, quotes a letter from the queen to Charles, saying Cavendish cannot rejoin his army till he has buried his wife. Is-Eliz was laid to rest in the family tomb at Bolsover. A fact about the Notes in Plowden's book: a large percentage of them are derived from letters sent home to Venice from the Venetian embassy in England during the civil conflict. (CSP Venetian.)

401 Bolsover Castle. Once a Norman castle, its renovation was begun by William's father, Charles, and continued by William and his bride.

402 L. P. Smith. op. cit., vol 1, p 165. On 16 May Ven. 1619, Harry left Venice, traveling with Queen Anne's cousin, Duke Joachim Ernest of Holstein, to Munich and Augsburg.

403 L. P. Smith. op. cit., Appendix 3, p 474: de' Monti in charge of English affairs at Venice from May 1619 to March 1621. Wotton recommended him to the Doge as "persona assai practica e discreta . . ." Esp. Prin., May 5, 1619 [Filza 27, Registro 30]. Speech printed, CSP Venetian.

404 Kit's letters to Naunton, in Italian, preserved at Eton. Available in microfilm and in Letters and Dispatches of Sir Henry Wotton in the Years 1617-1620. The Roxburghe Club. Wm. Nichol, The Shakspeare [sic] Press, 1855.

405 CSP Venetian. xv, p 594. 26 August 1619. Letter from the Venetian sec'y in England, Pier Antonio Maroni, to the Council of X: George Abbot, Archbishop of Canterbury, told the Venetian Ambassador that the anonymous writer of news to di Dominis knew "all secrets" in Venice. Gregorio was betrayed, carelessly or deliberately.

406 DNB. Thomas Howard. Basil Montagu. Works of Francis Bacon. London: Wm. Pickering 1834. part I pp 226-230. Oct.-Nov. 1619. Good Tom Howard, Earl of Suffolk, examined in Star Chamber, charged with embezzlement. At first he says he'll speak out [then keeps silent to save the king's honor.] Bacon nasty; a painfully obvious frameup. The earl and his wife separately imprisoned in the Tower for eleven days; he's ordered to repay all he embezzled.

407 Letters and Dispatches of Sir Henry . . . op. cit., p 139, Sept. 1619. Ven. Gregorio writes Naunton thanking him for his humane letter of 26 August, comforting to Gregorio's family. (Did the baby die?)

408 Ibid. p 230, 231. Venice. autumn, 1620. Kit writes about the Valtellina in several dispatches—the Spanish want possession of the pass so they can move soldiers into Hapsburg territory to defeat Jas.'s son-in-law Frederick.

409 Ibid. pp 206-7. 14 Aug. Ven. 1620. Paul Pindar, retiring ambassador to Constantinople, leaves Venice today for England. Kit presents to him papers for knighthood.

410 Ibid. p 225, 226. Gregorio's Sept. 11 dispatch; also CSP Venetian. vol 16, pp 397 & 404.

411 CSP Ven. vol 16, p 405. Don Celso Galarato knows.

412 The last letter in Letters and Dispatches of Sir Henry Wotton. op. cit., pp 257-258, to Sec'y of State Robert Naunton from Gregorio, 29 January 1620 (1621, new style). All these letters from Gregorio are in "choice" Italian, in his own hand. A Charles Ré translation is offered in the text above. Kit was to be

granted a knighthood. He was not allowed to go to England for a ceremony; the papers were sent to Venice. (He refers to himself as "Sir Kit de' Monti, mean and shameless" late in Bargraves Polisie). Naunton, in persuading James to sign the papers, must have infuriated Bacon, for in that January Naunton was suddenly threatened with dismissal. Historians speculate he was punished for favoring Prince Charles' courtship of Henrietta Maria, which angered Spanish Ambassador Gondomar—but think how Bacon would feel, learning that Secretary Naunton approved not only a match between Charles and a French princess, but also honor for Gregorio, whom Bacon now fiercely hated. Naunton was shaken and his wife so stressed she had a miscarriage. Robert Naunton DNB.

413 John Taylor. Sir Gregory Nonsence His Newes from no place.

Printed at London, and are to bee sold betweene Charing Crosse, and Algate. 1700. [a jest] On the last page: *FINIS* Printed at *London* by *N.O.* 1622. Copy from Charles Hindley's Miscellanea Antiqua Anglicae, 1873, in the Folger Library.

414 Notes of the Debates in the House of Lords, specifically taken by Henry Elsing, Clerk of the Parliaments. AD 1621. Ed. Samuel Rawson Gardiner, esq. NY: AMS Press, 1968 (Camden Society 1870). pp 1 and 9.

415 Other sources for this proceeding re Bacon: Spedding, op. cit., vol 14. On p 226: James spoke in Lords, recognized them as a Supreme Court of Justice, confirmed their privileges, leaving judgement wholly to them. Hen busy through p 281.

Basil Montagu. The Works of Francis Bacon. London: Wm. Pickering, 1834. vol xvi, Part One. On p 353, in a verbose speech, Bacon inserts a story of a king who killed his son—hoping the words will scare James? Montagu offers a Journal of the Proceedings Against Lord Bacon. Note GGG. pp 699-742. The whole thing.

416 Spedding. op. cit., vol 14, p 280; Montague. op. cit., vol xvi Part 1, p 382. Thurs. 31 May: Bacon sends note to Jas., "Procure the warrant for my discharge this day."

417 Bargraves Polisie ciphers, ll. 187-198, 215, 220.

418 Letter to me from Dr. Maria Tiepolo, Director of Venetian Archives, 17 Feb. 1983 with Xerox of a tax notice 27 April, 1661 for Iseppo Monte q. Gregorio (filius quondam Gregorio). Iseppo lived at S. Luca in Calle dei Fabbri in his own house assessed at 40 ducats, proprietor of a shop at S. Salvador in the street of the Tinsmiths, valued at 75 ducats and with another house at S. Luca also in the Street of Fabbri assessed at 75 ducats.

419 Frances Berkeley Young. Mary Sidney . . . op. cit., p 117 says Mary died of smallpox in London 25 September 1621. A footnote gives ref. for three different dates for her death: "Brydges. Censura Literaria, p 148; Collins, Peerage, vol 3 p 123; Sydney Papers, vol 1, p 97. Memoir."

420 Plaster death masks were being made in Venice early in the 17th century, while in England the application of thin sheets of copper was still an accepted mask-making technique. The so-called Shakespeare plaster death mask is now at the Universitäts und Landesbibliothek, Schloss, Darmstadt, Germany. Long ago

Curator Irmgard Brüning sent me excellent negatives; front and three-quarter views as well as a view of the scratches on the edge, and I obtained clear 8x10's from the films. The naturally flowing moustache, handsome mouth, wide-spaced eyes are Kit's, as in his college portrait. A small scar (with two sutures) on the forehead is clearly visible in the Janssen portrait of "Shakespeare," or was, before restoration. Also apparent on the mask is the nasal cyst Kit writes about in ciphers. Though the mask is not recognized as Kit's—or Shakespeare's—by any scholar or English expert, the nasal cyst clinches provenance for me.

Who made this work? Pope-Henessy. Italian High Renaissance and Baroque Sculpture. London, 1963, lists two sculptors working in Venice at this time: p 413 Girolamo Campagna (1549—1625?) who made a monument and a posthumous statue, no doubt using death masks, and p 419 Niccolo Roccatagliata, who worked in Venice churches, 1593-1633.

CSP Ven. vol 15 p 197: On 20 April 1618 Harry was granted permission to visit the studio of Sig. Carlo Ruzini. A sculptor? An artist who knew sculptors? Also, on 3 Jan., 1619, CSP Ven. vol 15, p 426: Harry goes to visit the studio of Andrea Vendramin, to see the statues.

Frederick J. Pohl. "The Death Mask," The Shakespeare Quarterly, 12, 1961, pp 115-125, suggests that sculptor Gheeraerdt Janssen may have used the mask as model for the half-statue of "Shakespeare" on the Stratford cenotaph, but years later when its nose was broken the man hired to fix it just smoothed it and left it short, filling the space below it with an 18th century-style moustache, spoiling the likeness. The mask itself is as surely Marlowe's as the accepted portraits of Shakespeare are really pictures of Kit.

A photoprint of a painting of a very different Shakespeare was printed in the New York Times on 24 May, 2001—a painting proven to have been made early in the 17th century and owned by Mr. Lloyd Sullivan, a Canadian descendant of the painter. Could this work be a likeness of William? (Stephanie Nolen, et al. Shakespeare's Face. New York: Free Press: A Division of Simon and Schuster, 2002.)

421 L. P. Smith, op. cit., vol 1, pp 178-'9; vol 2, pp 218-219. Harry's letter to Sir George Calvert from Venice 16/26 Nov., 1621. "fevers . . . whereof we are willinger to impute the cause to the crudities of last years' wines than to our own immoderation . . . Two have I lost, one that was my steward heretofore . . . William Leete . . . . The other was poor Gregorio de' Monti . . . of whom I am to speak more in a dispatch wherewith I am now in travail . . ." Ibid. p 220. Harry to Calvert. Venice, 7/17 Dec, 1621. "I was preparing a dispatch for a gentleman bent homewards, of whom I made stay upon my last indisposition of body. He shall besides some strange things (which I mean to couch in cipher) bring with him . . ."

Ibid. p 220. Harry to Sir Walter Aston. 8/18 Dec. 1621. " . . . a Venetian, who had long served under Sir Dudley Carleton and me here, as secretary of the language or compliments, a place more easily supplied than when substance is vacant."

Also ibid. p 473, 474, (Appendix 3), a monograph on Gregorio de' Monti.

422 Italian Dictionary of National Biography. copy at FSU Library at Gainesville, FL. Celio Calcagnini studied humanities at Ferrara U under guidance of Battista Guarini, a forebear of Kit's spymaster Battista. Celio Calcagnini became professor of belles lettres at Ferrara, taught there till 1537 when he was succeded by G.B. Giraldi (Cinthio—who wrote the Hecatommithi, later a source for Kit's Measure for Measure and Othello). Next, our Battista Guarini's uncle Alessandro Guarini became the professor, relinquishing the chair c. 1556/'7 to nephew Battista Guarini.

423 Vittorio Rossi. Battista Guarini ed Il Pastor Fido. op. cit., Part One p 12. Guarini follows his uncle Alessandro in the cathedra di rettorica e poetica at Ferrara U, after Alessandro dies July 1556.

Borsetti's Ferrarese history of Padua U (Guarini's alma mater) states that by 1558 Guarini was a professor in the "studio patrio" at Ferrara U.

424 stewards. The Guarini home, la Guarina, was just outside the hamlet of San Bellino, north of Ferrara, c. eight miles SW of Venice. The Calcagninis lived near Fusignano, about ten miles south of Ferrara—and for three generations, the forebears of the poet Vincenzo Monti (b. Feb. 1754) worked for the Calcagnini as land-or-house stewards. Vincenzo Monti, like Kit and Guarini, was a politically motivated poet, probably in secret service.

425 L. P. Smith. op. cit., vol 2, p 225. Harry's steward Deering was his nephew. On 12/21 Jan., 1622, Harry writes Walter Aston a paragraph of news, then breaks off to say, "This much only have I obtained leave from my present griefs to tell your Lordship; my steward and kinsman being this very day taken from me . . ."

426 Arnold Harris Mathew. The Life of Sir Tobie . . . . op. cit., p 194. 28 Dec. Eng. 1621. Toby Mathew arrives at Dover. Commissioner of the Passage at Dover reports to Zouch. Digby writes to Zouch, "Let Toby Mathew come to attend his Majesty." The king seems pleased. Did Toby bring false news to the king re Spanish marriage? And news to Bacon re Venice wine job? Chamberlain to Carleton, op. cit., vol 2, p 419, Jan. 1622, re Toby: "At his last being here yt is saide (how truly I know not) that he got a great deale of monie by the Lord Chauncellors favor . . ." [Chamberlain is still calling Bacon Lord Chancellor.]

427 Spedding. op. cit., vol 14, p 324. A note to Bacon, 3 Jan. 1622: "About Saturday Mr. Burrows hopes to be at liberty to wait upon your Lordship." Mr. John Borough goes to Venice ostensibly to bid on the Barocci Library there for Bacon's pal Rob't Cotton; really to *heist Kit's scripts out of the English embassy house.*

Letter to me from M.A.F. Borrie, Assistant Keeper, British Library Dept. of MSS, 2 June 1981: "You are right in supposing that Cotton did not buy the Barocci library . . . (but) Borough was certainly commissioned by Cotton to buy MSS, since (Borough) says in his letter from Venice . . ." etc.

428 Borough is a known agent of Bacon: he's mentioned as middleman in a bribe discussed during Bacon's trial, and a man identified as "one near the

Ld. Chancellor" in Basil Montagu. The Works of Francis Bacon. op. cit., p 716-717.

429 Spedding's Works of Bacon. De Augmentis Scientiarium. vol 1, Appendix. pp 841-844. Anything you'd need to know about ciphers Bacon respected (not anagrams—he thought them childish toys) is offered here, with additional notes in the text, vol 1, pp 658-661. Three principal 16th century cipher-writers were: 1. J.B. Della Porta (a friend of Kit, in Naples). The author says, "The idea of a bi-literal alphabet, which Bacon seems to claim as his own, is employed, though in a different manner, by Porta." 2. Trithemius. Spedding explains, p 842, that to write the word "Trithemius" (a ten-letter word) in Trithemian cipher takes 15—count'em—15 words! And 3. Blaise de Vigenère. Spedding outlines Blaise de la Vigenère's method and concludes, "The transition from this to Bacon's cipher is so easy that the credit to him must be reduced."

430 Bacon claims AUTHORSHIP. Kit made Sonnet 135 so Shakespeare could say he was a sonneteer. But in these ciphers, Kit writes, ll.7 & 8, 9 & 10, "Then I C *Sh.*, fair and crass, give all R neat writin' t' the actors' theater as his ouun, 'n' *Bacon's!* Ye deed's a l-lie! A dead l-lie!"

431 Sir George Buc. DNB. p 171: "There accompanied the Cadiz expedition in 1596 a gentleman adventurer bearing the name of George Bucke . . ." This odd monograph contains, among several errors, serious misinformation about the date of the onset of Bucke's fatal illness; see Chamberlain to Carleton, ed. McClure. op. cit. vol 2 p 430. Chamberlain gets it right: In a postscript to his letter of *30 March, 1622* he states, "Poore Sir George Bucke master of the Revells is in his old age faln starke madd . . ."

432 Mark Eccles. Thomas Lodge and Other Elizabethans. ed. Charles Sisson. Cambridge, Mass: Harvard U Press, 1933. The 5th monograph: "Sir George Buc, Master of the Revels." On p 495 Eccles sounds dubious about the burning, but quotes Chalmers' paraphrase of an entry in Sir Henry Herbert. Supplemental Apology of the Dramatic Records of Henry Herbert, p 203: "that he had licensed, without a fee, Jugurth, an old play, allowed by Sir George Bucke, and burnt, with his other books." The only illustration of Buck's handwriting Eccles can show (opp. p 476) is a burnt fragment of a kind remembrance Buck wrote about Ned de Vere.

433 Later, during printing, a good copy of Troilus and Cressida became available and was stuffed into the Folio between Henry VIII and Coriolanus.

434 Charlton Hinman, ed. The Norton Facsimile, the First Folio of Shakespeare. NY: Paul Hamlin for W.W. Norton, 1968. Intro, p x. Hinman writes, "the First Folio was 'in press' for almost two years."

435 E.W.Smithson and Sir George Greenwood, Baconian Essays. Port Washington, NY: Kennikat Press, 1970 (1922). Smithson's essay, "The Masque of 'Time Vindicated,' pp 41-65, presents selections from Ben's work, verbatim. Smithson doesn't see that the dramatist is making fun of Bacon, but Ben's intent—and

intent to leak—is obvious. More could surely be gained from reading the original work.

436 Marchette Chute. Ben Jonson of Westminster. London: Robert Hale, 1954, p 276. "The year in which the Shakespeare folio was issued there was a fire in Ben Jonson's house and all the manuscripts in his desk were burned. Jonson wrote a remarkably good-natured poem on the subject, a mock-heroic attack on the god of fire that he called 'An Execration upon Vulcan.'"

Jonson DNB and others say Ben's *whole library* burned. Ben's poem is a lasting, lashing, bitter list of Bacon's crimes of arson. About the most recent; " . . . didst thou spye/ Any least loose, or scurrill paper lye/Concealed or kept there; that was fit to be /By thy owne vote, a Sacrifice to thee?" [*Yes*: Marlowe's scripts!] Few beside honest men of SSS could understand Ben's catalogue to come. First, Ben's desk: "parcell of a play/ Fitter to see the firelight, than the day" [whole *packages* of Kit's plays?] " . . . whereof thy right doth boast, / to sow Consumption every where thou go'st." [Bacon used arson as his shredder.] Ben lost "all/ The learned library of Don Quixot . . ." Ben says things in other houses might have been burned without much loss; doesn't think much of Bacon's interest in magic or the Rosy Crosse. But in Ben's library " . . . some parts/ There were of search and mistery in the Arts: /And the old Venusine in poetry" [Horace, but OED gives Venus as an error for Venice, with examples, and Ben could use double entendre.] Ben links cruel detail with mythology regarding Bacon's own conception as a baby. [Harry was more humane in ciphers for the epitaph he made for Bacon.] Ben recalls being sent by Bacon into the explosive Gunpowder Plot, digresses to mention quicksilver [Bacon's poison of choice was mercury sublimate], then hits into the awful Globe fire. He mentions that "He burnt that Idoll of the Revells too." [Buck's Revels Records and works, and his ruined person!] Next " . . . let Whitehall with Revells have to doe /Though but in dances it shall know thy power." [Aha! ruin of the Banquet Hall, with its record repository, at Whitehall!] Enough! He cracks about a Chancellor's duty.

437 DNB. Maximillian Colt. Roger Manwood's monument (planned 1591) may have been Maximillian Colt's earliest work—he was in his twenties. (He and Roger went to the same church, St. Bartholomew's, west London, near Roger's town house.) Later Colt made a monument for Queen Elizabeth's grave, and other good works. He married a girl named Geeraerts (of the Stratford cenotaph-sculptor's family?)

438 The Dramatic Works of William Davenant. 5 vols. Edinbugh: Wm. Paterson, 1872. vol 1, Prefatory Memoir, p xxviii. William went to London in 1622 to serve this lady. Born Frances Howard, daughter of Thomas Howard of Bindon, she was a friend of Good Tom's daughter, Frances Howard of Audley End (Isabel's sister-in-law), so probably through Isabel's influence he got the job.

439 Ibid. p xxiii.

440 William Davenant DNB. The first performance of The Siege of Rhodes, 1656, (BM copy) was epoch-making: sung in recitatif with music, clothed in scenery—and Mrs. Coleman, the first woman on an English stage, was in the cast.

441 The Dramatic Works of William Davenant. op. cit. Prefatory Memoir. p xxxix.

442 Alison Plowden. Henrietta Maria, Charles I's Indomitable Queen. op. cit. A picture of the queen's landing at Bridlington follows p 174, with picture of Henrietta Maria, a note she wrote to Wm. Cavendish, and a picture of Cavendish.

443 L. P. Smith. op. cit., vol 1, pp 191, 193. He debarked at Sandwich 25 Nov., reached London the next day.

444 Ibid. vol 1, pp 199-203 describe the contest, and Harry's settling-in.

445 G.P.V. Akrigg. Jacobean Pageant. op. cit., p 387 describes confused circumstances of these preparations for war.

446 C.C. Stopes. The Life of Henry . . . op. cit., p 460.

447 Ibid. p 466. Sweeping charges: Eglisham (sic) sent one petition to King Charles; one to Parliament. They are kept, Stopes says, in the Harleian Miscellany. II. 69-80. Many documents which touch Marlowe's life are kept here; Hen's death is relevant.

448 Basil Montague. The Works of Francis Bacon. op. cit., pp 446-447. Montague remembers to say that Dr. Witherborne, in the coach with Bacon, was one of King Charles' own doctors.

Daphne du Maurier. The Winding Stair. op. cit., pp 197-199 offers a sentimental interpretation.

449 L. P. Smith. op. cit., vol 1, p 218. "To my other Supervisor, Mr. Nicholas Pay, I leave my chest, or Cabinet of Instruments and Engines of all kinds of uses: in the lower box whereof, are some fit to be bequeathed to none but so entire an honest man as he is." (an Isaak Walton note in margin: "In it were Italian locks, Picklocks, Screws to force open doors, and many other things of worth and rarity.")

450 L. P. Smith. op. cit., vol 1, p 20. "the celebrated Manso, who, almost half a century later, acted as Milton's guide when he visited Naples." Manso was the steady nerve-center of the movement to resist advancement of the Pope's worldly power.

Ibid. vol 1, p 220, 1638. "The young poet John Milton was about to start on his Italian journey. But shortly before leaving Horton he was invited to meet the old Provost [Harry] . . . The talk was no doubt of Italy and poetry." Harry and Milton wrote to each other—Harry sent advice, including an admonition about his conduct in Rome: "I pensieri stretti e il viso sciolto." Milton, however, surprised everyone by not being discreet and staying undercover but by speaking right out for religious freedom. He came home a few months before Harry died, and later worked as foreign secretary for Cromwell. When the Royalists won, Milton would surely have been sacrificed had he not been saved and freed by, of all people, William Davenant. (monograph on Milton in Encyclopedia Brittanica, 1955 edition.: Milton had saved Davenant years before, when Sir William, imprisoned by Cromwell, was about to be hanged.)

451 Ibid. p 508.

452 Reliquiae Wottonianae. ed. Izaak Walton. First ed. 1651; eds. 1654, 1661, 1672, with early letters. Copies of some eds. available at Proquest, University Microfilms International. Ann Arbor, Michigan, USA.

Author's note: There may not be a notarized document proving Kit was Gregorio. I've found no easy way to cross the river, but a multitude of converging references can bring epiphany. And if we let him take us over his own bridges—his constructions of letters, those steganographic stories linked with his identities—Kit, Gregorio, Moth, Yat, Sancho, Christopher—we can view his life, peopled with lovers, friends, enemies, moving in patterns unthought-of before, linking the Globe and Venice. He wrote in a cipher, "At my show they kno."

Illustrations

fig 1 Marlowe. putative. detail. Courtesy of Master, Fellows and Scholars of Corpus Christi College, Cambridge. (With the same permission, a detail of the restored portrait appears on the cover of this book.)

Recovered from a pile of detritus in the courtyard by the Master's study at Corpus Christi during renovation in 1953, this painting displays an image inscribed ANNO DNI AETATIS SUE 21 1585. QUOD ME NUTRIT ME DESTRUIT. Adolescent Kit was already a skilled government honest-man, already feeling misgivings. He stood on the threshold of one long, challenging, enervating career as state secret servant—and as writer of inspired dramas. (*2 Parnassus*, 1599: "O, sweet Mr. Shakespeare! I'll have his picture in my study at the court!")

fig 2 Sir Roger Manwood. © National Portrait Gallery, London.

Sir Roger was Kit's beloved natural father, a judge of Dover Admiralty Court, Common Pleas and later Lord Chief Baron of Exchequer. His chain of office, given him by the queen, symbolized the historic union of the houses of York and Lancaster and served as inspiration for Kit's 3-part *Henry VI*. It was Sir Roger's death—his secret execution at order of the Archbishop Whitgift—which pushed Kit over the top into near-fatal public retaliation.

fig 3 Man with Earring. Collection unknown. photo © National Portrait Gallery, London.

M.H. Spielmann called this image the Zuccaro Shakespeare but doubted the attribution. Why? Because Zuccaro hadn't been in England when Shakespeare's age matched that of the sitter. Kit met Zuccaro not in England but in Madrid: in July 1587 they were together there, working for Walsingham.

In 1933 an art dealer in Germany, Hermann Rothschild, sent this photo to the National Gallery; the gallery didn't purchase the painting but kept the photo. Here's Kit in Madrid, tense and weary after adventuring under cover in Portugal and Spain since April.

fig 4. Shakespeare by Taylor (formerly called the Chandos Portrait). © The National Portrait Gallery, London.

From early childhood Kit went to sea at Dover. He sailed the Channel, the eastern Atlantic, Mediterranean, Adriatic, Aegean, and Black Sea; from Venice to Bermuda he convoyed four ships, and sailed back to Naples. In later life he owned a little ship. This portrait has often been criticized for its sailor-like qualities. Could the Taylor who made it have been John Taylor the Water-Poet—an SSS friend of Kit's who ran a water-coach?

fig 5 The Gaeta Miniature of Shakespeare. attributed to George Vertue. Courtesy the Folger Shakespeare Library.

This elegant tiny painting may be a copy of a life portrait dating from Kit's years working counterespionage as an intermittent secretary and a popular director of drama at the palace in Naples. Miniatures were easy to send home. Frontal baldness, large eyes, rizzio hair and earring are salient features.

fig 6 The Harley Miniature of Shakespeare. in a private collection.

Here the artist has provided a touch of extra hair on Kit's forehead, and he's wearing a ruff—unusual for him. He's prepared to be viewed by nobility.

M.H. Spielmann called this the Welbeck Abbey-Harley Miniature: Marlowe's daughter Iz-Elizabeth (adopted by William Basset) lived at Welbeck Abbey with her second husband, William Cavendish. Their great-granddaughter Henrietta Cavendish Holles may have given this miniature to her husband Edward Harley for his famous Harleian Collection.

fig 7 The Flower Portrait. reproduced with permission from the Royal Shakespeare Company.

Once believed to have been the model for the Droeshout engraving, this portrait is now firmly accepted as a 19th century painting. It offers a better likeness than the Droeshout. Shadows in my file suggest a Flower Portrait connection with the Bedell family; William Bedell was chaplain for English Ambassador Henry Wotton in Venice.

fig 8 The Droeshout Engraving.

This well-known, much maligned head-on-a-platter presents a not-bad view of Marlowe's facial characteristics. The engraver was young and deserves credit for what he did accomplish. (Enlargement suggests a faint line of cursive script across the upper left field.)

fig 9 The Venice Portrait. permission to reproduce from the Royal Shakespeare Company, Stratford-on-Avon.

When Micaela cooked for him, Gregorio gained weight.

A dated letter was inked on the back of this painting—not in Gregorio de' Monti's hand. The letter has been more or less effectively obliterated by several restorations of the fabric. The portrait once belonged to Rawdon Brown, for several years editor of the Calendars of English State Papers Venetian.

fig 10 The Arlaud-Duchange engraving of Shakespeare, sometimes found in Rowe's edition of *Shakespeare*, 1709. from *Shakespeare, 1700-1740*, by H.L. Ford, 1938.

This image is postmortem but a sensitive picture of an exhausted man. It's the only portrait I've found which suggests the sore on the side of Kit's nose (his right side) which is evident on his deathmask. Other pictures of Marlowe show him pre-cancerous, or he's been discreetly posed to show a three-quarter view of the left face. The sores, commonly called "rodent ulcers," are described by Kit as "amphicoelus cysts" in his ciphers for *Bargraves Polisie.*

fig 11 The Shakespeare Deathmask. photos from former Curator Irmgard Bröning and permission from Curator Silvia Uhlemann, Handschriften-und-Musikabteilung, Ausstelungen. Universitats-und Landesbibliothek, Darmstadt.

Its identity is disputed, but the mask is carefully kept in this library in Germany. Someone who'd been told it was the face of Shakespeare has scratched the date 1616 on the edge of the plaster—otherwise it's in fine shape, with a tiny scar and two sutures on the forehead, faintly visible here and described for me in a letter from Curator Bröning.

fig 12 This photo of the Deathmask shows the epithelioma, a basal-cell carcinoma, on the side of Kit's nose. At first sight I'd guessed the damage was an injury to the plaster, but both my dermatologist and other physicians have pronounced it a cancer. (And see figure 10.)

One reason experts can't believe the mask is Shakespeare's may be because Will Shakespeare died in Stratford-on-Avon in 1616, at a time when plaster deathmasks were almost unknown in England. Deathmasks of important personages there were still being made from thin sheets of copper. Marlowe, the real subject of this mask, died in Venice late in 1621, where skilled sculptors—known to Ambassador Wotton—were already working from plaster deathmasks, making memorial statues.

fig 13 The Shakespeare Monument. detail. in Trinity Church, Stratford-on-Avon. photo by Ballantine.

This cenotaph is believed to have been erected c. 1622 (Kit died 21 November 1621), with Kit's friends, including his half-brother Peter Manwood, contributing. Unfortunately the nose on the statue was broken years later, patched up shorter, and the moustache was turned up. The likeness was lost.

fig 14 Sir Roger Manwood's Monument in St. Stephen's Church outside Canterbury. detail. photo by Virginia Stern.

Kit's real father's cenotaph, extant, was made by Maximillian Coult, who later made Queen Elizabeth's monument. Here Sir Roger is carved in colored alabaster, in a pose very like his son's in the niche in Trinity Church, Stratford-on-Avon, where Kit, too, is surrounded by an arch and pillars. (See figure 13.)

fig 15 Shakespeare, The Sanders Portrait. by kind permission of Lloyd Sullivan.

Here's a portrait well-furnished with qualities pointing to its validity as an image of William Shakespeare himself. The sitter appears to have gray eyes and light brown hair. The painting is proven to have been made early in the seventeenth century—about 1603—and the present owners state that the artist was a forebear of theirs named John Sanders, a member of the King's Players. Kit wrote in ciphers for Sonnet 135: "Then I see Sh., *fair and crass*, give all R neat writin' t' the actors' theater as his ouun 'n' Bacon's! Ye deed's a l-lie! A dead l-lie!"

fig 16 Queen Elizabeth I, c. 1592. a portrait attributed to the studio of Marcus Gheeraerts the Younger. reproduced courtesy of the Elizabethan Gardens, Roanoke Island, NC.

This is how Elizabeth appeared about the time Kit wrote for her the descriptive, ciphered love-poem which saved his life: "Shall I Die/Shall I Fly?" In May 1593 his friend Henry Wriothesley delivered the verses to her, along with more of Kit's poems, and it was she who made his escape possible. She also saved him on at least two later occasions.

fig 17 The Palazzo da Silva, Cannaregio, near the Ponte degli Ormesani, by the gate to the Venice Ghetto. This sketch is reproduced courtesy of Peter Lauritzen, who lived in the palazzo on its piano nobile.

From late 1604 through 1610, the old-already palace (1468) served as English Embassy House, home to Ambassador Henry Wotton and intermittently to Secretary Gregorio de' Monti (Kit).

f

Marlowe's Ciphers

Translations by Roberta Ballantine

MARLOWE'S CIPHERS

Plaintext Titles Pages

The Birth of Merlin 183
Sir John Oldcastle 184
The Lord Cromwell 185
Selimus 186
Lust's Dominion, or, The Lascivious Queen 187
Arden of Fevershame 188
Locrine, A and Locrine, B 189
Dido 191
Timon 192
The Famous Victories 193
The Tragedie of Doctor Faustus 195
Measure for Measure 199
All's Well, that Ends Well 204
Henry V 206
Fair Em 233
Edward III 234
The Jew of Malta 235
Tamburlaine II 248
Sonnet 86 253
Sonnet 126 255
Titus Andronicus 257
Epitaph for Roger Manwood 258
Henry VI Part I 260
Henry VI Part II 263
Henry VI Part III 265
Sir Thomas More 291
Hero and Leander 292
The Passionate Shepherd 293
Loves Labour's Lost 295

The Tragedy of Richard The Third 320
Venus and Adonis 324
Lucrece 326
Sonnet 116 330
Two Gentlemen of Verona 332
The Taming of The Shrew 333
The Comedie of Errors 336
A Midsommer Nights Dreame 340
Prologue Romeo and Juliet 341
Romeo and Juliet 343
The Play of Pericles, Prince of Tyre, & C. 344
I Henry IV 346
The Merry Wives of Windsor 372
The Merchant of Venice 379
Much Adoe About Nothing, A 386
Much Adoe About Nothing, B 387
Much Adoe About Nothing, C 388
The Tragedie of Troylus and Cressida 389
The Tragedie of Troylus and Cressida 392
Sonnet 125 B 412
As You Like It 414
Twelfe Night, or What You Will 433
The Life and Death of King Richard The Second 437
The Life and Death of King John 439
The Tragedie of Othello 443
The Tragedy of Othello, The Moor of Venice 444
To The Deserving Author, by Cygnus 446
Hamlet 447
Hamlet, Prince of Denmark 448
The Tragedie of Macbeth 450
The Tragedie of King Lear 451
Mucedorus 453
The London Prodigall 454
The Pvritaine Widdow 455
The Merry Devill of Edmonton 456
The Tragedie of Anthonie, and Cleopatra 457
Madrigali Amorosi 458
A Yorkshire Tragedy 460
Noches de Invierno 461
Cymbeline 462
Don Quixote I 464
The Winters Tale 465

The Tragedie of Julius Caesar 474
A Fvnerall Elegye 476
The Tempest 480
The Famous History of The Life of King Henry The Eight 497
The Tragedy of Coriolanus 501
The Life of Tymon of Athens 502
The Two Noble Kinsmen 504
Salutation on de' Monti's Dispatches for Sec'y
of State Robert Naunton, 1619-1621 506
Captain John Bargrave. A Form of Polisie, by Ignotus. 507
Captain John Bargrave. A Form of Polisie, by Ignotus 508
Captain John Bargrave Letter to The Treasurer 545
You Meaner Beauties 546
Francis Bacon's Epitaph, St. Michael's Church, St. Albans 548
Shakespeare's Epitaphs 549

The Birth of Merlin. Quarto. 1662. By William Shakespear and William Rowley.
The Shakespeare Apocrypha. Ed. C. F. Tucker Brooke. Oxford: Clarendon, 1971. p 351.

THE BIRTH OF MERLIN

1 & 2

You teach me language, sir, as one that knows The Debt of Loue I owe unto her Vertues;	**Kit wove ye rough tale about th' demon uuho starts a gaon life, C, 'n' neuer sees the woe**

No mention of collaboration here.
When Kit as Gilbert Gifford wrote a book with "Gratley," not telling their real names, he admitted to the Inquisitors that they'd done it together.
When he worked on *Sir Thomas More*, Kit's ciphers said he made it "with others," not naming the writers who might get into trouble with the censor.
When John Fletcher and Kit collaborated on *The Two Noble Kinsmen*, Fletcher was mentioned up front as a friend and welcome helper. William Rowley may have redone *The Birth of Merlin* for a publisher who wanted some changes. Kit seems to have made this first draft as a youngster, addressing the ciphers to his natural father.

3 & 4

Wherin like a true Courtier I haue fed My self with hope of fair Success, and now	**of mother 'n' her child, uuho's a speakin' adult wi' few, few years. Fie! So U C, I enter cri—**

5 & 6

Attend your wisht consent to my long Suit. Believe me, youthful Lord,	**yin' for ye gusty state o' th' world, 'n' mi lo' lot—U bein' lost t' vue. Need U. Ch.M.**

gusty. Webster. blustery.
U. Kit is writing to his dad, Roger Manwood.

f
Only lines of dialogue are counted.

Sir John Oldcastle. Quarto. 1600.
The Shakespeare Apocrypha. Ed. C. F. Tucker Brooke. Oxford: Clarendon, 1971. p 129.

SIR JOHN OLDCASTLE

1 & 2

The doubtful Title (Gentlemen) prefixt Vpon the Argument we have in hand,	**Over time, Marlouue planned tv begin t' fix the pla, 'n' he'd hunt t' get the new f—**

X

There's more

The Lord Cromwell. Quarto.
The Shakespeare Apocrypha. Ed. C. F. Tucker Brooke. Oxford: Clarendon, 1971. p 16.

THE LORD CROMWELL

1 & 2

Come, masters, I thinke it be past fiue a clock; is it not time we were at worke:	**Kit M. wrote this Kent web plai t' ouercome a sick fear o' mi waitin' tests, Ceee?**

3 & 4

my old Master heele be stirring anon. I cannot tell whether my old master will be stirring or no:	**Ma 'n' Roger meet—insist ye Moth (who bled yl Latin) B trained, learn rhetoric 'n' more, till less wrong**

Moth. Early nickname for Kit (see the boy in *Loves Labour's Lost.* Kit was enchanted with the court entertainments of Ned de Vere.)
Ma 'n' Roger. Kit's father, Roger Manwood, and Kate Marley cooperate and enroll Kit in The King's School at Canterbury.

5 & 6

but I am sure I can hardly take my afternoones nap, for my young Maister Thomas,	**'s in my uuork. My school starts again before day, 'n' I'm t' meet th' men. Pray for a—an—au—**

my uuork. Already he thinks of writing as his work.
before day. Students arrived at the King's School for chapel at 6 AM—the H.M. came in at 7.

7 & 8

. . . he keepes such a quile in his studie, with the Sunne, and the Moone, and the seauen Starres,	**dience in the writin' dep't! No! Sad, he sank. He must haue ansuuers t' al questions, see.**

He, he, he!

X
There's more

Selimus. Quarto, 1594. Printed by Thomas Creede.
Copy in Folger Library.

SELIMUS

1 & 2

Leave me my Lords vntill I call you foorth,
For I am heavie and disconsolate

Chris M. made ye vvooly old drama (all of it! E-e-e!) for school. In it, an evil sultan

Chris. In his ciphered letter to half-sister Meg in the Two Gentlemen of Verona, Marlowe calls himself Chris.
vvooly. woolly. In ciphers, Marlowe habitually uses this word to mean rough.
for school. Alhough the King's School was known for presenting plays on the Almonry Chapel dais, no productions during the almost two years Kit studied there have been made public.

X
There's more

Lust's Dominion, or, The Lascivious Queen. Written by Christofer Marloe, Gent. Printed for F.K. and are to be sold at the sign of Ben Jonson's head, on the back-side of the Old Exchange. 1657. Ed. J. le Gay Brereton. Louvain: Uystpruyst, 1931.

LUST'S DOMINION, OR, THE LASCIVIOUS QUEEN

1 & 2

On me, do(e)s music spend this sound
on me that hate all unity: hah!
Zarack Baltazar?

Kit M. made this Hozannah ta plae at Dad's house. Name your best call, couzin, 'n' R sh—

3 & 4

My gracious Lord.
Are you there with your Beagles?
hark you slaves,
Did I not bind you

ot 'd raise it. Go ahead, you'd see, al right! Yes, you knouu nobody'll bury R service! I'm wha—

X

There's more

Years later, at the death of Philip II, Kit must have reworked this very early play—a fiction perhaps created when as a boy he was told he must never write about Queen Elizabeth's love for Philip or her affair with her "Moor" Walsingham. The retouched text retains Kit's youthful style, recalling the earnest child he'd been.

Arden of Fevershame. Quarto 1.
The Shakespeare Apocrypha. Ed. C. F. Tucker Brooke. Oxford: Clarendon, 1971. p 3.

ARDEN OF FEVERSHAME

1 & 2

Arden, cheere vp thy spirits and droup no more: My gratious Lord, the Duke of Sommerset,	**Marlouue made this true story from his dad Roger's Kentish record. Vpon my need t' ope p—**

3 & 4

Hath freely giuen to thee and to thy heyres, By letters patents from his Maiesty,	**apers, Father lets me see 'em, 'n' I dig out th' betrayal 'n' th' tests for ye hy hyt on the Yi—**

5 & 6

All the lands of the Abby of Fevershame. Heer are the deedes, sealed and subscribed	**d—al for th' deeds t' Fevershame lands. Alice bated, abused—she'l ne'er b-be free. Oy! She ha—**

7, 8 & 9

with his name and the kings: Read them, and leaue this melancholy moode. Francklin, thy love prolongs my weary lyfe.	**d lost t' insane greedy men, C, 'n' not t' her mad, chummy love. She'l walk alone t' hard hap on ye f-far, hy, hy gallows. I, I! In mi**

10 & 11

And but for thee how odious were this lyfe, That showes me nothing but torments my soule,	**home study: tutut! Mosby's h-h-hot loue interest begins wi' transfer of th' home land. Woe-Woe!**

In mi home study. Kit takes the records home to read them.

X

There's more

Locrine. Quarto. 1595.
The Shakespeare Apocrypha. Ed. C.F.Tucker Brooke. Oxford: Clarendon, 1971. p 39.

LOCRINE, A

1 & 2 A Might(y) Lion, ruler of the woods, Of wondrous strength and great proportion,	**Youthful Marlowe wrote th' gross nothing for 'is dad. Prai, don't go 'n' report on e—**
3 & 4 With hideous noyse scarring the trembling trees, With yelling clamors shaking all the earth,	**ach gag R slob Kit lets loose in th' mist! Wait! He'l learn, C, 'n' giue ye higher matter: shril 'n' shrewd, 'n' y'**

shril. shrill. Webster [archaic or poetic] keen, sharp, biting, poignant.

5 & 6 Traverst the groues, and chast the wandring beasts. Long did he raunge amid the shadie trees.	**answer ta hard studie; but Dad saves this ol' green thing, seen home-acted 'n' dear t' his heart. G-g-r!**
7 & 8 And drave the silly beasts before his face, When suddeinly from out a thornie bush,	**Dad's honest lawyer friends uuere al suited for the iob of actin' shabby Velshmen. H—**

X
There's more

LOCRINE, B

1 & 2 A Might(y) Lion, ruler of the woods, Of wondrous strength and great proportion,	**Youthful Marlowe wrote th' gross nothing for 'is dad. Prai, don't go 'n' report on e—**

3 & 4	
With hideous noyse scarring the trembling trees, With yelling clamors shaking all the earth,	**ach silly error in R hasty Gogmagog scenes, sith Kit made all the lines in Bene't while hurt. Th' wr—**

Bene't. The nickname for Kit's Cambridge College, Corpus Christi, which stood next to the church of St. Benedict.

5 & 6	
Trauerst the groues, and chast the wandring beasts. Long did he raunge amid the shadie trees,	**ong thrust I gaue didn't saue me, C, so here I rest, stasht 'n bed with a gashed leg 'n' head, t' read narr—**

gashed . . . head. Could this be how he got the scar on his forhead—a wound mended with two stiches which shows on his death mask?

7 & 8	
And drave the silly beasts before his face, When suddeinly from out a thornie bush,	**atiues o' famed British heroes whu sent a bad hunne t' fall o'er hy Douer clif 'n' dye. S.S. b—**

British heroes. Corineius—and his brother Brutus—are said to have thrown Gogmagog over the cliff at Dover.
S.S. secret service.

9 & 10	
A dreadfull Archer with his bow ybent, Wounded the Lion with a dismall shaft.	**elieues Chr.'s o' th' iob, Dad, while mi bad-off hand wants t' write all th' whurly dan—**

11 & 12	
So he him stroke that it drew forth the blood, And fild his furious heart with fretting yre;	**gers of battle. I think of this hurt i' th' trial sword-dash fooeedoee thru mi friend. Why R th' t—**

13 & 14	
But all in vaine he threateneth teeth and pawes, And sparkleth fire from forth his flaming eies,	**rue thrvsts th' hardest t' make? E-e-e! In th' heat I'm gripp'd bi foolish fear 'n' want a healin' feelen'. Flan—**

X

There's more

Dido, Queen of Carthage. Quarto.
Complete Works of Christopher Marlowe. Ed. Fredson Bowers. 2nd ed. vol 1, p 7.

DIDO

1 & 2

Come gentle Ganimede and play with me,
I love thee well, say Iuno what she will

Ch. M. made this ele-ele-elevated play to w-win U, 'n' he l-lays it on me while going aw—

X

There's More

Timon.
Victoria & Albert Museum. Dyce MS 52.

TIMON

1 & 2
Laches hast thou receav'd my rents?
Master I have,
And brought in sacks filled with goulden talents.

Kit Marlowe vvrit this tale re a sh-shy generous man, abandon'd, C, uuhen his last gelt had fled, C? C? Test—

X
There's more

Geoffrey Bullough, in *Narrative and Dramtic Sources of Shakespeare,* offers the full text of this well-made early play.

The Famous Victories.
The Case for Shakespeare's Authorship of The Famous Victories. Seymour Pitcher, 1961.

THE FAMOUS VICTORIES

1 & 2

Come away, Ned and Tom. / Here, my Lord. Come away, my lads. Tell me sirs, how much gold have you got.

Chr. M. made ye show—Gad's Hyl to Agyncourt—w-wi' my amee Hal (moue over, '*omme*!), 'n' y' Old Lad o' d' Castle.

de Vere was already Hal's prototype, and the Old Lad o' d' Castle was an early name for Falstaff—Roger Manwood. Marlowe is saying he worked with these two men to write this opus.

3 & 4

Faith, my lord, I have got five hundred pound.
But tell me, Tom, how much hast thou got?

We had grog to beat th' cold. Hot, I'd vvrite my lood stuff tha whole nite 'n' h-hump U, m-m!—

U. means Ned. See ciphers for *I Henry IV* and *Henry V.*

5 & 6

Faithe, my lord, some foure hundred pounde.
Foure hundred poundes! Bravely spoken, lads! But

so U'd prefer me. No uuorry; al seem'd fine. But U broke Nan's heart! She'l d-d-d-d-d-dy of no love—P-U! Phu!

Nan's heart. Ned's abandoned wife was Anne Cecil. Much later, Kit shows her sorrow and death in *Hamlet's* Ophelia.

7 & 8

tell me, sirs, think(e) you not that it was a villainous part of me to rob(be) my father's receivers?

We're all for hire to make nationalist plays t' B shouun before her maiesty's covrt. It's time tv

9 & 10

Why no, my lord, it was but a trick of youth. Faith(e), Ned, thou sayest true. But tell me, sirs,

finish yt at last—rehearse yt with Buck! Oy! A new thril for me! But uue'l study to do most

11 & 12

whereabouts are we? / My lord, we are now about a mile off London. But sirs, I marvel that Sir Iohn Oldcastle comes not away.	**o' ye direction o' her maiesty's actors: fast movin' lines—a lot o' lafs are needed now. How about a brawl o'er what Mum'll bruw,**

what Mum'll bruw. Scene 7.

13 & 14

Z'ounds! See where he comes./How now, Iockey, what news with thee? Faith(e), my lord, such news	**'ow twenty-od die to stake 'n' hew al ze Frenchmen? So, wow, whee—wi' his hy *success* here! Ho hum.**

f

Doctor Faustus. Quarto, 1593.
The Complete Works of Christopher Marlowe. Ed. Fredson Bowers. 2nd ed.

THE TRAGEDIE OF DOCTOR FAUSTUS

1 & 2

Not marching in the fields of Thrasimen,
Where Mars did mate the warlicke Carthagens,

While h-he was incarcerated, K. M. (Chr. M.) made this find of a German t-tale o' regrettin' sins. H-

3 & 4

Nor sporting in the dalliance of loue
In Courts of Kings, where state is ouerturn'd,

e writes it as a lo doctor lost in lvck 'n' errors 'n' one fiendish fee—not uurung i' the gap.

5 & 6

Nor in the pompe of proud audacious deeds,
Intends our Muse to vaunt his heavenly verse;

He'd invade, sever, resume, put himself douun, so ye end's not too sad. No! U R a hippocrite! A nu v—

7 & 8

Onely this, Gentles:we must now performe
The forme of Faustus fortunes, good or bad,

iew shows Faustus desperate, lonely; U see, not born demon, he f-f-forgot t' go from trum—

9 & 10

And now to patient iudgements we appeale,
And speake for Faustus in his infancie.

perie t' wickedness: he's not sinned enuf t' see awful damnation at *fin.* I O U, Pa-Papa, ag—

11 & 12

Now is he borne, of parents base of stocke,
In Germany, within a Towne cal'd Rhode:

ain, for teachin' not t' sign away freedom, as th' lo-brow creep's done! He knows bein'

13 & 14

At riper yeares to Wittenberg he went,
Whereas his kinsmen chiefly brought him up;

without power, U want h-help. Shy, he signs ye tricksie bargain, remember? Fie! Enter th'

15 & 16

So much he profits in Divinitie
The fruitfull plot of Scholerisme grac'd,

chief good spirits tu trie tu help him. No! Daft, he'll fuss 'n' frolic i' Rome, C? I'v—

17 & 18

That shortly he was grac'd with Doctors name,
Excelling all, whose sweete delight's dispute

e seen lewd, wag, magic shadows: don't expect a tr-true scholar! He's l-lost—his light witheld. Yet

19 & 20

In th' heavenly matters of Theologie,
Till swolne with cunning of a selfe conceit,

a genius flashes now 'n' then, only t-t' go calm, content wi' foolerie. Fie! It'l chil thee! U

21 & 22

His waxen wings did mount above his reach,
And melting, heauens conspir'd his overthrow:

view his acts as error, but no, in his dim mind he'd hug al experience as good, 'n' now hunts wha—

23 & 24

For falling to a divellish exercise,
And glutted now with learnings golden gifts,

t's extravagant, stuffing it all down wi' greed. I! 'N' life's end gliding close! Re: h-hollo

25 & 26

He surfets upon cursed Necromancie:
Nothing so sweet as Magicke is to him,

satisfaction: unregenerate, he sinkes in mud. C-come, choose to swim! Hug spr—

27 & 28

Which he preferres before his chiefest blisse,
And this the man that in his study sits.

ites who can reclaim thy sad spirit! Fie! Be free! Sh, sh, sh, sh, sh, sh! But he is fetterd in *ein* t—

29 & 30

Settle thy studies Faustus, and begin
To sound the depth of that thou wilt professe,

t-t-tense wish! One tu, tu hot desire: tu B adept at gusty puffs 'n' foolish deeds, so, al th' th—

. . . Sh, sh, sh, sh, sh, sh! the poet comforts Faustus, cradling him and telling him to accept these good sprites. Faustus won't do it.

31 & 32

Hauing commenc'd, be a Diuine in shew,
Yet levell at the end of every Art,

eology left behind, each eve he'd matriculate in mere vain new study, 'n'

33 & 34

And live and die in Aristotles workes.
Sweet *Analitikes*, tis thou hast ravisht me,

send his learin' slavish devil out in haste wi' triksie tasks to do'n' tear meat t' awe

35 & 36

Bene disserere est finis logices.
Is to dispute well Logickes chiefest end?

guests! Cost? He'l seek, spend, lose, sit friendless i' frigid cel. Ie, ie, ie—'n' bow t' ce—

37 & 38

Affoords this Art no greater miracle?
Then read no more, thou hast attain'd that end;

rtain damn'd death at th' arranged hour! Fool! No comfort here, i' th' nastee strait; teas—

Identifying with Faustus, Marlowe is sitting in a frigid cell facing almost certain execution at the hands of a Catholic League judge who believes Kit to be Gilbert Gifford, and Kit blames himself for his own foolery.

39 & 40

A greater subiect fitteth Faustus wit:
Bid *on kai me on* farewell, Galen come:

ing, MT work is o'er: th' bil's begun t' come due at last. Feature it! We face a finale.

41 & 42

Seeing *ubi desinit philosophus, ibi incipit medicus.*
Be a Phisitian Faustus, heape up gold,

Eclipst, he's gone! (big fuss!) I-I tu mai die. Houu t' escape this bad bishop's diuine iail? Pin-pin up

43 & 44

And be eterniz'd for some wondrous cure:
Summum bonum medicinae sanitas,

braue remember'd words o' comment to saue mi fazed uacuous mind! 'N' sin—'n' sin—

45 & 46

The end of Physicke is our bodies health:
Why Faustus, hast thou not attain'd that end?

they harp on that: "thy soul's sick t' death with sin!" So e'en if U had a hot bed U'd not use ta f—

47 & 48

Is not thy common talke sound Aphorismes?
Are not thy bils hung up as monuments,

uc 'n' masterbate. No! My most nonny iailer uud sh-shout: "Gism!" So no help-p! Kno that sm—

49 & 50

Wher(e)by whole Cities have escap't the plague,/And thousand desperate maladies beene cur'd?

el o' piss-dirtie wash water? UUe had plentee each seven-day! C, he's both clap-mad 'n' greedee ta B u—

51 & 52

Yet art thou still but Faustus, and a man. Couldst thou make men to live eternally,

ltra-dutiful to ye scummy knave he'd serue 'n' tattle to about small sin, 'n' altho' U at—

53 & 54

Or being dead, raise them to life againe, Then this profession were to be esteem'd.

tempt t' ignore him, soon he begins lewd threats, 'n' I fear a bad dose o' reefis tee. Eie!

55 & 56

Physicke farewell: where is Iustinian? *Si una eademque res legatur duobus, alter rem, alter valorem rei, &c.*[etc.]

A friend saves me quils! We read 'n' write! He'l bring U a saucy Merlot, tel U chileee tales o' Paris! "U" R mee? U Arre—Kit!

Kit! He's had too much saucy Merlot. The friend was Edward Grimston, and Kit incorporated bits of the chilly tales in *Measure for Measure,* one of the three plays he drafted in this jail.

f

Measure for Measure. First Folio of Shakespeare. Comedies, p 61.

MEASURE FOR MEASURE

1 & 2

My Lord. / Of Gouernment, the properties to vnfold,
Would seeme in me t' affect speech & [and] discourse,

Chr. M. made ye t-tale closed in French priests' prison. Fed rot-gut food, 'n' swept 'n' moued—E-e-e-e!—foul vom—

3 & 4

Since I am put to know, that your owne Science
Exceedes (in that) the lists of all aduice

it 'n' we-wee ouer t' city tank. Spent months til' I chose—I chose—a cu-cu exit as a dead fello, 'n'

5 & 6

My strength can giue you: then no more remaines
But that, to your sufficiency, as your worth is able,

came home a thin weary failure. No success! Yet for no reason I brot my best uuriting t' you. Th-thy gun—

7 & 8

And let them worke: The nature of our People,
Our Cities Institutions, and the Termes
For Common Iustice,/

's confiscated in the t-trap. I'de onlee luck to saue me—Oi, oi—up there i' th' muniment room. Wet-front trousers

9 & 10

y' are as pregnant in/As Art, and practice, hath inriched any
That we remember: There is our Commission,

were a hindrance, C? But no more than ye assassin reachin' th' top a' th' stair. I'm i' danger, C? I pray t' re-remem—

11 & 12

From which, we would not haue you warpe; call hither,/ I say, bid come before vs Angelo:

ber how t' hide. No light. Here he comes! Oi! A couple of 'em in ovr way! Say! A brawl! U'd C—Wulf

13 & 14

What figure of vs thinke you, he will beare. for you must know, we haue with speciall soule	**has a knife! Both hu-hug Kit vp ye wal. Woe! T' lose my life for clues I stole! I weave, ru-run! Wow! H—**

15 & 16

Elected him our absence to supply; Lent him our terror, drest him with our loue,	**ow t' elude 'em? I slip, recoup, shoue thru ye door, sl-lam it on 'em, return t' Cher. Th' bri—**

17 & 18

And giuen his Deputation all the Organs Of our owne powre: What thinke you of it?	**lliant run ends i' fear. O-o, I'ue a knife-wound showin'! How t' go out happy to the great**

19 & 20

If any in Vienna be of worth To vndergoe such ample grace, and honour, It is Lord Angelo.	**room bleeding ingloriovsly 'n' escape vnforgiven? I cd rot here! Whoa! An-an-an out! Daft h—**

21 & 22

Looke where he comes. Alwayes obedient to your Graces will I come to know your pleasure.	**auen—ye iail! Look! My couer's a priest: We'l do some cock wrong at ye whore house—We'l B lo, ere t—**

23 & 24

Angelo; There is a kinde of Character in thy life, That to th' obseruer, doth thy history Fully vnfold:	**h' fool h-h-hitters softly return t' byte, and in regret I'l ask ovt loud for iail at once! H-hey! Thy chafed,**

25 & 26

. . . Thy selfe, and thy belongings Are not thine owne so proper, as to waste	**bleeding pal wants ye safest, highest sort o' retreat now—No, no hope yn**

27 & 28

Thy selfe vpon thy vertues; they on thee: Heauen doth with vs, as we, with Torches doe	**rvshin' out: they'd waste thy wet peter, 'n' why choose t' die? H-have t' shun thee, fools! Eve—**

29 & 30

Not light them for themselues: For if our vertues Did not goe forth of vs, 'twere all alike	**n tho' th' stolid gendarme felt sorroful t' see our h-hot revel, I felt I gaue 'im soft work. Fev—**

31 & 32

As if we had them not: Spirits are not finely touch'd,
But to fine issues: nor nature never lends

erish 'n' fetter'd, I'm carted thru sno, sno, snow to ye *fleuve*, 'n' beast-priests' iail. U dean of huntin'

33 & 34

The smallest scruple of her excellence,
But like a thrifty goddesse, she determines

knouu Paris Chrystmas t' B frigid! E-e-e! See, he's left t' extreme cold, Hen. He's led t' *les* cell—

35 & 36

Her selfe the glory of a creditour,
Both thanks, and vse; but I do bend my speech

s deep i' ye b-bldg, t' reach my chosen door. V'd h-have thot—fire, blanket, rest! No! Suf—

37 & 38

To one that can my part in him advertise;
Hold therefore Angelo:

ferin!—my motto! On arrival I enter. Hope's dead: no heat! Get th' chal-

39 & 40

In our remoue, be thou at full, our selfe:
Mortallitie and Mercie in Vienna

luts movin'! U'l be learnin' fortitude here or leave life, man! O-o, ice, mi natur—

challuts. chalutz. Webster: a Jewish pioneer (Hebrew: a Jewish warrior)

41 & 42

Liue in thy tongue, and heart: Old Escalus
Though first in question, is thy secondary.
Take thy Commission.

al enemy, on th' shutter! Th' guard frees my hands, goes out. Kit stays in, quiet, lyin' on a cold cot. Oi! Chin is shiu—

43 & 44

Now good my Lord
Let there be some more test, made of my mettle,

ery. O, Mom told me we'l feel better some d-day! No more t' get th' mos—

45 & 46

Before so noble, and so great a figure
Be stamp't vpon it.
No more euasion:

t dangerous, frustrating iobs. So B brave—feel no open pain! Oe, Oe! Metamo—

47 & 48

We haue with a leauen'd, and prepared choice
Proceeded to you; therefore take your honors:

rphose a dark cold hour to one wi' hope for heauy thaw—U dance 'n' reuert ye deep ice to readee

49 & 50

Our haste from hence is of so quicke condition,/That it prefers it selfe, and leaues vnquestion'd

liquid drops o' deuu. U C, insanitee takes me. O, qvite insensate, I stretch on th' floor on f-fresh feca—

51 & 52

Matters of needfull value: We shall write to you/As time, and our concernings shall importune,

l matter—damp, tho' not for long. U ever lie alone smear'd in frosty shit? U C, I was unwell, Uncle. Sea,

53 & 54

How it goes with vs, and doe looke to Know/What doth befall you here. So fare you well:

I should wake, try to wash! O-o, no water! Weakly I get on th' bed, hold f-foul sleeve. O-o, who—

55 & 56

To th' hopefull execution doe I leaue you, Of your Commissions.
Yet giue leaue (my Lord,)

's at ye door? "O, good!" I yel. "Expect U R comin' in?" "U'l see! Leue—uoo! Moue, U filthy louse!" My faith

57 & 58

That we may bring you something on the way.
My haste may not admit it,

i' humanity's gone, yet who am I? So I try t' B game 'n' do what th' yat meant. My

59 & 60

Nor neede you (on mine honor) have to doe With any scruple: Your scope is as mine owne,

open wound yawns, yet nouu I stande. *No*, I slip, rise once more, hover, reach home—O no, ye

61 & 62

So to inforce, or qualifie the Lawes
As to your soule seemes good: give me your hand,

soiled floor hits me. A guarde enters ye room, watches ye sequel. I go, "O-o-o," as if nouu v—

63 & 64

Ile priuily away: I loue the people,
But doe not like to stage me to their eyes:

omit's ineuitable. O-o, great! He'l tell U t' keep ye pot, or he'l deuise a pye wi' it. Oy!

65 & 66

Though it doe well, I doe not rellish well
Their lowd applause, and Aues vehement:

So "*leue-vou.*" He held me o'er th' desired pot wi' a gentle hand. We put in al o' th' swill—all

67 & 68

Nor doe I thinke the man of safe discretion
That do's affect it. Once more fare you well.

remnants o' indiscretion. O, ere I left them, ye fuckin' fools offer'd a death act. Woe! Tho' a—

69 & 70

The heauens giue safety to your purposes.
Lead forth, and bring you back in happinesse.

n hour saued Kit, he cd B shut up as Gilbert Gif. for aye, 'n' neuer see his pappy! O, no! Say no t' ea—

71 & 72

I thanke you, fare you well.
I shall desire you, Sir, to giue me leave

rly release! Ye killers wait outside! O, agony! I loue *ma vie*! Uh, uh! Fe—

73 & 74

To have free speech with you; and it concernes me
To looke into the bottom of my place:

ar hants me: what if I bot freedom, not content t-to keep my cool? O, pleeese! Oi vey!

Ch-chou!

f

All's Well That Ends Well. First Folio of Shakespeare. Comedies, p 230.

ALL'S WELL, THAT ENDS WELL

1 & 2

In deliuering my sonne from me, I burie a second husband.
And I in going, Madam, weep ore my fathers death anew;

Chr. M. made this in iail. I pretend I'm somebody named G. Gifford 'n' giue nonny a-answers. O, wearee! UUhen bad men a—

nonny a-answers. Kit, under cover as Gilbert Gifford, was questioned in jail about Gifford's activities and his relations with "Gratley" (Thomas Lodge). Kit never blew his cover, never bad-mouthed his working partners. His answers can be read in Latin in the *Calendar of MSS of the Marquis of Salisbury* (Robt. Cecil) at Hatfield House, Pt. III, #715, calendared 14 August 1588 (Historical MSS Commission). Copy in the Folger Shakespeare Library.

3 & 4

but I must attend his maiestie's command, to whom I am now in Ward, euermore in subiection.

re houndin' U, 'n' vomit's near, U write t' mimic some acts o' the dim *bon maison.* I seem t' await bed w—

mimic some acts. While in jail Marlowe began to write *Measure for Measure,* a work reflecting facets of the bordello he visited on Christmas Eve, 1587.

5 & 6

You shall find of the King a husband, Madame, you sir a father. He that so generally is at all times good,

i' Flo. Go t' business, Flo! Ha, Ha, Ha, Ha! Someday! Tyl then, Hen, I'l uurite al da feo stories 'n' al da drama. Kyt M. (G.G.)

Flo. Florence Bacot, the Madame at the brothel in Longchamp where Kit's enemies had arranged for him to be murdered. Florence seems to have offered to take Gilbert Gifford in her care on parole. If she'd managed that, her bravos could have swiftly dispatched Marlowe. Much later, not realizing that Kit had escaped, she wrote to Walsingham's secretary Phelippes (CSP Dom. Addenda xxxi p.297), asking him to send her money to aid Gifford's trial. **feo.** (Sp.) ugly. **Hen.** As he often does, Kit is writing to Henry Wriothesley, but in the last cipher Kit speaks to another friend, Edward. **(G.G.)** (Gilbert Gifford)

7 & 8

must of necessitie hold his vertue to you, whose worthinesse would stirre it vp where it wanted rather then lack

No more ciphers here, Edw. Kit's leavin' for Dover. Wish U were s-sailin' too! Hey, U write! T-Tush! Watch the dust settle on 't!

f

Henry V. First Folio of Shakespeare. Histories, p 69.

HENRY V

Prologue

1 & 2	
O For a Muse of Fire, that would ascend The brightest Heaven of Invention:	**O, Marlowe fashioned the thing for a dishonest effect bvt uurote in a nev—**
3 & 4	
A Kingdome for a Stage, Princes to Act, And Monarchs to behold the swelling Scene.	**er seen stile so actors c'd make d' long-ago storie plain t' C ('n' "the women B hang'd," C?—Fah!)**

women B hang'd. Marlowe was writing a story of a misogynist very like Ned—Edward de Vere. The play of *Henry V* was first drafted about 1588, in Ned's image.

5 & 6	
Then should the Warlike Harry, like himselfe, Assume the Part of Mars, and at his heeles	**He dreams he's R ruler—takes part in shameful lo wheedles. O, I think he fails hys team tha—**
7 & 8	
(Leasht in, like Hounds) should Famine, Sword and Fire Crouch for employment. But pardon, Gentles all:	**t pens for his theatre: nouu he cl-claims he penn'd all d' good lines of Kit's drama, 'n'-'n' wd rob my fello uur—**
9 & 10	
The flat unraysed Spirits, that hath dar(e)d On this unworthy Scaffold(e), to bring forth(e)	**iters, too! Fui! It's hard t' deal with th' od French songs, 'n' da feelyn' U hap t-t' B Harry—for that's**
11 & 12	
So great an Obiect. Can this Cock(e)-Pit hold The vastie fields of France? Or may we cramme	**always i' mi head as I pen each broken scene t' grace him, t-tired of MT coo-coo tears. Tvff! Cl—**

13 & 14

Within this Woodden O, the very Caskes
That did affright the Ayre at Agincourt?

ear thot dies: he's insane, C? Hungry-fit, C? What t' do? Go ahead, Kit: write! I'd favor th' ty—

15 & 16

O pardon: since a crooked Figure may
Attest in little place a Million,

rant uictor's cold misogynie—I pen a lo MT lace triplet 'e'd like, 'n'—O, Fa-a-a!

17 & 18

And let us, Cyphers to this great Accompt,
On your imaginarie Forces worke.

'E, a roi, C, wants the play to make men proud of our crass Eng. history, C? I cri, "Get

19 & 20

Suppose within the Girdle of these Walls
Are now confin'd two mightie Monarchies,

wise! This man's a pig, C?" "No," he tels me, "Harrie did no wrong, C? How wil U plot those ten fief—

21 & 22

Whose high, vp-reared, and abutting Fronts,
The perillous narrow(e) Ocean parts asunder.

s th' ruler o' France wd give th' girl? 'N'—'n'—soon a uuar! Repeat stabs, 'n' now—heaps o' <u>their</u> dead! Pr—

23 & 24

Peece out our imperfections with your thoughts:
Into a thousand partes divide one Man,

isoners? Wipe 'em ovt, C, 'n' head t' home—happy uuid treasure 'n' douuer, 'n' coiti-gash not too fit t'

25 & 26

And make imaginarie Puissance.
Thinke when we talke of Horses, that you see them

serue a king, *non*!" E-e! That's how he'd make the scenes a fast wrap, man! Oi! Yet I like him. U

27 & 28

Printing their prowd Hoofes i' th' receiuing Earth: /For 'tis your thoughts that now must decke our Kings,

know I pen for his hi theatre, yet in spite o' th' horrid sick tantrums, we R friends, C? Oh, goot, gu-u-u-t grog. Th' u—

his hi theatre. The Secret Service Theatre Wing.

29 & 30

Carry them here and there: iumping o're Times;/Turning th' accomplishment of many yeeres

gly time forgotten, he, R rey prince, is the past master o' charm—h-hummin', e'en dancin, euery m—

31 & 32

Into an Howre-glasse: for the which supplie,
Admit me Chorus to this Historie;

inute, with foolish gait 'n' time, as we lurch home to roost. Sh! R I P! His head, presc—

33 & 34

Who, Prologue-like, your humble patience pray.
Gently to heare, kindly to judge our Play.

ient, hit ye pillow hard till ol' p-p urge began a glory dreame, 'n' you—uue—proue coohkey. Kyt.

HENRY V

Act One

1 & 2

My Lord, Ile tell you, that self Bill is vrg'd,
Which in th' eleventh year of ye last Kings reign

Marlowe rit ye stvffy thing. Go get l-lost, U! He l-liked Harry—I held y' vital scenes in line. He bl—

3 & 4

Was like, and had indeed against vs past,
But that the scambling and vnquiet time

eats a sad mess, 'n' I sweat 'n' cvt 'n' pen dai 'n' night t' give him da quiet talk—bad, but had l—

5 & 6

Did push it out of farther question.
But how my Lord shall we resist(e) it now?

ess odor than if he'd writ th' play himself. Don't U bouu to w-worries—let's quit

7 & 8

It must be thought on: if it passe against vs,
We loose the better half of our Possession:

th' effort—SSS uuants it now. So—its foolish hash pretense mai plai! So ebb, get out get ove—

SSS uuants it now. This is a State Secret Service play.

9 & 10

For all the Temporall Lands, which men devout
By Testament haue given to the Church,

r it! H-he's not God! Cull! Cut d' waste! Leave h-him! Learn t' elevate th' myth—pen for Bacon. U wh—

Leave h-him! Kit is writing for De Vere. **pen for Bacon**. Kit thinks of working for intellectual Francis. w. an m used upside down as w.

11 & 12

Would they strip from vs: being valu(e)d thus,
As much as would maintaine, to the Kings honor,

o'd make plays must studie, learn how best t' fashion them—no as-U-go, lovv, dri writin'! Ugh! 'N' huc—

learn how best t' fashion them. Kit begins to dream of making a big-time history.

13 & 14

Full fifteene Earles, and fifteene hundred Knight(e)s
Six thousand and two hundred good Esquires:

kster sel of d' English nation at war. So th' queen 'n' Essex uuil d-do d-different: ade, hug 'n' feed U! Find her

15 & 16

And to reliefe of Lazars, and weake age
Of indigent faint Soules, past corporall toyle,

a-a tale of Tudor folke. Yea, pen fites, 'n' waste, 'n' pillage! Ai! It's frozen on Dad's collar: Roge—

Dad's collar. Manwood's SS chain of office shown in his portrait in the National Portrait Gallery and on his likeness on his monument at St. Stephen's Church outside Canterbury. Robert J. Blackham. *The Story of the Temple, Gray's and Lincoln's Inn.* London: "The portcullis in the . . . collar refers to John of Gaunt, the loops to the Union of the Houses of York and Lancaster, and the rose is . . . the Tudor rose, as the Collar of SS was first given . . . by Queen Elizabeth. It was given in her reign to a Judge of Common Pleas, but since then has only been worn by the Lord Chief Justices."

17 & 18

A hundred Almes-houses, right well supply'd:
And to the Coffers of the King beside,

r's chain shows the Tudors speedily rise t' B th' head of al: plug 'em! Defend ol' Eng.! Fuk!

19 & 20

A thousand pounds by th' yeere. Thus runs the Bill.
This would drinke deepe. / 'Twould drinke the Cup and all.

I'd properly pen all th' seesaw uuars betuueen al d' h-hi old Tudors' kin, but U'd think they went 'n' closed d'-d' h—

21 & 22

But what prevention? / The King is full of grace, and faire regard.
And a true lover of the holy Church.

ostility, then began t' fight, o'er 'n' o'er. Ah! graue h-hack error! VVd U wait, fear for d' end, clap enuf? U'll ch—

lover of the holy Church. Shadows suggest that de Vere once gave Kit a Geneva Bible.

23 & 24

The courses of his youth promis'od it not./The breath no sooner lefte his Fathers body,

afe! It robs R sho. So, see me edit—I try to hold U on th' hi path—offer U short hot scenes, 'n' by

25 & 26

But that his wildnesse, mortify'd in him, Seemed to dye too: yea, at that very moment,

bits the due history's made total. Now, tho,' I'm meetin' ye heat of Ned's very mad, *w*itty

27 & 28

Consideration like an Angell came, And whipt th' offending Adam out of him;

identification with cold Hal 'n' the long-ago drama, speakin' enuf o' "damn fem—

29 & 30

Leauing his body as a Paradise, T'inuelop and containe Celestiall Spirits.

s"—Nan's pitiable special predilection "A sin leadin' ta gross loue." Ai! *Duty* ha—

31 & 32

Never was such a sodaine Scholler made: Never came Reformation in a Flood,

s made R Ned (who??) a Nemesis to save R Nan from a frolic in hel, Eve-clad, C? O-o! Are U

Eve-clad. It seems Nan undressed trying in vain to attract her husband Oxford. These lines date the situation before June 1588, when Anne Cecil drowned, a suicide, at Greenwich. See Hamlet's line, "Get thee to a nunnery," and later Ophelia's tragic death.

33 & 34

With such a heady currance scowring faults: Nor never Hidra-headed Wilfulnesse

sure frustrate Nan's headin' for hel, 'n' *he's* so wel? Dig hi Ned: he crav'd wa-wa, U C? U C? I'l cry

35 & 36

So soone did loose his Seat; and all at once: As in this King. / We are blessed in the Change.

Ai! ! Can 'e think she's bad? She's lost, alone, long-wedded to an ingrate ass! Cee? Oi! In his sole

37 & 38

Heare him but reason in Divinitie; And all-admiring(e), with an inward(e) wish

view, Nan's girl-behauior ended ani wish t' win her. Ai! railin', he'd admit mi tan—

39 & 40

You would desire the King were made a Prelate:
Heare him debate of Common-wealth Affaires;

's better than her fair self. We weaue on home. O, O—felt like a ready-made pig. Dad, haue merci! Wom—

Dad, haue merci! Kit's father Roger Manwood was encouraging Kit to be Ned's lover, thinking that if Prince Ned were to become king, Kit could be the favorite.

41 & 42

You would say(e), it hath been all in his study:
List his discourse of Warre, and you shall heare

en R euer hit by this cad roi who uses SS only as a uuay t' deuil al who hate his false lordly ind—

43 & 44

a fearefull Battaile rendred you in Musique.
Turne him to any Cause of Pollicy,

ictment of ya relatiues unable tu respond. He may acquire foul info—U'l read y' il

45 & 46

The Gordian Knot of it he will vnloose,
Familiar as his Garter: that when he speakes,

t-tales of a shameless fag reporter—a liar in ink. High Ned'l weave his thot into who k—

a liar in ink. Probably Anthony Munday, who came to those hangings to laugh.

47 & 48

The Ayre, a Charter'd Libertine, is still,
and the mute Wonder lurketh in men's eares,

ill'd, then he wd err: rant, tease, tu tar, incriminate th' blamelss kin! Oye, he's reuered:

49 & 50

To steal his sweet and honyed Sentences:
So that the Art(e) and Practique part of Life,

a hated prince, free t' lie t-to th' honest queen:
seed-words that plast a saint on ye scaf—

saint on ye scaffold! Edmund Campion, d., hanged, quartered, 1 Dec. 1581.

51 & 52

Must be the Mistresse to this Theorique.
Which is a wonder how his Grace should gleane it,

old! O, this queer roi has a-a smel. I guess there's somethin' wrong with hi*m*, U C: I bet he's tetch'd.

53 & 54

Since his addiction was to Courses vaine,
His Companies vnletter'd, rude, and shallow,

How cd this capricious, volatile man rvle a countrie? His sad nonnie SSS went dead, des—

55 & 56

His Houres fill'd up with Ryots, Banquets, Sports,
And never noted in him any studie,

pite th' queen's hy annual subsidy. He wastes til he's too poor t' fvnd us, 'n' I'm dri in R dr—

57 & 58

any retyrement, any sequestration,
From open Haunt(e)s and Popularitie.

eary house—no pay for any pla—'n' d' queerman'srant'n'repetitiontiesmet-tu—

59 & 60

The Strawberry growes vnderneath the Nettle,
And holesome Berryes thrive and ripen best,

write twenty hopelessly bad dramas, 'n' he's sent here to B R dear nevv brother, greetin' the ren—

61 & 62

Neighbour'd by Fruit of baser qualitie:
And so the Prince obscur(e)dhisConte mplation

ascence of English drama. Oi! 'n' th' fools R cheated, brot t' ruin—I, I, I! By Bu-bu, d' queen's top pri—

63 & 64

Vnder the Veyle of Wildnesse, which (no doubt)
Grew like the Summer Grasse, fastest by Night,

nce! What t' do? H-his mom feeds us, gives vs bed 'n' glug, 'n' finally we write th' best story re her kee—

65 & 66

Vnseene, yet cressive in his facultie.
It must be so; for Miracles are ceast:

ne sense of her mom's beauty 'n' cruel fate. I, I, I! I access it, vse vestal restric—

I access it. Marlowe made a very early play, Henry VIII, about the courtship of Ann Boleyn, her coronation, and the birth of Elizabeth.

67 & 68

And therefore we must needes admit the meanes,
How things are perfected. / But my good Lord:

tions, pen her fatal drama: how she met 'n' wed de crude greedy Hen, good free-tit mom tu Bess, te—

69 & 70	
How now for mittigation of this Bill, Vrg(e)d by the Commons? doth his Maiestie/ Incline to it, or no?	**nder childish memory of An's embrace 'n' loving smile. Too—Oi, oi! Both thots fit nothing! To wit: I wit—**
71 & 72	
He seemes indifferent: / Or rather swaying more vpon our part, Then cherishing th' exhibiters against vs:	**ness her harsh brief treatment o' hi progeny 'n' gvess she, too, was reiected—a hi grievin' infant. Thru R mix p—**
73 & 74	
For I haue made an offer to his Maiestie, Vpon our Spiritual Convocation,	**erhaps I can C a uuai to vvrite 'er pla after Ned's finisht moo-moo-looin'. O, fui!**
75 & 76	
And in regard of Causes now(e) in hand, Which I haue open'd to his Grace at large,	**We—I—pen later scenes: R giddi Harrie goes on to win, U C—duh fag cad! Oh, naah, naah!**
77 & 78	
As touching France, to give a greater Summe, Then ever at one time the Clergie yet	**An' after th' great vvin—E-e-e-e! Gee! Amen! I stem the joy, C? Tu greet a girl he courts 'n' com—**
79 & 80	
Did to his Predecessors part withall. How did this offer seem(e) receiv'd, my Lord?	**pels t' marry him withovt spelt words or deeds, C? She'd flee his roi-codified dra—**
81 & 82	
With good acceptance of his Maiestie: Saue that there was not time enough to heare,	**ma, giuen a chance t-to choose her own moue: she's fettered; he's a pig. Ai, ai, ai! The t-two t-t—**
83 & 84	
As I perceiu(e)d his Grace would faine haue done, The seueralls and vnhidden passages	**ogether' l rule England for ai! Hush! We've a sad, sad endin': he dies 'n' decaies. Pace. U puissa—**
85 & 86	
Of his true Titles to some certaine Dukedomes, And generally, to the Crowne and Seat of France,	**nt rulers, note: his odoriferous fake gain was later lost, yet—fa!—decent men accede to the demon—**

87 & 88

Deriv(e)d from Edward, his great Grandfather.
What was th(e) impediment that broke this off?

greedie pestiferovs demands from fag Harrie, 'n' what matter th' woe that th' fib hard-dik wd

89 & 90

The French Embassador vpon that instant Crav'd audience; and the houre I thinke is come,

impose on his subiects. Ha, ha, the men who never retvrned didn't reckon t' find that caa-caa

91 & 92

To giue him hearing: is it foure a Clock? It is. / Then goe we in, to know his Embassie:

rat so keen abovt ecksecuting—I, I, I, I! Whom? He's missing it al i' the fog! Woe! He nor I

93 & 94

Which I could with a ready guesse declare, Before the Frenchman speake a word of it.

can C how t' finish R awful epic: he wd leaue ye horror as dog meat—E-e-e! I'd hack d' best Fre—

95 & 96

Ile wait vpon you, and I long to heare it.
Where is my gracious Lord of Canterbury?

nchy no-love wu-scene for R MT Harry 'n' a poor lost lady tu await bed. I, I, I, I! Egregiou—

97 & 98

Not here in presence./ Send for him, good Vnckle.
Shall we call in th(e) Ambassador, my Leige?

s arrangein' serves t' lend hipe to R leman scene—small chance of bed-ioy! Who'll go hide? K.M.

99 & 100

Not yet, my Cousin: we would be resolv'd, Before we heare him, of some things of weight,

No, Hebe: ye rummy sluff'l seem better when I-we do't onstage wi' good voices. Hi-ho for w—

101 & 102

That taske our thoughts, concerning vs and France.
God and his Angels guard your sacred Throne,

el-trained SSS actors uuho can tvrn egregious fakery t' touch 'n' go, hard 'n' hot, 'n' add grand changes.

Marlowe pays tribute to the actors.

103 & 104

And make you long become it. / Sure we thanke you.
My learned Lord, we pray you to proceed,

We leaue ye MT uuork-booke to R good player co., 'N' Ce? O, man, ye new play hits! A ruddy dreem—'n'

105 & 106

And iustly and religiously vnfold(e),
Why the law Salike, that they haue in France,

each of us thinks h-he did it all alone! I'll never say d' awful truth 'n' get in ye way a' y—

107 & 108

Or should or should not barre vs in our Clayme:
And God forbid, my deare and faithfull Lord,

ell'd ynsults 'n' lood h-horrid humyliations. Dreadful man! A boor-bore crvd-oaf—a drudge for

109 & 110

That you should fashion, wrest(e) or bow your reading,
Or nicely charge your vnderstanding Soule,

color'd raw betrayals of innocent Goy religious dissenters. Ah, Ned! Oh, why don't U uuorry? U gave R h—

111 & 112

With opening Titles miscreate, whose right
Sutes not in native colours with the truth:

opeless he-re-ti-ti-ti-ti-ti-tics tv th' galows, when there was nothin' uurong—no crime! Thus t—

113 & 114

For God doth(e) know(e), how many now in health,
Shall drop their blood(e), in approbation

h' family'l hate th' rat who kils th' dear bro! O-O—no one'd win when Pop'd open d' loo 'n' grab—oi!

115 & 116

Of what your reverence shall incite vs to.
Therefore take heed(e) how you impawne our Person,

Ned enioys others' pain. We fear re my future: a lack o' protection here! He who loves th' Vere wou—

117 & 118

How you awake our sleeping Sword of Warre;
We charge you in the name of God take heed(e):

ld risk defamation, euen death. O, woe! He forewarns U—we cop ye keywee, g-go a hog-raw hour

119 & 120

For never two such Kingdomes did contend,
Without much fall of blood, whose guiltlesse drops

'n' sleep. Cu-cu, he rols me out of bed—thud—t't' shiver on th' cold f-floor, 'n' addled, I kiss mi own wogswog.

121 & 122

Are every one, a Woe, a fore Complaint,
'Gainst him, whose wrongs gives edge vnto the Swords,

Dawn: I'm sore, weary. 'E'd hvnt vvi' his falcon; so, eager t' get a heron, we go. E-e-e! Stop! I'm s-so wrong!

123 & 124

That makes such waste in briefe mortalitie.
Vnder this Coniuration, speake my Lord:

A storm here! He sent da man back. We come t' ye tavern t' drink R fil—a lout stops us: "Hi-i-i-i-i!"

125 & 126

For we will heare, note, and beleeve in heart,
That what you speake is in your Conscience washt,

He says, "We're real ole friends, 'n' how about a pint or two? 'N' chicken shit, U can't leave yit!" E-e-e! Ha! We

127 & 128

As pure as sinne with Baptisme
Then heare me gracious Soueraigne, & (and) you Peers

stop in surprise, C, 'n' he says, "Ai, ai, ai! Remember uuhen o' Pegasus went o'er th' edge, 'n' a—a—

129 & 130

That owe your selues, your liues, and services,
To this Imperiall throne. There is no barre

real steep ivy-stretch strain'd 'er ol' ass, 'n' U 'n' I, we brot 'er home i' th' uuee hours, realy slo. O, I—I

131 & 132

To make against your Highnesse Clayme to France,
But this which they produce from Pharamond,

chance t' say, 'Me, I'm cold!' We stop tu haue grog. O, my frins, each day I thank both U 'n' her, for R mistep! Ha'

133 & 134

In terram Salicam Mulieres ne succedaul,
No Woman shall succeed in Salike Land:

drinks uui' me!" Mean Ned, a clam, auerts 'is head in scorn. Silence. Clam. 'e allows all cu—

135 & 136

Which Salike Land, the French vniustly gloze
To be the Realme of France, and Pharamond

cu balk! I apologize 'n' say we'l rest h-here, 'n' Ned half-offer'd t' cave in 'n' hand me th' malt. O, Chr.!

137 & 138

The founder of this Law(e) and Female Barre.
Yet their owne Authors faithfully affirme,

Hello! He twist'd 'n' threuu it far away from my hand, 'n' I feel a hateful stare before I offer

139 & 140

That the land Salike is in Germanie,
Between the Flouds of Sala and of Elue:

talk. A fuss: in anger, he, Ned, *boot-n-shafted* me! Aie! I fell! He went outside, all a—

141 & 142

Where Charles the Great having subdu'd the Saxons,
There left behind and settled certaine French:

ghast at th' crude Chr. Seen bleedin' extravagantlee under th' table inside, C. "Sh-h, sh-h! We'd not refer f—

143 & 144

Who holding in distaine the German Women,
For some dishonest manners of their life,

rom now on to 'e mans error in falling on his shaft! Tho' he's demented, we feed him." I-I sign

145 & 146

Establisht then this Law; to wit, No Female
Should be Inheritrix in Salike Land:

I'l stand, 'n' R host aids me, but I'l not walk—I feel his extra blo in th' nee. I'l whet his a—

147 & 148

Which Salike (as I said) twixt
Elue and Sala,/Is at this day(e) in Germanie, call'd Meisen.

nger. Can I walk? I test—I-I miss! As I slid, he held me in a dance a' hye distaste. I wax all au—

149 & 150

Then doth it well appear the Salike Law(e)
Was not deuised for the Realme of France:

thoritee: "Ned, saue Kit at once or he'l f-f-fall dead! See, he's all ripp't raw 'n' wet!" Homewa—

151 & 152

Nor did the French possesse the Salike Land,/Vntill foure hundred one and twentie yeeres

rd Chr. rode, utterly weak. The nut feels no pain for his nonnie, senseless deed. 'N' add the vile

153 & 154

After defunction of King Pharamond,
Idly suppos'd the founder of this Law(e),

coldness of Ned toward ye ol' man uuho offer'd the drinks! P-U! Naif, I fight t' app—

155 & 156

Who died within the yeere of our Redemption,
Foure hundred twentie six(e): and Charles the Great

eer t' ride rite when I feel d' horse go her own uuay. If Ned expected me t' head to th' dri wash, no, I turn

157 & 158

Subdu'd the Saxons, and did feat the French
Beyond the River Sala, in the yeere

'n' trot—de-de-de-de—far auuay to d' bushes, faintin' 'n' breathless, C? He, ye Rex, 'n' I, de H-H—

159 & 160

Eight hundred five. Besides, their Writers say,
King Pepin, which deposed Childerike,

H-Hebe, ride: R pride kept vs goin'. We circled. It's dark . . . if I die . . . he . . . he signs: I push t' ye end. Wh—

161 & 162

Did as Heire Generall, being descended of Blithild, which was Daughter to King Clothair,

en we reach'd th' building I dragg'd 'n' fel on this straw, C? Diabolical, he shrieked, "Go!" He lied t'

163 & 164

Make Clayme and Title to the Crowne of France.
Hugh Capet also, who vsurpt the Crowne

the men: "Sweaty wretch—drank too mvch! He tripp't, fel, 'n' was cut. Fool! Churl! go on, C!" Ae, ae, ae!

165 & 166

Of Charles the Duke of Loraine, sole Heire male/Of the true Line and Stock of Charles the Great:

Can't drag! He cd kill U here—I can't flee! Oh, oh, uale! He leans o'er me—O, Kit, stal! 'e offers to-to refresh

167 & 168

To find(e) his Title with some shewes of truth,
Though in pure truth it was corrupt(e) and naught,

me wi grog! I was helped up t' rest, 'n' th' hot wounds uuere uuash't 'n' stitcht. I, I! In th' offer, th' tort ha—

169 & 170

Convey'd himselfe as th' Heire to th' Lady Lingare,
Daughter to Charlemaine, who was the Sonne

s faded away, 'n' al th' egregious crvelty made nothin'—now he'l restore me as th' h-hi letch—Oi! 'N' he a—

171 & 172
To Lewes the Emperour, and Lewes the Sonne
Of Charles the Great: also King Lewes the Tenth,

nnounc't we were t' restore a shaggee pla (eek!) he writ 'n' almost lost on the shelf. He tels he'd e—

173 & 174
Who was sole Heire to the Vsurper Capet,
Could not keepe quiet in his conscience, Ecce, veo. Behold, I see

dit what I prepare, 'n' we'l shouu it to the queen. O no, sick process! Ecce, veo his cleen

175 & 176
Wearing the Crowne of France, 'till satisfied,
That fair Queene Isabel, his Grandmother,

quiet manner's a big lie! After I, a friend, offer words, he'l cheat—start stealin,' hog-chewin'

177 & 178
Was Lineall of the Lady Ermangare,
Daughter to Charles the foresaid Duke of Loraine:

al changes. He'l hurl dread insults if I make an error, or defeated, flee a-away t' th' loo, go

179 & 180
By the which Marriage, the Lyne of Charles the Great
Was re-vnited to the Crowne of France.

hide from scorn. He's yl; I regret it, bvt why not fear the real Gew-hate factor, when—Chee! An ac—

181 & 182
So, that as cleare as is the Summers Sunne, King Pepins Title, and Hugh Capets Clayme,

t damagin' as a cut comes, then suppress't hate'l rise again, 'n' (stinky lech—P U!) He'l seem s—

183 & 184
King Lewes his satisfaction, all appeare
To hold in Right and Title of the Female:

o rite in his freakie p-p shaftie that soon I'll meet death falling at d' gallows! C: en—

185 & 186
so doe the Kings of France vnto this day(e).
Howbeit, they would hold(e) vp this Salique Law,

vision his awful ioy at seein' others dye. O, get back! Quash th' ol' thot! I'ue been thru more from him la—

187 & 188
To barre your Highnesse clayming from the Female,
and rather chuse to hide them in a Net(te),

egm seen in Ned after al that scorchin' hate yesterday? Th' hog! I'ue been thru more from him la—

189 & 190

Then amply to imbarre their crooked Titles,
Vsurpt from you and your Progenitors.

tely then a man cd take, but—horror! I grieve o'er d' miss't opportunity for sly promo. U R

191 & 192

May I with right and con(fid)ence make this claim?
The sinne vpon my head, dread Soueraigne:

to hear: Roger'd have me as Ned's aide if he's made king 'n' they aim t' put him down in ani cyclic n—

193 & 194

For in the Booke of Numbers is it writ,
When the man dyes, let the Inheritance

o-rite fuss. E'en first in birth 'n' ye lawe, how'dhemeetmenhott' thro' backeinni—

195 & 196

Descend(e) vnto the Daughter. Gracious Lord,
Stand(e) for your owne, vnwind(e) your bloody Flagge,

nny tu nowhere? I feel sorry for d' snob. 'N' dad wd ayd d' vnsocial creature: he'd love U tu get go-go-go

197 & 198

Looke back into your mightie ancestors:
Goe my dread Lord, to your great Grandsires Tombe,

t' get ryd o' Ned's mean habits in good games o' dice! O, O, Ay! Til some error brot ugly terror, C: kuak!!

kuak! onomatapoetic word for thwack?

199 & 200

From whom you clayme; inuoke his Warlike Spirit,
And your Great Vncles, Edward the Black Prince,

We'l always haue a hard-up look: I'm t' B D' gym cocksucker drifter to my snarlin' nowhere prince. I've i—

201 & 202

Who on the French ground(e) play'd a Tragedie,
Making defeat on the full Power of France:

mprou'd nothin'—no hope! Get free—clear off, C? Gee, Kit, why flag now? D' U fear d' late Anne? Hard!

d' late Anne? Marlowe is recalling autumn, 1588. When he returned to England from Paris he learned Oxford's abandoned wife Anne had died on 6 June. While in Paris, Marlowe had written All's Well for Ned, trying to teach Ned to be kinder to his wife, but now it was too late—she was gone.

203 & 204

Whiles his most(e) mightie Father on a Hill
Stood smiling, to behold(e) his Lyons Whelpe

She's gone. Sillie—lost for ay! Th' ill S.O.B. won't lament! Pig! He'l do it! Hide him—show him she—

205 & 206

Forrage in blood(e) of French(e) Nobilitie.
O Noble English, that could entertaine

'd been hurt 'n' left t' die in grief, C? He'l regret he bot a lo, lo nonni liason! O, O, O, Fie! B ac—

207 & 208

With halfe their Forces, the full pride of France,
And let another halfe stand laughing by(e),

cepting of d' fatal error! U both regret d' way Ann's death'l finallie affect us: I'l flee, 'n' h-h-h-h-he

209 & 210

All out of worke, and cold for action.
Awake remembrance of these valiant dead,

went off sick. Freed, I learn'd abovt law, made a lot o' hack drama, 'n' once, to reueal o—

learn'd about law. off-hand acceptance of an opportunity for legal study—at Clement's Inn?

211 & 212

And with your puissant arme renew their Feats:
You are their Heire, you sit vpon their Throne;

pinions dear t' Father's heart, I writ an o'er-th'-top essay. They worry uuhen I never uurite home. I—

o'er-th'-top essay. Theses Martinianae—Kit's contribution to the Marprelate Papers. **uurite home**. To the Marleys in Canterbury.

213 & 214

The Blood(e) and Courage that renowned them,
runs in your Veines: and my thrice-puissant(e) Liege

'd a hit, 'n' was bein' such a greedy egotist only Hen rever'd me: I dreamt o' nonni uuealth, C? Neuer stop

I'd a hit. Tamburlaine, at the Rose Theater on the Bankside.

215 & 216

Is in the very May-Morne of his Youth,
Ripe for Exploits and mightie Enterprises.

'n' see ye extent of my vtter foolishness! Riding mi hi horse, I-I hope tu marry a p-pri—

217 & 218

Your Brother Kings and Monarchs of the Earth(e).
Doe all expect, that you should rowse your selfe,

ncess: th' louely dark-eyed poetess at th' gamin' house—oy! 'N' oh! U offer her all th' extra U cd borrow or

219 & 220

As did the former Lyons of your Blood(e).
They know(e) your Grace hath cause, and means, and might;

earn. Many nyghts she 'n' I made l'amour tyl d' break o' day, C, when oh, so sore, I'd haue t' go off o'er t' d' Cu—

221 & 222

So hath your Highnesse: neuer King of England
Had Nobles richer, and more loyall subiect(e)s,

t. I begin t' C no free release: I'm kyll'd! She's a hore, 'n' U R such an asshole! Nobody'l gain! Go! H-hundre—

d' Cut. A street on the Bankside near the Rose Theater.

223 & 224

Whose hearts have left their bodyes here in England,
And lye pavillion'd in the fields of France.

ds of hi lovers have lain in h-her elegant bed. She'd ne'er wed any lo city person, 'n' I'l flee afta th' dif—

hi lovers. Emilia Bassano was the mistress of the Lord Chamberlain.

225 & 226

O let their bodyes follow my deare Liege
With Blood(e)s, and Sword(e) and Fire, to win your Right.

fuse agony o'desire is ended. W-wit addl'd, I groan before her, try to B worthwhile, yet I'm lo, lo, lo.

227 & 228

In ayde whereof, we of the Spiritualitie
Will rayse your Highnesse suche a mightie Summe,

Yet together, she laughs al nite, 'n' I h-hope she'll use me f-foreuer. I, I, I! U C, I'd miss ye way I'm raw wi'

229 & 230

As never did the cleergie at one time
Bring to any of your ancestors.

activity. 'N' it costs! Yet, in error, a green fool Hebe gaue on demand. R s—

231 & 232

We must not onely arme t' invade the French,
But lay downe our proportion(e)s, to defende

trip-affectation veers toward dreem o' honest loue. E-e! R U nonny? But n-no! Weep! Hy M.D. told

233 & 234

Against the Scot, who will make roade vpon vs,
With(e) all advantages.

vs she was pregnant! She hated Kit! "Avv, O-o-o!" 'N' call'd 'im "all wet!" I go awa' t'

235 & 236

They of those Marches, gracious Soueraign,
Shall be a Wall sufficient to defend(e)

C, C? So she g-gets off wi' Hen 'n' later lies, sayin' he father'd mi bastard. UUoe! Fool! U clea—

sayin' he father'd mi bastard. Em seduced Hen; he took her to a lodge called Whitly on his Southampton estate. Kit writes about the affair in L's L's Lost, in the heartbroken last lines of Act III (First Folio):

> "A whitly wanton, with a veluet brow,
> With two pitch bals stuck in her face for eyes.
> I, and by heauen, one that wil doe the deede,
> Though Argus were her Eunuch and her garde.
> And I to sigh for her, to watch for her,
> To pray for her, go to: it is a plague
> That Cupid will impose for my neglect,
> Of his almighty dreadful little might.
> Well, I will loue, write, sigh, pray, shue, grone,
> Some men must loue my Lady, and some Jone."

Marlowe alerted Hen's watchdog Florio, and Hen was promptly sent off (August '92) to study at Oxford (C.C. Stopes. The Life of Henry, Third Earl of Southampton. p. 50. Whitely, p. 27). Em, hoping for child support, tried to make Hen believe *he* had fathered her unborn child. In spite of what Marlowe told him, Hen felt responsible and must have offered funds privately. In 1604 her husband Fonso seems to have pressed for more; in that year Hen gave Alfonso Lanier 6d. on every load of hay, 3d. on every load of straw brought into London and Westminster until 1624. (A.L. Rowse. Intro. The Poems of Shakespeare's Dark Lady. NY: Clarkson Potter, p 19.)

237 & 238

Our in-land from the pilfering Borderers.
We do not meane the coursing snatchers onely,

forgot 'n' inform Hen o' Em's repellent habit o' lyin': he's generous; I'm crude, 'n' O! darn scared!

239 & 240

But feare the maine intendment of the Scot,
Who hath been still a giddy neighbour to vs;

She'd wed Lanier, refuse me sight o' th' tit-babe, tho' Hen can go in 'n' out any time. Bvt he told F—

241 & 242	
For you shall reade, that my great Grandfather Neuer went with his forces into France,	**onso that if he, that rat, 'd rescue 'n' marry her, ye child'l ne'er suffer want. O, wait! O, gag! Fren—**
243 & 244	
But that the Scot on his vnfurnisht Kingdome, Came pouring like the Tyde into a breach(e),	**chie, th' reekie t-tosspot fool, might drink uuhat Hen 'n' I give, 'n' my babe cd starue! O, can't th' n—**
245 & 246	
With ample and brim fulnesse of his force, Galling the gleaned Land(e) with hot Affraye	**ew *flagship iob* start now? Em 'n' I'd marry, 'n' glad t' flee, sail off t' Uenice—Hen half-glad. He's he—**
247 & 248	
Girding with grievous siege, Castles and Townes: That England being emptie of defence,	**re. She eiects me, C? 'N' w-weds fat Fonsi! Egregious ending! I pledge t' begin again that vntold**
249 & 250	
Hath shooke and trembled at th' ill neighbourhood. She hath bin the(n) more fear'd the(n) harm(e)d, my Liege	**dream o' honest study I left b-behind: Let th' h-hore go! Remember mi Dad 'n' learn th' H-H-Halakah! Oi! Get h-hone—**
251 & 252	
For heare her but exampl'd by her selfe, When all her Chevalrie hath been in France,	**st! Ha! Error! I'm tv fall 'n' be an exile, C: "Aye, U can ne'er be freed!" Blah! We prefer h-h-h-h-h-hel!**
253 & 254	
and shee a mourning Widdow of her Nobles, Shee hath herselfe not onely well defended,	**Dead, I sail, 'n' free slaues wrongly held. O, don't see h-h-h-how t' free *me*, d' d' nonnee flown Hebe!**
255 & 256	
But taken and impounded as a Stray, The King of Scots; whom shee did send to France,	**Ransom saues me—I ship out, go fast t' Candy 'n' back. I wed—don't kno th-h d-dates! Ne'er def—**

Candy. Candia, Crete. See ciphers, 3 Henry VI. This message in a late rewrite of Henry V is a pale memoir of events in 1593/4.

257 & 258

To fill King(e) Edwards fame with prisoner King(e)s,/And make their Chronicle as rich(e) with prayse,

ame her! Danger, C—she's promised! We go—sail, fly! We dockt 'n' ran with kin t' seek th' friar 'n' chapel! I, I, I! Ri—

dockt 'n' ran with kin. Marlowe sailed from Candia to Venice with his bride, Marina Cicogna, and her aunt who was her nurse. They docked (on the Lido?) at evening (ciphers in 3 Henry VI) and married at a church of St Mary before sailing across the lagoon to the city in the dark, guided by bellbouys (ciphers, 3 Henry VI).

259 & 260

As is the Owse and bottome of the Sea With sunken Wrack(e), and sum-lesse Treasuries.

ta in her sweet best. (O, O! U must kno a krass sea-snatch.) We wed, 'n' rest i' d' familee's house.

261 & 262

But there's a saying very old and true, If that you will France win, then with Scotland first begin.

we'l g-go find a hut-stand to B R own, near the university; she'l sew, 'n' I'l try t' teach a difficult binary

263 & 264

For once the Eagle (England) being in prey, To her Vnguarded Nest(e), the Weazell (Scot)

theological theory wi' zeal, 'n' t' heal d' grudges, see? 'N' t' B open, C? 'N' never negate need fr—

265 & 266

Comes sneaking, and so sucks her Princely Egges,
Playing the Mouse in absence of the Cat,

om ye nonny past—'n' gee, gee, B glad for her louing kiss 'n' this success, C? Hen, speak t' me, Ace! I C, a—

267 & 268

to tame and hauocke more then she can eate.
It followes the (n)u, the Cat must stay at home,

fta uue wed, that the theme o' man's loue-cantata is ne'er lost, C? My thots ha'e come t' kno, ahe—

the u. The n is printed upside-down. I think it's meant to be used as an n and also as a u.

269 & 270

Yet that is but a crush'd necessity,
Since we have lockes to safegard necessaries,

ad, ye essence of what ye lass thinks, See?Bring it t' succeed as it occurs t' her. Saue a

271 & 272

And pretty traps to catch the petty theeves
While that the Armed hand doth fight abroad,

tear for the end o' th'—th'—th'—th'—th'—th' happy attractive plan! By October-t-time, she was dead, dead! Reg—

273 & 274

Th(e) aduised head defends it selfe at home:
For gouernment, though high, and low, and lower,

ret, greef sent me low, so long ago! R infant saved me—I had t' h-hold 'n' feed it. H-how? U'd h-have d-d—

So long ago! This reminiscence was perhaps created as he prepared Henry V for inclusion in a folio proposed by Edward Blount, c. 1618.

275 & 276

Put into parts, doth keepe in one consent,
Congreeing in a full and natural close, like Musicke.

one it easier. A gentle couu gaue milk to feed R apt little child, 'n' I n-n-kno success, 'n' n-n-kno appro—

277 & 278

Therefore doth heaven divide
The state of man in diverse functions,

achin' d' adversitee o' fatherhood is somethin' different, nevv, tu ente—

279 & 280

Setting endevour in continual motion:
To which is fixed as an ayme or butt,

rtain. I—uue—soon exit Italy 'n' go to find 'n' stawi Manco, much th' best Done'er I'v—

281 & 282

Obedience for so worke the Hony Bees,
Creatures that by a rule in Nature teach(e)

e seen. We care for th' babe uuhile others tryck 'n' betray us! E-e-e! O, I can't read on! Hot—

283 & 284

The Act of Order to a peopled Kingdome,
They have a King, and Officers of sorts,

hate! O, O, O! D' man's gov't. pay confiscated, in odd freakish error. He fot, kept gleef—

freakish error. William Byron. Cervantes, A Biography. NY: Doubleday, 1978, explicates these errors on pp. 374-376. On p. 375: "(Cervantes) will be bedevilled . . . for years afterward and made to suffer centuries of accusation of muddleheadedness, dishonesty, irresponsibility—none of them true . . . . he should have returned to Madrid with a decent profit for his ninety-day commission of just under 50,000 maravedis (about 1,450 reales). Instead, because of . . . royal auditors, he was a loser in time, money and reputation. A review of his accounts will measure both the depth of his indignation and the breadth of the wrong done him."

285 & 286

Where some like magistrates correct at home:
Others, like Merchants venter Trade abroad:

vl creditors awae. Here came aid th' Resistance sent to K.! Al goes better. O, m-mark th' error he m—

287 & 288

Others, like Souldiers armed in their stings,
Make boote vpon the Summers Velvet buddes:

ade. Less, even less then meek—dim, dvmb, 'e paid out the govt.'s boorish mis-uuritten errors! Kl—

289 & 290

Which pillage, they with merry march(e) bring home;
To the Tent-royal of their Emperor;

eerly he let go th' cheater who hit him—a poor plan! We both feer him, 'n' grim, I try t' C my err—

291 & 292

Who busied in his Maiesties surveyes
The singing Masons building roofes of Gold,

or, givin' money for a non-debt. I sho him: suggest dis fuss is sillie. We begin de sho a' su—

293 & 294

The civil Citizens kneading vp the hony;
The poore Mechanicke Porters, crowding in

per Eng. storm. H-he—we—vvork t' spoil cannon in Cádiz, C? H-he kept goin,' C? I, I! Chee! R identity?

295 & 296

Their heavy burthens at his narrow gate:
The sad-ey(e)d Iustice with his surly humme

Ammo stewards, viewin' al the hi hi hi guns t' B sure they're ready t' trust, C? Hu, ha! His eye

297 & 298

Delivering ore to Executors pale,
The lazie yawning Drone: I this inferre,

tels size o' d' openin' on every gun. He fitted each in error wi' il, extra large i—

299 & 300

That many things having full reference
To one content, may work contrariously,

ron ammo, so anyone trying t-t' shoot the heavy gun wil fail, C? 'N' after R recent luck, 'n'

301 & 302

As many Arrowes loosed severall wayes come to one marke: as many wayes meet(e) in one towne,

need o' money, we want some reales sent soon. We covnt ye weeks. A-ay, ay! Error! A-a measli smal mo—

303 & 304

As many fresh streames meet(e) in one salt(e) sea;
as many Lynes close in the Dials center:

ney order comes. He 'n' I necessarilee eat less meat, 'n' at last he says, "Man, if Lent's ye man's

305 & 306

So may a thousand(e) actions once a foote
And in one purpose, and be all well borne

time for absolution, Sancho Peon, we're double-clean: paso nonnee ensalada today."

307 & 308

Without defeat. Therefore to France, my Liege,
Divide your happy England into foure,

We uuait—no raid. No food, only one egg. Cheerful, 'e freed me t' try thievery: daft, I tap Phi—

309 & 310

Whereof, take you one quarter into France,
And you withall shall make all Gallia shake.

l's method o' conquest: take all! We'l al eat like a king! An error: on a hy, hy wal, I haue a fal! Fru—

311 & 312

If we with thrice such powers left at home,
Cannot defend our owne doores from the dogge,

galitee's d' word! The good ships come, 'n' we offer R effort 'n' aid, C? 'N' we're h-hot, 'n' cut 'em out! Oh, we

313 & 314

Let us be worried, and our Nation lose
The name of hardinesse and policie.

bear o'er nouu, fire their ships. Moodee, al de land-cannon stai silent. We do

315 & 316

Call in the Messengers sent by the Dolphin.
Now we are resolv'(e)d, and by God's helpe

deeds! Bvt Ralegh spoils R cool landin'. He goes—why?—between ye spread men 'n' th' hy slen—

317 & 318

And yours, the noble sinewes of our power,
France being ours, wee'l bend it to our Awe,

der peninsula. Huffee boor! R beau souldiers R lost in ye water! We go on, C? Won, to be new

Huffee boor. An angry exchange with Ralegh, who sailed his ship in between the peninsula and the loaded wading men, drowning some of them.

319 & 320

Or breake it all to peeces. Or there wee'l sit,
(Ruling in large and ample Emperie,

masters. I pack 'n' put mi dear girl in R li'l boat, 'n' go t' reelee help 'er. Woe! a reelee e—

321 & 322
Ore France, and all her (almost) Kingly Dukedomes)
Or lay these bones in an vnworthy Vrne,

levatin' change! She'l be wi' ye admyral 'n' me at Avdley End: She'l not kno—kno R s-sorro 'n' furor.

323 & 324
Tomblesse, with no remembrance over them:
Either our History shall with full mouth(e)

Beech bum, I'l stay t' hover ouer her h-home 'til I'm sent t' sel th' Erl's loot (from R humane, w-wi—

325 & 326
Speak freely of our Act(e)s, or else our Grave/Like Turkish mute, shall haue a tonguelesse mouth,

lee foray) at Venice. UUe seek t' sel R take at a huge gross profit—R share o' lousee hulls. U'l kum hom-

hulls. Essex was allowed to sell two? ships captured at Cádiz.

327 & 328
Not worshipt with a waxen Epitaph(e).
Now are we well prepard to know the pleasure

e (ha, ha!), 'n' Essex 'l wr-wr-write—want t' plan a trip to help keep d' Pope out o' R wai when we o—

home (ha ha!). Kit dreams of staying "home" awhile at Audley End with Isabel.

329 & 330
Of our faire Cosin Dolphin(e): for we heare
Your greeting(e) is from him, not from the King.

ffer help to Guarini's ninny high duke Cesario. O-o, he wrote me. I go into Rome fr-from Fer—

331 & 332
May't please your Maiestie to give us leave
Freely to render what we have in charge:

arra t' discover ye holy fee re the whole uuest area. Wee mvl, imagine past negative y—

Wee mvl. We mull. Think it over.

333 & 334
Or shall we sparingly shew you farre off
The Dolphin's meaning, and our Embassie.

ears' fruitless bargaining. Wd offerin' more money help us now? Ha, ha! Sh! Sly olde Pa

335 & 336
We are no Tyrant, but a Christian King(e)
Vnto whose grace our passion is as subiect(e)

wants cash ta couer waitin' proiects. UUe agree, 'n' sore Gvarini 'n' I take b-booty (Sh!) s-sn—

337 & 338
As is our wretches fettered in our prisons,
Therefore with franke and with vncurbed plainnesse,

ail-pace t' the west. Horrors! The coffer drops in a riuer t' sink! We turn, see shinin' under d' waves, 'n' bef—

339 & 340

Tell vs the Dolphins minde. / Thus than in few: Your Highnesse lately sending into France,	**ore we can save it, it's gone—suuept along—fed t' th' ninny, ninny, streem! H-h-hell! Shd—shd I l-lif—**

341 & 342

Did claime some certaine Dukedomes in the right/Of your great Predecessor, King Edward the third.	**t in some kind of catcher? Oy! Go get R casket! Retrieue R treasure! I swim-I'm in a d-d-d-d-d-deep hole! Gr! H-he**

343 & 344

In answer of which claime, The Prince our Master Sayes, that you Savour(e) too much of your youth,	**cals: "Hu, Huu!" I C ye chest, thrown out on a strip of shore, no worse for uuear! I may have it yet—may com—**

345 & 346

and bids you be advis'd: There's nought in France, That can be with a nimble Galliard wonne:	**e out easy. D' ninni current won't let me tovch d' edge! I saw R shining habbadabbah fall in da—**

habbadabbah. a nonsense palindrome.

347 & 348

You cannot revell into Dukedomes there. He therefore sends you meeter for your spirit.	**uuater, sinkyn! Oy! I push over horrid muddy rotten roots. E-e-e-e-e-e, 'n' feel R chest, left moore—**

moored. held by cables: here, by the rotos.

349 & 350

This tun of Treasure; and in lieu of this, Desires you let the dukedomes that you claime	**d in ye uueeds. Haul'd out. Al its mess clean'd off, I tie it on R horse tu hike tu Rome. That's ye**

351 & 352

Heare no more of you. This the Dolphin speakes. What Treasure Vncle? / Tennis balls, my Liege.	**story o' my swim in the river before I see the old pop 'n' he glances at all th' uueal 'n' shakes 'n'**

uueal. Webster 2. [obs.] wealth; riches.

353 & 354

Weare glad the Dolphin is so pleasant with vs, His Present, and your paines we thank you for:	**agrees to R stipvlations 'n' we head away happy, R hearts ful o' kindness. Now he, d' ole shep, intui—**

shep. shepherd.

355 & 356
When we have matcht our Rackets to these Balles,
We will in France (by God's grace) play(e) a set,

tively felt we conceal something. He cals us back: we're t' show we pay'd R share t' enter La Baga

357 & 358
Shall strike his fathers Crowne into the hazard(e).
Tell him, he(e) hath made a match with such a Wrangler,

Secreta. We assure him we did. Ha, Ha! He smiles. We thankt him 'n' left th' Alcazar. H-h-horror! Th' late light can

359 & 360
That all the Court(e)s of France will be(e) disturb'd
With Chaces. and we vnderstand(e) him well,

fool! We came near t' fallin' in th' river at d' street's end, but C, he'd bless'd U all, C, which wd awe th'

361 & 362
How he comes o're vs with our wilder dayes,
Not measuring what vse we made of them.

devils on th' way. We moved: rode far t' rest, ho hum-m, at Guarini's home. W-we chose swee—

363 & 364
We neuer valew'd this poore seate of England,
And therefore living hence, did giue our selfe

t sleepe, restoring worn nerves: we had ached enough in de effort. Did uue fail? I'le leave 'n' goe

365 & 366
To barbarous license: As 'tis ever common,
That men are merriest, when they are from home.

t' Ferarra—move there t' listen t' news o' my success at Rome. No! I hear—hear mi name more hobb—

367 & 368
But tell the Dolphin, I will keepe my State,
Be like a King, and shew my sayle of Greatnesse,

led: th' west'l B held in ye state, 'n' al ye rest goes to King Papa's family! E-e-e! 'N' he'l kwiklie bum

369 & 370
When I do rowse me in my Throne of France.
For that I have layd by my Maiestie,

from Cesare in hy, hy Modena. I fear d' fat yat who bites in envy to orewhelm mi

371 & 372

And plodded like a man for working dayes:
But I will rise there with so full a glorie,

hard work for Guarin'. Likely we'l lose out altogether. Bad piss! Did I mind if all we en—

plaintext: wishful thinking for Ned deVere, the secret prince.

373 & 374

That I will dazle all the eyes of France,
Yes strike the Dolphin blinde to looke on vs,

visiond were stopt? OK—I hiked off in a total daze, then heer th' yells 'n' calls: ye ol' bell—

OK. Startling to see this bit of slang, which has always been considered American.

X
There's more

Fair Em. Quarto.
The Shakespeare Apocrypha. Ed. C. F. Tucker Brooke. Oxford: Clarendon, 1971. p 287.

FAIR EM

1 & 2
What meanes faire Britaines mighty Conqueror
So suddenly to cast away his staffe,

Chr. Marlowe questions sad state after his young f-friend came in with a base toy. Say

X
There's more

Edward III. Quarto.
The Shakespeare Apocrypha. Ed. C. F. Tucker Brooke. Oxford: Clarendon, 1971. p 69.

EDWARD III

1 & 2

Robert of Artoys, banisht though thou be From Fraunce, thy natiue Country, yet with vs

Chr. M. wrote this fou-fou for Bacon, but he, bein' yn a hurry, starts t-to tout ye heavy thing

Kit wrote this after the Babington case broke, 1586/'87.

X
There's more

The Jew of Malta. Quarto. 1633.
Complete Works of Christopher Marlowe. Ed. Fredson Bowers. 2nd ed. p 263.

THE JEW OF MALTA

1 & 2

Albeit the world thinke Machevill is dead, Yet was his soule but flowne beyond the Alpes,

Hidden at ye Blue Vale, lost, banished clown-wit Kit remade this lowest of Hebe plays. U'l he—

3 & 4

And now the Guize is dead, is come from France
To view this Land, and frolicke with his friends.

ar how a hore trick'd Ithimore. Death mvscled in, dancin' 'n' f-f-f-fussin' wi' ze old Iew onstage. Is de—

the Guize. Died on Christmas Eve, 1588.

5 & 6

To some perhaps my name is odious,
But such as loue me, gard me from their tongues,

ath our dusty home? Is no progress possible for us? Come in, Mama; meet th' Geu *U*made!

7 & 8

And let them know that I am Macheuill,
And weigh not men, and therefore not mens words.

He'l hide snares 'n' do mortal damage t' th' enemie. Who d' U mean, that clown Kit, 'n' not Wm.? Fren—

Wm. This is a rewrite, after banishment. Kit thinks of Shakespeare?

9 & 10

Admir'd I am of those that hate me most,
Though some speake openly against my bookes,

ds think him lost, but see, he appears again, to shame th' feo Goy M.D's. O, Kate, O, M-mam, ye, too

feo Goy M.D.'s. ugly gentile doctors.

11 & 12

Yet will they reade me, and thereby attaine to Peters Chayre: And when they cast me off,

thot mee dead, yet C, thy bastard's here, home free. Free! An' he—Will—ye yat captain—went yn t—

13 & 14

Are poyson'd by my climing followers.
I count Religion but a childish Toy,

o town—left me (Chr. M.) ill aboard ship, ill 'n' unconscious, by God! O, Ge! Iy, iy! I try

15 & 16

And hold there is no sinne but Ignorance.
Birds of the Aire will tell of murders past;

t' crawl out o' d' narro bed 'n' get t' shore. I rise, slip 'n' lie still—need a bon ami—f-frend! Hush!

17 & 18

I am asham'd to heare such fooleries.
Many will talke of Title to a Crowne:

Men come—take me t' a doctor's house, al-all weary 'n' sweati. Ai! I roll off th' hi

19 & 20

What right had Caesar to the Empery?
Might first made Kings, and Lawes were then most sure

stretcher, hit th' rug, then weakly raise mi moist head 'n' grasp d' Gew men's feet. O, what drama! S—

21 & 22

When like the Dracos they were writ in blood.
Hence comes it, that a strong built Citadell

lidin' under the doctor's table, I start t' groan—shake wi' chill. I blow on my wet teeth. Cheece!

23 & 24

Commands much more then letters can import:
Which maxime had Phaleris obseru'd,

Exhausted, h-hot, I'm put in a warm bed, 'n' Doc calls mi Mom. She comes t' her charmin' repr—

25 & 26

H'had neuer bellowed in a brasen bull
Of great ones enuy; o' th poore petty wites,

obate 'n' stays to be a louin' n-nurse. O, I feel better, 'n' h-howwd U repay her? Pledge lo—

27 & 28

Let me be enuy'd and not pittied!
But whither am I bound, I come not, I,

uin' aid to her 'til the end o' time. B-b-but I may die now, C? Put end to me, 'n'

29 & 30

To reade a lecture here in Britanie,
But to present the Tragedy of a lew,

I'd neuer do it. So, wearee, feelin' better, I go t' Canterbury heat at her tap

Canterbury heat. Kit came home from the Paris jail at end of August, 1588. Canterbury is in the southeast part of England (a region favored by warmth-loving Romans in the old days).

31 & 32

Who smiles to see how full his bags are cramb'd,
Which mony was not got without my meanes.

house. I rest while Mom tends bar. A Goy-fag-sot blows in. Shye, he wants hot chow; Mam wil cum

33 & 34

I craue but this, Grace him as he deserues,
And let him not be entertain'd the worse

t' get readie-made stew. Th' shie lush can be seen steerin' ouer t' d' bar, mouin' th' chair

35 & 36

Because he favours me.
So that of th(i)s much that returne was made:

out ahead. He must reach th' counter, wash fast, sit, before Mam vues

37 & 38

And of the third part of the Persian ships,
There was the venture summ'd and satisfied.

his fat hands, t' deem him readi t' eat her stew. (She pvts heart 'n' fuss intu preparin' d' food.)

39 & 40

As for those Samnites, and the men of Uzz,/That bought my Spanish(e) Oyles, and Wines of Greece,

Ye man giues money 'n' soon—'n'then—Oops! He fals head-first t' th' stew—'iz face to B shmear'd! U gaze, s—

41 & 42

Here haue I purst their paltry silverlings.
Fye; what a trouble tis to count this trash.

orry! O, hel! In fury th' leerin' bul hits Cate wi' th' plate! "U souse!" I grasp his hat, tear't, trust—

43 & 44

Well fare the Arabians, who so richly pay
The things they traffique for with wedge of gold,

ing power. F-fear th' edgey castaway wil bite. He has th' sign of th' hot old wolf. Her frail query

45 & 46

Where of a man may easily in a day
Tell that which may maintaine him all his life.

came: "Alas, what ails me? 'N' I feel filthy! Let him alone!" I hit him hard: Wam! "Ay, ay, ay!" 'N' in

47 & 48	
The needy groome that neuer fingred groat, Would make a miracle of thus much coyne:	**agony he f-fel on th' ground, leaky chin couered wi' our meat—Mom's great cured meat! The**

49 & 50	
But he whose steele-bard coffers are cramb'd full, and all his life time hath bin tired,	**old lush-sot dreams in bubbles. After I fr-freed Ma 'n' bathed her, I call th' elf—watch. Ei, ei!**

elf-watch. The watchman was a little man.

51 & 52	
Wearying his fingers ends with telling it, Would in his age be loath to labour so,	**What t' du wi' ye insensate weight o' floor'd Giu boor? I'l get a sling. He'l B snarlin' his**

53 & 54	
And for a pound to sweat himselfe to death:/Giue me the Merchants of the Indian Mynes,	**oaths. Haue t' get 'im out! Mom stands wan 'n' defeated, 'n'-'n' ye timid officer's no help. He hear—**

55 & 56	
That trade in mettall of the purest mould, The wealthy Moore, that in the Easterne rockes	**s a D.T. cry, 'n' tells me, "look, treat!" We three tie a rope ta the man's feet 'n' haul him tu th' door. The**

D.T. delerium tremens.

57 & 58	
Withoute controule can picke his riches up, and in his house heape pearle like pibble-stones,	**torn trousers show his blue, blue knees. O, he's in pain, appealin'! I check d' cheap cloth, put—Ei, ie, ie!**

Withoute controule can pick his riches up. Kit thinks of Alvaro Mendes, rich merchant who lives in Kent, friend and in-law of Roger Manwood and Walsingham. Mendes owned the diamond mines of Narsinga in India.

59 & 60	
Receive them free, and sell them by the weight; Bags of fiery Opals, Saphires, Amatists,	**This Gew's m-met a bad hurt! He'l B a cripple for aie! Finisht! See, s-e-e-e ye ghastly stream of**

61 & 62	
Iacints, hard Topas, grasse-greene Emeraulds, Beauteous Rubyes, sparkling Diamonds,	**black blood! Ae, ae! Disgust! Pus s-stainin' ye gross harem pants. U—U need a rare Dr.'s regime!**

63 & 64

Andseildsenecostlystonesofsogreatprice,
As one of them indifferently rated,

Cart 'im off t' die slo? O, don't! Try care, 'n' see if a feelin' response sends th' edgey snot a l—

65 & 66

And of a Carrect of this quantity,
May serve in perill of calamity

ift—a quieter, less frantic mood. The yat lay in pain. A cry—cal—from U,

67 & 68

To ransome great Kings from captivity.
This is the ware wherin consists my wealth:

Mom: "Can't ye carry 'im straight t' Iohn's shop, 'n' I'l wash 'is wet knees?" We trie. At first U go

69 & 70

And thus me thinkes should men of iudgement frame
Their meanes of traffique from the vulgar trade,

t' Iohn. H-he agreed, lift'd R nouu-quiet madman so Mama's fem efforts uud free 'n' right th' knees after emvl—

71 & 72

And as their wealth increaseth, so inclose
Infinite riches in a little roome.

sion has cleaned more filth. Cate in control, 'n' I enter ta assist her. Wil he—? I, I, Ie!

73 & 74

But now how stands the wind?
Into what corner peeres my Halcions bill?

Th' wry blood 'n' urine spews in an il h-hot W.C. stream down on blithe Cate's

75 & 76

Ha, to the East? yes: See how stands the Vanes?
East and by-South: why then I hope my ships

best shoes. She unties them, steps out away 'n' washed on! Ys the yat past aid, Hen? Oy, H-h-he

Hen. Henry Wriothesley. Kit often writes to this Cambridge friend.

77 & 78

I sent for Egypt and the bordering Iles
Are gotten up by Nilus winding bankes:

open'd eyes 'n' begg'd for red grog, speakin' Latin in th' best, best winnin' uuay, til' R

79 & 80

Mine Argosie from Alexandria,
Loaden with Spice and Silkes, now under saile,

iaws relax 'n' drop. Insane! Odd! Like a medic, I fear loss, 'n' giue him water alone. Sn—

81 & 82

Are smoothly gliding downe by Candie shoare
To Malta, through our Mediterranean sea.

arlin' starts again! Mom, ye true Dr., goes ahead. We get him into bed al clean 'n' dry. Hoo hoo, U R

into bed. At this time the Marleys rented a big place in the middle of town which housed John's shoe-shop and where Kate took room-and-boarders and kept a small tavern.

83 & 84

But who comes heare? How now.
Barabas, Thy ships are safe, riding in Malta Rhode:

t' hear his name! His cheap gay shirt shows an awful boar embroidered on two ba—

85 & 86

And all the Merchants with other Merchandize/Are safe arriu'd, and haue sent me to know

rs on the arm, 'n' ouer a red fez, the name "Hot Will, Shake Mi Sacred Heart!" (Cut Nan dead!) What in—

87 & 88

Whether your selfe will come and custome them.
The ships are safe thou saist, and richly fraught.

anity! Il, he must suffer, forget, sleep, rest, cancel 'e mad show o' his red h-h-hot chemistry. What a lauu

89 & 90

They are. / Why then goe bid them come ashore,
And bring with them their bils of entry:

wd say o' holdin' him here? E-e! Who brot him here at th' first, C? 'N' the bang-byte-greetin' my

91 & 92

I hope our credit in the Custome-house
Will serue as well as I were present there.

Ma receiued shows his true rip-torn-cut hopeless state. E-e-e-e! Will he euer win, or l—

93 & 94

Goe send 'um threescore Camels, thirty mules,
And twenty Waggons to bring up the ware.

et us B on edge? I suggest we cart him away t' rot—or shd we relent 'n' help ye gros MT man? U C, n—

The author is not stalling, just making it bitterly clear that he could have destroyed Shakespeare early on.

95 & 96

But art thou master in a ship of mine,
And is thy credit not enough for that?

ot attacht t' sense, I try t' nurse him—bend 'n' drop him to 'n' fro. Ai, Ai! Houu th' fag

bend 'n' drop him. physical therapy.

97 & 98

The very Custome barely comes to more
Then many Merchants of the Towne are worth,

's torn! Tho' he moves now, he can't stay alone. We C frothy matter here, but ere my Mom re-c—

99 & 100

And therefore farre exceeds my credit, Sir.
Goe tell 'em the Jew of Malta sent thee, man:

leans ye damaged ioints h-he'l meet R tests, free o' error 'n' extreme effect. I watch lamed

101 & 102

Tush, who amongst 'em knowes not Barrabas?
I goe. / So then, there's somewhat come.

motions—mark t' see how soon th' snob can go home. He trusts me; w-we agree. Shabat—

103 & 104

Sirra, which of my ships art thou Master of?
Of the Speranza, Sir. / And saw'st thou not/ Mine Argosie at Alexandria?

h is th' day t' fare forth. I prepare t-t' cast out 'n' shun th' s-swan wazir—for ai! Ai, ai, ai! Mom's good RX 'n' moral sense has

swan. In secret service jargon, a swan is a male whore.
wazir. The invalid arrived wearing Turkish pants.

105 & 106

Thou couldst not come from Egypt, or by Caire,
But at the entry there, into the sea,

left 'im better, so by now he can go out 'n' try that post road home. Ie-e-e! T-try, C? The cr—

107 & 108

Where Nilus payes his tribute to the maine,
Thou needs must saile by Alexandria.

ude shit! Let's see! It's late—he's turnin' in at a bar. Ei, ei! (He's da man who'l B my proxy!) UUe

109 & 110

I neither saw them, nor inquir'd of them.
But this we heard some of our sea-men say,

soon see him return tu the road wi' a fem friend. Bi th' moon she requests him away.

111 & 112	
They wondred how you durst with so much wealth Trust such a crazed Vessell, and so farre.	**Uncle 'n' th' murderous shrew lvrch'd across ye road. The two faded, lost i' th' hazy waste. U-U-sw—**
113 & 114	
Tush, they are wise; I know her and her strength: But goe, goe thou thy wayes, discharge thy Ship,	**ine! T' hasten t' destroy thy good knee repairs wi' this sweet shy whore! Ugh, ugh, ugh! By the chara—**
115 & 116	
And bid my Factor bring his loading in. And yet I wonder at this Argosie.	**de, a big asignation in ye bog. Wham! 'N' a sad cry—her foot slid in dirt—dirt 'n'**
117 & 118	
Thine Argosie from Alexandria, Know Barabas, doth ride in Malta Rhode,	**water! Horror! Hear her! Mam is sinkin'! Go—'n' extend aid—all aid! A bo-boat! Daf—**
119 & 120	
Laden with riches, and exceeding store Of Persian silkes, of gold, and Orient Perle.	**t fools, t' leap in R swale! I look 'n' see no sign except her head. I find d-de ridge near R sc—**
121 & 122	
How chance you came not with those other ships That sail'd by Egypt? / Sir we saw 'em not.	**rub woods 'n' approach ye woman. She swims in th' t-toilet as ye-ye hog watches the chitt—**
123 & 124	
Belike they coasted round by Candie shoare About their Oyles, or other businesses.	**erin' slut sink. Oy! I hold out a dead branch to her: she sees it, beats ouer. See ye boob cry!**
125 & 126	
But 'twas ill done of you to come so farre Without the ayd or conduct of their ships.	**I pull, try to free her o' mud. Too hot hot-nut, coo-coo W.S. waits by th' side, sufferin'. A cad,**
127 & 128	
Sir, we were wafted by a Spanish Fleet That neuer left vs till within a league,	**dear Will! I strive, al wet, 'n' it baffles U, pal, th' way he neuer gets his feet wet! An—**

129 & 130
That had the Gallies of the Turke in chase.
On they were going up to Sicily:

y one else I kno wd haue helpt to fish her out! At last I get hy: Gig-catch her! I

Gig-catch. Webster. a rowboat used for racing, or a long, light ship's boat.

131 & 132
Well, goe / And bid the Merchants and my men dispatch
And come ashore and see the fraught discharg'd.

edge near, 'n' Cher scrambled in, almost dead. She, coated with th' muddy sand, 'n' he, th' cheap fag, in orgasm.

133 & 134
I goe. / Thus trowles our fortune in by land and Sea,
And thus are we on every side inrich'd:

I led ye shiverin', wrung out creature onto ye road. She ran—fast as wind! Undone, he slid b—

135 & 136
These are the Blessings promis'd to the Iewes,
And herein was old Abrams happinesse:

ehind some trees, 'n' I heard a s-splash—was *'e* in the bog? O, please! He'd better swim! R.I.P., sans

137 & 138
What more may Heauen doe for earthly man
Then thus to powre out plenty in their laps,

any hope o' help! Rant-nut, U deserue t' lie in the trap, lost to harm, away from thy home, 'n' we'—

139 & 140
Ripping the bowels of the earth for them,
Making the Sea their seruant, and the winds

d ignore it. I h-hear weak shouts, 'n' mi heart bleeds. I f-fret 'n' hasten t' greet th' man who p-p'—

141 & 142
To drive their substance with successefull blasts?
Who hateth me but for my happiness?

d on Mother's shoes. He's passive i' th' water. "Can't U climb thru th' swill t' escape, Bub? Tuff!" Ys 'e

143 & 144
Or who is honour'd now but for his wealth?
Rather had I a Iew be hated thus,

awash? Oh, rouu! Wish he'd bob! Now I hear his frothin' throat-rattle! Wd U dee—

145 & 146
Then pittied in a Christian poverty:
For I can see no fruits in all their faith,

p-dive far 'n' stay there? No trace? If I—I C a foot risin' up, then I'l—I'l hasten in th' tri—

147 & 148

But malice, falshood, and excessive pride,/Which me thinkes fits not their profession.	**cksie boat t' heave him in. Does he stil exist? I fume, 'n' press forward slo, C, 'n' chop in fetid h—**

149 & 150

Happily some haplesse man hath conscience, And for his conscience liues in beggery.	**oles—chop, 'n' chop, in ye gassy bog. Aha! A hit! I feel his presence under me, 'n' C—'n' C—lisis came, 'n'**

lisis. Greek. lysis. a freeing-up, an improvement, a loosening.

151 & 152

They say we are a scatter'd Nation: I cannot tell, but we have scambled up	**ye divin' nut rose up breathless 'n' claw-claw'd t' attach t' ye boat 'n' me—Ae! Ae!**

153 & 154

More wealth by farre then those that brag of faith./There's Kirriah Iairim, the great Iew of Greece	**The boat's gone! We share th' water. I try t' float free ere he grab me. I greet him. o, rich affair! Hark! Th' i-i-**

Kirriah Iairim. City of Woods, a town near Jerusalem. Kit is thinking of his dad, Manwood.

155 & 156

Obed in Bairseth, Nones in Portugall, My selfe in Malta, some in Italy,	**diot let me pull 'im to shore! (Ye fat-bal ninny's in insane orgasm.) I, able**

Nones. Nuñes.

157 & 158

Many in France, and wealthy every one: I, wealthier farre then any Christian.	**t' swim, carry 'n' leave ye ninny hi, dry. I hear a whine—a fret-note—he can't lean far**

159 & 160

I must confesse we come not to be Kings: That's not our fault: Alas, our number's few,	**enuf t' reach 'is floatin' bottle. 'E goes ouer! Wow! Fuck! Smart moue! Must B 's Ann's not s—**

Does Kit want to make us so sick of Shakespeare that we won't want any more of him? **Ann.** Ann Hathaway, Shakespeare's wife.

161 & 162

And Crownes come either by succession Or urg'd by force; and nothing violent,	**tandin' by t' aid ye fool cob. C, on th' scene he's growin' ever more gross 'n' cu-cu: drin—**

cob. Webster. a chunky horse, a lump, a male swan.

163 & 164

Oft haue I heard tell, can be permanent.
Give vs a peaceful rule, make Christians Kings,

kin' bottle-ale I th' suuamp, he vvhines, "Releree . . . " 'n' sinks again. Clap-mad, C? Gee! Al f-fracture—

165 & 166

That thirst so much for Principality.
I have no charge, nor many children,

d mental activity, tho' imperfect in origin, can h-h-harro U, sharply, C? No shr—

167 & 168

But one sole Daughter, whom I hold as deare
As Agamemnon did his Iphigen:

il anger, no s-shoutin' wd haue alter'd him. Dim-headed S.O.B., again he goes mop-

169 & 170

And all I haue is hers. But who comes here?
Tush, tell not me 'twas done of policie.

in'—now about th' wench that almost died. I reach for his sleeue. Puleese! Sl-loom!

171 & 172

Come therefore let us goe to Barrabas;
For he can counsell best in these affaires;

He fals—I go to th' bottom! O, cuss! Brace! He releases U! O, flee, ere 'e can transfer brain f—

173 & 174

And here he comes. / Why, how now Countrymen?
Why flocke you thus to me in multitudes?

euer to U! Why not swim out fresh now 'n' leaue him hot? No! Mom wdn't lyke such dycey che—

175 & 176

What accident's betided to the Iewes?
A fleet of warlike gallyes, Barabas,

esey acts. With fear, I get Sh. ta wade back t' drie land, so I feel able ta blow e—

177 & 178

Are come from Turkey, and lye in our Rhode:/ And they this day sit in the Counsell-house

asily auuay to hurry home. I need food, rest. Shit! Don't! U can't! He'l cry more! E-e! He'l sink 'n' d—

179 & 180

To entertaine them and their embassie.
Why let 'em come, so they come not to warre;

rown. O, come on, trie t' meet 'n' lead the MT sot o'er t' the nearby hiway. Seems each time

181 & 182

Or let 'em warre, so we be conquerors:
Nay, let 'em combat, conquer, and kill all,

we start, ye noble q-queer turns back, C? I'm all alone on R road. We'l come more l—

183 & 184

So they spare me, my daughter, and my wealth.
Were it for confirmation of a League,

eisurely! Win! Stay together on th' road! Where'l ye cad turn off? O, I'm agape! A fem-ma'm

185 & 186

They would not come in warlike manner thus.
I fear their comming will afflict us all.

ran t' greet 'im, 'n' all smiles, he uuent rockin' away—for wild flamin' hot chow, U C. I felt mil—

187 & 188

Fond men, what dreame you of their multitudes?
What need they treat of peace that are in league?

dly hopeful he'd stay wi' the fem. I turn toward Cate. I'm far out, hauen't eaten—need ta get home ere a

189 & 190

The Turkes and those of Malta are in league.
Tut, tut, there is some other matter in't.

faintness tether me. I hear a shout. The MT D.T. ogre o'ertakes me! I'ue run out a' all t-t-t-t—

191 & 192

Why, Barabas, they come for peace or warre.
Happily for neither, but to passe along

act: "Goe h-h-home!" I snap. "Please, bro, can't I borrow t' eat supper before y' hy far away? R l—

193 & 194

Towards Venice by the Adriatick Sea;
With whom they haue attempted many times,

ast trip made thee my bro, Kit! Aid mee now, as U have, C?" In this w-way, yet, the MT cad, the

195 & 196

But never could effect their Stratagem.
And very wisely sayd, it may be so.

mad bull, goes off t' eat stew yet, vvi' my recruited cash, as I, needy, try a bren—

197 & 198

But there's a meeting in the Senate-house,
And all the Iewes in Malta must be there.

t twig 'n' a shel in mi mouth 'n' beat it, lest he return! E-e-e! Let Shabath end as U see me ea—

199 & 200

Umh; All the Iewes in Malta must be there?
I, like enough, why then let every man

gerly hikein' home t' Ma'm, 'n' t' meet th' heat a' her heavenly stew! I'l liue wel, 'n' U sub—

201 & 202

Prouide him, and be there for fashion-sake.
If any thing shall there concerne our state

mit t' ordinary fare, Hen. Hopeful t' a'riue before th' kitchen's cold, I go nea-nea-near Sh-Sh.'s

Hen. Hen Wriothesley. **Sh-Sh.'s.** Sh-Shakespeare's

203 & 204

Assure your selues I'le look—unto myselfe.
I know you will; well brethren let us goe.

mire. Whose? Soon—you'll guess—I sank l-l-l-l-low, wet t' ye knee, but roue free o' ye suuill. R—

205 & 206

Let's take our leaues; Farewell good Barabas.
Doe so; Farewell Zaareth, farewell Temainte.

est later! Dark woods—a haze falls o'er R riuer below. An eagle. O, let a few leaues be a meal t-t' f—

207 & 208

And Barabas now search this secret out.
Summon thy sences, call thy wits together:

ill me. I s-stand at ye gate 'n' C R house on R street.
But who's that who chances by Ma's, scr—

ye gate. Canterbury was an ancient walled and gated city. Kit, standing at the West Gate, could see down the high street to the old two-story place the Marleys rented near midtown, on the right side, by St. Mary Breadman.

209 & 210

These silly men mistake the matter cleane.
Long to the Turke did Malta contribute;

atchin' at th' door? It's t-true, C! Let me leaue Kent, 'n' sly, mad Sh.'ll meet me in a bog tree! Kit

211 & 212

Which Tribute all in policie, I feare,
The Turkes haue let increase to such a summe,

All these clues reueal th' front man t' be: Wm. Shakespeare, C? I-i-i! I-i-i! I cu-cut out h-here!

f

Tamburlaine II. Quarto.
Complete Works of Christopher Marlowe. Ed. Fredson Bowers. 2nd ed. p 151.

TAMBURLAINE II

THE PROLOGUE

1 & 2
The generall welcomes Tamburlain receiv'd,
When he arrived last upon our stage,

Marlowe pens th' sad tale. Ecce! Th' ruler's goin' t' uuage blind war merrilee! Hovv nea—

3 & 4
Hath made our Poet pen his second part,
Wher death cuts off the progres of his pomp,

t! H-he'd go off 'n' propose other p.p. murders! A sho of death, C, was therapeutic t' him, 'n' esp—

p.p. piss-poor.

5 & 6
And murdrous Fates throwes al his triumphs down.
But what became of faire Zenocrate,

ousal of a princess was a bizarre act for th' one mutt who murdered maidens. But th' fem h—

fem. w inverts to m.

7, 8 & 9
And with how manie cities sacrifice
He celebrated her said funerall,
Himselfe in presence shal unfold at large.

ad dignitie as a slaue. She's won his heart, 'n' he freed her—welcome t' B his fecund female partner fer all 'n' ai (ill, C? IC, IC!).

THE PLAY

1 & 2
Egregious Viceroyes of these Eastern parts
Plac'd by the issue of great Baiazeth,

Chr.'s past-age story is too eager! See, if ye beavtiful Zenocrate's death grips U, Hebe,

Egregious. A favorite word of Marlowe's. Humorously used by Dickens in double-entendre stories about Marlowe.

3 & 4

And sacred Lord, the mighty Calapine:
Who lives in Egypt, prisoner to that slave,

th' gradval insanity o' th' crvel man's deeds ys not clear i' th' plaie. I wrote P.P.! O, he g—

5 & 6

Which kept his father in an yron cage:
Now have we marcht from faire Natolia

ot a train o' captive men. H-h-ha! Age 'n' worry'l win, 'n' wreck him. his fear of each fat

7 & 8

Two hundred leagues, and on Danubius banks,
Our warlike hoste in compleat armour rest,

son's lack o' hubris (E-e!) degraded his own rauu pouuer t' make MT war. It rolls unto an end, ban—

9 & 10

Where Sigismond the king of Hungary
Should meet our person to conclude a truce.

ning more egregious tuuists, C—C? He look'd only for death, 'n' now he's here, put mad, U C, r—

11 & 12

What? Shall we parle with the Christian,
Or crosse the streame, and meet him in the field?

e her death, which defeats him with that tall horror 'n' incessant MT miserie. We'l please

13 & 14

King of Natolia, let us treat of peace,
We all are glutted with the Christians blood,

all with trick death, but the ill pagan's sufferin' is not clear. E-e! We, too, led a goat to

15 & 16

And have a greater foe to fight against
Proud Tamburlaine, that now in Asia,

slaughter, for th' death of a great ego—an end apart—now must B in vain. Ai, ai, ai! T—

17 & 18

Neere Guyrons head doth set his conquering feet
And means to fire Turkie as he goes:

ried onstage, th' queer hack thing hits, 'ndeed, soon eueryone refers to me as a genius. F—

Turkie. Kit's own spelling in this place in the work, as shown in Octavo 4, 1606.

19 & 20

Gainst him my Lord must you addresse your power. Besides, king Sigismond hath brought from Christendome,	**ame! Fie! I rob mi high study t' uurite plays, B homo, drink 'n' do gross SS deeds. This angers my mom 'n' Roger, who'd cut**

21 & 22

More then his Camp of stout Hungarians, Sclavonians, Almain Rutters, Muffes, and Danes,	**me off, leavin' me a shunn'd lonesome ass, uuho in grim pain turns t' C a tart, C? Hard 'n' fast as s—**

23 & 24

That with the Holbard, Lance, and murthering Axe, Will hazard that we might with surety hold.	**in! What a woman! All I'd C, thru the dazle, was her extremely h-hot bright light that drain'd U wh—**

What a woman! Emilia Bassano, mistress of Sir Henry Carey, Lord Chamberlain, who'd provided her with a villa in Shoreditch where she was hostess for a little gambling club.

25 & 26

Though from the shortest Northern Paralell, Vast Gruntland compast with the frozen sea,	**en she laugh'd. She amazes me, 'n' R lunatic love grows. Th-th-tho' a front for her p.p. salon, t-t-t-tr-tr—**

Th-th-tho'. His stammering worsens with emotion. Melodrama.
A front. Emilia fronted for Fonzie Lanier and Fonzie Ferrobosco, who ran the club, presumably for Carey.

27 & 28

Inhabited with tall and sturdy men, Gyants as big as hugie Ploypheme:	**uly she's a great lady inhabiting a motley disguise (p.p.? b.m.!), 'n' when th' dat—**

great lady. At first Kit half-believed this. He wrote her a beautiful poem, Hero and Leander; she was its protagonist. Few people read the double entendre: this votary of Venus was a prostitute.

29 & 30

Millions of souldiers cut the Artick line, Bringing the strength of Europe to these Armes:	**es of our meetings R recall'd, I think she's been engagin' others. O, I C—from tuuist t' tilt, her plo—**

31 & 32

Our Turky blades shal glide through al their throats,
And make this champion mead a bloody Fen.

ts brot trouble: I lost Dad's chain—glug—tryin' t' h-help make a lad free o' a mad h-h-h-hook. Many aduise R

glug. Kit uses this term in ciphers to suggest he was drunk at the scene he describes.

I lost Dad's chain. Kit, thinking he couldn't lose, wagered Roger's gold chain at Emilia's club, but she cheated. The loss of the chain sparked events that led to Roger Manwood's downfall, and then to Kit's.

free o' a mad h-h-h-hook. Kit made the wager trying to help Hen Wriothesley prepare to pay a fine of £5000 imposed because Hen refused to marry Elizabeth Vere (Hen's secret half-sister). Hen himself was a product of incest, and his marriage to Elizabeth would have been a dangerous liaison—the fine was preferable. **R.** our.

33 & 34

Danubius stream that runs to Trebizon,
Shall carie wrapt within his scarlet waves,

hastie escape, but crass, I wait late, mi browz stain'd, shvn al truth, 'n' roast in hel! Wurr

35 & 36

As martiall presents to our friends at home,
The slaughtered bodies of these Christians.

ie hit me as Dad tries tu restore th' lost gold chain. He has seen mi faults 'n' past errors o' feb—

37 & 38

The Terrene main wherein Danubius fals,
Shall by this battell be the bloody Sea.

rile youth, 'n' feels I'm a worthless, shabby, thieuin' bastard Hebe—all bad—'n' lent t' e—

39 & 40

The wandring Sailers of proud Italy,
Shall meet tose Christians fleeting with the tyde.

gregious d-defense o' my l-lawless action. "I-I-I was t-t-tryin t' h-h-help a friend there! Th-th'-*last*

41 & 42

Beating in heaps against their Argosies,
and make faire Europe mounted on her bull,

thing I'd e'er plan in an age—age—uud B to harm or sneer at mi kin-father! O, belieue!" So pass

43 & 44

Trapt with the wealth and riches of the world,
alight and weare a woful mourning weed.

on ahead; put al new 'n' right—O, forget me awful error—that deed which wil lead t' what new s—

45 & 46

Yet stout Orcanes, Prorex of the world, Since Tamburlaine hath mustred all his men,

orrow—relentless harm, U C? Al my buddin' hope lost in extreme shifts! No trace a' that u—

47 & 48

Marching from Cairon northward with his camp,
To Alexandria, and the frontier townes,

n-earn'd confidence. Ha! I *w*as arrogant, mi low woman thirsti for th' extra pitch, 'n' harrow'd,

49 & 50

Meaning to make a conquest of our land:
Tis requisit to parle for a peace

I accede to a request for more, 'n' a gaf alters p-plai t' mi quietus. No, no, no!! Ka—

m as *w*.

gaf. gaff. a hook. slang (circus, carny, English), a cheat, trick.

51 & 52

With Sigismond the king of Hungary:
and save our forces for the hot assaults

te, shocked 'n' sovr, hates it. Lost in a fog, I go far away t' gross nu (h-h-hum) friends. U

53 & 54

Proud Tamburlaine intends Natolia.
Viceroy of Byron, wisely hast thou said:

C, I try an SS iob wi' an evil lyin' rat uuho sent me ta pryson! O, U Dad, O Father—I'd B lo—

evil lyin' rat. Richard Baines, sent to Flushing in Jan. 1591/2 (supposedly to help Kit investigate counterfeiting by William Stanley and renegade soldiers?) Someone (Ned? Burley?) paid Baines to turn on Kit, blow Kit's most famous cover-name and accuse him of coining. Apparently in real life this happened *before* the loss of Roger's chain at the gambling club on 1 April, 1591/2, as evidenced by records of the privy council. The dates may have been transposed in Kit's own memory, or he could have altered chronology for dramatic effect—a tool he used in Shakespeare history plays.

55 & 56

My realme, the Center of our Empery.
Once lost, All Turkie would be overthrowne:

st, broken, if U hadn't come t' help me to rule, renew my career. U were l-lovely! O, root—

X

There's more

Shake-speares Sonnets. Quarto, 1609. George Eld for T.T.

SONNET 86

1 & 2

Was it the proud full saile of his great verse,
Bound for the prize of (all-too-precious) you,

Chr. uurote th' foolish wails. O, Barnzee really got U to piss, lad! U—U! Proof of first deep vei—

Barnzee. Barnaby Barnes. The most inventive poet of his day, an alcoholic member of SSS, Barnaby eventually gave up all three occupations to become a minister.

3 & 4

That did my ripe thoughts in my brain inhearce,
Making their tomb the wombe wherein they grew?

n o' heat in thy spent heart! Why wd he—Kit—chide U bi not agreeing wi' him? Grr—Remember th' time amb—

5 & 6

Was it his spirit, by spirits taught to write
Aboue a mortall pitch(e), that struck(e) me(e) dead(e)?

assadors askt your ma Libbi t' wed? She gaue them a price with her picture t' tittilate, so t' pit

by spirits taught to write. The State Secret Service brothers were nicknamed spirits.
Libbi. Queen Elizabeth's private nickname.

7 & 8

No, neither he(e) nor his compeer(e)s by night
Giving him ayd(e), my verse astonished.

hi one on hi one. I cdn't emerge t' vie! Hys verse, his rhythms, began deep in orgasm: I, I!

9 & 10

He, nor that affable familiar ghost(e)
Which nightly gulls him with intelligence,

What metric magic! We'll h-h-hail th' laughing, fire-flashing boy! Fie! Th' ill note sent

11 & 12

As victors of my silence cannot boast,	**to 'im in secret was not from Kit! Before**
I was not sick of any feare from thence,	**any of vs can safely snatch occasione**

13 & 14

But when your countenance fil'd up his line,	**t-t-t' b-blame any one, we'd let fall no**
Then lackt I matter, that infeebled mine.	**inuectiue! Find his name, C? 'N' th-then**
	uue'l chide R rep.! Kit.

rep. reprobate.

f

Shake-Speares Sonnets. Quarto, 1609. George Eld for T.T.

SONNET 126

1 & 2

O Thou my lovely Boy who in thy power, Doest hould times fickle glasse, his fickle, howers:

Chr. M. writ, hopein' t' see U. Sly, I'l hyde til they go. I'l lose 'em—walk off de bvsy show. So, ho! U cook,

3 & 4

Who hast by wayning growne, and therein shou'st,
Thy lovers withering, as thy sweet selfe grow'st.

'n' after eatin' wee'l do a story-show, stay 'n' rest, 'n' begin t'—shhh—whist! G-gr! Why? Why not? I guess wee R lov—

5 & 6

If Nature (soveraine misteres over wrack[e])
As thou goest onwards still will plucke thee backe,

ers! Svre U know it—sailin' so far t'-t' Greece 'n' back, time was we saved each other. Look, uue slept till R

7 & 8

She keepes thee to this purpose, that her skill./May time disgrace, and wretched mynuit kill.

ship sailed! Capt. Kester 'n' Kit ye kid were (shh) still loue-dreamin' at port. See me get h-h-y! Much t'

9 & 10

Yet fear her O thou minnion of her pleasure, she may detaine, but not still keepe her tre[a]sure!

reliue: R Irish days—Perrot 'n' Sorlee Boy. E-e-e-e-e! Al I kno U taut me then. One mustn't f-fear the h-hap

11 & 12

Her Audite (though delayd) answer'd must be,
And her Quietus is to render thee.

that brot R queer loue: It was a deer, needed deed. A iust rhythm shunn'd giues h—

13 & 14
(   )
(   )

( ) The last two lines of this poem are lost. The quarto prints parentheses.

The poem was made for Christopher Carleill, Captain Kester, Francis Walsingham's step-son and son-in-law who sailed to Constantinople in 1577/'8 with Kit, then a shipboy and probably a doer for cargo of Thomas Gresham.
In 1584 Kit was with Carleill at Coleraine, and they took part in a campaign against Sorley Boy Mac Donnell, who was badly treated by Lord Deputy Perrot.
For years Carleill was captain of the Tiger, and he went to the Caribbean with Drake. The poem may have been provided to the publisher by Carleill's widow, Mary Walsingham, for his DNB biographer writes, "she was still living in 1609" (the date of publication of the Sonnets).

f

Titus Andronicus. First Folio of Shakespeare. Tragedies, p 31.

TITUS ANDRONICUS

1 & 2

Noble Patricians, Patrons of my right,
Defend the iustice of my Cause with Armes.

U can see Christopher Marley's name here, but I can find it? Sad iff my wits go to pot.

3 & 4

And Countrey-men, my louing Followers,
Pleade my Successiue Title with your Swords.

'E told me men fuc'd this lood piece I wrote years ago. Yur cuss 'n' slur won't sully my wine.

5 & 6

I was the first-borne Sonne, that was the last
That wore the Imperiall Diadem of Rome:

Ferdinando flees to Lathom, where he awaits this steamie Roman writ that lets prob—

7 & 8

Then let my Fathers Honours liue in me,
Nor wrong mine Age with this indignitie.

ity slide into th' riuer. As I'm writing one, he's home, hunting for new meaning: Let h—

9 & 10

Romaines, Friends, Followers, Fauourers of my Right:
If euer Basianus, Casars Sonne,

ands be shourn off in coarsest way! Mirrour gore! More slaine! Less f-fuss! *Ravia! Fine!*

Lathom. Ferdinando Stanley's country home, in Lancashire

Ravia! Italian. Ravvia! Arrange it!

Fine. The end.

f

Epitaph for Roger Manwood by Christopher Marlowe
Orthography from Mark Eccles' article in *Notes and Queries*, July 1935. p 40.

EPITAPH FOR ROGER MANWOOD

Capital letters (excluding the title): N E I A L V S N I P O A M P L I M T D V F	**Laf, Pap! I've lost V 'n' mi mind.**
Capital letters (including the title): I R M R C B N E I A L V S N I P O A M P L I M T D V F	**Pap's front 'n' bvm crvelli maim'd. I-i!**
Capital letters (left margin, incl. title) I R N E V I P O M L I M V F	**I pile furi on 'vmm.**
Title: In obitum honoratissimi viri Rogeri Manwood militis quaestorii Reginalis Capitalis Baronis	**I lost mi pa, slain in bravo horror. O, wail! I, I, I! Mi aim is to assist reuenge. I can't quit, so I'd bring mi Roi.**
1 & 2 Noctiuagi terror, ganeonis triste flagellum Et Iovis Alcides, rigido vulturq*ue* Latroni	**Anger against 'im for our satiric vvritings led to a cruel end. O, I loue 'is grit! I'l quote—tell U**
3 & 4 Vrnâ subtegitur, Sceleru*m* gaudete Nepotes. Insons luctifica sparsis cervice capillia	**o' success o' fierce prelates against Pa—ruinin' 'im vvi' crude l-lies, C, as 'e turns i' clip-gut beat—**
5 & 6 Plange, fori lumen venerandae gloria legis Occidit. heu secu*m* effoetas Acherontis ad oras	**ing, done i' secret, causin' death. O, mae mi curses fal on al cruel aged hie prelates! O, fa! No forgiv—**
7 & 8 Multa abiit virtus. Protot virtutibus vni Livor parce viro: non audacissimus esto	**in' re 'is controversial satiric vvrit—iust movv 'im douun, as U'l B brot past piti to a uu—**

9 & 10 Illius in cineres, cujus tot millia vultus Mortalium attoniut: sic cum Te nuncia Ditis	**allouu o' militant, rectitudinus injustice tu tilt uui' social miscriants 'n' mum vices. L—**
11 & 12 Vulneret exanguis, foeliciter ossa quiescant Famaq*ue* marmorei superet monumenta sepulchri.	**eaue Pa restin'! O, cease suspense—no criminal! Feuu equal 'im fur smart. Gone! Quit mi text. Love, Chr. Mar.**

f

Henry VI, Part I. First Folio of Shakespeare. Histories, p 96.

HENRY VI PART I

1 & 2

Hvng be ÿ heauens with black, yield day to night; Comets importing change of Times and States,

Kit M. penn'd this trilogy because of his dad's symbolic chain. Then, to avenge ÿ game that went g—

his dad's symbolic chain. Roger Manwood's gold chain of office, seen on his portrait in the National Portrait Gallery and on the bust on his monument outside Canterbury. A. Wraight and Virginia F. Stern. In Search of Christopher Marlowe. New York: The Vanguard Press. 1965, p. 34. Robert J. Blackham. The Story of the Temple, Gray's and Lincoln's Inn. London: Samson Low, Marston, n.d.: "The significance of the letters S S has been hotly disputed. The portcullis in the . . . collar refers to John of Gaunt, the loops to the union of the Houses of York and Lancaster, and the rose is, of course, the Tudor rose."

3 & 4

Brandish your crystall Tresses in the Skie, And with them scourge the bad reuolting Stars,

oring his dad's name, Kit bitterly teased th' Church t' show yts error in all ages. But SSS uener—

goring his dad's name. Before executing Roger on 14 Dec. 1592, Whitgift launched a campaign of character-assassination to destroy the image of this popular liberal judge. Catherine Drinker Bowen. *The Lion and the Throne.* Boston: Little, Brown. 1957, p. 65. She writes of the 1570's: "These great ones walked and talked in the garden . . . Sir Nicholas Bacon . . . Sir Thomas Bromley . . . Mr. Justice Manwood, beloved wherever he went . . ."

5 & 6

That haue consented vnto Henries death: King Henry the Fift, too famous to liue long,

ated the clergy—had entire faith in those fools o' Kent—tut! UUhen fine hvmans go to no

7 & 8

England ne're lost a King of so much worth. England ne're had a King vntill his time:

Matin—not a "deadlih sin"—nor need these gvll-men hang i' gags, or "rot in hell!" Fuck W.! Kn—

Fuck W.! Powel Mills Dawley. John Whitgift and the English Reformation. N.Y.: Scribner's, 1954, offers a largely sympathetic view of the archbishop.

9 & 10

Vertue he had, deseruing to command,
His brandish't Sword did blinde men with his beames,

owing o' th' vnreasoned, inhumane deeds—th' B.C. Bible shredded—Dad writ his satires. "Mum him!"

th' B.C. Bible shredded. Whitgift disliked the Old Testament, punished ministers who read any version but the Authorized Bishops' Bible.

Dad writ his satires. Even now the public doesn't know Manwood was the mover behind the privately printed "Marprelate Papers" which were distributed at court in 1588 and 1589, causing laughter and consternation. Four of these he wrote himself: "The Epistle," "The Epitome," "Hay Any Work for Cooper" and "The Protestation" are in his Falstaffian style. It looks as if Kit wrote "Theses Martinianae" trying to preserve Roger's anonymity. "Schoolpoints" seems to have been created by a puritan divine—Roger wanted those minsters to have a chance to say what they believed—and the slimy "Reproof" was written by a *provocateur* who managed to betray several workers on the project. The set of pamphlets available from The Scolar Press Limited, 93 Hunslet Road, Leeds 10, England, can be found in college libraries.

11 & 12

His Armes spred wider then a Dragons Wings:
His sparkling Eyes, repleat with wrathfull fire

Angered, th' snarling prelate issued warrant for R.M.'s death. His ill wishes whip my grief! Pesk—

th' snarling prelate. In a monograph in Dictionary of National Biography, Sidney Lee writes of the archbishop: "In his examination of prisoners he showed a brutal insolence which is alien to all modern conceptions of justice or religion." There were many questionable executions—people publicly hanged or secretly killed in jail or at home. G. B. Harrison, An Elizabethan Journal, Being a Record of Those Things Most Talked about During the Years 1591-1594. N.Y.: Cosmopolitan Book Corp. 1929: "27 February, 1593: . . . a Barrowist, having died in Newgate, his body was taken by his friends and enclosed in a coffin which they laid at the door of Justice Young, bearing this inscription:

'This is . . . the last of sixteen or seventeen which that great enemy of God, the Archbishop of Canterbury, with his High Commissioners, have murthered in Newgate within these five years, manifestly for the testimony of Jesus Christ. His soul is now with the Lord; and his blood crieth for speedy vengeance against that great enemy of the saints . . . '"

Whitgift thought he was cleaning up. Roger and many good lawmen saw trouble ahead.

my. Marlowe turns a W upside down to make an M.

13 & 14

More dazled and droue back his Enemies,
Then mid-day Sunne, fierce bent against their faces.

i craze for reuenge makes my drama touch Dad's fetid death-bed in slie *scenae*, 'n' nine, ten bish—

15 & 16

What should I say? His Deeds exceed all speech:
He ne're lift vp his Hand, but conquered.

ops 'n' a deacon, vpset, hurriedly exit th' queen's hall. See, chiefs wud heed Dad's belch! Hi—

exit th' queen's hall. The great hall of the palace of Hampton Court, where the Countess of Pembroke's Players performed scenes from Marlowe's play, an early Henry VI, on Twelfth Night, 1592/ 3.

17 & 18

We mourne in black, why mourn we not in blood?
Henry is dead, and neuer shall reuiue:

s horrid murder must be reueal'd—'n' can be, when "low kin"—hey, nonnie! Now all you, *adieu*!

f

Henry VI, Part II. First Folio of Shakespeare. Histories, p 120.

HENRY VI PART II

1 & 2

As by your high Imperiall Maiesty, I had in charge at my depart for France,	**I' bitter tearful fray, mi Pop hears Archdeacon Redman say, "Ay, higgily him!**

Archdeacon Redman. Dr. William Redman, Archdeacon of Canterbury (DNB), was apparently delegated to oversee the rewriting of Roger Manwood's will (signed two days before Manwood's death. Lewis J. M. Grant. Christopher Marlowe, the Ghost Writer. Orillia, Canada: Stubley Press, 1970, p 212) and to manage details of Manwood's execution.

Higgily. Higgle. OED. to strive for petty advantage in bargaining.

3 & 4

As Procurator to your Excellence, To marry Princes Margaret for your Grace;	**N' extra money to Ruy Lopes for greasie crap. C, tru martyr! C, rare courage! Color**

Lopes was the queen's own physician. Marlowe may suggest that Archdeacon Redman paid for extra damage to Manwood.

5 & 6

So in the Famous Ancient City, Toures, In presence of the Kings of France, and Sicill,	**couers his face. C, ye M.D. (giant ninni-ninni) curses in fear lest the flo stop. Took feca—**

7 & 8

The Dukes of Orleance, Calaber, Britaigne, and Alanson, Seuen Earles, twelue Barons, & [= and] twenty reuerend Bishops	**l waste, let with the blood, an' rubbed it all ouer Roger. Fie! A sad, an unnecessary processa, bann'd an' neuer seen! Keen!**

Keen! OED: To utter the keen, Irish lamentation for the dead.

9 & 10

I haue perform'd my Taske, and was espous'd, And humbly now vpon my bended knee	**Ye shibbuleth: Forsaken Dad's moans made no demand. Even puppy M.D. Ruy knew wo—**

Ye shibbuleth. shibboleth, a Hebrew word. OED 'stream in flood' . . . as the slaughter took place at the fords of Jordan. Also OED The Hebrew word used by Jephthah as a test-word to distinguish the fleeing Ephraimites (who could not pronounce the sh) from his own men (Judges xii, 4-6).

11. & 12

In sight of England, and her Lordly Peeres, Deliuer vp my title in the Queene	**nder at the iudge's fortitvde—'n' here ye shlemiel quipped, "No general yll in n—**

13 & 14

To your most gracious hands, that are the Substance Of that great Shadow I did represent:	**onconformist iudges has to be cured, whereas . . . Stop! I start to taste ratty red dung! Ha, Ha, Ha!"**

15 & 16

The happiest Gift, that euer Marquesse gaue, The Fairest Queene, that euer King receiu'd.	**The crude queer hasn't quit, kuts a gut again, tu get his fee. I' fear, Peter hears 'im: "Tee Hee!" Pe—**

Peter hears 'im. Peter Manwood, Marlowe's half-brother—a legitimate son of Roger.

17 & 18

Suffolke arise. Welcome Queene Margaret, I can expresse no kinder signe of Loue	**luic pain's gone now, as life fades. One request: "O couer me! Greek Mar-lex reeks!"** ***Fine.***

Greek Mar-lex reeks! Roger's joking: Dark, with aquiline nose, he looked Greek. In The Jew of Malta: "Kirriah Iairim, the great Jew of Greece." The name means "City of Woods." John Bakeless. Tragicall History of Christopher Marlowe. Westport CT: Greenwood Press, 1970, vol 1.

f

Henry VI, Part III. First Folio of Shakespeare. Histories, pp 147-150.

HENRY VI PART III

1 & 2

I Wonder how the King escap'd our hands?
While we pursu'd the Horsmen of ye North,

Defiant onstage, I spelt *my* doom—huh huh! Whips 'n' horrors were decreed, U know, 'n' h—

Defiant onstage. In the third part of this First Folio trilogy Kit writes (Act 1, scene 1, ll. 161, 162), "May that ground gape, and swallow me alive, where I shall kneel to him that slew my father!"

3 & 4

He slyly stole away, and left his men:
Whereat the great Lord of Northumberland,

hellish flame was threatened. Before long U warn they'll destroy my art and oth—

5 & 6

Whose Warlike eares could neuer brooke retreat,
Chear'd vp the drouping Army, and himselfe.

er things: drama, verse. O, U! Help! O, Help! We wait a month for deadly raid, ere Buck re-reckons Reue—

Buck. A year older than Kit, George Buck worked at the Revels Office—kept playscripts there, did some directing and later became Master of the Revels. A friend to Kit and Tom Watson, Buck lived with Segar the watercolorist. This mention of Buck as a Revels Office worker in 1593 antedates other references to him in that place.

7 & 8

Lord Clifford and Lord Stafford all abrest
Charg'd our maine Battailes Front: and breaking in,

ls records, leauing Dido 'n' other drama in a far corner for filing-stab—all to B blank'd—dratted. Aff—

filing stab. In those days, to file something meant to spindle it.
dratted. God-rotted.

9 & 10

Were by the Swords of common Souldiers slaine.
Lord Staffords Father, Duke of Buckingham,

ected by mi fear, Buck hid th' MSS. Fool raiders look'd, grew sour and soon left us safe from Wh. N—

11 & 12

Is either slaine or wounded dangerous. I cleft his Beauer with a down-right blow:

o hint o' a schedul'd trial. We wait to begin defense. When will U arriue, God! SS horrib—

13 & 14

That this is true (Father) behold his blood.
And Brother, here's the Earle of Wiltshires (blood,

lie hesitant to aid, for fear o' Wh.'s dred toll o' death. But ere brother broils, thei'l be—Sh, Sh, Shh!

15 & 16

Whom I encountred as the Battels ioyn'd.
Speake thou for me, and tell them what I did.

They ask for 'n' receiue mi banishment. Wh. plans to do a hit. To mutate th' deed, we'll do d—

Wh . . . . hit. Whitgift intends to murder Marlowe, using a hit man.

17 & 18

Richard hath best deseru'd of all my sonnes:
But is your Grace dead, my Lord of Somerset?

eseru'd deceit: th' borro*w*'d body of a dirty hang'd shyster-man serues as me, U C, for all sol—

19 & 20

Such hope haue all the line of Iohn of Gaunt.
Thus do I hope to shake King Henries head.

ution to this charade. Shaken, I peek, and so hug U, 'n' slip off aliue. Ho Ho Ho, He He He! Ten gl—

21 & 22

And so doe I, victorious Prince of Yorke.
Before I see thee seated in that Throne,

asses o' beer i' the eve, U C, 'n' hidden Kit's noo tooo ready for the trip to France! Ei, Ei!

23 & 24

Which now the House of Lancaster vsurpes,
I vow by Heauen, these eyes shall neuer close.

We pass by Henry ov Navarre: I, th' chef's clown, shoue now, cleaue to his heel lest he use seu—

Very probably Kit was directed by his chiefs, Bacon & Essex, to deliver a message to Navarre at a prearranged time at St. Denis.

25 & 26

This is the Pallace of the fearefull King, And
this the Regall Seat: possesse it Yorke,

ere action. G! He hath all th' slips against deliuery of peskee letters t' his loss: fake f—

He's kidding. Navarre was expecting—maybe even waiting for this message from Essex. In June '93 Essex writes Phelippes: Why hasn't William Walton sailed? This is important: tell him to get going! (CSP Dom. Eliz. 1591-'94). Wm. Walton of the Salamander pirated with Edward Marlowe in the Mayflower, out of Deptford.

27 & 28

For this is thine, and not King Henries Heires.
Assist me then, sweet Warwick, and I will,

friends want aid, 'n' enemies write lies . . . Cease! He has long known this Kit with Irish str—

long known. Kit was with Navarre in 1591, with Essex.

29 & 30

or hither we haue broken in by force.
Wee'le all assist you: he that flyes, shall dye.

eak! "Hey, hey, C here! See th' braue allies' offer to stand by you! No shit, we shall! Will fr—

Irish streak. worth study: Kit's mother's dad, Wm. Arthur, was born, I believe, of seafaring folks near Bristol, across St George's Channel from Ireland. Kit's real father Manwood's mother was Catherine Galloway—an Irish-sounding name.

31 & 32

Thankes gentle Norfolke, stay by me my Lords,
And souldiers stay and lodge by me this Night.

iends forget the mad days so long ago? 'Slyd, yes! U 'n' Robin 'n' Kit all brested th' enemy!" My talk sh—

'Slyd. His eyelid—a mild epithet.
Robin. Essex.

33 & 34

And when the King comes, offer him no violence,
Vnlesse he seeke to thrust you out perforce.

akes his effort to resiste me, 'n' grown undulee chumee, he looks vp over ye note o' th' chief, 'n' C, n—

chumee. chummy—college slang.

35 & 36

The Queene this day here holds her Parliament,
But little thinkes we shall be of her counsaile,

ow he smiles, at last quite sure o' U—a little needed help—a shiny brother in th' bleak French hel. H—

37 & 38

By words or blowes here let vs winne our right.
Arm'd as we are, let's stay within this House.

e says, "Sta!"—I hear! So in th' morn, rested, I s-set out by river to where wagons R held. Wh., will U B w—

From St. Denis Kit skirted the closed city of Paris and took passage on the coche de l'eau down the Seine and Yonne, probably as far as Bassau. Wh. is still Whitgift.

39 & 40

The bloody Parliament shall this be call'd,
Vnlesse Plantagenet, Duke of Yorke, be King,

aiting at the bend, to kill "le Kloon?" O, can svbterfuge help break a deadly spell? Shy men s—

shy men. Here he helps us pin down this phrase by using bashful in the next line.

41 & 42

And bashfull Henry depos'd, whose Cowardize
Hath made vs by-words to our enemies.

tay clear! We SS don't shoue Liza—'n' we avoid her odd byshops on her M.'s famed bed. Wh., R U—

bed. He suggests her M. (her Majesty) is in bed with (colluding with) her bishops? Or is her bed famed because she has shared it, tho' she claims to be a virgin?

43 & 44

Then leaue me not, my Lords be resolute,
I meane to take possession of my Right.

threatening her M. so U may kill e'en more? Yes, Pest! O, to be so smal 'n' to see U do it! F—

threatening. Whitgift blackmailed the queen so he could continue his inquisition. He was getting rid of Puritans, Marranos.

45 & 46

Neither the King, nor he that loues him best,
The prowdest hee that holds vp Lancaster,

or sins, provd prelate, U'll answer to God. H-H-H-H-Hie thee! That thin testament becks thee!

47 & 48

Dares stirre a Wing, if Warwick shake his Bells.
Ile plant Plantage et, root him vp who dares:

Wagons R slow. Press'd, I take horse 'n' ride clip-trip (h-half-kilt) t' Geneva, where I await a man's bl—

49 & 50

Resolue thee Richard, clayme the English Crowne.
My Lords, looke where the sturdie Rebell

essed aid. Cleuer Harry 'n' I slow-climb to th' heights, hurry down. Look! See me stretch! Le-Le Re-Le-Ree!

Harry. Kit was to meet Harry Wotton at Isaac Casaubon's house in Geneva. Harry was away but soon returned, and they crossed the Alps together.
Le-Le Re-Le-Ree! downhill skiing.

51 & 52

Euen in the Chayre of State: belike he meanes,
Backt by the power of Warwicke, that false Peere,

Blese ye camper who hie-kickt a bal t' the spot where Cheefe 'n' Kyt wave, fainte t' be free a' sno.! Rea-

camper. OED. a football player!

53 & 54

To aspire vnto the Crowne and reigne as King.
Earle of Northumberland, he slew thy Father,

ching Mantuah, Harry rides west alone, 'n' T. Lodge 'n' Kit R off to Veronah. We sleep near there, b—

Harry rides west alone. to Genoa, then back to Geneva.
T. Lodge. author Thomas Lodge, an SSS honest man.

55 & 56

And thine, Lord Clifford, & (and) you both haue vow'd reuenge
On him, his sonnes, his fauorites and his friends.

ed with fleas, 'n' fast-ride in sun—no snouu—to find an odd slimy riuer barge 'n' head for Venice. Hi Ho, Hosh Dosh!

57 & 58

If I be not, Heauens be reueng'd on me.
The hope thereof, makes Clifford mourne in steele.

UUe meet cheefe Guarini 'n' soon he hires me t' do one f—bolde prison breake. Th' f—element f—

59 & 60

What, shall we suffer this? lets pluck him down,
My heart for anger burnes, I cannot brooke it.

or th' mission? Folly! A barber enters t' attend all U Gew prisoners who—when—Fuk! Fuk! Catch him!

barber. Kit pretends to be a barber sent from English Embassy in Constantinople to a fortress still standing north of the city. In CSP Venetian, vol 9, 1593, the prison is called the Tower of the Black Sea. In a letter sent to me 11/ 26/ '84 by Cengiz Taner, Regional Director of Culture, Istanbul, he says, "by the Tower of the Black Sea the Ambassador must have meant Rumeli Hisar . . . Its north tower was used as a prison, especially for members of foreign embassies."

61 & 62

Be patient, gentle Earle of Westmerland.
Patience is for Poultroones, such as he

I cut th' floor. As th' ensign sleeps, we leap free out a *w*indow to a sere brent place. En—

cut the floor. They had to go through (It was wooden) to descend to an available window. **ensign.** OED. formerly a commissioned officer of the lowest grade in the infantry. Here, a Janissary (Kit must have drugged him). The word ensign is used with double entendre, "to point out," as a watchman. **sere.** dry, parched.
brent. OED. steep, lofty. brant, obs. They'd have landed in the dry inner courtyard, which contained a hill and a small mosque where the Janissaries were gathered for Friday worship.

63 & 64

He durst not sit there, had your Father liu'd.
My gracious lord, here in the Parliament

trap'd here in a yard? UUe're not lost: through a hi hole I thrust my fine secrit ladder, m—

They head for the top of the crenellated wall S of the E tower, facing the Bosporus.

65 & 66

Let vs assayle the Family of Yorke.
Well hast thou spoken, Cousin be it so.

akin' a way. UUe easily climb t' th' top 'n' look over t' see—s-s-s-*see*—oh, th' folly! F—

67 & 68

Ah, know you not the Citie fauours them,
And they haue troupes of Souldiers at their beck?

ar, far downe is the uu-uuater 'n' the tiny sloop I hired to take us to safety. Oh-h, chuck me! Obe—

Far, far downe. About 40 feet.

69 & 70

But when the Duke is slaine, they'le quickly flye.
Farre be the thought of this from Henries heart,

ying necessity, I hook th' silk lader t' one queer rib. We truly feel uue R t' be mash't. The fhh-fhh-fathe—

one queer rib. In 1452 Mehmet II Fatih constructed Rumeli Hisar out of of a concrete aggregate incorporating chunks of ancient buildings. There are many Byzantine fragments in the walls—columns, architraves, capitals—so there were projections on which Kit could climb to fasten his ladder.

71 & 72

To make a Shambles of the Parliament House.
Cousin of Exeter, frownes, words, and threats,

r o' fools starts off—then as prime beau silk extends, other men come down. Ah-ah—water saue—

water. In 1593, the water was right there at the bottom of the wall. The esplanade wasn't put in till 1954.

73 & 74

Shallbe the Warre that Henry meanes to vse.
Thou factious Duke of Yorke descend my Throne,

s vs, 'n' the honest monkey-foote lader destroyed, uue swim to reach the—uhh, leaky—craft nearb—

75 & 76

And kneele for grace and mercie, at my feete,
I am thy Soueraigne. I am thine.

y 'n' to hide there under a saile. Fifteen men! May *w*e not grace a racke! Ei! Magi—

Fifteen men. CSP Venetian, vol. 9. ***w*e.** M as W.
grace a racke. If they were caught now, they might all be tortured to death.

77 & 78

For shame come downe, he made the Duke of Yorke.
It was my Inheritance, as the Earledome was.

c sail, hide them today! Are we redeem'd or forsaken? O, now I see 'em—watchmen! They shake famou—

79 & 80

Thy Father was a Traytor to the Crowne.
Exeter thou art a Traytor to the Crowne,

s new toy èxecutor: we can't tarry there to hear th' horror of a rat-tat-tat! They wo—

81 & 82

In following this vsurping Henry.
Whom should hee follow, but his naturall King?

n't shoot us: we fly along th' flow 'n' slowlih, in dim hush, begin repairing ovr hull. Uk—

fly along. The current there is very fast.

83 & 84

True Clifford, that's Richard Duke of Yorke, and shall I stand, and thou sit in my Throne.

ase is out for our reclamation at th' officers' hands. I'll thank th' rudder 'n' th' kind Dy-Dy!

Ukase. an imperial decree. **Dy-Dy.** The kind boatman (?) who steers the craft?

85 & 86

It must and shall be so, content thy selfe.
Be Duke of Lancaster, let him be King.

Th' men safe in outbound craft, I'l go t' heed th' bell. It's my knell, see: Ass! T' be ackn—

Th' men safe. The fifteen men are stowed aboard two Venetian ships, the Liona and the Silvestra, but Kit must return as barber to the English embassy so the ambassador will not suffer. Fearful, Ambassador Barton refuses to help Kit and surrenders him to the Wazir: Kit is the "ass."

87 & 88

He is both King, and Duke of Lancaster,
And that the Lord of Westmerland shall maintiane.

owledged the men's uisitor 'll free th' kind, kind ambassador o' th' tall fate th' Hannan can a—

Hannan. A Turkish official. Kit resents this call—the ambassador technically has diplomatic immunity but fears the Sultan's anger.

89 & 90

And Warwick shall disproue it. You forget,
That we are those which chas'd you from the field,

ssign. Th' wadir cals. He doth talk a fierce way. I protest: "H-how would I free 'em? U C, th' hour of day

91 & 92

And slew your Fathers, and with Colours spread
Marcht through the Citie to the Pallace Gates.

precludes my attendance there!" "Ha! A guard saw th' sail at th' shore put forth with lo' cries o' 'Go! Cl—

93 & 94

Yes Warwicke, I remember it to my griefe,/And by his Soule, thou and thy House shall rue it.

ear out!' Were you there? You'll be dismember'd yf you lie!" C, I sh-sh-shake as I'm writing that n—

95 & 96

Plantagenet, of thee and these thy Sonnes,
Thy Kinsmen, and thy Friends, Ile haue more liues.

ote. On knees, sadly I admit sailing 'n' deny th' men uuere there. 'N' he has plenty of sense; th' fat h—

97 & 98

Then drops of bloud were in my Father's Veines.
Vrge it no more, lest that in stead of words,

og says, "Men moved under a sheet!" 'N' startled—don't rvn fro*m* it—"O," I offer, "it wil B those sheep!" R—

99 & 100

I send thee, Warwicke, such a Messenger,
As shall revenge his death, before I stirre.

ash statement! Chain'd, I grow wearee—feel Irish SSS 'I never B sau'd here i' Greek ches—

101 & 102

Poor Clifford, how I scorne his worthlesse Threats.
Will you we shew our Title to the Crowne?

oun, i' wet, wet hell o' prison with death or worse to follow. Yes, worse! C, he'l surch for th' tricsie

chesoun. OED. 1. occasion. 2. complaint, charge or accusation. [16th c. legal usage]. chesounable. liable to charge or accusation, blameable.

103 & 104

If not our Swords shall pleade it in the field. What Title hast thou Traytor to the Crowne?	**laddah the author used to lower all th' prisoners to th' water so efficiently (with it, not T—**

efficiently. Not used in Shakespeare plays, but in use in this sense (the ladder as agent) according to OED, in 1620—when this may have been written. Kit was still working on revisions when he died in 1621.

105 & 106

My Father was as thou art, Duke of Yorke, Thy grandfather Roger Mortimer, Earle of March.	**om or Harry's left t' get th' hook). Far i' fury, he may dare me to rearrange muck-threads of ar w—**

t' get th' hook. The sultan had a habit of impaling recalcitrant prisoners on hooks outside buildings and leaving them to die.
Muck-threads. wet remains of the ladder.
ar. our.

107 & 108

I am the Sonne of Henry the Fift, Who made the Dolphin and the French to stoupe,	**eft, 'n' what hope then? He'd remove th' iron chain that holds my f-f-foot? See, I penn'd**

weft. Webster. something woven [e.g. the ladder]. **f-f-foot.** Kit had a deformed foot that made him limp, and it was probably very painful to have an ankle-iron there.

109 & 110

and seiz'd vpon their Townes and Provinces. Talke not of France, sith thou hast lost it all.	**a note to Eliza there 'n th' prison, 'n' dast I put it, cover'd, i' th' vndone SSS sack? What fool, fall'n**

SSS sack. to reach the sack, he may have slipped his note to a visitor from the English embassy.

111 & 112

The Lord Protector lost it, and not I: When I was crown'd, I was but nine moneths old.	**in that hole, would hope to be ransom'd? Rest now, 'n' scorn it! Distance wil drown it! T—**

113 & 114

You are old enough now, and yet me thinkes you loose:	**o me, they sing, now, 'n' holy days R due: O! Neat-o! Looke U! Eu—**

holy days. The feast of Bairam was approaching. During those days everyone was kind and gentle.
Neat-o!. A slang expression that must have been current for centuries.

115 & 116

Father, teare the Crowne from the Vsurpers Head. Sweet Father doe so, set it on your Head.	**er see men freed, y'r torture sesa-a? Unheard-of, what? Devotees o' th' faith who respect orth—**

sesa-a. a phonetic spelling for Italian, cessa, cease? The extra a could be a sigh of relief.

117 & 118

Good brother, As thou lov'st and honorest Armes, Let's fight it out, and not stand cauilling thus.	**odocsi sai that during th' love-fest no one should go t' death, so all mi groans R but nut-rants. Th' t—**

119 & 120

Sound Drummes and Trumpets, and the King will flye. / Sonnes peace. Peace thou, and giue King Henry leave to speake.	**ruth is clear, tho': soon these depraued men'll attack 'n' flog my knees again 'n' keep me pissing. Ay, U—even U, wud depend**

121 & 122

Plantagenet shal speake first: Heare him Lords, and be you silent and attentiue too,	**on piss in a hell like that. Better than tears at least. No, I euen spray on 'em! God, U faded**

123 & 124

For he that interrupts him, shall not liue. Think'st thou, that I will leaue my Kingly Throne,	**then, 'n' that left thy son like kill-meat, hurt in their uillainous grasp. Mother, with thy lou—**

125 & 126

Wherein my Grandsire and my Father sat? No: first shall Warre vnpeople this my Realme;	**e, let me endvre th' s-sharp whirring pain till they ar' made weary, 'n' SSS may learn from of—**

127 & 128

I, and their Colours often borne in France, and now in England, to our hearts great sorrow,	**ficial code log of their torn, torn brauo's urgent need, 'n' aid's near, now—near, on th' Narrows.**

log. record-book. He sent his plea to Elizabeth in his official code, in the baga secreta.

129 & 130

shall be my Winding-sheet. Why faint you Lords?/My Ticles' (sic) good, and better farre then his.	**My wry dream ys true! An English boat bedect wi' fine sails shifted t' th' Golden Horn. Holy**

131 & 132

Prove it Henry, and thou shalt be King. Henry the Fourth by Conquest got the Crowne.	**day, Peteh! It brought queer, vnknown bonny gifts to the ruler's cort. Once he hath hy—**

Peteh. Phonetic spelling for Peter, Kit's half-brother, Peter Manwood.
gifts. CSP Venetian vol 9 tells about them in detail.

133 & 134

'Twas by Rebellion against his King. I know not what to say, my Titles weake:	**s lite toys in stow, I bet his men'll wake that broken Kit 'n' sing "Away, Away! Go!"**

lite. light. **in stow.** stowed, a sailor's term.

135 & 136

Tell me, may not a King adopt an heire? What then? And if he may, then I am (a) lawfull King:	**That day a man found me awake, penning, let me go free, "with Allah," I think—'n' all a' my thi—**

137 & 138

For Richard, in the view of many Lords, Resign'd the Crowne to Henry the Fourth,	**ngs, too. A sly note: "Tin hidd'n i' dri-vat. Hurry! Fence where worth more, for Chef R." H—**

Tin. Tin was in demand in Turkey; brass cannon were fashionable and there was much local copper but little tin.
Chef R. Probably SSS top nominal chief, Robert Cecil. The hidden tin may have been stolen from Elizabeth's cargo for the sultan.

139 & 140

Whose heire my Father was, and I am his. He rose against him, being his Soueraigne,	**e writes o' far-away Trebisond, near mines. As I'm an ass—"he-hi, he-hi, he-hi, he—" I mus' g-g-go!**

141 & 142

and made him to resigne his Crowne, perforce. Suppose, my Lords, he did it vnconstrayn'd,	**Near Sinope th' smelter-owners receive hidd'n SS cargo from us, hoddy-noddy. Map it, 'n' pic—**

143 & 144

Thinke you 'twere preiudiciall to his Crowne? No: for he could not so resigne his Crowne,	**ture us here in this weird chill spot: we C one hot cone. I, wood 'n' rock on fire is only a regu—**

145 & 146

But that the next Heire should succeed and reigne.
Art thou against vs, Duke of Exeter?

lar sight on this coast that even God neuer sauu. But Chef, U needed trade, *et exit Rex!* Kh—

et exit Rex! All the tin in the hold of the English ship was meant for the sultan from Elizabeth, but yes, the SSS chief stole some of it.
Chef. Chief.

147 & 148

His is the right, and therefore pardon me.
Why whisper you, my Lords, and answer not?

an wd trade wi' shorn hides. We refuse 'm, h-hoise t' go, then tarry 'n' play'd sorry on him. P—

shorn hides. On this coast there is still much trade in pigskin and in bristles for brushes.

149 & 150

My Conscience tells me he is lawfull King.
All will reuolt from me, and turne to him.

ulling out more skins, he'll offer al, 'n' we'll welcome 'em 'n' trade much illicit tyn. Mas—

Mas. "O Lord!" an expletive used by Kit in Dr. Faustus and apocryphal works.
Mas. in Spanish means but, yet, however.

151 & 152

Plantagenet, for all the Clayme thou lay'st,
Thinke not, that Henry shall be so depos'd.

Ha ha! Th' pyrate boards me t' open 'n' take all! "Not yet," I called, 'n' let fly th' guns. He shoots, l—

153 & 154

Depos'd he shall be, in despight of all.
Thou art deceiu'd:
Tis not they Southerne power

eaping about—hard to hit. He chose t' destroy the tiller; I'd defend, unless—oh! Pow! Slup!

155 & 156

Of Essex, Norfolke, Suffolke, nor of Kent,
Which makes thee thus presumtuous and prowd,

Look—enuf ruff-stuff! Knock 'm 'n deep water tu swim t' shore! A pox on duh losers' hopes! See, Kh—

157 & 158

Can set the Duke vp in despite of me.
King Henry, be thy Title right or wrong,

an, we don't seek dry hog skin here, or let U MT R tin cheep. Bvt, pig, get in thy fi—

159 & 160

Lord Clifford vowes to fight in thy defence:/May that ground gape, and swallow me aliue,

ne huff-fest 'n' contemplate what yovr mad idiocy has done t' good will: if we regard all U G—

161 & 162

Where i shall kneele to him that slew my Father.
Oh Clifford, how thy words reuiue my heart.

errys as criminal, look, what trade is left to try? H-h-h-h-huh? Moue! Fly, while we'd free thee, wom—

Gerrys. These people were Mongols who lived in big skin huts called Gers; that could be why he called them Gerrys. (also, what the English called Germans when they disliked them.)

163 & 164

Henry of Lancaster, resigne thy Crowne:
What mutter you, or what conspire you Lords?

an-cur! We go t' trade in honor! So we try t' sayl. We can't, for he rips our tymon-heel! U Chrys—

in honor! ? The tin they were to sell had been stolen from the queen.
tymon. OED. The rudder of a ship. When he went overboard the khan didn't swim for shore but attacked the boat.

165 & 166

Doe right vnto this Princely Duke of Yorke,
or I will fill the House with armed men,

tian friends, look! Wd you tvrn th' other cheek? Hell! Will I murder 'em? O, fig! O, shit! Yep! I

167 & 168

And ouer the Chayre of State, where now he sits,
Write up his Title with vsurping blood.

chide th' drippin' wet rats on shore. No hits; we waste shot. But hey, we'll reuive! I go aft. R U

169 & 170

My Lord of Warwick, heare but one word,
Let me for this my life time reigne as King.

familiar with rudders, Meg? This one broke off, 'n' my crew got more teake. Will ye in—

Meg. His half-sister, Meg Marley. He talks to her several times in these ciphers (here, in The Two Gentlemen, in Antony and Cleopatra, and ?).

171 & 172

Confirme the Crowne to me and to mine Heires,
And thou shalt reigne in quiet while thou liv'st.

uent a new heel, men? Then we sail in quiet fog, C, t' leave this horrid monster, 'n' rid o' him, to touch i—

173 & 174

I am content: Richard Plantagent
Enioy the Kingdome after my decease.

n at a port 'n' try t' find a kind merchant. E-e-e-e-e! Cyclone ahead! Go set me gim—

175 & 176

What wrong is this vnto the Prince, your Sonne?
What good is this to England, and himselfe?

mals! Ho! It's in sight, 'n' 'fore it hits 'n' we go agrovnd in sand, put down the sheet anchor! Yo! We'l

177 & 178

Base, fearefull, and despayring Henry.
How hast thou iniur'd both thy selfe and vs?

bare th' spars 'n' let her yaw i' the rough—huff, then sail on ye flvd as day is done, 'n' dub

179 & 180

I cannot stay to heare these Articles. Nor I.
Come Cousin, let vs tell the Queene these Newes.

our hurt . . . O silly ass! This is n-n-n-n-not a sqvall! Here it c-c-c-comes! E-e-e-e-e-e-e-e-e-e-e! What t-t-t-to

181 & 182

Farwell faint-hearted and degenerate King,
In whose cold blood no sparke of Honor bides.

do? An idiot fear o' the end: We'll drown! Gear-ropes on deck break: tin bales slide off! H-Hang on!

183 & 184

Be thou a prey vn to the House of Yorke,
And dye in Bands, for this vnmanly deed.

th' bar breaks my ship. No one drouuns. Have no tyn left, tho'. Oy vey! Dead indeed, f—

Oy vey! Leo Rosten, in The Joys of Yiddish, writes: Oy vay! is the short form of "oy vay iz mir," an omnibus phrase for everything from personal pain to emphatic condolences. (Vay comes from the German, weh, meaning "woe").

185 & 186

In dreadfull Warre may'st thou be ouercome,
Or live in peace abandon'd and despis'd.

or wd proud chef euer believe ye storm claim'd tin? No! A sad end, abandon'd à l'eau. R.I.P. S—

187 & 188

Turne this way Henry, and regard them not. they seeke reuenge, and therefore will not yeeld.

o we're hungry 'n' wet 'n' need ayd t' refit here. Elemental! Let ye good natur'd khan—yes, he, this err—

189 & 190

Ah Exeter. Why should you sigh, my Lord? Not for myselfe Lord Warwick, but my Sonne,

or-sod fool, fix th' boat 'n' in return dredge all he wyshes o' yucky, slummy ore! W-why m—

191 & 192

Whom I vnnaturally shall dis-inherite. But be it as it may: I here entayle

ust I let him see our strait? Ay, Ay! The men'll *m*end ye ribbin' 'n' th' hvll! Ai, Ai! A—

193 & 194

The Crowne to thee and to thine Heires for ever, Conditionally, that heere thou take an Oath,

ll ten trie to cut 'n' fit teak into the toe. Very hard here, eatin' sea-chowder 'n' tea—'n' oh, oh, oh, oh, ea—

tea. some infusion of local leaves. There are still plantations of a native tea near Sinope. **toe.** the prow? or stern? OED 1643, Sandys' translation of *Oedipus*: about the mast the youthfull ivy twine, the lofty toe imbras'd with clustered vines. 1869 Sir E.J. Reed. *Shipbuilding*. The aftermost rivets were driven through the thin part of the toe and knocked down in a countersink.

195 & 196

To cease this Ciuill Warre: and whil'st I liue, To honor me as thy King, and Soueraigne:

ch man giues his strength 'n' skill an' at last we row clear out in ye road. Hi-o! Ei! *Video* i—

197 & 198

And neyther by Treason nor Hostilitie, To seeke to put me downe, and reigne thy selfe.

ndeed, *miseria probat fortes uiros*! We look, 'n' yet eyes deny the thing that none let en—

In De Providentia, Seneca wrote, "Ignis aurum probat, miseria fortes viros." (Misery proves strong men.)

199 & 200

This Oath I willingly take, and will performe,/Long liue King Henry: Plantagenet embrace him.

tertaine in hope: we see lying there, gone aground, grimy flab tin, all pack't in a hill! M'm, will kh—

201 & 202

And long liue thou, and these thy forward Sonnes.
Now Yorke and Lancaster are reconcil'd.

an, so greedy, euer trade for awkwardly situated ore-cache? Still—sh, lad—'n' on 'n' on 'n' on 'n' on. Ch—

203 & 204

Accurst be he, that seekes to make them foes.
Farewell my gracious Lord, Ile to my Castle.

ild! So we must get ore back t' sell at some city. Cash, see? After th' fall, make recouery. Oh, me!

205 & 206

And Ile keepe London with my Souldiers.
and I to Norfolke with my followers.

Know remedy: dry off our tin 'n' lade it, piled low, so low, on th' keel, 'n' hoise sail. M—

207 & 208

And I vnto the Sea, from whence I came.
And I with griefe and sorrow to the Court.

i mission ended! I return to Venice, go off—Ho! What an arrow!—t' watch Crete. Head m—

209 & 210

Heere comes the Queene,
Whose lookes bewray her anger:
Ile steale away.
Exeter so will I.

an Essex buys low all o' Crete's qweere weake wine t' sell horror-high at home. Eye-e-e! Ai-e-e-e!

Essex. Essex & Bacon were partners in a foreign secret service, and Essex wanted money to put into the enterprise. He had the lease of the farm of sweet wines in England.

211 & 212

Nay, goe not from me, I will follow thee.
Be patient gentle Queene, and I will stay.

You see, Hen—I, agent, bring payment 'n' will lade all loot. We lie-to, e'en qwite MT, off

Hen. Kit is writing to his friend Henry Wriothesley.
lie-to. a seaman's term. waiting.

213 & 214

Who can be patient in such extreames?
Ah wretched man, would I had dy'de a Maid.

th' Mercado. At palace window I see a maid; her hidd'n beauty enchants me. "Dux, wh—

Dux. The duke in 1593/ '94 was Zuan (Giovanni) Domenico Cicogna, q. Gerolamo. (q., quondam, here stands for son of). Maria Francesca Tiepolo, Director of the State Archive, Venice, wrote to me that Candia was recovering from a bad year. The duke was glad to make this wine-deal.

215 & 216

and neuer seene thee, neuer borne thee Sonne,/Seeing thou hast prov'd so vnnaturall a Father.

o's she I see up there, so neat? Her husband'l neuer neuer need t' go an' love another rvf-teat Nan, 'n'

217 & 218

Hath he deserv'd to loose his Birth-right thus?/Hadst thou but lou'd him halfe so well as I,

what a mother she'd B! I'd tell her so, uh hvh! I'l 'fold this beauteous lass! Oh, durst I go thith—

219 & 220

Or felt that paine which I did for him once,
Or nourisht him, as I did with my blood,

er, Milord?" "Oh, no: i' faith, my child is betroth'd wife to Counti Paris, whom I did h-han—

Counti Paris. Dr. Tiepolo sent me information on 23 December 1982: an inventory of public representatives in Candia (Crete) 1592-1595, showing that Avogadro Paris, q. Pompeo, was elected one of three treasurers on 26 January 1592. He was to have served until 1595, but refused. The name is a coincidence, because in a source for Kit's Romeo and Juliet, Wm. Painter's Palace of Pleasure, 1567, Juliet's fiancé is Count Paris, and even before this, in Arthur Brooke's Tragicall Historye of Romeo and Juliet, 1562, the fiancé is—Paris! (line 1882.)

221 & 222

Thou wouldst have left thy dearest heart-blood there,
Rather th(a)n haue made that sauage Duke thine Heire,

d authority tu manage business here. He hath a deed to take her heart foreuer—to th' death. We'l all have th' dut—

223 & 224

And dis-inherited thine onely Sonne.
Father, you cannot dis-inherite me:

y to honor 'n' trust 'n' send mi neat childe in-in-in-into her fee-day!" I see he'd a—

in-in-in-into. The duke is sobbing—he'll lose his girl and pay a big dowry.

225 & 226

If you be King, why should not I succeede?
Pardon me Margaret, pardon me sweet Sonne,

lready set th' wedding day before seein' outcome as wrong, ram-sick phenomenon. P-uu!

227 & 228

The Earle of Warwick and the Duke enforc't me.
Enforc't thee? Art thou King, and wilt be forc't?

Now I let th' Duke know that hateful fee need not B, C, if I treat, arrange, C? "Reform th' dower, C? C? K—

Reform th' dower. He's thinking to make the dowry so low Paris won't want to marry.

229 & 230

I shame to heare thee speake: ah timorous Wretch,
Thou hast vndone thy selfe, thy Sonne, and me,

eep economy th' deal 'n' she stays home free!" Ha! 'n' I thot that I had seamen's work houres! "Th' event U

231 & 232

and giu'n vnto the House of Yorke such head,/ As thou shalt reigne but by their sufferance.

fear is but changeable in future. Oh, oh! Don't vse your shy daughter, then, as fee to such kin!"

233 & 234

To entayle him and his Heires vnto the Crowne,
What is it, but to make thy Sepulcher,

I sent mi hair bracelet 'n' a love-note hy tu her. She spoke tu me at th' hy window, stitch—

th' hy window. In Erotokritos, a famed popular poem Kit wrote in sailors' Greek, we learn this window was in her sewing room. The hair bracelet is mentioned in the ballad, too.

235 & 236

And creepe into it farre before thy time?
Warwick is Chancelor, and the Lord of Callice,

ery in hand. Nearbi, her old Ama listen'd. O, I cri woe, C: plae th' ol' water-trick, etc., C, for effec—

237 & 238

Sterne Falconbridge commands the Narrow Seas,
The Duke is made Protector of the Realme,

t, then swear t' free her from th' damned mercenari bed-contract. So goes a lood ass like me—P-U!

239 & 240

and yet shalt thou be safe? Such safetie findes
The trembling Lambe, environned with Wolves.

Th' ladin' finish't, nvrse 'n' Rita fly uuith me. She has on wedding-best. We've left! O, cease to blame, b—

In Noches de Invierno, a book in Spanish that Kit wrote for his daughter, and also in his Greek ballad Erotokritos, we see Rita's pearl-covered wedding gown. In Cervantes' "Spanish English Girl" we see it cut down to fit Rita's little daughter.

241 & 242

Had I beene there, which am a silly Woman,
The Souldiers should haue toss'd me on their Pikes,

ecause both Rita 'n' nurse made milk ready while I laded wine—so simple, see? Ho, ho, ho! Sh! Shut th'

243 & 244

Before I would haue granted to that Act.
But thou preferr'st thy Life, before thine Honor.

hatch, for we sail on th' tide, free o' bother after yon/foreland bight. Butt-out there, U repu—

bight. Webster. akin to Dutch & German bucht, a bay. 3. a curve in a river coastline, etc. 4. a bay.

butt. Webster. ME. butten, to drive, thrust. 2. to move or drive headfirst.

245 & 246

And seeing thou do'st, I here divorce my selfe,
Both from thy table Henry, and thy Bed,

gnant sly doubt! On, t' Venice! Oye: she disobey'd her father, fled her home t' B my Rita! H—

247 & 248

Vntill that Act of Parliament be repeal'd,
Whereby my Sonne is disinherited!

ow c'd I send her home tyed in a net t' B pvnished 'n' marry Paris? Better if I tell all

249 & 250

The Northerne Lords, that have forsworne thy colours,
Will follow mine, if once they see them spread:

when we reach Venice. Her lost father soon may relent 'n' let us wed. Oh, Ho! I'm still de fool of th' story! A pr—

Note that ll. 249, 250, 251, 252 should be deciphered as a unit. An A and an R cross over.

251 & 252

And spread they shall be, to thy soule disgrace,
And vtter ruine of the House of Yorke.

yncesse uued a lo sailor? O, Ney, Ney! Tho' Kit loved her best, her fat hog father'd part us! D—

253 & 254

Thus doe I leaue thee: Come Sonne let's away,
Our Army is ready; come, wee'le after them.

o we deem hym ruler o' our liues? No! Oye: his element's far away. C de tame cat tease thee!

255 & 256

Stay gentle Margaret, and heare me speake.
Thou hast spoke too much already: get thee gone.

At edge o' th' great lagoon uue stop 'n' marry, at Sta. Marya. On deck, see th' sleek page—me! He, he, he! T—

Sta. Marya. A church of Santa Maria was built on the Lido years later—maybe it replaced an earlier one? They probably did go to the Lido; later we learn that the nurse lived there, and she may have wanted the ceremony at her church.

257 & 258

Gentle Sonne Edward, thou wilt stay me?
I, to be murther'd by his Enemies.

hen my men draw wine 'n' greet th'bride thus: "Liue ye to best old time, so as

259 & 260

When I returne with victorie to the field,
Ile see your Grace: till then, Ile follow her.

to regenerate th' love thy lord will trulie offer U." "Well enow!" I crie: "Hie, hie!" It's nice—th'

261 & 262

Come Sonne away, we may not linger thus.
Poore Queene,
How loue to me, and to her Sonne,

general toast—tho' th' poem's queer. "Here now, come on, yu!" We sail on a moon-down eue, yn en—

263 & 264

Hath made her breake out into termes of Rage.
Reueng'd may she be on that hatefull Duke,

folding fog: hard t' see the markers on our uuay, but hear the bel 'n' heed thee, Mama Kate. Te—

Kate. Kate may have given him special warnings about the fog bell off Dover. He has spoken now to Hen, Meg, Peter, Kate and Francis Bacon. Letters home!

265 & 266

Whose haughtie spirit, winged with desire,
Will cost my Crowne, and like an emptie Eagle,

dious tacking, 'n' at last at midnight we moor de ship well in here, wi' ye Gew crew's help. Ie, ie!

267 & 268

Tyre on the flesh of me, and of my Sonne.
The losse of those three Lords torments my heart:

My lady's free, not some stolen loot: her honest desyre's for me, see? Tho' th' man offer th'-th' n—

Tyre. Webster. tire. to seize or tear at something.

269 & 270

Ile write vnto them, and entreat them faire;
Come Cousin, you shall be the Messenger.

otion, Rita cements it: her letters tel me we can have money from a bundle she hugs. Ie!

notion. She brought not only her wedding dress but her dowry, too. Was the man's "notion" simply matrimony or a suggestion she take her dowry along? Kit the gold-digger?

271 & 272

And I, I hope, shall reconcile them all.
Brother, though I bee youngest, giue mee leaue.

Enough t' buy a home 'n' liuing here. O cease t' blame: it is the legal loue-price held on her.

273 & 274

No, I can better play the Orator.
But I haue reasons strong and forceable.

O see, Rita's pregnant, 'n' babe to arriue for us yn October. Can the halt old a—

275 & 276

Why how now Sonnes, and Brother, at a strife?
What is your Quarrell? how began it first?

unty aid th' birth wi' a swill of bru? Great honor's shown t' her. No, no! Reqwest a safer way!

aunty. the nurse. A 'no' could go before great honors shown to her, but it was likely that Rita deferred to her, and Kit—after the fact—was apprehensive. I believe he wrote this story as a memoir. The Henry VI plays, though staged early in different form and with different titles, were never in print as Henry the Sixth, Parts 1, 2, 3, until the First Folio.

277 & 278

No Quarrell, but a slight Contention.
About what / About that which concernes your Grace and vs.

A call, but a question, C? Can I go 'n' leave Rita yn our house 'n' trust that crone, C, who'd grow t' B th' ban-h—

279 & 280

The Crowne of England, Father, which is yours.
Mine Boy? not till King Henry be dead.

ound here? Th' Chef at Rome becks now, 'n' yf a brother needs ayd, I go willingly in—in th'

281 & 282

Your Right depends not on his life, or death.
Now you are Heire, therefore enioy it now:

store to find 'n' get de way. Oh, hurry! Depart now. Ho! 'N' return here soon! Oh, I fly! O, ie-ie, ie-ie!

283 & 284

by giuing the House of Lancaster leaue to breathe,
It will out-runne you, Father, in the end.

In th' E. College I aduise th' bros. We 'n' they agree on a honey final flauor in th' butter (Et tu-u-u—).

E. English. There were English Roman Catholic colleges operating in France, Spain and Italy, and in each there were SSS agents on the watch.
final flauor. hiding the mercury sublinate. Shadows show that in 1585 Francis Washingham had sent Kit to kill this man, Dr. Allen, in Reims, but at that time Kit had given him half the dose, hoping he'd live and reform.

285 & 286

I tooke an Oath, that hee should quietly reigne.
But for a Kingdome any Oath may be broken:

A Kent knight (me, by Hob), rode out o' Rome barely a tenth of a league ahead o' th' ynquisition. K—

Hob. A name for Puck, a devilish imp. Fynes Moryson wrote in his Itinerary (p.159) that in 1594 a young English spy left Rome pursued by the Inquisition as far as Siena and then headed for Padua in such haste "as he seemed to fly over the Appenine without wings."

287 & 288

I would breake a thousand Oathes, to reigne one yeere.
No: God forbid your Grace should be forsworne.

now houu I fly toward Rita o'er rocks, 'n' on sodden ground. Here's our babe's day of birth! O, Geee! O, Geee! Lea—

289 & 290

I shall be, if I clayme by open Warre.
Ile proue the contrary, if you'le heare mee speake.

rn ye way! E-e! Hell! I seek, reach our home i' time: special preparation for ye babe, fully

291 & 292

Thou canst not, Sonne: it is impossible.
An Oath is of no moment, being not tooke

anticipating th' weak but insistent monotones soon to B one of home's lo nois—

*w*eak. m used upside down as w.

293 & 294

Before a true and lawfull Magistrate,
That hath authoritie ouer him that sweares.

es. Th' labor ouer, U greet th' new life that hath arriued. Atta Rita! What a famous smile!

295 & 296

Henry had none, but did vsurpe the place.
Then seeing 'twas he that made you to depose,

Heavy hemorrhage, 'n' can't stop yt! Nu hope—we need U! But she slips to death, indeed. Deat—

297 & 298

Your Oath, my Lord, is vaine and friuolous. therefore to Armes: and Father doe but thinke,

h! Save 'er! Tried! O, to lose Rita! Ama hies to fynd food for th' neuuborn. Try near: haue U milk? D—

299 & 300

How sweet(e) a thing it is to weare a Crowne, Within whose Circuit is Elizium,

ear Eliza, we must wean her. We choose t' trust this cow, C. I-I go in: I-I-I win th' wi—

301 & 302

And all that poets faine of Blisse and Ioy. Why doe we linger thus? I cannot rest,

llin' aid o' this spotty friend, 'n' th' bonny child eats wel 'n' grows fat. Ae, ae, ae! So U e—

303 & 304

Vntill the White Rose that I weare, be dy'de. Euen in the luke-warme blood of Henries heart.

ndure th' early death, her work-thimble ever on th' table. Ie! A sweet new life needs U, tho'. O, I, I!

305 & 306

Richard ynough: I will be King, or dye. Brother, thou shalt to London presently,

I go to work in Spain: hot, dry hell! Babe 'n' nurse go too. Ye yl trull hinder'd th' Chr—

Spain. Cervantes invited the little family to stay with him in Seville. Cervantes wrote about this nurse (as the 'afflicted matron') and Kit's courtship in Crete, in DQ 2, Chapter 38 and into 39 (Shelton), leaving out Rita's death.

307 & 308

and whet on Warwick, to this Enterprise. Thou Richard shalt to the Duke of Norfolke,

istian color she knew I'd created for our household, 'n' kept wearin' th'-th'-that forkt-w—

309 & 310

and tell him priuily of our intent. You Edward shall unto my Lord Cobham,

aist, to B call'd my whore in th' report R lad mail'd you on my neuufound ill h—

forked-waist. A sexy style. He writes to Francis Bacon? R lad. This could be Bacon's cousin Cooke, who may have come down to collect plays and pay for the Cardinal Allen job?

311 & 312

With whom the Kentishmen will willingly rise. In them I trust, for they are Souldiers,

elth. Error! I' truth, I'm well in Seuille with this thin SSS friend I know, who met me gayly,

Error! Refers to the messenger's misinformation plus the necessary misspelling of "health."
this thin SSS friend. Miguel Cervantes.

313 & 314
Wittie, courteous, liberall, full of spirit. While you are thus imploy'd, what resteth more?

stutter'd his offer to share home with my people. I wis I call it braue. O, will our trull yet u—

stutter'd. Cervantes was a famous stammerer.
The outside lines here honor not only Kit's Kentish compatriots but also his thin friend.

315 & 316
But that I seeke occasion how to rise,
And yet the King not priuie to my Drift,

p-root my design t' take a ten-week study in th' best church? I ran to it: O, fie! Oi! Oi!

317 & 318
Nor any of the House of Lancaster.
But stay, what Newes? Why comm'st thou in such poste?

I watcht th' hasty Ama waue 'n' cuss 'n' stone 'n' run our moo-cow off the holy steps. Ye best h—

319 & 320
The Queene, / With all the Northerne Earles and Lords,
Intend here to beseige you in your Castle.

old—Eee!—was to reach t' th' harness I see trailing behind our Queeney. O, relent 'n' let her do yt, unle—

321 & 322
She is hard by, with twentie thousand men:
And therefore fortifie your Hold, my Lord.

ss she'd run too far behind the harried ruminant, who did fly with ye lyt feet o' more o—

323 & 324
I, with my Sword. What? thinkst thou, that we feare them?
Edward and Richard, you shall stay with me,

ft-seen racers. Will she head home? Run away? What idiot wd wait! Sh! Kyt doth wryt U th' drama with th'

325 & 326
My Brother Mountague shall poste to London,
Let Noble Warwicke, Cobham, and the rest,

trull's wild escapade 'n' tell o' my MT babe's hunger 'n' then o' th' moo-cow o'ertaken. O, both ar—

327 & 328
Whom we haue left Protectors of the King,
With powrefull Pollicie strengthen themselues,

e hurt. This nurse must go home! How? Alone? She'll weep, 'n' Kit'll offer t' go with 'er, etc., etc. I flew p-p—

329 & 330

And trust not simple Henry, nor his Oathes. Brother, I goe: Ile winne them, feare it not.

ast mts. wi' her, 'n' sail t' Genoa 'n' post for Lido, her home. But yn error I hie in th' tent, 'n'—E-e-e!—

331 & 332

And thus most humbly I doe take my leaue. Sir Iohn, and Sir Hugh Mortimer, mine Vncles,

she's bathin'! She roughly screams "U klouun!" Thinkin' I'm doom'd, I retreat, leave m-my-mind—

333 & 334

You are come to Sandall in a happie houre, The armie of the Queene meane to beseige vs.

Eeeeeee!—'n' run! So the floosee queene Ama appears, C, laughin' at my too-timid behavior. H—

Again the outside words relate to the cipher: Kit is beseiged.
Sandall. The Duke of York is in Sandal Castle near Wakefield, Yorkshire.
queene. prostitute, Elizabethan slang.

335 & 336

Shee shall not neede, wee'le meete her in the field.
What with fiue thousand men?

auin' to defend mieself then, I tel her that in the house she'l hae me—we'l e'en wed w—

337 & 338

I, with fiue hundred, Father, for a neede.
A Woman's generall: what should we feare?

hen we arriue, a low lie t' hasten us on our merree wae, delighted. F-fah and f-fah! Wd

339 & 340

I heare their Drummes:
Let's set our men in order,
And issue forth, and bid them Battaile straight.

I start for mi trim babe at night, unseen, or uud this Ama hold me in her dreaded site, t' rest her sel—

341 & 342

Fiue men to twentie: though the oddes be great,
I doubt not, Vncle, of our Victorie.

f on an i-idiot—etc! Tvt, tvt, U! Our child needs U now. Get home to her! Goe—before U be It!

343 & 344

Many a battaile haue I wonne in France. When as the Enemie hath beene tenne to one:

We haue a hey nonnee nonnee in the tent. Ha'e no fear—at last, C, I'm e'en with mi ane babe.

345 & 346

Why should I not now haue the like successe.
Ah, whither shall I flye, to scape their hands?

Oh, child, child! Hoy, she tels o' her uenture to th' Spanish escuela while Kit was away, 'n' she f—

Hoy. Sp. Today.

347 & 348

Ah, Tutor, looke where bloody Clifford comes.
Chaplaine away, thy Priesthood saues thy life.

ill'd our Spanish home with the lot of pretty local words she heard off-key: "Boca i-ee. Y uaya co—. . ."

Boca i-ee. Sp., Boca allí. mouth here. (touching her father's mouth)
Y uaya co (n). and go with.

349 & 350

As for the brat of this accursed Duke,
Whose Father slew(e) my Father, he shall dye.

Seated here, she f-fills th' breach of my sad heart. After her study, we walk.

351 & 352

And I, my Lord, will beare him company./
Souldiers, away with him.

I bid U all—What?—Why? No more are my ciphers in my dam' swill! Adio!

f

Sir Thomas More.
The Shakespeare Apocrypha. Ed. C. F. Tucker Brooke. Oxford: Clarendon, 1971. p 385

SIR THOMAS MORE

1 & 2
Whether wilt thou hale me?
Whether I please; thou art my prize, and I pleade purchase of thee.

Marlowe thrust forth his hated, mazed play—writ with help—in hope a' peace. "E-e-e! He'l hurt U! E-e-e!"

Kit doesn't harm co-writers on this work by identifying them.
The play shows how Sir Thomas More's fall parallels Sir Roger Manwood's. The work, censored by Master of Revels Edward Tilney, remained unpublished till 1844, saved in twenty paste-up sheets in the collection of Edward Harley, Second Earl of Oxford, husband of Marlowe's great-great granddaughter. (Her great-grandmother was Isabel-Elizabeth Basset Cavendish, adopted as a child by the Bassets.)

f

Hero and Leander: Quarto.
Complete Works of Christopher Marlowe. Ed. Fredson Bowers, 2nd ed.

HERO AND LEANDER

First Sestyad, lines 1 & 2:

On Hellespont guilt(y) of True-loves blood, In view and opposit(e) two citties stood,	**The YAT sings o' love's end: best love put down, left cold. O, O, *Oi*! Stil I write t' U—I ope-open**

YAT. Yataghan, a mean Turkish knife—a nickname Emilia used for Marlowe.

X

There's more

Third Sestyard, lines 1 & 2:

New light giues new directions, Fortunes new To fashion our indevours that ensue,	**George touch'd these orfan lines sent to U, set in his winnin' words. Nouu, after U view**

George. To cover for Kit, George Chapman pretended he'd written the last part of this poem. George divided the work into 'sestiads', added touches here and there.
orfan. orphan.

X

There's more

a reconstruction of a 4-stanza lyric in Bodleian MSS Rawl. Poetry.
Complete Works of Christopher Marlowe. Ed. Fredson Bowers, 2nd ed. p 535.

THE PASSIONATE SHEPHERD

1 & 2

Come live with mee and be my loue	**We met, 'n' Marlove made U this, leauin'**
And we will all the pleasures proue	**R woo place. Ye bell peel'd while su—**

3 & 4

That Vallies, groves, hills and fieldes,	**nset flooded ye woodes. VVe ran along the**
Woods, or steepie mountaine yeeldes.	**hill trail—U passed me—I, I! Let's see, is**

5 & 6

And wee will sit upon the Rocks,	**it a race for kisses? D-do U flee?**
Seeing the Sheepheards feede the(i)r flocks,	**Heedless—shit!!—we keel o'er, 'n' git the p-p, 'n' when ch—**

7 & 8

By(e) shallow(e) Riuers, to whose falls,	**ase's o'er, more hugs! L-L-L-L-Libby, I won't**
Melodious Byrd(e)s sing Madrigalls	**go away from U ere I d-d-die! All's S-s-s-sh—**

Libby. Queen Elizabeth's private nickname.

9 & 10

And I will make you beds of Roses,	**rouded in a fog as U kiss me 'n' we part.**
and a thousand fragrant posies,	**I'l B lost—no, dead—as far's any ho—**

11 & 12

A cap of flowers, and a kirtle,	**ly mad prelate knows. But after I sail, wd**
Imbroydred all with leaues of Mirtle.	**mi ladie feel a horror of cl—**

holy mad prelate. Whitgift. Elizabeth has saved Kit, who'll sail, from Whitgift's hit.

13 & 14

A belte of Strawe, and Yvie buds,	**ub poet-lads that send bad dactil verse**
With Corall claspes and amber studs,	**far across ye sea, 'n' will bum w—**

club poet lads. Kit is a club-footed poet—and to Elizabeth, a lad—and he's making a half-joke about his broken-footed dactyl verse.

15 & 16

And if these things thy minde may moue,	**hat gov'ment funds they need? O, m-m-mi**
Then live with mee, and bee my loue.	**lady, I'ue been thine: Smile! Ha'e with ye!**

Over centuries this poem has been published with several inferior added stanzas. I can find no ciphers inside those extra stanzas, but in the four-stanza form printed here the ciphers link sensibly. Each line, too, has four beats.

f

Loves Labour's Lost. First Folio of Shakespeare. Comedies, pp 122-125.

LOVES LABOUR'S LOST

1 & 2

Let Fame, that all hunt after in their liues, Liue registred vpon our brazen Tombes,	**Marlouue made this iesting plaie anent Hen's revel for Eliza, but th' tr-tr-trouble (f—**

anent. Webster. ME. in line with, respecting, about.
Hen. Kit's friend Henry Wriothesley, Third Earl of Southampton
Eliza. Elizabeth Vere, Ned de Vere and Anne Cecil's daughter, Wm. Cecil's granddaughter.

3 & 4

And then grace vs in the disgrace of death: When spight of cormorant deuouring Time,	**its 'n' fits o' ire) gave Hen sudden courage to forgo th' marriage match; 'n' chid, he went 'n' p'd.**

chid. Webster. chided. scolded, upbraided. **p'd.** paid.
Wm. Cecil, Lord Burghley, did try to make Hen (himself a product of incest) marry his own half-sister, Elizabeth de Vere, and when Hen refused, made him pay a £5,000 fine. Father Garnet's note in a script preserved in Archives of the English Jesuits at Stonyhurtst, and quoted by G.P.V. Akrigg in Shakespeare and the Earl of Southampton. Cambridge MA: Harvard U Press, pp. 39-40. The money was to go to Burghley in one chunk when Hen came of age in 1594. (He was a Queen's Ward in Burghley's care). Stonyhurst MSS. 19 Nov. 1594. Hen didn't crumble, the marriage didn't take place, and this play had to be revised.

5 & 6

Th' endeuour of this present breath may buy: That honour which shall bate his sythes keene edge,	**Kit alter'd bans 'n' bed t' hints o' future MT years. So how's th' change? Ye be Phhhhhhreeee! Stay!! I loue U.**

Kit found out that Hen was the son of Ned de Vere and his mother Queen Elizabeth, and Kit told Hen, not only to prevent a weird union with Ned's legitimate daughter, but because Kit didn't want Hen to marry, in spite of the sonnets Kit had written to Hen about wedded bliss—sonnets contracted for by Ned.

7 & 8

And make vs heyres of all eternitie. Therefore braue Conquerours, for so you are,	**A fool t' require you to marry a Vere sister! Fah! No cruder fool has euer been seen! K-**

9 & 10

That warre against your owne affections, And the huge Armie of the worlds desires.	**nowledge o' wrong arriued iust in time for Hen t' wrest free o' th' shaft day! *Cessa*! Aaah!**

Mary Browne knew she'd reared a changeling—that the boy was Queen Elizabeth's child—but Mary, her family and Hen had believed Hen's natural father was Leicester. Now Hen discovers the truth.

***Cessa*! Aaah!** Enough already! (It. cessare, to cease)

11 & 12

Our late edict shall strongly stand in force, Nauar shall be the wonder of the world.	**Henry's dad's his brother, too! W. Cecil ran t' follow Ned's neat daughter 'n' flout all real**

Kit spells it out, but in this postscript the nouns can be scrambled; he's telling us it's a mess.

13 & 14

Our Court shall be a little Achademe, Still and contemplatiue in liuing Art.	**concerns o' ill th' match uud entail. A motiue? Spell it G-r-e-e-d! Ai! Until a brat all**

G-r-e-e-d! Wm. Cecil, Hen's guardian, Elizabeth Vere's grandfather, saw the match as financially good for the Cecils, besides adding to the family store of royal blood.

15 & 16

You three, Berowne, Dumaine, and Longauill, Haue sworne for three yeeres terme, to liue with me:	**misgotten's here! Then wd any memory—all uain reuelree—relieue th' fear, th' burden? O woe, woe! I O U**

17 & 18

My fellow Schollers, and to keepe those statutes
That are recorded in this scedule heere.

m' life, Hen, see? So altho' sworn to keep yr. dad's secret, I had to tell U the clear truth, see—see? Cd

19 & 20

Your oathes are past, and now subscribe your names:
That his owne hand may strike his honour downe,

I do otherwise? Any man o' honor wd do th' same when he hears o' sick trespass 'n' yu ar in a sour bunt. Ay, but

bunt. OED. the bagging part of a fish net, the bottom part of an eel-trap, the bag, pouch or middle part of a sail. Kit was a sailor.

21 & 22

That violates the smallest branch heerein:
If you are arm'd to doe, as sworne to do,

love more than duty steer'd me, so I bet R.'s chaine an' lost it! Fah! There's a low road! O! A—

R.'s chaine. Roger's gold chain of office. Kit thought he knew a sure way to win and help Hen pay his fine.

23 & 24

Subscribe to your deepe oathes, and keepe it to.
I am resolu'd, 'tis but a three yeeres fast:

s I took de father's chaine t' playe, I seemed to b-be so sure o' ye rebate I uud press t' treat U.

25 & 26

The minde shall banquet, though the body pine,
Fat paunches haue leane pates: and dainty bits,

Th' hunch fail'd. Hope ended in that quiet toss 'n' a base laugh. But then a deep, an e'en abysmal pity

Perhaps not just a hunch but loaded dice? And Kit's girlfriend Emilia made a dice-switch so her nightclub would win? In The Comedy of Errors, she is the abyssal-abbess.

27 & 28

Make rich the ribs, but bankerout the wits.
My louing Lord, Dumane is mortified,

came; I'l B shamed foreuer by th' bunt o' this ugli error. U didn't know mi mistake: it

For details of the loss of Roger's chain and events that followed: his monograph in *DNB* and Registers of the Acts of Privy Council, vol. 22, 1591-92, new series, pp 380-381, 449-51. A version of this episode was set down a decade later in John Manningham's Diary. Folio 70, November 1602, p 91: "Lord Cheife Baron Manwood understanding that his soone had sold his chayne to a goldsmith" [the man was Emilia's fence, Roger Underwood] "sent for the goldsmith, willed him to bring the chayne, enquired where he bought it. He told, in his house. The Baron desired to see it, and put it in his pocket, telling him it was not lawfully bought." [Manwood was correct about the illegality of high-stakes gambling, and in 1591 Elizabeth required that this law be more strictly enforced. G.B. Harrison. An Elizabethan Journal, 1591-94. NY: Cosmopolitan Books, 1929, p 38.] "The goldsmith sued the Lord, and fearing the issue would prove against him, obtained the councel's letters to the Lord, who answered, 'malas causas habentes semper fugiunt ad potentes. Ubi non valet veritas, prevalet authoritas. Currat Lex, Vivat Rex, and soe fare you well, my lords'; but he was commit." [The fence Underwood had appealed to Emilia's patron and lover Henry Carey, Lord Chamberlain Hunsdon, a council member.]

29 & 30

The grosser manner of these worlds delights,	**was ment to lower th' Vere fine when**
He throwes vpon the grosse worlds baser slaues:	**brother's due date's here. So regard: phhss!! Loss, loss, loss! G-gr!**

ment. meant. As long as a word is understandable when read aloud in dialogue or cipher, the spelling will pass muster for Kit—he's a dramatist.
phhss!! onomatopoeic fizzle. The air leaves the balloon.
G-gr! A stammered growl. Kit's many stammered utterances suggest that he had an intermittant speech defect, and in a late cipher he admits it.

31 & 32

To loue, to wealth, to pompe, I pine and die,	**Th' high man who saued U, little lo ill idiot,**
With all these liuing in Philosophie.	**was the Pope. Nope, nope, nope! I-I-lie! It**

33 & 34

I can but say their protestation ouer,	**was Roger: Oye! Euer an artist uuith dice,**
So much, deare Liege, I haue already sworne.	**at Emilia's he opened lo on Barcabudee. She, uery**

35 & 36

That is, to liue and study heere three yeares.	**hot, casts hi t' uuin, reset t' cast another**
But there are other strict obseruances:	**try, but he sees her error: a die-tylter! E-e!**

reset. In Barcabudi, the shooter retains the dice and continues to shoot as long as he wins. John Scarne, Scarne on Dice, 8th ed., NY: Crown, 1980. The "passage" in Kit's early play Sir John Oldcastle [Act 4. 01-43 fol.] is like Barcabudi (probably originally called Barcabougi).
die-tylter. In Barcabudi, one pair of dice is used, but each player casts from his own dice-cup; Emilia's was gaffed.
(Lines 33, 34, 35, 36 are deciphered together: from 35, 36 B U D E E & E go back to 33, 34.)

37 & 38

As not to see a woman in that terme, Which I hope well is not enrolled there.	**A waie to slide, not roll her settlers—each one with hi on top. Hen, Emma went**

39 & 40

And one day in a we ke to touch no foode: and but one meale on euery day beside:	**wilde! Denounced my father: "EeeeOOO—EeeeOOO—bad, bad . . . " 'n' Kyt an idyot, 'n' U—'n' *U* as an**

41 & 42

The which I hope is not enrolled there. and then to sleepe but three houres in the night,	**inept Hen. She'll lose! He'd th' right to shoot true new dice, 'n' the pair enter, both hi. He euen**

43 & 44

and not be seene to winke of all the day. When I was wont to thinke no harme all night,	**bets his take. He won 'n' won, 'n' at length de winner took al! Emilia howl'd at fate! Hey, non!**

45 & 46

And make a darke night too of halfe the day: Which I hope well is not enrolled there.	**Few knew, like me, th' plot facin' Roger—a hard deal to end at his death in ho-holy holee—**

Few knew. But since mid-1589, probably every member of the marriage-connected families of Walter Mildmay (d. 31 May, 1589), Francis Walsingham (d. 6 April, 1590), Thomas Randolph (d. 8 June, 1590), and Roger Manwood (d. 14 Dec., 1592), knew that all four men were doomed victims of Archbishop Whitgift's inquisition against Marranos and Puritans.

47 & 48

O, these are barren taskes, too hard to keepe, Not to see Ladies, study, fast, not sleepe.	**ass, prelate ordered, poke-a-stake ass-bleedin'. The note to you: not for the State SS! E-e!**

Incensed, Kit presented his play Edward II at Hampton Court on Dec. 27, '92. (Edward died stabbed through the anus.) Here in cipher Kit spells it out—no wonder those executions were kept secret. This play was to have been suppressed: only two copies have been found in early (1594) edition, one in Switzerland at the Zentralbibliothek, Zurich, one in Germany at the Landesbibliothek of Cassel. Edward II is a Pembroke play: Mary Herbert, a faithful friend, helped Kit.

49 & 50

Your oath is past, to passe away from these. Let me say no my Leidge, and if you please,	**O dam fatso sinful oppressiue prelate, may ya dye soon! Get ye away to shit-hel! Ames—**

51 & 52

I onely swore to study with your grace, And stay heere in your Court for three yeeres space.	**sage: U crude clown curate, O say yer prayers ere we hurry thee to ioin ye rest of th' idyots on**

53 & 54

You swore to that, Berowne, and to the rest. By yea and nay sir, than I swore in iest.	**Hades' outer shore, to be bayoneted in eternity wi' a rain o tynny hot straws. Was**

bayoneted. OED. bayonet . . . possible that the word may be a dimin. of O.F. bayon, baion, "arrow or shaft of a crossbow." "1. a short flat dagger. 1611 Cotgr., "bayonette, a kind of small flat pocket dagger, furnished with knives."

55 & 56

What is the end of study, let me know? Why that to know which else wee should not know.	**thy hate so low thou knockt Dad, who fel down to his knees, 'n' then U slew hym, wet, wet wi'**

Dr. Lopes did the slaying but Whitgift ordered the execution.

57 & 58

Things hid [and-&] bard (you meane) frõ cõmon sense I, that is studies god-like recompence.	**blood 'n' feces—th' paid assassin a uicious rotten demented Greek medic M.G. in hy honor,**

medic. Dr. Ruy Lopes.
M.G. a joke? Medical Grifter? Medical Greek?
in hy honor. Lopes was the queen's own doctor. She probably trusted him to perform gently.

59 & 60

Come on them, I will sweare to studie so, To know the thing I am forbid to know:	**'n' smother'd in secret? O, but I know who sent a man to kill! O! Whitgift—Woe, O, o! Die!**

61 & 62

As thus, to study where I well may dine,
When I to fast expressely am forbid.

Essex saw your sly Dr.-in-fee bleed hys father-i'-law to death. I spit on U: M-m-tw!

father-in-law. Essex and Frances Walsingham Sidney had just been married when Dr. Lopes came to the house in Seething Lane on the night of 5 April, 1590. By early morning of the 6th, Sir Francis Walsingham was dead.

63 & 64

Or studie where to meet some Mistresse fine,
When Mistresses from common sense are hid.

Two other SSS honest men were so murdered i' secret m-miserie: foes o' this insane femme's m—

Two other SSS honest men. Two others were Walter Mildmay, Roger's chief at Exchequer, and Thomas Randolph, diplomat, ambassador and postmaster (who once, long before, had hired Wm. Shakespeare).
The **insane femme** must be the queen, who let Whitgift rule her by threatening to reveal truth about her children.

65 & 66

Or hauing sworne too hard a keeping oath,
Studie to breake it, and not breake my troth.

ad rotten Goyan bishop, who'd break the rank 'n' take euerie good Torah minister, tout à-

The privately executed men were Marranos, as were many public servants in Elizabeth's day. Her mother was a Marrano, and Elizabeth once said, "I will never forget my people." But these men endangered Whitgift's view of Anglican theocracy.

67 & 68

If studies gaine be thus, and this be so,
Studie knowes that which yet it doth not know,

gout, t' undo th' best boys in SS. Did he euen think what he was doin'? Oi! Th' sick, fat, twiste—

think what he was doin'? Whitgift must have believed he was getting rid of a cell of conniving secret Jews who threatened his own position. After all, Roger wrote the best of the Marpreplate Papers.

69 & 70

Sweare me to this, and I will nere say no.
These be the stops that hinder studie quite,

d rat! Attend! Beth hates him, yet she's powerless to deter his inquisition. Wel, e'en U a—

71 & 72

And traine our intellects to vaine delight, Why? All delights are vaine, and that most vaine	**llow the vile rat-sin ta go unmentioned. Add t' this that ya receive all his late raving 'n' end a—**

73 & 74

Which with paine purchas'd, doth inherit paine, As painefully to poare vpon a Booke,	**ttendin' t' confer wi' your pappa's killer. Oie! Open vp, Bacon! What d'U hope? Ha ha ha! Shi-i-i—**

75 & 76

To seeke the light of truth, while truth the while Doth falsely blinde the eyesight of his looke:	**t! Look out, little Yid! Seek refuge, or th' Whitgift'll whet his teeth i' thy flesh 'n' blood! He, he, he, he! As**

Bacon. Francis Bacon, natural son of Francis Walsingham and the queen (Bacon conceived on the night of the Moorish Dance).

77 & 78

Light seeking light, doth light of light beguile: So ere you finde where light in darkenesse lies,	**I like U, knowe that he feels delight only in higgling her for little hedge-heresies. O, big disgust! E—**

Yid. Kit teases Bacon about his Jewishness.
The outside lines speak to the suppressed truth of the ciphers.

79 & 80

Your light growes darke by losing of your eyes. Studie me how to please the eye indeede,	**uery one is wary o' de beast: Look out for ye med i' th night, ye giddy geese! He'l peel us worse**

81 & 82

By fixing it vpon a fairer eye, Who dazling so, that eye shall be his heed,	**than Eliza. So exit i' line, V bad boys, t' feel hys fag-hog hired ire! Pay when**

83 & 84

And giue him light that it was blinded by. Studie is like the heauens glorious Sunne,	**it starts; when it ends, U'll be high SSS kill-meat in uieuu: dead on th' bed, I, yi! Gag! Hen, I-O-U!**

85 & 86

That will not be deepe search'd with fawncy lookes:
Small haue continual plodders euer wonne,

Know Lopes is a n-nasty accomplice who hurt all he bled, 'n' a dew-filter he's not. Euen loue wd dare t'

87 & 88

Saue base authoritie from others Bookes.
These earthly Godfathers of heauens lights,

hate this gross killer; he gets a fee for subhuman behauior. Easy to see he trod soft at ho—

base authoritie from others Bookes. from academic researchers' works.

89 & 90

That giue a name to euery fixed Starre,
Hauenomoreprofitoftheirshiningnights,

me, uuith great pretension ou horror at mi father's death. Oh, sing in ye exit, Feagin! F—

Feagin. Long before Dickens, Feagin was a theatrical villain.

91 & 92

Then those that walke and wot not what they are.
Too much to know, is to know nought but fame.

eign U R honest on oath, 'n'—oh! Watch out! K-tw, K-tw! Amnesty o' wealth to B due to th' woman, tho,' Kate, f—

K-tw K-tw. Kit spits at Lopes-Feagin.
Amnesty. Lopes' widow Sara received his estate. Lopes was convicted and hanged, not for these murders, but on a different, imagined charge, trumped up by sons and a son-in-law of men he killed (Bacon, Walsingham's bastard; Robert Devereux, Walsingham's son-in-law; Kit, Roger Manwood's bastard). For the legend the young men created, Lewis Wolfe, "Jews in Elizabethan England." Transactions of the Jewish Historical Society of England, vol. 11, xi, 1927, 91 pp. **Kate.** Kit speaks to his mother, Kate, who may have said, "think of that man's poor wife." This cipher may be reminiscent; Lopes is said to have died on the scaffold 7 June, 1594, after being convicted 28 February 1594. (Was it really '93?).

93 & 94

And euery Godfather can giue a name.
How well hee's read, to reason against reading.

or she's di innocent—unaware o' her greedy man's fee'd outrage. What a legend! Ai! Al aga—

95 & 96

Proceeded well, to stop all good proceeding.
Hee weedes the corne, and still lets grow the weeding.

inst odds, we'll protect her lone right to her place. We *do* do good deeds, C! 'N' all weeping—Ee-Ee—Lest Gew

97 & 98

The Spring is neare when Greene geese are a breeding.
How followes that?
Fit in his place and time.

ambassador here open, enter, higgle 'n' resist the final decree i' the Lopes hanging. We few wait in 'e—

Gew ambassador. Judah Serfatim, envoy from Alvaro Mendes, powerful Jewish adviser to the Turkish sultan. Ruy Lopes was Alvaro Mendes' brother-in-law. Lewis Wolfe. "Jews in Elizabethan England."

99 & 100

In reason nothing. / Something then in rime.
Berowne is like an enuious sneaping Frost,

I's torment as the Gew begins asking for reprieue. So, he must "hei-a-nonni, nonni, nonni-i-i . . . "

nonni. The nonnis represent the envoy's statement of his case for Lopes.

101 & 102

That bites the first borne infants of the Spring.
Wel, say I am, why should proud Summer boast,

In spite o' his plea, th' enuoy's first effort was rumored lost, 'n' by mi thrum th' b-beast was hang'd.

by mi thrum. at my insistence. It must have been '93.

103 & 104

Before the Birds haue any cause to sing?
Why should I ioy in any abortiue birth?

But I found no ioyi' this hy reuenge I craued, as it was both base 'n' horrible. Ay! Hy!

Hy! Lopes must have been hanged high, to swing in the wind, so his friends would be unable to pull his legs and hasten his death.

105 & 106

At Christmas I no more desire a Rose,
Then with a Snow in Mayes new(e) fangled showes:

Now I regret my SSS role in his death, for a man was wasted, see, 'n' in time, each one who's

107 & 108
Butlike of each thing that in season growes.
So you to studie now it is too late.

sau'd is giuen grace to see th' way to take th' blot o' sin out o' his life—sin now too, t—

109 & 110
That were to clymbe ore the house to vnlocke the gate.
Well, sit you out: go home Berowne: adue.

oo—t' couch wyth. O, better leaue all to heaven, where th' soul goes to meet iudgement. Work, obey

—. (unspeakable.)

111 & 112
No my good Lord, I haue sworn to stay with you.
And though I haue for barbarisme spoke more,

thy Lord! O, do not wish harm to your enemies! Ay, know God is master o' purge! O ha, ha! O fau rubbi—

113 & 114
Then for that Angell knowledge you can say,/Yet confident Ile keepe what I haue sworne,

sh, inuented t' keep safely in control all who wd gouge an eye for an eye, Cate! We think tha—

115 & 116
And bide the pennance of each three yeares day(s).
Giue me the paper, let me reade the same,

t repentance redeems a base man e'en afta a guilty deed. Heed *me*, Christopher, ye ape! (He, he!)

The s is needed to make the joke. (Even Christopher, ye ape, can be redeemed.)

117 & 118
And to the strictest decrees Ile write my name.
How well this yeelding rescues thee from shame.

Tho' remade whitest, my soiourn's finisht, C? I descend t' hell t' wrestle th' Gew, release my cream. Eee!)

119 & 120
Item. That no woman shall come within a mile of my Court.
Hath this bin proclaimed? / Foure dayes agoe.

I'm here, tho', facin' deuil Whitgift. O, I can't stomach th' loose ymmoral man's beratin' o' me! O, wd he play au—

121 &122

On paine of loosing her tongue.
Who deuis'd this penaltie? / Marry that did I.

ght fair at tilt, O, I'd surprise his stupid head with all mi neat, deep theology—no nonee-nonee, see?

123 & 124

Sweete Lord, and why?
To fright them hence with that dread penaltie,
A dangerous law against gentilitie.

Awful man! He'd decree that all who pen worthily against his ranting shd get a degree o' tit-tat, 'n' die wet! Ei—

125 & 126

If any man be seene to talke with a woman within the tearme of three yeares, hee shall indure

ther death or banishment is my true lot, Hen—e'en within a week! The fee for my sin! Waaaaaeeell!

127 & 128

. . . such publique shame as the rest of the Court shall possibly deuise.
This article my Liedge your selfe must breake,

UUill U see life gush from me, or cd a royal edict saue me? By th' Bible, as he supports th' kill, SSS stays it. Reech the quee—

129 & 130

For well you know here comes in Embassie
The French Kings daughter, with your selfe to speake:

n—let her know of my reuerse, 'n' beseech her t' aid th' escape from English soil o' a suk-fuk Gew toy wi'

131 & 132

A Maide of grace and compleate maiestie,
About surrender vp of Aquitaine:

one part poet. UUi'out a qveen's aid, fear I'm a dead man. If Gabriel come, "rescat—

133 & 134

To her decrepit, sicke, and bed-rid Father.
Therefore this Article is made in vaine,

ti!" I crie! Please ask for aid! I'm destined for death, Hen! I'd trie t' breech her cvnt. Rea—

rescatti. an imperative Italian form. A resa is the surrender of an insurance form. In modern It., a command to make such a surrender would be "riscatti." Kit was familiar with terms of shipping agents, and he and Hen were studying with Florio, learning to speak Italian.

135 & 136

Or vainly comes th' admired Princesse hither./What say you Lords? / Why, this was quite forgot.	**d her my secret fly-away poem now: show her al that I hid i' th' SSS codes! So U qvit, 'arry, I go t' ruin!**

Fly-away poem. Kit's love poem for Queen Elizabeth: "Shall I die, shall I fly . . ." An imperfect copy in Bodleian MSS, Rawlinson Poetry 160, folios 108, 109. The amanuensis who made the copy (maybe forty years after the poem was created) didn't know the original contained three or more kinds of ciphers, so he innocently altered the spelling. Troublesome but not irreparable. (The other extant copy, in Yale U Beineke Library, is corrupt: recovery of ciphered messages from its stanzas would be impossible.) one message spells Elizabeth, one is a compound anagrammatic acrostic, one an interior poem pleading for exile.

137 & 138

So Studie euermore is ouershot, While it doth study to haue what it would,	**Wow! See how th' uuhite-liuer idiot's arested—hauled to th' dusty room o' iust—**

arested. arrested. **dusty room.** The Star Chamber at Westminster? or was the council meeting at Nonsuch because of plague in London??

139 & 140

It doth forget to doe the thing it should: And when it hath the thing it hunteth most,	**tified lies t' hear th' t-ten aged men shouting. Hot, hot, hot! God! Thud! Hint, hint t-to th' wh—**

According to A.D. Wraight. In Search of Christopher Marlowe. NY: Vanguard 1965, the justices were 8: Whitgift, Ferdinando Stanley, Henry Carey, Thomas Sackville, William Cecil (Burghley), John Pickering, John Wolley and John Fortescue.

141 & 142

'Tis won as townes with fire, so won, so lost. We must of force dispense with this Decree,	**ite idiot. See them scowlin'. "This case referred off to SSS. Stop!" 'N' I shout, "C, we w-w-won! WON!"**

143 & 144

She must lye here on meere necessitie. Necessity will make vs all forsworne	**Know: in ease-recess th' sinful wretch—me—tries leavin' ye smelly room. See, see? L—**

145 & 146

Three thousand times within this three yeeres space:
For euery man with his affects is borne,

est I run off, th' watch stays me, 'n' from need, see, I try to piss in a shrub, ere wet, I scare the Hi Hi Hee.

Hi Hi Hee. Whitgift, president of the Chamber.

147 & 148

Not by might mast(e)red, but by speciall grace.If I breake faith, this word shall breake for me,

Tho' back fast, I'm embarrass'd by mi reekee flood which grieues th' fragile plant bitterly. Ba—

149 & 150

I am forsworne on meere necessitie.
So to the Lawes at large I write my name,

rely time ta register mi name when I was sweatin'—Oee Oee! Across from ten ol'

151 & 152

andhethatbreakesthemintheleastdegree,
Stands in attainder of eternall shame.

fakers that e'en restate 'n' sort all mi bad deeds in the greatest detail. Ahh, men, Hen—an'

153 & 154

Suggestions are to others as to me:
But I beleeue although I seeme so loth,

th' hot uote's to banish me. So I loose a gush, beg Iesus, tell o' mute regret. Aee!

155 & 156

I am the last that will last keepe his oth.
But is there no quicke recreation granted?

But no escape. I'm t-to sail in th' week—th' queen's orders—all at her charge. I like that. It t—

queen's orders. Eleanor Bull at Deptford, who sheltered SSS during this covert mission, was a friend of Elizabeth's nurse Blanche Parry; the ship on which Kit embarked (owned by a sailing partner of a Marlowe), was hired by the queen and Essex to carry a message to Navarre. The queen's coroner handled the cover-up after Kit's 'death.'

157 & 158

I that there is, our Court you know is hanted
With a refined trauailer of Spaine,

urn'd out she's a friend to Kit in his trauail. I o-owe her! How tu pay 'er a fee? Can I t-tr—

159 & 160

Amaninalltheworld'snewfashionplanted,
That hath a mint of phrases in his braine

ade mi small nonni-whip for half her banner aid? Has she intent to nap awhile, as that st—

161 & 162

One, who the musicke of his owne vaine tongue,
Doth ravish like inchanting harmonie;

ud enters, shakin' again? He comes to view the fine nice-lookin' virgin woman. Ho, ho, hu! Th'

163 & 164

A man of complements whom right and wrong
Haue chose as vmpire of their mutinie.

ladie shows me a thing or two, C? Ma'm proves a high hope for feminine cunt-art. Men mu—

165 & 166

This childe of fancie that Armado hight,
For interim to our studies shall relate,

st learn, C, from ladies' dance, Hi-ho, th' thrusts of loue—I—that aid their fragile moti—

167 & 168

In high-borne words the worth of many a Knight:
From tawnie Spaine lost in the worlds debate.

ons, 'n' best respond to them. I, I! Women of hy birth tend to fail 'n' withdraw; eager girls—aha!—know h—

169 & 170

How you delight my Lords, I know(e) not
But I protest I loue to heare him lie,

ow to make loue merrilie 'n' speedilie, with no hoity-toity or ughs, but hold

171 & 172

And I will vse him for my Minstrelsie.
Armado is a most illustrious wight,

fast, not t' miss a madli rollin' ride tv orgasm. I, so where is my wish? U illumi—

173 & 174

A man of fire, new words, fashions owne Knight.
Costard the swaine and he, shall be our sport,

nate passion, know how t' bring sense t' feed a forlorn sensual act. Ho! If we'd rid harm, wash, Ho!

175 & 176

And so to studie, three yeeres is but short.
Which is the Dukes owne person.
This fellow, What would'st?

So then your dance'll flow betide. I know those rushie steps, so wide. See, U start with two: sh, sh, the dru—

177 & 178

I my selfe reprehend his owne person, for I am his graces Tharborough: But I would see his own person in flesh and blood.

mming of your shoes begins. We dance, so slowli—faster, now: leap 'n' hop 'n' rub upon heart's desired h-hor, so brieflie h-hired.

179 & 180

This is he. / Signeor Arme, Arme commends you: Ther's villanie abroad, this letter will tell you more.	**So ere time is lost, U lead me into yovr shelter'd lair. We harbor, 'n' lie laughin' there—commit sly sma—**

181 & 182

Sir the Contempts thereof are as touching mee. A letter from the magnificent Armado.	**l 'citements to desire. I gage th heat, commence mi art—th star euent. Horror! A nap-off fem!**

183 & 184

How low soeuer the matter, I hope in God for high words./A high hope for a low heauen, God grant vs patience.	**Sleep wasn't part o' ovr agreement! Faced w-with failure, priggish, I g-go, "Hoo-hoo, Hoo-hoo." Then when U'd heard**

185 & 186

To heare, or forbeare hearing. To heare meekely sir, and to laugh moderately, or to forbeare both.	**me, U bare yr fair bosom, rearrange the gold hair 'n' freely take a breath t' reelee toot: "Hoo-hoo!" Orde—**

187 & 188

Well sir, be it as the stile shall giue vs cause to clime in the merrinesse. The matter is to me sir, as concerning Iaquenetta.	**er's here again: we hug in silence. I seem to sense in U a small reserve: tobacco scents that hair. I'll request time t' limit its t—**

tobacco. OED. tobacco. R. Cecil, 1600, in Cal. Carew MSS III485: "I have sent you tobacco . . ." (in this modern spelling).

189 & 190

The manner of it is, I was taken with the manner. In what manner? / In manner and forme following sir all those three.	**art whiff. No need! Mi leman toss't th' wig awaie, 'n' real hair's there, worn real short, 'n' I like that fine. Mmm! Nonne—nann!**

191 & 192

I was seene with her in the Mannor house, sitting with her vpon the forme, and taken following her into the Parke:	**So find us—thee 'n' me—at th' hot work! Imagine th' happiness! We like it hot in here, 'n' we haue no fear t' rol, right? 'N' renown—**

193 & 194

which put together is in manuer and forme following. Now sir, for the manner; it is the manner of a man to speake to a woman,

ed foreigners can't enter now! No—wait! Th' arras shook! Who was th' impolite Tom in th' opening? 'E ran off! U R a fine leman, M'am! Mu—

195 & 196

. . . for the forme in some forme. /For the following sir. / As it shall follow in my correction and God defend the right.

st some fool sentinal come in to watch in wonder the high rollers' gooood ffffffrree rolling 'mid th' dreary mi—

197 & 198

Will you heare this Letter with attention?
As we would heare an Oracle.
Such is the simplicitie of man to harken after the flesh.

nisters' reception-closet? U distrust me, fear for your safetie: I'm ilicit, 'n' I know how t' hate the law! Ah ha, ah ha, Helen! We let all the

199 & 200

Great Deputie, the Welkins Vicegerent, and sole dominator of Nauar, my soules earths God,

souldiers go home. 'Deed, I'll ravish U for my own need to taste a stranger—'n' keep U intact, age—

201 & 202

. . . and bodies fostring patrone:
Not a VVord of Costard yet. / So it is. / It may be so: but if he say it is so, he is in telling true: but so.

less in this magic net of loue. Great beauty's brief. In sooth, it does soon pass avvay if it's not restor'd by ridin'. But to do it

203 & 204

Peace, / Be to me, and euery man that dares not fight. / No words, / Of other mens secrets I beseech you.

may be hard to contriue. That princess o' Troy needed th sea-foe's semen, but we can go home free, s—

205 & 206

So it is besieged with sable coloured melancholie,
I did commend the blacke oppressing humour

ans seruitude or loneliness. C, we might B so happie U'd make me th' big clodsie hor, C: I'd come boldlie

207 & 208

. . . to the most wholesome Physicke of thy health-giving ayre: And as I am a Gentleman, betooke my selfe to walke: the time When?

as thy fool t' make songs, then weakly kneel 'n' whisper t' thee of my hot loue. O, I'd beg thee, Ma'm, to agitate me anew as I clime hy, h—

209 & 210

about the eixt houre, When beasts most grase, birds best pecke, and men sit downe to that nourishment which is called supper.

igh, to extreme happiness—'n' I thot I'd die o' th' loue-bbbbush's ssuck! When dear arms R stretched out to me, I want t' escape laws 'n' en—

nourishment. spelled nonrishment in the Folio.

211 & 212

So much for the time When. Now for the ground Which? which I meane I walke upon, it is ycliped, Thy Parke.

sconce myself here in your priuate life. Oh, C, I'm hooked! I think that great wh-wh-wh-whuppin' wd come in

213 & 214

Then for the place. Where? Where I meane I did encounter that obscene and most preposterous euent

handee another time. C, U showed me hope, so I can't be cuntent t' prefer another pet louer wi' red 'nees. S—

215 & 216

. . . that draweth from my snow-white pen the ebon coloured Inke, which heere thou viewest, beholdest, suruayest, or seest.

tay mi worthless punishment: I'd be your best hor! We cd love each other to the end. U see, what our two keen fires—these wh—

217 & 218

But to the place Where? It standeth North North-east and by East from the West corner of thy curious knotted garden;

ite hot desires—cd do t-t' break our hearts—else each nonny nonn wd whet us t' go to further battery, after th' Moth capt'n

Moth. a nickname for Kit, early and late.

219 & 220

There did I see that low spirited Swaine, that base Minow of thy myrth / Mee? / That unletered small knowing soule /

has sailed awai at thy order—gone foreuer! O, I blush! Help me t' sta hidden 'n' seek t' w-win thy sweet little toit, M-m-m. 'N'

221 & 222

Me? / that shallow vassall / Still mee? / Which as I remember, hight Costard, / O me / sorted and consorted contrary . . .

bring mi ram arrow ride in secret t' V that had most shamelessly concocted al hell t' do t' Marlowe's asse. Ohh!

t' Marlowe's asse. Elizabeth was whipping him; her first love had been a rough pirate, Admiral Thomas Seymour.

223 & 224

. . . to thy established proclaymed Edict and Continet, Cannon: Which with, o with, but with this I passion to say wherewith:

Nowhere cd I hope t' cohabit with a lady with thy passion and wry inuention. Show me how I cd still be the "Citt-Citt," sans th'

225 & 226

With a wench. / With a childe of our Grandmother Eue, a female; or for thy more sweet understanding a woman:

sweet hidden louer who gaue me that name! What other can Eros offer with mi mind on your danger? Law craf—

your danger. The queen was being blackmailed: the man behind the arras was spying on her, not for her.

227 & 228

. . . him, I (as my euer esteemed dutie prickes me on) haue sent to thee, to receive the meed of punishment by thy sweet Graces Officer

ts no protection from th' wicked threat. See, Ma'm, euen here spies haue come t' be his eyes—'n' C, Evy, I'd set thee free if U'd giue me tyme

229 & 230

Anthony Dull, a man of good repute, carriage, bearing, & estimation. / Me, an't shall please you? I am Anthony Dull.

& a little sublimated mercury. I'd go all alone—a personal h-hush gig, Ma'am—a priuate nonny-non, t' do at no fee. Ay!

sublimated mercury. The instrument of choice for SSS hush-gigs.
gig. OED. sb.III 6a. A fancy joke, whim (today, musicians' slang for a short job.)

231 & 232

For Iaquenetta (so is the weaker uessell called) which I apprehended with the aforesaid Swaine, I keeper her

No! U said. "I fear he'l kil thee! Escape awaee!" "H-how?" "Sh! Sh! If Kit wd pretend t' die in a closet quarrel, R.I.P.!" Here we see a

233 & 234

as a uessell of thy Lawes furie, and shall at the least of thy sweet notice, bring her to triall.

day when Whitgift'll control th' state: all base sons'll feel the earth's ease—Ai, Ai! So yr future

235 & 236

Thine in all complements of deuoted and heart-burning heat of dutie. / Don Adriana de Armado.

might B sad indeed: U dare not demote him for fear the old idiot'll traduce U 'n' open a na-na-na-na.

237 & 238

This is not so well as i looked for, but the best that euer I heard. / I the best, for the worst. But sirra, What say you to this?	**Order that he read his Bible to learn uerses about th' boy who set out t' uisit two 'alf-sisters of his? Ryte? How's that! Kit.**

learn verses. John, chapters 11 and 12, and Luke, chapter 10, especially verse 22. Kit sees Martha and Mary and Lazarus as Jesus's half-siblings, his mother's children. Jesus has a different father. And if Jesus's father is God, Jesus is one of those "base sons" that Whitgift hates. So there! Kit signs this.

239 & 240

Sir I confesse the Wench. / Did you hear the Proclamation? / I doe confesse much of the hearing it, but little of the marking of it.	**So fare thee wel! May good fortune proue infinite for thee! Thanks for th' chance t' B close t' U, Ma'm. I—I C it's th' end: I C I'l—hi-hie. God's**

241 & 242

It was proclaimed a yeeres imprisonment to bee taken with a Wench. / I was taken with none sir, I was taken with a Damosell.	**will B done. I can't vvin, so let me keep thy kinkie whip as memento o' a cherished time! Not resistant ta wa-wa, I wear a raw ass.**

kinkie. OED. "kinky. US colloq. queer, eccentric, crochety." But here it's English.

243 & 244

Well, it was proclaimed Damosell. / This was no Damosell neyther sir, shee was a Virgin. / It is so varried to, for it was proclaimed Virgin.	**V tell me t' go. "If V R apprehended on my shores, death will come to V at once! Sail, sail, sail awai! I wisss-wisss-God! I'm irrrrrational! I wd**

245 & 246

If it were, I denie her Virginitie: I was taken with a Maide. / This Maid will not serue your turne sir.	**live with ye. Irreleuant! Merrie winner Whitgift wd rid me o' U—assassinate U i' the dark o' nite! I! I, i, i!"**

247 & 248

This Maide will serue my turne sir. / Sir I will pronounce your sentence: you shall fast a Weeke with Branne and water.	**U lead us; I follow U down th' secret stair. There we kiss, 'n' in a ninny uein I say, "I'll always remember U." Then we part, corre—**

249 & 250

I had rather pray a Moneth with Mutton and Porridge. / And Don Armado shall be your keeper. My Lord Berowne, see him deliver'd ore,	**spondin' by wauin' til I'm out o' ken o' my Eden 'n' my dear, dear, dear dread trollop. Th' harrowed-up delights are a horror, Ma'm. Hee hee! Br—**

251 & 252

And goe we Lords to put in practice that, Which each to other(s) hath so strongly sworne.

othels carry gentler hores! C? Wet, C! How can I hope t' sit down again? Had U stopt short, tho',

253 & 254

Ile lay my head to any good man's hat, These oathes and lawes will proue an idle scorne. Sirra, come on.

I'd start away high 'n' dry. Yoo hold all ease as wel, so U can claim me, heart 'n' sole, 'n' I'd repeat soon. No eme—

255 & 256

I suffer for the truth sir: for true it is, I was taken with Iaquenetta, and iaquenetta is a true girle,

rald is worth a taste o' a queer queen's fair tit-tit-t-tits when U R afire. Neuer again t' fuk U i' this fire

257 & 258

. . . and I therefore welcome the sowre cup of prosperitie, affliction may one day smile againe, and vntill then sit downe sorrow.

is an affliction, so let me dream that one day I-I'l find V 'n' we'l lie together once more, happy in R resort of piss! O C, U and me, We-We. (or:)

He makes another cipher out of the same letters:

257 & 258—another version:

. . . and I therefore welcome the sowre cup of prosperitie, affliction may one day smile againe, and vntill then sit downe sorrow.

is a sorrow, so let me dream that one day I'l find V, C, 'n' we'l lie together once more, happy in R final effort. U need to cow-piss, 'n' I—I wea—

259 & 260

Boy, what signe is it when a man of great spirit growes melancholy?
A great signe, sir, that he will looke sad.

r bloody stripes on my ass. What a strange relation, rightlie known as a female witch-gig! Oh, sweet hag, Ile i—

261 & 262

Why? Sadnesse is one and the selfe-same thing deare impe. / No no, O Lord sir no. How canst thou part sadnesse and melancholy

gnore my pain. My odd passion for thee renders me senseless. It shows how th' honied heat calls, an' can lead U on to send an a—

263 & 264

. . . my tender Iuuenall? / By a familiar demonstration of the working, my tough signeur. / Why tough signeur? Why tough signeur?

nswer as burning hot—eagerly engage U on my way t' hide, fuk U 'n' forgiue thy rough rood insult. Tho' I gain my MT wish t' rule, I'm

265 & 266

Why tender Iuuenall? Why tender Iuuenall? / I spoke it tender Iuuenall, as a congruent apathaton, appertaining to thy young daies,

sure I'd end up happy in all outrageous deeds wi ye little ninny-nanny-whip. Haue I courage t' leaue a letter thanking U, 'n' not to rat a

267 & 268

. . . which we may nominate tender. / And I tough signeur, as an appertinent title to your olde time, which we may name tough.

lot o' our secret man-woman sharing, lying hidden? How wi' deep throat 'n' much pantin' U ate me wet, then gaue my teat—I—I—yie!

269 & 270

Pretty and apt. / How meane you, sir, I pretty, and my saying apt? Or I apt, and my saying prettie?

Yea, Dame, U astonish'd me wi' gay tit-tat, I not prepar'd t' grasp 'n' pry into ye in my apparent y-y—

271 & 272

Thou pretty because little. / Little pretty because little: wherefore apt? / and therefore apt, because quicke.

ieldin' queerly t' that teat. But base tho' I B, I rose up, up properly t' free thee. 'Twas all real fukee, etc. etc. etc. etc.

273 & 274

Speake you this in my praise Master? / In thy condigne praise. / I will praise an Eele with the same praise.

Ah, sweet princess golden hair, in haste I'm on my mery way past Priapus, 'n' still shakee. Repeat? Iiiii-eee!!

275 & 276

What? That an Eele is ingenuous. / That an Eele is quicke. / I doe say thou art quicke in answeres. Thou heat'st my bloud.

Th' day t' sail is nigh, when SSS hears o' a hit to kill me. Aeeeee! Quakin,' I send a tout t' touch U, our queen. Yea, but we can't

277 & 278

I am answer'd sir. / I loue not to be crost. /He speakes the meere contrary, crosses loue not him.

reach U! O, where R U? At sea? My O so recent-hired killer comes—steps in to breast me soon. Is not

killer. Perhaps Whitgift has approached Robin Poley, the queen's trusted messenger, now sailing home from the Hague, offering to pay him for killing Kit, but Poley will notify SSS. Kit must seem to die, but how?

279 & 280

I haue promis'd to study iii yeres with the Duke. / You may doe it in an houre sir. Impossible. / How many is one thrice told?

th' suruiual o' thy toy-boy louer o' some interest? U deem'd Kit a happy idiot; now SSS needs aid. In rime, I crie: Hi! I'm hi! O, why

281 & 282

I am ill at reckning, it fits the spirit of a Tapster. / You are a gentleman and a gamester sir.

ignore my distress? I'm no lame saint! That appalling taut fear creates a reek, if I 'gin t' rat.

'gin t' rat. He threatens to use leverage, like the villain Whitgift himself!

283 & 284

I confesse both, they are both the varnish of a compleat man. / Then I am sure you know how much the grosse summe of deus-ace amounts to.

Now U stop my fear: our hot chum Robin comes home to aid U, so a H-Hebe State SS (mute Moth) might weave off t' sneak across ye Channel. U 'n' he

285 & 286

It doth amount to one more then two. Which the base vulgar call three. /True.

together—U, he 'n' th' coroner saue th' Moth, 'n' Cate'l love U al. I admit we brot th' w—

287 & 288

Why sir is this such a peece of study? Now here's three studied, ere you'll thrice wink,

orst conuict corse t' lie here fur review while shy Kit wended easy tu his ship. Yesh, d—

corse. In contemporary use, corpse. **Yesh.** He's drunk. See ciphers, Venus & Adonis, ll 17-18, "diluting beer with mother's tears," and ll 19, 20, 21, 22 ciphers: "ten glasses o' beer i' the eve, U C, 'n' hidden Kit's noo tooo ready for the trip to France."

289 & 290

. . . & how easie it is to put yeres to the word three, and study three yeeres in two words, the dancing horse will tell you.

eer lady, R gratitude is endless. Euil is destroyed, & hope returns. Thy toy wil show thee worth, tho' woe, woe! I can't ent—

291 & 292

A most fine Figure. / To proue you a Cypher. I will heer upon confesse i am in loue:

er your imp. house. I'l go a*w*ay 'n' serue U in other places wi' effectiue info on pol—

imp. Short for imperial. m as *w*.

293 & 294

. . . and as it is base for a Souldier to loue; so am I in loue with a base wench.

itical matters abroad: I'l fin' a wai so SSS'l B wise, Hoo-Hoo! Euen U-U need a

I'l fin'. Still drunk, he talks as he goes to the ship.

295 & 296

If drawing my sword against the humour of affection, would deliuer mee from the reprobate thought of it,

report of foreign affairs before they might touch our island home t' damage U, whom we find true. It would t—

297 & 298

I would take Desire prisoner, and ransome him to any French Courtier for a new deuis'd curtsie.

ake discretion, patience, worry, watchfulness, 'n' sometimes a horrid darin' deed for U. I rue our n—

299 & 300

I thinke scorne to sign, me thinkes I should out-sweare Cupid. Comfort me Boy, What great men haue beene in loue?

ight of passions, as now I O U, 'n' memory won't let me aid other kings. I'd be checkt. U uuere mine, brach, tho' U tel H—

brach. bitch

301 & 302

Hercules Master. / Most sweete Hercules: more authority deare Boy, name more: and sweet my childe

-en th' heretic's loue-labor's lost. My sad eyes dim; U neuer cared? C, my memorees worree me. What that e—

303 & 304

. . . let them be men of good repute and carriage. / Sampson Master, he was a man of good carriage, great carriage:

ncounter meant to me defies description: A regal caper? A gross reward o' rage? A bare fag-hag ham-ma'm? Go to e—

305 & 306

. . . for hee carried the Towne-gates on his backe like a Porter: and he was in loue. O well-knit Sampson, strong ioynted Sampson;

each possible perspectiue: look: none shows the whole story o' Kit 'n' a great kween at rest in 'er grand salon. Ma'm, I find an od—

307 & 308

I doe excell thee in my rapier, as much as thou didst mee in carrying gates. I am in loue too.

d discrepancy in our eualuation o' this night. I hold it a gem: a sexy miracle! Eros et me! Mee!

309 & 310

Who was Sampson's loue my deare Moth? A woman Master. / Of what complexion? / Of all the foure, or the three,

A most extraordinary happenstance, Ma'm: the fool Moth shows loue for th' flame, who loues a we-we more.

311 & 312

. . . or the two, or one of the foure. / Tell me precisely of what complexion? / Of the sea-water Greene sir.

Tho' we met as result of prolix poem I (a cheeter) sent yoo, reel affection trooleh grew, whereon f—

prolix poem. He refers to "Shall I die."

313 & 314
Is that one of the foure complexions? As I haue read, sir, and the best of them too.

ine memories exist of a pure loue, not hashishheat'd: so that fee cd not 'a' bro't fo—

fee. The emerald she gave him.

315 & 316
Greene is indeed the colour of Louers: but to haue a Loue of that colour, methinkes Sampson had small reason for it.

rth such deep admiration, such restless mournful beds! Look, Hoo-Hoo, it's reallee too late t' ignore mee nouu. An affa—

317, 318 & 319
He surely affected her for her wit. / It was so sir, for she had a greene wit. / My Loue is most immaculate white and red.

ir so free, so fresh for us can't wither. Tho' U left me, thy hi royal art's euer with m-me, We-We! Glad? I'm a sad case indeed! I

320 & 321
Most immaculate thoughts Master, are mask'd vnder such colours. / Define, define, well educated infant.

must sail to a far land, destined to a sad life: me severed from U. C, C: th' loue went thru us cheek-dancing! M-m!

322 & 323
My fathers witte, and my mothers toungue assist mee. / Sweet inuocation of a childe, most pretty and patheticall.

Farewel, Ma'm! I leaue, appointed t' scatter secret designs. Time may not soon heal this wound that thy oft-mystic—

324 & 325
If shee be made of white and red, Her faults will nere be knowne: For blush-in cheekes by faults are bred,

al ruff-bed h-h-handlin' laid on me. See, I feel ye stil, 'n' know we sure shared the b-best bare free-fuck. We bro—

326 & 327
And feares by pale white showne:
Then if she feare, or be to blame,
By this you shall not know,

t all our fibs, then honesty won. Fear ye won't be able to answer me. Sad if I lose ye. Be h-h-h-hap . . . K.

f

The Tragedy of Richard the Third. First Folio of Shakespeare. Histories, p 173.

THE TRAGEDY OF RICHARD THE THIRD

1 & 2

Now is the Winter of our Discontent,
Made glorious Summer by this Son of Yorke:

In this thing Kit Marlowe wrote of Robert C.'s demon rise, 'n' some fouy-douys on us:

Robert C. Robert Cecil. Francis Bacon asked for this play to demonize Rob't Cecil.
fouy-douys. Tricks Cecil played to put down Bacon, Essex and Kit.

3 & 4

And all the clouds that lowr'd vpon our house
In the deepe bosome of the Ocean buried.

How, on false claim 'n' deuious plot, no doubt he'l euer be protected 'n' heard as he doth vo—

5 & 6

Now are our browes bound with Victorious Wreathes,
Our bruised armes hung vp for Monuments;

mit forth his envious words to undermine our progress. S.O.B.! Au unaware, we borrow much but nev—

7 & 8

Our sterne Alarums chang'd to merry Meetings;
Our dreadfull Marches, to delightfull Measures.

er get money that's due us, C. Marlo's messages R all left undeliuer'd. Crude, grim rat, huh! Normal for

9 & 10

Grim visag'd Warre, hath smooth'd his wrinkled Front:
And now, in stead of mounting Barbed Steeds,

a bitter man who grew to feel his mother wrong'd, abandon'd him as Tudor kin. Saddest findings svr—

State Secret Service (SSS) chief Robert Cecil was a secret son of the queen.

11 & 12

To fright the Soules of fearfull Aduersaries,
He capers nimbly in a Ladies Chamber,

round him before birth: her illness clearly damages his fetus. Result: a cape of a fai—

damages his fetus. Queen Elizabeth suffered measles and smallpox at Hampton Court, Oct. 1562.

15 & 16

to the lasciuious pleasing of a Lute.
But I, that am not shap'd for sportiue trickes,

ntlie odorous cartilaginous mass ouer his back. "Please tu put that off i' the pitt."

Please. The child speaks.

17 & 18

Nor made to court an amorous Looking-glasse:
I, that am Rudely stampt, and want loues Maiesty,

No way to remoue it! O, it sticks there and gro*u*es most naturally—a mound past all a gaon M.D.'s au—

gaon. Hebrew. genius, learned.
M.D.'s. medical doctor's

19 & 20

To strut before a wonton ambling Nymph:
I, that am curtail'd of this faire Proportion,

thority of Phs. Stil, it cannot preuent growth of a brain able to doom an *imprimatur.* F—

Phs. physic. ***imprimatur.*** (Kit's own) license for publication.

21 & 22

Cheated of Feature by dissembling Nature,
deform'd, vn-finish'd, sent before my time

ie! He did free me (cut off, dry), but gives my drama, stolen, to his friend, 'n' banns me!! Feet, B

23 & 24

Into this breathing World, scarse halfe made vp,
And that so lamely and vnfashionable,

fast 'n' send me far; this brooding devil has a privy leman 'n' wants a battle! Hold hoe! A chal—

leman. OED early Middle English, lover. Kit sees Shakespeare as Robert Cecil's lover.

25 & 26

That dogges barke at me, as I halt by them.
Why I (in this weake piping time of Peace)

lenge: Shakespeare, he against me, to act it i' th' gym: we both wyki-pap him i' bed. A fit—

gym. in the buff, naked. Kit makes it childish—ridiculous!

27 & 28

Haue no delight to passe away the time,
Vnlesse to see my Shadow in the Sunne,

ing way to settle that madman's insane dispute. Ho ho, Hee hee! U see vs so newly

29 & 30

And descant on mine owne Deformity and therefore, since I cannot proue a Louer,

fed or striuen—'n' I a winner! Cecil not to deede any drama to fops or con-men. Heauen

fops. fools, in 16th c. use.
con-men. altered form of 'cony-catcher; a cheater, hoaxer.

31 & 32

To entertaine these faire well spoken dayes,
I am determined to proue a Villaine,

relent! Witnes I'm alive! Please, defend me ere I die: Kit, an author o' plays! To rate one

33 & 34

And hate the idle pleasures of these dayes.
Plots haue I laide, Inductions dangerous,

unuuorthy of authorship deed? That's an asinine idea. All plaies seceded to "less dege—

35 & 36

By drunken Prophesies, libels, and Dreames,
To set my Brother Clarence and the King

nerate brother," like coddl'd ninny Shakespeare? Yes, men, hatred stings me: b-blur! Cop

brother. fellow SSS member (Shakespeare). **b-blur.** the sailors' raspberry.

37 & 38

In deadly hate, the one against the other:
And if King Edward be as true and iust,

drunke Ned's ioint, and rot, banished! He held fate. Haue wit, get set, try again! A da—

drunke Ned. Edward de Vere, who might have saved Kit.

39 & 40

As I am Subtle, False, and Treacherous,
This day should Clarence closely be mew'd vp:

y of retribution's ahead, so these dull dumps can be cleared away, chvms, else call s—

41 & 42

About a Prophesie, which sayes that G,
Of Edwards heyres the murtherer shall be.

ome chef brothers to write it all: say, sad he pray'd as he grew up, but here, hah, he's s—

chef. chief. often spelled this way in the ciphers.
he. refers to Robert Cecil.

43 & 44

Diue thoughts downe to my soule, here Clarence comes.
Brother, good day: What meanes this armed guard

et to wrong mee, destroy author identity, all because o' a damned dog-whore's greed. He's rham's chum.
Chou

f

Venus and Adonis. 1593 printing.

VENUS AND ADONIS

1 & 2
Even as the sunne with purple-colourd face,
Had tane his last leaue of the weeping morne,

Christopher Marlowe penned U this tale. We can't save the devil. He's e'en gone off up a luna—

3 & 4
Rose-cheek'd Adonis hied him to the chase
Hunting he loued, but loue he laught to scorne;

tic road to liue out there, shunn'd. Hee Hee! C th' ghost! His good name has been killed, U C: hou—

5 & 6
Sick-thoughted Venus makes amaine vnto him,
And like a bold-fac'd suter ginnes to woo him.

rlie sound a knel. But soft! Kit can gain this good name, even tho' U mask'd him wi' mvch ado! See:

7 & 8
Thrise fairer then myselfe, (thus she began)
The fields chiefe flower, sweet aboue compare,

wheneuer better plays R best, each will hide his name for some of us t' see, if th' cheef agree. F—

9 & 10
Staine to all Nimphs, more louely then a man,
More white, and red, then doues, or roses are:

ollo, m-men, to see three words that haue stayed all unseen, imprisoned on a mirror: A Hen—

11 & 12
Nature that made thee with her selfe at strife,
Saith that the world hath ending with thy life.

ry, a friend, with this his theme gift: that neat wet laddah that will set the author free. The hen—

13 & 14	
Vouchsafe thou wonder to alight thy steed, And raine his proud head to the saddle bow,	**chman goes away tu be alone. Adio, friends! Oh, this deep huddled sorro— that thov, the dut—**

laddah. Henry Wriothesley gave Kit a silk-gut ladder with which to rescue men from a Turkish jail.

m. He puts a W upside down to make the M in henchman.

15 & 16	
If thou wilt daine this favor, for thy meed A thousand honie secrets shalt thou know.	**iful sweet thin hickory rod, hath no wai to saue th' author 'n' end shame! So set off, dilut—**

17 & 18	
Here come and sit, where never serpent hisses, And being set, Ile smother thee with kisses.	**ing beer with mother's tears (Drinks in dispute). See, see, s-e-e-e where the Channel tosses him!**

f

Lucrece. Quarto. facimile of 1st printing. 1594. Scolar Press.

LUCRECE

1 & 2

From the besieged Ardea all in post, Borne by the trustlesse wings of false desire,	**See, banished 'n' disguised for aye, Marlowe pens this tale. Fog, tell forest trees: B br—**

3 & 4

Lust-breathed Tarqvin, leaues the Roman host, And to Colatium beares the lightlesse fire,	**others t' this man in quest o' shelter. He's brave but fragil—cast, 'mated, to lie alone here. Dual**

5 & 6

VVhich in pale embers hid, lurkes to aspire, And girdle with embracing flames, the wast	**risk: with MT head he slips in a cave, but wonder be, G.G., a friendli camper, saves him. Tell Rh—**

camper. in contemporary usage, a football player, according to O.E.D. Someone strong and good-hearted came by on the trail, kicking a ball!

7 & 8

Of Colatines fair loue, Lvcrece the chast. Hap'ly that name of chast, vnhap'ly set	**aetia her Alps' chyll effect can't stop this travel-man; he can choose to fly! Hav U,**

9 & 10

This batelesse edge on his keene appetite: VVhen Colatine vnwisely did not let,	**Ted, Steve—seen an event i' th' eve, lately? Opened a pit—been sick in high still woods?**

11 & 12

To praise the cleare vnmatched red and white, VVhich triumpht in that skie of his delight:	**Kit vvaits i' th' road 'n' sees traget to th' citie ahead in th' nice w.c. puddle-river. Flemm: Ph-h-h-h-h!**

traget. Venetian slang for traghetto, a ferry.
w.c. O.E.D. lists no w.c. before the 18th c.; this book was printed in 1594, when public notice of John Harington's water closet was a thing of the future.
Ph-h-h-h-h. Kit spits in the dirty river.

The earliest known impression of the first printing, a copy held at the Bodleian Library, contains clearly defined begin-quotation-marks before scattered lines of verse—marks which identify a series of anagrams continuing Marlowe's secret letter to Henry Wriothesley. Here are the printed verses, their hidden messages revealed:

87 & 88

"For vnstaind thoughts do seldom dream on euill. "Birds neuer lim'd, no secret bushes feare:	**U blind, U dear blind friend, Christofer's name has gone to moulde mud, vseless to restore.**

460

"Such shadowes are the weake brains forgeries,	**As we C th' broad shore, a few seek SS Guarini here**.

shore. Adriatic shore.
SS. secret service.
Guarini. Until his death, Battista Guarini was Marlowe's friend and Italian spy-master. In a letter from the bishop of Rimini to Cardinal Millino, Battista Guarini is mentioned as having worked with Gregorio de' Monti (Marlowe's Italian name). The letter is all about Gregorio, and characterizes him as a spy. CSP Venetian, vol. 15, Appendix One, Jan. 1617. Fatally poisoned in Rome, Battista returned to Venice and died in Gregorio's arms, 7 Oct. 1612. Vittorio Rossi. Battista Guarini ed il Pastor Fido, studio biografico critico. Turin: Ermanno Loescher, 1886.

528

"A little harme done to a great good end,	**One led to him at a great olde garden, to**

530

"The poysonous simple sometime is compacted	**apply to the missions. C me commit due esposeo.**

due esposeo. He advances himself properly.

580

"Tears harden lust, though marble were with rayning. (sic)	**He hath arranged to tell us names i' th' web. Grin! Wurry!**

831

"How he in peace is wounded not in warre.	**Now we're hie paid in new ducats. Hore? No!**

832

"Alas how manie beare such shamefull blowes.	**All's humble business, weal or woe. Ha! Am a chef!**

867

"The sweets we wish for, turne to lothed sowr(e)s,

We set forth down low, wet streets, er' his house-

868

"Even in the moment that we call them ours.

vu loom i' th' canal where th' tenements met.

1109

"For mirth doth search the bottome of annoy,

Now on f-foot he trod the stair to hy chamber.

1110

"Sad soules are slaine in merrie companie,

Mi mission: release a dunce, a prisoner. Ale

1111

"Grief best is pleased with griefes societie;

is so bad we piss freelie i' th' street. Fig! I C Gee!

Gee! Guarini, who watches his agents urinate in the canal.

1112

"True sorrow then is feelinglie suffiz'd

Ferrie's E Z. I find right useful new tools.

new tools. He shops for his mission.

1113

"VVhen with like semblance it is simpathiz'd.

I vvait, bill'd t' take ship. His men wish me cenz.

bill'd. He's on the passenger bill.
cenz. sense. Guarini's men hope he'll be cautious.

1114

"Tis double death to drowne in ken of shore,

No one knows th' bolde idea fur t'other side.

1115

"He ten times pines, that pines beholding food,

I, so if it's destined to be no help-p, then hang me.

1116

"To see the salue doth make the wound ake more:

Knowe U: hee hath address't to make loue to mee.

1117

"Great Griefe greeues most at that wold do it good;

So haue t' sail t-t' dodge free. Wrote G. Great God! Omit.

1118

"Deepe woes roll forward like a gentle flood,

O, I f-fled, let go, no look rearward. Speede well!

1125

"A woefull Hostesse brookes not merrie guests.

O, Bus, sail me to see these Turks R growne fooles!

Bus. buss. the type of ship Marlowe's grandfather Arthur would have sailed in, out of Dover: 50 to 70 tons or larger, about 50 feet along the bottom, like a Venetian marciliana. The buss described and illustrated in Gordon Grant and Henry Culver. The Book of Old Ships. NY: Bonanza Books, 1924. The marciliana described in Frederic C. Lane. Venice, A Maritime Republic. Baltimore: Johns Hopkins U Press, 1973, also, Wilfred Brulez, ed. Marchands Flamands à Venise, Vol. I. Bruxelles: L'institute historique Belge de rome, 1965, prints many entries about these popular ships.

1127

"Distres likes dùps whè time is kept with teares. (sic)

H.: I miss deeds that we're u-ster, like wet p-piss. Kit.

wet p-piss. Urine was used to strengthen the silk-gut ladder which Hen gave Kit for his mission, a ladder featured in later ciphers. Urea is a component of hair conditioners and strengtheners of wood fibers.

f

Shake-speares Sonnets. Quarto 1609. George Eld for T.T.

SONNET 116

The plaintext is famous for its use of nautical metaphor.

1 & 2

Let me not to the marriage of true mindes
Admit impediments, loue is not loue

Sea-demon Marlouue penn'd this. I got it al t' fit rite, see, 'n' rime, too! U led m-me to m—

3 & 4

Which alters when it alteration findes,
Or bends with the remouer to remoue.

end mie ruf measure—now it reads clearlie. Brother Wotton, e'en with his thot, h—

5 & 6

O no, it is an euer fixed marke
That lookes on tempests and is neuer shaken;

e aided this sonnet's form on R uuai to make an exit 'n' skee o'er th' Alps. Knees

7 & 8

It is the sta(rre) to euery wandring bar(que)
Whose worths vnknowne, although his highth be taken.

bent, we SSS go o'er h-h-h-h-high snow t' Italian border, where we quit at night 'n' hvrry t' take a skouue, 'n'

9 & 10

Lou(e)'s not Time's foole, though rosie lips and cheeks
Within his bending sickles compasse come,

go slo to Milon 'n' on t' pledge SSS help to Mantua's checkk'd forces. We see him—his uoice is shie, 'n' I, I, b—

11 & 12

Loue alters not with his br(i)efe houres and weekes,
But bears it out euen to the edge of doome.

eing a fool, said, "Not t' be worried—bet U feel better nouu we SSS'ue made it here!" U thot hee shook

13 & 14

If this be error and vpon mee proued,	**wi' horror. 'E bouued deep, man, 'n'**
I neuer writ, nor no man euer loued.	**referr'd us to a privee nonni reuel!**
	Monti

f

Two Gentlemen of Verona. First Folio of Shakespeare. Comedies, p 20.

TWO GENTLEMEN OF VERONA

1 & 2

Cease to perswade, My louing Protheus, Home-keeping youth, haue euer homely wits,	**Even without a home, your pet Chris Marloe pens you this play, Meg. See how ye duke go—**

Meg. Kit's half-sister, Margaret Marley, a year younger than he. He also addresses her in *Anthony and Cleopatra* and other ciphers.

3 & 4

Wer't not affection chaines thy tender dayes To the sweet glaunces of thy honour'd Loue,	**eth to find that incony ladder? C Ualentyne's gaffe—e'en th' wyt's sorrow! So chou to U! Tee hee!**

incony. English slang for French, inconnue.

These ciphers are for Kit's family—the hidden message is short, because figuring it would be hard for them. There's a farewell to his family in the plaintext (Act II sc. 3—farewell—the Duke's speech, Act II, Sc. 1, lines 153 fol.)

f

The Taming of the Shrew. First Folio of Shakespeare. Comedies, p 208.

THE TAMING OF THE SHREW

1 & 2

Ile pheeze you infaith.
A paire of stockes you rogue.
Y'are a baggage, the Slies are no Rogues. Looke

So all the uuork of Gregorio is by Shakespeare? No! That is a crazy gag in a pig-eye, U! Fool-eee Ou-eee!

in a pig-eye. children's slang: something incredible.

3 & 4

in the Chronicles, we came in with Richard Conqueror: therefore Paucas pallabris, let the world slide: Sessa.

If Christopher Marlowe can't be seen with his pen, he'll request use o' his alien alias t' record dra*m*a, or DCCL cr—

alien alias. In Italy he called himself Gregorio de' Monti. ***m*.** w used as m.
DCCL. 750.

5 & 6

You will not pay for the glasses you haue burst?
No, not a deniere: go by S. Ieronimie, goe to thy cold bed, and warme thee.

owns per annum for the loss o' hys byline to their unreasonable game. O, you decide, he'l agree to it—but do it de Goy way.

crown. OED: from the 15th to the 18th c, the common English name for the Fr(ench) **ecu . . .** a coin . . . of Great Britain of the value of 5 shillings (c. a quarter of a pound). Kit was asking for about £187 a year.
Goy. a non-Jew.

7 & 8

I know my remedie, I must go fetch the Headborough.
Third, or fourth, or fift Borough, Ile answere him by Law.

O, their theft o' my author'd words bids me break U off! Ile begin a life with more honour, whych might regrou—

9 & 10

Ile not budge an inch boy: Let him come, and kindly.
Huntsman I charge thee, tender wel my hounds,

u 'n' mend my credit without any stinking English ayd. He-U! No mob *here*'l cal me dead hel bent on Ch—

regrouu. He uses 2 u's to make a w. **He—U!** Hey, you!

11 & 12

Brach Meriman, the poore Curre is imbost,
And couple Clowder with the deepe-mouth'd brach,

urch destruction, archbishop murder 'n' more! I-I'd tel the world what became o' Pop—he became

Pop. Roger Manwood, Marlowe's natural father.

13 & 14

Saws't thou not boy how Siluer made it good
at the hedge corner, in the couldest fault,

a hidden martyr caught in the net fools woue—lost, bled to his death-rest. We go to couu—

uu. makes a w.

15 & 16

I would not loose the dogge for twentie pound.
Why Belman is as good as he my Lord,

ard's graue if we do not spell out his ghastly doom below: Oye! One good M.D. went in h—

Oye! OED: oye, apparently alteration of oyes, oyez, intransitive and substantive (from old French, oyez, hear ye!).
M.D. Ruy Lopes, the queen's physician.

17 & 18

He cried vpon it at the meerest losse
And twice to day pick'd out the dullest sent.

ate tu Dad's house to ope a vein, etc., 'n' emit red shyt. C, Peter told! 'E witness'd th' kill, C;

Peter. Marlowe's half brother, a legitimate son of Judge Manwood. The doctor made the death as painful as possible. Afterwards, Bacon and Essex hated Dr. Lopes and finally hounded him to death, for Bacon was Walsingham's natural son and Essex Walsingham's son-in-law. Whitgift wanted Manwood and the others bled to death, and Elizabeth, blackmailed, was forced to accede.

19 & 20

Trust me, I take him for the better dogge.
Thou art a Foole, if Eccho were as fleete,

th' corse reek't o' filth. Mi mother Cate, euer braue, washt it al off to de feet. Gee, O, G—

Mi mother Cate. The Kate in this play resembles Kit's mother, Katherine Arthur Marley from Dover, a spirited woman.

21 & 22

I would esteeme him worth a dozen such: But sup them well, and looke vnto them all,

ee! Now th' hot buz starts: M-m-m! What land U weeded! Look U on such love! "Let him lie! Ple—

23 & 24

To morrow I intend to hunt againe.
I will my Lord.
What's heere? One dead, or drunke?,

ase do not take him yet to ground, to where dread raine 'n' moulde will win in horr—

please do not take him yet. Kate didn't approve of entombment on the day of death.

25 & 26

See doth he breath?/He breath's my Lord. Were he not warm'd with Ale, this were a bed but cold

id certainty, where he shal B held, B humble, B rotted there, as death's reward. Woe, woe!" Moth—

27 & 28

. . . To sleep so soundly.
Oh monstrous beast, how like a swine he lyes./Grim death, how foule and loathsome

er smooth'd an' smooth'd h-his brow; wet eyes made unwise louing looks as she left ye house. No, all Plato

29 & 30

. . . is thine image:
sirs, I will practice on this drunken man.
What thinke you, if he were conuey'd to bed,

wrote o' that white stainles loue is confuted by her man an' his hidden eugenic prickywiki. Remin-

eugenic. After all, it helped make Kit.

31 & 32

Wrap'd in sweet cloathes: Rings put vpon his fingers:
a most delicious banquet by his bed,

iscence 's requiem:
Snow blows that day he goes up to find Gabriel, 'n' B sav'd. ('tis shit pun.) R.I.P.

's. his.

f

The Comedie of Errors. First Folio Of Shakespeare. Comedies, p 85.

THE COMEDIE OF ERRORS

1 & 2

Proceed Solinus to procure my fall, Andbythedoomeofdeathendwoesandall.

An odd play by lost dead Christopher Marlowe came of need of son to leuel und—

3 & 4

Merchant of Siracusa, plead no more. I am not partiall to infringe our Lawes;

ue criminal charges laid on a fine proponent of iust law: Late mars morator,

Late mars morator. A really broad controversy was put on the shelf—postponed. It became the English civil war.

5 & 6

The enmity and discord which of late Sprung from the rancorous outrage of your Duke,

for enmity rose, U C, when Dad Roger chose to speak out for th' dum or unfairly chain'd. Tug—

Dad. Kit's natural dad was a learned jurist, Sir Roger Manwood. **dum.** dumb, silenced. This anagram is about suppression and wrongful imprisonment of puritans as heretics. Roger began the "Marprelate Papers" in defense of those people, and Kit helped him.

7 & 8

To Merchants our well-dealing Countrimen/Who wanting gilders to redeeme their liues,

ged to hanging without trial, called new heretics or worse, more die: silent, mum. Unrelen—

9 & 10

Haue seal'd his rigorous statutes with their blouds,/Excludes all pitty from our threatning lookes:

ting authority orders Roger's priuate execution: he's bled to death. So lul, luhl, with last kiss. Famous

11 & 12

For since the mortal (l) and intestine jarres Twixt thy seditious Countrimen and vs,

ones executed: UUalter M., Francis W., 'n' Tomas R. So drin-tin-tin-tin! This is th' year to die!

Famous ones executed: Like Roger, these were Marranos and the queen's near helpers: Walter Mildmay, d. 31 May 1589. (Francis Walsingham's brother-in-law, Roger's chief at Exchequer, a puritan.) Francis Walsingham, d. 6 April 1590. (Roger's mentor, Elizabeth's secretary and chief of Secret Service.) Thomas Randolph, an ambassador and Postmaster of England, d. 8 June, 1590. (married first, Thomas Walsingham's sister Anne, later m. Ursula Coppinger, related to Roger's second wife.) Roger Manwood, Chief Baron of Exchequer and last of the four to be murdered, d. 14 December 1592, anniversary of death of Sir John Oldcastle, a freethinker.
This is the year. It's fashionable to die now. Really, it took 3 1/2 years to dispatch these friends.

13 & 14

It hath in solemne Synodes beene decreed, Both by the Siracusians and our selues,	**Emilia stole the chayne, 'n' Dad but couered his son's errant business need. yes, he bo—**

the chayne. Roger's gold chain of office, which Kit stupidly wagered at Emilia's nightclub, hoping to win money to help Hen Wriothesley pay a fine soon to be due because Hen refused to marry his secret half-sister. Kit had informed Hen of the incest which would have been involved in the marriage.

15 & 16

To admit no trafficke to our aduere townes: Nay more, if any borne at Ephesus	**re a burden, paid th' fee for my moonstruck sins at Eue's too, too neat winery. Faa!**

Eue's . . . winery. Emilia Bassano, bankrolled by Henry Carey, the Lord Chamberlain, was hostess of a nightclub at Shoreditch.

17 & 18

Be seene at any siracusian Marts and Fayres: Againe, if any Siracusian borne	**"In Canaan, in Canaan," Marina says, "Sir Roger's free, fit, best in Yauue's eyes." A bad**

Marina. Marlowe's first wife was Marina Cicogna, daughter of G. Domenico Cicogna, Duke of Crete. Kit eloped with her from Candia. He's writing this play in Padua, summer, 1594.

19 & 20

Come to the Bay of Ephesus, he dies: His goods confiscate to the Dukes dispose,	**toss o' th' dice took my hope of deep business, gaue choice: th' SSS, o' death. Fie! Des—**

SSS. State Secret Service.

21 & 22

Vnlesse a thousand markes be leuied
To quit the penalty, and to ransome him:

pite banishment, all quests—love, sun, ioy—are here, and th' mean to make do. Stud—

mean. OED. agency or course of action, by the employment of which some object may be attained.

23 & 24

Thy substance, valued at the highest rate,
Cannot amount vnto a hundred Markes,

dy at U, home to that married angel as heaven's red svn sank. Tututut! Both chance 'n'

25 & 26

Therefore by Law thou art condemn'd to die.
Yet this my comfort, when your words are done,

fate were truly friends when we did run to each other at my home's door: C, my boot trod on y—

27 & 28

My woes end likewise with the euening Sonne.
Well Siracusian; say in briefe the cause

e head of liue snake I wisse I in no wyse saw, slumbering in ye street. Ha! Eel-thin, U C, 'n' we c—

wisse. OED. wisse, wysse. of a certainty, for certain.

29 & 30

Why thou departedst from thy natiue home?
And for what cause thou cam'st to Ephesus.

ut 'n' dispatched th' poor raw meat for safety. U Hu! What ho—aye! Most stout, she e'en, much

lines 29, 30, 31, 32 seem to be ciphered together as a unit; a "d" from line 29 is used in the following cipher (31, 32).

31 & 32

A heauier taske could not haue beene impos'd,
Thn I to speake my griefs vnspeakable:

embolded (safe, unbitten), applies to make a' the corse's heavy skin a keep-guerdon. Ei! Ha'U

embolded. made bold. **corse.** OED. corpse. **keep-guerdon.** a present, keepsake.

33 & 34

Yet that the world may witnesse that my end/ Was wrought by nature, not by vile offence,

ever seen a doughty lady sew before yu? Ably stitch th' remnant 'n' waft it to me? Why not? T'w—

35 & 36

Ile utter what my sorrow giues me leaue.
In Syracusa was I borne, and wedde

as wonder indeed tu see ioy in her great braua muscular smyle as we two, wi—

37 & 38

Vnto a woman, happy but for me, And by me; had not our hap beene bad:

th' p-propah demeanah, movnt away to mad, no-obey, b-banner bed! F . . . U, U!

f

Midsommer Nights Dreame. First Folio of Shakespeare. Comedies, p 145.

A MIDSOMMER NIGHTS DREAME

1 & 2

Now faire Hippolita, our nuptiall houre
Drawes on apace: foure happy daies bring in

Her newborn on th' pillouu, a young wife is iust dead. "Papa, papa," in ilirare of reproach.

ilirare. probably ululare. wail, howl. This play's ciphers have no byline.

3 & 4

Another Moon: but oh, me thinkes, how slow
This old Moon wanes; She lingers my desires

Hemorrhage! No, it ys not so! A new slush—her best smile dims—look now . . . Oh! The demon wins!

5 & 6

Like to a Step-dame, or a Dowager,
Long withering out a yong mans revennew.

Great woe around me. Grinning death—so wrong—takes mi love away. Let open

7 & 8

Foure daies wil quickly steep the˜selues in nights
Foure nights wil quickly dreame away the time:

a crypt—see the ugly chill. Leaue mi fit wife inside? Don't question: stay, hug, kiss her. Le Requiem. Awkw—

9 & 10

And then the Moone, like to a siluer bow,
Now bent in heauen, shal behold the night

ard then, at home, Hen, I hold the babe who liues to look at new things: "N-n-n-n!" Belieue

11 & 12

Of our solemnities.
Go Philostrate,
Stirre vp the Athenian youth to merriments,

me, she lights mi life, restor's mi sanity. O, out on U! Hav to prepare their rott'n note . . . .

f

Romeo and Juliet. Prolog, facsimile. Quarto 2, p A2

PROLOGUE ROMEO AND JULIET

1, 2 & 3

Two housholds both alike in dignitie,
(In faire Verona where we lay our Scene)
From auncient grudge, breake to new mutinie,

As Grego de' Monti, Kit Marlowe wrote anew his chidin' tale o' a kin-feud goin' t' swift ruin. I-e-e-e! No cure! Ah, he'l even B ouer-run by

4, 5 & 6

Where ciuill bloud makes ciuill hands vncleane:
From forth the fatall loynes of these two foes,
A paire of starre-crost louers, take their life:

his uuoe: forever full of loue, he feels lo, so lo—stares at the M T place where all efforts fail'd, 'n' heart-sick, he saw Rita die. Ink can try t' climb on ro—

7, 8 & 9

Whose misaduentur'd pittious ouerthrowes,
Doth with their death burie their Parents strife.
The fearfull passage of their death-markt loue,

tten lies—Phhh!!! But truth is apart. Aliue, it sings—oft it weaues itself. U do hear from me th' idea of how t' auert th' spark o' rude disorder, there where

10, 11 & 12

And the continuance of their Parents rage:
Which but their childrens end nought could remoue:
Is now the two houres trafficque of our Stage

anger stirr'd. No gain in th' futile heat! Foolish feud! Th' word's negotiate: restore th' wouen peace. B sure how U act, C, 'n' confound th' church requiem.

13 & 14

The which if you with patient eares attend, What heare shall misse, our toyle shall strive to mend.

Wait! Fate alters mortal ways. *U* need t' plan: *She* has her own moues. U try: cold, *She'*l hit, hit, hit, hit! I-e-e-e!

She. Fate

f

Translation © R. Ballantine

Romeo and Juliet. First Folio of Shakespeare. Tragedies, p 53.

ROMEO AND JULIET

1 & 2, 3, 4, 5 & 6

Gregory: a' my word wee'l not carry coales.
No, for then we should be Colliars.
I mean, if we be in choller, wee'l draw.
I, While you liue, draw your neck out o' th' Collar.
I strike quickly, being mou'd.
But thou art not quickly mou'd to strike.

Crosse beyond a wall; call Gregory de' Monti ye author here. Wolf nor crow nor brother who kill'd my na<u>m</u>e will care what you'ue called <u>m</u>e. Curious if I lie. But mi Kit-quill touched on Uerona's begrimed story o' kin kut to ye quick. T—

Gregory de'Monti. Kit's new name in Italy.
<u>m</u>. w used for m is underlined.

7 & 8

A dog of the house of Mountague, moues me.
To moue is to stir: and to be valiant, is to stand:

o see mi name hide on a verse—O good! But I am glad too soon! Tut! To U it's a shout-stufft name—

9 & 10

Therefore, if thou art mou'd, thou runst away.
A dogge of that house shall moue me to stand.

a mouthful, though mine to use for aye. So do U trust me now? Does God th' father hear at-at al?

X

There's more

The Play of Pericles, Prince of Tyre, & C. Quarto, 1609. A2.
Shakespeare's Plays in Quarto. Ed. Michael H.J.B. Allen and Kenneth Muir. U. of C. Press. p 751.

THE PLAY OF PERICLES, PRINCE OF TYRE, & C.

1 & 2

To sing a Song that [of] old was sung,	**'N' w-woe! After Rita's death, Monti sang**
From ashes, auntient Gower is come,	**this long-ago song, C? Some o' us suf—**

Quarto One is the best copy extant. G.B. Evans says, "that old" means "that *of* old" (and here "of" is needed for the cipher).

Rita. Kit's first wife, who died after childbirth late in October 1594.

Monti. Kit in exile had a new name: Gregorio de' Monti.

3 & 4

Assuming mans infirmities,	**fer silent; my pain sings a sad serenade:**
To glad your eare, and please your eyes:	**O my glorious Rita, may uue e—**

5 & 6

It hath been sung at feastiuals,	**uer B as one in my song: I steadfast 'n'**
On Ember eues, and Holy dayes:	**duely able t' saue thee. Hah!**

7 & 8

And Lords and Ladyes in their liues,	**Irrational 'n' odd, th' soul reassur'd i'**
Haue red it for restoratiues:	**fantasy: there, deuils die ere**

9 & 10

The purchase is to make men glorious,	**th' tale's o'er. Iniquitous pouuer shouun**
Et bonum quo Antiquius eo melius:	**in some bleak game CMs quite om—**

CMs. seems. This is early work.

A thought about Ned de Vere's and Elizabeth's incestuous relationship is reflected in the outfront story.

11 & 12

If you, borne in those latter times,	**inous, yet th' prince escapes to marry, the**
When Witts more ripe, accept my rimes;	**il wife to B immers't in more wet**

13 & 14
And that to heare an old(e) man sing,
May to your Wishes pleasure bring:

than anyone wd possibly liue through, 'n' Marina emerges to a trade as

Marina. Rita's real name.

15 & 16
I life would wish, and that I might
Waste it for you, like Taper light.

foul as filth—remains lily white. Her dad—Tut! A pig who got wet! I-I! Kit.

17 & 18
This Antioch, then Antiochus the Great,
Buylt vp this Citie, for his chiefest Seat;

(C, confvsion reigns i' tatters: Hi-he, hi-he, hi-he! At last, uh, fit t' B tacit, ye chuse t' stop!)

Hi-he . . . Kit is an ass, braying.

f

I Henry IV. First Folio of Shakespeare. Histories, pp 46-51.

I HENRY IV

1 & 2

So shaken as we are, so wan with care, finde we a time for frighted Peace to pant,	**Kit M. penn'd this show of war, peace, fat Ned 'n' Roger to ease a ceasefire wait-awh—**

In these ciphers, there's often a resonance between out-front and secret lines. **Fat Ned.** Edward de Vere, 17th Earl of Oxford (and the queen's eldest secret son), is Hal in the play; Sir Roger Manwood is Falstaff. **ceasefire.** a lull in the 1596 Cadiz raid.

3 & 4

And breath shortwinded accents of new broils To be commenc'd in Stronds a-farre remote:	**ile before an order came t' shoot once more 'n'-win-n-n-n th' fort. SSS'd made a start, C: we'd cribb'd**

SSS. English State Secret Service. At Cadiz in '96, Marlowe and Cervantes, working for the Service and pretending to be ordnance officers, rearranged cannon balls in the Spanish forts so the ammunition wouldn't fit and the guns couldn't shoot.

5 & 6

No more the thirsty entrance of this Soile, Shall daube her lippes with her owne childrens blood:	**uniforms, entered 'n' piled all th' worst balls beside the hi stations here, C? Ho, ho, ho, he! Clown rey, R.I.P.!**

7 & 8

No more shall trenching Warre channell her fields, Nor bruise her Flowrets with the Armed hoofes	**Hal, th' crown h-heel, refused t-t' reward Falstaf 'n' scorns him when he neels. (No ogre more horrible i' ril—**

9 & 10

Of hostile paces. Those opposed eyes, Which like the Meteors of a troubled Heauen,	**ed-up days then ill iesters who speak the simple truth, Cee?) So, "Hoo hee?" O-o! "Be off o' Cae—**

then. than. a contemporary spelling.
Hoo hee? Who he? Hal pretends he doesn't know Falstaff any more, dismisses him just as Ned de Vere turned his back on Roger—and Kit.

11 & 12

All of one Nature, of one Substance bred, did lately meete in the intestine shocke,	**sar's toes! I don't need a banterin' clouun. I mock ye! I'l not e'en see thee bled!" That f-fle—**

see thee bled. Hal as Ned; Ned ignored Roger's execution-by-bleeding.

13 & 14

And furious cloze of civill Butchery, Shall now in mutuall well-beseeming rankes	**edglin' monarch betrays 'n' sullies a fine wize servant, C? Lull lull . . . O! Fucke him! Bow ou—**

Lull, lull. Kit tries to comfort his father.
Fucke him! Hal-Ned.

15 & 16

march all one way, and be no more oppos'd Against Acquaintance, Kindred, and Allies.	**t, ape—so quick t' grasp a dear old dyin' one's crown! An animal came 'n' laid a blade on Hen—**

Hen. Henry IV in the play. Did Ned, insane, threaten Elizabeth like this? In Famous Victories (An early play made by Marlowe for Ned's Revels Co.), Sc. 6: "Enter the Prince, with a dagger in his hand." Was Holinshed Marlowe's source? He's thinking of 1 & 2 Henry IV as one story.

17 & 18

The edge of Warre, like an ill-sheathed knife, No more shall cut his Master. Therefore Friends,	**off Hen! O horrid greed! He relented: reflects till his father wakes. He makes a last reunion. Mi—**

19 & 20

As farre as to the Sepulcher of Christ, Whose Souldier now vnder whose blessed Crosse	**racles do occur, Bvt here, see, his swine's prowess fools us ere worn old father's death: Sh—**

21 & 22

We are impressed and ingag'd to fight, Forthwith a power of English shall we leuie,	**ould he fear or hope his dad's nap is final? Will w-w-wet regret get him a gifte o' Hen's g—**

w-w-wet. use of Kit's stammer to epitomize a tearful scene between father and son.

23 & 24

Whose armes were moulded in their Mothers wombe, To chace these Pagans in those holy Fields,	**old, gemmed crowne? Now, before it's too late, lean ouer his chest, whispah thy shame. See him dres—**

25 & 26

Ouer whose Acres walk'd those blessed feete/Which fourteen hundred yeares ago were nail'd	**s reform wi' words o' loue. Hurry, Hal; U need his assent! Bend to degrade; he's weak, Cee! Th' fecal—Eee!**

Bend. Hal kneels beside his dad.

All this time Kit is telling the suppressed story of the death of Henry IV, which occurs at the end of Part Two. Ben Jonson was right: Kit divided the play into Parts One and Two only because it was so long.

27 & 28

For our aduantage on the bitter Crosse. But this our purpose is a tweluemonth old;	**Raue on, U! Press on to Ierusalem to hear Gabriel's horn, C! But it's odd—the two of U putt—**

29 & 30

And bootlesse 'tis to tell you we will go: Therefore we meete not now. Then let me heare	**in' "neel-to-feet" ahead o' worthee men who smote lo blows t-to let ye rule. Get reel, swine! T—**

Marlowe thinks of Hal abandoning Falstaff, and the King's lines, "By whose fell working, I was first advanc'd, And by whose power I might well lodge a fear, to be againe displac'd. Which to avoid, I cut them off."

31 & 32

Of you my gentle Cousin Westmerland, What yesternight our Councell did decree,	**o desert old seruants, C, might run in your dull fam'lee, C, yet—C, C!! Ye won i' the end! Woe! G—**

33 & 34

In forwarding this deere expedience. My Liege: This haste was hot in question,	**greed seems th' quality we need for winning *ici*. Hi-ho! Hasten to express it!**

35 & 36

And many limits of the Charge set downe But yesternight: when all athwart there came	**Idea: Loyalty B damn'd! Watch green, mean Marlo, th' new Chef: it's true he gets wet i' th' rain at Seh—.**

37 & 38

A Post from Wales, loaden with heavy Newes; Whose worst was, That the Noble Mortimer,

vil, 'n' stands awae at sea o' the morrow, t' re-stow balls i' th' enemy fort. Whee! Pow! Show me h—

stands awae. An old term for 'sails off.'

t' re-stow balls. He recalls moving Spanish cannon balls to the wrong stations.

Whee! Pow! Kit joined the English in the shootout at Cadiz—bullets whizzed by.

39 & 40

Leading the men of Herefordshire to fight Against the irregular and wilde Glendower,

—ow greed dragged this irreligious friend of England t' the hell o'war 'n' hate, after he min

41 & 42

Was by the rude hands of that Welshman taken,
And a thousand of his peoplebutchered:

ed th' secret store of th' enemy plan—'n' afta (ha, ha, ha, U du know)—he'd plot bad business? Haw! D—

43 & 44

Vpon whose dead corpes there was such misuse,
Such beastly, shameless transformation,

on't U C? A base smash-traitor wd never shew himself so: ache to help your cause, spend SSS sm—

smash-traitor. in modern terms, a saboteur. Some English suspected Kit of treachery because he worked with a Spanish partner (Cervantes, a wild idealist who believed that working against inquisition-loving Philip II was striking a blow for freedom).

45 & 46

By those Welshwomen done, as may not be (Without much shame) re told or spoken of.

art-money with care, send U notes, sweat th' enemy mobs! Ho, hoo! U F . . . . S.O.B.! Who'll do K.P.? Me!

smart-money. OED. 1. a sum of money paid to sailors, soldiers, workmen, as compensation for disablement or injuries while on duty or at work. OED's first example is 1693.

K.P. kitchen-police.

47 & 48

It seemes then, that the tidings of this broile,
Brake off our business for the Holy Land.

If this is soon ouer, I'l bring Isabel t-to some safe Hebe nest 'n' hurtle off t' the dark they'd h—

soon ouer. The Cadiz raid ended Aug. 1596. Marlowe's daughter Isabel was 22 months old when he took her to live at the admiral's house (Good Tom Howard, admiral of the third squadron of this expedition. Later he'd be Earl of Suffolk.)

49 & 50

This matcht with other like, my gracious Lord, Farre more vneuen and vnwelcome Newes	**ave me haunt. Let me know your thots—wd I come t' England in error, which false Vere's crim—**

51 & 52

Came from the North, and thus it did report: On Holy-roode day, the gallant Hot spurre there,	**inal mind cd use t' damage R plans? Th' fool, the rotter—hated horror! Don't hope to hurry ye The—**

53 & 54

Young Harry Percy, and braue Archibald, that euer-valiant and approoued Scot,	**ater construction; dry Bear Garden property available! Ah, houu can U pay? Had d'—**

55 & 56

At Holmedon met, where they did spend A sad and bloody houre:	**Uere held on, al wd B done. He's odd-odd, 'n' may yet promise that ha—**

The Holywell Theater lease was to expire in late March or early April, 1597. C.C. Stopes. Burbage and Shakespeare's Stage. 1913, 1970, p 66. Notice on her page 76, the mysterious William Smith who helped on moving night, 28 Dec. 1598, and brought money. (the loan from Ned de Vere, at last?)

57 & 58

As by discharge of their Artillerie, And shape of likely-hood the newes was told:	**If he said he'd bring i' loan. O, it wd cost less t' redo ye shell—keep it for a year. Ha, Ha! W—**

59 & 60

For he that brought them, in the very heate And pride of their contention, did take horse,	**e cd get dead drop on them: H-h-o! h-h-h-o! Ferry it o'er the river at nite 'n' situate it on the bank f—**

61 & 62

Vncertaine of the issue any way. Heere is a deere and true industrious friend:	**ar awaie 'n' rent-free. They cdn't do us any hurt, see? Our deed's enuf, sans Vere! I, I! I, I! I—**

Our deed's. They possessed a deed to the building itself?

63 & 64

Sir Walter Blunt, new lighted from his Horse,
Strain'd with the variation of each soyle,

f we go on from there, dry, renovate 'n' do business—what a theatrical thrill! I, I—whilst his

65 & 66

Betwixt that Holmedon, and this Seat of ours:
and he hath brought vs smooth and welcomes newes.

abandonment o' SSS wd B a shame. Th' chef dreams, studies on how he'l give th' extra loot to th' nut who'—

Th' chef dreams. Here Kit changes the subject suddenly, writing of Essex's intentions at Cadiz.
loot. Much booty was being taken from Cadiz.

67 & 68

The Earle of Dowglas is discomfited,
Ten thousand bold Scots, two and twenty Knights

d set us back! He'll dishonor England! Dogmatic effete idiot! 'N' what's t-t-to do t' wyn? S.O.S.! Sw—

idiot. The idiot was Ralegh, who wanted to stop debarcation for Cadiz town and push on into the harbor next to the Spanish ships. (John Winton. Sir Walter Ralegh. NY: Coward, McCann & Geoghegan. 1975, pp 178-192.)

69 & 70

Balk'd in their owne blood did Sir Walter see
On Holmedons Plaines. Of Prisoners, Hotspurre tooke

an-hore! Let 'im frisk bi, press on past R town 'n' spoil R landin'! O, Look out! He breeds lies! Here, we do, do, do!

Swan-hore. Henry S. A. Becket, The Dictionary of Espionage. NY: Stein & Day, 1986. p 160: "Male prositutes, both straight and homosexual, are known as swans."
He breeds lies. True: the only account of the Cadiz raid is Ralegh's own. He did push past the landing operation and claimed it was doomed by an Atlantic swell. He could have ruined it with the wake of his ship. Cervantes was there and used the scene of confusion and men in the water in his Viaje del Parnaso.

71 & 72

Mordake Earle of Fife, and eldest sonne
To beaten Dowglas, and the Earle of Atholl,

Demon Walter, deaf to reason, fled off t' gaine th' lead—'n' broken, he stood alee, as all e—

73 & 74

Of Murry, Angus, and Monteith.
And is not this an honourable spoyle?

nter on a good tide 'n' shoot at sum nearby ships. In an hour, all my fun

75 & 76

A gallant prize? Ha Cosin, is it not?
Infaith it is.
A Conquest for a Prince to boast of.

is quasht: O! I notice a pair o' fires start to zip along aft, 'n' in bi th' fo'cas'le! Actin' on

77 & 78

Yea, there thou mak'st me sad, & mak'st me sin,
In enuy, that my Lord Northumberland

a mad try, I send sails t' th' dek t' smother th' burn—& hear my name. Aye look, 'n' U men tum—

79 & 80

Should be the Father of so blest a Sonne:
A Sonne, who is the Theame of Honors tongue;

ble free 'n' soon beat those flames t' death usin' wet rags. So ho ho, ho ho! Enuf o' th' nonse—

81 & 82

Among'st a Groue, the very straightest Plant,/Who is sweet Fortunes Minion, and her Pride:

nse, 'n' on with this pen-review o' th' play. Meet Dad as aggressiue hero—from rat-stunt to ring—

83 & 84

Whilst I by looking on the praise of him,
See Ryot and Dishonor staine the brow

leader—who tried (oi, oi, oi!) t' make Hal honestbyshowingbonny,honestspiritsfr—

85 & 86

Ofmyyong Harry. O thatit could be prou'd,
That some Night-tripping-Faiery, had exchang'd

om rough xperience—no dry propah toady, but a man, a cad—o' nitty-gritty h-h-higgles. Th' diff—

a cad. OED cad 1. obs. a familiar spirit. 5. a fellow of low vulgar manners and behaviors. Appears to have arisen at the universities as sense 4. low fellows who hang about the colleges to provide Etonians with things neccessary to assist their sports. [How about—caddy?]

87 & 88

In Cradle-clothes, our Children where they lay,
and call'd mine Percy, his Plantagenet:

erent, liuely teacher cd help Hal learn, change, rid him o' condescendin' ways—all prytt—

condescendin' ways. Close reading of the plaintext above displays Hal's truly despicable condescension.

89 & 90

Then would I haue his Harry, and he mine: but let him from my thoughts. What thinke you Coze

y mannahs, cold, self-entwined thot! Oi! Make him euer hearty with bout-hourz i' th' gym (Uh-huh),

cold, self-entwined thot. Later, Ned becomes Hamlet.
bout. OED. A round at any kind of exercise. A turn or spell of work; as much of an action as performed at one time.
gym. OED. Short for gymnasium or with meaning, naked. A place for practice of or instruction in athletic exercises. Kit also speaks of "acted in the gym" in his ciphered lines 25, 26 in Richard III. He means "naked" there—maybe here, too.

91 & 92

Of this young Percies pride? The Prisoners
Which he in this aduenture hath surpriz'd,

with increas'd SSS hope driuin' dis uenture t' prepare th' youth for his high prize, 'n' che—

93 & 94

To his owne vse he keepes, and sends me word
I shall haue none but Mordake Earle of Fife.

erful aid o' workmen in d' open field, al seems assured, bvt when he sees a hook—a fee—O, then

Thinking of a time when Elizabeth asked Roger Manwood to look after Ned? Roger hoped that if Ned became king, he and Kit would profit. Uh huh . . .

95 & 96

This is his Vncles teaching. This is Worcester
Maleuolent to you in all Aspects:

his chums change to coarse, vncouth, wastin', ill-pleasin' lesser lites. Oi! yet it's t—

This may be the whole story for fictional Hal; for real Ned de Vere there was more: Vere turned against Kit and Roger because Kit told Hen Wriothesley the truth—that the girl Ned asked him to marry was Hen's own half-sister—so Hen balked, spoiling the plan.

97 & 98

Which makes him prune himselfe, and bristle vp
The crest of Youth against your Dignity.

rue their plans were immoderately ambitious—th' syc hopes f-fuckin' high. Nvthing stay'd

99 & 100

But I have sent for him to answer this:
And for this cause a-while we must neglect

th' same: in time, Hal wd forget his best realist teacher 'n' was usin' few uncouth, vo—

101 & 102

Our holy purpose to Ierusalem. Cosin, on Wednesday next, our Councell we will hold	**latile, wooly uolenteers. He excell'd in war 'n' od'ly wd oppose Moor sinners. Chouu! C U!**

wooly. In ciphers, Kit uses this word to mean rough. **wd oppose Moor sinners.** Hal and his father had been planning a crusade to Jerusalem. **od'ly.** An inside irony? Falstaff is Roger, and Roger's Jewish forebears may have come from Moorea. (Queen Elizabeth called Walsingham, a Jewish friend of Roger's, her "Moor," and Roger, too, may have had a "Moorish" reputation).

103 & 104

At Windsor, and so informe the Lords: But come your selfe with speed to vs againe,	**No! No more codes! Wish you wd let me stop and rest free; I value this brain. G. D. Fatso**

105 & 106

For more is to be said, and to be done, Then out of anger can be vttered. I will my Liege.	**wants more of it then I can deliuer. O, G, O, G; I bleed for my deniable debt! Vote treason**

107 & 108

Now Hal, what time of day is it Lad? Thou art so fat-witted with drinking of olde Sacke,	**out! Won't he C I'm loyal t' England? Oi! What w'd it take t' show off th' dri s . . . as a fake? I did tri!**

Fatso? In Hamlet, V, ii, l. 287, Hamlet's mother speaks of him as fat—and in Kit's mind Hamlet, like Hal, was Ned, indeed a true prince—eldest son of Queen Elizabeth, born when she was a princess. (His father Admiral Thomas Seymour.)

109 & 110

. . . and vnbuttoning thee after Supper, and sleeping vpon Benches in the afternoone,	**I began Ned th' Prince 'n' Roger Falstaf 'n' then soon—tush!—penn'd U pee pee. I vvant one t' B**

in the plaintext: Sacke, and sleeping vpon Benches. Roger, a judge, kept a roast capon-leg and sacke beside him at work, and had been known to doze on his official bench in the afternoon.

111 & 112

that thou hast for'gotten to demand that truly, which thou wouldest truely know. What a diuell . . .	**strate, one deuious: U'l all no which! That frothy, muddy laughter that Hal knew how t-t-to do t-t-t'U, w—**

13 & 114

. . . hast thou to do with the time of the day? Vnlesse houres were cups of Sacke, and minutes Capons,

ith such mean scorn. Peeee-uu! 'N' dad-Falstaf's h-honest t-tricksee ways do show them up! I vote to o—

115 & 116

and clockes the tongues of Bawdes, and dialls the signes
of Leaping-houses, and the blessed Sunne himself a faire

utface Hal's mindless bleats before Dad's kind, engagin' speech, so no one uud fail t' see d' shoe's last. When English af—

117 & 118

hot Wench in flame-coloured Taffata; I see no reason,
why thou shouldest bee so superfluous to demand the time of the day.

fords such neat, fit means t-to show off a foul man, it ioyes the author's heart! U C, Ned, you owe me, 'n' h-hope's dead, but loue led ele—

119 & 120

Indeed you come neere me now Hal, for we that take Purses,
go by the Moone and seuen Starres, and not by Phoebus hee,

ments o' poesy to these words. My dreams o' you as a friend 'n' helper are gone now: then, tho', each kneuu U'd bee beaten be—

Plaintext: we that take Purses, go by the Moone. Roger worked at Exchequer, the financial arm of government, for the queen, who was often called Diana the moon goddess.

121 & 122

. . . that wand'ring Knight so faire. And I prythee sweet Wagge, when thou art King, as God save thy Grace . . .

fore U'd even think t' grasp thy crown. Didn't wee wink—ha ha—at the shaggie, raw, stagey aggregations

123 & 124

Maiesty I should say, for Grace thou wilte haue none.
What, none? / No, not so much as will serue to be Prologue to an Egge and Butter.

o' tales U showed your mother, who saw ye goin' on 'n' on alone, pitiable, laughable, 'n' suggested a concert of ten authors t' vvrite em?

Kit is disingenuous. These were authors hired for the Theatre Wing, and Ned was their chief, at £1,000 a year. (John Lyly, Tom Nashe, Robin Greene, Sam Daniel, George Chapman, Tom Lodge, Nathan Field, Tom Kyd, George Peele and Kit?)

125 & 126

Well, how then? Come, roundly, roundly. / Marry then, sweet(e) Wagge, when thou art King, let not vs that are Squires of the Nights bodie,

We tvtors taught our leader t' shine for th' queen, 'n' while traces o' my long-gone style adher'd t' his M T work, wily, he began on . . . hum . . . 'n—

W upside down for *M*, or M for W, will be underlined here.

127 & 128

. . . bee call'd Theeves of the Dayes beautie. Let vs be Dianaes Forresters, Gentlemen of the Shade, Minions of the Moone:

ot-honest liftin' of some o' my best dialogue. E-e-e! VVe all resented that breech, see, 'n' feared h-he'd been one fat-ass mis—

Falstaff keeps pounding home his jest about sly financial managers in Exchequer working for Elizabeth, the moon goddess.

129 & 130

. . . and let men say, we be men of good Gouernment, being gouerned as the Sea is, by our noble and chast mistris

erable, sad waste o' time, but SSS hired us, 'n' euen tho' Ned left, good nabob Regina's money came in, 'n' ye grog 'n' m—

nabob. OED. the title of Mohammedan officials who acted as deputy governors in the Mogul Empire. 2. A person of high rank or great wealth.

Elizabeth herself hired the writers to make plays for SSS Theatre Wing, which she'd created on advice of Wm. Pickering, who told her about French and Italian writers and actors working under cover for their governments, as spies.

grog. Sailors' term for spirits mixed with water, used here 172 years prior to first OED example.

131 & 132

. . . the Moone, vnder whose countenance we steale.
Thou say'st well, and it holds well too:

eals, 'n' candy, too. We ten vote to write some howls on Ned 'n' that loue-*m*ess he cal'd hell. U

hell. Ned wrote a poem (extant) about his affair with his mother. Hen Wriothesley was the child of that liason.

133 & 134

for the fortune of vs that are the Moones men, doth ebbe and flow like the Sea, beeing gouerned as the Sea is,

know that sad tale of his mother's need: from venal strife—E-e-e-e-e!—on her bed, Fatso begot thin Hen. So uague be—

He's spelling it out. Here's the lowdown: **Fatso begot.**

venal. OED. exposed or offered for sale (A bargain was made). This word, too, is used here long before first example in OED.

135 & 136

. . . by the moone: as for proofe. Now a purse of Gold most resolutely snatch'd on Monday night,

comes sure: Hen's Regina's own frog-boy—th' son of Ma'm 'n' Ned! Do tell! O Happy Day! Toot fur loot!

frog-boy. hidden, disguised prince. **Toot fur loot!** Ask for inheritance!

137 & 138

. . . and most dissolutely spent on Tuesday Morning; got with swearing, Lay by: and spent with crying, Bring in:

Angel changeling, do try t' bring *one* winnin' way into thy gross, dim-twin dad's style: try t' B passin' up some u—

dim-twin. Ned de Vere was a twin. He and Edward Manners, later Earl of Rutland, were born to Elizabeth while she was a princess in house arrest at Hatfield. First-born Ned was the dimmer twin. His birth-cry may have been stifled to prevent her jailers, the Tyrwhits, from hearing it.

139 & 140

. . . now, in as low an ebbe as the foot of the Ladder, and by and by in as high a flow as the ridge

nheard-of good deed of th' fat rat. While he wins in any base way, he's not all bad; no big bas—

141 & 142

. . . of the Gallowes. / Thou say'st true Lad: and is not my Hostesse of the Tauerne a most sweet Wench?

tard, either: He stands low, weasel-cheats on foot-heels to seem a man, 'n' oft hugs yu to test yu, Sw—

143 & 144

As is the hony, my old Lad of the Castle: and is not a Buffe Ierkin a most sweet robe of durance?

earin' he's thy stout friend for aye! O, man, it cd be al off, as soon as U cd ha' been wed. Lost, like M T

my old Lad of the Castle. Some readers believe revising editors forgot to delete these words (Oldcastle was Falstaff's name in the early version), but Kit retained the phrase to keep the cipher and give a hint of Falstaff as Roger. Roger idolized John Oldcastle, an earnest lollard influential in the passage of the act of Praemunire of 16 Richard II, and erstwhile friend of Henry V. In the early 1400's, Oldcastle lived at Cooling Castle (in the marsh below Roger's Gad's Hill house), and acted as lay preacher in the churches of Hoo, Halsted, Cooling and Chalk, avowing that a man could go on pilgrimage and be damned, or stay home and be saved; that images were not to be worshipped; that he was ready to believe what God wished him to believe, but that the pope or prelates had no power to determine such things. Oldcastle, declared a heretic, was cruelly executed on 14 Dec. 1417, 175 years to the day before Sir Roger Manwood was privately executed (in the manner of the murder of Edward II).

145 & 146

How now? how now mad Wagge? What in thy quips and thy quiddities? What a plague haue I to doe

hope. Ie! U'd hate it 'n' wish he w'd q-quit 'n' go away, away—auaunt! Whom do pigs lodge, with tho'? Dawn

147 & 148

. . . with a Buffe-Ierkin? / Why, what a poxe haue I to doe with my Hostesse of the Tauerne?

shows fat-nut weauin' at ye hore-house door, with th' key, th fee . . . a fib! We expiate him.

149 & 150

Well, thou hast call'd her to a reck'ning many a time and oft. / Did I euer call for thee to pay thy part?

Cooky cad, he left us with all th' rent, 'n' Ma Hell had t' pay, after a lot o' recrimination. Get ready, dup—

Ma Hell. Queen Elizabeth. Ned referred to his affair with her as hell.
left us with all th' rent. Mark Eccles' essay on George Buck in Thomas Lodge and Other Elizabethans, ed. Chas. J. Sisson. Cambridge: Harvard U Press, 1933, p. 465, and Dorothy and Charlton Ogburn. This Star of England. Westport, CT: Greenwood Press, 1972, p. 930-31. The hostess was Julie Arthur Penn Hicks; the house was on St. Peter's Hill between Paul's Wharf and Paul's Chain. Once the home of postmaster-ambassador Thomas Randolph, after his death there, his widow leased half to Julie Arthur, who may have been a relative of Kit's mother. (Years later Kit sent a viola from Venice to Mike Hicks, this woman's son.) Mark Eccles says this 13th century house stood in the same block as the house in Dicken's Little Dorrit which fell down at the end of the story. I believe it was the same house.

151 & 152

No, Ile giue thee thy due, thou hast paid al there. / Ye(s) and elsewhere, so farre as my Coine would stretch,

plicitous souse, ere I show ye as U are—tel the world of thy need 'n' shame! Aye! C'd truth denigrate a h-heel?

153 & 154

. . . and where it would not, I haue vs'd my credit. / Yea, and so us'd it, that were it heere apparant,

To Ned: ye used yr mother 'n' said Dad had U vote in a tie ere that win! What crap! R.I.P? Ule Sweat!

155 & 156

. . . That thou art Heire apparant. But I prythee sweet Wag, shall there be Gallowes standing in England when thou art King?

That habit o' lying t' ruin Regina's honest helpers—what pleasure d' U get, neelin' an awkward leg t' Beth at the wrong path? A

157 & 158

. . . and resolution thus fobb'd as it is, with the rustie curbe of old Father Anticke the Law?

stretch o' truth w'd B allowed, but sinister hateful fabrication on his eue of death is k—

eue of death. just before Roger's secret execution.

159 & 160

doe not thou when thou art a King, hang a Theefe. / No, thou shalt. / Shall I? O rare! Ile be a braue Iudge.

in to a degenerate fool's rush t' the kil. Ha ha ha! U are an ignorant tool! W'd Beth belieue U, a hog hu

tool. (of John Whitgift)

161 & 162

Thou iudgest false already. I meane, thou shalt haue the hanging of the Theeues, and so become a rare Hangman.

has betrayed good men, not enemies—all undeseruing o' th' charges U use t' tangle them. O, ha ha ha ha ha! A fate fiue

163 & 164

Well Hal, well: and in some sort it iumpes with my humour, as well as waiting in the Court, I can tell you.

loyal men met due t' your misanthropic machinations. R U sane? W-will lies get U loue, whilst all with w—

165 & 166

For obtaining of suites? / Yea, for obtaining of suites, whereof the Hangman hath no leane Wardrobe.

ronged ones i' thy web shun thee as if unfit for hate? Sooo, Ile begin: bring wrath for Nan—me too! Faaaa!!

Nan. Ned's first wife, Anne Cecil, was so badly treated by him (publicly scorned and lied-about) that she died of a broken heart (an insane suicide in the river at Greenwich?) Circumstances of her death were not made public but are displayed in Hamlet as Ophelia's death. Ned & Kit were lovers in the early Boar's Head days, but when Kit helped Roger with satires about prelates, Ned turned against Kit—hated him, too, for spoiling Ned's plan for an incestuous marriage between his secret son and legitimate daughter. **shun thee.** A fact reflected for centuries in the emptiness of Ned's public biography. Many unpleasant facts about Ned's character were suppressed, probably because of Ned's blood-relation to the Queen. The cloud of mystery surrounding de Vere first made researchers looking for "the real Shakespeare" think this might be the man.

167 & 168

I am as Melancholly as a Gyb-Cat, or a lugg'd Beare. / Or an old Lyon, or a Louers Lute.

O, scorn your ma'm, laugh at all real, steady, caring loue! A gay boar'll soon bleed,

169 & 170

Yea, or the Drone of a Lincolnshire Bagpipe. / What say'st thou to a Hare, or the Melancholly of Moore-Ditch?

when frantic hounds catch him by his throat for a meal. O, O! th' poor, poor thing'll realee lose today! Yeeea!

171 & 172

Thou hast the most vnsauoury similes, and art indeed the most comparatiue rascallest sweet yong Prince.

Massive lies on Nan, 'n' th' crude aim t' sell thy daughter t' th' secret son at a price—O, it seems so uuop-tawdry! A mo—

Massive lies. Ned's lies about Nan are history, and his aim to sell his daughter Elizabeth to young Wriothsley is also recorded.
wop-tawdry. Kit thought Ned's actions suggested those of some contemporary Italians.

173 & 174

But Hal, I prythee, trouble me no more with vanity, I wold thou and I knew,

re vain poobah man neuer liu'd, but I'm yr o<u>w</u>n yll Moth, tied t' thee. Who? Kit.

poobah. One who'd be a potentate.
Moth. The character Moth in Love's Labor's Lost was Kit, and he was the hero of his Erotokritos, where he carries a banner with a moth on it at the tournament.

175 & 176

. . . where a Commodity of good names were to be bought: an olde Lord of the Councell rated me the other day

We won, 'n' fled for ye road to get my girl home. Both sad to leaue our dear Manco to bleed. He'd come to the ch—

Kit changes the subject, going back to the Cadiz raid. He wanted his daughter Isabel, almost two years old, to be reared in England.
Manco: Cervantes' nickname.

177 & 178

. . . in the street about you sir: but I mark'd him not, and yet hee talk'd very wisely, but I regarded him not,

ild's house—I think ouertly—t' try t' see her, 'n' had been wounded by my guard. E-e! I'm Kit, but I am a traitor t—

179 & 180

. . . and yet he talkt wisely, and in the street too. / Thou didst well: for no man regards it.

o no honest man. Th' wet hurt dress'd, I said farewel, led girly 'n' took ye t-t-t-tide at lan—

honest man. The secret service term for an undercover agent. Kit was not about to abandon his friend Cervantes. **t-t-t-tide.** Like Kit, Cervantes stammered.

181 & 182

O, thou hast damnable iteration, and art indeede able to corrupt a Saint. Thou hast done . . .

d-pan. Aboard, I thot t' uuas a treat t' see Isabel toddlin' around 'n' hear th' men cooin' to the a—

land-pan. The oblong flat promontory west of the city.
Aboard. They went aboard Good Tom Howard's flagship, the Golden Lion.

183 & 184

. . . much harme vnto me Hall, God forgiue thee for it. Before I knew thee Hal,

greeable cute girl, who, free o' fear, talkt to 'em of home 'n' me. Uh hvh! I hid, 'n'

cute. OED. aphetic form of acute—first OED instance of use, 1731.

185 & 186

I knew nothing: and now I am (if a man shold speake truly) little better then one of the wicked.

she told th' men how Pa waked her t' get ready t' clime in-into a skiff alone, unknown, Ei! 'n' let it B

187 & 188

I must giue ouer this life, and I will giue it ouer: and I do not. I am a Villaine.

tow'd along on a line after his ouun. Ei, Ei, Ei! Mi little girl, U <u>viuidas mi uida</u>!

189 & 190

Ile be damn'd for neuer a King's sonne in Christendome. / Where shall wee take a purse to morrow, Jacke?

On mi knees I implore Lord Howard t-t' take Isabel, for her sake 'n' mine, 'n' so succeed. Near U, we agree, 'n' wh—

Lord Howard. Admiral Thomas Howard. Isabel spent the rest of her childhood at his home, Audley End. Her first husband was this Thomas Howard's third son, Henry, who died of poison during Bacon's "damage control," late in 1616.

191 & 192

Where thou wilt Lad, Ile make one: and I doe not, call me Villaine, and baffle me.

ile we are al landin', U came, lookt ill at me, 'n' went off home—Avdlie End. Ah, I bled.

193 & 194

I see a good amendment of life in Thee: From Praying to Purse taking. / Why, Hal, 'tis my Vocation Hal:

Yet I strongly need t' aim—fast—at a safe home for you, with kind, loving, rich people. I am no mean Gh—

195 & 196

Tis' no sin for a man to labour in his Vocation. / Now shall wc know if Gads hill haue set a Watch.

etto man, a sinful freak who chains his girl to B sold at auction. No law shows I have won a <u>nil</u>

197 & 198

O, if men were to be saued by merit, what hole in Hell were hot enough for him?	**obstat t' rear U, my own girl. Oh, believe me, mi own feelin' for thhhheeee wd—Oh!**

nil obstat. a legal term meaning no objection to, nothing in the way of. (Literary censors used it, giving permission to publish.)

199 & 200

This is the most omnipotent Villaine, that euer cryed, Stand, to a true man. / Good morrow, Ned.	**In England I hid out at her home til' SS sent me to roam Venice to try to draw ten maps o' d' rout—**

201 & 202

Good morrow sweet Hal. What saies Monsieur Remorse? What sayes Sir Iohn Sacke and Sugar: Iacke?	**es o' th' city, 'n' to work SSS wi' Guarini. I swear he looks much shamed, more aged. A war erases reason. A**

203 & 204

How agrees the Diuell and thee about thy Soule, that thou soldest him on Good-Friday last,	**battle o' deals at Rome had left only a shred o' th' o-old wit. Yet O, he shouus U that he's guiding**

Guarini. Guarini worked under cover for the duke of Ferarra.
Rome. Rome was preparing to take over Ferarra in 1597-'98, and England was anti-Rome.

205 & 206

. . . for a Cup of Madera, and a cold Capons legge? / Sir Iohn stands to his word, the diuel shall haue his bargaine,	**policie wi' all care—unpaid, as added burden—'n' th' last seal'd affair going to ash so soon. Rush! Reach home! Gh—**

207 & 208

. . . for he was neuer yet a Breaker of Prouerbs: He will giue the diuell his due. Then art thou damn'd	**osts harrow him in bed: who'd euer belieue he'd tuueak'd th' great nose, freely refutin' all U Phar—**

209 & 210

. . . for keeping thy word with the diuell. /Else he had damn'd for cozening the diuell. / But my Lads, my Lads,	**isees long-held MT, MT, MT, words! Eliza'd gladly help thy hidden worth, if before day U cd leaue kin 'n' hu—**

kin. Guarini, a widower, was living at his country place, la Guarina, with three of his sons and a daughter-in-law. Vittorio Rossi. Battista Guarini ed il pastor Fido, studio biografico critico. Turin: Ermanno Loescher, 1886, p 104: Guarini's daughter Anna had married; Victoria was away in service of Lucrizia d'Este, and Guarina had become a nun.

211 & 212

. . . to morrow morning, by foure a clocke early at Gads hill, there are Pilgrimes going to Canterbury	**rry to England t' begin a tight SS career. I'l B your real employer. Go for it! Look: much wrong—a-a crime—**

213 & 214

. . . with rich Offerings, and Traders riding to London with fat Purses. I haue vizards for you all;	**t' hide, when th' dear Liza wd honor U. I cried, I uuas so sorry t' find V so frail 'n' grasping for flatt—**

215 & 216

. . . you haue horses for your selues: Gads-hill lyes to night in Rochester, I haue bespoke Supper	**ery. SSS shill! You hide all U knouu o' th' pope. Get busy! Share! Giue hope t' Fonso's heir Cesare! Re-r—**

Pope Clement VIII (Ippolito Aldobrandisi) was refusing to recognize Cesare as duke of all Ferrara.

217 & 218

to morrow in Eastcheape; we may doe it as secure as sleepe: if you will go, I will stuffe your Purses.	**ehearse! Try again t' effect some deal wi' your pope! Wil U use my SSS? Cooperate! Ile follow U. I wis U R s—**

your pope. Pope Clement VIII, a friend to Cardinal Allen, was unfriendly to Queen Elizabeth. He burned philosopher Giordano Bruno at the stake and fostered English Colleges of Catholic Studies in European cities.

219 & 220

. . . full of Crownes: if you will not, tarry at home and be hang'd. / Hear ye Yedward, if I tarry at home and go not,	**hy in referring t' that odd, all-day meeting at Rome—fools wud fly away in horror—yet how, on a bed, can U af—**

221 & 222

. . . Ile hang you for going. / You will chops / Hal, wilt thou make one? Who, I rob? I a Theefe? Not I.	**fect gouernment? All I know is, U 'n' I go high: I leap with Hoo-Hoo, U bow to ye holy ear. Afli—**

Hoo-Hoo. Kit's nickname for Queen Elizabeth, taken from an incident in a night of love together described in Loves Labour's Lost ciphers.

223 & 224

There's neither honesty, manhood, nor good fellowship in thee, nor thou cam'st not of the blood-royall,	**cted 'n' lonely rulers, 'n' prelates too, often lie with strange bad friends—tho' not my Hoo-Hoo! H-Hoo H-Hoo! M—**

225 & 226

. . . if thou dar'st not stand for ten shillings. / Well then, once in my dayes Ile be a mad-cap.

any indiscretions R slufft in a shadow'd pall, negated by time's loth element o' chan—

loth. OED. repulsive, hateful, loathsome. 1592 example: "relaxment from loth prison strong".

227 & 228

Why, that's well said. / Well, come what will, Ile tarry at home. Ile be a Traitor then, when thou art King.

ce; th' others R awkwardly lit bi th' same element. Yet U, who'l win a trial with a new, all-too-high relat—

229 & 230

I care not. / Sir Iohn, I prythee leaue the Prince & (and) me alone, I will lay him downe

ion . . . T' discouer thy happie ioy-ride wil harm thine own clean name—E-e-e! All in rel—

231 & 232

such reasons for this aduenture, that he shall go. / Well, maist thou haue the Spirit of perswasion;

igion won't falter, so thou shalt liue much oppress't, in th' shades o' failure. Hear me! Haue that SSS r—

233 & 234

and he the eares of profiting that what thou speakest, may moue; and what he heares may be beleeued,

eport sent with strategy. U haue shaken ye ham; he'd hope t' meet, see? Wd a hit B an affordable moue? A hea—

235 & 236

that the true Prince, may (for recreation sake) proue a false theefe; for the poore abuses of the time, want countenance.

rtless one, but with it, U may check the threat to Ferrara 'n' effect a mean t' open resistance. Raue on! Fooeee! U hope for pea—

237 & 238

Farwell, you shall finde me in Eastcheape. / Farwell the latter Spring. Farewell, Alhollown Summer.

ce, arriued at less from effort than release o' all thy raw spleen 'n' phlegm. Wil U win 'em all? Well, half—

239 & 240

Now, my good sweet Hony Lord, ride with vs to morrow. I haue a iest to execute, that I cannot manage alone.

hearted trial's no solution. To extradite the man won't gaine U victory. So change ye m-mode! O, hew a wo-wo—

241 & 242
Falstaffe, Haruey, Rossill, and Gadshill, shall robbe those men that wee haue already way-layde,

oden horse: seem friendly, but get ready t' resist all foul deals by law. Laf: "Ha, ha, ha, ha, ha!" Say, "All we

243 & 244
. . . your selfe and I, wil not be there: and when they haue the booty, if you and I do not rob them,

need is aid t' bend to reformation—Bu-boo h-hoo—'n' then with thy hy loue we'l defeat any rey U

245 & 246
. . . cut this head from my shoulders. / But how shal(l) we part with them in setting forth? / Why, we wil(l) set forth

w-w-w-w-wish t' enslaue. Th'-th'-th'-price is only th'-th'-th' freedom of Ferrara." H-humm! this wd B too silly t' get us l—

247 & 248
before or after them, and appoint them a place of meeting, wherin it is our pleasure to faile;

oose, but perhaps in pitie he'l offer a deal for maintainin' a peaceful merger. Th' more we tott—

249 & 250
and then will they aduenture vpon the exploit themselues, which they shall haue no sooner atchieued,

er 'n' weep, th' more he'll condescend t' help U, so lately his love. Then he'd post a what-uuhy-'n'-uuhen at a hi-i exit.

hi-i exit. There'd be a papal pronouncement from a high balcony.

251 & 252
but wee'l set vpon them. / I, but tis like that they will know vs by our horses, by our habits,

(Bulky, he shows best at some very hi openin'.) Bvt wil U bow t-tu use this brotherly talk? It

253 & 254
and by euery other appointment to be our selues. Tut our horses they shall not see,

may lead us to another, better solution. Sh! Ye pope's no stony brute: Sh! U'l reuere the

255 & 256
Ile tye them in the wood, our vizards wee will change after wee leave them: and sirrah, I haue Cases of Buckram

memorie o' thy high love, as I think of Eliza 'n' me—a dual fact. Sh!! Their reserue was bent—reduced. We crave a law we

Sh!! Guarini keeps interrupting.

257 & 258

for the nonce, to immaske our noted outward garments. / But I doubt they will be too hard for vs.

cd use t' guard Ferrara's freedom. Withovt it, there's only one month to talk 'ob-nob to 'im. Wd U B ou—

'ob-nob. OED. Hob-nob. have or have not. (In Twelfth Night, "Hob, nob, is his word: giv't or take 't".)

259 & 260

Well, for two of them, I know them to bee as true bred Cowards as euer turn'd backe:

tsmarted 'n' sulk, or use brainwork to effect a better deal? Who'd B couer? Who? Me! We—

261 & 262

. . . and for the third if he fight longer then he sees reason, Ile forswear Armes.

'l restore him in his age—afford free flesh to renew, regain th' dash! There's no

263 & 264

the vertue of this Iest will be, the incomprehensible lyes that this fat Rogue will tell vs,

legal solvtion. It mvst lie between his sheets. Our last try will be t' hire th' cheep hit. U'l f-fe—

cheep hit. It must be cheap, a gesture that would fail—just to prove to Duke Cesare that they were trying.

265 & 266 & 267

when we meete at Supper: how thirty at least he fought with, what Wardes, what blowes, what extremities he endured; and in the reproofe of this, lyes the iest.

el sure, then, that we'ue done what we might do to aid Ferrara. Essex sent me t' help with this. He protests we do best in life if we put wrath away, tho' where the hy—

268 & 269

Well, Ile goe with thee, prouide vs all things necessary, and meete me to morrow night in Eastcheape,

est people R inuolued there's always something t' hate 'n' some congenialitie. We dream we'l get rich—h—

270 & 271

there Ile sup. Farewell. / Farewell, my Lord. / I know you all, and will awhile vphold

ave us a wonderful merry life—deal power, pay no toll. Hell, we'll walk d' hi hill wi—

272 & 273
The vnyoak'd humor of your idlenesse: Yet heerin will I imitate the Sunne,

th hy disdain for those not i' th' know. U see me reveal my i-ill enuy 'n' ire t' eue—

274 & 275
Who doth permit the base contagious cloudes To smother vp his Beauty from the world,

ry good brother there. Don't U C it? Svch low habits show me up as a stupid fool Moth. Meet e—

Moth. Kit's nickname again.

276 & 277
That when he please againe to be himselfe, Being wanted, he may be more wondred at,

mergent problem with a new one: fawn on him—heady, see? Get a bad bite—ease the deal h—

278 & 279
By breaking through the foule and vgly mists Of vapours, that did seeme to strangle him.

e'd impose. Think of al R means—any, hy or lovv! Grab fate, hold tight, thrust, dig, beg! U must see

280 & 281
If all the yeare were playing holidaies, To sport, would be as tedious as to worke;

how desperate is Ferrara! Will we let it be lost, as U say? Ile pay U! Think! Go! Doo! Doo! E—

282 & 283
But when they seldome come, they wisht-for come, And nothing pleaseth but rare accidents.

uery bit o' th' state needn't go Roman: much cd be Cesare's with one payment of th' well-hid ches—

284 & 285
So when this loose behauior I throw off, And pay the debt I neuer promised;

ts of treasure in his house, paid before the end o' th' year. Do whip 'im on: blow

th' year. It's 1597.

286 & 287
By how much better then my word I am, By so much shall I falsifie mens hopes,

flames—warm him—sway him, U C, so he'l send Chubby of Rome plenty o' th' best—hi i—

288 & 289

and like bright Mettall on a sullen ground: My reformation glittering o're my fault,

n regular market ualue, only no more entailment! D' startling gift might B d' oil for ly—

290 & 291

Shall shew more goodly, and attract more eyes, Then that which hath no foyle to set it off.

sis of the dilemma: ergo, tho' chatter, tattle, n ye dry oath o' laws fayl, fetch th' one show no h—

lysis. A letting go, freeing up, getting well.

292 & 293

Ile so offend, to make offence a skill, redeeming time, when men thinke least I will.

agiolater wd hate. He'l feel mock milk of kindness 'n' settle, if onlie we fee 'im. Men in

hagiolater. A saint-worshipper.

294 & 295

My blood hath beene too cold and temperate, Vnapt to stirre at these indignities,

a hi position, beset, vnderstand th' import o' money to a great deed. I bet he can't tell

296 & 297

and you haue found me; for accordingly, You tread vpon my patience: But be sure,

houu often fortvne douun'd a papal dream. You're edgy 'n' cryin' b-cause ye bot mi c—

298 & 299

I will from henceforth rather be mySelfe, Mighty, and to befear'd, then my condition

ool manner as intolerance of thy mild bid t' meet hym. Why B reticent, if h-he'd go fer fr—

300 & 301

Which hath beene smooth as Oyle, soft as yong Downe, and therefore lost that Title of respect,

iendly terms? Retreat 'n' siege o' th' town's not th' death of hope, C: choose th' affable way t' loose sh—

302 & 303

Which the proud soule ne're payes, but to the proud. Our house (my Soueraigne Liege) little deserues

ut doors, bring home news o' good ripe ualue t' your petty Cesare: he'l uuish t' see U'; he'l pile th' seuered

304 & 305

The scourge of greatnesse to be vsed on it, and that same greatnesse too, which our owne hands

heads of assassinated couriers who brought sad news—an' honor V 'n' me, Cee? Get thee gone to tête à tê—

306 & 307

Have holpe to make so portly. / My Lord. / Worcester get thee gone: for I do see

te! O, try woookeee love—sodomy, C? Propose federal rights; he'l grant them! E—

308 & 309

Danger and disobedience in thine eye. O sir, your presence is too bold and peremptory,

nter his brain—bend it! No! Present your good pen's comedy o' L'Idropica, and I'd see ye ere e—

L'Idropica. Discussed in Vittorio Rossi. *Battista Guarini,* p 19-82. In 1584 Guarini sent this comedy to Mantua, where the MS was lost. It was finally played in Mantua in 1608! (In 1593 Guarini had published a synopsis of the play. Was he reconstructing it?) It was first printed at Ciotti Press, Venice, 1613, and Kit as Gregorio de' Monti wrote the preface. (Gamba, Serie #4, No. 1939).

310 & 311

And Maiestie might neuer yet endure
The moody Frontier of a seruant brow,

ffusiue admirers o' theatre begin t' o'er-run ye at Rome: he wd note di Monty, 'n' a—

312 & 313

You haue good leaue to leaue vs. When we need
Your vse and counsell, we shall send for you.

ssure we'll haue any good deal we'd choose, euen to y' whole value, 'n' U'l say, "Free us novv!" "Done!"

314 & 315

You were about to speake. / Yea, my good Lord. Those Prisoners in your Highnesse demanded.

says ye ogre pope, 'n' we return, kissed, bathed in glorious honor, the doom-day saued! Oy, me! E—

316 & 317

Which Harry Percy heere at Holmedon tooke,
Were (as he sayes) not with such strength denied

'en U cd see these R h-hy dreams! Th' only h-hot idea is th' hog, C? otherwise we are wreckt, 'n' no re—

318 & 319

As was deliuered to your Maiesty:
Who either through enuy or misprision,

dress. Ay, hurry! Present him wi' restoratiue gold! Yoo-hoo! I wis U haue men t' i—

Yoo-hoo! Guarini is dozing off. **I wis.** I know.

320 & 321

Was guilty of this fault; and not my Sonne
My Liege, I did deny no Prisoners.

nsure timely deliuery of d' gift t' the nonny nonny pissa wissa idol o' d' mag—

322 & 323

But, I remember when the fight was done,
When I was dry with Rage, and extreame Toyle,

neii. Hurry! Dare t' greet that Hebe; get Modena from him, 'n' Essex'l aid ye 'n' be w-w-w-w-what

324 & 325

Breathlesse, and Faint, leaning vpon my Sword,
Came there a certaine Lord, neat and trimly drest;

ye wanted him t' B: a great friend, 'n' send hope at last, lest sly Ran-Ran-Ranvccio redeem more land. It

Ranvccio. Ranuccio Farnese was the duke of Parma, west of Ferrara. Parma was already a favored papal state, and it was feared Ranuccio might reach out at the time of takeover and snatch Modina and Reggio. A Prince of Mantua, by Maria Bellonci. NY: Harcourt, Brace, 1956, p 177: "to [Cesare], Clement VIII conceded Modena and Reggio with their surrounding territory, together with the title of Duke." This author says that at the papal celebration in Ferrara, Ranuccio's bearing was "rigid." (His nose was out of joint.)

326 & 327

Fresh as a Bride-groome, and his Chin new reapt,
Shew'd like a stubble Land at Haruest home.

wd B like Parma t' reach ouer 'n' grab al that land. See, U assist him 'n' his Hebe deeds when, for o—

328 & 329

He was perfumed like a Milliner,
And 'twixt his Finger and his Thumbe, he held

uertimid dealin,' U R shakin' wi' f-fear i' bed. Essex'l lend help! M-man! Get wi' th' h-h-h—

330 & 331

A Pouncet-box: which euer and anon
He gaue his Nose, and took't away againe:

i stakes! Honor cd B won again, in a coup! AAAAAgh! They'ue uexed thee, 'n' now on

332 & 333

Who therewith angry, when it next came there,
Tooke it in Snuffe: and still he smil'd and talk'd:

de wreck-edge, don't hesitate! Let's hasten! I, man! Hurry! Think of Modena 'n' what'll fix it! Win the l—

334 & 335

And as the Souldiers bare dead bodies by,
He call'd them vntaught Knaues,
Vnmannerly.

ast bad hand, 'n' save all ye uuest borderland t' B Cesare's gnat-hive 'n' mile-hy dukedom! 'N' h—

gnat-hive. The city of Modena lies in a damp plain. In those old days, mosquitos were called gnats.
mile-hy. The western border lay in the Apennines.
dukedom. The pope let Cesare keep the title of duke.

336 & 337

To bring a slouenly vnhandsome Coarse
Betwixt the Winde, and his Nobility.

ow can U ably debate me? Essex'l hy-honor it! Write ovt 'n' sign this bid on land in

338 & 339

With many Holiday and Lady tearme
He question'd me: Among the rest, demanded

ye west-most quarter, 'n' hie to meet him. Needy, he'll mind ya. Ha! And God-damn da ad—

340 & 341

My Prisoners, in your Maiesties behalfe.
I then, all-smarting, with my wounds being cold,

uerse Farnesii o' Parma! So, t' horse, 'n' begin y' muddy climb, hill 'n' glen! *Ioy* waits in th' west! M.

f

The Merry Wives of Windsor. First Folio of Shakespeare. Comedies, p 39.

THE MERRY WIVES OF WINDSOR

1 & 2

Sir Hugh, perswade me not: I will make a Star-Chamber matter of it, if hee were twenty Sir Iohn

U C, Marlowe made this froth as better pastime for her maiesty while her kin were waiting, n—

3 & 4

Falstoffs, he shall not abuse Robert Shallow Esquire. / In the County of Glocester, Iustice of Peace and Coram.

eruous, for th' queen's decision about a f-fall marriage—possibly a waste of herself. No! C, C, C! Not t' lose t' th' leche—

5 & 6

I (Cosen Slender) and Cust-alorum. I, and Rotolorum too: and a Gentleman borne (Master Parson)

r's greed! No, no! A representation o' our old bull man o' mammon, s-sent to a canard, cd result in a

7 & 8

who writes himselfe Armigero, in any Bill, Warrant, Quittance, or Obligation, Armigero.

right queenly answer to that ignorant Roman frog-worm, C, or . . . alarm! Bewail! I-I-I-I-I! See lib—

9 & 10

I that I doe, and haue done anytime these three hundred yeeres. / All his successors

ertiesshriueled, e'en lost in hard edicts—nay, ye'd neuer so shame us to death, C! He, ha!

11 & 12

(gone before him) hath don't: and all his Ancestors (that come after him) may: they may

Thy fresh calm may yet see th' danger i' th' man's mad machination befor too late—Ohh!

13 & 14

give the dozen White Luces in their Coate. It is an olde Coate. The dozen white

Now to uiew 'n' detect the zenith o' his crazed heated ilicit loue o' gain. See, the

15 & 16

Lowses doe become an old Coat well: it agrees well passant: it is a familiar beast	**fat asse will melt, 'n' treble wins o'er bass, as Meg, Alice stop a local toad. Ai! (Oi!) We de—**

Meg, Alice. Margaret Page and Alice Ford. In late 16th century, Pages, Fords, Cobhams, Lucys, attended churches around Roger Manwood's place at Shorne. Hasted's Kent. vol.III, pp 178-181. (In legend young 'Shakespeare' shot a deer belonging to a man named Lucy; Kit in Kent may have been the culprit.) Ibid. vol. III, p 451: in Shorne Church, "on the north wall a large monument, with the arms argent, on a bend sable, three birds of the field membred gules, and seven other quarterings, for George Page, attorney at law," and his wife and relatives. He died in 1613. George Page has a leading role in this play. Roger Manwood's Shorne house was on Gad's Hill, and William Brooke, Lord Cobham, the Lord Chamberlain of Elizabeth's household featured in these ciphers, was a near neighbor to the south.

17 & 18

to man, and signifies loue. The Luce is the fresh-fish, the salt-fish, is an old Coate.	**ride his selfish moues—still, as he hath said, no one's an angel! If U C f-fit to set the**

19 & 20

I may quarter (Coz). / You may, by marrying. / It is marring, indeed, if he quarter it.	**foreign chum-rat aside by my airy quiz—A-a . . . I quit! I'm trying t' remedy an error:**

chum-rat. an unsuitable suitor. **by.** by means of. **airy quiz.** The "froth" of the play.

21 & 22

Not a whit. / Yes per-lady: if he ha's a quarter of your coat, there is but three Skirts	**i' this opera, Fatso's so bad I'l try ta saue th' rhetor t' hy-fuck the weary queen. I err!**

Fatso. Falstaff here is the queen's fat suitor?

23 & 24

for yourselfe in my simple coniectures; but that is all one: if Sir Iohn Falstaffe	**Tasteless iest! Mi play's ful of rich efrontery—I'm an infantile boor! Helo, U suffic—**

25 & 26

have committed disparagements vnto you, I am of the Church and will be glad	**ient fool! U damn' angel! What cd U do t' me, Cobham, V cad? I sail my ship t' greet her; U**

27 & 28

to do my beneuolence, to make attonements and compremises betweene you. the Couucell shall heare it,	**haue spoilt the innocent melody between us, you nastee Brooke! So, come t' me, tell me, teach me—can U read l—**

29 & 30

it is a Riot! It is not meet the Councell heare a Riot: there is no feare of Got in a Riot: the Counsell	**oue's lorn frolic, or the last touching erotic chat, tête à tête? O, hear its final minor note—Ie, ie, ie!**

31 & 32

(looke you) shall desire to heare the feare of Got, and not to heare a Riot: take your viza-ments in that.	**Too eazy to hate thee, Kentish dog! Our heavenly efforts at a-a-amelioration R lost, ruined, here! O tak—**

Kentish dog. Lord Cobham as Manwood's Shorne neighbor. Lewis J.M. Grant. Christopher Marlowe, the Ghost-writer . . . Orillia, Canada: Stubley Press, 1970, p 213.

33 & 34

Ha; o' my life, if I were yong againe, the sword should end it. / It is petter that friends is the sword, and end it:	**e thy wild defiant idiot righteousness, ride t' Shorne 'n' stay there hiding. Please don't w-wait for me! If Da—**

35 & 36

and there is also another deuice in my praine, which peraduenture prings goot discretions with it.	**d were there, then nothin' c'd saue ye—thin, piss-poor addlepate saintie! Catching us i-in our mirror! Wig**

37 & 38

There is Anne Page, which is daughter to Master Thomas Page which is pretty virginity. / Mistris Anne Page	**'n' mi hat, garments—hers, mine—toss't t' th' rug again in disarray. We pee-pee *ici* that hot piss which gaue ye pig R**

ye pig. The intruder was fired from his job as Chamberlain in April 1597, which scholars see as composition date for Merry Wives.

39 & 40

she has browne haire, and speakes small like a woman. / It is that ferry person for all the orld,	**lair-spoor. Astonish'd, ye worm spoke, shakin' at that raw smell: "Release h-her, bare fall'n fiend,**

41 & 42

as iust as you will desire, and seuen hundred pounds of Moneyes, and Gold, and Siluer, is her Grand-sire

or feel deseru'd death!" "Leaue us," I snarl, "U sad spoiler!" Now he grins 'n' grins, 'n' says, "Did I ynuade Sodom, und

43 & 44

vpon his deathsbed, (Got deliuer to a ioyfull resurrections) giue, when she is able

who's this old griege U led here? I-I thot t'uuas our lady, see? Piss on! B free 'n' B cleavin'

griege. grieche. grey-hair.

45 & 46

to ouertake seuenteene yeeres old. It were a goot motion, if we leaue our pribbles and prabbles,

to Eue! Ride—No fear! I won't stop U, Kit, but leaue no spoor o' beer—mi Bess (a leer) w'd B angry at le—le . . . E-e-e-e!

E-e-e-e! Brooke recognizes the queen.

47 & 48

and desire a marriage betweene Master Abraham, and Mistris Anne Page. / Did her Grand-sire

Mi dear tired riding mistress heard, sighed, 'n' began t' weep—aa-e—as a bad man ran. "A mere erran—

49 & 50

leaue her seauen hundred pound?
I, and her father is make her a petter penny. I know

t hunk—'n' d-dear lady. I reuere U, 'n' see, h-happier times R ahead, 'n' take hope now, 'n' neuer f—

51 & 52

the young Gentlewoman, she had good gifts. / Seuen hundred pounds, and possibilities, is goot gifts.

ear, U possess infinite beauty!" "No, I'ue aged!" "Sh, sh, mi delight!" "G-G-G-God! No! Stop, son! Find th' towels! Sound

53 & 54

Wel, let vs see honest Mr. Page: is Falstaffe there? / Shall I tell you a lye?

retreat! Hellish ye way loue leaves me at last. I'll go . . . " 'N' she f-f-flees t' sp—

55 & 56

I doe despise a lyer, as I doe despise one that is false, or as I despise one that is not true:

in a-a-a hopeless fantasy o' loue. Distrait, dress opened, she stops t' rest—I see Dido. Ei, ei, ei!

Dido. Kit wrote a play about Dido while he was at Cambridge.

57 & 58

the Knight Sir Iohn is there, and I beseech you be ruled by your well-willers: I will peat the doore for Mr.—

Rudely thinking o' past rides there where we were, softly I call, "L-Libby, R U mi Hoo-Hoo?" I see her turn. I'd be l—

59 & 60

What hoa? Got-please your house heere. Who's there? Here is go't's plessing and your friend,

oath t' leaue her s-so unrestored—th' gypsy Regina whose loue I hoped for, s-shewing her se—

61 & 62

and Iustice Shallow, and heere yong Master Slender, that peraduentures shall tell you another tale, if

lf distress'd, nearly unhinged. "It's too late t' reach me at all." 'N' she wept. "Leaue, 'n' U'l ha-haue dry sorro." "Let an e—

63 & 64

matters grow to your likings. / I am glad to see your Worships well: I thanke you for my Venison Master Shallow.

gregious interrvption ruin thy m-most rowdy skill? We'll stay!" Hoo-Hoo says, "Woe, I'm left weak as a rag—U men R so l—

65 & 66

Master Page, I am glad to see you: much good doe it your good heart: I wish'd your Venison better,

ight you're never cool, but I, heated, reminded o' my poor aged state, I say, 'Go!' I must go! O, sad! U, who R

67 & 68

it was ill kill'd: how doth good Mistresse Page? and I thank you alwaies with my heart, la; with my heart.

a lad, go with a miss who'd loue thee! Take thy titilatin' lips 'n' say what ye mirror will show me: 'Hag!' Add k—

69 & 70

Sir, I thanke you. / Sir I thanke you; by yea, and no I doe. / I am glad to see you, good Master Slender.

keyhole-artist Brooke—he made me dread ye last day o' destiny! 'N' U R so yong, unsung—I . . . A-ai! Oi, oi!"

71 & 72

How do's your fallow Greyhound, Sir, I heard say he was out-run on Cotsall. / It could not be iudg'd

"Hoo-Hoo, let's not wait—all's wel, lady—ye cad's gone! Houu cd R diddy art B UUrong for us? I wish U no r—

73 & 74

Sir. / You'll not confesse: you'll not confesse. / That he will not, 'tis your fault, 'tis your fault:

eturn of any foolish stunt! To wish to fly 'n' leaue us! Let's rally—focus on R loue, solicit yt, t'

75 & 76

'tis a good dogge. / A Cur, Sir. / Sir: hee's a good dog, and a faire dog, can there be more said? he is good, and faire

restore order! De sad oaf's disgrace is of no danger t' us! Hoo-Hoo-Hag: Bridge! Engage! Dig! Add! Come! Ai! Ai! Ai!

77 & 78

Is Sir Iohn Falstaffe heere? / Sir, hee is within: and I would I could doe a good office be tweene you.

We're lost in each other—O, wild distress! I see ye fool hiding! We haue an audience! O, fub off, Fido! I, I!

79 & 0

It is spoke as a Christiane ought to speake. He hath wrong'd me (Master Page.)

T' saue her, how can I hit th' gross peeper t' make him go? I take a pass. God sent a—

81& 82

Sir, he doth in some sort confesse it. If it be confessed, it is not redressed:

n end to Fido's idiot interference before it cost SSS to hide SSS! His mere s—

cost SSS. Brooke was a State Secret Service brother and should have protected the queen and Kit. If he'd exposed Marlowe there'd have been terrible trouble.

83 & 84

is not that so (M. Page?) he hath wrong'd me, indeed he hath, at a word he hath: beleeue me,

tare had hampered me; now, tho', he seems hidden, gone, ha, ha! But gee—while at that hot

85 & 86

Robert Shallow, Esquire, saith he is wronged. / Here comes Sir Iohn.
Now, Master Shallow,

ass-dancin' I hear th' boorish gross queer stir somewhere. More? Now we wil lose al th' h—

87 & 88

you'll complaine of me to the King? Knight, you haue beaten my men, kill'd
my deere, and broke open my Lodge.

appy time I intended for th' lady! No, no! My keen anger bloomed—I'll kyll meek Cobham! H-Hey, out, U monkee! U egg—

89 & 90

But not kiss'd your Keepers daughter?
Tut, a pin: this shall be answer(e)d.
I will answer it straight.

head SSS braggart! T' strew despair o'er beauty! "U think U'l walk?" I shout. "Die, 'n' R. in P.!" Th' little s-swine

91 & 92

I haue done all this: That is now answer'd.
The Councell shall know this.

shows, turns slow t' hie awai alone—'n' I hit th' head—th' skull—E-e! Anno DCCLL!

Anno DCCLL. like a savage act, A.D. 800.

93 & 94

'Twere better for you if it were known in councell: You'll be laugh'd at. / Pauca verba; (Sir Iohn) good worts.

Ye poor fool fel unconscious. O, he'll B dead! W-we giue lovin' care t'-t' ye br-broken hurt r-rat, wa-waiting tu

95 & 96

Good worts? Good Cabidge; Slender, I broke your head: what matter haue you against me?

see hym struggle to rise. Too b-bad, Cad! We gaue hym a rag o'er th' wound—a drink, too! O, I ade—

97 & 98

Marry, sir, I haue matter in my head against you, and against your cony-catching Rascalls, Bardolf, Nym, and Pistoll.

d 'im tu 'is cl-clo-closet, 'n' by plan th' gross idiot turn'd around, hit me, man, 'n' r-ran! Y-y-y-ye friggin' a-a-a-a-a-a-a-assal! Chr. M.

f

The Merchant of Venice. First Folio of Shakespeare. Comedies, pp 163-162 (sic).

THE MERCHANT OF VENICE

1 & 2

In sooth I know not why I am so sad,
It wearies me: you say it wearies you;

Monti wrote this story o' a weakness. Oi, oi, oi! We Yids haue ways U may, in

Monti. Christopher Marlowe, aka Gregorio de' Monti of Venice.
We Yids. His natural father, Roger Manwood, was Jewish.

3 & 4

But how I caught it, found it, or came by it,/What stuffe 'tis made of, wherof it is borne,

ignorance, see as bad behauior, tho' it B our od' fit custom. Tut! Whiff my f-fit wit, whet—

Whiff. OED. to inhale, sniff.

5 & 6

I am to learne: and such a Want-wit sadnesse makes of mee,
That I haue much ado to know my selfe.

ted wi' sufferin' those MT customs. Makes me wish to heaue 'em all 'n' make a dance today! Oh, na-naa!

7 & 8

Your minde is tossing on the Ocean,
There where your Argosies with portly saile

Ye Iew is less greedy than other operators who ruine him to liue on ratsy coins. G—

9 & 10

Like Signiors and rich Burgers on the flood,
Or as it were the Pageants of the sea,

hetto Iews reside i' Uenice, held as th' bankers for al' th' Antonios or Frogges. Prag—

Frogges. In those days many French merchants were trading and living at Venice.

11 & 12

Do ouer-peere the pettie Traffiquers
That curtsie to them, do them reuerence

matic men e-euer uote t' proffer credit to those that reside here. The queer put

13 & 14

As they fly by them with their wouen wings.
Beleeue me sir, had I such venture forth,

seal vnwisely tu his merry oath, which then grew tu destroy him. But fie! He, euen bef—

merry oath. Israel Abrahams. ***Jewish Life in the Middle Ages.*** Society & Meridian Books, n.d., p 110. Abrahams (not mentioning this play) says according to Jewish law a public vow could not be annulled. Shylock took his merry oath to the notary. Marlowe scatters hints through the play—oath, oath, promise—over and over.

15 & 16

The better part of my affections, would
Be with my hopes abroad. I should be still

ore he made th' public writ, th' sly fool saw th' loan tested off as debit. U B my probe: I

17 & 18

Plucking the grasse to know where sits the winde,
Peering in Maps for ports, and peers, and rodes:

Think th' creep,so p-press'd, lost his iudgement in anger, 'n' dead wrong, swore afore a witness. Keep pr—

19 & 20

and euery obiect that might make me feare
Misfortune to my ventures, out of doubt

eiudice at bay before U: th' man's not out for revenge, yet he'd take it—mum, mum—for's tot—

21 & 22

Would make me sad. / My winde cooling my broth,
Would blow me to an Ague, when I thought

aly holding to ye Iew law. Mum, not breaking d' unwelcome oath he hugs. Mum! Bow dowd to

23 & 24

What harme a winde too great might doe at sea.
I should not see the sandie houre-glasse runne,

O-a-t-h! U see, he's demented, letting his goods go tu the hated man whose loan was in arrear. Ei! U R a

O-a-t-h. Shylock made the Oath his God.

25 & 26

but I should thinke of shallows, and of flats,
And see my wealthy Andrew docks in sand(e),

witness to a madness, born as he was kickt, hounded in a sly way. Tho' full, he'l fade 'n' fold. D—

27 & 28

Vailing her high top lower then her ribs
To k(y)sse her buriall; should I goe to Church

epriv'd o' th' oath, there's no wish t' kill or rob. He'll go liue uh beggar, shun ye rich Chris—

29 & 30

And see the holy edifice of stone,
And not bethinke me straight of dangerous rocks,

tians. Silent, by God forsaken, he's sued, checkt, doomed to enter on a foreign faith he

31 & 32

Which touching but my gentle Vessels side
Would scatter all her spices on the streame,

despises—yi! Al becavse, witless, he held t' th' letter o' his law, C, 'n' n-nouu, C, m-must go greet Chr—

33 & 34

Enrobe the roring waters with my silkes,
And in a word, but euen now worth this,

ist 'n' betray heritage, or inuoke ruin, wrestle wi' th' worst 'n' B damned. Who won, sh—

35 & 36

And now worth nothing. Shall I haue the thought
To thinke on this, and shall I lacke the thought

ackled Iew or—oh-h-h!—the sli hot gallants who'ue got his gain 'n' hauen't thankt th' thin hound, loth t'-

37 & 38

That such a thing be chaunc'd would make me sad?
But tell not me, I know Anthonio

t' admit he's indeed a human being? 'N' those who look t' ban a cut-out chunk, C—all M T w—

39 & 40

Is sad to thinke vpon his merchandize.
Beleeue me no, I thanke my fortune for it,

ords: foes kneuu if an avthorized notary kept the note in his m-minee-chimblee

m-minee-chimblee. In Marlowe's day the notaries sat on the Rialto, each behind his own table under a loggia near the bankers. The originals of their documents, the testamenti, were chronologically filed, probably by putting each face down into a tall rectangular box with an open top on the sidewalk, beside the table, from which they recovered their bundles at the end of the day. These boxes would resemble mini-chimneys. Wilfred Brulez. Marchands Flamands à Venise. v. 1, Rome: Inst. Historique Belge de Rome Tome IV, 1965, introduction.

41 & 42

My ventures are not in one bottome trusted,
Nor to one place; nor is my whole estate

'twas lauu, not some potential mvrder, 'n' now sober, they resent it, too—yet no one, cree—

w. m used as w. And does sober here mean simply serious? or were they a bit drunk in Scene i?

43 & 44

Vpon the fortune of this present yeere: Therefore my merchandize makes me not sad.

P or Tony, makes an effort t'compromize 'n' resist th' heavyfees due re the end here. Men

45 & 46

Why then you are in loue. / Fie, fie. / Not in loue neither: then let vs say you are sad

who hide loyalty t' another avthority suffer 'n' lie, see—euen I, euen I (as ye noun).

Shylock hid the fact that the Jewish law meant more to him than the laws of Venice. **euen I.** Marlowe the spy.

47 & 48

Because you are not merry; and 'twere as easie
For you to laugh and leape, and say you are merry

Racey, seamy, arrogant wop Tony had no fear o' disaster ere ye year's end. UUoe! Maybe U R all uuea—

49 & 50

Because you are not sad. Now by two-headed Ianus,
Nature hath fram'd strange fellowes in her time.

ry of these ruminations, so I'l grant you rest after we'ue watched a woman heal a bad Hebe 'n' sudden

51 & 52

Some that will euermore peepe through their eyes,
And laugh like Parrats at a bag-piper.

horror is harmless: he agreed t' giue up property 'n' get wet. Ai, ai! But he'll make a plea: the pa—

get wet. He'll be baptised.

53 & 54

And other of such vinegar aspect,
That they'll not shew their teeth in way of smile,

yments in little pieces over th' years, t' let th' wincehound go forth safe, what? Ha, ha!

55 & 56

Though Nestor sweare the iest be laughable.
Heere comes Bassanio, / Your most noble Kinsman,

See, when the bubble moon shines on the Rialto, reason's iust a sorry game o' blame. Ugh! Take sec—

57 & 58

Gratiano, and Lorenso. Faryewell, / We leaue you now with better company. I would haue staid till I had made you merry,

ond uiew o' ye wily Iew: O, O—*Oui*! Hatred, blame R always mutually repaid, C, 'n' relating to a defense led Harry Wotton, a hum—

59 & 60

If worthier friends had not preuented me. Your worth is very deere in my regard.

anist, t' write o' reformin' perversity in men: why, ergo, he'd hurry ouer dreaded def—

Harry Wotton. Marlowe had known Wotton since 1593, perhaps earlier. In 1604 he became English ambassador at Venice, and Marlowe, as Gregorio de' Monti, served many years as Wotton's secretary.

61 & 62

I take it your owne business calls on you, And you embrace th' occasion to depart.

ects to praise kind, carin', louin' souls, see: O, boot beauty away! C, C, deny human root—

63 & 64

Good morrow, my good Lords. Good signiors both, when shall we laugh? say, when?

s o' aggression, while odd Gregory shows brutally doom'd man, who—Oh! How long

65 & 66

You grow exceeding strange: must it be so? Wee'll make our leysures to attend on yours.

must Kit try tu coax morals out o' an egregious blow tu needy lender? We see no egrees. Y—

67 & 68

My Lord Bassanio, since you haue found Anthonio We two will leaue you, but at dinner time

et do as U w'd be done by is a winnin' moral theme in this uuoolly cautionary tale. Now feuu o—

69 & 70

I pray you haue in minde where we must meete. / I will not faile you.

f us liue with that ol' premium rule in mind. Aye, aye! Woe, woe! In ye e—

71 & 72

You looke not well signior Anthonio, You haue too much respect vpon the world:

nd now, we see too much risk in every prouocation, 'n' U hope to gull th' too loyal ho—

73 & 74

They loose it that doe buy it with much care,
Beleeue me you are maruellously chang'd

nest dealer. Houu could beauty euer claim this game o' th' yll oath to be mercy? Ye uiew h—

75 & 76

I hold the world but as the world, Gratiano,
A stage, where euery man must play a part,

onor as th' wage-leuy o' gain? That really merits Pluto's dread breath: P-U! Warm death, w—

77 & 78

And mine a sad one.
Let me play the foole,/With mirth and laughter let old wrinckles come,

hich corrupts all men who'd entertain it! Let fame alone, 'n' take my old saw he deem'd illog—

79 & 80

and let my Liuer rather heate with wine,
Then my heart coole with mortifying grones.

ical—the fit theme, th' Golden Rule! Yet—mean rats are winning! Oh, why worry; their time o'

81 & 82

Why should a man whose bloud(e) is warme within,
Sit like his Grandsire, cut in Alabaster?

gain wil B cut short by their own senseless demands. Oh, I haue dark hair—must I wail? Wail

The author thinks of anti-Semitism in relation to characters in the play, but there may be a second thought, if this is a letter to Kit's SSS superior Bacon: he and Marlowe both have Jewish blood, and both are discriminated against by Burghley and Robert Cecil, nominal chiefs of State Secret Service.

83 & 84

Sleepe when he wakes? and creep into the laundies
By being peeuish? I tell thee what Anthonio,

denial that the agnostic philosophy had been the best? We hew in line; U keep reuisin' anew—E-e-e!

85 & 86

I loue thee, and it is my loue that speakes:
There are a sort of men, whose visages

Fatso hates vs, so no work uue initiate to get ahead pleases him. See, he merely r—

Fatso. Lord Burghley? or Robert Cecil?

87 & 88

Do creame and mantle like a standing pond
And do a wilfull stilnesse entertaine,

efered an all-silent landing to a damn'd powerless toadie like me—U can't stand in n—

89 & 90

With purpose to be drest in an opinion Of wisedome, grauity, profound conceit,	**eed o' funds 'n' hope to *escribir*. Oi! Do trust me! On our own, we can't pay t' go pi-pi. Fini.**

we. Kit and Cervantes, working out of Seville, went to Cádiz, trying to prepare a quiet, easy landing for the English invaders who arrived there in June 1596. Fini. But there's a poststscript below:

91 & 92

As who should say, I am fit an Oracle, And when I ope my lips, let no dogge barke.	**Nay—alas! No more ciphers! 'N' liue in hope o' a day we'l flog th' swag S.O.B. Dead Kit M.**

f

Much Adoe About Nothing. First Folio of Shakespeare. Comedies, p 101.

MUCH ADOE ABOUT NOTHING, A

1 & 2 I Learne in this Letter, that Don Peter of Arragon, comes this night to Messina.	**Christopher Marloe made this art in anger, to set this fool gent in 'is net—a net**
3 & 4 He is very neere by this: he was not three Leagues off when I left him.	**he wove belieuing the wearisome yffy street lies. The fresh Ann h-h—**
5 & 6 How many Gentlemen haue you lost in this action? But few of any sort, and none of name.	**ad been tru, 'n' yet he saw only th' fals game, 'n' O, I cannot win him soon enuff to any moue to**
7 & 8 A victorie is twice it selfe, when the atchieuer brings home full numbers: I finde heere,	**see truth before ruining his love, 'n' e'en her life, with a slimie brutish act. Ecce! Fide me! W—**
9 & 10 That Don Peter hath bestowed much honor on a yong Florentine, called Claudio.	**hat an argument! Both ride in to th' country place, 'n' he deals lo—how lo! End of Code.**

f

Much Adoe About Nothing, A

Much Adoe About Nothing. First Folio of Shakespeare. Comedies, p 101.

MUCH ADOE ABOUT NOTHING, B

1 & 2

I Learne in this Letter,
that Don Peter of Arragon, comes this night to Messina.
He is very neere by this:

Monti pens this froth re an inocent's sly betrayal: her time on earth—her egregiovs death. I see in it st—

3 & 4

he was not three Leagues off when I left him./How many Gentlemen have you lost in this action?

ealthy foolishness with a woeful result: he came in heet envf to hit a woman—then my going en—

5 & 6

But few of any sort, and none of name. A victorie is twice it selfe, when the atchieuer

abled his crime, for now it's out 'n' ouer, C, 'n' yet the fat shit can waive f-e-e-e-e-e, 'n' wait on f—

7 & 8

brings home full numbers: I finde heere, that Don Peter hath bestowed much hono(u)r

auor here, C? No, the snuff's not punished, but who'd remember a thin bled girl, tho'? He? Me!

9 & 10

on a yong Florentine, called Claudio. Much deseru'd on his part, and equally remembred

'N' dead Anna: my queer play'd saue U from Ercol's lood coital crime, 'n' U 'n' he'll B right.

De End.

f

Much Adoe About Nothing. First Folio of Shakespeare. Comedies, p 101.

MUCH ADOE ABOUT NOTHING, C

1 & 2

I Learne in this Letter, that Don Peter of Arragon, comes this night to Messina. He is very neere by this:

Greg made this merry sho o' infinite insanity, hopin' t' serve t' teache better sense to all others in R ha—

3 & 4

hewasnotthreeLeaguesoffwhenIlefthim. How many Gentlemen have you lost in this action?

lf—male society re: young love—its gain 'n' loss, how t' meet in a huff to mate—he he he! What 'n' when in

5 & 6

But few of any sort and none of name. A Victorie is twice it selfe, when the atchieuer

courtin' season t' believe, 'n' when t' dout th' chancie story of a faint fem! Ie, ie! Few are w—

7 & 8

brings home full numbers: I finde heere, thatDonPeterhathbestowedmuchhonor

illin' t' wait for huge reason t' sho thru, come t' h-her defense, 'n' bend R phubbed homme

9 & 10

on a yong Florentine, called Claudio. Much deseru'd on his part, and equally remembred

t' leaue lo nonsenseical MCCL behauior 'n' return a good man. All d-d-d-did query my free ph—

MCCL. A.D. 1250: medieval behavior.

11 & 12

by Don Pedro, he hath borne himselfe beyond the promise of his age, doing in the figure of a Lambe,

antasy o' ye fobb'd off, beseiged girl disappearin' 'n' returnin' t' life. M-M-M Good! Ho-ho-ho! He-he-he! Hebe.

f

The Tragedie of Troylus and Cressida. First Folio of Shakespeare. Tragedies, p 369.
(between *Henry VIII* and *Coriolanus.* second page marked 79, the third, 80; no other pagination.)

THE TRAGEDIE OF TROYLUS AND CRESSIDA

Prologue

1 & 2

In Troy there lyes the Scene: from Iles of Greece
The Princes Orgillous, their high blood chaf'd

Fool G. Monti pens the Irish satire. C, C, C-E: hellish bloody errors fly high enough t' referee! Detec—

3 & 4

Have to the Port of Athens sent their shippes
Fraught with the ministers and instruments

t th' note o' satire. Tush! These men that prepare 'n' perish die not in th' high war—in M T fvss-fuss t'

5 & 6

Of cruell Warre: Sixty and nine that wore
Their Crownets Regall, from th' Athenian baye

rob a fello fall'n warrior-man, C? 'N' a wretched Essex euer waitin' t' try ye great h-h-hit, 'n' not

7 & 8

Put forth(e) towarde Phrygia, and their vow is made
To ransacke Troy, within whose strong emures

findin' any good reason to attack. So we rest up, worry, revue, miss what e'er h-horrid hap we might, 't-'t

9 & 10

The rauish'd Helen, Menelaus Queene,
With wanton Paris sleepes, and that's the Quarrell.

quell these wild queer warriors that hem us in ahead 'n' tease us, 'n' happen t' shell an' ente—

11 & 12	
To Tenedos they come, And the deepe-drawing Barke do there disgorge	**r R night camp wi' no thot o' ar tents. E-e-e-e-e! Oh, d-do seek, beg ye d-degraded**
13 & 14	
Their warlike frautage: now on Dardan Plaines The fresh and yet unbruised Greekes do pitch	**kinky creeps t' wait 'til dawn before shootin' at us. Gr! Gr! UUe need R sleep! A dear friend h-h-had an**
15 & 16	
Their brave Pavillions. Priams six(e)-gated City,/Dardan and Timbria, Helias, Chetas, Troien,	**old horse at his tent; Irish experts came 'n' stabb'd it dead. 'arry gave alarm in panic: I, I, I! Vali—**
17 & 18	
And Antenonidus with massie Staples and corresponsive and fulfilling Bolts	**ant men l-leapt to his aid—no s-sign of bad interlopers! We cuss'd 'n' fuss'd, all in uain.**
19 & 20	
Stirre up the sonnes of Troy. Now Expectation tickling skittish spirit(e)s	**At first light I went to seek kerns. Oi, Oi! I crept thru copse 'n' spinny to six st—**
21 & 22	
On one and other side, Troian and Greeke, Sets all on hazard. And hither am I come,	**akes, each holdin' its dead man's head on a thong. Me retaliate? I r-r-reezon: No. No. Dr—**
23 & 24	
A Prologue arm'd, but not in confidence Of Authors pen, or Actors voyce; but suited	**udgin' staffer's mi iob, not chancey one-person uuar, C? U've redoubl'd a t-troop co. t-to**
25 & 26	
In like conditions, as our Argument; To tell you (faire Beholders) that our Play(e)	**defeat th' hot sauages, 'n' uue'l kil all, 'n' proue mordant Boyle's in error, C? Yo! To it! I, I!**

mordant Boyle. Richard Boyle, the most powerful Englishman in Ireland, is being sarcastic about Essex's generalship.

27 & 28

Leapes ore the uaunt(e) and firstlings of those broyles,
Beginning in the middle; starting thence away,

Greg must pass all day in a tent, writin' 'n' sending off notes, trying t' saue Robin. He, he, he! O, he'll debate ice—

29 & 30

To what may be digested in a Play:
Like, or finde fault, do as your pleasures are,
Now good, or bad, 'tis but the chance of Warre.

y letters Libby sent re R—R—procrastination. We'l put a good face on th' dubious delays, forge ahead! Do! Make headwai! Aw, Fou.

Greg. Kit's Italian name. **Libby.** Queen Elizabeth.

f

The Tragedie of Troylus and Cressida. First Folio of Shakespeare. Tragedies, p 369.
(between *Henry VIII* and *Coriolanus.* second page marked 79, the third, 80; no other pagination.)

THE TRAGEDIE OF TROYLUS AND CRESSIDA

Scaena Prima

1 & 2	
Call here my Varlet, Ile vnarme againe. Why should I warre without the wals of Troy(e)	**Marlow writ thy comedy to try 'n' elevate a low Irish failure, 'n' leave laughs where a h—**
3 & 4	
That finde such cruell battell here within? Each Troian that is master of his heart,	**h-h-hurtful battle scar lies on Irish heather. To imitate the ancient war cd let shaf—**
5 & 6	
Let him to field, Troylus alas hath none. Will this geere nere be mended?	**ts o' light on R mean liues here, filled wi' demented broyles that he'l nea—**
7 & 8	
The Greeks are strong, and skilful to their strength, Fierce to their skill, and to their fiercenesse Valiant:	**rlie ignore 'til check't. Then, angered, he'l s-stir—take lives of his truest fighters—dare t' kil fer no reason, 'n' att—**
9 & 10	
But I am weaker then a woman's teare; Tamer then sleep, fonder then ignorance;	**ack wrong—R hit unplanned—'n' we remain to breathe! Those men R a fast team! E-e-e-e—**
11 & 12	
Lesse valiant then the Virgin in the night And skillesse as vnpractis'd Infancie.	**e-e! They advanced, singin', lavghin' 'n' teasin', 'n' their knives 'n' spears flasht, C, 'til, slit—**

13 & 14

Well, I haue told you enough of this: For my part, Ile not meddle nor make no farther.

tin' 'n' slammin', they hit R men hard. We fled. They ouerlooked R offer to go u-up alo-alo—

15 & 16

Hee that will haue a Cake out of the Wheate, Must needes tarry the grinding./ Haue I not tarried?

ne o'er the hil—they stuck with U 'til we turn'd—Grrr! 'N' hit 'em good! Aha! The natiues fade! Aee, Aee! At a

17 & 18

(E)i the grinding; but you must tarry the bolting(e).
Have I not tarried? /(E)i the boultinge:

signal, they h-hied o'er ye brae. Tu lie in R torn tent taught U t' B bitter. I! U've mi good nig—

19 & 20

but you must tarry the leau'ing.
Still haue I tarried.
I, to the leauening, but heere's yet in the word hereafter,

ht suueete hug, yet heare thy horrid groans 'til mornin' lite. A braue try. U failed—ineuitable. E-e-e! Trust th' wet

21 & 22

the Kneading, the making of the Cake, the heating of the Ouen, and the Baking; nay,

fog t' hide th' men hiking ahead in the fen. They take back a neat gun. Gee, thank no o—

23 & 24

you must stay the cooling, too, or you may chance to burne your lips. Patience her selfe,

ther general, only ye shy Robin for mouin' us aliue to-to occupy that spot! Cease my euoc—

25 & 26

what Goddesse ere she be,
Doth lesser blench at sufferance, then I doe: At Priam's Royall Table

ation o' failure: al sh'd be better, now R cheef's able, ready t' respond. Hate'll get 'em, C—He had s-s-s-se—

27 & 28

doe I sit;
And when faire Cressid comes into my thoughts,
So (Traitor) then she comes, when she is thence.

een the enemy in action (cuss 'em!), 'n' decided it was worthe a fight t' restore 'im, since sh-sh-sho-sho-short o'

29 & 30

Well: / She look'd yesternight fairer, then euer I saw her looke,
Or any woman else.

annihilation, ye kooks'l see real defeat here: We R grown more—U R lost! Why, he's el—

31 & 32

I was about to tell thee, when my heart, As wedged with a sigh, would rive in twaine,

ated bi the thot o' engagement. We wait al day while d' Irish hurl w-wuv notes. As I we—

33 & 34

Least Hector, or my Father should perceive me: /I have (as when the Sunne doth light a-scorne)

nt t' the loo, their gun-fyre comes clean across th' dale t' h-h-h-harm us! We respond (E-e-e-e) vvi' a hi

35 & 36

Buried this sigh, in wrinkle of a smile:
But sorrow, that is couch'd in seeming gladnesse,

uollie. Shock'd, thei began running madli towards us, in soft scree. I wis this's grim, Hebe!

37 & 38

Is like that mirth, Fate turnes to sudden sadnesse.
And her haire were not somewhat darker then Helen's,

These men take kniues in their teeth 'n' dash—dash—t' raw horror, t' defend Eire's deare stones. Man, shall U tw—

39 & 40

well go too, there were no more comparison between the Women. But for my part she is my Kinswoman,

yst strong purpose into mere nonny woo-woo? A meek mom'l B fierce at her home's threat! W-wil we B men

41 & 42

I would not (as they tearme it) praise it, but I wold some-body had heard(e) her talke

who'll see they R desperate idiots, 'n' make a deal—treat with th' dumb boor? Ai! Do yu i—

th' dumb boor. Hugh O'Neil, Earl of Tyrone, chief of the rebels.

43 & 44

yesterday(e) as I did: I will not dis-praise your sister Cassandra's wit(te), but—
Oh Pandarus!

ntend iust to repeatedly resist his stupid aduances? Alas, R war is awry! I, yi! I'd B so sad—or

45 & 46

I tell thee Pandarus;
When I doe tell thee, there my hopes lye drown'd: Reply not in how many Fadomes deepe

disappointed. Why not hurry t' hew 'em? Or let's tel ye leadah if he'l parlee, we'l not deny some needed hope, 'n' m—

47 & 48

They lye indrench'd. I tell thee, I am mad In Cressids love. Thou answer'st she is Faire,

anie'l want cessation o' th' mindless hits. He'd revere thy merciful deed as shylie R i—

49 & 50

Powrst in the open Vlcer of my heart,
Her Eyes, her Haire, her Cheeke, her Gate, her Voice,

nept warriors meet coy regretfvl kerns. He he he, he he he—*ho*, I ache! They recover! repai—

51 & 52

Handlest in thy discourse. O that her Hand(e) (In whose comparison all whites are Inke)

r their weapons 'n' attack us all in new order. Yes, th' season o' death is comin'. I'l h-h-h-hide

53 & 54

Writing their owne reproach; to whose soft seizure, The Cygnets Downe is harsh, and spirit of Sense

in th' first good-sized cote we pass tonight! C, I refuse t' hew, harrow 'n' worry these Irish nonnees. A spe—

55 & 5th'

Hard as the palme of Plough-man. This thou tel'st me:
As true thou tel'st me, when I say I love her:

l o' movin' thru deep marsh. At first lite we must stop, 'n' E-e-e! He-Hel! A host o' them laugh at us—al hy

57 & 58

But saying thus, instead of Oyle and Balme, Thou lai'st in every gash that love hath given me,

On th' hil ahead. We go t' shelter in a uuood, but stil many fal, many give ye stab ta these sing—

59 & 60

The Knife that made it. / I speake no more then truth. /Thou do'st not speake so much. / Faith, Ile not meddle in't:

in,' leapin' madmen, suddenlee on us. Th' trees make it hard to shoot them. I keep off, out in a th-th-thicket, t-to

61 & 62

Let her be as shee is, if she be faire, tis the better for her; and she be not, she has the mends in her own hands.

hit 'n' stab the rebel Irish before I enter the fen wood, headin' after R men, see? Bastahd sh-sh-sh-sh-sheenees!

63 & 64

Good(e) Pandarus: How now Pandarus? I have had my Labour for my travell, ill thought on of her,

So they ran. U R afraid—dvmm—no loud hash hero! A valuable opportunity g-gone for all wh-who'd

65 & 66

and ill thought on of you: Gone betweene and betweene, but small thankes for my labour.

beat ye kerns about a bit ere all the fen-wood belonged t' them. Go slowly nouu, fun-man, 'n' h—

67 & 68

What art thou angry Pandarus? what with me? / Because she's Kinne to me, therefore shee's not

ap t' confuse th' base enemy: wait, t' rod, harrow, 'n' hurt as th' weakest ones emerge in haste. Huh?

69 & 70

so faire as Helen, and she were not kin to me, she would be as faire on Friday, as Helen is on Sunday.

E-e-e-e-e! Yn fear, R own men dash out o'er land. Sly, I hide alone, safe in this bush. So now a friend asks a-

71 & 72

But what care I? I care not and she were a Black-a-Moore, 'tis all one to me.

bout what he calls mi lack o' action. It met a need, bro: we're a rea-reason—

73 & 74

Say I she is not faire? / I doe not care whether you doe or no. Shee's a Foole to stay behinde her Father:

in' sort: I had fear. Now hear Robin say, "Ye deserters'l die!" Oh-oh! He's h-hot t' effect it! No!! Easy, U! A-e-e-e! O-o-o!

75 & 76

Let her to the Greeks, and so Ile tell her the next time I see her: for my part,

Essex' terror! He'l kil the tenth o' the fettered, loyal men! He agrees t' rip mi

77 & 78

Ile meddle nor make no more i' th' matter. Pandarus? /Not I. /Sweete Pandarus. Pray you

medal 'n' let me stay—ye rest o' R troop must d-die! I know him! Ae! Run around near—appea—

79 & 80

speake no more to me, I will leave all as I found it, and there an end.

l to 'im: don't kil fine men! We'l deal, 'n' aid, save, restore U! A-a lean hope

81 & 82

Peace you vngracious Clamors, peace rude sounds, Fooles on both sides, Helen must needs be faire,

fades, 'n' you open on a r-rabble o' R souldiers left hangin' dead. I uueep to see svch success. O, come, sme—

83 & 84

When with your bloud(e) you daily paint her thus. I cannot fight vpon this Argument:

l th' stench o' futile death! In vain U hang'd them up! Yo! Hurry, now, wi' a big pit, 'n' you! Stor—

85 & 86

It is too starv'd a subiect for my Sword, But Pandarus: O Gods! How do you plague me?

m comes—do it fast! O-o! Drop ghastly bodies into ye broad grave! U, U, U! Dust wraps U. Wo—

87 & 88

I cannot come to Cressid but by Pandar, And he's as teachy to be woo'd to woe,

e! Mad! Sad! O, O! Innocent boys bow to death t' obey. So draw th' curtain, C, escape!

89 & 90

As she is stubborne, chast(e), against all suite.
Tell me Apollo for thy Daphnes Love

Shun th' scene! Dash to a ballroom in a lovely house. A lapse is legal—t' rest, t' fib, t' s—

91 & 92

What Cressid is, what Pandar, and what we: Her bed is India, there she lies, a Pearle,

pend a spel rehearsin' what's t' B, here i' this raw, wide wilderness. Aah, aah! Dedicat—

93 & 94

Between oar Ilium, and where shee recides Let it be cald the wild(e) and wandring flood,

e months ahead to deeds o' daring! "We'l defeat each uile rebel! We rewind: I'l dril t' win, C? 'N' B

I'l dril t' win. Essex doesn't have as many men as Tyrone, and not many ideas.

95 & 96

Our selfe the Merchant, and this sayling Pandar,
Our doubtfull hope, our convoy and our Barke.

sure of a plan t' harrouu 'n' bring dul paddy kerns to heel 'n' dash to honorable victory! Fa! Come uu—

honorable. Honor was Robin's watchword.

97 & 98	
How now Prince Troylus? Wherefore not a field? Because not there; this woman's answer sorts.	**i' us, t' see how we, sorry now, shal renew, crown the action 'n' pass on t' be master o' the field, for U R**
99 & 100	
For womanish it is to be from thence: What news Aeneas from the field to day?	**to win in th' end, wi fame for al t' see! Hi ho, 'n' away from these soft beds t' more ac—**
101 & 102	
That Paris is returned home, and hurt. By whom Aeneas? / Troylus by Menelaus.	**tiue pursuit o' R honor's trust!" (Lahdeedah!) "Hear, me, my ablest base man; wyn yn**
103 & 104	
Let Paris bleed, 'tis but a fear to scorne, Paris is gor'd with Menelaus horne.	**Eire, I gain at home! Her distress't frown eras' d, al places'l B open to us, but Ir—**
105 & 106	
Harke what good(e) sport(e) is out of Towne to day/ Better at home if would I might were may:	**ish fagots wait. U go meet 'em: I take th' proud one to a low death ere he wd try t' B Roy of mi wo—**

proud one. The earl of Tyrone.

107 & 108	
But to the sport abroad, are you bound thither? In all swift hast. / Come goe wee then togither.	**rld 'n' show me the beaten general uui' a dearth o' troops to fight. I hate the twisty boor, but—co—**
109 & 110	
Who were those went by? / Queen Hecuba, and Heller And whether go they? / Vp to the Easterne Tower,	**uld we treat—'n' placate R queen? Why, then we'd agree to no new hvrt. So when th' Hebe—" "O?" "O, yes, the Hebe—**

111 & 112

Whose height commands as subiect all the vaile,
To see the battell: Hector whose pacience,

pens each wise article o' cessation t' touch him, we'l B able t' go home! He'l have t' C the deale's st-

113 & 114

Is as a Vertue fixt, to day was mou'd:
He chides Andromache and strooke his Armorer,

rictures ar dead seriovs. He—my shado aide—can make us a firm text." "Who?" O, don't sho ar

115 & 116

And like as there were husbandry in Warre
Before the Sunne rose, hee was harnest lyte,

hidden assets—no leak before ye treaty's writ! Run! Release Nash, 'n' Hebe here, U 'n' he wra-wr—

Nash. Tom Nash, a staffer for Essex, as were Kit and Tom Lodge and Harry Wotton.

117 & 118

And to the field goes he; where euery flower
Did as a Prophet weepe what it forsaw,

ap up the war! We hope t' sail away fore'er, free o' wild fighters (E-e!) who'd not heed dest—

119 & 120

In Hectors wrath. / What was his cause of anger?
The noise goe's this; / There is among the Greeks,

ruction o' homes 'n' estates!"

Can writers reason wi' the high, h-hawkish foes—these aggregates

destruction o' homes 'n' estates. the end of a long speech by Essex.
Can writers. the start of Kit's own thought.

121 & 122

A Lord of Troian blood(e), Nephew to Hector,
They call him Aiax. / Good; and what of him?

of exceptional warmen (who don't retreat i' fog, I'm told)? Oh, oh! Ha, ha, ha! I'l B a cloddy o—

123 & 124

They say he is a very man per se and stands alone.
So do all men, vnlesse they are drunke, sicke, or have no legges.

l' sap to demand surrender, as they heal 'n' vvin every day! Nashe 'n' Kyt'l share a keene loss, see? O, no logic-message

125 & 126

This man Lady, hath rob'd many beasts of their particular additions, he is as valiant as the Lyon,

that'l dissvade, pacify the hot Irish. Tom 'n' I try R brains—hash ideas—al, al, al, not to B used. Nay, a man

127 & 128

churlish as the Beare, slow as the Elephant: a man into whom nature hath so crowded humors,

neuer had such a h-h-hard trial. We meant wel, but each h-h-hope was soon lost. No rest. A storm im—

129 & 130

that his valour is crusht into folly, his folly sauced with discretion: there is no man hath a vertue

minent: h-h-hi wind tears R odious, fatuous, illicit treaty! O, C hovv th' ceaseless rain h-h-hurts all of yt!

131 & 132

that he hath not a glimpse of, not any man an attaint, but he carries some staine of it.

No use. Again, th' same tinny hipe: another batch of fit, neat, MT, total shit. A more sanat—

133 & 134

He is melancholy without cause, and merry against the haire, hee hath the ioyntes of every thing,

ive tone was used, tho': only a cease-fire treaty sought, Ce, 'n' a near-year time limit. H-h-h-h-h-hey!! Night

sanative. (Webster) healing.

135 & 136

but every thing so out of ioynte, that hee is a gowtie Briareus, many hand(e)s and no vse;

's gone. Robin's not satisfied; he'd have us uurite more. By evening, we no that ya-yat oath:

137 & 138

or purblinded Argus, all eyes and no sight. But how should this man that makes me smile, make Hector angry?

"Damn Authoritarians!" (Sh, sh, sh!) We wryte: Eire t' block kerns, giue up land, guns, go home. Oh, m-m-mad! All bodes yl-

139 & 140

They say he yesterday cop'd Hector in the battell and stroke him downe, the distaind & (and) shame whereof,

hit, yl-hit, for lastin' peace between h-heated nations who don't see e-each other's d-darker myths. My daddy

141 & 142

hath euer since kept Hector fasting and waking.
Who comes here? Madam your Vncle Pandarus.

says, do t' each man like U'd have other men treat U, 'n' swap, 'n' win, 'n' check egregious crap from da h—

143 & 144

Hectors a gallant man. / As may be in the world Lady. / What's that? What's that? Good morrow(e) Vncle Pandarus.

igh clod. But at last yt dawns on Tom an' Moth: R harsh treaty's a legal sham! No one wd wrap a wretched vala—

145 & 146

Good morrow(e) Cozen Cressid: what do you talke of? good morrow(e) Alexander: how do you Cozen?

nce o' my words 'n' fool guarded Eyre, who'd wreck our game—exact a dozen o' hiz worst, loo—oo-oood

147 & 148

When were you at Illium? / This morning Vncle.
What were you talking of when I came? Was Hector arm(e)d

conditions ere we may go home, C. I'l take R general what we frame, 'n' Tyrone wil have wun us, chum, with il

149 & 150

and gon ere yea came to Illium? Hellen was not vp? was she?
Hector was gone but Hellen was not vp?

consent soon t' deny U his law signatvre. But how else can he manage to appear level, mellow, wh—

151 & 152

E'ene so, Hector was stirring early. That were we talking of, and of his anger.

ile looking for a way t' start another sewer fight? 'E'd change, snare, 'n' rise w—

153 & 154

Was he angry? / So he says here. True he was so; I know the cause too, heele lay about him to day

ith al his kerns to win you—but what else are you to say or do? Heeaah we see a game o' chess: he

155 & 156

I can tell them that, and there's Troylus will not come farre behind him. Let them take heede of Troylus;

'll checkmate, defeat us! R stateside'll ne'er win th' holy hoot till he B found in error. He may meet that MT

157 & 158

I can tell them that too. / What is he angry too?
Who Troylus? Troylus is the better man of the two.

toy treaty with laughter—home free—as he, Robin, twists, totally lost. Oh, can't U hew t' th' monoto—

159 & 160

Oh Iupiter; there's no comparison. / What not betweene Troylus and Hector? do you know a man if you see him?

nous iob o' war? Tyrone's out ahead of us. What wil he concede? Nothin', man! So keepe tryin'! Meet him! Try, U

161 & 162

I, if I ever saw him before and knew him. Well, I say Troylus is Troylus. / Then you say as I say,

sissy, make-believe souldier! No more wishy-washy 'esitation! Fury! Finality! Rush away! L—

163 & 164

For I am sure he is not Hector. / No not Hector is not Troylus in some degrees.

eaue Tyrone mired 'n' lost! Rise 'n' shine! Ch-choose to-to striue! 'N' go from stro—

165 & 166

'Tis iust, to each of them he is himselfe. Himselfe? alas poore Troylus I would he were.

ll to liuelie march-step! Use haste! Show th' feo foe we're thy souldiers! Safe i' mi hi mo—

feo. ugly.

167 & 168

So he is. / Condition I had gone barefoote to India. / He is not Hector. Himselfe? nor hee's not himselfe,

ral region, I—*I*, an idiot, offer al those demented sentences to mi hi chief, he so bent on his Hoo-Hoo's

169 & 170

would a were himselfe: well, the Gods are aboue, time must friend or end: well Troylus well,

dim view of R deeds t' stall all ye low rebels. E-e-e! He would sail 'n' tel her o' wrong tu R few mum

171 & 172

I would my heart were in her body; no, Hector is not a better man then Troylus. Excuse me.

member-souls who'd need extra time to breech 'n' try to clean euerythin' out. Ay, who R si—

173 & 174

He is elder. / Pardon me, pardon me. Th' others not come too't, you shall tell me another tale	**lent men 'n' try to stop a lot o' death-horror here. E-e-e! So all can sail the puddle home t' mom.**

175 & 176

when th'others come too't: Hector shall not haue his will this yeare. / He shall not neede it	**O-o! Humane H. Wotton 'n' slo T. Nash criticised i' th' last letters. What R ye? O, hel! O, hel! H-h-hel! E-e-e!**

177 & 178

if he haue his owne. / Nor his qualities. No matter./ Nor his beautie. /T'would not become him,	**O-o! Th' Cobra Queen wants us not t' sail R men home until we'ue had more hi, hi, hi fites! O, I! 'Bie!**

179 & 180

his own's better. / You haue no iudgement Neece; Hellen her selfe swore th'other day	**No more new cyfers here. Too sad, Hen. A sweet louin' girl used by thee. Then U'l heet he-**

181 & 182

that Troylus for a browne favour (for so 'tis I must confesse) not browne neither.	**r as substitute, 'n' now leave her to morn for a feo S.O.B. Sorry U scorn th' fit wife; not**

th' fit wife. Elizabeth Vernon, whom Hen married in 1598.

183 & 184

No, but browne. / Faith to say truth, browne and not browne. / To say the truth, true and not true.	**a year wed, 'n' U with th' babe, too! But no: U, R hot stud, trot on t' taste 'n' try a new front—'n' burn her! O!**

185 & 186

She prais'd his complexion aboue Paris. Why, Paris hath colour inough. / So, he(e) has.	**Hi, ho—Essex's war a loss—home to angry Bess—choppin' up her poor child. Ai, ai, ai! U-huh!**

187 & 188

Then Troylus should haue too much, if she prasi'd him aboue, his complexion is higher then his, he hauing colour	**U i' th' Tower! I beg o' Ned a clean place for his child. No sign. H-H-H-Hoo—H-H-H-Hoo's my last resort! I sue: Mix hipe uui' mush**

189 & 190

enough, and the other higher, is too flaming a praise for a good complexion, I had as lieve

ado; I go alone 'n' hug her good—chide her—o-o! Express mi faith i' maternal love, in spight of a—a—

191 & 192

Hellens golden tongue had commended Troylus for a copper nose. / I sweare to you,

necessary anomaly. Feer sweeps ouer me—good God! I told uh lood ol' cunt "repent!" 'N' h—

193 & 194

I thinke Hellen loues him better then Paris. / Then shee's a merry Greeke indeed.

ere she relents, sends Kit tu Italy—t' be a religion-keeper! H-he, h-he! Hen, remind me

195 & 196

Nay I am sure she does, she came to him th' other day into the compast window, and you know

to pen th' deeds o' waste 'n' death in Eire. I'm Kyt. Who? A sour homo cynic who'd shout away man's

W. M is used for W.
compast window. bay window.

197 & 198

he has not past three or foure haires on his chinne. / Indeed a Tapsters Arithmetique may soone bring

dignity in sneerin' critiques of motiues 'n' methods. He's poor—near bare—'n' hee has a rare hope that as th—

199 & 200

his particulars therein, to a totall. / Why he is very yong, and yet will he within three pound

y nation wins, U'l try to change th' hi hi law so people wd truly share. I, I! They'd never alter thi—

201 & 202

lift as much as his brother Hector. / Is he so young a man, and so old(e) a lifter? / But to prove to you

s incessant itch for pouuer that rules some men, Bo: they grab first! O, Lady Hoo-Hoo, toda U viola—

203 & 204

that Hellen loves him, she came and puts me her white hand to his cloven chin. / Iuno have mercy,

te natural law: a mom sh'dn't chop her son t' death! 'N' see, 'n'-'n' see—U'll vievv him! O, hi yie—him! Ch-ch-chee!

205 & 206

how came it cloven? / Why you know 'tis dimpled, I think his smyling becomes him better then any man

Imminent: My trip t' Venice, t' sho new SS ye Catholic way. Hen needs my aid now, tho'. Bob'l mug, k-kil him, h—

Bob. Robert Cecil, who with Bacon has masterminded this overthrow of siblings and half-siblings.

207 & 208

in all Phrigia. / Oh he smiles valiantly. Dooes hee not? / Oh, yes, and 'twere a clow'd in Autumne.

elpless Hen, al alone in this ol' Tower. V may decide ta stay wi' him or go h-haue a nonni duel

209 & 210

Why go to then, but to prove to you that Hellen loves Troylus. / Troylus wil stand to thee Proofe, if youle proove it so.

'n'—oo-oo!—lose al! But O, Hen, to survive, wryte to her lots—lots—of lovin', hopeful, witty letters, euery day! Hop to 't! Go! Put hy

211 & 212

Troylus? Why he esteemes her no more then I esteeme an addle egge. / If you love an addle egge

themes in wi' da laughs, ere U ladle on ye goode love. Ne'er forget that! See, ye need my gems! Hee—

213 & 214

as well as you love an idle head, you would eate chickens i' th' shell. / I cannot chuse

hee, Kit's teachin' U how t' loue d' lady—loue, loue a hi, hi lady! 'N' C, C, C: a lone slave's new SS

215 & 216

but laugh to thinke how she tickled his chin, indeed shee has a marvel's white hand I must needs confesse.

goes to Venice in a week. Write to Kit 'n' tel him al the neuus, C? H-he'd B sad, sad. C; he's sh-shad! I'l miss U, H-Hen! Done. F—

217 & 218

Without the racke. / And she takes vpon her to spie a white hair on his chinne. Alas poor chin?

ree, I've had t-to speak: I teach R nu SS how a h-hot sharp iron wil open inkie notes 'n' catch a hi h—

219 & 220

many a wart is richer. / But there was such laughing, Queene Hecuba laught that her eyes ran ore.

eretic enemy writing carelessly about R great queen H-hu-H-ha. Aha, Aha! But C, R guest has run: we h—

221 & 222

With milstones. / and Cassandra laught. But there was more temperate fire vnder the pot of her eyes:	**ave ta follow him, obserue, frustrate him, wryte and send that ciphered report. Geee, 'n' that's SS, man!**

that's SS. Kit is tutoring neophyte secret-servicemen, in Italy, 1601-1602, for Elizabeth.

223 & 224

did her eyes run ore too? / And Hector laught. At what was all this laughing? Marry at the white haire	**We go t' Uenice, where Rita lies. Sad, halt, I return t' thy last grim ho<u>m</u>e at th' Laguna. Ah, ah, ah, d' hy odor r—**

ho*<u>m</u>*e. W is used as m.

225 & 226

that Hellen spied on Troylus chin. / And 't had beene a greene haire, I should haue laught too.	**rushes out uuhen, that e'en, I enter t' hold thy poor bones. Gee, gee, and all da air had a hi chill, 'n'**

227 & 228

They laught not so much at the haire, as at his pretty answere. What was his answere?	**I, th' Yat, wept ta see her worn remains—swore t' sta th' night—wash à l'eau, assay each uh th'**

sta th' night. Kit is characterized in several Ben Jonson plays. In The Poetaster, Horace says, "Our melancholic friend Poropertius, Hath closed himself up in his Cynthia's tomb, and will by no entreaties be drawn thence." **uh th.'** of the.

229 & 230

Quoth(e) shee, heere's but two and fifty haires on your chinne; and one of them is white. / This is her question.	**stars ouerhead before restin' in (yes, Hen, in) this quiet house o' death, 'n' wi' thots of my honie wife t' quench h—**

231 & 232

Thats true, make no question of that, two and fiftie haires quoth hee, and one white, that white haire is my Father,	**ot question: is my wife safe in here, in utter quiet? Her father did kno of this wet, wet toom. Then aah, aah, that hath a—**

Her father. Duke Giandomenico Cicogna.

233 & 234

and all the rest are his Sonnes. Iupiter quoth she, which of these haires is Paris, my husband? The forked one,	**s-sad end: bitter, he'd not take her in his uault. Fy! Perhaps now he's free o' queer sh-shit, so I can sho him her sail—**

235 & 236

quoth hee pluckt out and give it him: but there was such laughing, and Hellen so blusht, and Paris so chaft,

wrapp't squalid shack, 'n' he c'n go lade a shelf in th' closet h-hive-tomb uuith th' lost daughter, 'n' uue gain, súb—

237 & 238

and all the rest so laught, that it past. So let it now, For it has beene a great while going by.

ito, an end t' all th' worrie about th' ghastlee plight. Go, go, win Rita a safe nest! These salty b—

239 & 240

Well Cozen, I told you a thing yesterday, think on't. / So I does. / Ile be sworne tis true, he will weepe you, an'twere a man borne in Aprill.

eaches R hazardous. Stil, pileing'll let al B dry on top. Yes, now I know: I rite ye uault. Need ye man to see it! I bow: wil he en-enter now, or—

241 & 242

And Ile spring vp in his reares, and t'were a nettle against May. / Harke they are comming from the field, shal (l) we stand vp

tvrn away, repell'd? He s-saw Rita—he lifted his davghter, 'n' in tears he faced me: "P-prego, I'm a man alone: my girl stinks—tanne—

243 & 244

here and see them, as they passe toward Illium, good Neece do, sweet Neece Cressida. / At your pleasure.

d, salted—aee, peeeeu! Stessa! She can rest in de uault wi' her poor dear mother. Yes, yes, come, we cd go. An il—

245 & 246

Heere, heere, here's an excellent place, heere we may see most brauely, Ile tel you them all by their names,

hap met thy man Essex ere ye came here! E-e-e-e-e-e! 'N' U still loyal! How clever—really smart—t' be here! He'l be in—

247 & 248

as they passe by, but marke Troylus aboue the rest. Speake not so low'd. That's Aeneas, is not that a braue man,

terr'd sans peer honor, as she was. A-a-ay!" UUe set out yn hys boat t' th' tomb isle. Sun kept me able to take a basta—

249 & 250

hee's one of the flowers of Troy I can—you, but marke Troylus, you shal see anon. / Who's that? / That's Antenor, he has a shrow'd wit

'd. Oy! Ow! Fuk! We reach shore. Rita yn hys arms, he turns into th' uault, 'n' now, oh, we set her on a shelf to stay, safe at last! O-o-o-o—h! Be—

251 & 252

I can tell you, and hee's a man good inough, hee's one o' the soundest iudgement in Troy whosoever, and a proper man of person:

fore we go, he opens her gouun, so th' rottenness'l dry. And so uue leave, hopin' a Goy peace'd dominate this damn nonnie room a—

hopin'. Cicogna must have said a Christian prayer as they departed.

253 & 254

when comes Troylus? Ile shew you Troylus anon, if hee see me, you shall see him nod at me.

thousand years. Now, immune to ye noisome smell o' y-ye shelues, we face R hi loue: Hel's th—

255 & 256

Will he giue you the nod? / You shall see. / If he do, the rich shall haue more./ that's Hector, that, that, looke you,

is view o' forever: th' last load lately stack't. Oh, h-here it comes: Oh, h-h-h-h-h-h-hell!Yet uue go out t' enioy al a' d'

257 & 258

that there's a fellow. Goe thy way Hector, there's a braue man, Neece, O braue Hector! Looke how hee lookes?

color as we roe the boat. The man forgets the uault: "Ahoy!" He works ye oar t' check a lone Hebe who (e-e-e-e!) rel—

259 & 260

there's a countenance; ist not a brave man? O brave man! / Is a not? It dooes a mans heart good, looke you

eases content o' iordan. O, stinky! And rouu to miss that charge, man! E-e-e-e! On R bovv, man! A-a-o-o-o-! Blat!

261 & 262

what hacks are on his Helmet, looke you yonder, do you see? Looke you there? There's no iesting, laying on,

Yo! Yn town h-he asks me to share dinner: h-h-he orders gooey eel. I sit, l-look; you knouu I can't eat gooey eel.

263 & 264

tak't off who ill as they say, there be hacks. / Be those with Swords? / Swords, any thing he cares not, and the divell come to him,

No chow, 'n' soon Cicogna says farewel. Tired, I walk t' my SSS, relieved that b-bless't dad took thy sweet Rita h-h-h-h-h-home. Th' fe—

265 & 266

it's all one, by Gods lid it dooes ones heart good(e). Yonder comes Paris, yonder comes Paris: looke yee yonder Neece, ist not a gallant man to,

llo's decent at last! Ye day o'er, I rest—dream o' Rita's restoration. O-oh, soon I'l employ ye nonny SS: cd I keep 'em engaged in a good old scene o' ob—

267 & 268

ist not? Why this is brave now: who said he came hurt home today? Hee's not hurt, why this will do

edience t' th' dim-wit Roman-style oblation rites, t' aid H-h-h-hoo H-h-h-hoo's SS? We R w-w-way tu shy: U v—

obedience. Webster 2. "in the Roman Catholic church, a.) the Church's jurisdiction. b.) all those who submit to this jurisdiction." [obedients?] **Hoo Hoo.** Kit's nickname for Queen Elizabeth.

269 & 270

Hellen's heart good(e) now, ha? / Would I could see Troylus now, you shall (see) Troylus anon. / Who's that? / That's Hellenus,

ue, learn rytuals, don't enter yn! We hesitate tu long. Let's allow U all ye dull dances! Sh, sh! Oh, oh! Who? U! Hoo-Hoo's SS! Wo—

271 & 272

I maruell where Troylus is, that's Helenus, I thinke he went not forth to day: that's Hellenus. / Can Hellenus fight Vncle?

n't U get sense? 'N' when U feel like it, sun, neel, so then we'll sail home t' catch all the traitors for th' hi lady! Uh, hvh! Try, sun!

273 & 274

Hellenus no: yes heele fight indifferent, well, I maruell where Troylus is; harke, do you not haere the people

U! I'l help U learn t' use thy Latin, kno 'n' enter all ye worship forms, defer to ye fool hi, hi heels. E-e-e-e-e! We'l hug R de—

275 & 276

Crie Troylus? Hellenus is a Priest. / What sneaking fellow comes yonder? / Where? Yonder? That's Daephobus, Tis Troylus!

ceit—use yt as an illusion to help our state wi' yntelligence for R worst dread problems. Aye, sh, sh, sh, sh! 'N' ye'd wrek ou—

277 & 278

Ther's a man, Neece, hem, Brave Troylus, the Prince of Chivalrie. /Peace, for shame, peace. / Marke him, not him: O brave Troylus:

r plan here! I! if U can't C the reason for R hi scheme—play a part, C? Act like Rome is home! "Oy, Hebe, vve must have more beer, man."

279 & 280

looke well vpon him Neece, looke you how his Sword is bloudied, and his Helme more hackt then Hectors, and how he lookes,

Look, look—we come to help SS, not to chase hookers 'n' drink all de beer in Venice. I smell U wd hie home—oh-h-h, who'd sho U de way?

281 & 282

and how he goes. O admirable youth! he ne're saw three and twenty. Go thy way Troylus, go thy way, had I a sister

Now, this'l B a year o' serious learnin': how t' wryt home, what t' say, when t' say yt—a good-deed Greg ta ayd ye! "Huh? he—

283 & 284

were a Grace, or a daughter a Goddesse, hee should take his choice. O admirable man! Paris? Paris is durt to him,

's a mad drag egghead who misst or lost euerie chance he had. He'l aid us t' stop or break up crimes? Ai, ai!" "O, dear, I r—

285 & 286

and I warrant, Helen to change, would give money to boot. / Heere come more. / Asses, fooles, dolts, chaffe and bran;

egret accedin' to SS. Can we bow t' ye fool homo bastard, 'n' leave? Go home free?" "It's so far, man, 'n' he'l hold on, under ea—

287 & 288

chaffe and bran; porredge after meat. I could live and dye i' th' eyes of Troylus. Ne're looke, ne're looke; the Eagles are gon,

ch bad SS rule." "Let's ride o'er the Alp, to F-France, 'n' let old hag-man Gregorio rave!" E-e-e! I kno ye keen dolour of defeat, 'n' ye yea—

289 & 290

Crowes and Dawes, Crowes and Dawes: I had rather be such a man as Troylus, then Agamemnon, and all Greece.

r's s-study-course ends. What a shame—a waste! A doge'l call a nonnie dance, 'n' we can go! Remember da hard, raw h—

291 & 292

There is among the Greekes Achilles, a better man then Troylus./ Achilles? A Dray-man, a Porter, a very Camell.

ap Cicogna gave me in other years? Here he ayds me: he talks ta all R youths, tells 'em t' care, learn, 'n' B alert. I'm r—

293 & 294

Well, well. / Well, well? Why have you any discretion? have you any eyes? Do you know what a man is?

eliev'd when I know all you men'l stay ye school year—U won't hy away, now, will U? We see yv al had

295 & 296

Is not birth, b(e)auty, good shape, discourse, manhood, learning, gentlenesse, vertue, youth, liberality, and so forth:

thots of rashly goin' t' Eng. prematurely, but no, uue bros.'d have good learnin' in this ol' city at de seashore, 'n' beside,

297 & 298

the Spice, and salt that seasons a man? I(e), a minc'd man, and then to be bak'd with no Date in the pye,

add th' swimmin', th' neatest in Italy! At ease, men! "O, that sad nonnee pinchback, he's not a bad peda—

pinchback. pinchbeck. a cheapskate. (OED. 1545, ELYOT *Dict. Aridus homo.* A drye fellowe, of whom nothyng may be gotten.)

299 & 300

for then the mans dates out. / You are such another woman, one knowes not at which ward you lye. / Vpon my backe,

phile; he's a bad cock-svcker!" "O, man, what R we to do here, away from home?" Why, U nonny nut-ass—toot a nonny tuueet!

301 & 302

to defend my belly; vpon my wit, to defend my wiles; vppon my secrecy, to defend mine honesty; my Maske, to defend my beauty,

O, yes, 'n' Daddy needes t' C lots of fit development:
wit-ymprovements made yn U m-men. Holdin' off my weepyn', d' ye C? Bye-bye. Kyt M.

f

Shake-speares Sonnets. Quarto, 1609. George Eld for T.T.

SONNET 125 B

1 & 2

Wer(e)'t (a)ught to me I bore the canopy,/
With my extern the outward honoring,

Greg wrote th' rhyme. Note th' thin texture o' each word! I may bow out—pen an i—

3 & 4

Or layd great bases for eternity,
Which proves more short then wast(e) or ruining?

diotic report for Robyn. He wants a heavy list o' R men's error in th' huge egress t'wa—

Greg. Marlowe's Italian name. **Robyn.** Robert Devereux, Earl of Essex. Marlowe's in Ireland with Essex, and some of Essex's troops ran away from Irish attacking forces.

5 & 6

Haue I not seene dwellers on forme and fauor
Lose all, and more by paying too much rent

rd defeat. No! Betray 'n' hang poor souldiers? No, no! Let 'em live safe! We'l only hear U comman—

7 & 8

For compound sweet. Forgoing simple fauor,
Pittifull thriuors in their gazing spent.

d whipping! Stop! Realize! If more lives R lost, uuinning's farther off, C? G-go out on M.T. trip—

Essex intends to hang 10% of the 250 soldiers who ran away.

9 & 10

Noe, let me be obsequious in thy heart,/
And take thou my oblation, poor but free,

s, let thy poor queen mom uuait for letters! O, think a-about ye end, Bobbie hon! Ea—

11 & 12

Which is not mixt with seconds, knows no art,
But mutuall render onley me for thee.

ch nonny error stokes th' enmitie at home with extra fuel, 'n' wd U B lost in d'low scum?

13 &14	
Hence, thou subornd Informer, a trew soule When most impeacht, stands least in thy controule.	**B lost in d' swan-'n'-sparrouus, C? Try nouu, man, for when d' clem hits, then it's too late! Oe! Tee hee! Chr. M.**

Swan-'n'-sparrows. SSS slang for male and female prostitutes. **clem.** the put-down, the damper, the squelch.

f

As You Like It. First Folio of Shakespeare. Comedies, pp 185-187.

AS YOU LIKE IT

1 & 2

As I remember Adam, it was vpon this fashion bequeathed me by will, but poore a thousand Crownes,

A demonic Marlowe's hidden here, t' pen U this babble about a quest for answers, so I may vow I map th'

3 & 4

. . . and as thou saist, charged my brother on his blessing to breed mee well:

whole range o' human desyres. I cribb'd Lodge; he's not t' blame! I stress tha—

5 & 6

. . . and there begins my sadnesse: My brother Iaques he keepes at schoole, and report speakes goldnely of his profit:

t Lodge inspired me, tho' these ramblin' shypboy's peek-peek scenes aren't a quarter so good as his Rosalynde. He, eff—

7 & 8

. . . for my part, he keepes me rustically at home, or (to speak more properly) staies me

ortless, makes a loue-story to cherish from merely ratty pappee-mamee pork pie!

pork pie. Thomas Lodge's source was the Tale of Gamelyn, a bloody fourteenth century poem.

9 & 10

. . . heere at home vnkept: for call you that keeping for a gentleman of my birth

Not long ago, after the affair, much peeve pikt them, 'n' my lonely heart broke.

pikt. piqued. There was bad feeling over the source of this play. Tom Lodge and Kit had worked together since the '80's, in Paris and Reims, and in the summer of '93 they'd gone together from Mantua through Verona to Venice. They'd written a book together for Francis Walsingham, Kit as a ringer for Gilbert Gifford, Tom using the name Edward Gratley. Gratley translates to 'try Lage.' In London at that time, 'Lodge' was mispronounced, and often written, 'Large.' (Ann Bacon's letter to Francis: "tell Large to go home, he's a married man.")

11 & 12

. . . that differs not from the stalling of an Oxe? his horses are bred better, for besides that they are faire with their feeding,

I thot he'd long been my friend—a brother, right? Both with Essex' staff, far 'n' fast t' Irish soil. Did he see a fat fee? Rattee error! E—

13 & 14

they are taught their mannage, and to that end Riders deerely hir'd: but I (his brother) gaine nothing

gregious idea! Ohhhh! It ne'er enter'd my brain or heart t' steal thy giant better art! Hidden, I'd hang un—

15 & 16

vnder him but growth, for the which his animals on his dunghils are as much bound to him as I:

notic'd, as U R lost in honor's magic feast. Wahhhhhh! Hush! I give U th' bid, mi slumber man in row D!

slumber man. Lodge, at a performance of As You Like It, must have fallen asleep in the fourth row. Kit rewrote the first part of this play after the show appeared on stage in London.

17 & 18

besides this nothing that he so plentifully giues me, the something that nature gaue mee,

Hi hi hum! The time stagnates. Only note th' date! If the neuu age must begin here, Let's go piss. L—

neuu age. new age. It's 1600. He ushers in the 17th century.

19 & 20

his countenance seemes to take from me: hee lets mee feede with his Hindes, barres mee the place of a brother,

let's be friends, so we can help make a-an Irish truce here, see—or some Hebe-fem-moon (hee hee) c'd fail t' meet th' test.

Hebe-fem-moon. Queen Elizabeth.

21 & 22

and as much as in him lies, mines my gentility with my education. This is it Adam that grieues me,

They'ue enuenom'd this lady's mind, set her against a chummi way t' mitigate th' claims 'n'—isms. I-I-I-I!

They've envenom'd. Cecil and Bacon had worked to turn Elizabeth against Essex and his Irish treaty.

chummi. chummy. Cambridge slang, used much earlier than first instance in O.E.D.

23 & 24

and the spirit of my Father, which I thinke is within mee, begins to mutinie against this seruitude.

In th' hy bags, did U see their mean twists t' gain power o'er th' feminine uue? It's his fit makin'. Hitch it i—

in th' hy bags. in the dispatches from England sent by baga secreta and handled by Essex's staff in Ireland (Tom Lodge and Kit).
his fit makin'. his style, probably Robert Cecil's.

25 & 26

I will no longer endure it, though yet I know no wise rememdy how to auiod it.

nto thy design: don't deny i-it! He wil lie more to haue our uiew look wrong. Wi—

Hitch it into thy design. Tom Lodge is preparing the Irish treaty for submission; Cecil wants it thrown out.

27 & 28

Yonder comes my Master, your brother. Goe a-part Adam, and thou shalt heare how he will shake me vp.

ll argument persuade hy Ma'm o' th' worth o' peace, or, as we try, does th' mamaboy kid snare her love, hah?

mamaboy kid. Robert Cecil, Elizabeth's crippled, favored son.

29 & 30

Now Sir, what make you heere?
Nothing: I am not taught to make any thing.

We must get her attention now: make our man into a hot high king. Ya, yah!

31 & 32

What mar you then sir? / Marry, sir, I am helping you to mar that which God made,

I<u>*m*</u>agine th' rage: ratty room, 'n' mama with muss'd hair! Oy! Hurry! Do help him at c—

As soon as he came back to London, Essex went to Elizabeth in early morning, caught her en deshabille, without her wig, and began to tell her his side of the Irish-truce story.

33 & 34

. . . a poore vnworthy brother of yours with idlenesse. / Marry sir be better employed, and be naught a while.

ountin' blessings here, not to repel Beth day by day with ever more horrid sour fop blather. We're away m—

35 & 36

Shall I keepe your hogs, and eat huskes with them? What prodigall portion haue I spent,

ore. Aduise him tu keep an eye on th' shallo, th' dangerous, law pig—he's happli th' worst. Kit.

law pig. Bacon, who prosecuted his own half-brother, Essex.

37 & 38

that I should come to such penury? / Know you where you are sir? / O sir, very well

The play's your own, t' cherish or destroy. Where are U? Ink cools my love. U, U, U I w—

39 & 40

heere in your Orchard. / Know you before whom sir?
I, better than him I am before knowes mee:

'd rest with foreuer: I'm shy 'n' choke; ye make me one braue Moor boor breathin' fire when I wo—

I'm shy 'n' choke. He may think of his stammering.

41 & 42

I know you are my eldest brother, and in the gentle condition of bloud you should so know me:

uld drown in loue. You're th' best one, I-I realise, 'n' soon U'l B gone. O, don't mock thy K. Do defy what m—

43 & 44

the courtesie of nations allowes you my better, in that you are the first borne,

any men say—I! Let's each liue 'n' B free! O, stow it! To you, that's free thot, not error. I, bu—

45 & 46

but the same tradition takes not away my bloud, were there twenty brothers betwixt vs:

t think: rowdy, ratty, stew-meat beds may not B elevatin' us to the best with our Rex: we're ba—

stew-meat beds. In those days, houses of prostitution were called the stews.

47 & 48

I haue as much of my father in mee, as you, albeit I confess your coming before me is neerer to his reuerence.

ttling for her t' receiue nice Robin in hi fauor; if she sees us as mere mean, chafee, crummy bums—Ay! Eee! Ooooy!

49 & 50

What Boy. / Come, come elder brother, you are too yong in this. / Wilt thou lay hands on me villaine?

We try not to lose Robin, but a coy enemy'l destroy him. O, thru a deal he'l live on high! Now I'm a coa—

51 & 52

I am no villaine: I am the yongest sonne of Sir Rowland de Boys, he was my father, and he is thrice

rse, disgrvntled, ironic satirist—maybe. Oh, how'd ye feel if alone 'n' moanin'? Yea, th' hash was on me.

hash. army-issue hashish from the Irish campaign? Did Essex have some, too?

53 & 54

a villaine that saies such a father begot villaines: wert thou not my brother, I would not take this hand

Beau King Robin—vtterly lost at last! He's i' th' Tower, condemned t' await his fatal hour o' heat. Shh! U 'n' I live a—

55 & 56

from thy throat, till this other had puld out thy tongue for saying so, thou hast raild on thyselfe

t death's door if th' Youth stal us on a run. If only his royal mother'd see th' truth of that higgly plot!

th' Youth. Henry Wriothesley. **stal us on a run.** Wriothesley's plight may prevent Lodge and Kit from escaping. **higgly plot.** Cecil and Bacon lied, and drove Essex to his frantic march on the palace. Essex wanted to destroy them.

57 & 58

Sweet Masters bee patient, for your Fathers remembrance, be at accord. Let me goe I say.

Beery, at the street lamp, we dreamt o' crossing ye sea, before frustration came—came be—

59 & 60

I will not till I please: you shall heare mee: my father charg'd you in his will to giue me good education:

tween dim desire 'n' action: ugly fate allow'd my high lily t' close our gate o' hope. So U all hail him? I-I! Uere—

high lily. Hen, Earl of Southampton. Hen did frustrate Kit's escape; Kit couldn't leave him in the Tower threatened with death.
Uere. Vere. Edward de Vere, Earl of Oxford, Hen's half-brother and natural father.

61 & 62

you haue train'd me like a pezant, obscuring and hiding from me all gentleman-like qualities:

'l let Queen Eliza condemn their imprison'd boy t' death. I'l fail again. Glug. U saue 'im, 'n' make R nak—

63 & 64

the spirit of my father growes strong in mee, and I will no longer endure it: therefore allow me

ed effort win, 'n' she'l let 'im go free, tho' I'm reeling 'n' wrestling wi' death o'er our payment o' ars-rol—

65 & 66

such exercises as may become a gentleman, or giue mee the poore allottery my father left me

ling o'er Hebe Molly Ma'am, C, ta try ta free Southampton from Essex's guilty march, C? Eeeeeeeee!

67 & 68

by testament, with that I will goe buy my fortunes. / And what wilt thou do?

W-w-w-win! Mutter out: "it's best not t' behead al th' goy-lad youth in th' family."

goy-lad. Hen was Catholic, Essex, Catholic Church-tolerant. Other children of Elizabeth's with Catholic leanings came to sad ends, though not beheaded—Philip Howard in the Tower, Ferdinando Stanley poisoned.

69 & 70

beg when that is spent? Well sir, get you in. I will not long be troubled with you: you shall haue

Angel Bess 'n' I hide in th' lair wi' th' pillows, 'n' we woo. U'll say, "Loue? No—th' better glug," But th'—oy uey!

71 & 72

some part of your will, I pray you leaue me. I will no further offend you, then becomes me for my good.

I pled, 'n' our fool Hen remains full o' life i' th' Tower. By tomorrow U may escape—moue y' grey mud off o' ye.

73 & 74

Get you with him, you olde dogge. Is old dogge my reward: most true, I haue lost my teeth

Th' suruiuors rue it: goy, yid. Sold, MT, we go ye lo, dim way home, t' meet thee, old Death. G-g-go!

ye lo, dim way home. a dirge for defeat. Anthony Bacon died—a suicide? Henry Cuffe was executed, as were others. Henry Wotton quickly crossed the Channel. Tom Nashe died. Where's Tom Lodge? He survives.

75 & 76

in your service: God be with my olde master, he would not haue spoke such a word.

At Wilton I hide below t' pen a dark, sour comedy-revue show o' Cressyd. Ho hum—ueg—

Wilton. Kit's friend and lover, Mary Sidney Herbert, Lady Pembroke, is hiding Kit at her country place.

77 & 78

Is it euen so, begin you to grow vpon me? I will physicke your ranckenesse, and yet giue no

etable-seedy 'n' poor—Oy!—I'm accepting euil! No! Rise 'n' go t' young kin! I wish Vere knew us—oy! Su—

79 & 80

thousand crownes neyther: holla Dennis. Calls your worship? / Was not Charles the Dukes Wrastler heere

rreptitiously—Sh! We'd let th' earl know how Hen's saued, so he'd see our clear worth as crass n-n-n-nelly char—

81 & 82

to speake with me? / So please you, he is heere at the doore, and importunes accesse to you.

acters, 'n' he'd pay us wel to haue more such toy missions to peekapoo at desire. O, tee hee! E—

83 & 84

Call him in: 'twill be a good way: and tomorrow the wrastling is. / Good morrow to your worship.

gregious sin made th' poor lad, cast low wi' wrath into a horribly gloomy world, wi' no room t' w—

85 & 86

Good Mounsier charles: what's the new newes at the new Court? / There's no newes at the Court Sir,

rite, or euen welcome others. So haue courage, Hen, t' stand 'n' sit 'n' stare, 'n' th-th-tho' w-w-w-we recess,

stand 'n' sit 'n' stare. Later, Hen was given a comfortable apartment in the Tower.

87 & 88

but the olde newes: that is, the old Duke is banished by his yonger brother, the new Duke,

We'l soon return here t' aid thy English head by use o' th' best kind o' stud-bed with Hebe ke—

89 & 90

and three or foure louing Lords haue put themselues into voluntary exile with him, whose lands and reuenues

eper o' th' life-threads o' her many grouun sons. Essex dared al—lost! *U*wil liue, Hen; We loue U, 'n' I'm the' hound in rut at V—

91 & 92

enrich the new Duke, therefore he giues them good leaue to wander./Can you tell

ere, U C? Ere we leaue thee, U'l haue changed to fire-light 'n' desk-room! Why not? Noted

93 & 94

if Rosalind the Dukes daughter bee banished with her Father? / O no; for the Dukes daughter

inhabitants o' th' Tower haue liued here as k-kings, offered th' best, free o' d-d-dread. Uh huh! Gr—

95 & 96

her cosen so loues her, being euer from their Cradles bred together, that hee would haue followed

eat ones secluded haue studied. U'll learn t' write here. Chr. M. goes off, t' brew or beg or hore—Ho, Ho, Hee! L—

Kit will go to Ned de Vere to deal, to get Hen decent quarters in the Tower.

97 & 98

her exile, or haue died to stay behind her; she is at the Court, and no lesse beloued

et's see—Brother-Dad can uuin it! So, today our h-hero'll die. See this: he'd been laxe. He,

99 & 100

of her Vncle, then his owne daughter, and neuer two Ladies loued as they doe.

the cad, gaue her no lovin' words, no due attention. U sh'd heed her well. Ye safe—

Essex was reared by Elizabeth's cousin, Lettice Devereux, who was envious of the queen. He was taught to dislike his real mother Elizabeth, who loved and favored him. With her he was cool and resentful.

101 & 102

Where will the old Duke liue? / They say he is already in the Forrest of Arden, and a many

st way t' renew her dead loue is—offer your head—daily, hat in hand! Hasten: yel, "Kill me, er—

103 & 104

merry men with him; and there they liue like the old Robin Hood of England: they say

e I die here of th' shame 'n' regret I h-hold i' my h-heart! I lou'd my noble lady 'n' knew yt not!"

105 & 106

many yong Gentlemen flocke to him euery day, and fleet the time carelessly as they did

I'm glad you'll get t' stay safe, locked here i' th' ancient fort. Hey! Ned may lend me ye men ye

107 & 10

.in the golden world. / What, you wrastle to morrow before the new Duke. Marry doe I sir:

gaue him when U left town t' dare doom 'n' lose. Harrowed, worried, I'l borrow ye rest. Kyt

109 & 110

and I came to acquaint you with a matter: I am giuen sir secretly to vnderstand, that your yonger brother

Th' queen underwrote this year: uue'l go t' roam Venice to train my dandy attaboys to Christian trim. A grac—

attaboys. Ben Jonson was one of these young men who went to Venice with Kit to learn Catholicism for SSS. Ben went as "Mr. Fox." CSP Dom. Elizabeth, 1601, p 140, v. 6, v. CCLXXXII. no. 72. Acc't of intelligencers employed abroad this year and sums they have received: Mr. [Simon] Fox, in Venice, 20£.

111 & 112

Orlando hath a disposition to come in disguis'd against mee to try a fall: tomorrow sir	**ious crown spared this fool! Soon I'l stand again i' th' Rialto I t-t-trod years ago. Dim memo—**

Kit left Venice soon after his first wife's tragic death in childbirth in 1594. He returned briefly in 1597, '98, mapping the town, then worked with Guarini in Ferrara. (ciphers for I Henry IV).

113 & 114

I wrastle for my credit, and hee that escapes me without some broken limbe, shall acquit him well:	**ries stir'd. I weep so m-much th' quill shakes, for my Rita became all white, C: en-t-tombed at Hallowe'en.**

my Rita. Kit's wife Rita, Marina Cicogna, died of hemorrhage after childbirth in late October 1594. Ben Jonson, in Venice with Kit in 1601, 1602, must have heard this memory of Kit's, for Jonson writes, as Horace in Poetaster, "Our melancholic friend, Propertius, hath closed himself up in his Cynthia's tomb, and will by no entreaties be drawn thence." Act 3, l. 267. In 3 Henry VI, Kit says he stayed with Rita-Marina in her tomb. Ben Jonson also mentions a ring Marina gave Kit: In Every Man in his Humour, Stephano is Kit, who finds his lost purse, says he wouldn't have cared save for the ring "Marina sent me."

115 & 116

your brother is but young and tender, and for your loue I would bee loth to foyle him, as I must	**D-death, to undu-u-u your worst, I'l feed R liuely bonny babe at home. I'l s-sing for your mother, too.**

feed R . . . babe. Kit couldn't afford a wetnurse—he bought a cow.
S-sing for your mother. Songs for Rita-Marina are A Midsummer Night's Dream, Romeo and Juliet, Pericles, Erotokritos.

117 & 118

for my owne honour if hee come in: therefore out of my loue for you, I came hither to acquaint you withall,	**In Romeo 'n' Iuliet my effort t' uoice our queer emotion of too much ioy hath an ache for her. Why we fall, you**

119 & 120

that either you might stay him from his intendment, or brooke such disgrace well as he shall runne into,	**see, may haue t' do with Fortune's rollin' globe—damn her! 'Tis mere il chance, not the stars mouin' h-hi i' th' sky! Gr—**

Kit and Rita were not "starre-crost lovers," as he calls Romeo and Juliet in the quarto versions of his play. And in Midsummer Night's Dream, Kit blames himself—many times, between the lines—for Rita's death.

121 & 122

in that it is a thing of his owne search, and altogether against my will. / Charles,

ief, the il, th' tragic end 'n' loss I sing, al wil shame hi*m* to go rather than stay. Can a

him. Romeo died. Kit took the baby and went to Spain.

123 & 124

I thanke thee for thy loue to me, which thou shalt finde I will most kindly requite: I had myselfe

man stay to liue in th h-home of his dead loue, with their child? Is he queer t' flee? Know my Kit'l fly t'

125 & 126

notice of my Brothers purpose heerein, and haue by vnder-hand meanes laboured to disswade him from it, but he is resolute.

Sevil, t' stay free i' th' home of an honest man. Dumb, I'd depend on a horse carryin' me ouer bad riuer boulders, but see, we stop, h-hi.

home of an honest man. The honest man was Cervantes. Note early colloquial use of 'dumb.'

127 & 128

Ile tell thee, Charles, it is the stubbornest yong fellow of France, full of ambition, an enuious emulator

Nan crosses on a log with ye little babe. UUe let th' horses climb o'er a tuff uallie floor 'n' mount, feelin' fit.

129 & 130

of euery mans good parts, a secret & (and) villanous contriuer against mee his naturall brother:

UUe sail t' Valencia. Horrors! R f . . . . couu resists boardin'—'n' all R M T hope 'n' anger—t' stay at Genoa. Deem

couu resists. Their milk cow refuses to walk up the gangplank. She'd had enough already, crossing the Appenines.

131 & 132

therefore vse thy discretion, I had as liefe thou didst breake his necke as his finger. And thou wert best

it insane! UUater everywhere 'n' the babe has no food! Chris-s-t-t—free this child! God, strike Kit dead! Fie! She's

A double-edged cipher. (We hear the baby screaming.) Chris-s-t-t! Free Kit! God! Strike this child dead! Fie! She's—

133 & 134

looke to't; for if thou dost him any slight disgrace, or if hee doe not mightilie grace himselfe on thee,

tired. She took a little dose of grog, 'n' tho' hungry fel into rest. Ah, if I c'd goe hi aloft, she home, C? Ei, Ei! Imm—

135 & 136

hee will practice against thee by poyson, entrap thee by some treacherous deuice, and neuer leaue thee

ediate attention t' nourishment is necessary: a heauy brew o' clear uegee broth c'd help. Peel ye peach. Eue—

137 & 138

till he hath tane thy life by some indirect meanes or other: for I assure thee, (and almost with tears I speake it)

ry food Nan tried, th' stormy weather brot up—Ei, ei, ei! Till (SOS!) at last I-I flee th' rank cheesie mess (ha ha ha!) t' meet

139 & 140

there is not one so young, and so villanous this day liuing. I speake but brotherly of him but

bo'sun 'n' sailors tryin' t' stop a leak before yt got bad. I yell "Hu-Hu," 'n' go ioin 'em. U shove in this du—

141 & 142

should I anathomize him to thee as hee is, I must blush, and weepe, and thou must looke pale and wonder.

b-size 'n' poke it till it's tite. Now do another: Hem! Hum! Heh! 'N' soon—Aha! See how uue amass a muddle-puddle, a—

143 & 144

I am heartily glad I came hither to you: if hee come to morrow, Ile giue him his payment:

uoid al ye high water that might haue come in miles from ye home port. Ei, i, i! Ye lacrimo—

145 & 14

.if euer hee goe alone againe, Ile neuer wrastle for prize more: and so God keepe your worship.

se one slept on. Euery waue rolled 'n' poured foggie hazie air o'er her fair skin. We goe more pea—

147 & 148

Farewell good Charles. Now will I stirre this Gamester: I hope I shall see an end of him for my soule

cefully. A distant Spanish shore glimmers. Ere long we'l moor i' the swell of a road. How Irish I feel! E—

149 & 150

(yet I know not why) hates nothing more than he(e): yet hee's gentle, neuer school'd, and yet learned,

'en t' go o'er th' mountain, we'll need t' talk t' these strangers—indeed! How? "Hey, hey, hey, hey?" Can no one

151 & 152

full of noble deuise, of all sorts enchantingly beloued, and indeed so much in the heart of the world,

go on with us to th' road-end? If Nan'll lend reales dobles, I'll offer them 'n' can feed ye child. UUe bot us ho—

153 & 154

and especially of my owne people, who best know him, that I am, altogether misprised: but

rses, 'n' we start by moonlight, with a map. People beckon me—I deem yt a hold-up; a thief wil so

155 & 156

it shall not be so long, this wrastler shall cleare all: nothing remaines but that I kindle the boy

call, then rob. These, tho', B trauellers awaitin' daylight in a tent. Sh, sh! I'll go in, tell o' loss 'n' make br—

157 & 158

thither, which now Ile goe about. I pray thee Rosalind, sweet my Coz, be merry. Deere Cellia;

azen cries: "Aid my staruin' child! Help her to a cow! Go wi' me o'er ye hill to ye bee tree t' brew h—

159 & 160

I show more mirth then I am mistresse of, and would You yet were merrier: vnlesse you could teach me to forget

oney-m-mush t' end R anguish, or remit, O, remit—R cow!" We've set out for ye tree. Her death is so woefully close! I'm mad—

161 & 162

a banished father, you must not learne mee how to remember any extraordinary pleasure.

dened by worry; I lean arrear to lift a bee-nest 'n' expose the honey. A smart moue? Ha! A murmur

163 & 164

Heerein I see thou lous't mee not with the full waight that I loue thee; if my Vncle thy banished father

arose: bees settled on me 'n' hit, hit, hit, hit, hit, hit! We wage heavy uuar 'n' clout them on th' fly. I feel fulee h—

165 & 166

had banished thy Vncle the Duke my father, so thou hadst beene still with mee, I could haue taught my loue

eartless, takin' th' bee food. Do it! Ye child must eat, huh? Be made wel, uh-huh! Steal hunney! Go t' ye child! VVhat m—

167 & 168

to take thy father for mine; so wouldst thou, if the truth of thy loue to me were so righteously temper'd

ore t-t-t' do? I go off t' hide. Haue U euer felt ye hot hurt? I was lost—lost there. No rest! O, m-my mother, whup Kyt f—

169 & 170

as mine is to thee. / Well, I will forget the condition of my estate, to reioyce in yours. You know

or a fool! I find ye cow (ye town merchant sells one) I milk—in go ye sweets—I-I totter to you. The ui—

171 & 172

my Father hath no childe, but I, nor none is like to have; and truely when he dies, thou shalt be his heire,

tal neat fluid is welcome t' ye, babe. H-h-h-hooray! The uuorst is o'er, 'n' Dad's euen kneelin' t' th' h-h-h-h-hiier, in—

173 & 174

for what hee hath taken away from thy father perforce, I will render thee againe in affection:

ner hooray, a-a prayer, thankin' God for her fit life. Ie! I felt there what few men can teach: the awf—

175 & 176

by mine honor I will, and when I breake that oath, let mee turne monster: therefore my sweet Rose,

ul e-easy breath o' death with no restraynt—e'en here, when we're not lookin'. I'm blest t' m-mire R foe! M—

e-easy breath o' death. When Kit was a child in Canterbury, two little half-brothers died as babies, one at two weeks, one perhaps a month old. Kate may have given them "grog" to let them slip away easily, as Kit's own baby might have gone.

177 & 178

my deare Rose, be merry. / From henceforth I will Coz, and deuise sports: let me see,

ay ye ride from Uenice t' fresh horizons. Proceed: let R dreams seem so well met b—

Kit shows how people pray: first they thank God; say they have been blessed; then they ask for something, and soon they are telling Him what to do.

179 & 180

what thinke you of falling in Loue? Marry I prethee doe, to make sport withal: but loue

y reality that fortune'l smile! Amen! But w-wil God like or approue of Kit? Oh, no! "Haue the

His bitter heart shows; trouble ahead!

181 & 182

no man in good earnest, nor no further in sport neyther, then with safety of a pure blush

mountain rise steeper 'n' th' riuer run faster, 'n' poor Nan B lost on th' way," Oy! F . . . F . . . God! (he, he!)" 'N' th'

(he, he!). Just kidding.

183 & 184

thou maist in honor come off againe. What shall be our sport then? Let vs sit and mocke the good

forests blacker!" I go on, feelin' doom'd, 'n' see—Ho hoo! A path cuts thru th' main one. It mvst go al th' wa—

185 & 186

houswife Fortune from her wheele, that her gifts may henceforth bee bestowed equally. / I would wee could doe so:

y to some quiet hidden hotel where wee c'd rest 'n' feed ye babe. We follow it f-for h-hours! Woe! U'l laugh at mee for such

187 & 188

for her benefits are mightily misplaced, and the bountifull blinde woman doth most mistake in her gifts to women.

a wise fool! Pe-u! At dusk we'l find its end—an M T clearin'—nothin' t' shelter ye babe from th' night m-mist. Oh, grief! M-mi blood

189 & 190

'Tis true, for those that she makes faire, she scarce makes honest, (&) and those that she makes honest, she makes very illfauouredly.

rushes t-tu mi shaken heart. Milk—no food! Th' roof a starry sky. A trucvlent owl seeks t' shame me as, safe, he'd chastise: "He-e-e-!" S-see the ha—

191 & 192

Nay now thou goest from Fortune's office to natures:
Fortune reignes in gifts of the world, not in the lineaments

lf moon shine on horses 'n' MT cow out gettin' grass, Nan goin' off f'r water, elfin one free t' t-tout her identity. So feuu

193 & 194

of Nature. / No, when Nature hath made a faire creature, may she not by Fortune fall into the fire?

men haue been here that th' earth's a new audience for my innouatiue frontal foray. O, f-flatt'r R

195 & 196

though nature hath giuen vs wit to flout at Fortune, hath not Fortune sent in this foole to cut off

fool! UUhen it's lit we're off. Foot-foot it thrv th' forest to get Nan a tent—'n' h-hang th' cost! U uuin uuhat

197 & 198

the argument? / Indeed there is fortune too hard for nature when fortune makes natures naturall,

Fortune allows. UUe'ue made a run, found that tent in trade, 'n' Nan rests from her hike. Age, the terror

199 & 200

the cutter off of natures witte. Peraduenture this is not Fortunes work neither, but Natures,

of th' unfit, stares at her. I, u-unfit, cook 'n' serue, 'n' twist 'n' putter tu restore her before we'd uuant tu

201 & 202

who perceiueth our naturall wits too dull to reason of such goddesses, hath sent this Naturall for our whetstone.

s-start on th' siluan path ere food runs out. Saue th' horses! We'll go afoot. Th' wee child'l ride out o' th' sun. We run lost acr—

203 & 204

for alwaies the dulnesse of the foole, is the whetstone of the wits. How now Witte, whether wander you?

oss stones, see nothin' on the far side, h-hi or low. Woe! We towel tuf wet feet. Why trauel i' th' heat? Few do. Wh—

205 & 206

Mistresse, you must come away to your father. / Were you made the messenger? No by mine honor, but I was bid

y not moue ahead at sunset? So which is ye way t' goe? We'ue some doubts, 'n'—'n' you may remember mi f . . . . error. Bi str—

207 & 208

to come for you / Where learned you that oath foole? / Of a certain Knight, that swore by his Honour they were good

ategic tracin' we found th' way. After R feed 'n' a rest, we began th' hot, hot, hy, hy, miles o' heet. O, horror! O, U . . . Looky, U! Oooo!

209 & 210

Pan-cakes, and swore by his Honor the Mustard was naught: Now Ile stand to it, the Pancakes were naught, and the

We saw a man lyin' in th' path, stretched on th' ground near a rock. Was he dead? No, he was panting: "O take th' best! Su-su—

211 & 212

Mustard was good, and yet was not the Knight forsworne. / How proue you that in the great heape

suppose U stand 'n' take what ye want o' my things—I go now t' feed great Death. U who are th' horror o'

213 & 214

of your knowledge? / I marry, now vnmuzzle your wisdome. / Stand you both forth now: stroke your chinnes,

decent men, work on, U! Fil your bags! Try on my remnant shirts for size! O, U, U who drove down—why, U look—Oy! Z!

Z!. Delirious, the heat-stricken youth goes to sleep.

215 & 216

and sweare by your beards that I am a knaue. / By our beards (if we had them) thou art. / By my knauerie (if I had it)

I shade 'im, bathe his brow, wait for ye fried brayn t' uuake. Nan makes broth—but he may die. Ay! UU'd a ray dart e—

217 & 218

then I were: but if you sweare by that that is not, you are not forsworn: no more was this Knight swearing by his Honor,

asy restoration o' his sight 'n' sanity afore we must start on our hike—'n' who *R* U, booby nit-wit? Why 'n' wherefore began th—

The out front lines refer to Sir John Davies, a provocateur at the time of Essex's march to the palace, who did many dishonorable deeds before and after until the end of his life. Circa 1593 he and Kit had written a book together, one part Davies' Epigrammes, the other Certain of Ovids Elegies, translated by Christopher Marlowe. Davies referred to them as the pancakes and the mustard. The book was publicly burned by Archbishop Whitgift in 1599, but a copy was discovered bound with Venus and Adonis and The Passionate Pilgrim, and reprinted, edited by the discoverer, Charles Edmonds, in 1870 (A.D. Wraight. In Search of Christopher Marlowe. NY: Vanguard, 1965). Kit's allusion here makes it clear that the dishonorable man, who worked undercover to provoke Essex and his followers, was the Sir John who wrote the Epigrammes.

219 & 220

for he neuer had anie; or if he had, he had sworne it away, before euer he saw those Pancakes or that Mustard.

y feuer? Wait—I'ue found shirts here, 'n' *poems*! Ee! Search no farther! Ahaa! A broken heart w'd dash th' head! A wooe—

221 & 222

Prethee, who is't that thou means't? /One that old Fredericke your Father loues. My Fathers loue is enough

r, forsaken, goes far away t' die, Uh huh! Eyes open, he mutters: "I felt lost, crauin' her loue—thot—thot the demo—

223 & 224

to honor him enough; speake no more of him, you'l be whipt for taxation one of these daies. / The more pittie

ns took me! O, not eatin', exposed for too long t' th' hot sun, I may haue poor power t' frame mi hie hie hie hie—" Feb—

225 & 226

that fooles may not speak wisely, what Wisemen do foolishly. / By my troth thou saiest true: For, since the little wit

ril moans follow this shy utterance. We feed him ye last o' ye honey w-wi' milk, as it's th' best hope. T-t-tut! A fool story! I! 'T—

227 & 228

that fooles haue was silenced, the little foolerie that wise men haue makes a great shew;

is late. We ate. Can't leaue him, so heaue 'im on th' horse with Elf, see? Walk. Get ahead, test for sl—

229 & 230

Heere comes Monsieur the Beu. / With his mouthfull of newes. / Which he vvill put on vs, as Pigeons feed their young.

ides . . . "Help! Come! He's beginnin' t' fal!" VVi' muscle we lift 'n' sew him t' the horse. Rough here. UUhy no poste house? I vow fu—

231 & 232

Then shal we be newes—cram'd. /All the better: shalbe the more Marketable. Boon-iour Monsieur

rther on we'l see it—I'm at a lo ebb. Th' man wakes, moans: "No, but we'l hear the herder's bell ere U come b—

233 & 234

le Beu, what's the newes? / Faire Princesse, you have lost much good sport. / Sport: of what colour? / What colour Madame?

y a-a narrow stream. Watch, see? for crown-coppers, he'l guide U to the post house. But U cd also follow him to see—uh—a m—

235 & 236

How shall I aunswer you? / As wit and fortune will / Or as the destinies decrees. Well said, that was laid on

ountain hut." We start ahead in th' wild sierra: we all sway, slide, fall down in scree. O, so U do last wishes! E—

237 & 238

with a trowell. / Nay, if I keepe not my ranke. / Thou loosest thy old smell. you amaze me Ladies:

ons later, we met ye lone herdzman, who—(payd!)—took us t' ye M T mail house! I! Like ye last I! of all!

239 & 240

I would haue told you of good wrastling, which you haue lost the sight of. Yet tell vs the manner of the Wrastling.

We have no food. Th' lout herdsman offers little dry cuts o' goat, with stale hay. When uuill I get going south? Low hy—

going south. Looks as if he's heading west-southwest to Albacete, where he can get a road south.

241 & 242

I wil tell you the beginning: and if it please your Ladiships, you may see the end, for the best is yet to doe, and heere where you are,

waymen are on ye road: ye reyes dobles—uh huh—gone! I set ye tent 'n' fish—stupidly fall i' th' hole. We rise, eat. Ee-ie!—bite on a putrid dog!

putrid dog. roadkill.

243 & 244

they are comming to performe it. / Well, the beginning that is dead and buried. / There comes an old man,

Tremblin', th' madman said, "C mi home castle hidden nearby. Go there; ae'l not forget U!" We go, intrepid, en—

245 & 246

and his three sons. / I could match this beginning with an old tale. / Three proper young men, of excellent growth

couraged, 'n' there behind trees is th' castle! M-most willing, we approach th' lodge 'n' try tu go in. Oh, no! N-n-nix! Flee! "H—

247 & 248

and presence. / With bils on their neckes: Be it knowne vnto all men by these presents. / The eldest of the three,
wrastled with Charles

onn!" He spoke t' th' bear. "She's chained, C? 'T's safe t' enter wi' th' babe now. Keep her stil-l-l-l, C! Sh!" 'N' silent, he led everyone in t' rest-t-t. W-we'd rem—

249 & 250

the Dukes Wrastler, which Charles in a moment threw him, and broke three of his ribbes, that there is little hope of life in him:

ember that th' rest of R life. Th' parents kiss him. We reek but bathe (chilli-i-i-i), eat, feed M-moo 'n' R thin h-h-h-h-horses. We l-lie down. Car—

251 & 252

So he seru'd the second, and so the third: yonder they lie, the poore old man their Father, making such

denio's true, sad story c'd make me a tenth good play—not couert, hidden or Irish-shhhh. There! Hen, feel

Irish-shhhh. That play was Troilus & Cressida, about rotten happenings in the '99 Irish campaign.

253 & 254

. . . pittiful dole ouer them, that all the beholders take his part with weeping. Alas. But what is the sport

sure there'd B but smal thot of *us* as th' parallel tale. Strange tho', how we aid it! Tip: hit'l wipe hit! Keep th'—

hit'l wipe hit! Sounds like a sinister SSS proverb; here he suggests a stage hit about a faraway Spanish story will wipe out suspicions about Kit, Emelia, and Hen?

255 & 256

Monsieur, that the Ladies haue lost? / Why this that I speake of.? Thus men may grow wiser euery day.

hope for times ahead; th' readin' may assist U. Giue loue t' her always, 'n' shew some t' thy Kit thru ye

her. the queen. See cipher here in As You Like It, ll. 97-104: Kit's advice to Hen about how to treat his natural mother.

257 & 258

It is the first time that euer I heard breaking of ribbes was sport for Ladies. / Or, I, I promise thee.

grapeuine. Did 'Orio miss letters? I saw Babe at h-her home. Bitter pie starts off for Eire.

Irish Kit.

'Orio. Gregorio (de' Monti). Kit's Italian name. **at h-her home.** Isabel-Elizabeth, Kit's daughter, is living at Audley End with good Tom Howard as Kit writes this cipher. **Bitter pie.** A badly revised peace treaty is going back to Ireland.

259 & 260

But is there any else longs to see this broken Musicke in his sides? Is there yet another doates vpon rib-breaking?

No more ciphers, see? Hen, uue leave today. H-hail 'n' goodbye! S-see, s-see, s-see? Inn-inn-gratt—sr—b-br—br—Kit—Kit! O, shit, it's Kit!

f

Twelfe Night, Or what you will. First Folio of Shakespeare. Comedies, p 255.

TWELFE NIGHT, OR WHAT YOU WILL

1 & 2

If Musicke be the food of Loue, play on,
Giue me excesse of it: that surfetting,

Kit M. begs too much of his lady loue: giue fee of praise to unfit scene text? Fe—

3 & 4

The appetite may sicken, and so dye.
That straine agen, it had a dying fall:

el a—a sinking sensation deep i' my heart: th' neat, daft, hy-gaited Lady P. act—

5 & 6

O, it came ore my eare, like the sweet sound
That breathes vpon a ban[c]ke of Violets;

s a noble maid vvhose wit took her t' ape a brother: faces alike, eyes meet t' encount—

7 & 8

Stealing, and giuing Odour. Enough, no more,
'Tis not so sweet now, as it was before.

er one another afta being lost in waues. Some insist good God is gone! No! R U tu w—w—

9 & 10

O spirit of Loue, how quicke and fresh art thou,
That notwithstanding thy capacitie,

ithout faith t' see His good work is part of th' reunion? Thy cap wil quit at th' end, C? Can a—

11 & 12

Receiueth as the Sea. Nought enters there,
Of what validity, and pitch so ere,

n actor direct th' show? To see th' hair aids th' play—giues the event a feuer ne'e—

13 & 14

But falles into abatement, and low price
Euen in a minute; so full of shapes is fancie,

r felt in all th' past scenes—iust a fit bono finale, see? 'N' U'd leaue wi' cap on? No, Ma'm! Fie! Bu—

15 & 16

That it, alone, is high fantasticall./ Will you go hunt my Lord?/ What Curio?/

t try it! Fling it! Ah, all that colour! Nouu this is how we'l go, mi lady! Ah, can

17 & 18

The Hart./Why so I do, the Noblest that I haue:/O when mine eyes did see Oliuia first,

't we feel th' hushed thril when they see ye best! O, I had a most radiant uision! Oi, oi!

19 & 20

Me thought she purg'd the ayre of pestilence
That instant was I turn'd into a Hart.

My heart aches at this sight: Let no Spring dare t' fade it! Then turn t' one who put U a—

21 & 22

And my desires, like fell and cruell hound[e]s,
Ere since pursue me. How now what newes from her?

head o' SSS duties, who'll ne'er whisper any lewd offense, ne'er make U endure mi clown rule. Chr. M.

23 & 24

So please my Lord, I might not be admitted,
But from her handmaid do returne this answer:

You're in mi heart, but I don't dare dream. Mi pen shal bring thee t' me, shadow'd, from old st-st—

25 & 26

The Element it selfe, till seuen yeares heate,
Shall not behold her face at ample view:

arlit moments beside the leuel water. Thy face shone: I, a heel, felt heaven. Please tell

27 & 28

But like a Cloystresse she will vailed walke,
And water once a day her Chamber round

what made our love increase e'en as Kit chided? Why? Let's B reasonable: wd a lull carry k—

29 & 30

With eye-offending brine: all this to
Season/A brothers dead loue, which she would keepe fresh

nowledge? A poor rouer can't always B free, so it's best finished, lest h-h-he'd feed on U like h-h-he wi—

31 & 32

And lasting, in her sad remembrance.
O she that hath a heart of that fine frame

th time might learn t' do. Ah, a bitter end for an actress 'n' her man, as he, ha ha, affe—

in her sad remembrance. Mary Sidney Herbert mourned brother Philip Sidney for years.

33 & 34

To pay this debt of loue but to a brother,
How will she loue, when the rich golden shaft

cts hot loue, 'n' feels guilt. Ha! Both pay for this behauior! Woe! He who'd let troth blend w—

35 & 36	
Hath kill'd the flocke of all affections else That liue in her. When Liuer, Braine, and Heart,	**ith a false declaration o' fealtie can ne'er B kind t' h-her, who thinks all uuell. If he left her**

37 & 38	
These soueraigne thrones, are all supply(e)d and fill'd Her sweete perfections with one selfe king:	**alone, she, faithful 'n' patient, wd wait on edge for his return, keeping her eyes clos'd, see? Less repell—**

39 & 40	
Away before me, to sweet beds of Flowres, Loue-thoughts lye rich, when canopy'd with bowres.	**ed by wd-be louers than loyal to her creep. O, we must ban this effect! I show ye how we forgo sw—**

41 & 42	
What Country (Friends) is this? / This is Illyria Ladie. / And what should I do in Illyria?	**orn, uain fidelity: stay assur'd, child, this wil rid ye o' all oaths in law 'n' its hi, hi rid—**

43 & 44	
My brother he is in Elizium, / Perchance he is not drown'd: What thinke you saylers?	**in' check, 'n' e'en our Eliza's rant! Best stay the prim widow, only h—hurry—h-hide some i—**

45 & 46	
It is perchance that you your selfe were saued. O my poore brother, and so perchance may he be.	**ntimate, braue sweet ioys t' cheer U 'n' reduce ye balance of ye sad horror. Choose more happy ph—**

ye sad horror. Mary's royal mother's relentless anger, or death of Mary's daughter on the day of her second son's birth, or her husband's last will—or?

47 & 48	
True Madam, and to comfort you with chance, Assure yourselfe, after our ship did split,	**ysic (R present loue) t' cure U of dread o' that royal shadow! Cast out dim fears! Hump M.! <u>Fini.</u>**

49 & 50	
When you, and those poore number saued with you, Hung on our driuing boate: I saw your brother	**I go now: Goodbye, sweet Mary, 'n' no awaitin' th' Boor o' Douer's return! I pray U 'n' Hu-Hu do euer hush, bu—**

th' Boor o' Douer. Kit, a sea captain, called Dover his home port.
Hu-Hu. Kit's nickname for Queen Elizabeth. He explains in ciphers for L's L's Lost.

51 & 52

Most provident in perill, binde himselfe (Courage and hope both teaching him the practice)

t before scourgin' the Hebe, please recall mi chipped, impotent, vagrant condition, mi h-h-hid—

53 & 54

To a strong Maste, that liu'd vpon the sea: Where like Orion on the Dolphines backe,

den sorro that leaves me incapable o' liuing here. O, know that, 'n' so—heed th' Post! Kit

f

Life and Death of King Richard the Second. First Folio of Shakespeare. Histories, p 23.

THE LIFE AND DEATH OF KING RICHARD THE SECOND

1 & 2

Old Iohn of Gaunt, time-honoured Lancaster, hast thou according to thy oath and band	**Undaunted, Marlo author'd this no-action tale of good-bad Ryche, 'n' things that on a cho—**

3 & 4

Brought hither Henry Herford thy bold son: Heere to make good ye boistrous, late appeale,	**ral readin' seem egregious to those prepar'd t' hound Rob, ye boy rebel—oh, oh—they that flok h—**

egregious. Kit uses this word in All's Well, Henry V, Cymbaline—and in Othello, "**egregiously.**" The term may have amused Dickens; in his mystery, Edwin Drood, which contains many allusions to Kit, the lawyer is named Mr. Grewgious.
Rob, ye boy rebel. Robin Devereux. Some hearers thought this play of Richard the Second encouraged rebellion.

5 & 6

Which then our leysure would not let vs, heare, Against the Duke of Norfolke, Thomas Mowbray?	**urtfuly arovnd the earl. U see, they wait, asking for the worst. Oh, he'l be known a hoodlum! Cosme—**

asking. Kit thinks of the provocateurs who encouraged Essex to march toward the palace.
hoodlum. (Its use here is early and may be controversial, but here it is.)

7, 8 & 9

I haue my Liege. Tell me moreover, hast thou sounded him, If he appeale the Duke on ancient malice,	**tised tale o' ye <u>w</u>alk t' th' palace is a lie. He held good chief men at home, 'n' U uuere neuer V.I.P., 'n' he immo—**

<u>w.</u> m upside down to make w. **U.** Kit's writing to Hen Wriothesley.
V.I.P. very important person.

10 & 11

Or worthily as a good subiect should
On some knowne ground of treacherie in him.

bilis'd 'em there, in fear o' death, while U cross't, cryin' "Go! Good work!" Oh, moans! Nouu no

U cross't. U stands for Hen.

The rebels headed first into town from Essex's house, then towards Whitehall, on 7 Feb. 1601 n.s.

12 & 13

As neere as I could sift him on that argument,
On some apparant danger seene in him,

one appears ignorant of Hen's eager inuoluement in this damned matter. His masca—

Hen went to the Tower for this ill-fated adventure. Robin was executed.

14 & 15

Aym'd at your Highnesse, no inueterate malice.
Then call them to our presence face to face,

rade of chaste, fragile innocence may conuince a mother t' shelue U, yet she'l operate t' tam—

a mother t' shelue U. Hen's mother (Queen Elizabeth) shelved him in the Tower.

16 & 17

And frowning brow to brow, our selues will heare
Th' accuser, and the accused, freely speake;

e, check 'n' peer far into U sly rebels who'd sugar-coat 'n' defend coarse behauiors. U R all w-w-wet!

all w-w-wet. all wet. an old slang term denoting unacceptable behavior, derived from infantalism. At the time of the Walk, Hen was 27, Essex 34, (Kit a day over 37), and Kit here calls Essex, Rob, ye boy rebel.

18 & 19

High stomack' d are they both, and full of ire,
In rage, deaf as the sea; hastie as fire.

U see Rob has failed 'n' he's going t' die for his rash act—yet—Faa! He had me, after al. Kit

The out-front lines come close to the ciphers.

f

The Life and Death of King John. First Folio of Shakespeare. Histories.

THE LIFE AND DEATH OF KING JOHN

1 & 2

Now say Chatillion, what would France with vs?
Thus (after greeting) speakes the King of France,

As ol' Gregorio, Kit chang'd this play t' show U th' f-fat effete uncle's vice: 'N' what a sinner! Wreak'n w—

3, 4 & 5

In my behauiour to the Maiesty,
The borrowed Maiesty of England heere.
A strange beginning: borrowed Maiesty?

rath o'er ye boy Arthur, 'n' h-harming England by ye swift wedding! E-e! Imagine, too, a better obese man o' serious mite:

6 & 7

Silence (good mother) heare the Embassy.
Philip of France, in right and true behalfe

His being sarcastic 'n' of leuel head helped bring home a fine trophy after the more

a fine trophy. "Austria's head."

8 & 9

Of thy deceased brother, Geffreyes sonne,
Arthur Plantaginet, laies most lawfull claime

stupid moues of all others—French 'n' English—brot t' intercede. A flame eats away fragyl ele—

10 & 11

To this faire Iland, and the Territories:
To Ireland, Poyctiers, Aniowe, Terayne, Maine,

ments into eternity 'n' old-fashioned warriors don't reach a partial treaty! Ei, ei, ei ei!

12 & 13

Desiring thee to lay aside the sword
Which swaies vsurpingly these seuerall titles,

Tho' disgustin' silliness resolues th' day, we view ye head with great respect. Are hills

ye head. see Act III, scene 2.

14 & 15

And put the same into yong Arthurs hand, Thy Nephew, and right royall Soueraine.	**that we paint as grh-h-hann' mountains truly so grand, or are they deuelop'd in ye h—**

we paint. Kit may be a painter. See his Erotocritos, in which he leaves his writings and paintings in a little shed in care of his mother. Also ciphers in 3 Henry VI, when Kit's art, drama and other things are to be destroyed.

16 & 17

What followes if we disallow of this? The proud controle of fierce and bloudy warre,	**eat o' th' deed? Low falls can be pictur'd as hi-flowin' floods. We worry for th' wile of Euro-**

18 & 19

To inforce these rights, so forcibly withheld, Heere haue we war for war, & (and) bloud for bloud,	**fooler false friend, Lou, who bought R easy loue after horrid threats ebb'd. How cd we win? Chri-**

20 & 21

Controlement for controlement: so answer France. Then take my Kings defiance from my mouth,	**stian reticence sets out t' harm th' deal. Knock off ye fool comment! Frame no merger! Wyn-n-nn, or m-**

reticence. OED says "reticence" not in common use until after 1830, but: 1603, Holland. Plutarch's Mor 841 (R), "Many times, I wis a smile, a reticence or keeping silence, may well express a speech, and make it more emphatical."

22 & 23

The farthest limit of my Embassie. Beare mine to him, and so depart in peace,	**aintain preparedness to stem a tide of blame at home re chief, sith by imme—**

re. ablative of L. *res*, thing, affair: "in the matter of, referring to." Used in legal papers.

24 & 25

Be thou as lightning in the eies of France; For ere thou canst report, I will be there:	**nse error he'l alienate th' subiects. U C, th' fool hath no peer: one gift writ in brief ge—**

26 & 27

The thunder of my Cannon shall be heard. So hence: be thou the trumpet of our wrath,	**nerates th' hatred of loyal men. But at home none preferr'd th' cub, tho' such who unhe—**

Kit reviews the story. **the cub.** Arthur, the king's nephew.

28 & 29

And sullen presage of your owne decay:
An honourable conduct let him haue,

eded help th' crouwn feel shame in young Art's end—alone, U C, a royal cub on a uo—

30 & 31

Pembroke looke too't: farewell Chattilion.
What now my sonne, haue I not euer said

luntary airie leap to town, he who in time cd haue been free, lost al. O, O! K. knows too m—

K. king.

32 & 33

How that ambitious Constance would not cease
Till she had kindled France and all the world,

uch o' stranded lad's abuse t' claim total innocence i' th' free death on th' wall. Who knows? Did all

He's chewing his way through the plot.

34 & 35

Vpon the right and party of her sonne.
This might haue beene preuented, and made whole

the men's brvte threats fade, Hen? Or did one hang on, leading th' pup to iump? Anywhere he e—

Hen. Kit writes to his friend, Hen Wriothesley.

36 & 37

With very easie arguments of loue,
Which now the mannage of two kingdomes must

lects to goe, enemies surrovnde him. Now, what if Fat Ma wake hym? Who's gon-e git U nu?

Fat Ma. Kit suggests that Eleanor may have frightened the boy—that the determinative threat may not have come from Hubert or John.

38 & 39

With fearefull bloudy issue arbitrate.
Our strong possession, and our right for vs.

Does Elinor so terrify Art he springs off to die? Tush! Wil U go as Ur Boar's subaltvrn? U?

This is a private letter to Hen. Kit is chiding him: will Hen let himself be intimidated by his Boar? The Boar is Ned de Vere, Hen's sinister natural brother-dad.

40 & 41

Your strong posession, much more then your right,
Or else it must go wrong with you and me,

He ignored U. N-now, O woe! His gross aggression turns to U! Thy memory o' him protects U. Truly, M.

42 & 43

So much my conscience whispers in your eare,/Which none but heauen, and you and I, shall heare.

(Read the plaintext as the final inner message.)

f

The Tragedie of Othello. First Folio of Shakespeare. Tragedies, p 310.

THE TRAGEDIE OF OTHELLO

1 & 2

Neuer tell me, I take it much vnkindly
That thou Iago who hast had my purse

Kit Marlowe told this story that came living. Take heed—'n' pu-hu—hu! Amen.

f

The Tragedy of Othello. Quarto I. 1622.

THE TRAGEDY OF OTHELLO, THE MOOR OF VENICE

1 & 2

Tush, neuer tell me, I take it much vnkindly That you Iago, who has had my purse	**Kit Marlowe hath spvn yu this story: old, yt came liuing. Uhu-hu! Take heed! Amen!**

Old, yt came liuing. The plot of the Moor of Venice is an old one, but Marlowe was inspired by a contemporary tragedy. Oh-oh! It'll happen again.

3 & 4

As if the strings were thine, shoulds't know of this. S'blood, but you will not heare me,	**So safe in bed she submits to guiltful Trotti, who kills her there—hys own Ann! Woe! Do—**

The steward at the Zenzalino lodge wrote eyewitness details to Duke Cesare. Vittorio Rossi. Battista Guarini ed Il Pastor Fido. Doc. XXI, p 290. Torino: Ermano Loescher, 1886.

5 & 6

If euer I did dreame of such a matter, abhorre me. Thou toldst me, thou didst hold him in thy hate.	**th this mudded true death remind U of a tedioso authored her-him story? Both teach me: m'fallii.**

tedioso. Italian. tedious.
m'fallii. I failed. He tried to stop Trotti (ciphers for Much Ado).

7 & 8

Despise me if I doe not: three great ones of the Citty In personall suite to make me his Leiutenant,	**To mourne his loste childe, Guarini makes Anne's fitte epitaphe noted in ye streete. Fools meet it—**

epitaphe. Guarini set it up in the church.
Fools. Duke Cesare, protecting Trotti, ordered it torn down.

9 & 10

Oft capt to him, and by the faith of man,
I know my price, I am worth no worse a place.

look, broach, destroy it—with no pity for th' innocent wiffe. "Paw! Mama Mamah!"
PACE.

f

A Prefatory Poem for Ben Jonson's Sejanus

TO THE DESERVING AUTHOR, BY CYGNUS

1 & 2	
When I respect thy Argument, I see An image of those Times; but when I view	**Chr. (MA) pens homage t' Ben's wit. He wove integrity intu his weft, U see? E-e! I ma-**
3 & 4	
The wit, the workmanship, so rich, so true, The Times themselues do seem retrieu'd to me.	**de hot errors i' mie Em-T work. U march wi' smooth steps tu the end. U'l see Hi, hi esteem! Test-**

X

There's more

In November 1604, Ben Jonson sold Sejanus to Edward Blount.

Hamlet. Quarto. 1604.

HAMLET

1 & 2

Whose there? Nay answere me. Stand and vnfolde your selfe. Long live the King,

Kit Marlowe wrote of Ned's degenerate h-hy life, 'n' Ann, no less sad, yn huge vvel—

X

There's more

Hamlet, Prince of Denmark. First Folio of Shakespeare. Tragedies, p 152.

HAMLET, PRINCE OF DENMARK

1 & 2

Who's there? / Nay, answer me: Stand & (and) vnfold yourselfe.
Long liue the King. / Barnardo? / He.

Here Kit Marlowe wrote of Ned de Vere's heh nonny nonnys. Alban is glad th' drug's flaua

Alban. Francis Bacon was created Viscount St. Alban early in 1621—Kit's last year of life.
heh nonny nonnys. OED. formerly often used to cover indelicate allusions.

3 & 4

You come most carefully vpon your houre. 'Tis now strook twelve, get thee to bed, Francisco.

permits general use. Vere so cooly beckon'd Francis out to the roof to low-cut hym. You'v wet.

Marlowe leaves us in the dark: Who cut who? Exploitation of an anagrammatic flaw: when two proper nouns are used, they can be exchanged. But Francis never had any children.

5 & 6

For this releefe much thankes: 'tis bitter cold, And I am sicke at heart. / Haue you had quiet Guard?

Here, haf disguis'd, are Burhley, his An, a Cecil. Add to Uere his fukt Queen Mother—Atomick! T-ta T-ta!

7 & 8

Not a mouse stirring.
Well, goodnight. If you do meet Horatio and Marcellus, the Riuals of my Watch, bid them make hast.

So Hamlet hath not left his duty to tomorrow, but his reuenge gathers many drug-dead kin-fools: Cecil! Mamma! Wail: O, I, I!

Mamma. Robert Cecil was 'kin' to the queen; he and Vere were among her secret sons.

9 & 10

I thinke I heare them. Stand: who's there? Friends to this ground. / And Liege-men to the Dane.

See, Dad, I writ it famous; the king was e'en hostage i' th' net, 'n' her hidden hore Ned nelt to her.

f

The Tragedie of Macbeth. First Folio of Shakespeare. Tragedies, p 131.

THE TRAGEDIE OF MACBETH

1 & 2

When shall we three meet againe? In Thunder, Lightning, or in Raine?	**'N' heare U, Hen: He, Marlowe, writes again, enditing her nell in the thing.**

Hen. Henry Wriothesley. **enditing.** an old form of inditing.
her nell. Lady Macbeth's death-knell.

3 & 4

When the Hurley-burley's done, When the Battailes' lost, and wonne.	**She droue her husband to sin, 'n' e'en all th' way to hell, between wyt 'n'**

5 & 6

That will be ere the set of Sunne. Where the place? / Vpon the Heath.	**the waste. But e'en then she 'n' her hero wept to call Fate vile. He ph—**

7 & 8

There to meet with Macbeth. I come, Gray-Malkin. Padock calls anon: faire is foule, and foule is faire.	**ysic'd her to silence, fought to keep a human life alreadie lost in infamie. Black morrow came afta.**

physic'd her to silence. part of the story not seen by playgoers. When Lady Macbeth began to talk, walking in her sleep, her husband, who loved her, arranged for the doctor to put her to sleep forever.

9 & 10

Houer through the fogge and filthie ayre. What bloody man is that? he can report,	**Gone to bloud: A change i' th' pyg. (My thral foreuer, for I honed, whet th' hit.) Aaah, rest.**

Gone to bloud. Macbeth—and Kit's experience in Vicenza, Easter 1605.

f

The Tragedie of King Lear. The First Folio of Shakespeare. Tragedies, p 283.

THE TRAGEDIE OF KING LEAR

1 & 2
I thought the King had more affected the Duke of Albany, then Cornwall. It did alwayes seeme so to vs:

Kit Marlowe made al these mad scenes. Ay, he can iuggle too. He fovnd foot-traks by th' elf-hithe, didn't U?

hithe. harbor.

3 & 4
But now in the diuision of the Kingdome, it appeares not which of the Dukes hee valewes most,

Th' theme he penn'd is not so od; th' king is old, U C: A few of us mai take his trip. Th' woven web: I O U—E-e-e!!

5 & 6
for qualities are so weigh'd, that curiosity in neither,
can make choise of eithers moity.

Mi critics question th' easy way he forsooke Cordelia. I grant U, neat if he tie her to his mi—

7 & 8
Is not this your Son, my Lord?
His breeding, Sir, hath bin at my charge

sery. Instead, he turn'd to honor his bitchy Goniril's sham brag. My i—

9 & 10
I haue so often blush'd to acknowledge him that now I am braz'd too't.
I cannot conceiue you.
Sir, this yong Fellowes mother could;

ntent was to haue father fool'd—like my own Iudge Roger Manwood. To best th' buz, I lost him in a uocal cyclone. O, C! I count'd his shoe

uocal cyclone. Kit and his dad, Roger, had a terrible argument after Kit lost Roger's gold chain at Emilia's nightclub. ("How sharper than a serpent's tooth it is/ To have a thankless child.")

11 & 12

where-vpon she grew round womb'd, and had indeede (Sir)
A Sonne for her Cradle, ere she had a husband for her bed.

her friend when he 'n' she were porn-mad—bed-bare 'n' free. God holds 'is shroud. No one ever had such a braw, dear dad.

his shoe her friend. Kit suggests love was born between his natural father, Roger, and his mother, Kate, when Roger brought his shoes for repair into a shop where Kate's husband's worked. **braw.** (Scottish) excellent. The play was made after James' accession.

f

Mucedorus. Quarto. 1598.
The Shakespeare Apocrypha. Ed. C. F. Tucker Brooke. Oxford: Clarendon, 1971. p 105.

MUCEDORUS

1 & 2

Most sacred Maiestie, whose great desertes Thy Subiect England, nay, the World, admires:

C. Marlowe cries theme o' death 'n' desert danger—later assists shy mates tu end wi' bed ioy. G—

This work was Marlowe's most popular play ever: in his lifetime, ten quartos, and seven more after he died—a play that could be produced at home—a romantic melodrama suitable for eight persons.

X

There's more

The London Prodigall. Quarto.
The Shakespeare Apocrypha. Ed. C. F. Tucker Brooke. Oxford: Clarendon, 1971. p 193.

THE LONDON PRODIGALL

1 & 2

Brother, from Venice, being thus disguisde,	**Gregorio d' Monti uurote this cheesy bomb**
I come to proue the humours of my sonne.	**for his friends vp home 'n' some 'cute neuu**

X

There's more

The Pvritaine Widdow. Quarto.
The Shakespeare Apocrypha. Ed. C. F. Tucker Brooke. Oxford: Clarendon, 1971.

THE PVRITAINE WIDDOW

1 & 2
Enter the Lady Widdow—Plus, her two Daughters
Franke and Moll, her husbands Brother an old Knight

K. Marlowe noodled th' raw pla. A better one's bann'd. G-r-r-r! 'N' U think I had dyed t' flout greed! Sh-sh-sh! Whu'l

X
There's more

The Merry Devill of Edmonton. Quarto.
The Shakespeare Apocrypha. Ed. C. F. Tucker Brooke. Oxford: Clarendon, 1971. p 265.

THE MERRY DEVILL OF EDMONTON

1 & 2

Your silence and attention, worthy friends,
That your free spirits may with more pleasing sense

SS misread, ignored Chr. Marlowe's ninny-uuit play for years—no fit presentation. Yet it sheweth te—

SS misread. The Secret Service was afraid of the Merry Devill, thinking Marlowe was leaking their methods, because in this play a character pretends to be a priest. Ciphers for The Pvritaine Widdow suggest he wrote the two plays together. The Widdow allowed, the Merry Devill was banned.

X

There's More

The Tragedie of Antonie, and Cleopatra. The First Folio. Tragedies, p. 340.

THE TRAGEDIE OF ANTHONIE, AND CLEOPATRA

1 & 2

Nay, but this dotage of our Generals Ore-flowes the measure: those his goodly eyes	**Fool! Betyusold author Gregory de' Monti's he-she tale, fou-ago. See, the answer is yes!**

fou-ago. a crazy while ago.

3 & 4

That o're the Files and Musters of the Warre, Haue glowed like plated Mars: now bend, now turne	**Deaf to reason, Shakespeare did—to frugal Blunt—to win a row when the men were thrumed t' sell.**

Blunt. Edward Blount, publisher.
thrumed. thrummed. Webster. to tell, in a monotonous, tiresome way.

5 & 6

The Office and Deuotion of their view Vpon a Tawny Front. His Captaines heart,	**"Cease to pen," they notified th' author, who answer'd in ire, "Can't nap-off. Vivo! Fiat!"**

Vivo! Fiat! I'm alive! Let it be! Kit can't stop writing.

7 & 8

Which in the scuffles of great Fights hath burst The Buckles on his brest, reneages all temper,	**But th' finish't plai of great hearts has been better lik't. Fresh flesh, 'n', C, Meg, C? Cleo's—guess whu! Rh—**

Meg. Kit's half-sister. **guess whu!** there's always been speculation about the identity of the author's model for Cleopatra.

9 & 10

And is become the Bellowes and the Fan/ To coole a Gypsies Lust. Looke where they come:	**apsody to loue, hearts in hell-heat. Scenes flash by—E-e-e! (We let king be cowed, C, t' moo-moo.)**

f

Lyrics,Claudio Monteverdi's *Madrigali Amorosi. The Eighth Book of Madrigals, 1638.* from *Historical Anthology of Music*, The Bach Guild.

MADRIGALI AMOROSI

No. 4 Ninfa che Scalza il Piede

1 & 2
Ninfa che scalza il piede e sciolta il crine
Te ne vai di doglia in bando

'N' since Clavdio hir'd "Anon" t' pen, if it's ilegible—O, cancel! Ai, ai! Dead lazie

X
There's more

No. 8 Perche t'en Fuggi

1 & 2
Perche t'en fuggi O Fillide?
Ohimè, deh Filli ascoltami

Monti reflect Claudio's melodie? Phff! A hi-higglie lie!

3 & 4, 5, 6 & 7
E quei belli occhi voltami
Già belva non son io
Nè serpe squallido.
Aminta io son se ben
Son magro e pallido.

On quiet Lido beach I sing o' livelie love, on a rime spellin' quest. No one's near—al, al gon, C? "Amo, amo—" O, b-bad piss! I—

8, 9 & 10
Quelle mie calde lagrime
che da quest' occhi ogn 'hor
Si veggon pieovere

I quel ire, 'n' goe pledge mai qveer cloud-echo ta C.M.'s clear shine. Oh, go, give

C.M.'s. Claudio Monteverdi's.

11, 12 & 13
Han forza di commovere
Ogni piu duro cor
Spietato e rigido.

poor, poco, ignorant uuords for great mvzic. Oi! Idea: hide 'em i—

14, 15 & 16
Ma'l tuo non già che più
D'un giaccio frigido
Mentre spargendo indarno

n a changing flo o' voices: Onto d' grim putrid, pour d' incendiarie! Manage—

17, 18 & 19
A l'aura pianti e lamenti
Indarno il cor distruggesi
Filli più ratta fuggesi

long uouuels fer al a' U singers. Plan t' git at d' fragil' pair'd rime—ai! I C initiati—

20, 21, 22 & 23
Ne i sospir che dal cor
Si dolenti escono
Non voci o priegi i piè
Fugaci arrestano

on in a guild of liricists! No, I oppose the process! Convinced, I groan "e-e-e," or cri, "a-a-i!"

f

A Yorkshire Tragedy.
The Shakespeare Apocrypha. Ed. C. F. Tucker Brooke. Oxford: Clarendon, 1971. p 251.

A YORKSHIRE TRAGEDY

1 & 2
Sirrah Raph, my yong Mistrisse is in such a pittifull passionate humor for the long absence of her loue

R Gregorio Monti pens a true piece of life about this s-sousy shril snarlin' h-hateful psycho man, a shrim—

R. our.
psycho. Very early use of this word.

X
There's more

Noches de Invierno. por Antonio de Eslava. Pamplona: Carlos de Labayan, 1609.

NOCHES DE INVIERNO

(The Dedication)

A Dios doy gracias, (señor Fabricio) de la buena ocasion que se ofrece con vuestra venerable presencia, para gozar en esta sitio de los apazibles rayos del Sol. Hurta(n)dome aueys

So Gregory de' Monti penned al ov these crazee colloquies for ye consideration of R Eliza Basset's brain. Uarious severe appraisals ov loue, decency 'n' reason are discussed. Baa-ae Baa-ae!

Eliza Basset. Elizabeth (Isabel) Basset was Marlowe's daughter, born at the end of October, 1594, in Padua. Her mother, Kit's first wife, was Marina (Rita) Cicogna, daughter of the Duke of Crete, G. Domenico Cicogna q. Gerolomo, who opposed her marrige to Kit. Early in 1594 the young couple eloped to Venice.
Marina died in childbirth, and Kit took Isabel to Seville, where he, the baby and her nurse lived with Cervantes. The child's first language was Spanish. After the Cádiz raid of 1596, Kit took her to England to be reared in the home of Good Tom Howard, who later became earl of Suffolk. Isabel was adopted as replacement for a dead baby by William and Judith Basset, family friends of the Howards and the Browns (the viscounts Montague).

f

The Tragedie of Cymbeline. First Folio of Shakespeare. Tragedies, p 369.

CYMBELINE

1 & 2

You do not meet a man but Frownes.
Our bloods no more obey the Heavens
Then our Courtiers:

Chr. Marlowe uurote this too-broad nonny before he uuas sent to be ye monster-demon. O, U ov—

3 & 4

Still seeme, as do's the Kings.
But what's the matter?/His daughter,
and the heire of 'skingdome

ersee th' remake o' this mouldie SSS thing Ned wrote (I'd gag). He thankt me, but half-hated it. SSS

5 & 6

(whom
He purpos'd to his wiues sole
Sonne, a Widdow
That late he married) hath referr'd herselfe

needed drama, so I rewrote the show. A ualid reproof wd hurt me less than shrewish pheelth. O, if

SSS needed drama. The poet speaks of the Theater Wing.

7 & 8

Vnto a poore, but worthy Gentleman.
She's wedded,
Her husband banish'd; she imprison'd, all

truly good pla men shot words 'n' ideas at him, he'd B less svperior then. He wd ebb, 'n' unhand a

9 & 10

Is outward sorrow though I thinke the King
Be touch'd at very heart.
None but the King?

groggy hack uuith a wink, 'n' t'take on th' writer uuho'd B nothin' short o' de best *e-ver*! Eith—

e-ver. This is a joke Ned liked to use to identify himself.

11 & 12

He that hath lost her too; so is the Queene,
That most desir'd the Match. but not a Courtier,

er he'l require some insane match or choose a dated shouu t-t-t-t-t-to be hasht, th-th-tho' it

insane match. The marriage de Vere wanted to make between his daughter Elizabeth and Hen Wriothesley, Earl of Southampton—insane because it would have been incestuous; Hen was the girl's secret half-brother. This cipher dates Cymbeline's first draft c. 1592.

X
There's More

Don Quixote, Part One, Chapter One, Editio Princeps of 1612.
transl. Thomas Shelton. NY: AMS Press 1967. (London: David Nutt, 1896)

DON QUIXOTE I

1 & 2

There lived not long since in a certaine vilage of the Mancha, the name wherof I purposely omit, a Yeoman

Chr. Marlowe English'd the vvhole tale for U, Manco—not an easy feat! Ei, ei, ei, ei! many a pen gone t'pot in mi chr—

3 & 4

of their calling that use to pile up in their hals old(e) Launces, Halbards, Morrions, and such other armours and weapons.

onicle o' th' mad aduentures of a great don 'n' a smal Sancho! Hush! Wait! Printed properlie, it shall run i' los corrales. Hush! B—

Manco. Sp. maimed. Cervantes' nickname; his left hand was crippled. The adventures are mad—Quixote is a great don—Marlowe is Sancho. Cervantes must want the work to be a play; los corrales were the playhouses of Madrid. Marlowe says the book should come first, then the play.

X
There's more

The Winters Tale. First Folio of Shakespeare. Comedies, p 277.

THE WINTERS TALE

1 & 2

If you shall chance (Camillo) to visit Bohemia, on the like occasion whereon my seruices are now on foot,

Marlowe wrote this foolish fable. Coy Micaela thinks U may choose to live ouer eons—a nonni choice! 'N' C, I

Micaela. Micaela Lujan, former mistress of Lope de Vega. Lujan was a premiere actress in Madrid and star of the Sanchez Theater Company working in Naples for the court of Viceroy Pedro de Castro, 7th Count of Lemos. (This letter was written August 1610 from Naples.)

3 & 4

You shall see (as I have said) great difference betwixt our Bohemia, and your Sicilia.

wish it cd be true! If I labor, uueary al day, she has excelent vagani for mi ease. I do so i—

vagani. It. rambling walks. Also an English anagram.

5 & 6

I thinke, this comming Summer, the King of Sicilia meanes to pay Bohemia the Visitation, which hee iustly owes him.

ncline to Micaela! She's the most famous singing beauty in ye theateh—mi hostes to mi hi, hi prickiwikie—mi ho-hvm wi'

7 & 8

Wherein our Entertainment shall shame vs: we will be iustified in our Loues: for indeed—

rest. We run, swim alone. She feeds me. I read t' her, 'n' I tel tales of how I liued—'n' o' U 'n' Lib. U R invi—

o' U. owe you. **Lib.** Queen Elizabeth's private nickname. Marlowe is writing to Hen Wriothesley, Elizabeth's youngest son; together they saved Kit's life.

9 & 10

'Beseech you—
Verely I speake it in the freedom of my knowledge: we cannot with such magnificence—in so rare—

t'd t' come 'n' visit us here. Ai! A rough honest welcome—we like gypsy wine 'n' beer—no fin-fan fee! Democracy! I cheek—

no fin-fan fee! They don't pay a liquor tax to Spain. fin-fan? flim-flam? The Spanish government was stealing the Neapolitans blind. Everything was taxed. See Symonds, Renaissance in Italy, vol. II, p. 530: "The rising of Masaniello in Naples was simply due to the exasperation of the common folk at having even fruit and vegetables taxed." (mid 1600s).

11, 12:

I know not what to say—Wee will giue you sleepie Drinkes, that your Sences (vn-intelligent of our insufficience)

ily offer hospitality, knowing U—U can soiourn elegantly elsewhere. O, I test, seek t' win U now—if I succeed, invent

13 & 14

May, though they cannot prayse vs, as little accuse vs.
You pay a great deale to deare, for what's given freely.

a way t' force U t' leaue England avvhile; you'd C that Naples possesses great charm. Ay, ay! Try to giue th' feo Rey

15 & 16

'Beleeue me, I speake as my vnderstanding instructs me, and as mine honestie puts it to vtterance.

ye slip, vndaunted, 'n' come t' rest 'n' bring th' dear missus t' mi sunnie steep cove! Ae, ae! I ask ta meet ten

dear missus. Hen was married to Elizabeth Vernon.

17 & 18

Sicilia cannot shew himselfe ouer-kind to Bohemia: They were trayn'd together in their Child-hoods;

Englishmen who wdn't be o'erioyed t' take their restoratiue holiday on this shore, Hen. If I cd claim ch—

19 & 20

and there rooted betwixt them then such an affection, which cannot chuse but braunch now. Since, their more

oice, I'd exit th' S. Seruice 'n' announce th' n-new iob of father, C? Worth much more then t' be a hunter 'n' catch th' bad sw—

21 & 22

mature Dignities, and Royall Necessities, made seperation of their Societie, their Encounters

arms o' euil doers. None can see th' nature o' mi presence here. Instead, it's as if I lie i' d' Goy citie t'-t' tr—

23 & 24

(though not Personall) hath been Royally attornyed with enter-change of Gifts, Letters, louing Embassies,	**y a new life in art there, 'n' t-to ayd th' elegant Lemos. No! I'll obserue, get hys plans for hot aggression—but th' ch—**

Lemos. Pedro de Castro, the seventh Count of Lemos, had just come to Naples as Viceroy. He brought with him many artistic people, playwrights, poets and performers, and expected to set up an academy of arts in Naples. Lemos had been Cervantes' patron, but at the last moment Cervantes was told he could not be part of the entourage, that he was too old and ill. Possibly he was abandoned because Lemos' advisor, Quevedo, rightly suspected that Cervantes was a double agent.

25 & 26

that they haue seem'd to be together, though absent: shooke hands as ouer a Vast; and embrac'd as it were	**ances o' th' Moth's o'erthrow R so great that in mad haste she takes ye bad Hebe to B a neuu dad—she gave ut—**

Moth. an old nickname for Kit. **she.** Micaela.

27 & 28

from the ends of opposed winds. The Heauens continue their Loues. I thinke there is not in the World,	**most thot t' this known idee: U liue on in those U procreate. 'N' while I fend deeds, she pines for her Hon t'**

known idee. In 1591, Kit made seventeen sonnets for Hen, explaining the benefits of fatherhood.

29 & 30

either Malice or Matter, to alter it. You have an vnspeakable comfort of your young Prince Mamillius:	**greet an infant chip o' hymself—born a vvriter! O, Micaela, I'm too late—U R, too—to make ye replica! U R sly! U mu—**

31 & 32

it is a Gentleman of the greatest Promise, that ever came into my Note. I very well agree with you,	**st see eye to eye! We R romantic, immensely unfit to rear a little one. We might grovv t' hate a phagi—**

33 & 34

in the hopes of him: it is a gallant Child; one that (indeed) Physicks the Subiect,	**ology dictatin' sin applicable t' U! I hate cheek 'n' sh-shit hid in these methods! F—**

I hate. He thinks about the difficulties of rearing a Catholic family—feels that the priests are voracious, cheeky and mealy-mouthed. Does he invent the word phagiology?

35 & 36

makes old hearts fresh: they that went on Crutches ere he was borne, desire yet their life,

ree the innocent child t' seek the mother's sweet breast, free of their hard, surly ways! A he—

37 & 38

to see him a Man. Would they else be content to die? Yes; if there were no other excuse,

retic, excessiue Moth father wd be most hard on the new little ones—O! E-e-e-e! 'N' you! Eye

Moth. He'll always be fluttering around.

39 & 40

why they should desire to live. If the King had no Sonne, they would desire to live on Crutches.

sh'd think o' thy safety in our love together, C? We don't need children—O, yes, we do! Sh! Sh! I'l live! U—I—U!

41 & 42 (Scene 2)

till he had one. Nine Changes of the Watry-Starre hath been the Shepheard's Note,

Children! 'N' her eyes shone. So I go t' B a father! Ha, ha! We need help—th' tart 'n' th' tease! 'N'

43 & 44

Since we haue left our Throne
Without a Burthen: Time as long againe
Would be fill'd vp

danger around us—what fun! We hope th' little bug wil come before I sail, 'n' 'til then—O! U've a

danger. Not only could Marlowe be exposed as a spy for England, but Micaela could be exposed as a defected Spanish spy.

45 & 46

(my Brother) with our Thanks
And yet we should for perpetuitie,
Goe hence in debt:

welcome dip waiting for U here by R Kit-nest. Don't destroy R h-hope! But the heauen

47 & 48

and therefore, like a Cypher (yet standing in rich place) I multiply
With one we thanke you,

we feel—i-it cd appear t' you an ugly, dirty shoreline, C? Then, Hen—Hen—know mi plea: Charity! Kit

49 & 50

many thousands moe,
That goe before it.
Stay your Thanks a while, and pay them when you part.

th'-th'-th' madman, Kit yn paradyse, says farewel to U! I hope to go by way o' the nu San Remo hauen, t'

by way of the nu San Remo hauen. In May 1611 Kit is to sail to England from Venice for Ambassador Carlton, with gifts for Carlton's friends.

51 & 52 Sir, that's to morrow: I am question'd by my feares, of what may chance, Or breed vpon our absence,	**find men t' trim ye boat. Hope my babe's a seaman who cd foray or succor, not a queer SS writer. Hov-**
53 & 54 that may blow No sneaping Winds at home, to make vs say, This is put forth too truly:	**v t' giue youth o'er to th' pain of harsh SS? No past SS man may want to do it. Will Kyt M. be**
55 & 56 besides, I haue stay'd To tyre your Royaltie. We are tougher (Brother) Then you can put vs to't.	**teaching hys babe uuays to waste evil doers? Noe, you'd rather rot! Yet I hope t' try our utter**
57 & 58 No longer stay. One Seue' night longer. Very sooth, to morrow. Wee'le part the time betweene's then:	**nonnee soon, so R little one's here by May, when I, lost tramp, go north. We've got t' get U wet here ere 'e**
59 & 60 and in that Ile no gaine-saying. Presse me not ('beseech you) so: There is no Tongue that moves;	**'s born. No hitch! Suuimming neat-o here in al seasons, e'en at night! Aee! O, God! Steep test!! Oy vey!**
61 & 62 none, none i' th' World(e) So soone as yours, could win me: so it should now,	**Ooo! So nouu, due t' sea-swels 'n' declines in slow-ooo rhythm—no drownin'!**
63 & 64 Were there necessitie in your request, although 'Twere needful I deny'd it. My Affaires	**I hear Queuedo advises Lemos t' try t' fry free Venice 'n' win ye reward. If the English let te—**

65 & 66

Doe even drag me home-ward: which to hinder,
Were (in your Love) a whip to me; my stay

nder aid to a weary Ve-Veneto, who'd help? "Who? I—me—G.Monti!" "Who? My Chris, ye dreamer?" "U

67 & 68

To you a charge, and Trouble: to save both,
Farewell (our Brother.)
Tongue-tyed our queene? Speake you.

knouu ye treachery?" "O?" "Our queere hore fled to Naples." "O!" "But he'l bust a gut to brew yer advantage!" "O-o-o!"

69 & 70

I had thought (Sir) to have held my peace, vntill
You had drawne Oathes from him, not to stay: you (Sir)

Micaela 'n' I wait as my-my hidden plan evolves: th'-th'-th'-th'-th'-th' h-hot idea, too gros for your ears! Do yu, u—

71 & 72

Charge him too coldly. Tell him, you are sure
All in 'Bohemia's well: this satisfaction

ndah oath, agree to B still? I'l say t' Lemos, "I'l fire mi city arsenal—I'l choose how much U'l

73 & 74

The by-gone-day proclaym'd, say this to him,
He's beat from his best ward.
Well said, Hermione.

pay my bad men who'l aid me as doers—t' B in de city t' blow a great fire! Sh-sh-shhh! Yer tool is me!"

75 & 76

To tell, he longs to see his Sonne, were strong: But let him say so then, and let him goe;

But no—I'll need to h-hire honest Englishmen—yes, SSS! To go to th' arsenal. We'l meet to g-

77 & 78

But let him sweare so, and he shall not stay,
Wee'l thwack him hence with Distaffes,

o as bad seamen—without Italian friends, see? What'l check them? Sh-sh! We-we'l flyt' th'

79 & 80

Yet of your Royall presence, Ile adventure
The borrow of a Weeke. When at Bohemia

city! O, wee'l warn Duke 'n' al before U Hebe enemy arrive! Try to float ashore! Whoopee!

81 & 82

You take my Lord, Ile give him my Commission,
To let him there a Moneth, behind the Gest

Ye elegant Viceroy Lemos is held mum. Months go by! Do it! Think a thot—hire me! (hi time, me—

83 & 84

Prefix'd for's parting: yet (good-deed) Leontes,
I love thee not a Iarre o' th' Clock, behind

ntor pooba!) He decided to send ye gallies to fight th' Tvrk or Dane—for experience! I lo-

85 & 86

What Lady she her Lord. You'le stay?
No, Madame.
Nay, but you will?
I may not verely.

se my mad idea: R Veneto may not B all threaten'd. So why wil all o' yu yu yu royal h-

87 & 88

Verely? You put me off with limber Vowes: but I,
Though you would seek t' vnsphere the Stars with Oaths,

ighs help my bibulous hope o' futvre defense re ivst a wet mystery threat? Wow! Who'l shoot Kit? U, U, U! Th' V-

89 & 90

Should yet say, Sir, no going. Verely
You shall not goe; a Ladyes Verely is

eneto land-hold allouus very slo going o'er Rhaetia. Y-yes, give sly SS y-y—

very slo going. The Spanish troops, brought by sea to Venice, could (if the Veneto were captured) take their time crossing the Hapsburg Alps. They could even carry heavy equipment on their way to the Netherlands and across to England.

91 & 92

As potent as a Lords. Will you goe yet?
Force me to keepe you as a Prisoner,

our trust, for England's at risk, Cee? O-o-o-o! Please say yea to my pleee, wi' op—

93 & 94

Not like a Guest: so you shall pay your Fees
When you depart, and save your Thanks.
How say you?

portune ayd. Look: you'l saue ye shy Veneto to disgust ye sharks, 'n' uue'l away, away, h-Ho! for Span—

95 & 96

My Prisoner? or my Guest? by your dread Verely,
One of them you shall be.
Your Guest then, Madame:

ish tourneys out on ye deep green sea—BUUMMM! May they flee ovr broad gold shore! U'l try my yar—

97 & 98

To be your Prisoner, should be to import offending;
Which is for me, lesse easie to commit,

e ship! We'l hound 'm to Naples for I! but mi SSS R goin' home too, free i' secret by rode, C? If mi too-

99 & 100

Thenyoutopunish. / NotyourGaolerthen, But your kind Hostesse. Come, Ile question you

too plan seems quite noony to you—shh!! C th' uirtue: no one gets kilt or euen bruis'd! You hy-

101 & 102

Of my Lords Tricks, and yours when you were Boyes:/You were pretty Lordings then? / We were (faire Queene)

ones'l send your fit men—where? Here! Yu know, y-ye few actors I'ue requested t' play ye wrongdoers. B worri—

103 & 104

Two Lads, that thought there was no more behind,
But such a day to morrow, as to day,

ed re Eng. Wonder, but B cautious. Do th' wash too smoothly t' start a mad, hy-oath war. H-

105 & 106

And to be Boy eternall. / Was not my Lord The veryer Wag o' th' two? / We were as twyn'd Lambs,

ow else wd we send 'em to an yl retreat? Ay may B wrong, bvt stay low—we'l both trade on R h-

107 & 108

that did frisk i' th' Sun, / And bleat th(e) one at the other: / what we chang'd, / Was Innocence, for Innocence:

earin' new accounts of change in their condition. We'd beck al th' hated fat ass' who'd enter th' net, 'n' h—

109 & 110

We knew not / The Doctrine of ill-doing, nor dream'd / That any did: Had we pursu'd that life,

hundreds'l come, for they're planning the dark deed now. Do hold—wait tu win it at a fit d—

111 & 112

And our weake Spirits, ne're been higher rear'd
With stronger blood, we should have answer'd Heaven

ate when—aha! We'd shovv their own egregious, brainless plan—shredded, ruin'd! O, brother, ere we are kn—

113 & 114

Boldly, not guilty: the imposition clear'd, Hereditarie ours. / By this we gather

own t' B spoilers, their ill charade uud go smoothly. Then—I, yi! B ready t' get rite i—

115 & 116

You have tript since. / O my most sacred Lady. Temptations have since then been borne to's: for

nto th' act: mercenaries slip avvay—no fires—enemy ships can B booted out. Others deem yt not

117 & 118
In those vnfledg'd dayes, was my Wife a Girle;
Your precious selfe had then not cross'd the eyes

suffycient pay fur their evil scheme—th' doers al goin' away—no gorey deeds t' show. D' less seen, d'

119 & 120
Of my young Play-fellow. / Grace to boot:
Of this make no conclusion, least you say

best cart 'em off 'n' let 'em go, now. Spain'l soon kil al yu yu yu yoo yoo fools! Th' ca-ca G—

121 & 122
Your Queene and I are Devils: yet goe on,
Th' offences we have made you doe, wee'le answere,

ery fools'l get dead now, for sure. U ce-hee-eee-eee! Hey, U! We'd wave a nonny, qviet, "Adios." Amen.

123 & 124
If you first sinn'd with vs: and that with vs
You did continue fault; and that you slip't not

I C th' day is finisht. Adio, until U hunt 'n' find a way t' shoot down to Naples. Du try! Svvift, utt—

125 & 126
With any, but with vs. / Is he woon yet?
Hee'le stay (my Lord.) / At my request, he would not.

er ruin's ye only way t' quell those ydiots, who must B met at the end wi' th' Yaweh ov

127 & 128
Hermione (my dearest) thou never spoak'st
To better purpose. / Never? / Never, but once.

Iustyce on rum breaks 'n' retreat. He votes; vve don't rub pepper on the sore—ee! Monte

129 & 130
What? Haue I twice said well? when was't before?
I prethee tell me; cram's with prayse, and make's

No MT ciphers, C? Fie! Let me eat 'n' sleep awhile! W-where's my shawl t' wear—"wea-ah!" Die, U bastard! Kit

wea-ah. He makes fun of Hen's accent.

f

The Tragedie of Julius Caesar. First Folio of Shakespeare. Tragedies, p 109.

THE TRAGEDIE OF JULIUS CAESAR

1 & 2

Hence: home you idle Creatures, get you home:
Is this a Holiday? What, know you not

C, e'en yet ye author's named Kit Marlowe; at his show they no! Oui oui, le chou d' goy! H—

no. know. **chou.** French. cabbage, or darling, dear.
goy. a non-Jew; King James? The king likes the show?

3 & 4

(Being Mechanicall) you ought not walke
Vpon a labouring day, without the signe

e would play to a king 'n' give no name. Aha! But this *chou* beggary will continue, tho'.

chou beggary. He's in England, living on cabbage (This play performed at court 1612/13. E.K. Chambers. Shakespeare Facts and Problems, vol. 1, p. 397).

5 & 6

Of your profession? Speake, what Trade art thou?
Why, Sir, a Carpenter.
Where is thy Leather Apron, and thy Rule?

O, I C th' top head! Work appears: U! Here, U! Don't tarry! Hurry, Harry! Then, after ye show 'n' a fire, we set sail to Naples.

top head. Francis Bacon, now chief of SSS (Robert Cecil is dead).
Harry. Henry Wotton, ambassador at the English embassy at Venice, called to England by Bacon.
set sail to Naples. See the epilogue to The Tempest, another of Kit's plays performed before the king while Kit was in England that spring. In that epilogue Kit says if he can't get a pardon, he's going back to Naples. At this time Hen Wriothesley sets sail too, perhaps with Kit. they may talk about Hen's property on Bermuda, needy settlers there, and how Kit might go to help them.

7 & 8

What dost thou with thy best Apparrell on?
You sir, what Trade are you?

A notable delay! Th' sea water pours thruout th' ship today—worry with

9 & 10

Truely Sir, in respect of a fine Workman,	**caulk for a seam—cruel slime—but by ye**
I am but as you would say, a Cobler.	**sirrau we soon find a way into port.**

sirrau. sirocco? (He's telling us he's a seaman by trade.)

f

A Fvnerall Elegye in Memory of Vertuous Maister William Peeter. by W.S.
Text in the Bodleian Library, and Donald W. Foster. *Elegy by W.S.* Newark: U. of Delaware Press. Associated U Presses, 1989.

A FVNERALL ELEGYE

The Epistle

1 & 2

The loue I bore to your brother, and will doe to his memory, hath crav'd from me	**Oh, Marlo must drum on a hot lie t-t' hide ye low hit our boor cheef made by error.**

3 & 4

this last duty of a friend; I am heerin but a second to the priviledge of *Truth*, who can warrant	**Cecil order'd us t' Deuon for a hy tit-tat iob 'n' wd grant this nana Peter a role. Hush! We muff it! Ah, I—**

Cecil. Robert Cecil was still Secret Service chief. Thomas Thorpe registered Kit's poem on 13 February, 1611/'12, and it came off the George Eld press after 25 March 1612. Cecil died in May.

5 & 6

more in his behalfe, then I vndertook to deliuer. Exercise in this kind I will little affect,	**i-i-i! Th' dreadful exit of the lost criminal, see? Everi one there felt ill, sicken'd bi knowin' th'**

7 & 8

and am lesse adicted to, but there must be miracle in that labour, which to witnesse	**woe, th' miserable circumstances inuolued. I! At th' bitter end, we SS bot a halt—made th'**

9 & 10

my remembrance to this departed Gentleman, I would not willingly vndergoe:	**newly-ruined man's death a God-given mercy. L-low l-lo grime t-t-t' be printed on me:**

11 & 12

yet what-soeuer is heere done, is done to him, and to him onely. For whom, and whose sake,

th' wounded sinner (me) now knows h-hy SS lied to me. I seem to die, too. O, O, ye fear! Hear: "Ha, Ha!

13 & 14

I will not forget to remember any friendly respects to you, or to any of those

Ye will fight any fool SS points out! Try for ye better record, man! One more to e—

15 & 16

that haue lou'd him for himselfe, and himselfe for his deserts.

liminate! He, he! Striue for fauor!" I fled—fled! H-h-h-hot s-sad m-mess!

The Elegy (for SSS eyes)

1 & 2

Since Time, and his predestinated end,
Abridg'd the circuit of his hope-full dayes,

'N' C, dire-chided Francis had dutiful G. de' Monti indite these lies ere hys p p boat sa—

3 & 4

Whiles both his *Youth* and *Vertue* did intend,
the good indeuor's, of deseruing praise:

il'd: subverting 'is pen, I, so others shoud neuer finde how the dead youth died. No tragi—

5 & 6

What memorable monument can last,
Whereon to build his neuer blemisht name?

c waste. Ha! Lull me no more; he built his own demise! Men, mar 'n' burn that name; to be

Francis. Bacon. **built his own demise.** This sounds like Bacon's view; the youth was going to talk.

7 & 8

but his owne worth, wherein his life was grac't?
Sith as it euer hee maintain'd the same.

lost in ignominie is its fate. Ha, hum 'n' haw, sir; receiue the weather's wash: be the 'drat. W—

'drat. Webster. God-rot.

9 & 10

Obliuion in the darkest day to come,
When sinne shall tread on merit in the dust;

hat would teach a man to desert kind SS brothers—I, 'n' not liue 'n' die only in them? Ei—

11 & 12

Cannot rase out the lamentable tombe
Of his Short-liu'd desert's: but still they must

ther stay or leaue sans MT conuerse, to B less li'ble to th' stab (not t' emit th' humid flud).

A miniature story inside the Elegy is identified by otherwise meaningless quotation marks (") before each line of verse in which a cipher is hidden. This part is meant to be read by family and friends, not SSS.

95 & 96

"But suting so his habit and desire
"As that his *Vertue* was his best *Attire.*

Hear U: itt was that he in a' his disguises observ'd at that bitter business.

165 & 166

"Whereof as many as shall heare that sadnesse
"Wil blame ye or es hard fate, the others madnese.

Mas, 'a seems ye ashen fool hath fear. He went arear to share small ale, distress'd by what he'd seen.

187 & 188

"Who cã māk friendship, in those times of change,
"Admired more for being firme then strange.

He drinks with a friend. Danger's imminent. He's gone for home. A groom, Bisham, t' effect a price.

245 & 246

"In minds from whence endeavor doth proceed,
"A ready will is taken for the deed.

Deceit shadowd 'im. Stricken from th' rear—new open'd vein—he fell dead on ye road.

255 & 256

"So in his mischiefes is the world accurst,
"It picks out matter to informe the worst.

Commission complete, th' cur-witt turns—whist! Rides off to seek his traitor-cash. I-e!

345 & 346

"So hence forth all (great glory to his blood)
"Shall be but Seconds to him being good.

There's no blood-gold at the inn! C, his foolish labor got hym doublecrosst. Beg-a-leg!

beg-a-leg. Archaic slang? It may mean that the groom is so broke he'll have to beg a leg to walk away.

347 & 348

"The wicked end their honor with their sinne,
"In death, which only then the good begin.

To hide the bones, he wedged th' horrid n-new thing in a tiny niche-hole in th' white rock.

357 & 358

"His vnfain'd friendship where it least was sought.
"Him to a fatall time-lesse ruine brought.

Th' hateful friend far-spies th' hole as us'd. Unwilling to mitigate, he serves a writ on Bisham.

455 & 456

"Whence when he fals, who did erewhile aspire,
"Fals deeper downe, for that he climed higher.

Where dread law cals th' groom to die, when wel-plac'd friend is free, we finish—phhee-he-he-he!

461 & 462

"And those are much more noble in the mind.
"Then many that haue nobleness by kind.

Many nonneh men can't belieue this handmade h-hambone story. So, blur! The End. Kit.

blur! The poet was a sailor, and blur was the sailor's raspberry (our Bronx cheer), given in derision through the 'trumpet,' or megaphone, ship to ship, when the other ship did something noxious. Lord Say and Sele's letter to Cecil from Dunkirk, 20 April 1605: "their contempt using no acknowledgment or respect to the Lion's Whelp, our Captain of her gave the Hollanders the blurr, as the seamen term it, which the Hollanders returned again . . ." H.M.C. Salisbury MS XVI, 146. "Blur" is a popular band in England.

nonneh. O.E.D. nonny-nonny. A meaningless refrain formerly used to cover indelicate allusions.

Kit. The author, Kit Marlowe, who has just told the real story, signs his real name.

f

The Tempest. First Folio of Shakespeare. Comedies, pp 1-3.

THE TEMPEST

1 & 2

Bote-swaine. / Here Master: What cheere? / Good: Speake to th' Mariners: fall too't, yarely,

E-e-e-e! Here's Marlowe's patch'd tale for Isabel 'n' Henry's marriage, that took ye two to

Isabel 'n' Henry's marriage. Kit's daughter Isabel-Elizabeth and young Henry Howard, third son of the Earl of Suffolk, were married in 1613.

3 & 4

. . . or we run our selues a ground, bestirre, bestirre.
Heigh my hearts, cheerely, cheerely my harts:

heights ere SS brot trouble. Henry, I regret my Rey's cruel lie—he's euer shamed! O, Rey, U R an arch w—

SS brot trouble. Involved in damage-control after the Prince of Wales' murder, Bacon's SSS victimized some of its own workers, including this Henry Howard's own sister Frances. In Oct. 1616 this Henry may have been about to defend her when he died "sodainly at the table." The Letters of John Chamberlain, (dated 12 Oct. 1616). Ed., Mc Clure. Westport, CT: Geenwood. 1979. vol 2, p 24.

5 & 6

yare, yare: Take in the toppe-sale:
Tend to the Masters whistle: Blow till thou burst thy winde, if roome enough.

illful murderer, hopin' to wrest money out o' thy pet son's death! What gain is that, ye low beast? Here, like bette—

7 & 8

Good Boteswaine haue care: Where's the Master? Play the men.
I pray now keepe below.

r men, ye need help to keep th' secret; U R a mess! Ai! Go weep! Betray al who bow in awe! Oh, a

9 & 10

Where is the Master, Boson? / Do you not heare him? You marre our labour, Keepe your Cabines:

crime o' yours has robb'd 'n' hurt us! It's our hope t' make o' ye a more honorable Rey—ai! We euen e-

11 & 12

you do asist the storme. / Nay, good be patient. / When the Sea is: hence, what cares these roarers for the name of King?	**efface thy arrant shame, cook'd by hot persuasion (he he he). Now, tho', we're in a sore distress't state o' engagement. I—**

hot persuasion. Bacon may have persuaded James to order that death.

13 & 14

to Cabine; silence: trouble vs not. Good, yet remember whom thou hast aboord.	**'m in hel! Bacon ouer us: he told me not t' save goy-Bob's record! I row the MT boat, e—**

Bacon. In 1613, SS chief Bacon planned to take many unwanted records to be burned in the Globe.
goy-Bob's record. records of Robert Devereux, 2nd Earl of Essex. Essex's records would have been among those Bacon would destroy, for they'd show extenuating circumstances and some good things that Robin had done, though Bacon had mercilessly prosecuted and destroyed him.

15 & 16

None that I more loue then my selfe. You are a Counsellor, if you can command these Elements to silence,	**nslaued. Ye chef means to fire ye theater, 'n' not let us lo, lo men come in close t' reclaim 'n' saue. Oh, you men, o—**

chef. chief. refers to Francis Bacon.

17 & 18

. . . and worke the peace of the present, wee will not hand a rope more, vse your authoritie;	**pe th' deep vault! Take ye records awaie, free! No! We won't let him trash our honor! Ei! Open**

19 & 20

If you cannot, giue thankes you haue liu'd so long, and make your selfe readie in your Cabine	**uuhen he's gone auuay! Kit'l rouu ye records back again on ye flood 'n' saue 'em! Ay! I'd not lie! Fini!**

on ye flood. Upriver to Denmark House (Somerset House), as the tide comes in.
Fini! A done deal!

21 & 22

for the mischance of the houre, if it so hap. Cheerely good hearts: out of our way I say.	**I fear our chef's a traitor t' ye state. I hope he'l soon rue his mad chef-chug! Oy, oy! Who, fo—**

23 & 24

I haue great comfort from this fellow: methinks he hath no drowning marke vpon him,	**r th' fee of a lo' king, w'd wreck 'n' rvin th' pattern of English historie? Mom, O Mom! Ha, ha! Hum—**

Mom, O Mom! What would Bacon's mother, Elizabeth, have thought of the way he was behaving? How would his good foster mother Ann Bacon have reacted?

25 & 26

. . . his complexion is perfect Gallowes: stand fast good Fate to his hanging, make the rope	**iliating good fag helpers can seem expedient now. Later, tho', cast-off saps might hook s—**

27 & 28

of his destiny our cable, for our owne doth little aduantage: If he be not borne to bee hang'd,	**udden reuenge out o' a boat in brine. Oh, then, al bets wd be off! Oh, grief! Al thy redaction lost! O,**

hook. There must have been such a heavy bale of state papers that Kit would have to unload with a crane-hook.

in brine. He's thinking he'll take the records which Bacon would have destroyed back to safety in his boat on the flood (when the brine comes upriver from the sea) and then Bacon can't rewrite English history as he's planning to do.

29 & 30

our case is miserable. / Downe with the top-Mast: yare, lower, lower, bring her to Try	**I row, row, row t' saue, so th' crime may be brot t' light ere year's end! Phew! Roast in 'ell!**

31 & 32

with Maine-course. A plague—vpon this howling: they are lowder then the weather, or our office: yet againe?	**I-e! No one hateful ruler may toy wi' th' great huge hive of neat English records we own, which appear to tie a**

33 & 34

What do you heere? Shal we giue ore and drowne, haue you a minde to sinke? / A poxe o' your throat,	**knot in history. O, U uain Rey, we'l see U pay! O, row an extra hour—we haue to do a good deed—Ha! Me! He'—**

we have to do a good deed. Henry Wriothesley (Hen) is with Kit in the boat.

35 & 36

. . . you bawling, blasphemous incharitable Dog. / Worke you then. / Hang cur, hang, you whoreson insolent	**s so bad other h-h-high killers now seem loueable. N-n-n-nay, I groan, U cut your own gay cub owing to a ph—**

37 & 38

Noyse-maker, we are lesse afraid to be drownde, then thou art. / Ile warrant him for drowning, though the Ship

lepbotomy that w-weaken'd th' lad for a hit. He had a s-strong digestion. He's merrie 'n' free now. I raue 'n' row. Hurr—

phlepbotomy. An early spelling? (phleps means a vein.)

39 & 40

. . . were no stronger then a Nutt-shell, and as leaky as an vnstanched wench. / Lay her a hold, a hold,

y! Shallow—we shal run agrovnd! "Al h-hands t' y' crane! Take care not t' lean, Hen, lest—" O sad end! H-Hen

41 & 42

. . . set her two courses off to Sea againe, lay her off, / All lost, to prayers, to prayers, all lost.

falls to th' water as y-ye loose crane lifts all our great papers to safe shore. Tools for y—

43 & 44

What must our mouths be cold? / The King, and Prince, at prayers, let's assist them, for our case is as theirs.

e work are at hand: Royal An has much care for us. Hen, stress't, climbs up o'er th' edge t' sit i' mist. I s-stop tu s—

An. They're unlading at Denmark House (Somerset House); Queen Anne, who lives there, has invited them.

45 & 46

I am out of patience. / We are meerly cheated of our liues by drunkards,
This wide-chopt-rascall,

teady my crane, 'n' ask hi*m* t' tie off. Oops—he rose up well ouer R heads! "Cut R cable," I cried madli. Tau—

47 &48

. . . would thou mightst lye drowning the washing of ten Tides. / Hee'l be hang'd yet,

t line seuer'd 'n' h-h-he shot down again, t' this muddy boggy wet well. O, get th' fine

49 & 50

Though euery drop of water sweare against it.
And gape at wids't to glut him. Mercy on vs.

papers t' dry ground—tru safe seclusion. We go ta aid wet Hen: he m-might try ta go ovt awai

51 & 52

We split, we split, Farewell my wife, and children,
Farewell brother: we split, we split, we split.

helpless, t' B l-lost in ye w-wild riparian tide-crest. Well, w-we w-wept all P.M. fer his life—wept fer

53 & 54

Let's all sink with' King / Let's take leaue of him.
Now would I give a thousand furlongs

a needless loss—till at last, look! We see 'im laughing at a window! F-fie! I knouu th' rough funk

funk. Webster. Flemish fonck [?]. dismay, via thieves' slang and college slang.

55 & 56

. . . for an Acre of barren ground: Long heath, Browne firrs, any thing; the wills aboue be done,

of anger: Hen left us 'n' had a safe bath 'n' change in R lobby, 'n' bi error we worried too long. R U

57 & 58

but I would faine dye a dry death.
If by your Art (my deerest father) you haue

aware o ye tide-run i' th' riuer? My buffeted body has to defy hy uuater al day

59 & 60

Put the wild waters in this Rore; alay them: The skye it seemes would poure down stinking pitch,

while he rests inside. He kept me here! What'l I do now? God, my spent spirit can't sail, row! Tut! Kyt uu—

61 & 62

But that the Sea, mounting to th' welkins cheeke,
Dashes the fire out, Oh, I haue suffered

d B a fool t' rush awai. Go in, Kit, rest, then take Hen uuith U. He's esteem'd the cheef of th' seu—

63 & 64

With those that I saw suffer. A braue vessell (Who had no doubt some noble creature in her)

eral investors in th' beautiful Bermuthas—he who'l forsee what c'd B o'er th' sea waues. O, don'—

65 & 66

Dash'd all to peeces: O the cry did knocke
Against my very heart: poore soules, they perish'd.

t spoil yovr chance to sail there! See me chargin' o'er ye deep sea! Hold th' sad spyt, k-kyd! Do U r—

Hold as in hold the mayo. **spyt.** spite. Kit wanted to go to Bermuda, and he did go, in 1614.

67 & 68

Had I byn any God of power, I would
Haue sunke the Sea within the Earth, or ere

esent dear Hen, who saued your life? No! Hi, hi, hu! I know how t' repay a great debt!

saued your life? In 1593 Hen delivered Kit's ciphered love letter to the queen (Bodleian MSS, Rawlinson poetry 160, fols. 108, 109), which gained Kit a long personal relationship with Elizabeth and banishment instead of death for him.

69 & 70

It should the good Ship so haue swallow'd, and/The fraughting Soules within her./ Be collected,

U'd sail a ship t' the New World, C, loaded with goods for Hen's colonists! Bet I'll haue the huge hug

71 & 72

No more amazement: Tell your pitteous heart There's no harme done. O woe, the day.

that Hen rezerues—then, O wondrous day, he'l relent, ope it to me at m-my room. O, A-e, A-e!

73 & 74

No harme: I haue done nothing, but in care of thee (Of thee my deere one; thee my daughter) who

U'd haue t' go o'er there, tho', 'n' heed th' reef—'n' home again—a thief o' my time ere we'd be—Nonny! Chou!

75 & 76

Art ignorant of what thou art.
naught knowing Of whence I am: nor that I am more better

No! No more t' tag afta a rat! Forget him! We tire, 'n' go back on th' riuer w-without th' man, 'n' han—

77 & 78

Then Prospero, Master of a full poore cell, And thy no greater Father. / More to know

g y' stream! From nowhere, fool Hen appear'd: he lept on astern—to rock, t' roll! O featur—

79 & 80

Did neuer medle with my thoughts.
Tis time / I should informe thee farther: Lend thy hand

e th' return to ye flow—diuided. He seem'd ashamed o' my filth, 'n' his G. d. il intent h-hurt me thr—

81 & 82

And plucke my Magick garment from me: So,
Lye there my Art: wipe thou thine eyes, haue comfort,

u 'n' thru. I say, "what kept thee so long?" C 'im mock my grief: "Medler man, ye pry after me too much!" A-ee!

83 & 84

The direfull spectacle of the wracke which touch'd
The very vertue of compassion in thee:

Oh! How c'd I have shipp't water o'er mi knee to his clean dry clothes? Cut th' clever effect! Fuu-e

85 & 86

I haue with such prouision in mine Art
So safely ordered, that there is no soule

on your spite! Hen hurt his arm, see? I-it's held in a Dr.'s cast t' heal, renew. Oi, oi, U-U-foo—

87 & 88

No not so much perdition as an hayre
Betid to any creature in the vessell

I, he shd B at home restin' in peace, not annoy'd o'er ye uuaves—'n' I'l start to cri.

89 & 90

Which thou heardst cry, which thou saw'st sinke: Sit downe, For thou must now know farther.

Sh-h! Chuck it, C? D-don't show U R aware it's unsafe t' trie to hurry home now! Think of how th sw—sw—

91 & 92

You haue often / Begun to tell me what I am, but stopt
And left me to a bootelesse Inquisition,

ift flo against us outdoes mi talent 'n' physique—it'l moue the boat out e'en ta be blown to mee—

93 & 94

Concluding, stay: not yet. / The howr's now come
The very minute byds thee ope thine eare,

t our end. The hope: when we come close to it, ye bridge stanchion myt stay U 'n' Hen. Trve, ye

95 & 96

Obey, and be attentiue. Canst thou remember
A time before we came vnto this Cell?

tvb may crash, 'n' we'l meet t' lie at bottom. U emit a screech: "E-e-e-e!" No, no! U b-be a friend t'

97 & 98

I doe not thinke thou canst, for then thou was't not
Out three yeeres old. / Certainely Sir, I can.

Hen, 'n' hold fast til ye tide turns. O, horrors! E-e! Can we take ye hit? No, no! The contact tore us! U—I—It

99 & 100

By what? by any other house, or person?
Of any thing the Image, tell me, that

opens a great hole, but we hang in there. M-y-y-y-y! Hot bail! No rest! Th' fathom—

101 & 102

Hath kept with thy remembrance.
Tis farre off: And rather like a dreame, then an assurance

s hide a ferry near here. R U different? H-Ha ha! We can B lost in a snap! Take the tack m-m-matter—R

103 & 104

That my remembrance warrants: Had I not
Fowre, or fiue women once, that tended me?

we not mad? Not t' come home, 'n' t' head ye boat t' crash in ruff water? We're weird, man! Ner—

105 & 106
Thou hadst; and more Miranda: But how is it/That this liues in thy minde? What seest thou els

eus, turn th' tide! It's not too late t' save us il hot bastards waitin' midway! Shhhhhh! My need m—

107 & 108
In the dark backward and Abisme of Time? Yf thou remembrest ought ere thou cam'st here,

ust wait for the dumb riuer's hard rage t' cease—then I'd t-take my Hen b-back home. O, me! From

109 & 110
How thou cam'st here thou maist. / But that I doe not. / Twelue yere since (Miranda)

nowhere came a loose tree t'hit us astern with heauy "Cium-m!" I don't doubt that

111 & 112
Twelue yere since, / Thy father was the Duke of Millaine and / A Prince of power. Sir, are you not my Father?

ye craft wd haue sunk, if ye awful rear impact hadn't set her free t' spin. I hear ye yowl to me: "O-o-o!" 'n' I relen—

113 & 114
Thy Mother was a peece of vertue, and She said thou wast my daughter; and thy father

t. Shyt! Wee see thee, f-far away! Are U doomed t' destrvction? Ah, U grasp my h-hand. Uh, that

relent. He stops bailing.

115 & 116
Was Duke of Millaine, and his onely heire,/And Princesse; no worse Issued. O the heauens,

pulls me o'er south. I hold Hen, 'n' we descend awash in a free sieue. Is sinkin' R end? Yes! O-o-a-a!

117 & 118
What fowle play had we, that we came from thence?
Or blessed was't we did? / Both, both, my Girle.

Before the flow slow'd, blest boatmen heed R plight: C them watch, head away toward ye swim—

119 & 120
By fowle-play (as thou saist) were we heau'd thence,
But blessedly holpe hither. / O my heart bleedes

min', helpless, half-dead blobs out there i' ye waues. They row t' ye rescue—sweep ahead! They'll both B

121 & 122

To thinke o' th' teene that I haue turn'd you to,
Which is from my remembrance, please you, farther;

t-tryin' t' moue out here t' intercept us before we sink i' th'-the flood. Hear my h-heart, Mama—you can h—

Mama. Kit's mother died in 1605; this is 1613.

123 & 124

My brother and thy vncle, call'd Anthonio:
I pray thee marke me, that a brother should

ave thy child! But, aha! Ye trailer-boatmen come t' troll ye dark depths, on 'n' on—R h-harm h—

t' troll. The boatmen trolled—trawled—with a trailing drag. Webster. trawl. doubtful late ME trawelle; prob. var. of trail, 1. a large baglike net dragged by a boat along the bottom of a fishing bank.

125 & 126

Be so perfidious: he, whom next thy selfe
Of all the world I lou'd, and to him put

as help! Oh, oh, oh! Th' expedient follow-net'l lift, rid us of some muddy water! I, bu—

follow-net. the trawl-net.

127 & 128

The mannage of my state, as at that time
Through all the signories it was the first,

t life is missing heere! They MT R lungs of more mist-Aaaaaaaagh! H-H-Hen's t-t-t-t-t-t-to—

129 & 130

And Prospero, the prime Duke being so reputed
In dignity; and for the liberall Artes,

o soaked! Terrified, I push 'n' pull in dread, tryin' t' get some proper breathing. Need a bl—

131 & 132

Without a paralell; those being all my studie,
The Gouernment I cast vpon my brother,

ast o' clovdy, glug, spit-out water, 'n' t-then maybe he'll breathe some air. U R limpin' on the

133 & 134

And to my State grew strnager, being transported
And rapt in secret studies, thy false vncle

edge t' stand, C, 'n' instead, ye trip 'n' fall—'n' a great brown tide presses, rushes ovt, C—t' grant my tear—

135 & 136

(Do'st thou attend me?) / Sir, most heedefully.
Being once perfected how to graunt suites,

ful prayer! We R saued! "These good men did not count th' cost. Let's see fit t' giue them bon—

137 & 138

how to deny them: who t'aduance, and who
To trash for ouer-topping; new created

o good reward th' men here cd appreciate!" "So, what do they want? Tuf!" "No, not *now*! U h—

139 & 140

The creatures that were mine, I say, or chang'd 'em,
Or els new form'd 'em' hauing both the key,

aue enough money t' get them a new trailer, C? Remember how they dash'd to R sinkie crash! F—

141 & 142

Of Officer, and office, set all hearts i' th state
To what tune pleas'd his eare, that now he was

f-feature th' case with no net: oh, oh, t' drift lifeless, lost! What a-a scene of despair! A-a! Th' wate—

143 & 144

The Iuy which had hid my princely Trunck,/And suckt my verdure out on't: Thou attends't not?

r cd haue triumph'd o'er us, C? Uh! Don't think not t' treat kindly th' c-city men uuho sav'd ye! Wyt,

145 & 146

O good Sir, I doe. / I pray thee marke me:
I thus neglecting worldly ends, all dedicated

skill, etc.—aye, 'n' their God-led will t' agree and come to our aid—grip me, Hen! So, d-did ye s—

147 & 148

To closenes, and the bettering of my mind.
with that, which but by being so retir'd

ee th' MT net? They'd B so glad o' one which myt bring distant fish in better, C?" I bow: "U R

149 & 150

Ore-priz'd all popular rate: in my false brother
Awak'd an euill nature, and my trust

th' one t' return 'n' make a fit, properly amazin' lu-la, lu-la reward! Assuredly to B paid! R—

151 & 152

Like a good parent, did beget of him
A falsehood in it's contrarie, as great

espect a gift o' life 'n' air: rate it hi! Good times R ahead—sad 'n' bad R gone!" Kool

153 & 154

As my trust was, which had indeede no limit,
A confidence sans bound. He being thus
Lorded,

it, ere th' mad burnin' begins. Soon I must d-d-do it! He's ye law. No chance he'd fal dead. Such sin w—

155 & 156

Not onely with what my reuenew yeelded,
But what my power might els exact.
Like one

w-wil one day be examin'd y-yn clear light—no smoke! W-we hope t' tel U th' truth! My wee tee—

wil one day be examin'd. Bacon's motives in destroying the Globe will be examined. He would destroy evidence of his provocation of James: Bacon would have power over the King.

157 & 158

Who hauing into truth, by telling of it,
Made such a synner of his memorie

n's nothin', but what made ye rumor-monger steal th' high files? You C, if I-I no,

teen. Webster. injury, anger, grief.

ye rumor-monger. To achieve damage control, Bacon spread invidious rumors about Isabel's husband's sister, Frances. She, Bacon insinuated, was the only murderer of a man in the Tower named Thomas Overbury, who wanted to tell of her unsavory affairs. Not true, but Bacon made it seem so, and Bacon prosecuted and convicted her, though the King promised she would never be executed. She agreed to be a goat to save the king's name. (In fact, Overbury had threatened to leak the truth about Prince Henry's murder.)

159 & 160

To credite his owne lie, he did beleeue
He was indeede the Duke, out o' th'
Substitution

'n' tel th' truth, no one wd belieue it. O, what t' do? C, I'd bid—I seek—t' shouu U his deeds: I, I! E-e-e-e-e-e!

his. Bacon's.

161 & 162

And executing th outward face of Roialtie
With all prerogatiue: hence his Ambition
growing:

Go, go, go: If we explore frustrated hi, hi ambition, hate 'n' anger wil crawl out: it can't hide in caue

163 & 164

Do'st thou heare? / Your tale, Sir, would cure deafeness.
To have no Schreene between this part he plaid,

o' deceit foreuer. Two sad hits he planned led ta his neat secret power o'er th' Souse-Rey. (An able Hu-Hu u—

two sad hits. murders of Prince Henry and Thomas Overbury, who threatened to leak about Prince Henry's death. **th' Souse-Rey.** King James I.
Hu-Hu. Queen Elizabeth. The story of this nickname is told in ciphers for Love's Labor's Lost.

165 & 166

And him he plaid it for, he needes will be Absolute Millaine, Me (poore man) my Librarie

nintimidated by her son: new bad Roi fears him.) I, a member-pal, am i'-i' hell-'ell-'ell! Pee-uoo!

her son. Bacon was Elizabeth's son by Francis Walsingham.
new bad Roi. James.
member-pal. Kit was a longtime member of Bacon's SSS.

167 & 168

Was Dukedome large enough: of temporall roalties
He thinks me now incapable. Confederates

His fulsome web-control makes an innocent girl th' goat of a murder. We speak o' a dee-deep hell! A

an innocent girl. Frances Howard must have been told she must sacrifice herself to save the king's name. She received royal pardon, her name forever blackened. Her brother Henry died, perhaps because he tried to speak for her.

169 & 170

(so drie he was for Sway) with King of Naples
To giue him Annuall tribute, doe him homage

grim, awful, to me inhuman habit o' destroying helpers to aid his false king. He wo-woue a

inhuman. Bacon cruelly disposed of helpers. These people, hired by his SSS, were hanged to save the honor of the crown: Sir Gervase Helwys, installed as Lieutenent of the Tower; Richard Weston, underkeeper at the Tower; Anne Turner, mistress of Sir Arthur Mainwaring; James Franklin, apothecary. Frances Howard and Robert Carr were promised pardons and got them. GPV Akrigg. Jacobean Pageant. NY: Atheneum, 1974. Edward Le Comte. The Notorious Lady Essex. NY: Dial Press, 1969.

171 & 172

Subiect his Coronet, to his Crowne and bend The Dukedom yet vn bow'd (alas poore Millaine)

web a' lies 'n' couer'd Roial crime. He did bonny honest souls t' death. Woe! U don't pack me in to B

173 & 174

To most ignoble stooping. / Oh the heauens: Marke his condition, and th' euent, then tell me

one more lost honest agent (he-he!) sentenced to hang! I'm leauin'! I'm old—no hits! Kit put both

175 & 176

If this might be a brother. / I should sinne To thinke but Noblie of my Grandmother,

brain 'n' time on bleak rough SS hits. Oh, if I fire th' Globe, then I'd t-try t' bum home 'n' do

177 & 178

Good wombes haue borne bad sonnes. Now the Condition. This King of Naples being an Enemy

nothing: swim, read, sit i' the sun. N-no plays. Go on hikes. A good fond woman, C? Bene, bene, bene! O, B

179 & 180

To me inueterate, hearkens my Brothers suit,/Which was, That he in lieu o' th' premises,

sure—no mistake—this heat iob's th' last teen-sin I haue t' cope with here! Hurry! We're m-m—

181 & 182

Of homage, and I know not how much Tribute,
Should presently extirpate me and mine

akin' extreme news today, Hen: I'l get burnin' wad t' th' humid roof 'n' hope t' C a plume o' smo—

183 & 184

Out of the Dukedome, and confer faire Millaine
With all the Honors, on my brother: Whereon

ke, then flame. Our honest men'l watch for harm. Ready, I lie low on the roof. O-o, the burnin' died!

185 & 186

A treacherous Armie leuied, one midnight Fated to th' purpose, did Anthonio open

I re-ignite th' damp hard thatch, fan it. O, don't die! Unresolued, I pause, ope one more o—

187 & 188

The gates of Millaine, and i'th' dead of darkenesse/ The ministers for th' purpose hurried thence

ilee depression i' the roof t' fire. Sudden flames rise, run, race past me. H-Hen, I thank'd God the that—

189 & 190

me, and thy crying selfe. / Alack, for pitty.
I not remembering how I cride out then

ch was catchin', but ye-ye hot fire kept me from daring t' retire! O, I'll end ignomyn—

191 & 192

Will cry it ore againe: it is a hint
That wrings mine eyes too't. / Heare a little further,

iously railing at arson. With some water (tee hee) I reach air 'n' get t' thy lift-line. I t-tr—

193 & 194

and then I'le bring thee to the present businesse
Which now's vpon's: without the which, this Story

y t' grab the rope, but sh-sh-sh-sh-sh-shit, I s-slip, 'n' over I went, 'n' woe! I e'en went t' hit the countdown! Chie—

195 & 196

Were most impertinent. / Wherefore did they not / That houre destroy vs? / Well demanded wench:

f Wotton hvrried to med me while ye honest crew emptied R theatre. Th' wynd swel'd, an' endorse—

197 & 198

My Tale prouokes that question: Deare, they durst not,
So deare the loue my people bore me: nor set

d th' horror as ye dear ol' oyl'd house burns, 'n' my t-toe—repeat—t-toe skin peels: Eeee-oo! T-t-teum paquem.

199 & 200

a marke so bloudy on the businesse; but
With colours fairer, painted their foule ends.

Bi dark, ye hopeless buildin' was consumed. In tears of sorro uue left the hot ruin ta be

201 & 202

In few, they hurried vs a-boord a Barke,
Bore vs some Leagues to Sea, where they prepared

look't at o'er ye mud barrier by apes who'd have us preserve the browned ashes. E-e! A grief

mud barrier. The Globe Theater was in a muddy spot on the south bank of the Thames. The honest men must have made a mud wall to prevent the spread of flames.

203 & 204

A rotten carkasse of a Butt, not rigg'd,
Nor tackle, sayle, nor mast, the very rats

cloaks a ghastly site—a krater o' dust! After trayter Bacon's men R gone, rvn t-to

205 & 206

Instinctiuely haue quit it: There they hoyst vs
To cry(e) to th' Sea, that roard to vs; to sigh

get t-to our haul I hid at An's, reqvestin' her t-to save it i' secret. O, thy-thy-thy-thy stoic sou—

207 & 208

To th' windes, whose pitty sighing backe againe
didvsbutlouingwrong / Alack, what trouble

l brings advantage: hiding our haul, we wait—test ye sick, sobbing pig. How t' know the lout-cad—

sobbing pig. James.

209 & 210

Was I then to you? / O, a cherubin
Thou wast that did preserue me;
Thou didst smile,

's t-thot re Spain's entry here? Th' mad dad watches, but wd he loue it? Oui, oui, oui! Sm—

Spain's entry. James considers a Spanish match for his son Charles.

211 & 212

Infused with a fortitude from heauen,
When I haue deck'd the sea with drops full salt,

ile! U look'd in, 'n' when th' theatre was fast-fired, we saued dated files for H.M. Hu-Hu. Pictu—

H.M. Hu-Hu. Her Majesty Hu-Hu. Queen Elizabeth. She was dead, but some of these records were from years of her reign. Bacon would rewrite history.

213 & 214

Vnder my burthen groan'd, which rais'd in me
An vndergoing stomache, to beare vp

re Bacon reachin' hi heights 'n' great power n-novv, by drumming dread made to vns—

215 & 216

Against what should ensue.
How came we a shore?
By providence diuine, / Some food, we had,

eat cowed, bad Iames, who fears a no-hope day when his guilt—shoved—comes under uiew on

217 & 218

. . . and some fresh water, that A noble Neopolitan Gonzalo / Out of his Charity, (who being then appointed

al fronts. Oi! In a bad haze, he'l beg t' do anything to postpone or escape that awful time when no honor i—

219 & 220

Master of this designe) did giue vs, with Rich garments, linnens, stuffs, and necessaries

s seen in his dead face—nothin' t' revere: such smug, nasti, infradig grifts 'n' stews slide sm—

infradig. infradignitatem. Webster. beneath dignity. abbreviated infradig.

221 & 222

Which since haue steeded much, so of his gentlenesse
Knowing I lov'd my bookes, he furnishd me

elly schemes into his buffoon court! An knew o' his one huge wicked deed: she nudg's me. Sh! Sh! Me! I-I!

223 & 224

From mine owne Library, with volumes, that I prize aboue my Dukedome. / Would I might But euer see that man.

Wyl she bid me zip immediate reuenge? That nut-rut lout for a-a lamb? I knew she'd B home tomorrow. I-I'ue my vu—

225 & 226

Now I arise,
Sit still and heare the last of our sea-sorrow:/Heere in this Iland we arriu'd, and heere

lture worn e'en in error. Ae, ae! Al th' dear wants is a rite hidin' hole to saue his raw, sordid files. She

hidin' hole. Evidence suggests the Banquet House at Whitehall.

227 & 228

Haue I thy Schoolemaster, made thee more profit/Then other Princesse can, that haue more time

hopes that seen after centuries they'd proue a relic more h-historic than hammeee-ma'm to othe—

229 & 230

For vainer howres; and Tutors, not so carefull.
Hevens thank you for't. And now I pray you Sir,

r viewers. *Far years alter not a sour plot*! R voo nonny—nonny? H-h-he writ sick stuff! Adou, adou!

alter not a sour plot! Anne wanted James to be judged in the distant future, but . . .
nonny-nonny? Kit says, are you crazy? Bad is bad.
Danish Anne spoke little English. They seem to be talking in pidgin French.

231 & 232

For still 'tis beating in my minde; your reason For raysing this Sea-storme? / Know thus far forth,

So another generation'l iudge th' beast. Al my work is for nothin'. F-fr-frustration is my misssry.

233 & 234

By accident most strange, bountifull Fortune
(Now my deere Lady) hath mine enemies

Sailin' home duty-free t' n-new babe 'n' Micaela. Need her—my only good fit cunt. Must rest.

Micaela. Micaela Lujan, Kit's second wife, a famous Spanish actress who was in Naples with the Sanchez Company of players. For years she'd been the mistress of Lope de Vega.

235 & 236

Brought to this shore: and by my prescience I finde my Zenith doth depend vpon	**Goodbye, An. Don't U see yovr c-creep spends t' th' end? Find hyz mine i' th' h-hi brim pot!**

h-hi brim pot. treasure pot. In 1609 James had been given secret access to the treasury by Bacon, and James was mining it, à la the Trophonean Den. After a disagreement with Cecil, Bacon tried to improve his own state by calling "a Commission Touching the King's Service"—three meetings held at Michael Hicks' home. Spedding. Works of Bacon, vol. XI, p 131. Bacon got his idea of actually making a hole in the treasury from a legend he put in his book, De Sapientia Veterum.

237 & 238

A most auspitious starre, whose influence If now I court not, but omit; my fortunes	**But no mercy! "Poor Iames" must restore that s-stolen stuff now! "Oui, oui!" Fui! I can't win.**

"Poor Iames." conversation with Queen Anne continues.

239 & 240

Will euer after droope: heare cease more questions, Thou art inclinde to sleepe: tis a good dulnesse,	**So I relent, smile, prepare t' conceal saued files as she wished. "Goot!" No quarrel! Indeed, uue R toe to toe.**

241 & 242

and giue it way: I know thou canst not chuse: Come away, Seruant, come; I am ready now,	**O, An, I thot, ye'ue a wound: I kiss the tears 'n' go weauin' away toward ye anno MMMCCCC. U**

anno MMMCCCC. The year 3,400, when the time capsule might be opened.

243 & 244

Approach my Ariel. Come/ All haile, great Master, graue Sir, haile: I come	**release me—I'l sail home t' eat ye real magic caro rauioli. P-pra-agh! Chr. M.**

f

Henry VIII. First Folio of Shakespeare. Histories, p 205.

THE FAMOUS HISTORY OF THE LIFE OF KING HENRY THE EIGHT

Prologue

1 & 2

I Come no more to make you Laugh, Things now, That beare a Weighty, and a Serious Brow,	**Kit M. made the gunshot scene to burn th' Globe! Ai, ai, ai! O Woe, O Woe! Harry may wrong us a—**

3 & 4

Sad, high, and working, full of State and Woe: Such Noble Scaenes, as draw the Eye to flow	**bout ye firing: we all know he was told what he should do 'n' confess'd a strange case a' fe—**

5 & 6

We now present. Those that can Pitty, heere May (if they think it well) let fall a Teare,	**sterin' hate o' ye players' temple. What a fate, chief! Why not let Kit write—tell Ann the**

Aha! The original plan was to make Harry Wotton the goat—he must confess to arson. Kit says no! Let me write an accident into the play.
Ann. Ann Boleyn, a character in the play.

7 & 8

The Subiect will deserve it. Such as giue Their Money out of hope they may beleeue, May heere finde Truth too.	**shots R a greetin', but O! You smel ye thatch! I-e, i-e, i-e! Ye fire'l come with speed to burn uuhat U loued (he-he-e! My feet).**

shots R a greetin'. Shots were fired to greet King Henry the VIII in the play (Act 1, scene 4), and the concocted story was that these shots ignited the thatched roof of the theatre. (ciphers in The Tempest). To help start the fire, Kit had to be on the roof—he burned his feet.

9 & 10

. . . Those that come to see
Onely a show or two, and so agree
The Play may passe (If they be still, and willing,

So tho' Harry's not ye low goat, it happens al th' same, 'n' ye Globe flames to a sad, wet, illicit end. See who ye

goat. one who takes blame.

11 & 12

Ile undertake may see away their shilling
Richly in two short houres. Onely they

world'l see as maker o' all this: not Rey-Harry! Iust ye hot gun which hit in ye eye line

Rey-Harry. Was Harry playing King Henry VIII in the show? The burning was King James' fault—not Harry's; Bacon had ordered his agents to destroy papers incriminating King James.
eye line. The horizon line of the theatre? The shots hit the roof, but it was damp.

13 & 14

That come to heare a Merry, Bawdy Play,
A noyse of Targets: Or to see a Fellow

t' set ye ol' wet roof aflame at rat-Bacon's order. Whoa! My *play* here's ye goat! E—

15 & 16

In a long Motley Coate, garded with yellow,
Will be deceyu'd. For gentle Hearers, know

ach bro.'s guilty—all will regret ye crime. Why don't we follow good Anne? Take needed e—

17 & 18

To ranke our chosen Truth with such a show
As Foole, and Fight is, beside forfeyting

ualuation, then charge this beast-rey with his wickedness! Don't goof off, Frosh, or U

19 & 20

Our owne Braines, and the Opinion that we bring
To make that onely true, we now intend,

lose the way to bring out new truth re a knowne bad man. No, no, I'd not threaten: I-I weep in

onely true, we now intend. On the day the Globe burned this play was presented with title All Is True.
beast rey . . . bad man. See ciphers for The Tempest.

21 & 22

Will leaue us neuer an Understanding Friend.
Therefore, for Goodnesse sake, and as you are knowne

sorrow for those greedy needs 'n' ask return of R gold, leaked euen as we saue in uain. U lead Ann in nef—

return of R gold. Bacon is stealing money from the State treasury to give James (Bacon was inspired by the old legend of the Trophonean Den).
Ann. James's wife—the queen.

23 & 24

The First and Happiest Hearers of the Towne,/Be sad, as we would make ye. Thinke ye see	**arious ways she hated. We'd make the festered beef-pie plans known t' history. Ae! The e—**

25 & 26

The uery Persons of our Noble Story, As they were Liuing: Thinke you see them Great,	**ager sleuth's hot, yet must lose his errant prey foreuer. But Oi! Keen, I go on, when ye y—**

27 & 28

And follow'd with the generall throng, and sweat Of thousand Friends: Then, in a moment, see	**ears'l find me an old-fashion'd long-lost father who antedates th' new regime, 'n' th' wound ten—**

29 & 30

Howsoone this Mightinesse, meets Misery: And if you can be merry then, Ile say A man may weepe upon his Wedding day.	**ds t' B forgot in ye massiue waste, 'n' my cry o' payn's unheard. In deep midnight we men hoise my sails, 'n' hie away home. E-e-e!**

my sails. Kit was captain of his own little ship. He was going to Naples. (Hen Wriothesley, who sailed at that time, may have sailed part-way with him.)
E-e-e! a cry of pain.

Act 1, scene 1
1 & 2

Good morrow, and well met. How haue ye done Since last we saw in France? I thanke your Grace	**T' saue clean Harry from woe, low Kit resewed this ol' wonder in one day! Who can gage me? U can:**

old wonder. This play of Henry VIII, politically incorrect for James, had probably been kept for years at the bottom of Kit's trunk. **gage.** Webster. gauge.

3 & 4

Healthfull, and euer since a fresh Admirer Of what I saw there. / An vntimely Ague	**A drama neuer used gets a new scene wi' a live fire-arm that'll fal 'n' hit ye ruf! H-h-ho!**

5 & 6

Staid me a Prisoner in my Chamber, when Those Sunnes of Glory, those two Lights of Men	**An insult when ye Globe was fired! Hate yt! No hope for SSS. I'm goin' home, 'n' t-t' Rome SS. Chr. M.**

f

Coriolanus. First Folio of Shakespeare. Tragedies, p 1.

THE TRAGEDY OF CORIOLANUS

1 & 2
Before we proceed any further, heare me speake.
You are all resolu'd rather to dy then to famish?

Kit Marlowe's lyfe has euer been profoundly sad. Rope, heare me, you are the father to death. C, err—

3 & 4
First you know, Caius Martius is chiefe enemy to the people
Let vs kill him, and wee'l haue Corne at our own price.

ors have killed Kit's name in epic transport far from home. Cecil, I Cee U in it, yu-u-u, who we hate. Sleepe now; yu lost.

f

This play touches facets of the life of Robert Devereux, 2nd Earl of Essex.
Cecil. Kit resents what he considers Robert Cecil's slyly successful efforts to ruin gullible Essex—and harm Kit.
Sleepe now. Robert Cecil died, still chief of SSS, on 24 May 1612.

The Life of Tymon of Athens. First Folio of Shakespeare. Tragedies.

THE LIFE OF TYMON OF ATHENS

1 & 2

Good day Sir. / I am glad y'are well.
I haue not seene you long, how goes the World?

Laugh! Howl! Oldy Gregorio de' Monti has loosely wouen dyed water again. See,

3 & 4

It weares sir, as it growes,
I that's well knowne:/But what particular Rarity? What strange,

his witts rust away—loss irreparable. 'E waits to walk, run, charge in the water! Grant witt

5 & 6

Which manifold record not matches: see Magicke of Bounty, all these spirits thy power

to set surch t' shadow, catch 'n' kill his married wife before he goes to play Tymon! Men, pic—

married wife. Micaela. She came back, and things got better.

7 & 8

Hath coniur'd to attend. I know the Merchant.
I know them both; th' other's a Ieweller.

ture 'im, check'd, alone, then bemoan that horrid state! Now think he'l write th' hoot? W—

9 & 10

O 'tis a worthy Lord.
Nay that's most fixt.
A most incomparable man, breath'd as it were,

hat pla-man *in extremis* writes o' holiday? M-Manco! Brother's sad t-t-t-t-to B so far away!

Manco. Cervantes' nickname. He died in Madrid, in a diabetic coma, 13/23 April, 1616. Kit (his friend Sancho Panza) was far away in Italy./ **t-t-t-t-to.** Cervantes stammered.

11 & 12

To an vntyreable and continuate goodnesse: He passes./I haue a Iewell heere./O pray let's see't.	**Euen as hope was stale, as ye resolve to die alone in Spain, Sancho'l be there yet t' greet 'n' ade U.**

13 & 14

For the Lord Timon, sir? If he will touch the estimate. But for that—	**Wait for me t'—test! I'l arriue. U'l B seein' th-th-th-th' ol' Fido-foot. Chr. M.**

test. The old way to test diabetes was to taste the urine for sweetness.

f

The Two Noble Kinsmen. Quarto, 1634.
The Shakespeare Apocrypha. Ed. C. F. Tucker Brooke. Oxford: Clarendon, 1971. p 309.

THE TWO NOBLE KINSMEN

1 & 2
Roses their sharpe spines being gon,
Not royall in their smels alone

Iohn 'n' Monti pen this playe. I'l-lose sense, G-r-r-r-r—so, reasonable, he gits

Iohn. John Fletcher came to the English embassy in Venice in spring 1618 with the Queen's Players and his brother Nathan, who'd been Harry's chaplain. Old friends gathered in Venice then to help defeat the Spanish plot. After it was over, an afternoon playparty was held in the embassy house, where this farce by John and Kit was performed. Two noble kinsmen, Henry Wriothesley and Henry Vere, took the leading roles. Kit was having intermittent mental problems and this was probably his last dramatic work, though he was able to manage embassy business, prepare a tentative constitution for a proposed Virginia colony, and write to the Secretary of State for three and a half more years.

3 & 4
But in their hew. / Maiden Pinckes, of odour faint,
Dazies smel-lesse, yet most quaint

quietly t' work t' help me out as I toss at sea. Indeed he's a fine bon friend, C, 'n' mi Misuz

mi Misuz. Micaela Lujan, a famed Spanish actress, singer and dancer. They were church-married in 1616.

5 & 6
And sweet Time true.
Prim-rose first borne child of Ver,

acts to, 'n' seems freed from her terrible widouv trip, 'n' I—

7 & 8
Merry Spring times Herbinger
With her bels dimme.
Oxlips, in their Cradles growing,

'm the grim iailer (gr-gr-gr!) weddin' his miss, 'n' th' two Hens excel in R pri-prime roles. B-bye!

9 & 10
Mary-golds, on death beds blowing,
Larkes-heeles trymme.

(He's addled, no longer able t' make his Wm. S. rymes. Gr!) Oy, let B!

f

Letters and Dispatches of Sir Henry Wotton [and Gregory de' Monti].
London: Wm Nicholl. The Shakspeare [sic] Press, 1850. For the Roxeburghe Club.

SALUTATION ON DE' MONTI'S DISPATCHES FOR SEC'Y OF STATE ROBERT NAUNTON, 1619-1621

Illustrissimo Signore mio Signore sempre Osservandissimo.

I-e, U!
So Marlo pens, So d' Monti signs,
S-so Sir Roger lives i' mi rimes!

I-e, U! Hi, you! An informal inner salutation.
Here Marlowe enters his English and Italian names and mentions his natural dad Sir Roger (Sir John Falstaff) as part of Marlowe's dramatic poetry. The compromise of Kit's life is compressed into these lines.

The plaintext, Englished: "My most illustrious Lord, always most revered."

f

Captain John Bargrave's A Form of Polisie.
Papers of Lord Sackville at Knole Park, Kent. From print of Susan Myra Kingsbury. Records of The Virginia Co. of London, vol iv.

CAPTAIN JOHN BARGRAVE. A FORM OF POLISIE, BY IGNOTUS.

TITLE

A FORME OF POLISIE TO PLANTE AND GOVERNE MANY FAMILIES IN VIRGINEA, SOE AS IT SHALL NATURALLY DEPEND ONE THE SOVERAIGNETYE OF ENGLAND.

Monti penned this l-legal effort again (paid-aid), in response to the need for a nevv government. Yes, ye goal is e'en for all, all o' us, man! Ai, yai!

f

Captain John Bargrave. A Form of Polisie (by Ignotus). Papers of Lord Sackville at Knole Park, Kent. From print of Susan Myra Kingsbury. Records of the Virginia Co. of London, 1609-1626, vol iv, Washington D. C.: USA Print Office,1906-1935.

CAPTAIN JOHN BARGRAVE. A FORM OF POLISIE, BY IGNOTUS

1 & 2

Wheras we aswell by our Letters Patentes beareing date at Westminster the tenth daye of April	**Marloe writ this re: planting the yslandes so utterlee far away. Bad, wette weather 'n' pestes t' bee**

the yslandes. Marlowe first tried to make a Polisie for Bermuda. He rewrote it for a friend who wanted to start a Virginia colony.

3 & 4

in the fourth [4th] yeare of our reigne, as by diverse other Letters Patentes since that time graunted,	**o'ercome—hunger, e'en thirst. Profitable trading starts after harvest, Yu see? Ie, ie! Not e'en the duty—**

thirst. Much water on Bermuda was brackish; there were few good wells.

5 & 6

have given licence vnto diverse of our loveing subiectes named in those severall Patentes, to conduce and conduct[e]	**bound servants can produce vvealth out o' nothing for U. Cease, vain gentlemen! Desist—solve! Ecce! I tel evidence in code!**

Desist. The Adventurers' Co. in England wanted immediate profit.

7 & 8

severell coloneys of our loveing subiectes to abide in America, within thirty-four and forty-five degrees	**Al who R bound strive fiercely to B free, endure hard times tu gain love 'n' egality in society. So-o—vice offers i—**

9 & 10

of the equinoctiall, with diverse preheminences, liberties, and aucthorities as by the sayde Patentes appeareth,	**nstant aid. Apparent iustice quels the evil wretch, sends him far o'er sea t' start the happy colony. Bie, bie! I-e-e-e!! He die—**

sends him. King James favored sending criminals to the colony.

11 & 12

And whereas wee knoweing this derived aucthoritie from vs, to bee the efficient cause and the speciall meanes

s o' starvation. "Ungrateful stiff! Send a new man—wee deem each plai o' his dice worthie t' checke R hie debt. I've seen e—

Ungrateful . . . An Adventurer speaks.

13 & 14

wheareby wee shall attayne the endes proposed to ourselfe for the vndertakeing of the sayde plantaciouns,

verything now! Keepe that Naples dead-head off R turf—he'll see present ad hoc, blow a year's note into ye sea to s—

Naples dead-head. The stockholder criticises Kit.

15 & 16

did give likewise togeather with our first Patent certayne Articles and Instructions, theareby settleing

ave idiots by sending out—in error—a fleet they can't sail! Whate'er we spend is critical. Tut! I regret t' think steg—

17 & 18

downe our forme of government for the governeing of the sayde severall plantacions fitted at that time

anographers now manage the too, too slender finances of R yovthfvl firme—free t' meet t' vet U al—t' indite God!

steganographers. expert users of Kit's double-writing style.
vet. in sense medically diagnose, evaluate. Before leaving for Bermuda—and after his return—Kit had a job as reader in medicine at Padua University.
indite God! Some stockholder knew he was Kit Marlowe—once accused of heresy.

19 & 20

to those poore beginninges, and promiseing farther that as the Plantacion should encrease within the degrees

To permit th' presence on the isle of that spent hidden agent Sancho 'n' his hag wd B an egregious error, not easilie a—

Sancho. Kit was Sancho in Don Quixote: 10 chapters about Sancho's Island in Part II.

21 & 22

aforesayde, Wee, our heires or successours, would ordayne such farther instructions, lawes, constitutions, and ordinances,

ton'd for. Return this swan to 'is hideaway, 'n' case clos'd. I see serious loss yn our reuenue—hard for success o' crown credit at an u—

The stockholder still speaks. **swan.** secret service slang for a male whore.

23 & 24

for the better rule, order and governement of such as shall make plantacion theare as to us

nsettled hour for England. Ae-e! Al in R Co. must move—stretch to keep abreast of a harsh rule, an

25 & 26

our heires and successours shall from time to time be thought fitt and convenient, limiting our selves

illiterate bunglin' hedonistic Scottsman uuho rides ruf on U 'n' gets the most from creative evil. He's mos—

27 & 28

onely to frame them in substance consonant to the Lawes of England. And whereas we haue since contrarie

t intrigued ta watch any 'n' al new successes that cd offer him more hae nonnee nonnnee blow-arsse loot. Aae!"

29 & 30

to our first proceedeinges beene induced by severall Letters Patentes dated . . . to ordayne and institute

Suddenlee an end: a tied vote ript—al is eaten by ye crouun. D' gross pest dreads free election. Better not tit—

eaten by ye crouun. On 23 Nov. 1614, the Company became crown property.

31 & 32

severall orders of governementes, in our southerne and northerne plantacions now tearmed

le the firme—it cd soon go under, never t' return. O, present madness! We R so near a loan! One hovr, 'n' al

we. Looks as if Kit himself held a patent.

33 & 34

Virginea and New England, therein applieing our selves to the desires (and as wee feare, the private

wd have seen new funding approved. I'l sail, retire t' Naples, ignorant a' the heat 'n' duress. I-e-e, I-e-e-e! Grea—

35 & 36

endes) of the adventurers heare, which layeing the groundes of their governement accordeing to their private interest and severall ioyntestockes,

t tu ship home t' rest—greet R deer children—have her neare. Not understanding how far o'er ye ocean I've gone, U C, she asks if I got a letter sent to ye ile, 'n' C, vid—

37 & 38

have governed our free subiectes in Virginiea as if they were their servauntes, Wee knoweing thearefore,

e: a white tiny new infant. She feared he was sick, but vve gave grog, in error—error! U see, Hen, I strove—I-e-e-e-e—fiue

39 & 40

that thease severall formes of governementes doe breede distractions, as well amongst the adventurers	**hours t' restore warmth 'n' color, bvt instead, life fades gradvalee, soon ta meet 'n' greet death. Seems even less**

41 & 42

heare, as our loveing subiectes the personall planters, and vnderstandeing that the ioyntestockes of the Southerne Plantacion	**possible nou, hou hee happened to leave his life, tvrne so gently, so soon at rest, 'n' strange I ken actin' the crude R.N. Can't read that last**

R.N. Nurses had been graduated since 606 at the Hôtel Dieu at Paris, and records have been kept there by the Sisters of St. Augustine since the 12th century. Knights of St. John of Jerusalem also strictly regulated graduate nurses. There must have been registered nurses at Padua.

43 & 44

(whereon their governement heare by voices was founded) is now spent and gone, and the plantacion dothe	**withovt tears. O, Moth, I C U did do wrong! V left her 'n' went hae nonnee nonnee acros ye big sea, 'n' 'e happens dead.**

Moth. a nickname for Kit since childhood—daring hot adventure.

45 & 46

subsist onely of the ould planters now made free of severall private collonies, planted by Patentees	**VVe lost ye lone babe. Padua sent opportune offer o' medical readership, so in fall we sell, 'n' settle yn t' st—**

47 & 48

and of diverse publique servauntes, planted by the Collections and Lotteries, And that the plantacion is now soe strong	**ay in a tent near th' U. She quits Naples 'n' actin' to spend all dai with R babes. It grevv too cold to sleep out, so frends lend econ—**

49 & 50

that it is able to defend it selfe and fitt to put one the face of a commonwealth, Wee (being the politicke	**omic aid, 'n' then, onto a big, clean, tied-up boat, we take the helples familie of fit tots t' feed. No wet feet t' ch—**

tied-up boat. When Francis Drake was a child, he and his siblings lived on a boat tied up on the Medway. And later Kit puts this idea into the plaintext of the Polisie, suggesting that colonists might stay on boats till they could build on shore.

51 & 52

father of the whole and not lookeing one particulars in respect of it) considering and knoweing that the perfection and happinesse of a commonwealth,

il us. C, patient 'n' kind, she prepared hot food 'n' we ate together after work at nite. Long ago, C. Now I'm lonesome—no h-happiness left, 'n' if Chr. can die afta . . . No, no chi—

53 & 54

lyeth not soe much in the spaciousness of it, but first and principally in the governement, consisteing in the mutuall duties of commandeing

child's left alive. They'ue gone—gone ouerboard, off mi stupid ship, 'n' I'm insane—insane, 'n'-'n' she's gone t' N-Naples—lost t' M. C-cum, cum—try it! Cut it! No, hit it!

55 & 56

and obeyeing, next in possessing thinges plentifully, necessarie for the life of man, doe professe that next

No exit opens. Friends find 'n' bryng Chr. to 'is feet at hosp. Feel I'm a guest gainin' at ye host's expense, 'n' flee—l-lose

57 & 58

and immediately after the honour wee shall doe to God in converteing of the infidells to the knowledge and worshippe of Him,

my step—twisted 'n' fractured mi damned leg—no, no hope for Dr.'s fee: have to let it heal alone, if it will. I heede no God, know no high ho—

damned leg. This break actually happened a year later, in 1616—after he'd gone back to Naples, estranged from Micaela. He was working with the poets' clubs at the palace, and for Los Oziosos produced a farce about Orpheus, Euridice and Persephone in the underworld—the Duke of Estrada wrote a description: Kit, (as Secretary Antonio de Laredo), was playing Pluto. Standing at the top of the stage, he was being funny, and everyone was laughing when suddenly he twisted his leg and fell down on the other players.

59 & 60

we intend wholey the good of our subiects: first to the planters and adventurers, then to the planted, which wee would have soe cherished

pe. I retvrne to Naples. She's a stranger, C? When the viceroy left town, she was on board, C? I hide uhlone. Houu do U deel with defeet? Th'-th' tots wd d—

61 & 62

that they may prove planters themselves, and to that end endeavoureing to cause both England and Virginea,

ie over an' over yn my dumb head. That leg never heal'd, and she's gone out t' Spain. Don't eat, can't sleep at night—trav—

63 & 64

to endowe each other with their benefittes and profittes that theareby *layeing aside force and our coactive power*

el hard t' do. There's a bad fag new uiceroy here. Rode in pain—te-te-te-te—t' Venice for hot chow 'n' a iob at ye Ciotti Press. What f-

65 & 66

wee may *by our iustice and bountie* marrye and combinde those our provinces to us and our soveraignetye

uture y-year can ever bring such sorrow? Manco's dead in Madrid—no one to save 'im. I obey, I obey U 'n' put out t' see—

67 & 68

in naturall love and obedience, Wee will make this marriage our politicke and last end, to teach us

no return. Know U'l al B rid o' me. I'l make a sweet deal, C, sail 't' Antipodes, C, 'n' live in a caue—t' heed a right lo

69 & 70

what are the meanes that conduce to it, and to give both measure order and end to them. To which purpose

h-hot headed tomcat there who ses I'm non grata—'n' then, to weep! (poor damn'd outcast deceiver) But a true hi—

hot headed tomcat. The governor of Bermuda, Richard Moore.
ses. says.

71 & 72

not suffering any one to growe to greate, for feare of shaddoweing and hindering the rayes

gh wind ends ye heated fite, 'n' Gregorio fades, going far off to a new sorro. Aye! On return the an—

73 & 74

of our Maiestie to shine over all, *Wee will give to each planter advauncement in the governement,*

chor lets me go home t' pain. At d'Veneto, we earn more, C—'n' I lose everie tie—al, al in vain, when U left, Guv, t'

75 & 76

accordeing as hee shall give farthorance thereto. In regard thearfore this our soveraigne

sail t' Valencia 'n' that horrid Vega there. Gregorio's sad green hours o'erreach R affection. He, e—

Vega. Lope de Vega, her former lover, was waiting for Micaela at the Valencia dock; he called her la Loca (in his letters to his patron Sessa). **sad green hours.** time for jealous thoughts.

77 & 78

and uniteing power (and the facullties theareof taking theire roote from our maiestie in England) is to spread

mptied of al hope, thinks o' reuenge: resentment turns to hatred, 'n' lost in a drift o' woeful rage, 'e cried, "ai, ai, ai!" Gain'

79 & 80

it selfe amongst many *aswell differing in condition as severed in distance and place,* Wee

n' no sense, C, I left ye press t' go 'n' find Micaela's love-nest in a dreaded land. I imagine, C. W-wait f—

81 & 82

(findeing that nothing canne reduce this many into one againe but forme) doe ordayne one

or Manco t' send uuord—bring ye fag to the nag! No! He died, 'n' I'm hey nonnee nonnee. Ai, ai! Facit t-t—

83 & 84

setled and imoveable forme, to governe all the plantacions within the degrees aforesayde, *which forme*

imere **on the brain, I l-left, rode west. Soon a page came to say a wife 'n' her small child vvere on the edge of th' D—**

85 & 86

being maturely delibertated, ever one and the same, soe as wholely intendeing the end, it shall worke

olomites at an inn, 'n' wd the dad—me—hurry 'n' sled t' see ye babe. Ee-eee! I know all, 'n' go there t-t' give aid. She'll r—

87 & 88

noething but good theareto, wheareby yt shall not onely serve as a medicine to cure all the malignities

eturn! True! Stay there, Micaela—let B! I'l B coming!! Love yoo, Hon! The eagle's soaring to lead ye wai t'the inn! Shd

89 & 90

that the plantacion doth naturally bring with it, by reason of the distance of the place, but it shall alsoe by waye

we t-t-try for th' city? Can she be happy there? I-is th' babe well enuf to go? All day, thots about instant aid call in. A-a-h! Onl—

91 & 92

of right and interest procure us apt instrumentes for the form to worke by, and prepare matter of apt

y after hours of trek'in up a narro mt. road, I'm gone, C, bent ouer, not fit t' press farther. We p-pd. t' rest at emp—

trek'in. From Dutch trekkin, to draw, slowly and laborously, a wagon—or in this case, a sled.

93 & 94

condition for it to worke one, soe farr forth, as if wee laye the forme aright, to matter

ty r-rooms in a cote. I feel stiff. At dawn we hike i' the fo-fog 'n' meet t-terror—a horror too a-

95 & 96

soe capeable of it, wee may conclude that the properties of the forme must of necessitie followe.

awful to C. Mi horse impaled on the shelfe below screams in effort to escape, put ye ciottee feet o' o-

ciottee. ciotti, Italian. lame useless legs.

97 & 98

The matter thearefore whereone our forme must worke being the people and the place, which are to bee distinguished

ur sled which has gone down off the road. No hope t-t' bring the horse back up tu meet me—I wait, let him re-re-re-repeat! E-e-e-e-e!

99 & 100

and divided, and our soveraigne faculties limited to them by fundamentall lawes and order, Wee will first

Mad agony faded: 'e was silent, dead. Wee climb widout mi horse or sled. R final turn reveal'd d' inn ta vu. If I tell t—

widout, d'inn. A Kent accent.

101 & 102

giue lawes and order to the people, and then we will appoynte them their places, fortifications and manner

rue, a thot o' peace 'n' rest i' the inn now appeal'd more than greetin' mi own dear chyld! I spill'd sleet off, went apa—

103 & 104

of spreadeing. First thearefore that God maie the better give a blesseing to our endeavours, wee doe strictely

rt t' pisse, staggered in, fel at de hot stove fire, to be found bi Micaela. Gave her a hug, 'n' wee retired to ye resort o' es—

105 & 106

charge and commaund all our presidentes, councelles, magistrates, patriotes, governors, and ministers within

tranged 'n' reunited lovers. Passion, peace, warmth 'n' rest, till da child cries, 'n' we go to C our strong sea man. Ai! Misus

we. underlined m used as w.

107 & 108

our sayde severall collonies, respectively within their severall limittes and precinctes, that they with all

says she thot t' wait till ye snow receded. "Christ, that'll never happen!" I rave. "Come t' Venice! U R still reallie silly!" I—

109 & 110

diligent care and respect, doe provide that the true word and service of God and Christian	**'d race—race th' cold down 'n' ride post t' th' rapid river traget 'n' on to Venice. Deaf, I guessed I had**

111 & 112

faith bee preached planted and used, not onely within everie the sayde severall collonies, but alsoe	**no partner. I felt I was a creep, leauin' alone—e-e! Lost, isolated! But then, he—ye child—saved vs. He'd been odly**

113 & 114

as much as they may amongst the savage people, which doe or shall adioyne unto them, and border	**stil. He began to cry again. Soon my arms reached out t' hold hym. He stopped. Oh, shame! U'd leave an aw—**

115 & 116

uppon them, accordeing to the doctrine, rightes, religion, and eclesiasticall forme of governement now professed	**esome hole in three lives if U g-go off down de hil alone, C? O, don't do it, C! I regrett mi MT rage 'n' crass creep rant, C? 'N' open sp—**

117 & 118

and established in England. And because wee knowe that where Moses and Aaron agree not there religion	**ite! 'N' we talk 'n' decide ta go—she 'n' R babe on her horse, in least danger a' the dreadloess, me in a wagon—e-e! 'N' U wan—**

loess. (German. to loosen, dissolve). Unstable soil blown by the wind. Probably loess took the horse and sled over the edge on the way up.

119 & 120

will not onely bee scandalled but the soveraignetye must needes goe to wracke, therefore wee doe	**t warm den! Eee! Wee started. Eee! Wind chilled us! Go! Eee! By boots full o' sno. Reckon—eat at ye ten-hovr leg.**

By boots. His nose is stopped up. **leg.** Webster. a stage of a journey.

121 & 122

ordayne that whoesoever hee shall bee that shall refuse to bee governed by our eclesiasticall government	**Sheet sleet blevv o'er vs al day, 'n' finally—no rest—uuee came to a big log across the road h-h-h-here, between lo tree—**

123 & 124

established, he shall bee heald and esteemed as a register of our soveraigne power, commaundeing all our administers	**s—an immoveable mess! I unhitch, lead R horse around. We speed along de road until afar I see a blessed armee light. Go rest! E—**

armee light. at a military post? Kit and his party were coming from the German alps and were nearing the border of the Veneto.

125 & 126

of iustice, whome it shall concerne, not to suffer any person or persons to remaine or abide

ach turn brot us nearer, til soon we stopped R horses in firelite. O, O, man—I C on ye faces of men o'

127 & 128

within our sayde plantacions whoe shall professe any doctrine contrarie to oures, or shall

war h-honest c-care for R sorry party! Oasis! We all eat 'n' sleep till dai, 'n' shoue south—on 'n' on, C? Idio—

129 & 130

attempt to withdrawe any of our people inhabiteing or which shall inhabit within any of the sayde

t! I miss'd th' way t' th' traget! Hu-ha! I-I weep. Tho' I'd been a nonny fool, happily we row 'n' reach th' final boat. I, I!

131 & 132

colonies and plantacions (or any of the naturalls bordering one them) from the same governement

C the family rest upstairs at Venice—MT! N-n-no food, n-n-no grog, n-n-no heat! A bloodee shame! All me error!

133 & 134

or from their due allegeance to us our heires and successours, which persons soe often offendeing

Soon, R sudden success! A cheeree fire, h-hot food, soup, e-encouraging notes from Sir Henree W. lift us al!

Marlowe wrote to Harry Wotton on 7 October 1616, a letter preserved in English State Papers Venetian (99-21-X/lo9704). He wrote, "I have with me a wife, homely and poor [and Catholic, R.B.] . . . I beg you not to abandon me."

135 & 136

shall bee aprehended and imprisoned, untill hee shall throughly reforme himselfe or otherwise where the cause

Henree'll d-defend me, 'n' sith he'll hire me as his sec'y, we all prepare for a moue ouer to h-his h-house. We'll bring the trad—

137 & 138

shall require it to be banished Virginea and sent to England heare to receave condigne punishment,

e in quiet intelligence that he'd need in state seruice. Pavv rides hard; she, Nan 'n' R babe go along on mor—

quiet intelligence. In the letter sent to Wotton on 7 October, Marlowe includes bits of inside information about Roman and Spanish subjects.

Nan. Marlowe mentions the Spanish serving woman who accompanied Micaela from Madrid and who later returned to tell Lope about the journey, bringing him a letter from Kit and Micaela saying they were sorry.

139 & 140

for his or their offence or offences. And because wee are informed that some of the former governores	**e domestic broom efforts 'n' errands. Harree has given us a f-fine home here. O, o! We R free to effect or confo—**

141 & 142

both heare and in Virginea have contrarie to their patent, and our Royall instructions which tyed them to make	**und R promise to deliver al ye government news to Harry. I think I can't abide to hit, cheat or act an author in heat. H—**

143 & 144

their lawes consonant to the lawes of England, framed and caused to bee printed a certayne tyrannicall booke	**ow can we learn to earn R keep on th' leuel? No added dirt, no tricsie con games—ha! Laf! Stand ye best ya can, not t' be fal—**

best ya can. From now on, Kit will suffer from his badly broken leg.

145 & 146

of governement, which being sent into Virginea, and noe other supplies of foode or apparell sent either with them	**ling. Get a cane 'n' help poor Harrie wi' th' firewood 'n' even th' dishes. Be patient, love the misus, 'n' forget to mope! No frien—**

poor Harrie. By the end of 1616, no government money was coming as far as the English embassy at Venice.

147 & 148

or within 3 or 4 [three or four] yeares after them, wheareby many of you our subiectes, being forced	**d forgotten, a b-bear brot t' iustice, 'n' I'm free—free o' sorrow—each morn fresh wi'—Heye! Hae! Yu, yu, yu!**

a b-bear. Osuna-Pedro Tellez Girón? The Spanish plot is over.

149 & 150

to breake them for wante of foode and necessaires have miserablely lost their lives or bene brought into slaverie,	**Ye bear? Osuna! Together all R friends showed 'is beastlie scheme t' take the Veneto avvai from R noble bros! Oi, no relief**

151 & 152

and whereas this giveing life to lawes is one of the highest poyntes of our soveraignetye, given us from God	**until ye hi, hi aggressors meet defeat 'n' return to Naples in ye fog. So go, go, go! as vve finish'd, O, fie! How the wives**

meet defeat. Kit's successful plan for defusing Osuna's wicked plot is outlined before the fact in ciphers for The Winter's Tale. The plot was an idea of Quevedo's: capture Venice and the Veneto, move soliders into the city from Spanish warships, march them over Alps to Holland, sail across the Channel to occupy England. In May 1618 Quevedo came to Venice, believing the city was about to burn and be invaded by Spanish soldiers from the Adriatic. Instead, Kit's "mercenaries" suddenly disappeared, and Quevedo had to slip out of town.

153 & 154

to benifitte not to destroye our subiectes, wee shall hould our selfe guiltie of the iniurie done	**wait for th' ol' stutterer to sing this one silly bleedin' tune, "Deo-eo-eo-eo-eo!" Crude stuff, uuhile I, bie—**

155 & 156

if wee should not see it extreemely punished. And this being done in the face of our maiestie	**bad singin,' 'n' U, wi' Hosanah, expresst ioy, I found mi life reflected in the hot Te Deum! Estoeeeee!**

Hosanah. Gr. Hosanna. A shout of praise to God. **Te Deum.** An old Christian hymn beginning, "Te Deum laudamus," (we praise thee, O God). **Estoeeeee!** Sp. Estoy! I am! (Thy name is still Kit!)

157 & 158

what may wee hope for soe farr of if it bee not narrowely looked unto. Being	**We make a brief play for two Hen friends tonite. Go t' Harry 'n' bow, U fool! "Eo, eo, e-**

a brief play. The Two Noble Kinsmen, made with John Fletcher.
two Hen friends. Hen Wriothesley and Hen Vere, the 18th Earl of Oxford (Ned de Vere's legitimate son). These men came to Venice to help defuse the Spanish plot.

159 & 160

therfore most jealous of our honour in that kinde, wee doe straightely chardge and commaund	**o!" John Fletcher dared do most o' th' work—saued me to go free. Micaela uuas th' daughter in R ninny o—**

161 & 162

that noe instrument of our soveraigne power shall dare to encroach uppon any parte of our soveraignety,	**pus, 'n' ye two Hens act out rivals for her. O, I penned U a poor story! I regret a near vacant plot! O, hug me for an eon**

poor story. Exhausted by his efforts to destroy the Spanish plot, Kit made his part of the play a farce, with some poetry added at a later date.

163 & 164

further then they shall bee warranted by the councell of state, or by thease our orders and lawes now sett downe,

o' rest! Then wd each effort B a braue onward thrust? We'll neuer cheat or yeeld, 'n' let's say we'l do better soon! Has thy n—

165 & 166

uppon payne of high treason. And to the end this lawe shall bee the more strictley kept

arration stopp't? Wil U drop th' pen? No, Hebe, I'm not hasty. Ye'll see Kate, de cheef angel; th' sh—

167 & 168

wee will give the goodes of such offendoers to the publique treasurie makeing the publicke both iudge

ades o' U, lost Rita; U, Pop; mi sweet children . . . . O, if the Gew Queen's there—die kuuick—glug! I'l b-beg off, Eve—Beth—Hoo—

169 & 170

and iurie of this offence as will after appeare. Moreover because wee are fullye perswaided that wee can noe waye

Hoo! A-e-e-e-e-e! Beware! I'm far too weary for heaven; past deeds'l ruin al rest. Cd I stay wi' U, free 'n' peaceful? We'l win ape-face

171 & 172

better attayne unto thease our ende designed then by planteing of many private colonies, severed

again in R free solitude. Yet babes'l come—so no need t-t' vveep at the end—no grey rain at the end. Yu spent

win ape-face again. recall how we outwitted Osuna.

173 & 174

by distance and place, Wee therefore doe especially chargde, commaund and ordayne that all planters

years feeding a no account, harmed poet—no chance t' play lead parts when ye lame, addled bard cries "L-let

175 & 176

of what condition soever they bee, shall enter their names and subiect themselves under the government

Be!" 'N' sits al day on his house roof t' stare 'n' lament his decline 'n' need, but never tv emerge tv meet Cher. How the

177 & 178

of some one colonye or other, to bee governed accordeing to the rules and orders by us now sett downe

gloom seen round Dad hurt ye deer babes, we don't soon cee; ergo; covnt ye o-other sorrows I once felt not

179 & 180

uppon payne of being taken for rebbels and outlawes. And wee doe further charge and commaunde all our presidentes,

supreme—no! R poor sick needy babe wept 'n'fled from us ta plunge o'er da edge 'n' land on da street far below—'n' I h-haue uacan—

181 & 182

councelles and magistrates, within their iurisdictions, that onely the offences of tumultes, rebellions, conspiracies,

t uiew of sudden horror. Can this B? Micaela cannot stop screaming: she rushes to l-lift ye little one, 'n' I-I sense it is futile: C,

183 & 184

mutinies and seditions, such as shall come to that hight, that they shall prove dangerous to the state theare,

R dear little child's gone, so young! "O, Micaela," I stutter, "No hope t-t-t-t-t-t' s-s-s-s-save, 'n' U h-h-ha-hate h-ha-ha-hate me." I'd

185 & 186

togeather with murders, manslaughters, incest, rapes and adulteries, togeather with such offences as wee

press a chance t' asist her harrowing effort. We R stunn'd! At edge o' death, he l-liues, C! Gee, we must saue him strat—

187 & 188

by thease our lawes and orders, shall make fellonie or treason, to bee committed in those partes within the precinct

e! We stop, stoop to search t' find all the ill broken bones. There are none! It's a miracle—he's not t' d-die! We carry him t' measu—

189 & 190

of the degrees before mentioned, and noe other offences, shall bee punished by death without the benifitte

re how he'd use his limbs. I hoped he'd get to his feet but find each foot bent. Need an en-en-enabler for ye tot feet.

191 & 192

of clergie, except in the cause of manslaughter in which clergie is to be allowed. It followeth now

We made an excellent pair of shoes t' crouch-brace little ioints, C? Feet g-g-go, flie, hi 'n' lo! Wow! Uh, wil he—

193 & 194

that we sett downe thease our orders, degrees of councellers, magistrates, governors, and all	**fall once more? O, leave gross dread! Watch! Start to strengthen sound, sturdee legs! See, I wear ro—**

195 & 196

under officers belongeing to this our forme, which falls out, first to devide all our	**und hose, ful-cuff'd, to aide mi fool leg. C, I fear he inherits worst trouble: girls R not ov—**

197 & 198

adventureours into two orders, severing such as are free of our soyle and trade only,	**erly afflicted so R one daughter's saved. O, sad review o' nonny errors. Nouu U R to rest. A-e!**

199 & 200

from them that are citizens and free of our governement. Of the first order there are likewise 2 sortes	**U aid her sincere efforts t'-t'mend R son's ratzie feet ere h-he leaves R home fore'er. I'm growin' too fat t'-t' work.**

199 & 200

from them that are citizens and free of our governement. Of the first order there are likewise 2 sortes	**We now haue this good-sized familie to care for: one mirrors the fem; three freaks R not free e'en t' trvst t' tre—**

The author has made 2 anagrams from lines 199 & 200. He alerts the reader by putting in the outside message, "There are likewise 2 sortes" (Each of the inner messages uses letters T, W, O, instead of the numeral).

201 & 202

servauntes that haveing served out their time, and tenauntes that have estates in dependensie of their masters	**ad vvithout fear or aid. She sends me t' vieuu th' streets, then I meet her 'n' sit 'n' rest again, then eat pasta a' dente. Even s—**

203 & 204

and landlordes, togeather with freedome of trade, but have noe shares. The second sorte are such, whoe going	**uch gentle care doesn't bring me health. O-o-o-o, I groan, fret. Tho' she's stressed, no hard hate for dad. We weave due**

205 & 206

one their owne charges they gayne a share, and likewise freedome of trade but are not	**web of fear, care 'n' aid. Day 'n' night we R hostage to death: he slinks euer nearer to eye me. O**

207 & 208
citiezens till they have not carryed over two men. The second order of adventurers

let's stay t' see R dozen-toe chyldren racein' round each other wi' freedom t'vvin trve o—

209 & 210
are *such whoe appropriateing unto themselves their freedome, their landes and their degrees*

ptimum use o' their legs. Their heads appear t' have no horrid harrowing defects. Relent! See need e—

211 & 212
by purchase, they communicate either in the choice or participation of councells and magistracies

each of these R children has for U t' care, cope 'n' instigate happy sociable communication. I, I, I! Ecce! My t-tru—

213 & 214
and them wee call our citiezens, devideing them into 5 [five] degrees. The first degree is the patriot

st in their mental power haz grown: I lie here at fireside t' feed them, 'n' detect icie edge o' disgust e—

215 & 216
or patrition, they are such as are first named patentees in the particular plantacions of colonies, cities

uery time I slip, spil a spoonful in accident, C? Ae, Ae! I preach neatness to R tots. The attraction a' fash—

217 & 218
and corporations, thease shall bee such as haveing good estates in England they shall carrie

ionable dressin' holds R tiny girl hostage. She loves "pretend." She can act on stage. Aah-ha! A clue a—

219 & 220
or drawe over with them to the number of 300 [three hundred] men as their parteners and adherences

bout inherent tendencie! She's part of her mom's dream returned! Th' wonder: ha-have we erred at R h—

221 & 222
of whom they must bee protectors and for whose good abeareing they must bee pledges.

ope t' produce th' best sho home, 'n' dearest sho family? Greedy, we augment before we go t' sob—

223 & 224
The second degree are such as are admitted to bee of the order of governors by the patriot, whose name

er thot o' the fvture care o' these dear growing babes. Soon I heed a deep fear: necessary t' do more! Doth MT

225 & 226

being joyned in the patent, the power of chief governeing those colonies, if they bee thereunto	**hype hide free-fal nonnie poverty? No! Hoe! I go to connect gifts with the best neet job, 'n' gee! Her uie—**

hype. old slang still current: pretentious foolery.

227 & 228

elected shall be graunted unto them. Thease must likewise haue estates in England, either in land,	**w shocked me: she hates that I'll use de best Italian language t' uurite th' drei, dense 'n'-'n' elemental en—**

229 & 230

or money in banke, and they must carrie over, or send, as many men, as the patrition of the colonie	**dorsement o' ar inchoate embassy, I makin' up events to try 'n' credit ar noonah-moona lyfe here in**

makin' up events. When Kit (Gregorio de' Monti) died in Nov. 1621, his former SSS brother John Taylor the Water Poet wrote an arcane tribute to him entitled "Sir Gregory Nonsense, his Newes from no place." 1622.

231 & 232

and they canne agree to have their names soe put in. The patrition may alsoe at any time	**terra Venice. I mail notes to them 'n' to R. Naunton. They pay past time. He's ahead again. Ayee!**

233 & 234

after admitte as many into the colonie as hee please, they bringeing men to him	**I'm in charge of managein' the stil-open embassy here. Hate to mind it alone, yet te—**

In the Bodleian is an old semi-secret hierarchy of government workers in which "Shakespeare" is identified as the "writer of weekly reports." ("Great Assizes Holden in Parnassus by Appollo and his assessors." 1645. A copy in Durning Lawrence. Bacon is Shakespeare. N.Y.: John Mc Bride Co. 1910.) When Harry Wotton left Venice on 6 May, 1619, Kit was chargé d' affaires of the Venice embassy and had to write weekly reports to Secretary of State Robert Naunton.

235 & 236

to encrease his colonie. The 3rd[third] degree are such as shall bee maiores and aldermen in the foresayde	**n months ago Harry had ta leaue, so left here, Ae do best I can. Credence in me is less, see? I heed al horrid er-**

237 & 238
citties and corporacions, and they shall carrie over sixe men. The 4th[fourth] degree shall bee

rors o' chee-chee-cheeters from Austria 'n' Illyria, 'n' al R gossip o' de bann'd devil—he t-that exce—

239 & 240
common councellors, and they shall carrie over foure men. The 5th[fifth] degree are commoners,

ll'd at crime for ye Covncil of Ten. E-e-e! No more harm must reach England! See hours more of Chr.-

241 & 242
and they shall carrie over two men. And if any one shall comitte any act whearby

Cad's nonny news from nowhere—not Ilyria! But al—al a them here C that I came dayly a—

243 & 244
his life and goodes shall bee forfeited to us, though his life bee pardoned hee shall bee

t bag-deliuerie sho—listened for fools to feed us al de bad gossip 'n' libel. He-he-he-he-he! Fah!

245 & 246
suspended from his degree till hee hath brought over a certayne number of men, accordeing to

UUinter brot h-horror 'n' dread: no pay came, 'n' tu feed his familee Chr. needs t' beg-leg. U got some che-

247 & 248
the qualitie of his first degree, to restore him to his sayde degree agayne. Moreover,

ese, queer revolting fish, oat grits for 'em. Oi, oi! I hear: ye shy death does dare t' greet me!

249 & 250
wee ordayne that of all thease 5 [five] degrees, the eldest sonne onely shal bee of his fathers

No strength dealin' wi' fools 'n' troubles here. He feels defeated. He—he—he's lost at sea. Ay, Ay! Flee!

251 & 252
degree and the younger shall bee of the degree belowe it except they can rayse themselves by carrieing

Ye brach's grief exceeded mine. O, here, cheer U! Don't starve 'n' beg. E-e! Beg? I'l sel the news t' al that'l pay! Re ye goy

253 & 254
of of men. And further wee ordayne that the meanest servaunt that goeth (God soe blesseing him

bragger-man who left Rome—he'd send money t-t' read th' gist of hush events i' th' Ueneto 'n' at sea. A foe

255 & 256

and his endeavours, that hee canne purchase and estate in England or compasse to carrie over or drawe	**o' th' Vatican, we hear R dear crude preest's home's in England, 'n' so send each coranto via R post. Ae, ae, ae! R dun—**

crude preest. Marcantonio de Dominis, the ex-archbishop of Spolatro in Dalmatia, who left the Roman Catholic church to become Anglican and went to England, welcomed by the Archbishop of Canterbury. De Dominis read to everyone the private newsletters Kit sent. The Venetian ambassador was shocked—who'd know all these secrets of the Veneto? Who wrote these coranti? The Venetian State Inquisitors heard from their ambassador in London, and a man was found, don Celso Galarato, who said he knew the identity of the author of the newsletters. This don Celso had worked for de Dominis but has quarreled with him and is going home. When he reaches Brussels he'll tell the author's name, and things truly extraordinary. Kit's up the creek without a paddle.
coranto. a gazzetta, a newsletter. Coranto meant current news.

257 & 258

over with him of his friendes and adherences the number of three hundred men) he may become a lord	**sical friend reads them to eueryone, euen th' bad man from Venice. H-horror! He'd find me—h-he'd web-mesh**

259 & 260

patriot which is the greatest place the commonwealth canne beare. Now for the choice and election	**t' tangle me, C; scare th' familee, C? What to do? No cheer! No hope t' act 'n' win a better chance here. O, I-I spoil wh—**

261 & 262

of our officers, magistrates and governours, wee must beginne at the lowermost degree, sc:	**atever I start—no sense. Cash comes for R food, rest. Glug! We wait t' be found egregious. Men rem—**

He writes early in 1620.

263 & 264

the commoners that carrie over two men they shall choose out of themselves the burrowe houlders,	**ember yovthful svccesses. What I recall R a lot o' errors too h-hot to emend. U see, Mom, we thot h-here hun—**

265 & 266

surveyours of the high ways, and such like officers. And out of them that carrie foure men	**ger uuas in retreat, 'n' nouu, O, what a horrid mess, C? Chris t' die, U to fly home! F-feo f-fuks! Each hy**

267 & 268

they shall likewise choose their common councellers, churchwardens and such like officers.

hi-hi-hi one's read all ye c-c-c-c-coranti, C, 'n' sh-sh-shureli s-s-some one'll reueel who wrote 'um, C, C? F . . . k f . . . k, d—

269 & 270

The common councellers shall choose their aldermen and shreiffe out of them that carrie six men.

o U C? Harsher far then h-hel, shril torture'l end mi fool existence—send ma'm 'n' familee to c-chaos! To me, C,

271 & 272

The aldermen shall have a maior by turnes except some greate disabillitie happeneth and then

thei mean everything, 'n' to pass and leaue them—can't express it. I bleed. Ah! Al, al the mere broad phil—

273 & 274

the next in turne shall be maior. The Maior and aldermen shall choose their governour either out of them

osofical thots o' R meeting next in heaven I don't belieue—do U, Mother? H-hm? Al h-h-haue eternal r-r-r-rest. Marlo.

275 & 276

that bee admitted to bee of the order of governours by the patrition, or the patrition himselfe.

Spring: I'm stil free here, tryin' t' pen at home t' trade for food to eat. But too bad! Hi heet over the boi—

277 & 278

The maior and aldermen alsoe of severall corporation(s) shall have power to choose out of their corporation

ler has caused a flood, 'n' o-o, h-how t' repair 'n' clean it? 'N' o-o-o-o-o-o-o-o-o-o, 't vvas th' last sleep place of R merri, merri, rathe—

279 & 280

one of the order of governours or the patrition himselfe to bee of the provinciall coun(s)ell, which coun(s)ell

r rheumatic bitch: th' heeter—o-o-o-o-o-o-o-o-o—gave her sleep forev'r. N-n-not slow t' die, she flu off 'n' spun c-criei-i-n', l-l-l-l—

281 & 282

being all chosen out of the patritions and the order of governoures in everie province, and consisteing of

anded unconscious of vs on the floor—gone forever. Signorina Scala, R poor deer pet. I-I hie in t' get th' net 'n' be vi—

283 & 284

fiue, seuen, nine, eleuen, thirteen, or fifteen, they shall haue a monethly president

tally useful, Hen, in haulin' t-th' stuf from ye hot depths. Ninni-nin! E-e-e-e-e-e-e-e-e-e! R ear—

285 & 286

by turnes, whoe haueing two voices, hee shall for his moneth call and breake of all

s hear the awful screech of living steam as a new hole broke yn tha line! Hoo, bulldo—

287 & 288

assemblies, and untill the councell of union bee compleate, wee give them the same power which we doe

g! The net melts. U cee, an' I'm scalded. Each new burst o' steam wil help blow up mi lovein' home! E-e-e! One chief o'

289 & 290

give to our sayde councell of union, makeing all theire decrees to stand as lawe, till they are disanulled

flood-control arrived at last: he guided me, 'n' we cleaned ye stinking leauin's. I leaue U, call at ye Hotel Ross—

291 & 292

by us, by the generall parliament in Virginea or by the sayd councell of union, when it shall bee

i for mail. Ee! Harry'll soon B in Venice—his place a bubbley ruyn! What t' do? Ay, I'l get set 'n' hug 'n' n-neel—

293 & 294

compleate and in force, accordeing to our order now sett downe. This councell of union

'n' refuse perceiued guilt connected to a fool's accident wi' hot coal, 'n' on d' morrow noon R

295 & 296

being the most soveraigne councell wee will tearme a Syncretisme or councell of union

man comes in t' rent a better house—no fuss! ECCE! Lenience! All mi worry gone! C, love, I'll go wi' U—

297 & 298

with the councell of England and this councell shall be chosen onely out of the patriots of everie

to R Naples coue; then, one bold cool hush-effect, Hon, 'n' together we'l sail to Valencia—fly, childe, 'n' iust

299 & 300

province, by a component number of electours chosen out of the order of governoures which are not

snub Lope, C, bvt not too soon. Trust me, C, C? Free of uuorree—'n' no hye horror! Come down, C: hire a page 'n' five h—

301 & 302

patritions, one out of everie particular corporation, which electors shall bee chosen by the maior

orses 'n' reach the port, 'n' wee'l both retvrn to Harrie, C, C—C? But no, Micaela refuses to play. Oi, oi, oi! I plai ho—

303 & 304

and aldermen the maior haveing the casteing voice, and thease electoures shall choose four, three, two or one,

t necessitie: she demurs. Finallie we R agreed she'd go alone t' home theater 'n' not retvrn. Love? O, ha, ha, haa! U C, coo-co—

305 & 306

out of everie province as necessitie shall require. *This councell shall have three monthely presidentes,*

o Micaela uuon't cooperate, C, 'n' she shelves e'en this quiet try for her Spanish nevvs. Ei! I'll let her slide cleer

307 & 308

by alternate changes which untill wee have councellers wee will shew the manner of it by letters thus . . . .

out o my life! That silly babe's green-clean, C? Uh, she can't even steal th' news! Wel, Chr. wil write tu h-her, 'n' we'l e—

309 & 310

Thus the councell being of fifteen teens, if you order them in this sorte the same three men shall

uolue R reunion after th' fem's been home in th' city, 'n' has seen the ill effects o' d' shit-smel there. Tog—

311 & 312

not in five yeares space meete togeather to bee presidentes, whereas if they were to take their circularie

ether, she 'n' I, with a better effort at secret cooperation, may werk tv aid R English security. E-e-e-e-e-e-e-e-e! Spai—

313 & 314

courses, without changes, they should meete once everie five moneths. The presidentes being thus ordered

n's itching to move up t' England before we'd see their interest. UUe SS must choose ye h-hevee hod—shed R retice—

315 & 316

their three voices or two of them shall conclude all causes that shall bee controverted by equall voices

nce—create a scheme to foil the bastards. She cd tell us hot news o' all queer activity. O, lover, love Chr.! Oh, bull!

she cd tell us. If Micaela were to return to Madrid, a city hard to reach and the center of political planning in Spain, she'd learn news important to England.

317 & 318

and not concluded in the bodie of the councell, the eldest counceller of which presidentes shall summon and breake

U left, 'n' C, I uurote daielee. No response: all's ended, C! U no how I slid-d-d-d 'n' fell, bent 'n' broke that ancle. C-c-c-come h-h-h-home! St—

319 & 320

upp all assemblies, the number of this councell must bee seven, nine, eleven, thirteen or fifteen at the most	**op bein' th' cleenest Spanish nun! Can't U remember mi love? U baffle me—is the t-title of lover useless? Then ente—**

Spanish nun. To his patron Sessa, Lope wrote that la Loca said he "made love like a nun." Kit may have written to her using the language of this cipher, influencing her.

321 & 322

but in the minoritie of the plantacion three may serve without any presidentes, the elder counceller	**r the dreerie ol' convent t' find peace 'n' recall nothin' o' the times U suuam 'n' lay with thy beest. Ie, ie! Report—**

323 & 324

of the three to summon and breake of the assemblies. And our will and pleasure is that (besides the oath	**in' isn't a hel-sin! So take time, see? Tel us about th' bad stuff. Here, here, don't blame me! We had a hard loss. Poor**

325 & 326

of our supremacie which all our subiectes there shall be sworne to once everie yeare at the least)	**lost cherubim, swept away on th' river; ae, ae, lost for ae! O, uue R e'en aliue—Chr. here's the closest, C? I blee—**

327 & 328

there shall bee a particular oath framed, for all thease councells to take, viz: that all their decrees	**d. Reach, catch, hold, save—O, late! See them sink before R eies! U realize that U'll retroact th' fall, all apart**

329 & 330

shall bee made aswell for the uniteing of Virginea to the crowne of England as for the combindeing of the members to the whole,	**f-from realitee. It'l come t' U in dreams at night, Hon, 'n' tho' the babes have gone, we'll see them going fore'er, 'n' da f-fool wind blows. Ch-e-e!**

331 & 332

and that they will to their uttermost power endeavour to prevent all usurpation of, or encroachment uppon	**Hon, t' tel U to return home for R news was too cruel! Ae! Not proper t' put U in the vvay o' harm: I can't lend aid t' let opp—**

333 & 334

our soveraigne authoritie whatsoever. Reserveing therefore to ourselfe our most high absolute	**ortunitie show. O, I'm a beggarlie fool far over here, so houu t' get U to the Veneto? R Harrie reserves us s—**

R Harrie. Kit and Micaela were living in the English embassy house minding the store after Carleton left, and they were there when Harry returned to Venice just before Micaela went back to Spain with her theatrical company, the Sanchez Players. Harry Wotton himself may have suggested that it would be a good idea for Micaela to pick up some news in Madrid.

335 & 336

and perpetuall power of commaundeing and controuleing all, that thereby our commissions and writtes of iustice may spread

helter ouer at his palace, C? Get goin' soon now if U can. I'l find U at ye Brenner P-Pass and m-m-marry U! Al mi loue! Did t-two posts come t' dr—

337 & 338

themselves over everie person, and in everie place through our whole dominions there,

op mi letters over where U R singin'? O, don't scare me, Hon—respond! I'l leeve here heauie. VVho

339 & 340

we doe graunt that this soveraigne councell, shall have authoritie to unite in commaund, and to appoynte

can tel? Wil U travel or stay in Madrid? Months go past, C? I have no hope. Ai! Too late nouu, t' hug 'n' entice U 'neath de

341 & 342

the number of the forces, puteing the power of commaundeing them into one of our marshalls handes

couers, Hon. No, ma'm, U R a fem that flew from the nest, 'n' I'm d' fool t' go ridin' up here! No peace! She's gone, but h—

343 & 344

as cheife, to all by turnes, or to each one severally as occasion shall require, giveing them

ere's Chr., C? On a qvest for la Loca, on level trail, not climbing yet. E-e! He hears a guy sai, "Oui, she's

la Loca. Lope's name for Micaela when she came back from Naples to Spain, behaving oddly. Lope used this term repeatedly in letters to Sessa about the hard time she gave him.

345 & 346

our sayde councell likewise authoritie to proclaime warre and make peace with the naturralls

on ye mt., at rest " —wi' R child! Ei-e! Me a-a-a papa? C-count the weeks! Aid, lull, win her! U R so cruel! Look at R ire! A—

347 & 348

of the cuntrie, to taxe tributes as well for a treasurie for England as for Virginae, to dispose of the treasurie in Virginea

l's extraneous self-indulgence! Don't foster it! Get past it, see? Hon is a f-fit, brave wife. Go to her! U r-roar, "Ai, ai, ai!" in terror: R U eva—

349 & 350

as the councell in England have of the treasurie in England, To make contractes with the king or companie in England

ding goin' in sno t' get Hon 'n' R tinee child at th' teat? Aren't U glad Micaela's sick of Lope, 'n' U care, 'n' love her? Man, when cake ne—

351 & 352

and consenteing with them accordeingly to rate the prizes of comodities, which shall bee sent hither

eds t' B eaten it's soon enioy'd, 'n' if it pleezes Hon t' come home, that's g-great! I'll w-wait h-h-here, C-C-C? Hi 'n' dri! Chr.,

I'll w-wait h-h-here. He's joking. It's not just that he dreads the promised formal marriage. He can't walk on his broken ankle; he's going with a crutch, leery of starting up the mountain on an awful road. (Today it's still an awful road.)

353 & 354

or thither, to appoynte the places where the forces and colonies shall bee planted, to condemne

not feelin' happy, brot her throo sno to a chapel. So I met th' preest, 'n' th' cl-cl-cleen deed was done. Ae-e!

355 & 356

and pardon to banish, to confiscate, to proscribe accordeing to the laws ordayned, To call magistrates and governours

On th' cold, cold trip to Venice, I groan—"O-o!" 'N' R babe needs aid, C; 'N' U R so strong! It's good to rest at Harry's palace, C. Afta d' man saw

357 & 358

to accompt, *and in case of necessitie limiteing his time shorte and the place certayne to institute any*

ye child's state, he sent necessary hot food in time to saue it, I! 'N' C me—Cit-Cit—opening a clean apartment! It i—

359 & 360

one man that shall have soveraigne power as the dictatoures in Rome, and all this their authoritie

s spacious, elegant, 'n' we all toast in Harrie's heated Italian heaven! Oh, oh, troth, I'm married to U, th' ver—

361 & 362

and all thinges they have done theareby shall bee firme and of force till it be disanulled by us

y best uuife alive: gladly, incredibly, she left th' theata for R one lone babe 'n' me, and ill, she dash'd

363 & 364

and our councell in England. This councell of union cannot bee compleate, till there bee three provinces.

o'er the brent alps, close to leavin' life uuith an unborn child! Oe, oe! U'll e'en pardon nonnee me! C-c-c-cling t-t'

365 & 366

In the meane time the provinciall councell shall serve the turne, wee giveing them the sayde authoritie

Monti! Wrap him in love, etc., 'n' vve'l stai right here at th'-th' clean scene! Gee, I'm no heel, lady! See, I'l uurite thee u—

367 & 368

to exercise and use within their owne provinces. Now in regard the active and groweing quallitie

ncounted exit songs to sing right here in Venice! A queere cad-wit raw-paw, I'd win thie love! Carrie on!

369 & 370

lyeth in the well foundeing of private families, and collonies, wee (as a spurre to industrie, sheweing

we should stop Osuna: he wants t' defeat R Venice wi' fire, 'n' then go fer England! Ill! I, ie, ie! So I pray U'l smile

371 & 372

That the heades of thease colonies are sparkes derived from our hereditorie monarchie) doe give

at Kit-pirate readie t' go destroie R deer Venice as a mere chore for fool Osuna! H-he, h-hee! He's so dvm I'd

373 & 374

and graunte unto them and their heires for ever, the hereditorie commaund of the soveraigne forces, limiteing them to use

get him t' give me gold t' hire men t' fire th' citie on order. No need to use his navee, as the mad mercenaries ar h-hot enuf for our tu—

375 & 376

them onely in their owne collonies and in the wastes adioyneing to them, except they bee authorized to use them farther

rn. I'l need to sail north, size 'em up, get 'em set in the citee wi' U, mi wyfe, next to the arsenal, ready to act! Then, ho, ho, he, he, nobody

377 & 378

by the soueraigne councell of union, and to the end they shall onely employe this our sword and forces

'l find out: ye English actors'l B ye pyrates who'l come t' Venice for arson, 'n' on th deed-day, no one'l shouu!! He'l

379 & 380

to the supporteing of our soveraignetye and the mainetenaunce of our iustice theare, Wee will give them

C two men go to the Doge t' uncover a Spanish plot! Tuf! Hear ye alarm ring out: E-e-e-e-e-e! I finish it: We revieuu ten

381 & 382

for the reward of their service thease titles and honoures followeing. The degree it selfe because wee cannot

officers who said the invaders were all caught—sent to Frioolee for hangin'! E-e-e-e-e! But we'l not desert the secre—

Frioolee. Friuli, a city of the Veneto NE of Venice.

383 & 384

give them better names, they shall bee called Patriotes or patritions, when they are three hundred

t helpers. Ai! They go, rememberin' the heartbeat o' th island city we saved, 'n' the thunder a' steep roller—

387 & 388

strong and planted abroade then they shall bee tearmed knightes patriotes with the title of Sir.

s—hear them beat, beat on shore. I' th' dark wet street a gondola glides. Flares lit th' nippy nite, 'n' th' det—

387 & 388

When they have attayned to bee six hundred strong, at which number wee (intendeing everie

ermined buoy rings. When dawn tints R h-heaven, wee go t' bed. Even the day, here in the exact uti—

389 & 390

planter and servaunt to bee the father of a familie) doe stente the colonies that they shall not exceede

litarian apex o' trade, the music's a heartfelt shaft, 'n' ye feel the need to shovt, bleet 'n' dance on the ole toe—

391 & 392

above soe many families (or that another colonie hath issued out of them) our will and pleasure

s i' lovin' response. Al o' U men'l remember this city—a hauen of a too-sad fool author that U heal'd. We i—

393 & 394

is that their sonnes and heires shall bee then knightes patriotes and they themselves shall bee Barrons

ntend t' sho all Englishmen the best party here at Harrie's. He thinks their sli neat lesson saved babes, so he

395 & 396

and tearmed lord patriotes, their wifes and other children takeing their honoures and places accordeingly.

'd entertain wi' a play! Too tired t' do it alone—g-r-r-r—I ask Iohn Fletcher, "Cd U aide 'n' do al R gran' scenes? Shepherd me, C?" H—

397 & 398

In time of peace they shall bee and have the authoritie of our leiuetenauntes of sheires

e said yea, 'n' uue pen a farce: tuuo hi, hi nobles love the same lite shee, fite o'er her into th' aft—

399 & 400

in England, to appoynte the commaunders of our men at armes, see them trayned, to looke to their armes and watches.

ernoon. At the end a horse defeats the winner: he dies, 'n' ye loser gets ye madam. No, no! Tut, tut! Crackt moral! Mamma oppo—

401 & 402

In time of warre they shall bee charged with what number of men the councell of state shall thinke

ses th' tale o' chance, but finally takes th' role of mi daughter (nimble feet). I'm her clown-wit father. When th'

403 & 404

fitte. The patriot must bee allowed his leiuetenaunt aswell in cases of disabillitie, by nonage or impotencie,

lass lets a noble nut l-leaue a prison, 'n' ye friends, bedect wi' mail, fite to win th' beautie, I get coopt i' th' iail, see? Mo—

405 & 406

or in their abscence either about the busienes of the state theare, or about their private busienes in England,

re action: the Nan in love ebbs near insanitie before a doc restores her t' a better state. He gets U-U-U-U t' be hi-hi-hip,

407 & 408

but these leiutenauntes shall bee chosen by the order of aldermen out of the order of governoures the better

'n' freelee embrace thy husband-to-be before the uuedding! E-e-e! Horror! See another love-fest! Tut! Honour's lost! Lett—

409 & 410

to give the sayde order of aldermen content. And whereas the patriotes are the principalest ringleaders and greatest

he Roman priests rant! Love 'n' ioy are the greatest aid to health, 'n' priests R not perfect angels! We dread an aged creed, tied

411 & 412

adventurers, which carrie and drawe with them their freindes, kindred, followers and adherence out of their naturall

t' dark, unreal fear o' sin, when true freedom, half-hidden, awaits U here. Their crvell, horrid added writs that concern new i—

413 & 414

countrie to a place soe farr remoate, to be protected governed and cherished by them, Wee doe therefore will

nocent babes that die ere they're christened repeat th' dum error of a fool prelate, C, C?
We dodge love more. I owe

415 & 416

and commaund all our sayde patriotes, loveingly carefully and cheerefully to performe this their trust.

my life t' lovers: C, dear people louin'ly sau'd me from death—no ordinary cut! UUe English start t' rally after ch—

417 & 418

And wee doe ordayne that after admonition for being churlelish and negligent in that kinde,

alenge—'n' what loue cd remain after hidden, banished, nonney idiot Kit higgled 'n' tore at a front

419 & 420

they shall bee noted with a note of ignominie, if they shall not endeavour the helpeing and protecteing

given him in good faith to allow al of his plays t' be enioyed there in England? No pretence, then! The teeth U

421 & 422

any of their foresayde adherence, by all lawfull meanes they may, and this wee charge as well

showed yn selfish f-fury! Ae, ae! All ye edgey melodramatic letters! H-ha! Can an able hy law renew

423 & 424

all our presidentes councells and marshalls to looke carefully unto, the rather to drawe the Indyans to the like

a penitant's ryte to return to Kent 'n' liue or die? Cd loue defend Kyt? Shall he reach home, or shall a last slo, slo crawl u—

425 & 426

dependencye. And wee doe further ordayne that from the time that the patriot shall bee planted abroade,

nseam that man left here on trial t' be freed by dreaded death? Adio! Can ye weep no tear? Drop the h-hope U'l t-t-t—

427 & 428

his estate of inheritance in England, togeather with his honoures, titles and inheritance in Virginea, shall be soe united

aste good English ale again! 'N' th' brite, neet, lovin' actors sail auuai on R wind 'n tide. There! It's finisht! Rest, ninni! He, he, he! Chee!

429 & 430

and made one to him and his heires that he shall not sell the one without the other, and that sale

Here at home with mi ladie I need t' send al those hasht letters to Naunton: He ho-holds al th'-th' a-an—

431 & 432

to bee made by the consent of our councell of union in Virginea and our Virginea councell in England,

suuer to R n-need for food 'n' uuinter clothing. Can I give mi babe Cleo a n-nonny DCL-guinea lace? N-no! I love

DCL. 650. **guinea**. Webster. 21 shillings. A term used in giving prices of luxury items.

433 & 434

or the most parte of them, meeteing at their generall courtes and not otherwise. And if it happen that the patriot

mi children more than aniething. I don't want to see them get spoilt! U appear to fear t' protest a tort after the he-he—

435 & 436

doe dye leaveing noe heire male of his name then shall it goe to the female and their heires.

avy sorro of tots h-h-hi falling—E-E-E-E-E-E-E-E-E-E-E-E—'n' lost t' death. I'm here in h-hell again! In mad dem—

437 & 438

And the eldest daughter of the patrition, and the heires that shall challenge by the female side and their children shall beare

onic replai a' that terrible scene! Shh! B still! All their suffering's o'er, man, 'n' all that that ye had had—Gad!—deleted! Heed, h-heed, the ne—

439 & 440

the patriotes sirname, if they will inherite the sayde honoures and landes, which if they shall refuze that

ew family needz. Offer aid—insist on their learnin' t' read—teach, tell, haue h-hope! They're iust sh-sh-shy. What lit—

441 & 442

then the next of the kinde either by the father and then of the mothers side, takeing the patriotes

any brings is retention. Offer repetition to the defeated, 'n' take exam! H-he, h-he! Seek th'—th'—th'—th'—th' det—

443 & 444

adopted sirname shall enioye the sayde inheritance. And because wee knowe howe dangerous it will bee

ention o' rowdy swingin' scholars—ae, ae, ae—'til they all know the deep wide ABC's 'n' dead numbers! E-e-e-e-e! I haue

445 & 446

to the state to suffer thease greate honoures and inheritances, to bee conioyned either by combinations, leagues, and marriages,

to teach serious math so n-no hunger bites y-years ahead, an so I can see each one of 'em liuin' better before tainted rott'n Greg dies at—

447 & 448

wheareby some one familie may growe monsterous in the state, thearefore wee doe establish and ordayne

last—maybe a tin trade, a steward iob—O, no sly SS! Eeeeee! Hy modern news—writing here at home—a home free of ou—

449 & 450

that noe person planteing or inhabiteing within any of our provinces within the degrees

tright poverty: where hope can gro, gainin' profit with sensible use. Ai! Not tendin' a nonni he—

451 & 452

aforesayde shall make any leagues, combynacions or contractes either by worde or writeing,

ebe SS trace-iob for ye gaine o' some edgey criminal r-rat (RAT!) who'd ask U t' chase all ye nonny crow—

trace-iob. detective job.

453 & 454

or confirmeing them by oaths, offensive or defensive, to the mainetenaunce of any faction whatsoever, vppon payne

ds of enemies t' far-away cities 'n'-'n'— afta great effort, shoot every nonny-non one of 'em. Hee, hee! Mi hi-vp occv pation! Vnpub—

455 & 456

of forfeiteing their goodes and lives as fellons, and to prevente the combindeing and conioyneing of thease

lishable idiotic adventvres—fag hosts— no, I can't defend mi nonnie story. Gee, he'l get gone—poof! afore de nonnie f—

457 & 458

honouresinonehousebymarriageweedoe furthur ordayne that such eldest daughter

ryghtenin' rot shud gro 'n' uuear ar free youth down uui' debt here at home. Ae, heedl'ss a' cos—

459 & 460

or heire female as shall marrie with any patriott, or the heire of a patriott, shall disinable herselfe

t—i-in arrear t' try t' help their bleari father, far lost in a memorie disease. Ha, ha! hopeless fool, he'll wait

461 & 462

from inherriteing her fathers or predecessours patriotshippe thereby, except shee marryeing

in error t' see his MT existence change for better. Phi! Phi! He'd resist yr prayers. O, hug me! Prepare for

463 & 464

of a husband soe inamored with her that he shall sell or give away his owne patriotshippe

life without this worthless man. Don't weep—piss! R h-hi-lo years have al been good. A-ah, a-ah. R.I.P.

465 & 466

and soe shall take the sirname of his wife's auncester, he may by that meanes inable himselfe

ye late Sir Kit de'Monti, mean 'n shameless, left U. Hys ace wife, 'n' R babes alone. He has faith she ma—

Sir Kit de'Monti. He notices his knighthood.

467 & 468

to inherite her honoures and estate and soe by marryeing the inheritrix of the patriot, hee will bee

y understand he left not t' harm her or the babes. There's no phixin' ye rot area. Oi! I let it go. Ei, ei! When I re—

469 & 470

accompted a kinde husband, and that will be his portion. The principal intent of frameing

turn'd from sea it began, 'n' I thot, O, chap! 'N' it'd heal—bind, at least. No—I pick 'n' clip—find where amp—

471 & 472

This lawe being that noe one subiect shall either by purchase or any other meanes unite

hicoelous nasal cysts grow, 'n' I, beery 'n' euer inable t' stop the habit a' hurtin' 'em—e-e-e! The han—

amphicoelous. concave on both sides: hollow. This cyst visible on the Death Mask.

473 & 474

the forces, thearby to inable himselfe to bee stronger then any of his order. But to the end

d e'er at the sore, ye mind bereft of thot, he, the uacant boorish slob, briefly greets the nonn—

475 & 476

that love may bee mayntayned, and that theise degrees may not estrange the upper orders

y day, then, spent, subsides yn a tattered gloomy death-rot heap. Grr! E-e! Man, heave me! Entreat—

477 & 478

From the lower, wee wish that the heires and eldest sonnes of the upper orders may marrie

fate t' release me from years o' this h-hard-pressed writin'. Then when U'd let me see how R poor

479 & 480

with the daughters of the lower orders soe to rayse their wives fortunes. And that the daughters

strife turns t' ashen death without redress, O, I'd serve U farther—go the rest o' d' way—go to hel, whetha—

481 & 482

of the upper orders being heires may marrye with the sonnes of the lower orders, makeing choice

win or lose, hon femme: euer thy writer of greased dispatches 'n' horrific mangey book reports—he-hee!

greased dispatches. unctuous notes to the secretary of state.

483 & 484

of the most vertuous, soe as vertue may advance both men and woemen to marriages,

A dutee to write song's no vvorse then tu B a fat man. U've more o' me each day, Ma'm! Eros's

fat. The "Venice Portrait" (1621?) shows Marlowe a plump man.

485 & 486

and that all degrees may bee thereby bound together in the bonde of love that none

ode left V holy babees yn bed and then the iob ta rear 'em al on the edge o' rotten naught.

Eros's ode. Romantic love.

487 & 488

may be scorned but the scorner. To this end alsoe, although wee would not haue you

Celeb voce, U'l need to marry again—no other shot—tots need U. Bless U! You! Wh-what do h—

Celeb voce. Micala had been a celebrateed singer in Spanish and Neapolitan theater.

no other shot. No other way to meet this problem.

489 & 490

imitate the Irish in their wilde and barbarous maners, yet wee will commend one custome

ard times mean when the tots liue 'n' R learnin'? My dear, U'd best watch o'er 'em, so we'l B—O! I-I-I! I C I'm

491 & 492

of theires unto you, which is that the poorer sorte sueing to gett the nursing of the children

putting h-horny Gregorio into th' future! No! At rest, I'd not s-see, touch or feel thee, which is the s—

493 & 494

of the lordes and gentrie, and breedeing upp in their minoritie as their owne, this breedeing,

ad part o' dieing, for euen tho' I, Sir Greg M., 'd be liein' here t' spend eternitie, we'd be sharin' nothin'.

495 & 496

together with their custome, doth begett another nature in them to love their foster children.

Go t' Guarina; there's home there for U 'n' th' tots. Don't trie t' relive th' ol' t-time here—we tend to B ch-chi—

Guarina. The Guarini family country place outside San Bellino, southwest of Venice.

497 & 498

and brethren, as if they were naturally bread of the same parentes, and they are accompted most vile and base

ded by tha past. See ahead: R tads can possibly be three lean men 'n' a dear woman fleein' terror at th' mercy a' tuf ve—

499 & 500

that shall neglect any good opportunitie to shew their thankfullenesse thus begotten and bread

nal ouerlords. Oh, can't we giue th' babetots strength to stay independent al life long? Ahh, thus t' keep—

501 & 502

betweene the riche and poore. And because wee will give all furtherance of the spreadeing

U 'n' R babes free o' d' hel-woe fear that liued w-wi' Greg at Naples 'n' Venice. O, th' children—e-e-e-e! Pace . . .

503 & 504

of thease newe collonies wee doe thearefore ordayne and appoynte that all such servauntes

E-e-e-e-e-e! Hope al U tots fynd place as loyal servants to friends around here. O, Hon, can't we weathe—

505 & 506

that shall be carried at the carge of any adventurer or planter, both those servauntes that are soe carryed

r th' gale? Set a yat husband o'erboard ta enter th' deep here. Rvn, C: chart thy course, love, 'n' sail t' Ferrara! Soe ta, ta!

507 & 508

over and their servauntes, with their servauntes servauntes shall be tyed to plante in consortshippe

Sir Henry's here. So ta, ta t' U to! Nu Sir Christopher'l want tv bid thee al adiev. Psst! U'l resent open vanes, even

509 & 510

with their first masters and shall(e) rise and remove with them to plante a newe colonie

mi love 'n' patient ladee 'n' dear wife Micaela. I'm sorree. "N' so, 'n' O, th' th' th' th' th' last we-we: s-sir-r,

ladee. Kit is a knight; he can call his wife a lady.

511 & 512

when their foresayde masters shall bee enabled by our forme thereunto, which shall bee

best we be ready. No brash lul, C? Sell th' boat here, 'n' find more ways t' leaue R home. Sh-h! If e'er He—

513 & 514

After hee hath gayned and estate in England and is able to drawe over or carrie with him

n has aided vs, 'e'd do it now. Wait for Greg ta die, then, ai! Try 'n' heal th' breech, ere a-a-al manner

515 & 516

three hundred men, leaveing the collonie hee was first planted in three hundred strong or upwardes.

o' hesitation waste thee, 'n' U'l need t' decidewhat'sproper, mil-love—'n' U'lneed R Hen. Grr—Grrr! 'N' shh! A funded e—

517 & 518

The next magistracie is the governour, him wee ordayne after the death of the first patriott

xistence is mi wish for thee. A great friend, he'd manage to prorate it—thy futvre here—to th' tota—

519 & 520

to bee annuall by election, but dureing the life of the first patriott hee shall bee governour and afterwardes

l. Now he's freein' us of a huge traitor, but ere fal he'd aid U, love. Let it B for th' babes, C? One printed letter'l gayn ten a—

a huge traitor. Bacon's trial is in progress—May 1621.

521 & 522

his heires shall be honoured as head of that order but shall not govern unlesse he bee thereunto chosen.

vid readers, 'n' U'l soon B the able author o' the best neuus sheet for all o' England, C? 'N' h-here I rest, see? Ho, ho! Shh!

neuus sheet. Kit wants Micaela to write gazzettes for England.

523 & 524

The governours charge shall bee to see the lawes, decrees and orders aswell in the publique governement

Requite us! U can sho we were not a useless team! Believe: 'orlorn, brash old Greg needed thee as th' helper, C? 'N' gl-

525 & 526

of the colonie as in the private families observed hee shall controlle all men for breach of manners

gliomatovs, he'l slip to near coma 'n' V, dear, 'l finish all the notes for him so he'l be clean, clear 'n' free before

gliomatous. Webster. with a glioma, a tumor, usually of the brain or spinal cord, composed of tissue that forms the supporting structure of nerves.

527 & 528

and discipline first giveing them private admonition and afterwardes publique if they perscever

R deadline. Ace, I no U hate ye fringe nevves dispatches bvt do 'em wel, PDQ, as I-I'm nappin'. Grr! Tuf if it irrit—

529 & 530

in their misdemeanour. Hee togeather the maior, the shreife, the churchwarden, and one commoner chosen

ate Frances. R notes don't concern him. O, more 'n' more I resent that he—he, he, he, HE—hid mi Chr. Mar. I D: 'e woue a huge,

531 & 532

by the rest of the commoners, the governour haveing the casteing voice, they shall have power to indite

clever web to cheat me, *saying he authored mi Sh plays.* O, hovv to retort t' the feo egregiovs hit? 'N'-'n'-'n' I ce Hen

Hen. About now, in England, Hen is imprisoned (indirectly by Bacon).

533 & 534

for breach of lawes, and to suspend from degrees for breach . . . manners accordeing as in their discretion

has been arrested for prosecuting Francis in Lords: O! Some mad Bacon-anger stirred, which e'en f-forced a—

535 & 536

shall be thought meete. The next order that wee ordayne is the maior and aldermen, together

n extreme royal order t'-t' hold Hen tight at home. O, he's been released unharmed, t' get awai at the

537 & 538

wirh the shreif, all which 3(three) orders in matters of triall of life and death, we ordane

end of a month with d' friendly iailer. So wd he sail here for R late farewel chats? He, he! (titt'r.)

friendly iailer. Sir William Parkhurst, who'd worked at the embassy in Venice with Wotton and Kit. Hen's imprisonment ended 30th of August.

539 & 540

that they shall bee tryed either by the counsell of state or the provinciall councell, the jurie that tryeth

July's c-cold this yeere; he'll probably ne'er hear th' Yat's t-t-teeth chatter i' the rain. O, uuil he t-t-t-touch 'n' feel ol'

541 & 542

them beeing to bee of their own ranke and order, and in case where there are not soe many	**Kit? Beery breath fades as h-he'd read a once—winnin' remnant. E-e! No! Go home now—retreet o'er**

543 & 544

to bee founde, they shall bee supplied out of the order and ranke next beneath them.	**a snoee Alp, e'en to d' b-b-beautiful Eden foreuer lost t' rotten expended me. Ahhhhh! Kyt.**

545 & 546

And wee doe give as well to our provinciall councell as to this degree and order the jurisdiction	**No, Doctor Daniel, nothing here now—just a crude uglie l-larded old corpse. Let sea waves cover it! I, I, I.**

f

Captain John Bargrave's A Form of Polisie, by Ignotus.
Papers of Lord Sackville at Knole Park, Kent. From print of Susan Myra Kingsbury. Records of The Virginia Co. Vol. iv. #CDXVIII.

CAPTAIN JOHN BARGRAVE LETTER TO THE TREASURER

1 & 2

Right honorable after ten yeares service in the warres in the summer time, and at my studdy in the wynter,

'N' Monti, restin' here mum at Uenice, wrote this earnest letter t' aide hys dear friend Bargrave wyth hys mun—

X

There's more

Henry Wotton's Poem for Elizabeth Stuart. Logan Pearsall Smith. *Letters of Sir H.W.*

YOU MEANER BEAUTIES

1 & 2

You meaner beauties of the Night,
That poorly satisfy our eyes,

I, Henry, pen a toy gift uerse for you. O, stay at home, Elisabeth, t' su—

3, 4, 5, 6

More by(e) your number than your light,
You common people of the skies,
What are you when the Moon shall rise?
You curious chanters of the Wood,

bmerge thy sorrouu in some happy home time, 'n' look U—let your boys C enuf of children's natural ioy! (Chr. M. wrote that.) Oh, you see, hon, we show U Aeo—

thy sorrow. Married at 16 to teen-aged (handsome, manic-depressive, ambitious) Frederick, Elector Palatinate, Elizabeth Stuart moved with him to Heidelberg Castle. Intractable adolescents, they needed guidance. In denial about her pregnancy till her first baby actually arrived, struggling to manage an enormous household, the poor spoiled princess was overstressed, while Frederick busily comitted political suicide. **your boys.** By 1620, Elizabeth was the mother of a six-year-old and a three—year-old boy, a baby son and a little girl.

7, 8, 9, 10

That warble forth(e) dame Nature's layes,
Thinking your passions understood(e)
By your weak(e) accents; what's your praise
When Philomel her voice shall raise?

lus' sound: like an answer'd prayer, it begins to soothe thy sad heart. A nutritious motherly love wil shape 'n' cheer ye, C? Keep away from his raw sensual breach o'

Aeolus' sound. Aeolus was the Greek god of winds. Henry may have given the princess an aeolian harp, a toy popular at the time.

11 & 12

You violets that first appear(e),
By your pure purple mantle known,

your prim pure love. Stay—B patient! Know he'l return safe to U. Apply

13 & 14

Like the proud virgins of the year(e),	**yovrself: rough it! (He, he!) Pray don't**
As if the Spring were all your own;	**sink t' false weeping! I'l worrie! Are U**

A gentle resonance between plaintext and ciphers; Elizabeth was proud—she did think the Spring was all her own.

15 & 16

What are you when the Rose is blown(e)?	**a mere shy babe? No! Show us—let's see ye**
So when my Mistress shall be(e) seen(e)	**woman, 'n' we'l neel to her. I wish she, str—**

17 & 18

In form and beauty of her mind(e),	**ife-torn, th' enemy near, cd end her quest**
By Virtue first, then choice a Queen(e),	**for much ioy. Invite a babie, fu—**

strife-torn, th'enemy near. With some connivance, Elizabeth's husband Frederick had just been declared elected king of Bohemia, and to aid the new emperor, Maximillian of Bavaria was bringing forces to oust Frederick. Wotton was trying to negotiate a peaceful solution, suggesting that if Frederick were to pull out of Bohemia right away, he might keep the Palatinate. Frederick indignantly rejected the proposal and lost everything at the battle of the White Hill, 8 Nov. 1620.

19 & 20

Tell me if she were not design'd	**ll of his princely deeds, who'd neel—**
Th(e) eclipse and glory of her kind(e)?	**make thee free t' sing, not die! Gr.**

Gr. Gregorio? He must have given this poem to Henry to present to the princess. The old-fashioned extra e's throughout are needed to make the ciphers but don't change the sound.

f

Created by Sir Henry Wotton, 1626, and carved in stone.

FRANCIS BACON'S EPITAPH, ST. MICHAEL'S CHURCH, ST. ALBANS

QUI POSTQUAM OMNIA NATURALIS
SAPIENTLAE ET CIVILIS ARCANA
EVOLUISSET,
NATURAE DECRETUM EPLEVIT:
COMPOSITA SOLVANTUR.

Is our queen's poor, queer, unvvanted son t' sit in mama's lap at last? Accelerate time no more; it vvil slip past U, uui' lactic A-a-a-i!

the Latin, Englished: "After he'd unfolded all natural knowledge and civil secrets, he fulfilled nature's decree: "Dissolve, Compounds!"

f

Shakespeare Epitaphs. Trinity Church, Stratford-on-Avon.

SHAKESPEARE'S EPITAPHS

IVDICIO PYLIVM, GENIO SOCRATVM, ARTE MARONUM. TERRA TEGIT,
POPVLVS MAERET, OLYMPVS HABET.

The anagram:
Yes, eager t-to aid civic improvement, bright Marlove vvrote immortal plays and poems. Peta

PYLIVM. Pylius, a poetic form of the name Nestor. Nestor's father was a great judge, executed because he disagreed with the government. Nestor himself was to be executed but escaped. Kit experienced a parallel tribulation.

SOCRATVM. Socrates, a bi-sexual man who married late, had children, died by poison, loyal to his principals. So did Kit.

MARONUM. Like Kit, Virgilius Maro was a spy poet who made comical secret writing.

"Peta" was Kit's half-brother. (In his own ciphers, Kit made fun of Peter's accent.) Peter may have helped pay for the Stratford cenotaph, similar in design to their father's.

Below a half-statue of the poet in a niche, this poem was carved:

STAY PASSENGER, WHY GOEST THOV BY SO FAST?
READ IF THOV CANST, WHOM ENVIOVS DEATH HATH PLAST,
WITHIN THIS MONVMENT SHAKSPEARE: WITH WHOME,
QVICK NATVRE DIDE: WHOSE NAME DOTH DECK Y(s) TOMBE,
FAR MORE THEN COST: SIEH ALL, Y(T) HE HATH WRITT,
LEAVES LIVING ART, BVT PAGE, TO SERVE HIS WITT.

WAS MARLOVES STAR ENTOMBD, BY THIEVES,
WITHIN THIS CRYPT? THE EPITAPH Y(T) DECKS THIS CLOSE,
FRAGMENT THAT: SEE THROVGH, KNIT VP, THE WOOLSEY
WEAVES OF QVEEN DIDO, KING LEAR: IN BOTH, ONE AVTHOR
SHOWS, WHOSE ART HIS NAME WITH LOVE HATH WRIT:
THAT FACT MUST SAVE Y(s) DAMNED, SAVAGE WIT. H.

Floor Slab Message over Shakespeare's grave:

GOOD FREND FOR JESVS SAKE FORBEARE,
TO DIGG THE DVST ENCLOASED HEARE!
BLESTE BE Y(e) MAN Y(t) SPARES THES STONES,
AND CVRST BE HE Y(t) MOVES MY BONES.

BENEATH Y(e) CLOSE FIND MARLOVES VERSE,
NEAR SHAKESPEARES DVSTY BONES,
O Y(t) BRAGGART JESTE OF GODD BE CVRSD!
HE Y(t)S ENTOMBED OF THESE STONES. M.

A TIMELINE

Events that Touched Marlowe's Life

About dating: Conyers Read. Mr. Secretary Walsingham. Cambridge, MA: Harvard U Press, 1925: "documents dated in England after 1582 are dated 10 days earlier than they would be dated in Roman Catholic countries." All through the years of Marlowe's story, England used the old Julian calendar while most of Europe used the "New Style" Gregorian calendar after 1582. (20 May in England would be 30 May across the Channel.)

During Marlowe's years and later, the legal year in England began on 25 March. January 1590 New Style would be January 1589 in England. These facts help readers figure whether a text refers to a date in Julian (old) or Gregorian (new) style. In this timeline, New Style is used for the years, and for days of the month, Julian style in England, Gregorian in Europe—according to where the story moves.

1549 Oct. Twins (Ned de Vere, Ed Manners) b. to Elizabeth Tudor in house arrest at Hatfield. Father, Admiral Tom Seymour. See Marlowe. Dido. 1.01. ll. 106-108. Complete Plays of Chr. Marlowe. ed. Irving Ribner. NY: Odyssey Press 1963; shadows also show in Elizabeth Jenkins. Elizabeth the Great. NY: G.P. Putnam's Sons, 1967, pp 25, 27, 28, 31, 33; and in Donald Barr Chidsey. Elizabeth I, A Great Life in Brief. NY: Knopf, 1955, pp 13, 14.

1554 March Boy baby Philip Sidney b. to Elizabeth Tudor at Reicote. Father, Prince Philip of Spain. Martin Hume. Two English Queens and Philip. NY: G.P. Putnam's Sons, 1908. Hume makes it clear that nine months before this birth Philip came to England incognito with lawyers arranging a marriage contract for Mary. Elizabeth was locked up in the palace fearing for her life. Prince Philip became this baby's godfather.

1556 c. April Fraternal twins Mary de Vere, Philip Howard b. to Elizabeth Tudor at Hatfield. Father Prince Philip became the boy baby's godfather. (Twins conceived just before Philip left England in 1555.)

1558 c. March Boy baby Ferdinando Stanley b. to Elizabeth Tudor. Father was Philip, now king of Spain. Child conceived just before Philip's last goodbye to England, June 1557.

1559 May William Pickering, away from England during Queen-Mary-years, returns, talks privately with new Queen Eliz. DNB. William Pickering; and Wlliam Neville. Elizabeth the First; and also Elizabeth Jenkins. Elizabeth and Leicester. NY: Coward McCann, 1962.) Pickering must have informed the queen of privileged playing companies in France and Italy, government-subsidized companies in which spy-actors reported to their rulers. It seemed Elizabeth liked the idea:

1559 June The queen's lover Robert Dudley writes he has created a company of players, "and they are all honest men." C. C. Stopes. Burbage and Sh's Stage. NY: Haskell House, 1970, p 7. (Spies called themselves honest men.)

1560 Christmas Elizabeth Rex, Robert Dudley are secretly married at a house belonging to the earl of Pembroke. (Dudley DNB.)

1561 early Jan. Boy baby Francis Bacon b. to Queen Elizabeth Tudor at York House. (Newborn damaged—by Robert Dudley?) Father, Francis Walsingham. Baby conceived on night of Moorish and Queen Dance. E. K. Chambers. The Elizabethan Stage. Oxford: Clarendon, 1923. Appendix A, "A Court Calendar." Moorish and Queen p 78.

1561 27 Oct. Girl baby Mary Sidney Herbert b. to Queen Elizabeth Tudor at St. James (said to have been born far away). Father, Robert Dudley.

1562 probably late Dec. (no recorded birth date.) Crippled boy baby (Robert Cecil) b. to Queen Elizabeth Tudor after she suffered smallpox and measles at Hampton Court. Father, Robert Dudley.

1563 The new queen grants her loyal shadow Roger Manwood "the royal manor of St. Stephens or Hackington, Kent." Manwood DNB.

Also, Edward Foss. The Judges of England. NY: AMS Press 1966, vol 5.

1563 early May In woods above Dover, Kate Arthur Marley and Judge Roger Manwood participate in a "Monstrous Ransom;" and Christopher Marlowe is conceived. See the William 'Shakspeare' and William Rowley play, Birth of Merlin. Also many references to Manwood as Marlowe's father in Marlowe's ciphers. In The Diary of John Manningham, 1602-1603. ed. J. Bruce. Camden Society Pub., 1868, the entry at Nov. 1602 is a third-hand recollection of 1592: Manwood and "sonne," and the gold chain.

1563 Nov. Boy baby Robert Sidney b. to Queen Eliz. Tudor at Whitehall. Father, Robert Dudley.

1564 6 February Christopher Marley (Marlowe) born. John H. Ingram. Christopher Marlowe and his Associates. NY: Cooper Square Pub., 1970. (1904). His source: Rev. J.S. Sidebothem. Memorials of the Kings School, Canterbury. 1865. Students had to furnish proof of age before admission on the foundation. Kit(Christopher) born nine months after Roger's presence in Dover as judge of Admiralty Court.

Calendar of the Inner Temple Records, and Black & White Book of the Cinq Ports. Christopher born in a house (pic, Ingram. op. cit.) corner St. George's St. and St. George's Lane, Canterbury. A slight club foot from mother Kate Arthur. Ciphers, passim, Taming of The Shrew plaintext, and a discussion of Kit's own three boy-children with club feet in Bargraves Polisie ciphers.

1564 26 Feb. At church of St. George, Kit (all his life, this Christopher was known as Kit) is christened. Ingram. op. cit., and Bakeless. The Tragicall History of Christopher Marlowe, vol 1. Westport, CT: Greenwood Press, 1970. Today the register reads "Marlowe;" almost surely it has been renewed, copied, with name changed to Kit's later professional name.

1564 20 April Kit's legal father John Marley made freeman of the city and member of guild of shoemakers, three years before his apprenticeship was to have ended. Urry. Christopher Marlowe & Canterbury. London: Faber and Faber, 1988. Also Constance Kuriyama. Christopher Marlowe, A Renaissance Life, p xiii: John Marley, made freeman, paid a reduced fee of 4s 1 d.

1566 19 Nov. Boy baby Robert Devereux, to become second earl of Essex, b. to Queen Elizabeth Tudor, at Whitehall. Father Robert Dudley, now Earl of Leicester.

1568 28 August Kit's older half-sister Moll is buried in St. George's churchyard. (Bakeless. op. cit., vol 1.)

Dates for Kate's nine children (Bakeless. op. cit.):
Moll b. '62, d. Aug. '68.
Kit b. 6 Feb. '64, christened 26 Feb. '64. [d. Nov. 21-22, 1621 Gregorian, in Venice. R.B.]
Meg b. '65, m. John Jurdan, a tailor, June 1590.
baby son (no name) christened Hallowe'en '68, buried 5 Nov '68.
Joan b. Aug. '69, m. John More, shoemaker, April '82, d. Aug, '98.
Thomas b. & died '70.
Anne b. July '71. m. John Crawford, shoemaker, on 10 June 1593.
Dorothy b. Oct '73. m. Thos Cradwell, June '94.
Thomas (second of this name) b. April, '76. may have lived 28 years or more.

1568 Kit becomes mascot of a federation of city street-gangs. Antonio de Eslava [Kit]. Noches de Invierno. Pamplona: Carlos de Labayen, 1609. Near end of the year 1568 Kit is sent to sea with grandsire William Arthur of Dover, a ship's yeoman, clerk of the cargo.

Kit serves c. four years as ship-boy. Learns seamanship and shipping practices. Urry writes of grandfather—not enough. William Urry. Chr. Marlowe and Canterbury. Ed. A. Butcher. London: Faber and Faber, 1988. Numerous mentions of ships and voyages in Kit's ciphers, and Dover as home port. Excellent study of the playwright's seamanship by A.F. Falconer, Lieutenant Commander, Royal Naval Reserve. Shakespeare and the Sea. London: Constable, 1964. 155 pp of enlightening text.

1572 Kit, after accident on board, comes ashore, works as page for Roger Manwood or for Roger Manwood's patron, Sir Thomas Gresham, Queen's Merchant.

John William Burgon. The Life and Times of Sir Thomas Gresham. 2 vol. NY: Burt Franklin, 1965 (1839). Also Manwood DNB, Gresham DNB.

Edward Foss. The Judges of England, op. cit., vol 5.

A sideline: Burgon. op. cit., vol 2, p 461: Youthful Ned de Vere rents a town house from Thomas Gresham, in parish of Peter the Poor.

1572 June Kit's first theatrical role (?), sailor boy in Geo. Gascoigne's masque (included in An Hundredth Sundry Flowers) for double wedding at Southwark town house of Anthony Browne, Viscount Montague. Masque probably directed by Ned de Vere.

1572 24 August France. Francis Walsingham, English Ambassador in Paris, witnesses the St. Bartholomew's Day Massacre of Protestants there. Saves some lives. Walsingham DNB. Walsingham takes leave of absence from Paris job at end 1572 thru early 1573. Is this when his illegitimate son Ben Jonson is conceived? Mother an SSS (State Secret Service) agent?

1572 (to '77) Kit works as page for Gresham (?) at Bishopsgate, Osterley and Mayfield. Learns geography and shipping practices. (Writes boyish play, The Lord Cromwell.)

1573 first week Aug. Boy baby (her last—Henry Wriothesley) b. to Queen Elizabeth Tudor, at Thomas Gresham's Mayfield house on the East Rother. Father, Ned de Vere.

Kit could have been there at Mayfield when Elizabeth came to deliver.

E.K. Chambers. Eliz. Stage. "Court Calendar," for dates (probably 4, 5, 6 August) and extreme privacy of visit.

A letter to me 21 Nov. 1986 from occupant of Mayfield, Convent of the Holy Child, with pamphlet, pix, house-plan. Gresham built a private tower-stairway for Elizabeth's quiet visit (pix), and filled in some windows to improve privacy in her apartment(pix).

1573 Plans made for the first theater built in England to present plays only—no bulls and bears. Frances Yates. The Art of Memory. Chicago: U of Chicago Press, 1966, and

Richard Deacon. John Dee. London: Frederick Mulks, 1968. Theater to be erected in Shoreditch, on corner of property of Edward Manners. C. C. Stopes. Burbage and Sh's Stage. NY: Haskell House, 1970 (1913). There's design aid from John Dee, financial help from the queen. (Did Walsingham bring his natural son Francis Bacon to the planning meeting?)

Some time between 1573 & '76, Bakeless: The Marleys move from St. George's Parish to St. Andrew's, middle of Canterbury.

1573-77 Kit spends vacations from work at his dad Roger Manwood's three homes—at Hackington outside Canterbury, at Gad's Hill, Shorne, and in West Smithfield near London. Kit's earliest plays are presented in Roger's, and perhaps Gresham's, living rooms. Kit's ciphers are hidden in each "apocryphal" play printed by Tucker Brooke. The Shakespeare Apocrypha. Oxford: Clarendon, 1971 (1908).

1575

1575 spring Tin for the sultan—meeting of overt Jew Alvaro Mendes with Gresham, Francis Walsingham and Elizabeth at Gresham's Osterley estate. Resentful neighbors fire the fence. Kit could bring news. Gresham DNB, and E. K. Chambers. Eliz. Stage. "A Court Calendar," offer different dates.

1575 Kit's grandsire dies in Dover—Kate and Kit could be with him. They may bury him at sea ("full fadom five thy father lies") from the Harveys' longboat. Harveys are longtime sailor-friends in Folkestone (circulation of-the-blood man, and his father, brothers). Wm. Urry, TLS 13 Feb. 1964, p 136, and Wm. Harvey DNB.

1575 July Gresham attends the Killingworth (Kenilworth) Party to get Elizabeth's approval of his expense account—Kit goes with him as page, loves the shows—elements of them identifiable in Shakespeare plays. (John Nichols. Progresses of Elizabeth, vol 1.

E. K. Chambers. Eliz. Stage op. cit., also his William Shakespeare, A Study of Facts and Problems. Oxford, Clarendon, 1930.)

1575 Francis Bacon attends Trinity College, Cambridge, under care of John Whitgift. (Bacon bios: Montagu, Dixon, DNB.)

1576

1576 early April Lease signed for the Theater to be built on corner of land owned by Ned's twin Edward Manners, Third Earl of Rutland, but sub-lease apparently belongs to Giles Alleyn. (C. C. Stopes. Burbage and Sh.'s Stage. op. cit., p 19.) Construction begins.

1577

1577 From November till May 1578 Kit sails—Plymouth to Constantinople and back as ship boy and doer (?) for Gresham, at first aboard the Judith, then in the Tiger with Capt. Christopher (Kester) Carleill, Walsingham's young step-son son-in-law. (Gresham bio; Drake bios; Carleill DNB; Carleill portrait in Geo. Malcolm Thomson. Sir Francis Drake. NY: Wm. Morrow & Co. 1972. Cipher in Sh Sonnet 126 identifies Captain Kester and Kit as lovers—in Constantinople and later in Ireland.)

1578

1578 May. Kit back in England, home from Constantinople.

1578 June to November. Shadows: Kit as page, actor-writer for Ned de Vere (and probably Ned's lover) on Elizabeth's long Progress with Churchyard. (E.K. Chambers. Eliz. Stage. op. cit.; Nichol's Progresses, Churchyard's works in microfilm: The Turkish Boy and Young Mercury.)

1578 15 Nov. Roger knighted at Richmond. 17 Nov. Sir Roger Manwood becomes lord chief baron of Exchequer. (Kit, Ned deVere and Roger, together, write The Famous Victories.)

1579

1579 Jan. to December 1580 Almost two King's School years for Kit. He enters a month before his fifteenth birthday; later he wouldn't have been eligible. A scholarship arranged by Roger Manwood. Kit lives at home, writes Selimus (see microfilm from Folger copy, and Kit's ciphers), remembering his voyage to Greece in '77-'78. (Sonnet 126 cipher) Kit writes The Lord Cromwell, using his memories of the Mayfield ironworks, and may have sketched a near-pantomime with bits of schoolboy-sailor Greek dialogue—a proto-Erotokritos. (John Mavrogordato. The Erotokritos. London: Oxford U. Press, 1929), a play perhaps used as school production by Greek-scholar headmaster Gresshop, who may have taught Kit about the linked anagrams found in Greek tragedies. (Urry essay on Gresshop"s qualifications in Chr. Marlowe & Canterbury. op. cit., and also Thompson & Padover. Secret Diplomacy. (Appendix.) N.Y.: Frederick Ungar, 1965 (1937).

1579 February, new style: Francis Bacon's foster father Nathaniel dies, and in March, Francis, back from work with English embassy at Paris, learns Nicholas has left him a threadbare inheritance. Daphne du Maurier. Golden Lads. Garden City, NY: Doubleday, 1975. Bacon can live in Nicholas's chambers at Gray's Inn, which he does. Spedding, Ellis & Heath, Life and Letters . . . and other bios. Late in the year he's taken by his real father to a party at Barn Elms, Walsingham's country place, described in Read. Mr. Secretary Walsingham. Here Francis learns his mother the queen secretly married Robert Dudley in Dec. 1560, just before Francis was born. He figures that made him legitimate, puts him in line for the throne.

1579 With Roger's help John Marley begins a business as bondsman and continues in the profession till his death. At time of his death John is also parish clerk of St. Mary Bredman. Family must have moved again, from St. Andrew's. Bakeless, op. cit., is confused about this and dubious about John's literacy. (A parish clerk was necessarily literate, and several of John's signatures exist.)

1580

1580 Kit spends holidays from King's School at Roger's house, where plays The Lord Cromwell and an early draft of Lust's Dominion are produced as play-parties. (ciphers in these plays.)

1580 December Kit to Cambridge early, settles in ground-floor chamber at Bene't (Corpus Christi), meets steward Francis Kett, who becomes his tutor. Kit makes friends with older boys; puritans John Greenwood at Bene't, John Ap-Henry of Peterhouse, John Udall of Trinity; before long they will become victims of Archbishop Whitgift. (Udall in '92, the others in '93. DNB for all.) Kit to have a Parker Scholarship in Divinity; Manwood and Parker had been longtime friends. (Jas. Mc Mullen Rigg. Manwood DNB, and Manwood's letters to Parker in Parker Correspondence—Parker Society Papers—pp 187-192, 338, 405.)

1581

1581 Easter Francis Kett leaves for home in Norfolk. A free-thinker, he'll be burned alive by his bishop **January 1589**. (DNB.)

1582

1582 (or **'81**?) Kit meets Gabriel Harvey, fellow of Trinity Hall, a friend of poet Edmund Spenser—and recruiter for SSS? (Virginia Stern. Gabriel Harvey. Oxford: Clarendon, 1979, between the lines.) Gabriel shows Spenser's poems to Kit, helps him with writing and rhetoric, and in July 1582 may have involved him in overseas work for Francis Walsingham.

1582 July 17/27 to late August Europe. At Reims, Kit goes to see a man named Richard Baines, locked in local jail for trying to kill the president of Reims English Catholic College by poisoning the faculty soup. It seems Kit promised Harvey he'd free the prisoner, a not very good SSS agent. Kit suggests Baines might appeal to the Christian conscience of Dr. Allen, the president, and offer to work for him as double agent. Tom Walsingham appears (?) to help this happen and get Kit back to England. Reluctant, hating Kit, Baines agrees. (Kit turns up at Reims with assumed name: study dates in Douay Diaries.)

The First and Second Diaries of the English College, Douay, with Appendix of Unpublished Documents. London: David Nutt 1965 (1878). Years later Baines reappears, to twice betray Kit. Also, Wraight & Stern. In Search of Christopher Marlowe. NY: Vanguard, 1965.

1582 autumn to spring 1583 Kit studies hard, Gabriel helps him write. Scenes of Dido, Queen of Carthage are sketched, and perhaps now an outline of Arden of Feversham appears. Kit writes Locrine—a successful play-party melodrama produced at Roger's house (ciphers), and at holiday party at Bene't? Kit's school and college plays, identified in his ciphers, are absent from records of those institutions.

1583 10 March Walsingham carefully selects "honest men" for a Queen's Players' Co. (E. K. Chambers. Eliz. Stage. op. cit., vol 2, p 104.)

1583 Kit spends most of the year at Dr. Allen's Catholic College at Reims in France (European calendar), returning to Cambridge **near end Aug.** He and friends swim at Grantchester Pool, against rules made by Whitgift. (pic of pool: Noel Barwell. Cambridge. London & Glasgow: Blackie & Son, n.d. pix by E. W. Haslehust.)

1583 Roger Manwood buys rectory of Chalk Church on the Dover Road (Edward Hasted. History and Topographical Survey of the County of Kent. Simmons and Kirkby, 1790-1799, vol 3, p 469), from which Kit might someday minister to the parish. (A bas-relief of Puck is carved over the church-door.)

1583 winter Kit studies, translates Ovid's Amores and first part Lucan's Pharsalia. (Complete Works of Chr. M., 2nd edition. Ed. Fredson Bowers. Cambridge: Cambridge U, 1981.) Kit and Tom Nashe spend time at nearby inns where the girls are.

1584

1584 Feb., March Kit prepares for BA—an Act in the public schools; two debates, in each responding to 3 opponents; exams by tutor and headmaster; on Ash Wednesday a test in the schools by The Ould Batchelor. One more test, in Latin. He presents his supplicat, becomes a determiner. Palm Sunday at the U., BA's conferred on 231 grads. Kit is #199—makes BA in spite of extra-curricular work. Wraight & Stern. op. cit, and Benstead. Portrait of Cambridge, and Bakeless, etc.

1584 May through July Kit the graduate introduced around London by his dad Roger Manwood. Francis Walsingham will send Kit to Ireland to learn soldiering with Captain

Christopher (Kester) Carleill. (cipher, Sonnet 126.) Walsingham tells Kit to go back to Cambridge (he's studying for MA) and wait for a call.

1584 21 June Sir John Perrot, Elizabeth's pirate secret-half-bro who looks like Henry VIII, becomes lord deputy in Ireland. (Sir John Perrot DNB.)

1584 summer Sir John Perrot appoints Christopher (Kester) Carleill commander of the garrison of Coleraine and the district of Route, north Ireland. Carleill, Francis Walsingham's step-son and son-in-law, is now married to Mary Walsingham, Walsingham's younger daughter, who did *not* die as a child, as histories say. (Carleill DNB.)

1584 late Oct. At Bene't Kit gets word he's to ship out of Bristol to Coleraine. (Friends sign the Buttery book for him in his absence. Wraight and Stern. op. cit.)

1584 25 Oct. Kit sails for Ireland (calendar same as England's) in the Gift of God, Capt. Allerton, mate Sampson, old friend (mate on trip to Constantinople on the Tiger, 1577-78). At Coleraine Kit shares a cottage with Capt. Kester, learns about holding a fort. (CSP Ireland, and Sonnet 126 cipher.)

1584 Hallowe'en Wild Scots-Irish, masked, come to Kester's Coleraine headquarters, entertain with songs, bagpipes, story of Amleth-Hamlet (description of such men, Edward M. Hinton. Ireland through Tudor Eyes. Philadelphia: U of PA, 1935). Carleill, who has Scots forebears, is hospitable; his lieutenant Bagenall hates the whole thing.

1584 10 Nov. Carleill asked by Perrot to report in Dublin. (CSP Ireland.) Carleill takes the Tiger, and Kit and Sampson take two pinnaces down, all to be cleaned and refitted for coast-patrol. Garrison left in care of Lieut. Bagenall. (CSP Ireland.) In Dublin Kit and Carleill meet Perrot (Sonnet 126 cipher), his secretary Edmund Spenser, and pentagon-fort-designer Paul Ive? (shadows: Spenser DNB. Ive DNB.)

1584 end Nov. Carleill learns from Perrot that Bagenall (disobeying Carleill) took men from Coleraine and attacked Scots in the Glinns, mid-Nov. Badly defeated, Bagenall writes for shovels. Perrot, furious, says Carleill abandoned his post, sends him back to Coleraine. (CSP Ireland.)

1584 mid Dec. Carleill ordered from Coleraine to Dunanany with men and field guns. (CSP Ireland.) Kit goes along. Wm. Stanley, Bagenall, Fenton, Warren, Carleill beseige the castle. Big mess. Finally they get inside. Sorley Boy Mac Donnell (Sonnet 126 cipher, and CSP Ireland) and his men march in to save the Scots. Carleill captures Sorley Boy, spares his life. Awful cleanup. CSP confuses some dates.

1585

1585 Feb. Carleill relieved of his post by Perrot (CSP Ireland, and DNB), stays to defend Sorley Boy—no use—Perrot wanted his head. Kit sails for England, Canterbury, Cambridge.

1585 Feb.-April, May Kit studies 6 weeks, then crosses Channel on another job for Walsingham. Stays at Reims under cover. European calendar. First and Second Diaries of the English College at Douay. op. cit.

1585 end May Kit returns to Cambridge, then goes to London, checks with Walsingham who tells him to be at Barn Elms on **11 July**.

1585 11 July Her Majesty at Walsingham's Barn Elms on the Thames. (E.K.C. Eliz. Stage. op. cit., "A Court Calendar.") On this day Kit is probably told he's to waste Dr. William Allen.

1585 19 July France Kit's at the English College at Reims. Douay Diaries. op. cit. Besides the Dr. Allen job, Kit is to talk to Gilbert Gifford, a deacon there who's an agent for Walsingham—Kit delivers to this man a message about imprisoned Mary of Scotland.

1585 27 July France Hoping Dr. Allen might survive and reform, Kit gives the man only half the dose of mercury sublimate prescribed by Walsingham. (See Martin Haile. An Elizabethan Cardinal, William Allen. London: Sir Isaac Pitman, 1914.) Kit's method detailed in Ballantine, Honest Men.

1585 3 August France Allen has suffered intense illness, burned his papers, is carried to Spa. Haile. op. cit.

1585 August Eng. Kit back at Cambridge. Hen Wriothesley moves into St John's, registers on his twelfth birthday (numerous bios). A sizar at St. John's, Tom Nashe (an honest man), is chosen to be Hen's SSS guard.

1585 19 August, Canterbury. Is this the **August Sunday** on which Roger asks John Marley and Kit, with his uncle Thomas Arthur and brother-in-law John Moore, to witness the will of Katherine Benchkin, soon to be an in-law of Roger's? Kit's signature is here—his only publicly-known, English secretary-style handwriting. (Wraight & Stern, Bakeless, Urry, etc.) Kit, in Canterbury or at Roger's, now finishes (?) Arden of Feversham from Roger's case-books,.

1585 autumn Kit's famous portrait painted—at Cambridge?

1585 autumn France to Italy Alive, Dr Allen moves to Rome, stays till 1594 when SSS finally wastes him.

1585 late Oct. Eng. Walsingham shows Kit a letter from Mary of Scotland's secretary Thomas Morgan, written from the Bastille 15 Oct. 1585, introducing Gilbert Gifford to Mary as trustworthy. Gifford, erstwhile agent of Walsingham and alienated from family, has just killed himself in Paris. Walsingham wants Kit to be ringer for a big job. (between the lines, Conyers Read. Mr. Sec'y Walsingham and the Policy . . . op. cit.) Mary is to be led to believe she can send mail to her supporters uncensored by SSS.

1585 early Nov. Kit home from Cambridge (Attendance record, Wraight & Stern. op. cit.) to grow and groom hair and beard to resemble Gilbert Gifford's. Kit practices imitating Gilbert's voice and manner.

1585 end Nov. France, Eng. Kit goes to Paris with papers from Walsingham for Morgan. In Paris Kit picks up Gilbert's clothes, jewelry, returns to Rye on a French ship. (Conyers Read. op. cit.; Antonia Fraser. Mary, Queen of Scots. NY: Delacorte, 1969.)

1585 early Dec. Eng. Pretending to be Gilbert Gifford, Kit is arrested as he debarks at Rye—he's hustled to Walsingham. Everyone's told Kit is Gilbert G. In private, Kit tells Walsingham his idea of channeling Queen Mary's mail—in hollow bungs of her beer barrels.

1585 soon after Christmas, Eng. Walsingham's man Phelippes goes to Chartley, where Queen Mary is now held. Phelippes talks to her jailer Paulet. "Gilbert" talks to Catholic families in London (Read, Fraser et al), gets a letter addressed to Mary from French ambassador. "Gilbert" says he'll soon take the letter to her in person, in private.

1586

1586 16 Jan. Mon. (washday at Chartley) Eng. Kit swims icy moat, persuades laundresses to hide him in wet-wash basket. Unknowing guards come, carry loaded basket, leave it in Mary's wash lobby, go. Kit climbs kitchen stairs, persuades Mary she can send, receive mail via her new hollow beer bungs, swims back in dark (viewed by Mary), reaches Burston Inn feverish, delirious.

1586 Feb. France, Eng. Kit in Rouen, using name Jaques Colerain or Colerdin; can't call himself "Gilbert Gifford" here because Gilbert's cousin's in town. Colerdin stays with SSS Edward Gratley (Tom Lodge). They investigate opinions of expatriate Eng. Catholics. Tom is working on a play, The Wounds of Civil War, and starting to think about a novel, Rosalynde. (re these works: Edward Andrews Tenney. Thomas Lodge.

NY: Russell and Russell, 1969 (1935). Kit works on Edward III. After a week Kit goes to Paris, gets mail for Mary from Morgan and sails for home.

1586 May France Kit back to Paris as Gilbert Gifford, mail carrier to Mary's secretary Morgan. (Read. op. cit.; Fraser. op. cit.) Morgan introduces him to John Ballard, English priest, popish organizer who'd created a Catholic coalition. (DNB Ballard.) Kit goes with Ballard to his Paris lodgings. Ballard has seen the real Gilbert, wonders what this imposter is doing. He drugs Kit, searches his pack, steals his Gilbert code. (Read. op. cit.) Kit unsuspecting for too long: Spends weeks in Paris with Tom Lodge writing a book against the Reims English College, for Walsingham.

1586 12 June Eng. Kit to Eng. with Mary's mail and the finished propaganda book.

1586 26 June Eng. Elizabeth grants Ned de Vere £1000 per annum (probably for theater) under a Privy Seal Warrant, to be paid quarterly. (Alan H. Nelson. Monstrous Adversary. Liverpool: Liverpool U., 2003, p 301.)

1586 mid-June Eng. John Ballard has written two letters to Mary in stolen Gilbert Gifford code, tries to pass them in with the brewer at Burston Inn to see what will happen. Confusion in Walsingham's camp. (Read. op. cit.; Fraser. op. cit.) Kit is told, and told to find the priest.

1586 April—July Young Catholic activists meet around London, mostly at home of leader Sir Anthony Babington. They want to free Mary. Babington wants to go abroad, consult with Parma re coordinating troop movement with Elizabeth's sudden death. Looking for a passport, Babington approaches Robert Poley as a friend, not knowing he's SSS. (Read. op. cit.) Poley learns that Babington and priest Ballard are combining efforts. Poley points out to Kit the inn where Ballard's staying.

1586 9 July Kit and Ballard tough it out; Kit tells the man the case is about to break, offers him a passport good for sailing from any English port. Read. op. cit. knows about passport, but not who gave it to Ballard. (Kit has been staying in Phelippes' office and has secretly forged the passport—Phelippe is Customer of London, had blanks in his office.) Ballard refuses the offer, says he'll stay. Kit tells Walsingham he can't find Ballard.

1586 late July Queen Mary writes to Babington: Yes, do it—free me, kill Eliz! Phelippes has the letters and copies. Babington and Ballard are at large, but net is closing. (Read. op. cit.; Fraser. op. cit.)

1586 28 July Drake is at the Solent, back from the New World. (George Malcolm Thomson. Sir Francis Drake. NY: William Morrow, 1979.) Kit leaves work and goes to see if Captain Kester and Sampson are alive. They are. Kit must cross to France for last batch Mary's mail.

1586 3 Sept. Kit returns across Channel to Rye with letter from King Philip saying yes, it (Elizabeth's death) must be supported. Walsingham sends Kit home to Roger, saying it's over; go back to school.

1586 20 Sept. Conspirators cruelly executed. Kit at Cambridge puts a scene into Edward III about virtue of royal mercy. None was given.

1586 Nov. Hen, back at St. John's from visit with Elizabeth, tells Kit & Tom Nashe the queen has told him he—Hen—is her youngest child. And Philip Sidney's dead body is brought home from Arnhem. King Philip, furious that Elizabeth let their boy die, hastily moves to finish preparations for an Armada against her.

1586 Dec. Tom Nashe talks Kit into doing a job with him at Ashford for new Archbishop Whitgift, who's looking for clerics to persecute in his Court of High Commission. Nashe says all they have to do is make a phony report that will hurt no one and get free meals. An adventure at Ashford. Walsingham and Roger are angry.

1586 3 Dec. Mary of Scotland condemned to death. Roger on the panel. Elizabeth hesitates, talks mean to Walsingham.

1587

1587 spring. To aid Ned de Vere, who manages the SSS Theater Wing, his mother the queen hires ten University Wits to write plays for Ned. (cipher, 1 Henry IV.) These men could be: Robert Greene, Tom Lodge, Tom Nashe, George Peele, Sam Daniel, Tom Watson, Matthew Roydon, Kit, and two others. Ned reads Kit's Dido, Queen of Carthage, and loves it (Hamlet's remarks about this work may be close to Ned's). While Kit's away in Europe in spring '87, Ned produces a play at Ipswich, probably Dido, performed by his Children of the Queen's Chapel. Kit may ask Tom Nashe to go over and keep an eye on production.

1587 Jan. Walsingham plans: he wants Kit to "prove" to the real Gilbert Gifford's father that Walsingham didn't destroy the young man. Kit will make it seem Gilbert's alive, living in France: An SSS man at Reims, John Fixer, who became deacon there 19 December Gregorian, would serve as aid. (Douay Diary op. cit.) Kit has a plan; though he'd promised Kester to scout for Drake this spring in Lisbon, Kit might do the "proof" job first, at Reims. Walsingham wants him to go on to Paris later, to investigate the loyalty of the English ambassador and the first secretary at the embassy. If he has time after scouting for Drake, Kit might go to Madrid and help Walsingham's friend, the painter Zuccaro, Resistance SS from Italy who's in Madrid making paintings for Philip. (Spanish Cities of the Golden Age; the Views of Anton van den Wyngaerde. Berkeley: U of C Press, 1989.) They might learn more about Spain's plan to launch an Armada. Walsingham doesn't want much.

1587 14 March France Kit and John Fixer get Gilbert Gifford's name registered at Reims English College (Douay Diary) as having been ordained priest. A dangerous trick.

1587 31 March, Julian. Kit sails from le Havre for Lisbon to scout for Drake.

1587 11 & 12 April Europe Kit meets Miguel Cervantes (Manco) in Lisbon, "turns" him—finds out that 5 galleons loaded for the Armada are hiding at Cádiz harbor. Then Cervantes, on the run, goes first to Toledo and on to Seville, riding fast. Description of Manco's odd movements: William Byron. Cervantes, a Biography. Garden City, NY: Doubleday, 1978.

1587 19/29 April Drake successfully attacks Cádiz—"singes King Philip's beard." George Malcolm Thomson. op. cit.

1587 early June Europe Kit, listening on the dock at Lisbon, hears of the great galleon San Felipe coming from the East Indies loaded with treasure. Hiring a pinnace he sails to Ságres, tells Drake. Drake sets sail, intercepts this biggest prize of all time for England, captures the ship (Thomson. ibid.) and takes it to Plymouth, arriving late June 1587. Thomson, pp 212, 213, writes that "the official valuation of the San Felipe and her cargo was £114,000.* What it was in reality, heaven knows." At foot of p 213, Thomson notes, *"Say £3,000,000 today." (in 1972. In 2006, add a million?)

1587 June Spain Kit sails along N coast of Spain in Drake's hospital ship on its way home, debarks at Aviles as a shipwrecked nobleman, says he's Arthur Dudley, wants to go to Madrid to talk to Philip. Escorted to Madrid by police, Arthur Dudley gives long statement to Philip's English Secretary Engelfield. (the statement, complete, is extant, Simancas, and in Dorothy and Charlton Ogburn. This Star of England, Westport, CT: Greenwood Press, 1972). Arthur is housed in building next to the palace, where Walsingham's agent, painter Federigo Zuccaro, is staying. In the king's gallery of secular art, Zuccaro shows Kit Titian's paintings of Venus and Adonis and Tarquin and Lucrece; Kit later makes poems about these subjects for Hen.

1587 June Cambridge authorities would deny Kit his MA; he's absent and thought to be turned Catholic, studying at Reims.

1587 28 June A letter is sent from Privy Council to Cambridge, saying Marlowe has served his country well and is to have his MA. (Wraight & Stern. In Search of . . . op. cit.)

1587 July Kit graced with MA (NB—in absentia) by Cambridge U.

1587 July, August Madrid Arthur Dudley meets Philip, snoops around the palace with lock pick. There was a secret passage from Philip's study in the palace across to the studio of the painters next door. Philip liked to come and stand, hidden behind an arras, to watch the artists at work. (Geoffrey Parker, Philip II. Boston: Little, Brown, 1978.)

1587 Sept. Madrid Arthur Dudley leaves for France and the low countries (with police escort to Spanish border).

1587 12 Oct. Gregorian A letter from Robert Dudley's (Leicester's) secetary at Utrecht: "Morley" is bringing confidential dispatches to Burghley in London (Wraight & Stern. op. cit.)—to Burghley, because Walsingham is ill.

1587 20 Oct. Gregorian Kit zips back to Paris, starting job for Walsingham re doubtful honesty of people in the English embassy in Paris. (CSP Dom. Addenda Eliz. vol xxx, p 229.)

1587 26 Oct. /5 Nov. Kit as Gilbert Gifford has been propositioned by disloyal persons at the Eng. embassy in Paris: "exhorted to kill the Queen of England, with great promises . . ." (CSP Dom. Addenda Eliz. vol xxx, pp 229, 230.)

1587 November Paris Kit as Gilbert is snooping in Paris. Ambassador Stafford and First Secretary Lilly, both secret Catholic Leaguers, begin to suspect.

1587 Christmas Eve Paris Kit, still under cover as Gilbert Gifford, goes to a party in Longchamp at a brothel managed by Secretary Lilly's girlfriend, Madam Florence Bacot. Learning he's about to be wasted, Kit (still as Gilbert) declares he's a priest who has sinned in this house, and demands to be taken to the bishop's prison. He's carted to the Four de L'Evèque and locked up. (Gilbert Gifford DNB—but note, this essay is wrong in most places—and CSP Addenda Eliz. vol xxxi.) Kit has foiled the murder plot of the Leaguers but can't get out of prison.

1588

1588 Thurs. 14 Jan. Paris Edward Grimston, second secretary at English embassy, brings Gilbert 30 crowns for expenses. Grimston turns out to be a lifesaver—a true friend to Kit: Grimston works for Walsingham and knows the truth. He's a translator (did he bring the copy of Dr. Faustus, newly published in Paris in German, and read it to Kit?) Grimston also collects stories of "monstrous ransoms," such as the one Angelo proposes in Kit's Measure for Measure. Kit may have told Grimston that was how he, Kit, was conceived. (Re Edward Grimston: see his DNB. Also Geoffrey Bullough. Narrative & Dramatic Sources of Sh. NY: Columbia U, 1959-75. vol 2. Measure for Measure, p 406.)

1588 Paris To the prison, Four de l'Evèque, a new prefect comes, a Leaguer who discovers that "Gilbert Gifford" and Tom Lodge co-authored that book against the Catholic College at Reims. Kit makes difficult deposition. (extant—Calendar of MSS of Marquess of Salisbury at Hatfield. Part III #715, calendared 14 Aug, 1588, probably taken earlier.) Kit doesn't lie, doesn't blow his Gilbert cover or finger co-workers. "Gilbert" will almost certainly be condemned to death, and if he escapes to the street the Leaguers will murder him. (See his ciphers.)

1588 Feb. to August Paris Grimston brings paper, pens, Merlot and books to the prison. Kit writes Doctor Faustus, Measure For Measure (unfinished), and All's Well.

1588 6 June Eng. Ned's oft-abandoned wife, Anne Cecil de Vere, dies a suicide at Greenwich. (an event shadowed in Ophelia's death in Hamlet). Production of Kit's play All's Well is now impossible as the play's too close to the tragic end of Ned de Vere's marriage.

1588 19 July Eng. Drake at Plymouth. Spanish sails sighted at Scilly Isles. (Thomson. op. cit.)

1588 21/31 July Lineup for first fight with Spanish Armada—the Crescent formed.

1588 26 July Eng. Good Tom Howard knighted.

1588 27 July Eng. Ned de Vere, offered command of Harwich, sulks & refuses. J. Thomas Looney. Shakespeare Identified. ed. Ruth Loyd Miller. Kennikat Press, 1975, vol 1, p 513, and Alan H. Nelson. Monstrous Adversary. Liverpool: Liverpool U Press, 2003.

1588 6/16 August Fierce winds drive the Spanish ships north, helpless. English cease pusuit. (Garrett Mattingly. The Armada. Boston: Houghton Mifflin, 1959.) Kit's ciphers in Sonnet 107 and in the Jew of Malta rewrite are sympathetic to the lost Spanish sailors.

1588 8 August Eng. The queen at Tilbury, maybe with Ned. Someone misread Oxford as Ormond? Because "Ormond" carries sword of state this day, and that's Ned's job.

1588 26 Aug./5 Sept. A moon eclipse (Sonnet 107). It's all over.

1588 late August Paris To the bishop's prison: English secret agent Petruchio Ubaldini may send the potion smuggled in by Grimston. It makes Kit look dead. Kit's friends take his body away.

1588 end August Julian Kit, semi-conscious, is swept to Dover harbor in a small boat on the same winds that ruin Philip's Armada (ciphers. Jew of Malta); all through **September** Kit is home sick at Canterbury, Kate his nurse.

1588 4 September Robert Dudley, Earl of Leicester, dies of stomach-medication at his lodge at Cornbury. (Ned had a chance to make it happen.)

1588 mid-October While Kit was in Paris jail, his dad Roger had been distressed by Archbishop Whitgift's suppressive policy. Elizabeth, blackmailed by Whitgift, who has threatened to expose her as a mother, has been forced to give the man power negating English common law; his Court of High Commission never acquits an accused person. Frustrated, Roger resigns from the Commission and using byline Martin Marprelate, publishes a satirical attack on the bishops, the Epistle, first of several anonymous tracts written by Roger and other authors exposing the bishops' misbehavior. (William Pierce. An Historical Introduction to the Marprelate Controversy. London: Archibald Constable, 1918.)

1588 27 to 30 November The Epitome, another satiric essay by Roger, is distributed at court. Courtiers laugh, bishops are furious. (John Greenwood, a senior at Bene't the year Kit was a freshman, and Henry Barrowe, a lawyer friend of Roger's, have already been in jail more than a year now for opposing Whitgift.)

1589

1589 Jan. Francis Kett, Kit's friend who'd been steward and tutor at Corpus Christi College when Kit arrived there, is burned alive in Norwich. (Francis Kett DNB.) Another Cambridge acquaintance of Kit's, John Udall of Trinity College (MA 1584), enters the fray on Marprelates' side.

1589 Feb. A Marprelate paper by someone not Roger: "Minerall and Metaphysical Schoolpoints."

1589 March Roger's third anonymous paper printed: "Hay any Work for Cooper?" a response to "An Admonition to the People of England," published in January by Cooper, Bishop of Winchester.

1589 May Spain Cervantes may at last receive pay from Walsingham for service to English SSS: Cervantes suddenly has a lot of mysterious money. (Byron. Cervantes. op. cit.)

1589 31 May Eng. Sir Walter Mildmay, Sir Frank Walsingham's bro-in-law, Roger's chief at Exchequer and founder of a Puritan college at Cambridge, dies, brutally bled to death at Whitgift's order. (Mildmay DNB, and ciphers, Comedy of Errors.)

1589 12 July Eng. A provocateur, Job Throckmorton, pretends to befriend the Marprelate writers, inserts his own ersatz Marprelate essay among printed Marprelate papers, naming names, *revealing the identity* of several workers: "The Just Censure and Reproof." (Has any modern investigator noticed that he ratted?)

1589 5 July Kit is at Ferdinando Stanley's place at Lathom with Lord Ned and the players orphaned by Leicester's recent death (they now call themselves the Queen's Players). They're asking Ferdinando to be their patron. (E. K. Chambers. Eliz. Stage. vol 2, p 111.) Kit sees the Zodiac Screen at end of the great hall, uses it in Titus Andronicus, which he writes on contract for Ferdinando. (See ciphers inside this play.) Kit also noticies Job Throckmorton walking across the gallery above this screen, on his way to the earl of Derby's study.

1589 14 July Earl of Derby's officers arrest Marprelate printers, who are working (at Throckmorton's invitation) at a house near Manchester. John Penry, manager of this clandestine publishing enterprise, narrowly escapes arrest. (Pierce. Historical Intro. op. cit.) Kit warns him, but Penry will not believe the truth, blames Kit.

1589 Aug. From Paris, a letter from Flo Bacot, mistress of Lilly, the Leaguer secretary at English Embassy. (Walsingham can't fire Lilly and Ambassador Stafford; they're blackmailing the queen.) Flo writes to Walsingham's seretary Phelippes that Gilbert Gifford's case is soon coming up, so please send her "beaucoup d'argent" to help the poor boy make out (CSP Dom. Addenda Eliz. vol xxxi p 279). She doesn't realize Kit is long gone (that's because the Prévot was persuaded by Kit's friends to keep any money that came in for "Gilbert," not signing his death-certificate till just before Gilbert's trial—an old army trick called dead pay.)

1589 mid-Sept. Roger writes his last Marprelate essay, "The Protestation," tries to print it himself, is aided by Verstigan (a broadminded Catholic, cousin of Mrs. Crane who keeps a printing press. Verstigen, a printer-publisher, was in the Four de l'Evèque prison while Kit was there.)

1589 c. Sept. The queen increases subsidy for the ten University Wits (Kit among them) to help Ned with drama-writing for the Theater-Wing (shadows in drama-history, explicit ciphers in I Henry IV). Kit and Ned start a serious Henry V, and Kit goes to bed with Ned with approval of Roger, who reasons that if Ned becomes king, Kit could be king's favorite. (ciphers, Henry V.) Kit writes 1st draft King John for Ned?

1589 18 Sept. Coming out of Fisher's Folly, Ned de Vere's recently-sold mansion, Kit is attacked by William Bradley, son of a vintner in Gray's Inn Lane. Why, no one knows. My guess is that the man, who needs money, is a pursuivant for Whitgift, looking for Marprelate. Word has gone out that Marprelate is called Jaques, and that he's "halt, and clubfoot." (Wm. Pierce. op. cit.) Bradley may have called out, "Jaques!" and Kit, limping, turned around. They fight with rapiers—Kit's friend Watson comes out of the house, and Bradley, who knows and hates him, attacks him.

1589 18 Sept. continued. Kit, hoping to aid Watson, strikes down Bradley's sword, which badly wounds Watson. (Kit uses this sequence in his play Romeo and Juliet, when Mercutio is fatally hurt.) Watson kills Bradley—Kit and Watson are jailed in Newgate Prison. (Eccles. Christopher Marlowe in London. NY: Octagon Books, 1967.)

1589 1 Oct. Kit out on bail to appear at next sessions, before his dad.

1589 3 Dec. Kit appears at the Old Bailey, is dismissed, and on **12 Feb. 1590**, Watson, still suffering from his leg-wound, will be freed.

1589 Dec. In Newgate Prison, Tom Watson, working for Whitgift, is writing an anti-Marprelate tract. Kit and Tom Nashe, visiting, join him and turn the tract into a nonsense piece, with neat suggestion of the three authors' initials. (Elizabethan & Jacobean Pamphlets. ed. George Saintsbury. Freeport. NY: Books for Libraries Press, 1970 (1892).

1590

1590 Jan., new style. Tamburlaine I, Kit's first great stage success, has been playing at the Rose on the Bankside. Edward Alleyn is Tamburlaine, the Admiral's Company produces, and Kit is famous. It has gone to his head. (ciphers. Tamburlaine II.)

1590 24 Jan./3 Feb. In Paris, Secretary Lilly of English Embassy has written Gilbert's cousin Engelfield. (Walsingham still can't get rid of Lilly or Ambassador Stafford; they have leverage on the queen re her pregnancies; Stafford's mother was once in charge of dressing the queen.) Lilly has apparently written asking Engelfield for money to help Gilbert Gifford in his "upcoming trial." (Cal. Domestic Addenda Eliz vol xxxi, p 297.) The Leaguers in Paris English Embassy still don't know Kit escaped long ago. (note above, at **Aug. '89**)

1590 6 April Eng. Sir Francis Walsingham dies, rodded and bled to death by Dr. Ruy Lopes by secret order of Whitgift (ciphers, Comedy of Errors), after what seems to have been a desperate appeal. Walsingham's new son-in-law Robin Devereux is present at the murder, shocked. When night comes, Sir Francis is buried in Paules.

1590 May After Walsingham's death, Robin Devereux, Earl of Essex, Walsingham's son-in-law, and Francis Bacon, Walsingham's natural son, quickly move the man's files to Essex House—including names and addresses of excellent overseas agents. Bacon and Essex hire the best agents in London and start an unofficial foreign service, soon far outstripping the Cecils, supposed chiefs of diplomacy. (G.B. Harrison. The Life and Death of Robert Devereux, Earl of Essex. NY: Henry Holt, 1937.)

1590 8 June In his ancient house on St. Peter's hill, Thomas Randolph, former ambassador to Russia and Scotland, and Postmaster of England (and after Mildmay's death, Chancellor of Exchequer), dies, bled to death by Dr. Ruy Lopes by secret order of Whitgift. (Tom Walsingham is Randolph's bro-in-law, and Randolph's second wife is related to Roger's second wife.)

1590 summer Roger and Maximilian Colt, a young sculptor who lives near Roger's town house in West Smithfield, spend weeks designing a monument for Roger to be erected in St. Stephen's Church near Roger's Canterbury home.

1590 July After Randolph's death, his widow leases half their house on Peter's Hill to Julie Arthur Penn Hickes, who wants to run a boarding house. Tom Churchyard wonders if Ned could use it to house Theater Wing writers, since Ned has sold Fisher's Folly, wants a new place.

1590 14 August Tamburlaine the Great finally ends its run and is entered on the Stationers' Register. Kit has been living it up—not much money, but a famous artist.

1590 August Kit probably goes with friends Tom Watson, Nash and Sam Daniel to meet Mary Sidney Herbert at Cardiff Castle in Wales. Daniel will be tutor to her older son. (DNB.) Mary, a daughter of the queen, is a writer and translator in love with theater. She asks Kit to stay, and they begin a long, intermittant love affair.

1590 late Ned asks Kit to make sonnets for him about how good it is to get married and have a family. The poems will be given to Hen Wriothesley: Ned wants his legitimate daughter Elizabeth to marry Hen. Kit puts off starting the chore.

1591

1591 9 January. Kit and Tom Nashe are in Southampton with Hen. On this day, the corporation grants Hen "the freedom of the city." (C. C. Stopes. The Life of Henry, Third Earl of Southampton. NY: AMS Press, 1969, p 39.) Probably on 10 January Kit, Tom Nashe and Hen sail off in Hen's pinnace along south coast to Dover, stopping first at ruins of Beaulieu Abbey, now part of Hen's estate. Here they read on an old stone the date of death of Elinor of Aquitane: **1 April, 1204.** Kit writes it down to put in his play King John.

1591 March? In London, rehearsing The Second Seven Deadly Sins, Kit breaks his bad leg. Put in traction at Julie Arthur's Peter's Hill place, he helps roommate Tom

Kyd with Spanish Tragedy and a proto-Hamlet, and finishes his 17 sonnets for Ned, about marriage.

1591 July France Robin Devereux sails to France with soldiers to aid Henry of Navarre, and Kit goes too—before his leg is healed. Hen, forbidden to sail, stows away.

1591 August A play thought to have been an early Romeo and Juliet is produced at Easeborne, country home of the Viscount Montague, Hen's foster grandfather.

1591 late August through September Hen back early from France to see his mother the queen at Titchfield, 2 September. (E. K. Chambers. The Eliz. Stage. A Court Calendar.) Kit is soon drafted to play Nereus, swimming at a Progress party at Elvetham, 21 Sept.

1591 late autumn Kit learns about Hen's real parents from Roger: Hen is the son of Queen Elizabeth and Ned de Vere. Kit tells Hen the truth: If he were to marry his half-sister, Hen, himself a product of incest, would risk creating damaged children. Hen forgoes the match, though his guardian Burghley (who'd profit from the marriage—Elizabeth Vere is Burghley's granddaughter) is said to have set a fine of £5000 for Hen's refusal, due on the day he becomes 21. (G.P.V. Akrigg. Shakespeare and the Earl of Southampton. Cambridge, MA: Harvard U Press, 1968, pp 31-2, 39.)

1591 Nov.? Early Dec? Ned, furious that Hen Wriothesley has learned the truth about his parentage (and blaming Kit for telling), slams out of Julie Arthur's boarding house on Peter's Hill without having paid any rent. (Dorothy and Charlton Ogburn. This Star of England. Westport CT: Greenwood, 1972 pp 930-31 (confused by odd interpolaton); Mark Eccles' monograph on Sir George Buck, in Thomas Lodge and Other Elizabethans. ed. Sisson. Cambridge, MA: Harvard 1933, pp 464-5, gives a clearer picture; also Alan H. Nelson. Monstrous Adversary. op. cit., pp 328, 329.) Through with Theater Wing, burning with hatred for Kit, Ned goes away and marries Lady Elizabeth Trentham. Julie Arthur writes to Ned and the queen, asking for what's owed; the queen finally pays (Kit's ciphers, 1 Henry IV), but Julie fades away, perhaps because of stress, and her half of the big old house is taken over by her son Mike Hicks. (Mrs. William Hicks Beach. A Cotswold Family. p 71.)

1591 Dec. Burghley may punish Kit for telling Hen the truth by sending him to sea—or Kit sails away to evade Ned and Burghley's anger. It looks as if Kit is sailing with pals Carleill in the Tiger and Sampson in the Sampson, pursuing Spanish ships in the Channel. (Those two privateer ships are still out hunting together three months later—March '92 (Acts of the Privy Council, new series, vol 22, p 381: A ship called Tygure was out of Middleburgh or Flushing, with a ship called the Sampson.)

1592

1592 Jan. Kit puts in at Flushing and finds Richard (Bull) Baines waiting for him. (Baines, the man Kit had managed to free from jail at Reims, Aug. '82.) Kit and Baines seem to be partners listening for news of Parma's progress toward Rouen. Baines, probably hired by Ned and Burghley to damage Kit, suddenly accuses Kit of counterfeiting, calls him "Gilbert Gifford" in front of Governor Robert Sidney, (the confused amanuensis writes, "Gifford Gilbert." Baines may have been shouting, repeating the name.) Sidney sends both men home under guard. Mark Eccles, "Brief Lives" Studies in Philology. Chapel Hill, NC: U of NC, 1982, pp 89-90. Also a letter printed in English Historical Review, April 1976, pp 344-45.

A.D. Wraight, in The Story the Sonnets Tell. London: Adam Hart 1994, p 281, suggests that Kit may have been looking into the counterfeiting operations of William Stanley and his renegade soldiers in Holland.

1592 Feb., March Kit is trying to study law (cipher, Henry V)—at Clement's Inn? An old Inn of Chancery subsidiary to the Inner Temple, named for the guardian saint of sailors. Its records after 1583 are said to be lost. Kit's play The Jew of Malta is a hit, and Kit's a center of attention, beseiged by friends. He's in love with Emilia, hostess at a gambling cub in Shoreditch. He introduces her to Hen.

1592 31 March and 1 April Trying to win money to aid Hen with his upcoming fine-for-not-marrying, Kit stupidly wagers Roger's gold chain of office at gold-play, maybe cheating, thinking he couldn't lose. But Emilia, shareolder in the House, switches his dice, and he loses all—early AM, **1 April**.

1592 April In 1591, The queen had forbidden gambling (**6 June, 1591**. G.B. Harrison. An Elizabethan Journal. NY: Cosmopolitan Book Corp., 1929, p 38), though gold play—after-midnight high-stakes gambling—continued to be popular sub rosa. Of course Roger knows the law. Roger calls the fence, Roger Underwood (Registers of the Acts of Privy Council, vol 22, 1591, 92, new series, p 451) into chambers and pockets the chain, saying it's stolen property illegally sold—next time, the man will be prosecuted. Underwood appeals to Emilia and the club-owner himself, Henry Carey, Elizabeth's Lord Chamberlain, and Roger Manwood is called to appear before the privy council. He sends a letter furnished with a rhyme, amused that the council seriously considers the charge of a known dealer in stolen property, but Roger is sent into house arrest. Ten years later, in Manninghams' Diary (Diary of John Manningham 1602-1603. J. Bruce, ed. Camden Society Pub. 1868, entry Nov. 1592), Manningham, recalling Roger Manwood and sonne, retells this chain story, derived from Burghley's secretary Curle. Imperfect but interesting because Manningham identifies the youth who took the chain as Manwood's "sonne," so the relationship's in print to this day.

1592 9 May Kit, nauseated by his deed, which he can't call a crime but sees as a fatal error, takes refuge with new friends and morphine. In early morning 9 May he's with a group of young men singing and marching in Holywell. When the constable appears, the youths scatter—all but Kit, who's caught and promises to pay 20 pounds if he fails to keep the peace.

1592 14 May Roger has sent the Council a letter of submission and on 14 May appears before them (Registers of the Acts of Privy Council, op. cit., pp 449, 450) with the chain, which is taken from him and delivered to Lord Cobham to do with as he sees fit. Council determines that Roger, after paying the fence, and after Trinity term, must ride circuit as a justice of assize thru the little market towns of Berkshire. (Justices of assize were usually young judges of Queen's Bench.)

1592 summer Roger and Kit are alienated. Bacon and Essex's unofficial oversea operations are thriving; they want to present Elizabeth with their accomplishments at Christmas, but not before; they want to keep their growing list of achievemants to surprise her and gain funding. Tom Watson works for them oversea—maybe Kit could, too, but Bacon wants Kit as a writer here at home—secretarial work for Bacon but mostly playrwiting—propagandistic historical works. Kit has bones of Edward II, Richard II, Richard III, King John. Jew of Malta is ready to go, made along antisemitic lines Bacon has laid out.

1592 summer Kit doesn't know Emilia switched the dice that awful night. He feels he's married to her; they've started a baby. He tells her he'll have a steady job with Bacon, who plans to send him abroad. They'll have enough money to educate their child. She secretly scorns him as unstable, plans to gain child support by persuading Hen that he's the baby's father.

1592 August Emilia flirts with Hen, who takes her to Whitely, a lodge on his place near Titchfield (Whitely: GPV Akrigg. Shakespeare and the Earl of Southampton. Cambridge, MA: Harvard U, 1968, and C.C. Stopes. The Life of Henry, Third Earl of Southampton. Cambridge: Cambridge U. 1922/1969), for a weekend. Kit refers to this adventure obliquely in Loves Labour's Lost. (III. 1. ll.196-205) Kit alerts Hen's watchdog Florio, who tells Hen's foster mother Mary Browne. She quickly sends the youth off to Oxford. (ibid.)

1592 August At Windsor, Judge Manwood and corpulent Count Mömpelgard meet in Roger's court. Roger, told by the council to stick to the letter of the law, prosecutes the count for stealing horses from the Garter Inn: the host has told the count's men that they and their master were too heavy for the inn's horses, but the animals were taken anyway. Roger teases the tourists, reciting the law for horse-theft, and finally sends them off with instruction to rent dray horses. (shadows in Merry Wives of Windsor, mention in G. B. Harrison. An Elizabethan Journal. op. cit., pp 160 & 164, and E. K. Chambers. A Study of Wm. Sh. Facts and Problems, vol 1, pp 427, 428, and Roger's own A Petition Directed to her most excellent Maiesty. pp 29 fol. (copy in Henry Huntington Library, attributed to a Henry Barlowe—Roger's friend Henry Barrowe may have written the middle part of this petition.)

1592 September Kit goes with players to Canterbury to see Jew of Malta produced. He stays at home, meets old friend Wm. Corkine, who hates the play. They start a fight. He and Kit sue each other for assault but Kit drops charges. He appears in court 2 Oct., asks for a stay to prepare for Corkine's charge, but on 9 Oct. he and Corkine come back together (say they're friends?)—case dropped.

1592 15 Sept. Tom Watson has been abroad undercover for Bacon and Essex with mission to waste Parma. His chiefs don't want Elizabeth to know details till they reveal their oversea activities to her at Christmas, but a Customer has word of Watson's premature return, and the queen may become curious. Bacon writes suggestive letter this date re how to keep their agent quiet. (Spedding. op. cit.) Bacon may send his doctor to 'attend' Watson for old leg wound?

1592 26 September Watson buried. He has left a poem for Mary Sidney Herbert, with a note for Kit; Watson wanted Kit to see the work through the press and write a dedication, which he does. (Watson DNB, and Dedication in Complete Wks Chr. Marlowe. second ed., Ed. Fredson Bowers. vol 2, p 534.) Kit will take it to her this month.

1592 18 Oct. Emilia marries Fonsie Lanier at St. Botolph's Church, Aldgate. (The Poems of Aemilia Lanier, ed. Susanne Woods. NY: Oxford U Press, 1993, p xviii.) Kit's sorrow and chagrin are made clear by his ciphers in Sonnet 99. He'd believed they were married.

1592 Oct. Kit and Mary Herbert select two of Kit's plays for Hampton Court Christmas parties: her Pembroke Players are to make their first court appearances at these galas. Her dates, 26 Dec. and 6 Jan. (E. K. Chambers. Elizabethan Stage. op. cit. Appendix: "A Court Calendar.")

1592 early Nov. Roger has privately printed and delivered a last appeal to Elizabeth. It's anonymous, but he can't resist putting in a whimsical bit about horse-stealing, thinking of his court at Windsor in **August**, and Whitgift, as soon as he reads that part, knows it's by Roger.

1592 16 Nov. A letter from Privy Council at Hampton Court to the Lord Keeper: [paraphrase:] All officers and under-officers of the Courts of Records are to take the Oath of Supremacy, in its new form (which includes swearing the whole Book of

Common Prayer is the Word of God). Tell the judges of both benches and the Lord Chief Baron of Exchequer; any who refuse are to be sequestered from execution of their offices. Roger pledges allegiance to the queen but not to the prayerbook.

1592 late Nov. Roger can choose his date of death, any time within a month. Archdeacon Redman will help him revise his will, prepare. (Lewis J. M. Grant. Chistopher Marlowe, Ghost-Writer. Orillia, Ontario, Canada: Stubley Press, 1970, Part 2, p 212 fol.) Roger chooses anniversary of death of a man he admires, Sir John **Oldcastle, executed 14 Dec. 1417** for the same pseudo-crime for which Roger now stands condemned—speaking against inquisition. Roger decides to die at his Shorne house, so his wife won't know till later (?). Kate comes as housekeeper.

1592 10 December. At Chalk Church on the Dover Rd. Roger delivers a lay sermon on freedom from fear, keeping English Common Law above ecclesiastical dicta, and against rule by expediency. Kate is there.

1592 13 Dec.,late. Ruy Lopes, the queen's doctor, comes to rod and bleed Roger. He's brutal. Roger's son Peter is there with Roger's son-in-law John Leveson, Archdeacon Redman, Robert Poley as reporter for the archbishop, and Kate.

1592 14 Dec. Before one AM, Roger dies, and in the last minutes of this day he's buried in the Manwood vault at St. Stephens Church, Hackington, outside Canterbury. (His grave was robbed—when? All male corpses roughly removed, leaving the room in confusion. (Pix of chaos found by church-folk entering to dust the chamber are printed in The Kentish Gazette, 1962.)

1592 late Dec. Kit, sorrowful, creates an epitaphios for Roger, ciphered thruout in several directions (Marlowe's ciphers.) Eccles. "Chr. Marlowe in Kentish Tradition," N & Q, op. cit. Also Complete Works of Chr. Marlowe. Ed. Fred. Bowers. op. cit.) Kit and Mary Herbert work together to devise special, telling productions for the Pembroke plays at court at Christmas time.

1592 25 Dec. Bacon and Essex offer their Christmas present to Eliz—a review of their undercover accomplishments oversea. Impressive—awful—but the Cecils keep official, financial control of SSS. Deaths of three cardinals reported: Henry Wotton nicknames them in Logan Pearsall Smith. Life and Letters of Sir Henry Wotton. Oxford: Clarendon Press, 1907.)

1592 26 Dec. Mary's Pembroke Players perform Edward II at Hampton Court. E. K. Chambers. Eliz. Stage, Appendix A. op. cit., "A Court Calendar," p 107 identifies Pembroke Players as present at court on this date, and Edward II is known as a Pembroke play. Edward dies the same way Roger did, but offstage, and the show is seen to the end.

1593

1593 6 Jan. On Epiphany, the Twelfth Night of Christmas, a mix of scenes from the unpolished Henry VI plays is offered before queen and bishops in the Great Hall at Hampton Court. A simulacrum of Duke Humphrey's mutilated stinking body, murdered by order of a wicked prelate, is displayed downstage, and Kit speaks to the audience. (See ciphers for First Folio 3 Henry VI, first lines) Kit's doom is sealed as ten bishops get up and leave. The queen rises; the party's over. The queen never visits her daughter Mary Herbert again. Never again do Pembroke Players work at court. (Complete Wks. of Chr. M. 2nd Ed. ed. Fredson Bowers, vol 2, p 7: "The first state of the title page repeats the original statement that the play was acted by the earl of Pembroke's servants." And NB p 9: it is believed by critics that "printer's copy for the play was the promptbook itself, sold by Pembroke's company in the summer of 1593 when they ran into financial difficulties.")

1593 early Whitgift's men raid the Revels Office to destroy Kit's writings "and art," but are foiled by office-worker George Buck (ciphers). Jan., Feb., March go by; Kit is not arrested. In April plague hits London, so Bacon moves SS people to his agent Tom Walsingham's safe country place, Scadbury.

1593 early April Kit at Scadbury is working on "Hero and Leander," a funny, bitter memorial of Emilia and Kit's love and its ending. He has the first part on paper.

1593 early April Kit's first child is born—a boy, to Emilia Bassano Lanier. She names him Henry, suggesting to the world the father is her known lover, Henry Carey, Lord Hundsdon, and also suggesting to Hen Wriothesley the baby is his. Kit ciphers sonnets to Emilia about his love for the baby.

1593 19 May, Saturday Henry Maunder, messenger of Queen's Chamber, comes to Scadbury with warrant to take Kit to report to council at Nonsuch. (Wraight and Stern. In Search of . . . . op. cit., p 283.)

1593 20 May, Sunday morning Maunder and Kit ride first to Nonsuch, then to the goldsmith for bail assurance and on to Westminster, where Master William Mill, Clerk of Star Chamber, is doing extra work. Kit admits he owns the script to be produced as evidence of his heresy, thereby omitting days of rigamarole so he can go to meet the council (at Nonsuch?) on Wednesday, ore tenus, and hear the outcome of the case right there, from the mouths of the judges themselves. Kit finds Hen, gives him ciphered love poem for queen asking for banishment, not death. (A later copy of the poem, imperfect but reparable, is held in the Bodleian Library, Rawlinson Poetry MSS, folios 108, 109: "Shall I Die, Shall I Fly?" And Kit writes about it in ciphers, Ls L's Lost, as "my secret fly-away poem.") The queen reads, invites Kit for an interview.

1593 21 May, Monday Kit makes love to the queen at Nonsuch, is given assurances, an emerald and warnings. They forge a lasting friendship. (ciphers, Ls L's Lost, and queen's warning in Duke's mouth, The Two Gentlemen of Verona, III. 1. ll. 153 fol.)

1593 23 May, Wednesday Kit examined by council, Whitgift presiding. (Wraight and Stern. op. cit., and Ls L's Lost ciphered lines 137 fol.) That night weary Robin Poley, just returned from Scotland (Eugenie De Kalb. "Robert Poley's Movements as Court Messenger," RES, April, 1931), reveals that though Marlowe has been exiled by the queen, Whitgift has hired an agent (Poley?) to kill Kit before he can sail. Essex and Bacon plan to save Kit.

1593 24 May, Thursday SSS bros. plan, look for queen: she's nowhere!

1593 25 May, Friday Leaving 2 sonnets for queen, Kit rides to Canterbury to say goodbye to family.

1593 26 May, Sat. Kit's at home in Canterbury.

1593 27 May, Sun. Kit's back at Nonsuch. No queen.

1593 28 May, Mon. Queen's at Greenwich; ready to provide safehouse in Deptford belonging to Widow Elinor Whitney Bull, related to Elizabeth's old nurse. (Urry. Chr. Marlowe and Canterbury. op. cit.) Queen and SSS will also provide a hanged body.

1593 29 May, Tues. Poley and Kit ride to Deptford. Poley reserves a chamber for four men for tomorrow at Whitney-Bull's boarding house; the men to dine in their chamber. Kit, disguised as an old man, checks into another room there, using a pseudonym.

1593 30 May, Wed. Rob't Poley, with Tom Walsingham's man Ingram Frizer and Essex's man Nicholas Skeres, arrive at widow's with criminal's hanged body dressed in Kit's clothes, supported between them as if he were alive but falling-down drunk. The whole day's a plotted drama, with Kit as himself in plain sight later in own clothes and then again in disguise. At night, Kit in disguise checks out, boards ship or waits at Edward Marley's naval-stores warehoue at the dock. The men upstairs create a murder scene, stab the dead body dressed in Kit's clothes: the new wound must be above the neck, as the bruise from hangman's rope must be concealed from coroner's jury—by bandana or winding sheet. The widow calls police. (For study: J. Leslie Hotson. The Death of Christopher Marlowe. NY: Russell & Russell 1967 (1925).

1593 31 May, Thurs. A call for inquest jurors. Kit waits aboard ship—the Salamander? at the Edward Marley dock. (CSP Dom Eliz. 1591-'94, pp 138, 139: Wm. Walton's Salamander (which had been working with Edw. Marley's Mayflower), was waiting, according to CSP, to cross the Channel on a diplomatic mission.)

1593 1 June, Fri. Inquest. With some legerdemain the Queen's coroner determines Frizer killed Marlowe acting in self-defense, and the body is buried in churchyard of St. Nicholas, patron saint of thieves. (J. Leslie Hotson. The Death of Christopher Marlowe. op. cit.)

1593 2 June, Sat. Ship misses the tide because Kate shows up weeping. Last goodbyes. Kit gets drunk. (ciphers, 3 Henry VI, and Essex's note—hurry up and sail!—CSP Dom. Eliz. vol ccxlv p 358.)

1593 3 June, Sun. The Salamander? sails with Poley, Kit (aka Jaques Coderain? Codere? Colerain?) End of first half of Kit's life.

Second Half of Kit's Life Begins

1593 c.7/17 June France At St. Denis, Kit delivers message from Essex to Henry of Navarre, who asks him to stay and rest. (ciphers, 3 Henry VI.)

1593 8 June Eng. Poley's back at court with proof that Kit has left Eng.

1593 12 June Eng. Venus and Adonis goes on sale: "William Shakespeare" printed on dedication.

1593 c, 27 June? Europe After crossing France, Kit reaches Geneva. Stays at Professor Isaac Casaubon's house and there meets new SSS partner Henry Wotton; they cross Alps together, skiing part way. (ciphers, Sonnet 116.)

1593 c. 3? July Italy Harry and Kit reach Mantua with messages from Essex for Gonzaga, stay 2 days. (ciphers, Sonnet 116.) Kit works on Lucrece. Harry goes to Genoa. Kit meets old friend SSS Tom Lodge. As two gentlemen, they go through Verona and Padua to Venice.

1593 c.8 July. Venice Tom Lodge introduces Kit to Italian spymaster Battista Guarini, working for organized Resistance against temporal expansion of papal power. Kit is approved for job in Constantinople, buys supplies.

1593 c. 10 July. Ven. Kit ships out for Constantinople.

1593 20 Aug. Constantinople Marlowe arrives at Golden Horn, checks in with Ambassador Barton at English Embassy. (Detailed story in CSP Venetian vol. 9, without Kit's name. Further details in ciphers, 3 Henry VI.) Kit as barber visits prisoners at

Rumeli Hisar (CSP says Tower of the Black Sea, but in a letter to me 26 Nov. '89, Cengiz Taner, Regional Director of Culture, Istanbul, says political prisoners were kept on 7th floor of North Tower of Fortress of Rumeli Hisar. Have pix.) Kit was sent to save 1 prisoner but 18 are locked up together and 15 want to make the break. Kit has a concealable silk-gut ladder, gift of Hen. In his barber bag are saws; they cut floor. He returns on a Fri. when Janissaries are in their mosque praying. Prisoners go through floor, run down to first-story window, avoiding drugged watchman. Climbing out into the yard they clamber up rough retaining wall on Bosphorus edge, go 40' down silk ladder to water; swim to small boat to be swept downstream—all 15 escapees safely board Venetian ships Liona and Silvestra in the harbor.

1593 25 Aug. Constantinople Barton, fearing the Wazir, turns barber over to authorities. Kit is jailed, tortured till feast of Bairam. He writes in prison, sends message to Elizabeth, fears it won't help. But the queen, figuring Kit would be in trouble, has *already* sent a ship laden with knicknacks for the sultan, tin in the hold.

1593 17 thru 29 Sept. Constantinople The ship arrives, flags flying, is unloaded. Kit is ransomed, freed. (Many dispatches from Matheo Zane, Venetian Ambassador in Constantinople. CSP Venetian, vol 9.)

1593 c.1 Oct. Constantinople Kit has a note from SSS nominal head Robt. Cecil, who has stolen tin from Elizabeth's cargo and put it in secret place on the ship. Wants Kit to take it to a Black Sea city and sell it for Cecil's profit (ciphers). Kit rents a ship with 10 sailors, heads north. Writes in every spare moment.

1593 c.7 Oct. Black Sea Attacked by pirates near a copper smelter on south shore of the sea. Kit and sailors repair rudder, sail east into storm that rips the boat apart, leaves them unhurt but stranded on desolate shore without their tin. They eat fish, drink wild tea, rebuild.

1593 c. 2 Nov. Black Sea They get going. Miracle! On a sand bank they find the slimy tin. They sail to Trebisond, sell, get back to Constantinople without trouble (ciphers).

1593 c. 4 Nov. to 9 Dec. A passenger, Kit sails slowly back to Venice, writes a play on the way, disembarks at the city. Gives Spinola the banker The Two Gentlemen of Verona—and Lucrece? to send home in Essex's dispatch bag.

1593 15 Dec. Ven. Kit signs on as captain of a ship, owners Prospero Colombo and Francisco Rizzardi, to carry cargo to Crete and return with wine to be reshipped to England for Essex. Essex has lease of the farm of sweet wine (histories), wants to import a lot, plow profits into his new foreign service (ciphers). Against rules about not sailing in Dec., Kit as Giacomo Coderin sails down the Adriatic in the ship Rizzarda et Colomba, insured (cargo sardines & soap), bound for Crete. (Marchands Flamands à Venise. ed. Wilfred Brulet. Bruxelles, Rome: Academia Belgica. vol 1 p 162.) Storm off Cattaro—seen in trouble by others there. Puts in at Durres (forbidden Albanian port) which shelters them. Kit pumps bilge, replaces mast, fixes sliding deckhouse (narrative, Kit's Noches de Invierno por Antonio de Eslava. op. cit.)

1593 24 Dec. Durres They set off again.

1594

1594 4 Jan. Crete The Rizzarda et Colomba reaches Crete. Duke Zuan Cicogna gladly sells sweet wine (Malvesia) to Essex. Kit falls in love with the duke's daughter Marina. (list of all civil servants on Crete in **1593, '94**—duke, treasurer, etc.—sent to me by Dr. Maria Francesca Tiepolo, Director of the State Archive at the Frari in Venice.) Kit and Marina court through her sewing-room window, her nurse enchanted. Kit writes love-ballad to sing to Marina. She and her nurse sail away with Kit when lading is finished. Marina wears wedding dress, brings dowry. They make for Venice (ciphers).

1594 8 March Ven. Owners Francesco Rizzardi and Prospero Colombo, fearing their ship sank off Cattaro, apply for their insurance and soon offer salvage rights to Cattaro people. (Marchands Flamands à Venise. vol 1 op. cit., p 162.)

1594 8 March Ven. Kit stops at St. Mary's church (on the Lido?), where he and Marina (he calls her Rita) are wed, serenaded by his sailors. (ciphers, 3 Henry VI, and ciphers late rewrite Henry V.) He crosses lagoon, docks his ship at Venice in the night.

1594 March—late September Veneto Kit and Rita live a dream of happiness. Her dowry buys a little place in Padua. She keeps house, he studies at U (ciphers, Comedy of Errors) using name Scipio Monti? (register, Padua U law school, 1594.) Rita's pregnant.

1594 End September Italy SSS calls Kit to help with a hard job in Rome. SSS friends are already there at Cardinal Allen's place. Promising to be back when the baby's born, Kit rides to Rome.

1594 16 October Rome Dr Allen, now a cardinal, dies at his apt. on via Montserrat. Among his servants, two English: his chaplain Thos Honley from Milan (Tom Walsingham worked in Milan) and a new shoemaker, Wm. Warton (Kit?). Blind old Frank Engelfield is visiting. (Martin Haile, An English Cardinal. op. cit.) He may recognize the voice of "Arthur Dudley," English spy in Madrid in 1587.

1594 17 Oct. Italy A young English spy "flies" over the Apennines towards Padua, pursued by the Inquisition as far as Siena. (Fynes Moryson. Itinerary. unpublished chapters in Shakespeare's Europe. ed. Charles Hughes, 1903, p 159. Kit corroborates Moryson's story in ciphers, 3 Henry VI: Kit was the spy who flew.)

1594 25? Oct. Padua Kit reaches home.

1594 29 Oct. Padua Marina-Rita gives birth, hemorrhages, dies. Baby Isabel is healthy. With no money for wet nurse, Kit buys a cow, learns to milk.

1594 31 Oct. Venice. Because she eloped with Kit, Rita's father has refused to accept her body in the Cicogna family vault. Now Kit takes Rita's white corpse into a tomb he himself has made for her, on a lonesome beach where they'd watched the sails and run on the sand in the summer.

1594 1 Nov. Padua A messenger (Bacon's "Cousin Cooke"?) comes with pay, wants to take to Eng. Kit's SSS notes plus a play for Gray's Inn Christmas and another for Ned's daughter's wedding (not to Hen, but to William Stanley, sixth Earl of Derby). Kit must finish, polish plays.

1594 20 Nov. Padua The Messenger leaves on a rush (20-day) journey to Eng. with Comedy of Errors, M. Night's Dream, a printed copy Scipio's Dream for Bacon? and SSS notes in the secret bag.

1594 28 Dec. Eng. A performance of Comedy of Errors causes riot at Gray's Inn. (descriptions, Jas. Spedding, Ellis and Heath. Works of Francis Bacon [Life and Letters]. Also, E. J. Castle. Shakespeare, Bacon, Jonson and Greene, Port Washington, NY: Kennikat Press, 1970, and various other sources.)I believe this was due to the fact that The comedy was a sendup of a play Ned wrote years before (for Gray's Inn?—he was a member)—a work called the Historie of Error. You can tell from styles of verses and dialogue in Kit's comedy that he's spoofing Ned's early effort.

1595

1595 26 Jan. Eng. At Greenwich, before the queen, Elizabeth Vere marries the sixth earl of Derby. Looks like two other couples marry, too. A play, Midsummer Night's Dream? that evening at court. (J. Thomas Looney. Sh. Identified. ed. Ruth Miller. Kennikat Press, 1975, (1920) vol 1, p 521, and E. K. C. Eliz. Stage. op. cit., vol 4, p 109.)

1595 Jan. Feb., March, April Padua Unhinged, feeling guilty and sad, Kit tries to make out in Padua milking the cow, rewriting Romeo and Juliet, working on Pericles, rewriting King John. Someone in Spanish government hates Cervantes: he goes to Madrid, Toledo, Seville, trying to manage false accusations by the Treasury (we now know these people badly misconstrued his accounts) and to pay money they want. His banker goes bankrupt. (Byron. Cervantes, a Biography. Garden City, NY: Doubleday, 1978.) Cervantes asks Kit to bring his family to stay at his place in Seville, and Kit says yes.

1595 May Italy Looks as if this is when Kit sells his house in Padua, and with nurse, baby, cow and horses, starts for Spain, over the Apennines to Genoa. (reminiscent ciphers, As You Like It.)

1595 June Italy-Spain Kit probably travels most of this month—by ship to Valencia and horseback south to Sevilla. In ciphers (3 Henry VI and As You Like It) he recalls a hot trip. When he reaches Sevilla, apparently as broke as Cervantes, it looks as if he dashes all the way back to see rich Resistance spymaster Manso in Naples, or sends a request to get Cervantes out of hock. (Byron. Cervantes. op. cit., pp 375-6.)

1595 August Sevilla Cervantes begins paying, in driblets that keep coming, the money the treasury wrongly claims he owes. (Byron. Cervantes. ibid., pp 375, 376.) Kit and his family live at Cervantes' home, and Kit studies at a church in Seville, circuitously sending to Essex-Bacon notes of current Catholic politics.

1595 Sept.-Dec. Sevilla Kit's family is with Cervantes. Kit dashes off again—ciphers (3 Henry VI) tell us he takes the nurse back to her home on the Lido, but there's another reason? Soggy, rainy winter in Seville. Kit writes Richard II?

1596

1596 Jan. Venice Henry Hawkins, since December settled in Venice as newsman for England, writes home to Bacon's sec'y Anthony Bacon that he, Hawkins, has a correspondent in Spain (Kit? Cervantes?) and another in Rome (Anthony Bacon's letters at Lambeth).

1596 Jan. Sevilla News comes to Kit from Essex, who's planning a raid on Cádiz in late May or June. He wants Kit and Cervantes to scout the town, make things easy for an English win.

1596 Feb.—April Sevilla Soggy, rainy spring in Seville. Kit and Manco (Cervantes) stay home a lot with Isabel. This may be when Cervantes starts trying to teach Kit to write in Spanish.

1596 May Cádiz Through rain, Kit and Manco Cervantes sail to Cádiz, Manco disguised as an ordnance officer, Kit his aide. Ammunition is to be redeployed: the cannon balls are mixed-up, shifted to wrong stations so when Essex sails in the cannons can't shoot.

(ciphers, 1 Henry IV; rewrite, Henry V; and G.B. Harrison. Life and Death of Robert Devereux, Earl of Essex. N.Y. Henry Holt, 1937. p 114.)

1596 30 June Cádiz Essex's ships appear; the ammunition mixup works well. (Ibid. G.B. Harrison. Life and Death. p 114, and 1 Henry IV. Ciphers.) A fight; the English win, prepare to leave with loot.

1596 15 July Cádiz The English move out at night; Kit and Isabel say goodbye to Manco. Kit, in a longboat with others, Isabel by herself in a tiny boat pulled behind, go out to Admiral Thomas Howard's flagship, climb aboard. Kit begs the admiral to find a good home in England for his little girl, and Howard (the queen's "Good Tom") says he'll take care of her himself. (ciphers. 1 Henry IV.)

1596 Mid-August Eng. Kit and Isabel are at Good Tom's place, Audley End.

1596 Sept. till c. end May '97 Eng. Kit stays in England under cover as an Italian shipping agent working out of the Exchange, arranging for Essex's loot to be shipped to Venice for sale. (Much about Kit is only half-hidden in Poems of Joseph Hall. ed. Arnold Davenport AMS Press. 1969: Hall's Virgidemearum. Satires [6 books]. Bk. 6 pub. in 1598. Satire 1: "Tattelius, the new-come traveller, with his disguisèd coat, & ringèd ear, tramping the Bourse's marble twice a day.")

1597

1597 March or April Eng. Kit and the queen make love in her "lair" in the palace, and the Chamberlain Wm. Brooke, Lord Cobham, walks in on them, leaves and then returns to watch. Kit drags him out, hits him. Kit and queen bandage Brooke's head, give him a drink and Kit escorts him to his chamber, where Brooke turns around and hits Kit. (ciphers, Merry Wives of Windsor.)

1597 23 April Wm. Brooke, Lord Cobham, has been fired from his place as Elizabeth's Lord Chamberlain. George Carey, who will take the job, is created Knight of the Garter on 23 April, the night Merry Wives of Windsor is performed before Elizabeth at the Garter Feast at Westminster, one month before Carey's installation as Lord Chamberlain. This could be a Theater Wing celebration—everyone's glad Cobham is out. He hated the Chamberlain's Players he had to sponsor—tried to take away their water at their Blackfriars theater.

1597 mid-May Eng. Kit has been staying with Isabel at Good Tom's home at Audley End, and maybe at Mary Sidney Herbert's home at Wilton, writing The Merchant of Venice.

1597 20-22 July Eng. Tom Walsingham is now married to Audrey Shelton; on this day their home, Scadbury, is visited by the queen (E.K.C. Eliz. Stage. "A Court Calendar"). Robert Cecil must have been there, for on 24 July he writes of "the dancing at Lady Walsingham's" (P. M. Handover. The Second Cecil. p 157). Was only the Lady at home? Tom away on a job?

1597 23 August Padua Entry in Padua University Register (unnoticed by scholars?): Ottavio B. (Ottavio Baldi is Henry Wotton's Italian undercover name, known to historians), Henricus Cuffe (Henry Cuffe was a well-known secretary of Essex), and Franc Bocons (a not-so-pseudo pseudonym for Francis Bacon), all registered together to audit a law lecture at the college on 23 Aug., probably after attending Resistance meetings in the Grisons.

1597 3/13 Sept. Italy Kit sails back to Italy to sell in Venice two ships captured at the Cádiz raid last summer (ciphers, Henry V rewrite). Shadows suggest he leaves Eng. as factor for a shipment of cocchineal Essex captured at Cádiz. Sails to Sevilla, Cartagena, Leghorn (Gregorio Monleone in index, Marchands Flamands à Venise. op. cit., vol 1, p 262, #78) selling to a friend in Venice, Francisco Vrins. Kit debarks at Venice, sells the ships, rides to la Guarina to winter with spymaster Battista Guarini. Essex has sent Kit to help Guarini deal with the Pope.

1597 24 Sept. Eng. English Parliament opens—Bacon's not home yet.

1597 27 Sept. Eng. Both houses Parliament adjourned till 5 November—by Elizabeth, says Spedding—by mistake, says D'Ewes. (Is this to give Bacon time to get back and get with it?)

1597 30 Oct. Eng. Essex home from an Azores raid. Gets a letter from Henry Wotton re: Resistance doings in Chiavenna in the Grisons. That's where Wotton, Cuffe and Bacon have been.

1597 7 Nov. Eng. A 21-year-old judgement of Roger's against a man who didn't pay his rent is finally declared valid at a special meeting of all the judges of England, called by the queen. The man had appealed to Equity in Chancery, and there the case had lain undecided till the judges, Common-Law men like Roger, met this day. Roger won his case from his grave, and Kit couldn't let it go unnoticed: In his rewrite of I Henry IV, Act II. sc.2, Falstaff-Roger says, "no Equity stirring." (Chas. E. Phelps. Falstaff and Equity. Boston: Houghton Mifflin, 1901.) Phelps writes up the case, doesn't realize Roger is Falstaff—mistakenly thinks Falstaff would favor Equity.)

1597 Oct-Nov. Italy At La Guarina, Kit tries to help Guarini save part of Ferrara, about to be consumed whole by the Pope.

1597 Nov. Italy Together Kit and Guarini ride to Rome, pay the pope so he'll let Duke Cesare keep Modena and the rest of western Ferrara. A compromise victory. (ciphers, I Henry IV; rewrite ciphers, Henry V.)

1598

1598 4 May Italy Kit is still at La Guarina when Battista Guarini's daughter Ana is murdered by her own husband, Ercole Trotti, who says he believes her unfaithful; he's been tricked by an enemy. Trotti takes her to his hunting lodge at Zenzalino, kills her—not with a pillow, as in Kit's play, but with a knife. (Vittorio Rossi. Battista Guarini ed il Pastor Fido. Turin: Ermanno Loescher, 1886.) This source contains an eyewitness account of the murder, a letter (from the Zenzalino steward) which Kit later uses for touching detail of Desdemona's death. Kit writes Much Ado about Nothing re this killing. Incensed, he puts 3 ciphers in Much Ado and starts thinking about Othello.

1598 Eng. Bacon turns away from Essex—encourages the earl to give up diplomacy and concentrate on being a warrior. Slyly Bacon writes to Essex giving him wrong advice. Bacon has decided to team up with Robert Cecil, and together they mean to destroy their bro-half-bro; he's too close to the queen.

1598 end May to Dec.? Eng. Where's Kit? Shadows suggest he goes to England under cover—said to have performed as Stephano in Ben Jonon's first play, Every Man in his Humour, produced this year. He may be in town waiting to go to Ireland with Essex.

1598 Dec. Eng. The Theater in Holywell is in danger of being destroyed. At night, Chamberlain's Men move timbers of the Theater across the river to the Bankside, where they'll re-erect them to make the Globe. A mysterious man named William Smith comes to help them cross the water, brings money. (C. C. Stopes. Burbage and Shakespeare's Stage. op. cit, pp 74-77; and I Henry IV rewrite, ciphered lines 51-64 of up-front dialogue.)

1599

1599 Jan. Eng. The Theater re-constructed as the Globe, on the Bankside.

1599 10 Feb. Spain In Sevilla, styling himself "a servant of his Majesty," Cervantes takes notarized receipt of 90 ducats from don Juan de Cervantes, in repayment of a loan. No one knows who this don Juan de Cervantes might be. (Byron. Cervantes. op. cit.) I think Kit, in Eng., is already in pay of Essex, waiting to ship out for Ireland. Cervantes may have received pay for newsletters.

1599 20 Feb. Spain Treasury officials bill Cervantes for 27000 maravedis he'd paid years ago. (Byron. ibid.)

1599 16 April Eire After a rough crossing—Lord of Kildare's ship lost on the way—Essex lands forces at Dublin, intending to Subdue the Irish. Kit, Harry Wotton, Tom Lodge and Tom Nashe are with him as secretaries. (ciphers, Troilus and Cressida and As You Like It.) Kit sees writing on the wall; worst possible advice keeps arriving for gullible Essex from Bacon & Cecil.

1599 8 May Eng.—Eire Council in England allows Essex to go into Leinster. (Spedding vol ix p 137.) Essex goes *through* Leinster, into Munster.

1599 May Eire Edward Reynolds later said Piers Edmunds was Southampton's lover and corporal-general of horse—ate and slept in his tent. (Who was "Piers Penniless?" Tom Nashe?)

1599 3 July Eire Essex returns to Dublin with c. half his army. (Spedding. vol 9, p 138.) Because some of his soldiers ran away from an engagement, Essex decimates them (hangs one tenth of their number) for "discipline." (Is this one of Bacon-Cecil's suggestions?) No doubt other soldiers decided to leave because of this process. (Sonnet 125 B and ciphers in Troilus and Cressida.)

1599 5 Sept. Eire Essex refuses an offer to parley. (Spedding. vol 9.)

1599 6 Sept. Eire (ibid.) Essex offers to fight; Tyrone wants to talk.

1599 c. early Sept. Eire A truce made for 6 weeks with option for 6 more—and on, to Mayday next, not to be broken without 2 weeks' warning. (ibid.) Kit's ciphers in Troilus and Cressida say that he and Tom Nashe were employed by Essex to draft this "toy treaty." (G.B. Harrison. The Life and Death of Robert Devereux. op. cit., says Sir Warham Sentleger, Sir Wm. Constable and Henry Wotton met Tyrone's men in his camp to present this truce. Also see Logan Pearsall Smith. Life and Letters of Sir Henry Wotton. Oxford: Clarendon, 1907, vol 1)

1599 9 Sept. Eire Essex "dispersed his army; and went himself to take physic at Drogheda, while Tyrone retired with all his forces into the heart of his country." (Journal, "Nugae Antiquae." 1. p 301, and Spedding. vol 9, p 141.)

1599 14 Sept. Eng. From Nonsuch the queen writes an interminable letter telling Essex he's done everything wrong. (ciphers. Troilus and Cressida. Harrison. op. cit.)

1599 22 Sept. Eire Essex receives the queen's letter at Dublin. (ibid.)

1599 24 Sept. Eire Essex sails for England to explain to Elizabeth, and Harry Wotton comes bearing the treaty of truce to show the queen. Perhaps Harry stays in England until Nov. 1600, when he's said to have left for Italy. (L. P. Smith. op. cit., vol ii, p 36.)

1599 28 Sept. Eng. 10 AM To try to explain, Essex goes into the queen's chamber as she's dressing. Bacon and Cecil have already told her exactly what to think.

1599 Oct. Eng. Essex is staying at York House with Egerton, seeing no one. G. B. Harrison. op. cit., writes of Elizabeth: "her mind had been poisoned by the little Secretary with his suave, official subservience." Essex won't see his wife Frankie, afraid it would irritate the queen.

1599 28 November Eng. The queen visits Essex at York House. (E.K. Chambers. Eliz. Stage. "A Court Calendar.")

1599 29 November Eng. Essex censured in Star Chamber—Cecil speaks re Essex's coming home before he was bidden. Four days later his hundred sixty servants are dismissed.

1599 12 Dec. Eng. At last Frankie can see Essex. Sick in bed, he has to be lifted out to change the sheets. Elizabeth weeps when she hears.

1599 Dec. Eng. Essex won't listen to Kit's advice, so Kit's at Mary Sidney Herbert's place at Wilton, hiding out below stairs, writing As You Like It, starting Troilus and Cressida.

1600

1600 Eng. In this year Kit's daughter Isabel is adopted by Wm. and Judith Basset, friends of Viscount Montague and the Good Tom Howard family, with whom Isabel lives at Audley End. Judith Basset has lost a baby girl and can't have more children, and although Isabel is 4 years too old, she becomes Elizabeth Basset. Kit is grateful, puts a bit about Basset hounds in a rewrite of MN's D.

1600 Eng. In this year Kit takes some really old plays, perhaps out of his trunk at John and Kate's place in Canterbury, gives them to the players: Sir John Oldcastle to the Admiral's, Lord Cromwell to the Chamberlain's.

1600 Feb. Eng. Lord Mountjoy leaves to be Lord Deputy in Ireland—12,000 soldiers.

1600 5 June Eng. A judicial censure at York house for Essex. Bacon speaks last and long, attacking the earl. Essex boyish, abject. Apologetic. The commissioners order house arrest.

1600 22 July Eng. Kit's friend in Venice Francisco Vrins (bought cochineal from the Cádiz raid) sends power of attorney to Erasmo della Fontaina in London to talk to judges about getting back 405 cases of sugar stolen from the Santa Maria. Does Erasmo have dinner with Kit and Ben Jonson at Marco Lucchese's Italian restaurant? Cipriano Gabri, another Vrins agent, is in town and might join them. (Marchands Flamands à Venise. op. cit., vol 1, p 341, and Schoenbaum. A Documentary Life of Sh. NY: Oxford U Press, 1975, p.127: "Paolo Marco Lucchese . . . ran a restaurant in the parish of St. Olave . . . and lodged Italian visitors . . . . In Othello . . . the Duke asks, "Marcus Lucchese, is he not in town?")

1600 2 Oct. Eng. Essex, living quietly at Essex house, writes submissive letters to Eliz. (In ciphers As Y. L. It. Kit says he should have written *loving* letters.)

1600 30 Oct. Eng. The queen does not renew Essex's lease of the farm of sweet wines. He's broke.

1600 Nov. Eng. Looks as if Cuffe is secretly more loyal to Bacon than to Essex (Cuffe at Padua with Bacon while Essex was away in '97). Cuffe, as a secretary of Essex, brings groups of discontented people to Essex House, so that Essex seems to hold a rival, hostile court. Sir John Davies, a provocateur, puts into Essex's rather simple head the idea of forcing entry to the palace at Whitehall. (Davies, an awful man, is scorned in As You LikeIt. I. 2. lines 61 through 85, as the knight without honor. Years before, he and Kit made a book together, Epigrammes of Sir John Davies and Certaine of Ovid's Elegies, Translated by Christopher Marlowe. Davies calls them the Pancakes and the Mustard, and swears by his honor the pancakes were good and the mustard was naught. Touchstone avows the man has no honor to swear by. Somehow, after Essex is dead, Davies is kicked upstairs to live a long, increasingly dishonorable life, while Cuffe is abandoned to the gallows. (Bacon will do this again.) Ben Jonson's Cynthia's Revels premieres about this time and infuriates Kit; the play suggests Essex should die, and Kit is still trying to save him.

1600 Nov. Eng. Harry Wotton gets away—to Paris and Italy. (L. P. Smith. op. cit., vol 2, p 36.)

1601

1601 Jan. Eng. Mary Sidney Herbert becomes a widow.

1601 Jan. Eng. Kit makes Twelfth Night for Mary, for a play-party at Baynard's Castle. Olivia and Viola are roles suitable for her to play—she chooses Viola. (In loving ciphers for this play, Kit advises her to stay a widow.)

1601 Sunday, 8 Feb. Eng. Cecil and Bacon receive hourly news of a stir at Essex House; under cover they fan resentment. Supporters, provocateurs gather around Essex. The Lord Keeper, other important men come to ask what's wrong. Essex shouts that his life is sought-after—false letters have been written in his name! He locks the mediators in his study to be guarded by John Davies, says he'll be right back, rushes out with henchmen. Riot all day. At night he comes home chastened, goes out on the roof. His secret brother Robert Sidney talks Essex down, and he submits. (C. C. Stopes. The Life of Henry, The Third Earl. op. cit.)

1601 19 Feb. Eng. Essex and his loyal follower Hen Wriothesly are tried, and Ned de Vere serves as senior peer. Bacon prosecutes. Essex and Hen, convicted of treason, are sent to the Tower and sentenced to death.

1601 20 Feb. Eng. Abject, Essex fingers his loyal followers! Harry Wotton? Gone! Tom Lodge? Gone. Tom Nashe? Gone, too—to die at home. Kit's in town, scared, trying to save Hen's life (ciphers, As You Like It).

1601 24 Feb. Eng. Elizabeth, hoping Essex would send her a message, countermands execution order. No message. Execution on.

1601 25 Feb. Eng. Essex dies in blood, cool, brave, haughty.

1601 2 March Eng. Instigator John Davies writes Cecil: Davies has not had the help he expected from others [Bacon?] but owed everything to Cecil: "you gave order unto Sir Walter Rawley that if I were indicted, that it should be stayed . . ." (C.C. Stopes. The Life of Henry . . . p 223) Davies lives, others die later: In this year Love's Martyr is published by Robert Chester with poems by Shakespeare, Marston, George Chapman and Ben Jonson, all dedicated to Sir John Salisburie—nine years an Essex man, loyal to the end. Kit's Shakespeare poem was "The Phoenix and the Turtle," and Chester put a note up front: "Mar: Mutare dominum non potest liber notis." I read it:

"Marlowe: to change your master won't alter your free celebrity."

1601 early Eng. Kit has money trouble. (As Amorphous in Ben J.'s first draft of Cynthia's Revels, it seems Kit is earning his meals as a comedian at the Italian restaurant.)

1601 March Eng. Kit is called into the palace. The queen is good to him, and during a last assignation he persuades her not to kill Hen. (ciphers, AYLI.) The queen gives Kit a year's work inducting young actors and writers into SSS, taking them to Venice to learn Catholicism so they can come home, serve as chaplains in great houses, planted there to listen for signs of disloyalty. (ibid., and ciphers in Troilus and Cressida.) Ben Jonson goes as Simon Fox. (CSP list of intelligencers abroad in 1601.

vol CLXXXII, p 140, item 72.) Aurelian Townsend (David W. Davies. Elizabethans Errant. Ithaca, NY: Cornell U Press, 1967, p 198.) and John Fletcher (Sonnet 124 A ciphers.) go, too.

1601 June Venice Arriving in town with his band of neophyte SSS spirits, Kit goes to the beach to see the tomb he made for Rita in Nov. 1594. He goes inside. The water comes closer now. He puts the tomb up on pilings, finds Rita's father and asks him once more to take her body into the Cicogna family vault. The duke comes, looks, weeps and carries his daughter's remains to his boat; he and Kit row to the "tomb isle," and they lay Rita's body next to her mother's in the vault. (ciphers, Troilus and Cresida.)

1601 Venice Through the rest of this year Kit, working with the young SSS men in Italy, writes to Hen, encouraging him to read and write in the Tower, to write *loving* letters to the queen, and to decipher sonnets.

1601 Venice Ben Jonson writes a first draft of Volpone (?) and Poetaster, with characters Crispinus (Bacon), and Asinus Lupus (Ned, the asinine wolfish earl).

1601 9 Sept. Scotland. Sent by the Duke of Florence, Henry Wotton arrives (aka Ottavio Baldi) at Dumferline, to talk to King James and stay till spring. Cecil's spy Wilson doesn't know where Henry has gone . . . (Pearsall Smith, Life and Letters of Sir Henry W. vol 1, pp 41, 42)

1601 11 December Eng. William Basset, Elizabeth Basset's adopted father, is buried. A letter to me from the Staffordshire County Council, 19 Jan '83, states his burial is recorded in the Blore parish register: "Wyllm Basset esquyer buryed the xi[th] daye of December 1601." He left no will: Isabel-Elizabeth (Kit's daughter by Rita) becomes a ward of the queen.

1602

1602 Venice, Spring Ben Jonson as Simon Fox, still in Venice with Kit's group of SSS neophytes, goes with SSS brother-intern Aurelian Townsend to look into actions of a couple of con men who have hired a big house in town and are claiming to be alchemists. Ben starts to think of his play, The Alchemist? (David W. Davies. Elizabethans Errant, op. cit., p 148.)

1602 18 May Eng. Elizabeth Basset's wardship is sold to Henry, Lord Cobham, who keeps it two days, sells it to Walter Ralegh with Cecil as witness. On the day Ralegh buys the wardship he enters into agreement with Cecil providing that if Cecil should die within two years, Ralegh will transfer the wardship to Cecil's executors. This arrangement is explained at the beginning of the agreement: "the passing of which grant [to Ralegh] is truly meant to be in trust, and to the only use and behoof of him, the said Sir Robert Cecil and his assigns." Cecil wants the lucrative wardship, but since he's Master of Wards it wouldn't look right to grant it to himself. Cobham's and Ralegh's agreements are entered in official records, and Cecil executes a private trust with Ralegh, which, as a trust and not a re-sale, doesn't have to be put in official records. Judith Basset asks for Isabel-Elizabeth's wardship and is turned down. (Joel Hurstfield. The Queen's Wards. Cambridge, MA: Harvard U, 1958, pp 301-304.) Hurstfield wonders how many times Cecil performed this sort of trick. It was only by chance Hurstfield found the private papers. (H. M. C. Salisbury xii, 580-581; Hatfield deeds 192, 6 & 10.)

1602 early July Eng. Just returned from Italy, Kit and Ben Jonson write additions for Tom Kyd's Spanish Tragedy and split the fee. (Henslowe's diary, 24 June 1602, an *advance* of £10 to Ben for "adicyons" to Kyd's play. Kit thanks Ben in ciphers.)

1602 July Eng. When the SSS actor-writers get back from Italy with Kit, Good Tom tells him Cecil's in control of Isabel's wardship, and Kit is worried.

1602 31 July, or 1 or 2 Aug. Eng. The queen, a guest of Sir Thos. Egerton at Harefield, sees a preview of Kit's Othello, performed by Burbage's men. (John Payne Collier. New Particulars. p 57.) This play is the first draft, made while Kit was in Venice. Plot shows Eliz. how someone can be fooled into thinking a beloved person is bad. Is Kit present at the show? Does he talk to Elizabeth?

1602 28 December Eng. Good Tom Howard is acting Chamberlain of the Household.

1603

1603 14 Jan. Spain Royal auditors in Madrid still pester Cervantes about his 1594 accounts. They look for him, can't find him. (Byron. Cervantes.)

1603 Mon. 17 Jan. Eng. Elizabeth keeps a last appointment in town before going to Richmond to die: she comes to see Good Tom Howard (and Isabel-Elizabeth) at the Charter House. (E.K. C. Eliz. Stage: "A Court Calendar.") Kit may have been with them, and perhaps he told Cervantes, for Manco's description of the interview rings true, full of intimate detail and touching dialogue. (Novelas Ejemplares: "La Española Inglesa.") It seems that on this day Isabel is befriended by the queen, who straightens out the wardship, taking it from Cecil. At last she's wise to his dishonesty.

1603 21 Jan. Eng. The queen goes to Richmond, sits on pillows on the floor. Won't eat.

1603 Feb. Eng. Elizabeth has a sore throat. Won't get in bed.

1603 Wed. 23 March Eng. Elizabeth lifted into bed. Too late for broth. Whitgift comes to pray on his knees. Hours pass. Again and again he thinks she's gone and tries to leave the room. She moves her arm; he must go on praying.

1603 Thurs. 24 March, between 2 and 3 AM. Elizabeth dies.

1603 28 March Eng. From Gray's Inn? Francis Bacon sends letter to a Mr. Davis, gone to the king. The body of the letter is written by "one of his men." It ends: "so desiring you to be good to concealed poets, I continue Your very assured, Fr. Bacon" (Lambeth MSS 976, fol. 4.)

1603 March Eng. Bacon sends his favored agent Toby Mathew with a letter to King James. (DNB, and Arnold Harris Matthew. London: The Life of Sir Tobie Mathew. Elkin Mathews, 1907, pp 156, 157.)

1603 6? April Eng. Bacon writes Hen in the Tower: "I may safely be now that which I was truly before."

1603 10 April Eng. Hen released from the Tower.

1603 22 May Eng. Good Tom Howard becomes official Chamberlain of the Household.

1603 July Eng. Plague in London.

1603 2 July Windsor Eng. Prince Henry Stuart becomes Knight of the Garter, as do four young noblemen. One is Wm. Herbert. His mother, Mary Sidney Herbert, is here with daughter Anne (Frances Berkeley Young. Mary Sidney, Countess of Pembroke. London: David Nutt, 1912. pp 99, 100). Is Bacon here with sidekick Toby Mathew? [Did Toby say something rude to Mary? Like, "Well, Ma'am, aren't you the lucky bastard, to fall into such fortune?" Toby and Bacon weren't knights.]

1603 4 July Eng. Mary Sidney Herbert writes furious letter to Julius Caesar, asking for redress from insult given her by one Mathew. (ibid. excerpts.)

1603 7 July Eng. Hen Wriothesly made Captain of the Isle of Wight. He and Kit think maybe Kit could be governor-on-the-spot, if Kit can be pardoned. (Cervantes' last chapter, D.Q.I. Kit is Sancho Panza.)

1603 8 July Eng. Mary writes again, saying the *king* must be told what this Mathew has done. She did nothing malicious to Mathew. He's to receive no grace or place . . . [I put this in only because of story-line . . . could this be the same Mathew—since 1601

Bacon's catspaw—in years to come, the man Bacon would send to Italy just before the poisoning of Harry's embassy? No evidence here.]

Toby Mathew, 13 yrs younger than Kit, was Catholic intelligencer for Bacon. Banished from Eng., he gained re-entry several times. I think when Toby was in Florence he sent news to Eng. embassy at Venice by pigeon-post. He visited that embassy in 1612, when several agents went together in disguise, Venice-Naples, to attend a festival. Knighted 1623. Died at Eng. Cath. College at Ghent, 1655.

1603 23 July Eng. At Whitehall 300 knights created. Bacon's one, at last.

1603 25 July Eng. Because of plague in London, a quiet coronation at Westminster.

1603 26 Aug. Eng. James at Salisbury near Wilton. Mary Sidney Herbert writes to her son William asking him to bring the king to Wilton to see a performance of A Y L I. The letter contains words, "we have the man Shakespeare with us." (Gilbert Slater. Seven Sh's. London: Cecil Palmer, 1931, p 78.)

1603 29 Aug. Eng. The king sees A Y L I at Wilton. Did Mary suggest James should pardon Kit? He did not, but there may have been talk of a new Eng. embassy at Venice, to be set up next year.

1603 17 Nov. Eng. Ralegh has outlived his usefulness to Cecil. Anti-Spanish Ralegh gets in the way of Cecil-and-Bacon's plans to soften up Jas re Spain. Today at Wolverton Castle, Ralegh is tried for treason.

1603 Nov. to Dec. Eng. Kit's having a hard time—no steady work—shadows suggest he works as actor.

1603 5 Dec. Eng. Cecil tells Venetian envoy Nicolò Molin that Henry Wotton has been appointed ambassador to Venice. (CSP Venetian and L. P. Smith. Life and Letters of Sir H. W. op. cit., vol 1 p 45.)

1603 5 Dec. Eng. Ralegh sent to the Tower to stay 13 years.

1604

1604 14 Jan. Eng. James wants a new Bible: clergy convene at Hampton Court to work over prayer book and Scriptures.

1604 Jan.? Eng. To Dudley Carleton, secretary to earl of Northumberland (both friends of Kit's since 1592), J. Cardén writes how broke he is—landlord took his cloak—lend me one? (Kit? CSP Eliz Dom. Add. xxxvi p 452), Carleton went to work for Northumberland in Oct. 1603.

1604 24 Jan. Eng. Unexplained fire at Gray's Inn, where Bacon is living.

1604 6 Feb. Eng. Kit is 40 years old. He may be working as shipping agent out of the Exchange, for friends in Venice: Ben J. has written about how Kit, Amorphous, likes Italian food.

1604 29 Feb. Eng. John Whitgift, Archbishop of Canterbury, dies.

1604 March Eng.-Italy Kit hired by SSS to aid Henry Wotton in Venice: Kit will have a legitimate job as Harry's Italian Secretary of Compliments, Gregorio de' Monti. (L.P. Smith. Life and Letters. op. cit.: "bio" of Gregorio in vol 2, Appendix 3, pp 473, 474.) In March? Kit says goodbye to his folks at Canterbury (leaves them with an entertainment he has written for them, inside revised Jew of Malta), and heads for Venice to set things up for the new embassy.

1604 c. 20 April? Venice. Kit hires a house for the embassy—Palazzo da Silva in Cannaregio, near Ponte degli Ormesani—and a temporary place to live (the palazzo is unavailable till Dec.)—rents furniture from Jews in the Ghetto, a villa for Harry on the Brenta, writes to Cervantes, now in Madrid, settles down to rework Measure for Measure and Othello.

1604 24 June Eng. Ned de Vere dies at a house in Newington, Middlesex, after long illness (DNB) and is buried 6 July in the churchyard of St. John of Hackney (Alan H. Nelson. Monstrous Adversary. Liverpool: Liverpool University Press, 2003.) Ned's son Henry becomes 18th earl at age 13.

1604 c. end June Spain Manco Cervantes sells his finished Don Quixote I to Francisco Robles. Manco has worked 7 years on this book.

1604 8 July Eng. Harry Wotton knighted by the king. (L.P. Smith. vol 1, p 45.)

1604 19 July Eng. Sir Harry's at Dover, ready to sail. (ibid.)

1604 27 July Italy Duke of Urbino writes in his diary: Guarini has suddenly left town. (Battista Guarini has gone to Venice to see Kit?)

1604 late July Spain Cervantes moves to Valladolid (Byron, op. cit.), perhaps as paid observer for Kit. There, a great English-Spanish Peace Party is planned for 1605, and Kit is shaping up an info service for Harry. Kit will get some funding from Bacon. Manco's family will work.

1604 1 August Ven. Kit shows Guarini a script of Othello (about the murder of Guarini's daughter), sends the play to England, starts re-writing his play Leir for Mary Herbert. The post brings news of Ned's death, and Kit drops everything to revise Hamlet.

1604 23 Sept. Ven. Harry arrives (at Padua?) with his "family" of retainers. All wait, quiet, preparing for their giorno d'entrata later this month. (L.P. Smith. op. cit.)

1604 30 Sept. Ven. Harry, in gondola (followed by his train and all the English in Venice and Padua) is rowed to Isla San Spiritu, enters monastery garden to meet 60 Venetian senators. (ibid.)

1604 1 Oct. Ven. Giorno d'audienza for Harry. He speaks with the Doge in the Collegio. (pic and picturesque details. ibid. vol I pp 51-53.)

1604 2 Oct.? Ven. Kit sends revised Hamlet home, along with revised Measure for Measure.

1604 28 Oct. Eng. Promotions in the legal world: Bacon hopes for Solicitorship—loses again. Bacon is Nowhere. Frustration mounts.

1604 3 Nov. Eng. Othello is performed at Whitehall by King's Co. before Jas and Anne—much appreciated.

1604 2 Nov. Eng. Ben Jonson sells his first tragedy, Sejanus, to Edward Blount. (S.R. and EKC Eliz Stage vol 3 p 368) Kit, signing himself Cygnus, has written a preface.

1604 4 Nov. Eng. Merry Wives played at Whitehall by King's Co. Lots of laughs. Bacon depressed.

1604 26 Dec. Eng. Measure for Measure performed at court by King's Co.

1604 28 Dec. Eng. Comedy of Errors performed at court by King's Co. Everyone loves these plays.

1605

Some time this year, Kit's play, The London Prodigall, is performed by the King's Co.

1605 Jan. Ven. Through a glass darkly we see an emissary of Doge Grimani approach Harry to ask if he keeps a bravo. Would he do a job for the Doge—a personal job, but good for the State? Looks like an evil kinsman of the Doge, a man who lives with two sons in Vicenza, is extorting protection-money from the licensed houses of prostitution in Venice—bleeding a source of city revenue. Grimani doesn't want to prosecute, but if all three men were to die . . . . Harry asks Kit to do the hits, to help the standing of the new English embassy.

1605 23 Jan. Eng. John Marley makes his will. (printed, Wm. Urry. Christopher Marlowe and Canterbury. London: Faber and Faber, 1988, Appendix VI, and Wm. Urry. London TLS 13 Feb.1964.)

1605 25 Feb. Eng. Marlowe's legal father, John, dies. Buried Parish of St. George, where he and Kate set up housekeeping 44 years earlier. (ibid.)

1605 17 March Eng. Katherine Arthur (Marley, or is it spelled Marlowe?) makes her will (ibid.)—and dies, this day or the next.

1605 18? 19? March Eng. Katherine Arthur buried. In her will she asked to be buried "near where as my husbande . . . was buried," but instead, says David Riggs. The World of Chr. Marlowe. NY: Henry Holt, 2004. p 349, her daughters laid her to rest "in the nearby parish church of All Saints." Riggs offers no source.

1605 April Vicenza Kit will try to do the hit job, for Harry. Never seen on the street, the gangsters live in a guarded villa, but all citizens of the Republic must go to church on Easter. Kit hires two "broken men" to help him.

1605 10 April Vicenza Cavagion and his boys appear at the Duomo for Easter Mass; Kit kills the father with a knife. The sons elude the broken men. Kit gets his helpers away, down Carpan Street and across the bridge. (Venice. Consiglio X, Processi Criminali reg. 22, 9 April 1605. Street map, Vicenza. The Blue Guide: Muirhead's Northern Italy. London: Macmillan, 1924.) The Venice Recorder has put down the wrong date? 9 April. Harry says Easter Sunday, the 10th. Girolamo da Monte kills Mauritio Cavagion in front of Episcopal throne in the Cathedral of Vicenza. (CSP Ven. Writes it up later—1607, p 483.) Grimani is angry that the Cavagion boys are still alive, so Kit suggests a stakeout at an elegant bordello on Murano—the only place at which the sons are ever seen. Kit says he'll work things out when he returns from another job.

1605 9 June Valladolid Formal ratification of Eng.-Spanish Peace treaty, in Valladolid on Corpus Christi Day.

1605 10 June Valladolid Bullfight. The Great Elite enter the plaza in their splendid coaches. Thousands of jewels. Leading the parade is a Don Quixote on Rosinante, and before them comes a Sancho Panza on Dapple. (William Byron. Cervantes.)

1605 11 to 18 June Valladolid The English are entertained at a fabulous Peace Party: c. 400 English dignitaries and their SSS guards are here—among them friends of Kit's:

John and Jane Davenant from the St. George Tavern by the Old Bailey. They've moved to Oxford as student-watchers. On 11 June, Kit and Jane go to bed together and start a baby.

1605 12 June Spain to Italy Kit heads back to Venice to finish Cavagion job.

1605 27 June Valladolid Just before 11 PM, G. Espeleta and Cervantes fight with swords outside Manco's house. Espeleta, mortally wounded, is carried upstairs. (William Byron. Cervantes.) Was Manco hired to waste this man, or did Espeleta overhear something about Cervantes' English connections?

1605 14 July Murano Back in Venice, Kit, with hired men, sets up a stakeout at Murano bordello of Anzola Mazina. They wait.

1605 16 July Murano Kit had known an import-export man down the block, Carlo Helman, a friend who'd died last month. Kit visits his family, talks to their gatekeeper. The Cavagioni see Kit, recognize him, plan to *frame* him. (CSP Venetian 1607.)

1605 19 July Murano Kit wakes in his room at Anzola's to see a drugged child lying on his bed. (Unconscious, she's been brought upstairs in a large basket by the Cavagioni). Pig-blood has been poured on her; police are coming up the stairs. Kit, naked, escapes out the window, goes to the Helman family's gate.

"Ven. Consiglio X. 20 July 1605: In casa de Anzola Mazina, Augustin Carpan had carnal commerce with Antonia, daughter of Hieronimo Verglierzin & Iseppa Furlana, just 9 years old & not only deflowered but sodomized and damaged. Anzola Mazina jailed. Antonia given 500 ducats for dowry." [all Kit's money]. (CSP Venetian, 1607, [sic] in Italian—ed. noted it was too awful to print in English.) *Kit's been framed by the bad guys. Antonia was deflowered by her own dad Hieronimo, in hope of promised dowry.*

1605 21 July Ven. At the embassy house, Kit's room is cleaned out by police confiscating everything. Angry Doge is looking for Kit. He escapes to England with borrowed money.

1605 2 August Eng. In those old days, the ordinary post took 22 days Ven. to Eng. (L.P. Smith, op. cit.) Kit wd probably arrive at Dover c. 12 August, Gregorian, or *2 August, English time.* First thing he'd do would be go to see his sister Meg in Canterbury and find out how his folks came to die, and what was happening. While he was there it seems he took old work out of the trunkful of his writings at home: The London Prodigall, The Puritan Widdow, The Merry Devil—plays he touched up to give the players—and a reportorial drama about a fiendish psychopath, a work he rewrote naming it The Yorkshire Tragedy. In London he left three of the dramas with the King's Co. and one, The Puritan Widdow, with his friend John Marston.

1605 25 August Eng. Kit goes to friends in Oxford. King James is coming here for entertainments.

1605 27-30 August Eng. As James and family approach the city for fiesta they're greeted by Mathew Gwinne's device of three Sibyllae—this gives Kit idea for witches in Macbeth. (Riverside Shakespeare. Boston: Houghton Mifflin, 1974, p 1308, and Geoffrey Bullough. Narrative and Dramatic Sources, vol 7: "Macbeth" p 429-30.) Plays are given by Kit's friends. (4 accounts of this whole festival listed, E.K.C. Eliz. Stage. vol 1, p 130 footnote) Kit earns his keep. (Ibid. "provision was made for a magician." See Kit's ciphers in King Lear: "Ay, I can juggle, too.")

1605 1 Sept. Eng. In London, Kit sees Marston's Sophonisba played by the Children at Blackfriars—uses ideas in Macbeth, which he's quickly writing. (Geoffrey Bullough. op. cit., vol 7, p 425-6.)

1605 end Sept. Spain Kit's in Valladolid. Can't go back to Venice: Doge angry about the flubbed job. Kit stays with Cervantes till end of year—Manco tries to teach him how to write in Spanish, and Kit makes Milon y Berta, starts Noches de Invierno.

1605 3 Oct. Spain Harry Wotton's nephew Pickering is here in Valladolid (since Peace Party?) Sick. Gets fever. Gets worse.

1605 17 Oct. Valladolid Pickering receives Catholic last rites.

1605 18 Oct. Valladolid Pickering dies. Cervantes and Kit attend church funeral, and here Kit meets 7th Count of Lemos, Cervantes' patron.

1605 4 Nov. Eng. Ben Jonson (ersatz Catholic since returning with Kit from Italy in 1602), has been a spy in Gunpowder Plot, using bricklaying skills to take down walls in Parliament cellars to make suitable spaces for gunpowder placing. (Ballantine) Now B. Jonson fades, the scheme is exposed, and ringleaders are in custody. (Paul Durst. Intended Treason. NY: A.S. Barnes & Co. 1970.)

1605 3 Dec. Ven. Marino Grimani, the intransigent Doge, is dead in Venice. Kit can go back to the embassy.

1606

1606 Jan. Ven. New Doge Leonardo Donato, a Resistance man, is more friendly to Harry than to Paul V, the new Pope. Venice taxes the clergy, requires State permission for erection of churches & monasteries—and at end 1605 Venice has arrested two priests, refusing to hand them over to Rome. (sources for 1606 in L.P. Smith op. cit.)

1606 Jan. Ven. Kit back at the embassy, bringing with him framework of a book of stories in Spanish for Isabel-Elizabeth, Noches de Invierno. He's polishing Macbeth, finishing King Lear. Harry works with Venice's Theological Councillor Paolo Sarpi in the cause of temporal princes against papal aggression.

1606 Jan. Ven. Kit's friend in Mantua Giambattista Andreini, manager of acting troupes Gelosi and Fidele, sets his tragedy La Florinda in a Scottish castle in the woods. Has he seen script of Macbeth? (Winifred Smith. Italian Actors of the Renaissance. NY: Benj. Blom, 1968 (1930).

1606, n.s. 3 March Eng. Jane Davenant's new baby by Kit is christened in Oxford. His name is William. (Eyes like Kit's: adult pic in Richard Barber. Samuel Pepys, Esquire. London: pub. by the National Portrait Gallery, 1970. p 32.)

1606 17 April Italy Pope issues bull of Interdict & Excommunication for the Republic of Venice—20 days to repent. Venice issues edict: the bull is nothing; clergy should work as usual. Jesuits say no, are expelled.

1606 spring Guarini sent to Rome as secret observer for Venice—stays till a settlement is made. (Vittorio Rossi. Battista Guarini . . . op. cit.)

1606 c. April Ven. Looks like Kit's favorite old ship, the Tiger, stops at Venice on her way home to Portsmouth after a terrible trip to the east—how far east? (Macbeth I. 03. line 7.) Ship is a mess. Is Kit's friend Sampson aboard? (Mark Eccles. "Brief Lives" in Studies in Philology, 1982. Eccles says her captain was a John Davys. Also Geoffrey Bullough. op. cit., vol 7, p 427.)

1606 April—Aug. Ven. Harry's in heaven—rashly promises Donato there'll be lots of English aid. Suggests strengthening undercover union of Protestant Swiss and free north-Italian states. Sends Kit out to rob Catholic posts, using his old trick of removing wax with thin, hot shoemaker's knife. (L. P. Smith, and King Lear: "Leave, gentle wax . . .")

1606 10 May Eng. At a suggestion from Cecil that preference will come to Bacon after marrying Alice Barnham, Bacon does marry her. Nothing good happens.

1606 Sept. Ven. Since James has sent a letter saying he'll help all he can, Harry now formally declares forthcoming aid from England to Venice—ships, men.

1606 14 Oct. Ven. Venice is ready to say yes to Jas.'s "offer," but Jas. backs off, leaving Harry embarrassed.

1606 26 Dec. Eng. King Lear is played at court on St. Stephen's night.

1607

1607 7 July Italy (CSP Ven. 1607. vol 11, #21, p 11) Pope complains of pamphlets printed in English in Venice (CSP Ven. vol 11, #35, p 17), and Cardinal Borghese writes that Free-Thinkers meet in a big room in the fondaco della biancarie.

1607 summer Kit prints for Harry, robs the posts. At Colorno he stops to see Guarini's fellow spy, dedicated Resistance leader Countess of Sala, who sends messages to N. Italian dukes via her charming dwarves and midgets.

1607 August Eng. Toby Mathew turns up in England, Catholic, and is jailed but allowed to go with keeper to see his patron Bacon. (Spedding. op. cit., xi, p 8)

1607 August Ven. This may have been the month Sir Francis Verney was in Venice and found out Kit was alive. (Verney travelled on to Jerusalem, signed the Pilgims' Book there, 12 Oct.) Verney sent a four-line poem about Kit to Cecil: "Marlo the splendour of our worthlesse time . . ." (an anagram?) held in Cecil Papers 233/9, at Hatfield House. (mentioned by Eccles. Studies in Philology. 1982)

1607 Sept. Ven. Is Kit the "secretary" who sometimes goes to the Cabinet to speak for Harry? He'd have the best Italian. (CSP Ven. vol xi, p 34.) He goes again in Oct. Kit is working on Antony and Cleopatra.

1608

1608 8 Jan. Ven. The son of Julius Caesar, Master of Requests in Eng., is a youth called Juley Caesar, studying in Padua. On this day Juley is fatally impaled by his fencing teacher Brochetta (could this be the origin of the term en brochette?) Harry sends a secretary to Padua to investigate the death.

1608 20-25 Jan. Ven. Harry's sick in bed—a secretary (who?) deals with Juley Caesar's death at Cabinet, Collegio. Does Kit now start re-working his Julius Caesar?

1608 Jan? Ven. Kit sends first draft Antony and Cleopatra to King's Company.

1608 early Feb. Eng. Bacon writes his agent Toby Mathew in the Fleet. "Do not think me forgetful or altered towards you . . . " (and, equivocating) "Good Mr. Mathew, receive yourself back from these courses of perdition." (Spedding. op. cit.)

1608 Feb. Eng. (Chamberlain to Carleton. John Chamberlain. Letters. vol 1. ed. McClure. Westport, CT: Greenwood, 1979 (1939). Cecil says he hadn't known of Mathew's imprisonment, gives him 6 weeks to keave Eng. Meanwhile "to pick a friend of good account" where he may stay. Toby picks "Mr. Jones."

1608 11 April Ven. The Nuncio came to the Cabinet to say that two cases marked Books had been sent to English Ambassador Henry Wotton and his chaplain Bedell. The Nuncio thinks they must contain material concerning the English "Sect"—thinks books would soon to be distributed throughout the city to befog citizens. He said he would come back to report when he had proof of distribution. (CSP Ven. vol 11, p 121.) The contents of these boxes has never been made public. Is it possible they contained galleys of King James's Bible, then being created in England? The doctors of divinity working on that Bible were good theologians but not poets, and there are places of great beauty in the King James version. Gregorio de' Monti aka Christopher Marlowe, a student of theology and poet of considerable genius, was living at the embassy.

1608 20 May Eng. On Stationers' Register, Edward Blount enters "a booke Called Anthony and Cleopatra." Will Shakespeare has sold this play too soon—thinks it's badly put together and Kit should stop writing. (ciphers in rewritten script of this play.)

1608 late May, early June Mantua A famous festival: On 2 June Guarini, after 19 years, premieres his comedy, Idropica. Kit is there. Stage plays and music. "An entre'acte sent by Monco." (Leo Schrade. Monteverdi.) This must be Manco, who wrote entre'actes; eight have been translated. (S. Griswold Morley. The Interludes of Cervantes. Princeton, NJ: Princeton U. Press, 1948.) In Monteverdi's 8th Book of Madrigals are lyrics by Guarini, unascribed songs identifiable as Marlowe's by first-lines-anagrams, and others by Kit's friend G.B. Marino. These madrigals were probably part of the party. (The Bach Guild. Historical Anthology of Music. IV. The Baroque, Early and Middle. A. Music of Italy. 2. Secular Vocal Music.)

1608 June Eng. Getting money for insatiable King James is a major occupation for the English government. Cecil speaks at Custom House; lays £60,000 a year of impositions on merchants. (Spedding. op. cit., xi, p 157.)

1608 24 June Julian (4 July Gregorian) Ven. Oddball traveler Tom Coryate arrives in Venice from Padua to stay a month and a half at the embassy. He may be an SSS brother. A good writer, he kept a wonderful diary, published it (with some difficulty) after he got home. (Coryate's Crudities, pub. W.S. 1611) Enjoyed as comedy in England but a valuable handbook for travelers. The part about Venice is best—Kit showed him odd places around town, made up stories about them.

1608 16 July Eng. William Mylle, Clerk of Star Chamber, dies. Bacon has held reversion of the office for many years; he's sworn in as replacement on day of death. (Spedding. op. cit., xi, p 21.) At last all those records are in Bacon's trust. After dealing with what he wants to change or delete, Bacon will sell the office.

1608 19 August Eng. The "Kallender of Orders" is delivered to Bacon: Sentences, Decrees and Acts of Star Chamber, "engrossed in a fair book with the names of Lords and Judges and others present who gave their voices." Spedding says from beginning Henry VII to 30 Elizabeth. Were the last years of Elizabeth already missing? Today, *all* are missing.

1608 18 August, Gregorian Ven.—Eng. Coryate heads home from Venice—mission accomplished? Does he carry Kit's sonnets home, asking agent William Hall to collect more in England, give them all to Thos. Thorpe to publish? For money? Money is getting tight at the embassy.

1608 Sept. Ven. Kit leaves for Spain, pretending to be Antonio, a Spaniard, taking scripts of Don Quixote, translated, and Noches de Invierno to show Manco. Soon Noches is officially approved. (Aprovacion por Fray Gil Cordon para Noches de Invierno, por Antonio de Eslava.) In English cipher the book is dedicated to Kit's daughter Isabel-Elizabeth; anagram for her in first lines. Kit goes with Manco to see his patron count of Lemos, who says both Manco and Antonio can be part of the train of artists when Lemos goes to Naples as Viceroy in 1610. Kit heads for Venice—he's heard a whisper about a plan against the Veneto, a plot conceived by Francisco Quevedo, adviser to the duke of Osuna.

1609

1609 20 Feb. Eng. Marcantonio Correr, Ambassador from Venice to Eng., writes he was not invited to the Masque of the Queen, but she heeled him in. Anne was a kind friendly lady who loved theater. (CSP Foreign. Ven 1609, and Ida Sedgwick Proper. Our Elusive Willy. p 471.)

1609 April Eng. About now, Cecil is trying to cut back government expenses, disagrees with Bacon about how to get money for James—and Cecil hates Bacon's idea of an expensive peripatetic "scientific" college to mask SSS agents. Big fight.

1609 26 June Spain Kit's Noches de Invierno is published (in Pamplona, by Carlos de Labayen), with byline Antonio de Eslava and a second official approval, this one by Juan de Mendi. In this same year, 1609, there was a second printing.

1609 Sun. 6 August Eng. Bacon has made his own plan for furnishing James with funds: Researching old myths to make a book, he has found a tale about the Trophonian

Den: an ancient prince who needs money makes a hole in the wall of a treasury, takes out what he wants. 6 Aug. Bacon writes Mike Hicks (private banker): there'll be a meeting at Mike's house Tues. afternoon. All will have to eat with Mike, but he "may have allowance, the Exchequer being first full . . ." (Spedding. op. cit., xi, p 131.)

1609 Tues. 8 August Eng. "a commission touching King's service" is executed at Mike Hicks's house in afternoon and evening. (note to Sir John Bennet. Spedding. ibid.) Will Ben Jonson the brickworker open the Trophonian Den? Yes: There's an anonymous book, The Great Assizes Holden in Parnassus by Appollo and his Assessors. London: Richard Cotes for Edward Husbands, and are to be sold at his Shop in the Middle Temple, 1645. Several pp of this work are reprinted in Sir Edward Durning Lawrence. Bacon is Sh. NY: John Mc Bride, 1910, and in Gilbert Slater. Seven Shakespeares. op. cit.) Bacon, "The Lord Verulan" [sic], is "Chancellor of Parnassus," and below this title there's a list of workers in the field (SSS bros) with their occupations. William Davenant, Kit's son, is "the Scout". William "Shakespeere" is "the writer of weekly accounts" (Kit, when he was chargé d'affaires at the embassy?), and *Ben Johnson is Keeper of the Trophonian Denne.* Being a bricklayer and Bacon's (half-bro?) slave, Ben must have made an inconspicuous reclosable opening in the side of the treasury (&/or the mint), so treasure could be removed without walking in the door. Of course the scheme has awful repercussions, but Bacon himself will not be charged with these thefts.

1609 Thurs. 10 August Eng. Bacon writes Cecil re Mr. Chancellor, Mr. Att'y and "transportation of gold and silver." "The Frenchman never came or called about it. Henry Neville sent up a solicitor about it. Mr. Calvert says you want a copy of his answer." (Letter in State Papers printed in Wm. Hepworth Dixon. Personal History of Lord Bacon. Boston: Ticknor & Fields. 1861. pp 405-406.)

1609 11 Sept. Ven. Harry goes to Collegio and resigns his post because the Senate refused to accept James' book full of bigoted remarks re evil Catholics—his just-off-the-press work: Premonition to All Most Mighty Monarchs . . . . (L.P. Smith. op. cit., vol 1.) Donato away sick—when he comes back he persuades Harry to stay.

1609 Oct. Eng. Bacon's working on his book of myths, de Sapienta Veterum (thinking about Trophonean Den). In Feb. he sends a copy to Toby Mathew. Operation Vulcan appears in Bacon's mind.

1609 14 Nov. Toby leaves Milan to go to Spain. (L. P. Smith. vol 1, pp 476-7.)

1609 Eng. In this year the mysterious quarto, Shake-speare's Sonnets, is published, printed by G. Eld for T.T. [Thomas Thorpe], to be sold by William Aspley. Emilia is polishing her own book, to be published next year.

1610

1610 In this year another edition of Noches de Invierno is published, this one by Kit's old friend Roger Velpius in Brussels.

1610 6/16 Feb. Kit is 46.

1610 13 March Ven. Harry writes King James re Galileo's discoveries with telescope. (Galileo teaches at Padua U.)

1610 14 May Europe On this day Henry IV is murdered. Aided by Savoy, he had been preparing a strike on Milan that could knock Spain out of N. Italy. The death an immense setback for the Resistance, but workers don't give up.

1610 June Naples Kit, as Antonio de Laredo, goes to Naples to watch for arrival of new viceroy Pedro de Castro, Seventh Count of Lemos, who will come by sea.

1610 mid-June Naples Castro and his wife arrive with 15 galleys and a great train: Lots of poets, writers, the Sanchez Co. (premiere troupe of actors from Madrid), but no Manco; Quevedo has turned the count against him.

1610 same day, mid-June Naples Kit sees Micaela Lujan, star of the Sanchez Co., falls in love with her. They shack up at the beach.

1610 June, July, till late August Naples. They honeymoon, though day work takes her to the theater and Kit to the palace. He writes a play with a good role for her: Gregorio de' Monti. L'Ippolito. (First ed. 1611. The Folger has copy of third ed.: Pietro Baba pub., 1620.) A baby's on the way. Kit must check in at Venice by end August.

1610 27 Aug. Eng. Ann Cooke Bacon, Francis's dear foster mother, is buried.

1610 1 Sept. Ven. "Gregorio de' Monti" given power of attorney to recover bill of sale for freight of the Sant'Andrea (Captain John Allen, Scotsman). She brought salt from Trapani. The secretary may keep 100 ducats for his trouble. Giulio di Franceschi identifies the captain and "acts as translator" (because Gregorio is not supposed to know English). Marchands Flamands à Venise. op. cit., vol 2, p 302. #2643. Notary Spinelli #11932 f. 769. Kit is moonlighting.

1610 Sept. Ven. Kit sends to England his new Winter Night's Tale, along with a complete makeover of an old Ned de Vere play, which Kit names Cymbeline. (ciphers)

1610 Sept. Naples Kit goes back to Naples as Antonio.

1610 15 Oct. Ven. Guests arrive to stay at Harry's embassy (L.P. Smith vol 1, p 498 footnote): William Lord Cranborn (Cecil's son) and young Henry Howard (Good Tom's third son) are staying here. Henry has come to ask Kit for Isabel's hand in marriage. Both boys may be hoping to win her—she's rich—but Cecil's son soon retires to Padua, his nose out of joint. (L.P. Smith can't figure why.) Dr. Mat Lister has come with the boys and is looking out for them.

1610 22 Nov. Ven. Gregorio comes back to Ven. from Naples by way of Padua, brings letter from Dudley Carleton who waits in Padua for word that Harry's ready to leave town. Carleton will then come in to be ambassador.

1610 same day, 22 Nov., Ven. Young Henry Howard talks to Kit about marrying Isabel-Elizabeth, and Kit says yes.

1610 7 Dec. Ven. At farewell audience, Harry introduces new Ambassador Dudley Carleton.

1610 10 Dec. Ven. Harry leaves town.

1610 10? Dec. Ven. Dr. Matt Lister, Mary Herbert's new boyfriend, has brought to Ven. a packet of news for Kit (from Mary?), with a copy of William Strachy's letter from Virginia (I'm guessing that's how Kit gets to read it—it's addressed to an Excellent Lady), a letter about a shipwreck on Bermuda, with details Kit weaves into The Tempest, which he starts writing as soon as he gets back to Naples, dedicating it in cipher to his daughter Isabel-Elizabeth and young Henry Howard, who will be wed.

1611

1611 Jan. to May Naples Kit, as a secretary to Viceroy Lemos, encourages public works. Summer 1610 to summer 1616 are the only years in the history of the viceroyalty in which sensible public works are achieved. (D.A. Parrino. Teatro eroico e politico de governi de' Viceré Spagnoli di Napoli. Naples: Collana di cultura Napoletana, 1730. Essay on don Pietro Fernandez de Castro, Seventh Count of Lemos, p 88, and a list of public-spirited decrees, especially #12, re aqueducts.) I suspect Marlowe started these improvements; His natural father was a judge, and Kit had read The Governour.

1611 March? Ven. Kit sends a first draft of The Tempest north to the players.

1611 May Naples First baby for Micaela and Kit. Soon Kit sails to Eng. in his small ship (his intent ciphered in The Winter Night's Tale, written 1610), taking gifts to Eng. from Carleton?

1611 15 May Eng. The Winters Tale, called The Winter Nights Tale, plays at the Globe. (Note similarity of title to that of Kit's Spanish book of stories, Noches de Invierno.)

1611 midsummer Eng. Dr. Theodore Turquet de Mayerne installed as a physician for royal family. Diagnoses Cecil: he has a tumor. (G.P.V. Akrigg. Jacobean Pageant. NY: Atheneum, 1962/1974, p 107.)

1611 August Naples? Is Kit back in Naples? Probably, because in September at Naples he and Micaela start a new baby.

1611 1 Nov. Eng. First draft of The Tempest performed at court. Shadows suggest Bacon's in the cast here as Prospero, in carnation-colored stockings. Performed on Hallowmas Night at Whitehall. (Ida Sedgwick Proper. Our Elusive Willy. p 563, and The Riverside Shakespeare. Boston: Houghton Mifflin, 1974.)

1611 5 Nov. Eng. "Winter Night's Tale" entered in Account Book of Revels at court. (Proper. ibid. p 563.)

1611 Dec. Kit must be sailing for England again in his "p p" boat (cold trip!) He takes translation of Don Quixote I to be published for Manco.

1612

1612 Jan. Eng. Cecil isn't feeling well.

1612 Jan. Eng. Cecil may have found out about Trophonean Den operation. Something has gone wrong. Bacon tries to make up with Cecil, at same time trying for damage control at the small port of Exeter. What's going on? A plan to export silver bars (stolen from the mint) to France at a profit? Someone leaked? (Spedding)

1612 19 Jan. Eng. n.s. Stationers' Register: to Edward Blount & William Barret, The Delightful History of the wittie knight, Don Quixote.

1612 late Jan. Eng. Bacon sends Kit to Exeter for SSS job. Horrid confusion described in Kit's ciphers in his A Fvnerall Elegye in memory of the late Vertuous Maister William Peeter. by W. S. Imprinted at London by G. Eld, 1612 (after 25 March).

1612 Sat. 25 Jan. Eng. At Exeter, Kit walks into a scene of torture, dispatches the victim to end pain, is laughed at. William Peter, a shocked neophyte SSS bro, is present, wonders out loud if he should leave the secret service, is murdered on his way home by a groom promised payment by the local SSS chief, who later betrays the groom. (See Kit's ciphers.) A disgusting day.

1612 13 Feb. Eng. Stationers' Register: to Thos. Thorpe, the above Elegye. (Donald W. Foster. Elegy by W. S. Newark: U of Delaware Press, 1989.) Foster doesn't mention hidden content, seems not to know that the elegy is a poem secretly ordered by Bacon, who intended the work to show that William Peter had been struck down by a highwayman—could happen to anyone—nothing sinister afoot. But in cipher Kit manages to stuff his interminable Elygye with true horrid details. He sails for Naples, thinking to quit the service.

1612 Feb. Eng. Cecil loses interest in work.

1612 18 March Eng. Harry, who's been in England, sets out for Savoy with young noble riders and 50 beautiful gift horses, to deal for a Savoy princess as bride for Prince Henry. This trip touches Kit's later life-story, as one of the young riders is William Cavendish, who (in 1618) will become Isabel-Elizabeth's second husband.

1612 March Eng. People wonder why there's only a smidgin of silver in the mint, so Bacon writes a comic doubletalk Report: A Certificate to the Lords of the Council upon Information Touching the Scarcity of Silver. (Spedding. xi, pp 255-259). Cecil's fading.

1612 March Ven. Ambassador Carleton writes Chamberlain (Dudley Carleton to John Chamberlain. ed. Maurice Lee, Jr. NJ: Rutgers U. Press, 1972) about long uncomfortable winter—but now the sun brings lizards and nightingales. Carleton expects to see Peter Manwood's eldest son, Roger Manwood (Kit's 1/2 nephew), who's coming to Venice. (Kit's in Naples.)

1612 April Ven. Carleton writes (ibid.) about artist Tintoretto, son of the famous painter and very good himself, who may have painted the face of the Flower Portrait of Kit, called "Shakespeare," kept at Stratford-on-Avon. It has been revealed that the lower part of the portrait has been painted with modern paint.

1612 24 May Eng. between 1 and 2 PM, Cecil dies, at Marleborough Parsonage House.

1612 May Italy Inquisition moves into Colorno—Countess of Sala beheaded—her family executed, Resistance workers tortured and killed. What have they revealed? Is this the death-blow for the Resistance? Henry IV dead, Gonzaga dead, Leonardo Donato dead.

1612 16 June Eng. George Carey is new Master of Wards. Bacon had wanted the place.

1612 June Eng. (Spedding. xi, p 359.) Commissioners show James just how much money Prince Henry spends. Henry is called in to justify expenditures. Privately, Bacon explains to James how much he'd save without Henry.

1612 14 Aug. Italy Kit, who's been in Naples since spring, now checks in at Venice. (Carleton to Chamberlain. op. cit., p 132.) Toby Mathew and George Gage are at the embassy, leaving to go to Naples "to winter." Gregorio calls Toby "il veccio." They must be in disguise, and Kit must be going back with them to show them the pageant there. He'll return to Venice in Oct.

1612 22 Sept. Naples I think Kit writes and directs the great fiesta here—a mountain, elephants. Micaela must perform. Cervantes writes in his long poem, Viaje del Parnaso, that in a dream Promontorio helped Manco go to a good place to see it all.

1612 7 Oct. Ven. The fiesta finished, Kit has checked in at English embassy, then goes to his apartment in parish of San Moisé, where he finds Guarini, desperately ill. At 19 hours—7 PM—he dies, in Gregorio's arms. Battista is buried in church of San Mauritio. (Vittorio Rossi. Battista Guarini. op. cit.)

1612 12 Oct. Eng. Stationers' Reg.: Essays of Sir Francis Bacon, Knight, the King's Solicitor Gen'l. Bacon dedicates them to Prince Henry.

1612 Oct. **Eng.** Prince Henry says he feels fine. Plays tennis.

1612 Oct. Eng. Dr. Mayerne attends Prince Henry.

1612 Fri. 6 Nov. Eng. Prince Henry dies, 8 PM.

1612 13 Nov. Eng. Sir George Carey, (made Master of the Wards in June), is dead on this day, "of this new disease," says Chamberlain, writing 19 Nov. 1612. (Court and Times of James I. vol 1 p 208, and Spedding. xi, p 342.)

1612 Dec. Christmas time Eng. A performance at court of Kit's play, Cardenio, now lost. (E.K. Chambers. Eliz. Stage. vol iv, p 128.)

1613

1613 Jan. Kit sails north: His daughter Isabel-Elizabeth is marrying Good Tom's third son Henry, and Harry needs Kit in London; Harry's being attacked by Bacon. And with black clouds half-obscuring Prince Henry's recent death, James' daughter Elizabeth will wed the Elector Palatinate in London this spring—plays, masques, general rejoicing. (G. P. V. Akrigg. Jacobean Pageant. op. cit.)

1613 Feb. Eng. Tom Walsingham and wife Audrey are in charge of wardrobe. (details, John Bakeless. Tragicall Historie of Chr. M. op. cit., vol 1, p 165.) In the Banquet Hall at Whitehall they cut costumes for coming entertainments. And now, pipe rolls and other records Bacon would destroy are to be disguised with fabric, carted from the Banquet Hall Repository to the Great Wardrobe and stored in a secret underground passage for later disposal.

1613 11 Feb. London Fireworks.

1613 13 Feb. London River triumph.

1613 Sun. 14 Feb. Wedding, Elector Palatinate and Princess Elizabeth Stuart.

1613 Mon. 15 Feb. A George Chapman entertainment: Masque of the Middle Temple and Lincoln's Inn: (E.K. Chambers. Eliz. Stage. vol i, p 173, and vol iv, p 74) In the antimasque, shadows show Kit playing "Caprizzio, a Man of Wit." Masquers come in chariots from the house of the Master of the Rolls, with outriders. Moors hold the horses as all dismount in the Tiltyard. Play includes Virginians, a gold-mine mountain, antimasque with monkeys, Caprizzio and fire-juggling. James is so intrigued he asks the cast to a meal afterwards.

1613 Tues. 16 Feb. Beaumont's "Masque of the Inner Temple and Grays's Inn" comes by water, but James is too tired to watch it. Bacon has paid for part of it. (Think James is angry with Bacon—and scared, for James is now in a dangerous position as accessory in the secret matter of Prince Henry's death.)

1613 21 Feb. James does see Inner Temple Masque, and several of Kit's plays are performed this week. (Julius Caesar, Tempest, etc.)

1613 late Feb. At Wotton's lodging in King Street near Whitehall, Kit learns that Bacon has spoiled Harry's chance to become secetary of state by circulating Harry's old joke; "Who is an ambassador? A man sent to lie abroad for the good of his country." James is shocked. Harry also tells Kit that Bacon means to burn the Globe Theater, packed with unwanted government records he'll stash there. SSS bros are expected to cooperate.

1613 1 & 2 March Eng. Kit to Trinity College, Cambridge, with John Donne and Christopher Brooke, to see Adelphe, a play by Chris's brother Sam. Chris goes home and writes—The Ghost of Richard III.

1613 10 March Eng. Will Shakespeare signs up as ostensible owner of Blackfriars Gatehouse, fronting for Bacon, who has always wanted to own this place. Bacon's natural father Francis Walsingham lived here once and showed Bacon ancient secret passages to the Wardrobe and down to the river.

1613 24 March Eng. "Mr. Shakespeare" designs an "impresa" for the Earl of Rutland for a tilt at Whitehall. Receives xliiij (shillings?) in gold. Was it Kit? He could use the money. Richard Burbage painted it, also received xliiij. (Gilbert Slater. op. cit., and multiple sources.)

1613 April Eng. The unwanted records waiting in the Wardrobe are carried through a subterranean passage into seclusion at Bacon's Gatehouse. Next step—down to the river and over to the Globe basement.

1613 May Eng. Kit goes to see his half-sisters at Canterbury, gets his never-produced play Henry VIII out of his trunk? takes it back to London.

1613 May Eng. Kit goes to see his son Will Davenant, seven years old, at Oxford. Takes him to London to see a play.

1613 20 May Eng. Newlyweds Princess Elizabeth Stuart and the Elector Palatinate finally sail—they're going to Heidelberg. Lord and Lady Arundel go with them.

1613 June Eng. Commissioners working on James's budget make a Report (Spedding. op. cit. xi, p 360): "The Schedule: Improvements yearly. 1. In the return of the late Prince's revenue, if no part thereof be otherwise disposed . . . 50,000 l."

1613 8 June Eng. The King's Players perform Kit's Cardenio for the Savoyard envoy, Marchese di Villa.

1613 10 to 26 June Eng. Casually, a few at a time, wrapped as bolts of cloth, documents to be destroyed by Bacon are taken from the Gatehouse through the tunnel to Puddlewharf, then rowed across the Thames and stashed in the cellar of the Globe Theater, Bankside.

1613 27 June Eng. Bacon checks on everything in the Globe, goes home. (Kit's ciphers in rewrite of The Tempest.)

1613 28 June Eng. Early, Kit and Hen take big rowboat to Bankside. With help of SSS bros, they get documents into boat, head up river, aided by incoming tide, to Denmark House. (Somerset House, where Queen Anne lives.) Documents are safely landed at her "lobby," but Hen disappears—he broke his arm unlading with the crane. Kit thinks Hen's just inside cleaning up. Hen comes back too late—they're swept away by outgoing tide to shelter at the Bridge, but their boat is hit by a floating tree. Swamped, they're drowning, saved by fishermen who come with net. (ciphers in rewrite of The Tempest.)

1613 29 June Eng. A performance of Henry VIII, or All is True, starts at the Globe. The House is papered with SSS. Bacon had wanted Harry to say he set the theater on fire because he was angry with the players. Kit said no, not that—he's rewritten a scene in the show requiring a gun to go off—a burning wad landing on roof should start the fire. It doesn't, so Kit has to go up to get it going. Arsonist! Globe burns. (ciphers, ibid.)

1613 29 June, evening, Eng. At Denmark House, Kit talks to Queen Anne. He wants the recovered documents shown in public to reveal what James and Bacon have done. Sadly she says future generations should judge her husband. Kit puts the records back in a repository—in the Banquet Hall? (ciphers in the Folio Tempest.)

1613 30 June Eng. Kit boards his boat, sets sail for Naples (ciphers). Kit has left SSS. Hen, too, sails—does he go with Kit? No one knows where he went—gone a month or more. (C.C. Stopes. The Life of Henry, Third Earl . . . . , p 362.)

1613 July Naples Kit in Naples corresponds with Manco. Manco poor, needs help. Manco goes to Alcalá de Henares to join Tertiary Order of St. Francis, following example of his wife and sisters. He goes back to Madrid to find publisher for his Viaje del Parnaso.

1613 August Madrid Still hopeful, Cervantes dedicates his just-published Exemplary Stories to Lemos.

1613 Sept. Naples Kit in Naples sends money to Manco—as if it were a pension from Lemos?

1613 Oct. Ven. Kit checks in at Venice. As Gregorio de' Monti, he writes dedication for Guarini's incredibly convoluted comedy, Idropica, now posthumously published by Gio: Batt: Ciotti.

1613 Oct. Eng. Bacon's in hot water re Prince Henry's murder: Sir Thomas Overbury, secretary to the King's favorite, threatens to leak. Back in April Overbury was offered a place as ambassador far away, but said no—so he was put in the Tower and gradually poisoned to death. Dies in Oct. 1613, poisoned by Bacon-driven, simple-minded SSS workers. With aid of smarmy old Henry Howard (Good Tom's uncle), Bacon creates fanciful, heavily-embroidered Legends (Bacon loves doing this) implicating Howard's grandniece (Good Tom's daughter—Isabel-Elizabeth's sister-in-law) as the murderess. She has been divorced and will marry James' ex-favorite—*that* will catch the scandal-mongers. James promises that she and her new husband will not die if they agree to play the legend-game and keep his secret about Henry's death and Overbury's, but the disgusting charade goes on in the courts for the next two and a half years, Bacon prosecuting, carried away. Coke, hinting of Henry's murder, is quickly removed from the courtroom—and *Bacon abandons his SSS people to the gallows!* (State Trials. 13 James 1615, 14 Jas 1616. T. B. Howell. pub. Longman, Hurst, Rees, Orme & Browne et al.

1816.) See also Kit's explicit ciphers in his folio rewrite of The Tempest. I put this here because I don't want to mess with it at later dates—a few short mentions.

1613 25-26 Oct. Eng. The king must listen to Bacon, who schemes to gain the office of Attorney-General by pointing out that Coke, Chief Justice of Common Pleas, loves Common Law and so curtails the king's prerogative. Kick Coke upstairs to be Chief Justice of King's Bench (position open), where there'd be small opportunity to work against James' absolutism, and let present Attorney-General Hobart (mild and timid), be Chief Justice of Common Pleas, leaving the Attorney-Generalship open for Bacon to take.

1613 25 Oct. Eng. Coke, weeping, walks to other end of the hall to be Chief Justice King's Bench.

1613 26 Oct. Eng. H. Hobart made Chief Justice Common Pleas, F. Bacon, Attorney General, and Yelverton takes Bacon's place as Solicitor. (Akrigg. pp 289, 290, and Spedding. xi, p 390.)

1613 27 Oct. Eng. Chamberlain writes to Carleton: "There is a strong apprehension that little good is to be expected from this change, and that Bacon may prove to be a dangerous instrument." (CSP Dom. James I. vol xxiv # 89.)

1613 Nov. Italy Quevedo goes to Milan, reports to his patron Osuna in Sicily: "the [political] poison is coming from Venice; Venice is also poisoning Bohemia." (Luis Astrana Marin. La vida turbulenta de Quevedo. Madrid: Gran Capitán, 1945, p 209.)

1613 20 Dec. Ven. Carleton writes Chamberlain: (Dudley Carleton to . . . . Ed. Lee, op. cit.) Venice is dealing with the Grisons to renew alliance, because the Valtellina Pass is there, a vital link between Hapsburg possessions in Milan and the Tyrol.

1614

1614 Jan. Eng. At first sitting of Hilary term, Bacon holds forth on all degrees of murder. (Spedding. xi, pp 404, 405.)

1614 25 Feb. Ven. A bear chased by dogs tries to climb in a window at the Eng. embassy. (Carleton to Chamb. op. cit., p 158.)

1614 end March Naples Kit and Micaela start a new baby.

1614 May Italy Toby Mathew and George Gage, a couple of sinister men, become priests in Rome, ordained by Belarmine. (Arnold Harris Matthew. The Life of Sir Tobie Mathew op. cit., p 125.)

1614 7 June Eng. Parliament has been in wild confusion over how to supply James' always greater financial needs. James *dissolves* Parliament.

1614 13 July Eng. Good Tom Howard, who has been Chamberlain of the Household, is made Lord Treasurer (Akrigg. op. cit., p 95). This is a set-up; later, when it becomes evident there's not much left in the Treasury, he'll be accused of embezzlement.

From Oct. 1613 thru June 1614 Naples Kit's been working here, with Micaela and two babies. Now, early in July 1614, Kit writes to Manco, says farewell to Micaela and goes to Venice. With money from Hen, Kit buys two new marciliane for the earl, equips them with guns and good crews (Is one man his half-nephew, Roger Manwood?) heads for Tunis to hunt English pirates, backed by Hen's commission. (ciphers, Bargraves Polisie, also C. M. Senior, David & Charles Newton Abbot. A Nation of Pirates. London, Vancouver, NYC: Crane, Russak, 1976, pp 140, 141, re: English efforts to suppress English piracy. Between 1610 and 1614, commissions to capture pirates were granted to several port cities, "besides a joint commission for the Earl of Southampton [Hen] and the Mayor of Portsmouth.") Kit means to take what he catches, plus extra guns and food, to Hen's starving colonists on Bermuda, leaving the two marciliane with the Bermuda people and returning to Italy in the captured vessels. He captures two good ships. Dr. Maria Tiepolo, Director of the Archivio di Stato, Venezia, wrote me enclosing film of a letter sent from Domenico Domenici: Senato, Dispacci Firenze, filza xxix, cc. 132 r.—134 v. Venezia: 1614. 23 July "Monsu de' Monti's marsigliane have captured at Tunis an English [pirate] ship which was coming from Algiers with a great quantity of reales. He has also taken another good ship (a "buonavia") and a petache. (captured cargo to go to the Bermuda Company.) He is at Malta, and "is said to be arming all the vessels which he takes, and he thinks it to be to his advantage, as in the case of the English ship, that they should have 22 pieces of artillery; and that he intends to procure the abandonment of the affairs of Barbary." Poorly translated related copy is calendared in CSP Venetian 1614, and a footnote to that item is part of a letter, Carleton to Chamberlain, 15 July 1614, Eng. style: "We hear of an English ship, the Tiger, taken at Tunis by two marciliane sent out against pirates." (Copy of the complete letter in my file.)

1614 late July Malta Kit leaves Malta for the Atlantic and Bermuda: he's admiral of the little fleet, sailing in the buonavia; Captain Sampson aka Ali Reyes, in the Tiger, who turned out to be an old sailor-friend of Kit's, helps navigate, and the two new little ships, laden with food and bristling with guns, come along.

1614 early Sept. Bermuda Fair winds and good canvas: 5 weeks to Bermuda? The fleet docks at St. George Harbor, Somers Isles (Bermuda). Governor Richard Moore fears the raunchy armada, suspects the gift of the little ships. Marlowe shows letter from Hen directing administrative changes to aid the starving colonists; these "new things" the governor refuses to consider, challenging Kit to a sword fight.

1614 c. 12? Sept. Bermuda. Sampson and the Tiger shoot off to Virginia; Marlowe sails for home in the other captured pirate ship, the "buonavia," leaving the two marciliane for the colonists. John Smith. The General History of Virginia, New England, and the Summer Isles, 1624. (Birmingham: Edward Arber, 1884.) John Smith's honest early pages shadow forth the only sensible published account of the two little ships which Hen Wriothesly sent by Kit, though Marlowe makes it clear in ciphers. Bargraves Polisie. For Kit, hope of taking his family to live on Bermuda is fading.

1614 c. 20 Nov. Naples Kit is home with Micaela after storm-tossed weeks at sea. Their new baby, pale and tiny, dies in his arms. Kit is tapped to be chargé d'affaires at the embassy while Carleton must be away; Kit and Micaela sell their beach place, pack up and take the children to Venice. (ciphers. Bargraves Polisie.)

1614 28 Nov. Padua. Because Carleton's travel is delayed, he has arranged an interim job for Kit—a readership in medicine at Padua U (Carleton to Collegio. CSP Ven. xiii, pp 260-261: "There is a Venetian subject of foreign nation at U of Padua. He asks for an increase, not in salary, but of dignity. As he is of high character and a dear friend of mine, I recommend him . . ." and this note, Carleton to Collegio: "Dr. Gio. Prévotio asks for the readership in medicine rendered vacant by the death of Sig. Tarquinio Carpaneto . . ." (cover-names for Kit.) So Kit has held this job before. When? His family moves into a tent. (CSP Ven. and ciphers. Bargraves Polisie.)

1614 Dec. Padua Cold weather forces a shift for kit's family to quarters on a boat tied on the Brenta. (Couldn't Carlton could have arranged an apartment for the family?) The two children jump or fall into the swift stream and drown. Kit tries to commit suicide, spends time in a hospital. (ciphers. Bargraves Polisie.)

1615

1615 14 Feb. Ven. At Collegio Carleton announces that Gregorio's in charge of the embassy while he, Carleton, is away at Turin. Kit and Micaela stay at embassy house till mid-Sept.? when Carleton returns. Gregorio writes weekly letters to the secretary of state—where are they? (Gregorio's later letters to Secretary Robert Naunton are preserved at Eton.)

1615 14 March Eng. Isabel-Elizabeth goes to Cambridge to see Albumazar, a play of Kit's? (Chamberlain to Carleton. ed. McClure vol 1.) This play has been wrongly attributed to Tomkis, its copyist.

1615 16 April Eng. James actually gives some money, 100,000 crowns, to Savoy, to help Savoy resist Spain. (CSP Ven. vol xiii, p 417.)

1615 21 April Italy Lemos had been thinking of sending galleys to surprise Nice or Villa Franca, but now the plan is abandoned. (CSP Ven. vol xiii, p 420) Kit told Lemos to forget it? Kit must be checking in at Naples.

1615 1 June Italy Lemos decides to send his galleys to attack the Turks, not Savoy (ibid.). Savoy was prepared to fight, using Jas's 100,000 crowns. Kit, still in charge in Venice, zips back and forth to Naples.

1615 August Spain Lemos's fleet, instead of going to Turkey, goes to harbor at Sevilla: 20,000 men! The king doesn't know what to do with them. (Ambassador Foscarini, writing from Eng.)

1615 18 Sept. Ven. Carleton's back. Writes Chamberlain about bad effects of summer heat—pestilence. (Do Kit and Micaela stay on at the embassy? Looks like it.)

1615 Oct., Nov. Eng. Trials for SSS people snared by Bacon into helping kill Overbury: Bacon prosecutes: Richard Weston, Jervis Elwes, Anne Turner, James Franklin—all condemned to death.

1615 13 Nov. Eng. Ambassador from Venice Barbarigo writes home that Good Tom's second son (Isabel-Elizabeth's.'s husband's big brother) was thrown into prison on 11 Nov., implicated, Barbarigo implies, in the Overbury murder. Barbarigo also says that more than one Eng. minister is selling out to Spain. (Bacon has already made noticeable alliance with Spanish Ambassador Diego Sarmiento de Acuña.)

1615 20 Nov. Eng. The first of the SSS helpers prosecuted by Bacon is hanged—Jervis Elwes. (Guess Bacon thinks it keeps the man quiet.)

1616

1616 Jan. Eng. In this month, Francis Collins, Will Shakespeare's friend and lawyer, makes first draft of Shakespeare's will. (S. Schoenbaum. Wm. Sh., a Documentary Life. op. cit.)

1616 13 Jan. Eng. Ambassador Barbarigo writes home: Sir Robert Cotton (Bacon's friend) was arrested Sat. on charge of having given a state document to the present Spanish ambassador. (CSP Ven. vol xiv, p 104) Barbarigo is perceptive, but does he know his diplomatic dispatches are being read by Bacon's code-man Phelippes?

1616 6 March Eng. A meeting of the Virginia Co. is held, and a new list of shareholders issued. Was this when it was decided that Kit could not—could never be—governor of the Somers Isles Co.? (Susan Myra Kingsbury. Records of the Virginia Co. of London. vol 1 p 125, and Bargraves Polisie ciphers.)

1616 21 March Ven. At a very low ebb, Kit edits a book of poems contributed by Guarini's friends in his memory, makes sonnets for the work, gives it to Ciotti Press. Varie poesie di molti excellenti autori in morte del M. Illustre Sig. Cavalier Battista Guarini. Venice: Ciotti, 1616.)

1616 29 March/April 8 Carleton writes to Chamberlain from the Hague: "If you can give Gregorio any comfort I shall be very glad, for the poor man doth much languish after it." Chamberlain's brother was a stockholder in the Virginia Co. So was Hen! Why couldn't Hen do something? (James seems set against a pardon for Kit—he fears Bacon, who wants to suppress Kit and keep the authorship a secret forever?)

1616 23 April Madrid (Gregorian calendar) Manco dies, alone, in a diabetic coma.

1616 23 April Eng. (Julian Calendar) Will Shakespeare dies, at Stratford-on-Avon. ("the ghost in his own hamlet . . . .")

1616 early May Ven. The furnace blows up in the Eng. embassy house (no safety valve) ruining every room and killing Signora la Scala, Kit and Micaela's arthritic dog, who was sleeping on the boiler.

1616 mid-May Ven. Harry Wotton returns to be ambassador. No worry about the house—he rents a different one.

1616 14/24 May Carleton to Chamberlain, op. cit., p 201: "I shall be glad to hear from you whether Sir H.W. signed the letter in Gregorio's favor or let the suit fall, which I rather believe."

1616 24 May Eng. Isabel-Elizabeth's sister-in-law Frances Howard is tried in Eng. for Overbury murder. Lord High Steward's court. (State Trials. op. cit.) Kit must fear for Isabel.

1616 25 May Eng. Robert Carr tried for Overbury murder, Ld. High Steward's court. (State Trials. ibid., and L. P. Smith. vol ii, p 102.)

1616 May 28 Eng. Venetian Ambassador Barbarigo has been reporting the trials, now sends home a letter about Prince Henry's murder. Barbarigo gets a fever, is attended by Dr. Mayerne and dies, leaving his two little boys orphaned in London. They go home.

1616 9 June Eng Bacon sworn in as privy councillor after swift twist of James' arm. (by a letter, 30 May: Spedding. xii, p 349.)

1616 June Naples About mid-month the count of Lemos and his train will sail for Spain, but Micaela plans to stay with Kit in Venice. Harry and Kit suggest she should go to Madrid for news, bring it back. Hurt, she says Kit never really loved her; he's only using her, won't even marry her in the Church. Yes, she'll go, and not come back. Insulted, she disappears in Naples. Kit follows her; she won't see him. He works for the Ociosos Players Club, falls onstage, breaks his bad leg—no money for doctor. She sails away. Desolate, he rides in pain to Venice to Guarini's old apt., works for Ciotti Press, makes Timon of Athens, a rough rewrite of a better college play of his, Timon.

1616 c.20 June Lemos' party reaches Barcelona with Sanchez Co. Players, including Micaela. The company stays in Barcelona almost a month, playing comedies.

1616 24 June Ven. Harry and Carleton jointly petition for a gratuity for de' Monti. (CSP Ven.) Kit in bad shape.

1616. 30 June Eng. Coke suspended from his office: Bacon rides high.

1616 15 July Valencia Lope de Vega, Micaela's old lover, is in Valencia, waiting for Micaela's company to come from Barcelona—gets sick waiting—17 days. Micaela (Lope calls her "la Loca") arrives in Valencia, says cool hello to Lope, goes on to Madrid to work. (D. Cayetano Barrera. Nueva biografía de Lope de Vega. The Spanish Academy, 1890.)

1616 c.1 August Madrid At her theatre, Micaela gets letters from Kit saying please come home over the Brenner Pass; I-will-marry-you! (ciphers. Bargraves Polisie.) For 20 days, Lope tries to win her back. (Barrera. Nueva biografía. op. cit.)

1616 c. August 21 Madrid In disguise, Micaela, her maid and a page disappear from Madrid. They plan to ride over the mountains.

1616 1 Sept. Eng. Bacon has written Toby Mathew about possibility of his coming back to Eng., and Mathew replies: " . . . if his Majesty should make any difficulty, some such reply as is wont to come from you in such cases may have the power to discharge it." (Spedding. xiii, p 215.)

1616 5/15 Sept. The Hague Carleton to Chamberlain: "I send you a letter which I met with here on my return, from Gregorio at Venice, by which you will see in what ill state the poor man stands and how much worse he fares for his friends' recommendations." (Dudley Carleton to John Chamb. op. cit.)

1616 28 Sept. Naples The new viceroy, the duke of Osuna, parades through the city with sidekick Francisco Quevedo.

1616 1 Oct. Alps Micaela, pregnant with baby she and Kit started in Feb. (Kit doesn't know), rides up to the Brenner Pass with her party. Kit is not there. The travelers go down the hill to an inn—at Bolzano? The baby comes. The page goes to find Kit, who comes up. Reunion. (ciphers. Bargraves Polisie.)

1616 c.2 Oct. Dolomites Micaela and Kit are married by a priest at a chapel on the mountain. (Chance of finding chapel record?)

1616 7 Oct. Ven. From his bachelor apt. Kit sends a letter asking Harry not to abandon him—he's married! (Copy in Public Record Office, State Papers, reference SP 99-21-X/L09704, and in my file.) Harry keeps the letter, gives Kit and family a good apartment in the embassy house. (ciphers. Bargraves Polisie.)

1616 11 Oct. Ven (L. P. Smith. op. cit.) Harry writes Sec'y of State Ralph Winwood (with inclusions *privata*) saying his expense account will be presented by his attorney; it includes an allowance for Gregorio—30 ducats a month, less than the French king gives his Italian sec'y. A tribute to Gregorio for loyal service and "some hazards he hath run here, besides the spoiling of his fortune forever in all other places of Italie by this dependence." Harry suggests the King sign a few lines for Gregorio's better protection (think Harry sends suggestions) which will give him security and courage in his service. Harry writes, "With my solicitor, the merchant, Mr. Blunt [Blount] will likewise repair unto you with all due information . . . . I have written my solicitor to send me one hither whose hand I shall use in copying of some things; whom, if it shall please you to dispatch with a packet of those points I have now handled, your Honour shall do me a special favour. And he shall be brought to receive your pleasure by my said solicitor." Harry thinks of Kit cleaning up his scripts for a folio? Looks like Kit's old friend Ralph Crane is sent down to copy things: G. B. Evans, in The Riverside Shakespeare, op. cit., 1974, p 1636, states that it is now believed that scrivener Ralph Crane prepared at least 8 of the Folio versions of "Shakespeare" scripts:

> The Tempest [last ciphered rewrite c. 1615. R. B.]
> The Two Gentlemen of Verona
> Merry Wives
> The Winters Tale
> Measure for Measure
> Cymbeline
> Henry IV Part Two
> Tymon of Athens [written and ciphered 1616. R. B.]

1616 12 Oct. Eng. Letters of John Chamberlain. ed. Mc Clure, vol 2, p 24., Chamberlain writes Carleton: "Since I wrote last . . . Master Henry Howard died sodainly at the table without speaking one word as most say. His wife is thought to be with child, beeing a fresh, younge and rich widow." Isabel-Elizabeth's husband is dead! He had visited his sister in jail; had he made some brave noise that scared Bacon?

1616 25 Oct. Ven. Venice Cabinet fears Spanish aggression. If James can't help, Harry says, he himself will go to talk to German princes. (CSP Ven. vol xiv, pp 338, 339.)

1616 31 Oct. Ven. Council of X grants permission for the orphans of recently-dead Ambassador Barbarigo to visit Harry's house on Hallowe'en. (CSP Ven. vol xiv, p 339.)

1616 Oct. Nov. Dec. Madrid Lope writes his patron Sessa many bitter letters about la Loca, Micaela. (Barrera. Nueva Biografia de Lope . . . . op. cit.)

1616 30 Dec. From James, Gregorio gets cheery letter, which he copies. Sends original to his son Wm. Davenant. (Davenant bio. in The Dramatic Works of William Davenant. 5 vols. Edinburgh & London: Southeran, 1872) A copy of this letter, in Kit's Italian hand, is kept in the Public Record Office. SP 99-21-X/L09704. Will Davenant said he had a letter written to his father by the king.

1617

1617 28 Jan. Italy Cardinal Millino thinks of hiring Gregorio as intelligencer: Berlingerio Gessi, Bishop of Rimini, Papal Nuncio at Venice, writes that Gregorio lives—eats and sleeps—at English embassy, and worked for "Cavalier Guarino" before working for Wotton. Thinks he'd be a double agent. (28 Jan. Borghese, T 2, Vatican archive, and CSP Ven. vol xv, p 596, Appendix One.)

1617 early March Eng. James and his court prepare for a summertime in Scotland.

1617 7 March Eng. Bacon, moving up, becomes Lord Keeper of the Great Seal.

1617 14 March Eng. James and his entourage leave London for Scotland. Bacon is the most powerful man remaining in Eng.

1617 c.15 March Ven. Gregorio receives from James a "patent" confirming him in the service. (Gregorio has laid before the Doge a plan for protecting Venice—Quevedo's aggressive intent is now public—but the Doge won't approve Gregorio's scenario unless it's approved by James. The patent means James says yes.)

1617 22 March Ven. At the Collegio, Harry hands over Gregorio's patent (CSP Ven. vol 14, item 701, p 473.) Doge Bembo gives Gregorio permission to create a sting against would-be Spanish invaders.

1617 late March Naples Kit as Jakes-Pierre, crippled Normandy pirate, and Micaela, his homely pirate wife, privately interview Viceroy Osuna at the palace, outline a plot to savage Venice using mercenary agents—pirates who will burn the Arsenal at a signal, leaving the city helpless as troops of Spanish soldiers debark from Osuna's ships (soldiers who'll cross the lagoon in lighters, making the ashes of Venice their base for deployment north into friendly Hapsburg territory and on, to Holland, and who knows? perhaps to England). It's that first step, the fiery destruction of the city, that Jakes-Pierre can provide, given time and money. (D.A. Parrino. Teatro eroico è politico . . . . op. cit., vol 2, p 115.) Jakes will need money up front to get wheels turning, offers to leave his wife hostage. (ibid. p 116). Osuna, amused, says no collateral needed, gives cash; the pirate couple leaves.

1617 late March Eng. James is in Scotland; Bacon neglects to publish the king's contra-conspiracy proclamation telling the gentry to go home—not to hang around London.

1617 23 March Eng. Bacon writes to James re: sending warships to join with Spanish forces to extirpate pirates in Argier, a move that would leave the coasts of England unguarded.

1617 10 April Ven. Harry at Collegio with Queen Anne's cousin, Joachim Ernest, Duke of Holstein (come to aid Venice?).

1617 16 April Naples Quevedo, eager to subdue Venice, goes from Naples to Rome. (Luis Astrana Marin. La Vida Turbulenta de Quevedo. Madrid: Gran Capitan, 1945.)

1617 27 April Ven. The Doge rises to welcome Ned de Vere's son Henry Vere, 18th Earl of Oxford. (CSP Ven. vol xiv, p 495.) Secretly, Henry's here to help Venice and will bring 20 "mercenaries." Out loud, the Doge says everything is fine; thanks anyway, he needs no help.

1617 7 May Eng. As "Easter" Term starts, Bacon takes his seat in Chancery. (Spedding. xiii, p 181.)

1617 9 May Eng. Bacon, on sick leave from the Bench, drops out of sight for 10 days. (Spedding. xiii, p 200.) No one knows where he is.

1617 8/18 July Carleton at the Hague writes that Toby Mathew, who in June was "crazy at Louvain" is going to England. (Matthew. Life of Tobie Mathew. p 144.) Bacon is letting in the bad fairy while James is away.

1617 22 July Eng. Toby Mathew is staying "a kind of prisoner" with Bacon till the king comes back. (Spedding. xiii, p 216.)

1617 1 August Ven. Gieronimo Venier gets leave to meet twice with Henry Wotton, to rent him his house. (CSP Ven. vol xiv, p 562.) Is this note misplaced? Or does Harry need more room for Kit and family? A new baby will come c. Dec.

1617 11 August from Eng. A nasty letter to Doge & Council from Giovanni Lionello: Nobody likes Henry Wotton. Henry Wotton is a rat! All hateful things. Who is masterminding this character-assassination? Harry is getting the Treatment. Is Bacon frantic about possibility Harry may say something about Overbury case? Bacon has run the country for the last 5 months, has had a chance to devil his enemies. (CSP Ven. vol xiv, pp 74-76.) Re Spanish Plot: did Bacon approach Harry through Bedmar, asking for, or ordering, cooperation with Spain, only to be rebuffed by Harry? Lionello, secretary of the Venetian embassy in England, has collected all the unfavorable gossip about Wotton he could get together. Letter of Lionello, Ven. Arch. Communicate, Dec. 29, 1617. [Bacon stuff.]

1617 30 August Ven. Captain Jaques-Pierre (Kit) submits ten-page report to the Council of X with full details of a Spanish plot to take over Venice (CSP Ven. vol xiv, pp 590-591, and Aug. 30. Senato Secreta. Communicazione dal Cons. Dè X—Venice Archives.) Is Bacon seriously in on this plot? With Spanish Ambassador Sarmiento in London?

1617 31 August Eng. Bacon's safely at home at Gorhambury as James is returning from Scotland.

1617 2 Sept. Ven. A brief of Capt. "Jiques-Pierre," of 30 Aug., is to be sent to the Savii of the Cabinet, after enjoining secrecy. (CSP Ven. vol xv, p 2.)

1617 8 Sept. Eng. Queen Anne is wise—she has turned against the whole Spanish party. (CSP Ven. vol xv, p 6.)

1617 15 Sept. Eng. The king is back in London. (Spedding. xiii, p 250.)

1617 Sept. Naples Viceroy Osuna has sent an English merchant, Alex Rose, to England with money to buy 4 or 6 good ships to send to Naples with cover of salt fish—Osuna to use them to attack Venice. (CSP Ven. vol xv.)

1617 18 Oct. Eng. Chamberlain to Carleton (Matthew. Life of Sir Tobie Mathew. p 152.) re Toby's "nightly visits to the Spanish Ambassador Gondomar."

1617 27 Oct. Eng. Anti-Catholic Secretary of State Winwood gets sick. He dies **Nov. 1,** attended by Dr. Mayerne, according to CSP Ven. vol xv., but Encyc. Britt. says **27 Oct.**

1617 c. Oct. Ven. Kit and Micaela have a new baby girl, Cleo. Normal feet.

1617 Oct. Ven. In the Cabinet, the Senate asks Harry to ask James for immediate help; Don Pedro de Toledo threatens Venice from the west, Osuna is sending 22 ships against Venice from Naples. (CSP Ven. vol xv, p 34.)

1617 5 Nov. Ven. Harry to Collegio, says he sent info to Jas. by courier day before yesterday. Harry asks the Senate to decide on jobs for Henry Vere, Capt. Bell, John Vere. [They can bring men.] (ibid. p 39.)

1617 7 Nov. Naples An English ship is detained and armed at Naples against wishes of the owner, and Alex Rose is going to send galleons under cover of the fish trade; the religious of Malta are sending a galleon built in Amsterdam (ibid. p 40.)—all to attack Venice.

1617 14 Nov. Ven. Chris Surian writes about Carleton's friend and correspondent Pietro Asellinio, [sic] who frequents homes of French and English ambassadors at Venice. (CSP Ven. vol xv, pp 42, 43.) This Dr. Asselinau will have a role in the sting.

1617 1 Dec. Ven. Venetian Ambassador in England reports to the Doge: A "very leading member of the Privy Council" in London is bad-mouthing Harry. This man is saying Harry nightly secretly talks to the Spanish Ambassador in Venice and at a crucial time had withdrawn himself from the city. (CSP Ven. vol xv, pp 65-66.)

1617 13 Dec. Ven. The Senate reads to Harry a declaration—"that James's declarations and resolutions be no longer delayed, as it is impossible to place any trust in the promises of Spain." (CSP Ven. vol xv, p 71.)

1617 28 Dec. Ven. Harry to Collegio to hear that Osuna is readying a galleon for himself along with all galleys in the Arsenal of Naples. Harry wishes all a good New Year—rejoices that in the recent (Santa Croce) engagement, one of the English ships fired 400 cannon shot. (CSP Ven. vol xv, p 83.)

1617 Midnight, 16 Dec. Eng. Queen's Players have played their last date in Eng. for the next ten months—16 Dec. 1617 English is their last recorded performance till Oct. 1618. (John Tucker Murray. English Dramatic Companies, 1558-1642. vol 1. London: Constable, 1910.)

1617 18 Dec. Eng. (28 Dec. Gregorian) Venetian ambassador Piero Contarini and chaplain go up the secret stairs at Denmark House to see Queen Anne. (CSP Ven. vol xv, p 85.) She agrees to send the men of her Playing Co. to Venice to play "mercenaries" in Kit's sting.

1618

1618 1 Jan. Early A.M. Ven. Fierce fire in Harry's house, starting in storeroom for beams and boxes under the kitchen. Key on kitchen table; occupants must break down front door. (Harry's letter, L. P. Smith. op. cit., vol ii, p 125.) Embassy must move.

1618 7 Jan. Eng. Bacon is Lord Chancellor.

1618 22 Jan. Ven. Leave is granted for Harry to look at house of Zuan Antonio Valier, son of Piero—about renting it. (CSP Ven. vol xv, p 109.) See mention of later address of embassy: "to Gregorio de' Monti, sec'y of the ambassador of Eng. in San Mauricio, Venice." (ibid. p 323.)

1618 Jan. or early Feb. Eng. In 1618 the mayor of Exeter complained that Samuel Daniel was traveling with a patent for a theatrical company called The Children of Bristol, but had with him *men*—only 5 youths among them. (E. K. Chambers. Eliz. Stage. vol I, p 386.) The company is going to Venice to play the sting. Also, twenty players are coming subsidized by Hen (from Cambridge, under Henry Peyton?) and 20 come for Henry Vere. John Holland is in charge of all actors. Kit gives roles to friends: Henry Mainwaring, ex-pirate and best English sailor, unofficially directs the ships that will chase away Osuna's fleet. Dr. Asselinau of the French Embassy, as Regnault, will sit in Micaela's "Greek" restaurant over coffee, teaching French phrases to all actors who come. All player-mercenaries must register with Spanish Ambassador; they stay in unregistered pensions of Venetian Jews.

1618 16 March Ven. An hour before sunset, old pirate Doge Bembo dies.

1618 early April Italy As Jakes-Pierre, Kit and old friend ship-owner Prospero Colombo (disguised as 'Langlade') sail a boat of Prospero's to Brindisi, ride across to Naples to discuss the plot with Quevedo: Jakes-Pierre insists all mercenaries be paid before the burning. Then the three men—Quevedo comes too—cart the gold back to Brindisi, sail with it up the coast to Venice. Quevedo wants to be there on D-day. (Luis Astrana Marin. op. cit., pp 262, 263 foll. Marin contradicts himself, offering odd dates and fanciful reasons for the attempted attack on Venice, but these pp seem realistic.) Quevedo himself, (Obras Completas por don Francisco Quevedo y Villegas. Madrid: Aguilar, 1981) writes of "Jaques Pierres" in Tomo I p 792 and tells of the trip to Venice with "Xaquepierre and another janissery" in Tomo II p 876. He discusses the plot in Tomo II pp 934-955 and on p 943 mentions that Jaques-Pierre's nickname was "el Bornío." (Kit's college nickname, in Spanish—the Merlin, the littlest hawk)

1618 9/19 April Eng. Ships leave London for the Adriatic, to aid Venice: Colonel Henry Peyton with men; Capt. Bellingsley, Capt. Manwood. (CSP Ven. vol xv, p 196.) Mainwaring is already at Venice.

1618 24 April Ven. Council of X votes unanimously to send "copy of the advices presented by Capt. Jaques Pierre and Nicolo Renaldi about the designs of the Spaniards, and which Capt. J. P. says that he is about to send to his Most Christian Majesty [the king of France], if it please his Serenity, by Nicolo Renaldo" [sic] to the Savii of the Cabinet, after enjoining due secrecy. (ibid. p 207.)

1618 4 May Ven. Capt. Henry Bell sails from Venice with secret info for England. (Letters and Dispatches of Sir Henry Wotton, printed from originals at Eton. Roxburghe Club. London: Wm. Nicol, The Shakspeare [sic] Press. 1850. p 13.)

1618 12 May Ven. As close as I can get to D Day: Two well-dressed, booted Frenchmen step out of a boat, go in to see the Council; they are Baldesare Juven and Gabriel Montecasino (Kit) and they show a letter they received, saying there'll soon be a takeover in Venice, and to come for loot. They want to warn the Council, which thanks them. Later, Gabriel Montecasino is given £100. (Le pauvre abbé Saint Réal. Don Carlos, et La Conjuration des Espagnols contre la Republique de Venice. Facsimile of 1780 edition. Genève: Librerie Droz, S.A. 11 Rue Massot, 1977.) The part about the £100 is in the modern Notes by Andrée Mansau, p 642. The record, says Andrée, can be found in "le dossier du Conseil des Dix."

1618 12 May, late at night Under cover (with help from Kit?) Quevedo gets safely out of town, dressed as a beggar in raggedy clothes—his own account claims he evades two sinister assassins. (Marin. La Vida Turbulenta. op. cit., p 267.)

1618 12 May Ven. From the Council of X to the Capt. General at Sea: to be put to death "in such a manner as your prudence may suggest, without any display," Captain Jaques Pierre, Captain Langlad, & Rossetto, Capt. Jaques' sec'y. But the men who played these roles are really not harmed—not like the end of Bacon's big job. Kit's job is finished—his contract fulfilled, £100 (why £?) from Venice a modest payment. The mercenaries are said to be hanged at Friuli or strangled and thrown in deep canals, but really, the actors disappear to sail home with pay, happy memories and souvenirs.

1618 18 May Ven. Doge Nicolo Donato dies after only a month in office.

1618 23 May Ven. A body said to be Nicolo Regnault's hangs between the columns on the Piazzetta—it's truly the body of a condemned Uscock pirate executed in the prison.

1618 25 May Ven. Harry writes home to Good Tom (telling him he's threatened by Bacon?) (L.P. Smith. vol 2, p 440.) Said to be catalogued with Longleat MSS, Historical MSS, Rep. p 196, this letter is nowhere.

1618 25 May Ven. Harry writes to Thomas Lake re the "French" conspiracy in Venice. (Letters & Dispatches of Sir Henry Wotton. Roxburghe Club. op. cit., pp 17-18.)

1618 June Ven. The new doge is Antonio Priuli.

1618 2 June Ven. A note to the Venetian ambassador in Rome: the Spanish ambassador in Venice took part in a conspiracy against the city of Venice. It's all over now, and Venice has asked Spain to remove that ambassador. (CSP Ven. vol xv, p 226.)

1618 June Ven. Gregorio to the Cabinet on several days with different errands.

1618 14 June Ven. Spanish ex-ambassador Alfonso de la Cueva, Marqués de Bedmar, leaves Venice, heading for Milan in self-consciously casual style. (Marin. La Vida Turbulenta. op. cit., p 269.)

1618 15 June Ven. Fort of Vercelli is being returned to Savoy—Kit and helpers, by breaking up the plot in Venice, have broken a log-jam—Spain's giving way. (CSP Ven. vol xv, p 235.)

1618 June Ven. There are still several men from England at the embassy house here—men who participated in the sting—and everyone celebrates the end of the successful charade. Harry wants a play-party. Nathaniel Fletcher and his brother John are staying here, so John and Kit make a Marx Bros-like farce, The Two Noble Kinsmen: Micaela plays the Jailer's Daughter, Kit, the Jailer, and Hen and young Henry Vere are Noble Kinsmen.

1618 30 June Ven. By the end of this month, almost all English have gone home. Kit, who has had the best time of his life, is sad to think he'll never see these friends again. Hen is leaving. They sit on the Lido beach, talk about Bacon. Could his sinister proclivities be curbed? He's Lord Chamberlain and will sit in the House of Lords if there's another Parliament. Kit thinks of a rare MS held in the library of his Cambridge college, Corpus Christi—a MS showing precedent for the House of Lords to impeach one of its own. Could Bacon be restrained that way—not hurt, but kept away from the court and prevented from harming others? Something to think about.

1618 12 July Eng. Today, Bacon is Baron Verulam of Verulam.

1618 12 July Eng. Same day. Some one makes a complaint against Good Tom Howard, Earl of Suffolk, for misconduct in his place as Lord Treasurer. (Spedding. xiv, p 1.)

1618 9 August Ven. Harry's steward Will Leete writes from the embassy re Gregorio: "Gregorio is very thankfull to you for your good newes, hee hath delivered his pattent vnto my Lo: to send, hee is ready to serve you in all occasions, or else hee dissembles."

(Letters & Dispatches of Sir Henry Wotton. Roxburghe Club. op. cit., p 47.) This letter is addressed to a Mr. Bargrave, probably Captain John, brother of Isaac who'd been a chaplain at the embassy. For John, **over the next three years**, Kit wrote a "Polisie"—a constitution for a colony John wanted to start in Virginia.

1618 Aug. Eng. Toby Mathew writes a threatening letter to Bacon: Spanish Ambassador Gondomar wants Ralegh punished, or else. Aha! Bacon rules the king but Gondomar rules Bacon. (Matthew. The Life of Tobie . . . op. cit., pp 156, 157.) And since the Spanish Plot fizzled, Bacon's stock has gone down.

1618 Sept. Ven. Harry has been going to the Cabinet to stand up for his countrymen who he thinks have gotten raw deals. (Seems he doesn't much like the new Doge.) (CSP Venice. vol xv, pp 302-3.)

1618 1/10 Sept. The Hague Henry Vere offers to serve Venice again. (ibid. p 311.) In his train is his Venice girlfriend, la Gritti. (ibid. p 411.)

1618 Oct. Eng. Kit's daughter Isabel-Elizabeth remarries: handsome, wealthy young horseman William Cavendish, son of Bess of Hardwick's son Chas. (William is one of the youths Harry took to Savoy in 1612.)

1618 c. Oct. Ven. Micaela and Kit have a new baby boy with a club foot.

1618 1 Oct. Eng. Robert Naunton orders Toby Mathew out of England in 20 days—Toby complains he has four chancery suits pending. Toby encloses a note for James, today endorsed, "The King would not receive it." (Matthew. The Life of Sir Tobie . . . . op. cit., p 158.)

1618 7 Dec. Ven. Coming from Padua this night, one of Harry's household sees a great comet—all go up on the roof to watch till sunup. Speculation about its meaning. All catch cold. (L.P. Smith. Life & Letters. vol 2, p 160.)

1619

1619 3 Jan. Ven. Consiglio de X: "that leave be granted to Andrea Vendramin, son of Luca, to receive in his house the ambassador of England, for one occasion only, to see his study with the statues and figures and to pass the usual compliments." (CSP Ven. vol xv, p 426.) (A collector? A sculptor? Later made Kit's death-mask?)

1619 7 Jan. Ven. Harry to Collegio to deal about Henry Peyton's men and Sir Henry Mainwaring's offer to work for Venice. (Venice seems to be running out of money, or is Doge Priuli just stingy?)

1619 12 Jan. Eng. (Tues., 11 AM) "Fire at White-hall, which beginning in the banketting house hath quite consumed yt . . . One of the greatest losses spoken of, is the burning of all or most of the writings and papers belonging to the offices of the signet, privy seal and council chamber, which were under yt." And how about Star Chamber records? (Chamberlain to Carleton. ed. McClure. op. cit., vol 2, pp 201-202. Letter 313.) This letter was written four days after the fire—on 16 Jan., 1619. Bacon has found out that Queen Anne saved the papers that should have burned in the Globe fire! Privy council records burning today include years 1608 to 1613. (see Ida Sedgwick Proper. Our Elusive Willy. Dirigo Editions, Manchester, Maine. p 515.)

1619 5 Feb. Naples Spinelli, sec'y at Naples, writes that Sanson [sic] the pirate (must be Drake's, Carleill's & Kit's old friend Sampson) is making a mess of Naples shipping—the royal galleons can't get out of the harbor to fight him. (CSP Ven. vol xv, p 462.) This could be Kit and Harry's & Mainwaring's idea—Sampson working at Mainwaring's direction under cover for Venice, keeping Osuna out of the Adriatic, as they'd chased him out while defusing the Spanish Plot. (L.P. Smith. vol. 2, p 471-2.) Mainwaring wants to help Venice in 1619 and Doge tells him out front no position available, but gratefully pays him for past favors when he leaves. (Harry's letter in Letters & Dispatches. Roxburghe Club. op. cit., p 106. 12/22 Jan. 1619.)

1619 14 Feb. Ven. Harry's called to Collegio. Embarrassed, Harry must deal with James' inclination (pushed by Bacon) to join his newly refurbished fleet with Spain "to hunt down pirates." Harry speaks clear, says it would be bad for the Spanish to observe inside workings of the English fleet and learn its ways of fighting, and "to use the pretext of the pirates to enter these seas and proceed to Trieste would be a great affront. We shall serve as good spies for your Serenity." (CSP Ven. vol xv, p 495.)

1619 2 March Eng. Queen Anne dies, at Hampton Court. She thought she was recovering from gout but suddenly got very sick. Ambassador Antonio Donato in England wrote a letter about her which sounds as if she created her own death, but I suspect Bacon—he was so angry about her players' role in the Spanish Plot—and so furious about the saved Globe papers. Ambassador's letter worth reading. (CSP Ven. vol xv, pp 494, 495.)

1619 2 March to 13 May Eng. For 10-plus weeks, Queen Anne's body lay unburied. G.P.V. Akrigg. op. cit., calls this "one of the more bizarre interludes in the history of English royalty . . . Day succeeded day, week succeeded week, and finally month succeeded month." A mourning period? James was not mourning; James did what Bacon wanted, and Bacon wanted to leave Queen Anne nowhere. She's eviscerated, except for her heart, to slow decomposition; the rest of her is left in her private chambers in Denmark House (Somerset House), as time goes by. Bacon is *punishing the theatre people for what they did in Venice* last year to ruin the Spanish Plot, which he'd hoped might make him viceroy in a Spanish England. During the weeks Anne lies unburied, the theatres must be closed, and the players suffer increasing hardship. (G.P.V. Akrigg. op. cit., p 268.) Not till the anniversary of the sting in Venice can Anne's funeral preparations begin. She's laid to rest on **13 May, Julian**. The pace of life resumes; theatres open.

1619 12 April Ven. Receiving official news of Queen Anne's death, Harry spends his own money for weeds for his "family." (L.P. Smith. op. cit.) All at the embassy know how much she helped Venice and England.

1619 19 April Eng. Hen Wriothesley is sworn in as privy councillor. (C. C. Stopes. The Life of Henry . . . . op. cit.)

1619 For the rest of April Harry seems turned off on Venice government. He's leaving. (L.P. Smith. op. cit., vol 1.)

1619 5 May Ven. Harry at Collegio seems to be weeping. He says goodbye, presents Gregorio as his stand-in and goes.

1619 16 May Ven. Harry leaves Ven. for Padua and on, with Queen Anne's cousin Duke Joachim Ernest of Holstein. Going to Munich and Augsburg. (L.P. Smith. ibid.) Kit, holding down the embassy, starts a series of 60-odd letters in Italian to Secretary of State Robert Naunton. (Preserved at Eton, available in microfilm and in a book: Letters and Dispatches of Sir Henry Wotton in the Years 1617-1620. Pub. by the Roxburghe Club. Printed by Wm. Nichol, The Shakspeare [sic] Press, 1855.) The film and book inlude Kit's letters and those of several other people. Kit is ill—exhausted by last year's effort in Spanish Plot, unrelenting pain in his bad leg, and worsening memory problems. Sometimes Micaela helps him write.

1619 7 June Ven. Gregorio writes that Osuna has captured 3 Venetian galleys. (Letters and Dispatches. The Shakspeare Press, op. cit., p 131-132.)

1619 June, July Ven. Kit goes back and forth to Collegio. He's been writing newsy letters to a man who pays for them: Marcantonio di Dominis, ex-archbishop of Spolato, who left the Catholic Church and is living in England.

1619 26 August Eng. Geo. Abbot, Archbishop of Canterbury, betrays Gregorio, carelessly or deliberately, telling the Venetian Ambassador that the anonymous writer of news to di Dominis knows "all secrets" in Venice. (CSP Ven. vol xv, p 594. 26 Aug.—a letter from the Venetian secretary in England, Pier Antonio Maroni, to the Council of X.)

1619 Sept. Ven. Gregorio learns what Abbot told the ambassador. Gregorio is shocked, apprehensive; the letters to di Dominis were meant to be off the record.

1619 Sept. Ven. Gregorio writes Naunton thanking him for his humane letter of 26 August, comforting to his family. (Did Kit and Micaela lose a baby at birth?) Gregorio writes dispatches. (Letters and Dispatches. op. cit., p 139.) No mail comes into Venice; the mailman's in quarantine.

1619 Oct.-Nov. Eng. Charged with embezzlement, Good Tom is examined 11 days in Star Chamber. (Not guilty, he keeps quiet to save the king's 'honor.') Bacon says nasty things. A painfully obvious frameup. The earl and his wife separately imprisoned in the Tower for eleven days, and he's ordered to repay all he embezzled. (Thomas Howard DNB, also Basil Montagu. Works of Francis Bacon. Part I. London: Wm. Pickering, 1834. pp 226-230.)

1619 11 Dec. Ven. Gregorio finally gets the mailman out of quarantine with a small gratuity for the officer of the Dept. of Health. (Letters and Dispatches. op. cit., p 154.) Quiet, gloomy winter in Venice. No pay comes from England.

1620

1620 Jan. Ven. No money for Venice embassy. Food getting low. Naunton sends 200 lire sterling of his own money to help out. From now on Kit's grounded: walks around town on his bad leg with a crutch—goes to the post-office in the hotel Rossi for the mail—watches the babies: teaches the three and four year-olds alphabet and arithmetic, feeds the boy who's almost two. Lucky not much is going on in Venice. (ciphers, Bargraves Polisie.)

1620 7 Feb. Ven. New Venetian Ambassador Girolamo Lando in London mentions well-written newsletters that came to Di Dominis from Venice. (CSP Ven. vol xvi.)

1620 13 and 20 March Gregorio writes to Sec'y of State Naunton: the dragoman of the Venetian embassy in Constantinople has been beheaded by the chief Wazir—an affront to the Republic. (Letters and Dispatches. op. cit., pp 168-169.)

1620 24-28 April Adriatic. Osuna sends troops toward Trieste in a large galleon, with two Tartanes, but the galleys of Venice chase Osuna's ships into Manfredonia Harbor. They're hiding there. (ibid. pp 173-4.)

1620 15 July Ven. Paul Pindar lodging in Cannaregio, back from nine years' service as English ambassador at Constantinople. Gregorio goes to see him. (ibid. p 188, 17 July.)

1620 14 Aug. Ven. Pindar leaves Venice for England. James sent papers to be presented to Pindar, knighting him; Henry Peyton was supposed to do it, but didn't come ashore, so Kit gave them to Paul on **13 August.** (ibid. pp 206-7.) Today, Pindar's biographers wonder how and when he was knighted.

1620 21 Aug. Ven. Kit writes: The Turkish navy has entered the gulf on the way to Valona and has used generous terms of friendship, exchanging slaves, other courteous gifts. (ibid. pp 208-209.)

1620 4 Sept. Ven. Turks wipe out Manfredonia harbor! Awful! A deal with Venice? We'll forget the beheading if you'll get rid of Osuna's ships? (ibid. p 212.)

1620 c. Sept. Ven. b. to Micaela and Gregorio, their last child, a boy with clubfoot.

1620 autumn Ven. Kit writes about the Val Tellina—the Spanish want possession of the pass up there so they can move soldiers into Hapsburg territory to defeat James' son-in-law Frederick. (ibid. passim.)

1620 10 Sept. Ven. Prospero Colombo, who at the time of the Spanish Plot played a petardier who frequented the Spanish embassy, is shot at in Cannaregio by three young men from that embassy who recognized him. Prospero undamaged. (CSP Ven. vol xvi, pp 397 and 404.)

1620 11 Sept. Ven. Kit writes about Prospero's shooting: neighbors attacked the fleeing Spaniards, killed one, badly treated the others. (Letters and Dispatches. op. cit., p 226.) Kit had hoped no fatality would result from the Sting.

1620 17 Sept. Eng. The Venetian ambassador in Eng., Girolamo Lando, writes that a Don Celso Galato may soon tell identity of the author of the private news that came from Venice. (CSP Ven. vol xvi, p 405.) Kit is up the creek.

1620 21 Sept. Ven. Kit writes of troubles about the pass of the Val Telline—ends with " . . . supplicandola ad haver memoria de mi . . ." He's out of money. (Letters and Dispatches. op. cit., pp 231-232.)

1620 16 Oct. Ven. Kit writes that Catholic Leaguers want Venice to act with them against James' son-in-law Frederick. (ibid. pp 238-239.)

1620 autumn Europe Toby Mathew is at Rubens' place in Antwerp, dealing for a picture Carleton wants—the "Caccia." (Matthew. op. cit.) Toby repeatedly goes to Rubens; the painter is a spy for the Infanta (statement by Rory Howard, curator of a Rubens exhibit in NYC, April 1995, quoted by Lillian Ross in The New Yorker, 17 April, 1995) and James is hoping the Infanta will wed Prince Charles.

1620 29 Oct. Europe James' son-in-law Frederick is defeated at Prague. City returned to the Bavarians. Frederick is shown to have been dishonest; the Catholic world chortles.

1620 3 Nov. Eng. Isabel's new husband William Cavendish is made a viscount before the opening of Parliament. (Spedding. op. cit., xiv, p 158.) Are lords in the know lining up against Bacon's offenses?

1620 14 Nov. Eng. News of Frederick's defeat at Prague reaches England. Catholic Gondomar is so hated in London he applies for protection. A book: Vox Populi or News from Spain, warns England and the Netherlands against Spanish deceptions. (ibid. p 153.) Bacon thinks lavish discourse and bold censure should be suppressed. (ibid. pp 154-57.)

1621

1621 28 Jan. Rome Pope Paul V dies while celebrating the Victory of the White Mountain (Frederick's defeat).

1621 29 Jan. Ven. Kighthood for Gregorio. The last letter in the Roxburghe Club, Shakspeare Press collection of Letters and Dispatches, pp 257-258, is one to Secretary of State Robert Naunton from Gregorio, 29 January, 1620 (1621 New Style). A Charles Ré translation is offered here. All the letters from Gregorio to England are in "choice" (unctuous) Italian, in his own hand:

"Illustrious Lord, my most Reverend Lord.

With the mail of this week I have received a letter from your Most Illustrious Lordship of the 28th of last month [28 Dec. 1620] which has given me the greatest contentment, for it testifies that my humble services are viewed with favor by His Majesty. For this I render thanks first to God, then to His Majesty who has deigned to bestow on me such great honor; and I shall remain eternally obliged to Your Illustrious Lordship for what you have done on my behalf in securing the great favor of which I am the recipient. Thus, I pray God that I may be allowed to come and attend in person this ceremony, and humbly kiss His Majesty's feet. Meanwhile, I beg to remain in your good graces and to commend now my humble family to the benevolence of our Gracious Patron.

"The two Gentlemen whom your Most Illustrious Lordship has commended to me are today in Padua, where they wait. I shall serve them well and do everything in my power to implement their orders in all circumstances; the results you will see will be evidence of my zeal.

"Otherwise, there is nothing to report but that the projects of those gentlemen seem to advance rather slowly: they are waiting (as everyone seems to think) to see what the Most Christian King [the king of France] will do with regard to the answer that the Catholic King [the king of Spain] will give him. On the morning of the 20th of this month the Pope was victim of a most serious accident, so that now he is with fever; and according to the observations of the physicians, in general, in men of that advanced age, such accidents are messengers of death. I end here in kissing with reverence the hands of your Most Illustrious Lordship, praying God to grant you a long and happy life.

"Of your Most Illustrious lordship

I am your most humble and obedient

Gregorio de' Monti"

I've been told there was no registration of knighthoods in England at this date, but that the papers did come to Kit in Venice is corroborated: Immediately, Bacon became furious with Robert Naunton, who was summarily shelved and angrily threatened with dismissal. Shocked at the anger, his wife suffered a miscarriage. (Robert Naunton DNB.) Historians think Naunton might haave been punished because he favored Prince Charles' courtship of a French princess, thus angering Spanish Gondomar, though by this time Gondomar knew perfectly well the Infanta was already betrothed to a Hapsburg—the Emperor's son. Kit had sent word of this development (L. P. Smith, vol 2, p 226), but James was in denial.

In his last ciphers for Bargraves Polisie, ll. 465, 466, Kit wryly mentions "Ye late Sir Kit de' Monti, mean and shameless," and calls Micaela his "patient ladee." John Taylor the Water Poet, an honest man, wrote a 17-page sardonic encomium for Kit, published soon after his death:

SIR

Gregory Nonsence

His Newes from no place

On the title page is a false date: "Printed in London, and are to bee sold between Charing-Crosse, and Algate. 1700." (Maybe a cipher, surely a joke: Charing Cross was W. of London, Aldgate, E.) The real date of publication is printed on the back page: "FINIS. Printed at London by N.O. 1622." (a copy from Charles Hindley's Miscellanea Antiqua Anglicana, at the Folger Library.)

In the center of the title page are five weird names which together make this anagram: QUEER KIT M, HE HAS GONE UP TO SPY ON PLUTO—COACHMAN.

(John Taylor operated a water-coach on the Thames.) There are more ciphers in the body of the work, all of them beyond me.

1621 Tues. 30 Jan. Eng. After a seven-year recess, Parliament opens. The Lords will sit as a court of law, using old precedent contained in MSS given to Kit's college (Corpus Christi) by Mathew Parker. One is part of the St. Alban Chronicles, later edited and published as Chronicon Angliae; the other is the Anonimalle Chronicle, also important. They show the House of Lords able to try and impeach one of its own. (Colin C. G. Tite. Impeachment and Parliamentary Judicature in Early Stuart England. Gower St., London WCI: U of London, 1974.) Bacon now sits in the House of Lords.

1621 9 Feb. Rome Marcantonio di Dominis (the man who showed Kit's private newsletters to everyone) has a kinsman who has become Pope Gregory XV, and di Dominis rejoins the Church in Rome and does penance for his heresies. Gregorio is in bad trouble. He fears he could be tortured to death by inquisitors, his family left to starve. (ciphers, Bargraves Polisie.)

1621 28 Feb. Eng. Parliament: the Lower House sends a message to the Lords, asking for conference about a man of quality who'd have wronged his Majesty, disinherited his subjects, corrupted the Commonwealth.

1621 28 Feb. Eng. Parliament: John Churchill of Chancery to Grievance Committee: makes confessions for himself and everybody else in Chancery—determined not to sink alone.

1621 1 March. Eng. James writes to Bacon, warning him.

1621 15 March Eng. Conference of both Houses of Parliament. Hen makes his move quietly. (Spedding. vol 14, p 204.) The Lord Chancellor's behavior to be investigated. Some sources for Bacon's trial: Notes of the Debates in the House of Lords, officially taken by Henry Elsing, Clerk of the Parliaments. A.D. 1621. Ed. by Samuel Rawson Gardiner, esq. Printed for the Camden Soc. MDCCCLXX (1870.)
Basil Montagu. The Works of Francis Bacon. Part One. op. cit. On p 353, in a verbose speech, Bacon inserts a story of a king who killed his son—hoping the words will scare James? Basil Montagu offers a Journal of the Proceedings Against Lord Bacon. Note GGG. pp 699-742! The whole thing.

1621 17 March Eng. Bacon goes to bed sick; everything after that has to be done by letters and messengers. On this day Sir George Hastings leans over the bed, and Bacon says, "Sir George, I am sure that you love me . . . . I hear that one Aubrey intends to petition against me; he is a man that you have some interest in, you may take him off if you please." (Montagu.)

1621 8 March Venice. After a February trip over the Brenner Pass, Harry's back, to be ambassador again: four days' detention at Rovere by the governor, and twelve days' quarantine at Verona.

1621 27 March Eng. Parliament adjourns for Easter.

1621 29 March Ven. Only 19 senators show up to greet Harry at San Giorgio. England's stock is down due to James' son-in-law Frederick's underhanded attempt to take over Bohemia.

1621 Wed. 7 April Spain "Miercoles Santo." At last Osuna's in jail.

1621 15 April Ven. Harry has audience with the Doge, goes to Padua distressed, doesn't go to the palace again till Jan. 1622, to praise Gregorio after his death.

1621 1 May Eng. Bacon delivers up the Great Seal; he hopes that's the extent of his punishment. Hen Wriothesley moves unobtrusively, but he and Good Tom press ahead. (Spedding reports the whole thing. vol xiv, pp 196-201.)

1621 25 May Ven. Micaela takes Gregorio to Church of S. S. Giovanni e Paulo to hear Claudio Monteverdi's Requiem for Duke Cosmo II.

1621 Mon. 28 May Eng. Is this the day Bacon goes to the Tower? On **Sat. 2 June**, Chamberlain writes " . . . the beginning of the week . . ." (ed. Mc Clure. Chamberlain to Carleton. op. cit., vol 2, p 377, letter 383.)

1621 Thurs. 31 May. Eng. Bacon in the Tower sends this note to James, "Procure the warrant for my discharge this day." (Spedding. xiv, p 280, Montague, vol xvi part 1, p 382.) Bacon keeps his titles but can have no government employment, cannot be in Parliament or come within the verge. There's a fine. (James soon repeals the last punishment.)

1621 Sat. 2 June Eng. Bacon out today? So says Chamberlain to Carleton (Mc Clure. op. cit., vol 2, p 381, letter 384) "The Lord Chauncellor . . . getting the King's hand for his inlargement . . ."

1621 15 June Eng. James writes to the council from Greenwich: Hen Wriothesley is to be committed to charge of the Dean of Westminster. Sir Richard Weston to take him there; Hen not to see or speak to anyone but Weston and the Dean till further notice. Bacon must have insisted on this. (C. C. Stopes. The Life of Henry . . . . op. cit., p 406.) Bacon behind several June commitments. (ibid. p 406.)

1621 16 June Eng. Weston bows out as Hen's jailer and Sir William Parkhurst gets the job. He was once Harry's secretary at Venice and would have known Kit at least 1604-1610, so he and Hen have plenty to talk about. (Is Hen just doing James a favor?) Hen is allowed house-arrest in town and at Titchfield and full liberty by 30 Aug. (ibid. p 413.) Henry Vere also serves a short jail term.

1621 July Eng. Bacon, though no longer chief of SSS, works secretly with Phelippes trying to break the Venice code. Phelippes intercepts a note about the anonymous letters filled with Venice news sent to Di Dominis; name of author soon to be revealed. Bacon must figure that Kit, who'd worked so long for England, must not be examined by Venetian Inquisitors. He could reveal too much.

1621 8 July Ven. Harry reports he has received evidence that Philip III on his death-bed had determined to marry the Infanta not to Prince Charles of England, but to the Emperor's son. (footnote, L. P. Smith. op. cit., vol 2, p 226.) This report had been *ignored.* (It would be unwelcome to James.) How did Harry get the news? from Kit, always on the earie. Could this be one more reason Bacon would want to wipe out Kit and Harry?

1621 August? Eng. James sends secret word to Toby Mathew—at Rubens' house in Antwerp? Rubens has an inside line to the household of the Infanta, and James is anxious about current state of the Spanish match for Charles. Does Bacon shoot a message to Toby, about an extra job? Ride to Venice and take off those men at the embassy before you come home. I'll pay well. There'll be no trouble about your entering England: James wants your news of the Infanta.

1621 25 Sept. Eng. Mary Sidney Herbert dies of smallpox.

1621 14? Oct. The Veneto Harry takes his embassy "family" to his villa on the Brenta for Octoberfest. The vacationers carry with them wine from their cellar. (Kit and his family stay in town in their apartment at the embassy house.) Will Leete comes from Padua to Harry's villa for a party—everyone eats and drinks, and quite suddenly Will Leete dies. (L.P. Smith, op. cit., vols 1 and 2.)

1621 16 Oct. The Veneto Harry too sick to write. Dictates a letter: six are sick in bed at Padua. (ibid. vol 2.)

1621 21 November. Ven. At last, Harry and others drag home to Venice. Harry's cousin Edward Deering is carried upstairs.

1621 21 Nov. Ven. Gregorio and Micaela have been sick for weeks. Micaela is better, Gregorio worse. Late night or early AM 22 Nov., Christopher Marlowe, Sir Gregorio de' Monti, Kit, the Yat, the Moth, Merlin, Jakes-Pierre, the Hebe, dies in his apartment at the English embassy. Age 57 years, nine and a half months.

1621 26 Nov. Ven. Harry writes: I have lain under physic at Padova almost a month . . . . Two I have lost . . . .

1621 28 Dec. Eng. Toby Mathew arrives at Dover. Commissioner of the Passage at Dover reports to Zouch—Digby writes to Zouch, "Let Toby Mathew come to attend his Majesty." The king seems pleased. (Mathew. op. cit., p 194.) Did Toby bring false news to the king re Spanish marriage? And news to Bacon re Venice wine job?

1622

1622 Jan. Eng. (Chamberlain to Carleton, op. cit., vol 2, p 419) About Toby: "At his last being here yt is saide (how truly I know not) that he got a great deale of monie by the Lord Chauncellors favor . . ."

1622 Eng. In this year Ralph Crane writes a modest poem:

> "And some imployment hath my usefull *Pen,*
> "Had 'mongst these civill *well-deserving Men,*
> "That grace the *Stage* with *honour and delight,*
> "Of whose true *Honesties* I much could write
> "But will compris't (as in a Caske of Gold)
> "Vnder the *Kingly-service* they do hold."

T.W. Baldwin. The Organization and Personnel of the Shakespearean Company. Princeton U Press, 1954 (1927).

Ralph thinks of SS Theater Wing—his copyist job at Venice? Kit's recent death. Ralph's format was often used for anagram-letters. (I recently came across a fragile old one from my grandfather in this style.) Using the letters in the *underlined* parts of Ralph's poem, I found a message—checked it on the Anagram Checker on the internet. It reads:

KIT M. AGREED T' GO L-LIVE IN VENICE 'N' PENN'D GREAT SH SHOWES—HYS SONG'LL NEUER DIE.

1622 Jan. Eng. Plans for a Shakespeare monument are started, in Trinity Church at Stratford-on-Avon: Bacon wants to publicize the works, make them a nest for his own ciphers, intimating he, Bacon, created the plays anonymously. See ciphers for Kit's Sonnet 135: " . . . Then I C Sh., fair 'n' crass, giue all R neat writin' t' the actors' theater as his ouun—'n' Bacon's! A lie—a dead lie!" When Kit's friends learn of the monument they quietly offer to help. Mary Herbert's sons may have stepped up front; Kit's half-brother Peter Manwood, and Harry, Hen and others stay invisible, send design and money. Bacon accepts. Secretly (without Bacon's knowledge?) the monument becomes a remembrance for Kit.

1622 3 Jan. Eng. A note to Bacon: "About Saturday Mr. Burrows hopes to be at liberty to wait upon your Lordship." (Spedding. op. cit., xiv, p 324.) Mr. John Borough soon goes to Venice, ostensibly to bid on the Barocci Library there for Bacon's pal Rob't Cotton, really to *heist Kit's scripts out of the embassy house.* (Letter to me from M.A.F. Borrie, Assistant Keeper, British Library Dept. of MSS, 2 June 1981: "You are right in supposing that Cotton did not buy the Barocci library . . . [but] Borough was certainly commissioned by Cotton to buy MSS, since [Borough] says in his letter from Venice . . ." etc.) Borough is a known agent of Bacon: he's mentioned as middleman in a bribe discussed during Bacon's trial, and a man identifed as "one near the Ld. Chancellor." (Basil Montagu. The Works of Francis Bacon. op. cit., p 716-717.)

1622 29 Jan. Ven. The last victim of the bad wine, Harry's cousin and steward Edward Deering, who's been sick in bed all this time, dies, at the embassy house in Venice.

1622 22 Feb. Harry delivers a eulogy for Gregorio at the Collegio, a speech preserved in Venice Archives, Esp. Prin. Filza 29 Registro 32. Have copy.

1622 March Eng. In this month John Borough returns from Venice with a bundle of Marlowe's corrected MSS. It looks as if Bacon goes at once to George Buck, Master of the Revels, asks for more; tells him to issue certificates and submit to Stationers' Register the titles and the name of the publisher Bacon has selected. George, Kit's friend since 1591, knows Edward Blount has been buying from the players rights to publish the many plays Kit had been revising. Buck says since Bacon no longer has authority in the Theater Wing he should consult Blount about acquiring titles for registry. Bacon is furious. The Revels Office soon burns. (George Buck DNB. Henry Herbert's "Register" states that all Buck's office books were consumed by fire; all Buck's own unpublished works are just gone.)

1622 30 March Eng. (Chamberlain to Carleton. McClure. op. cit., vol 2, p 43.): Chamberlain writes, "Old Sir George Buck, master of the revels, has gone mad." It seems he quickly suffered an emotional breakdown, then a stroke.

1622 12 April Eng. The Guildhall jurors officially declare Buck insane. (Mark Eccles. "Sir George Buck, Master of the Revels," in Thomas Lodge and Other Elizabethans. ed. Chas. J. Sisson. Harvard U Press, 1933.) Buck soon dies.

1622 5 April Eng. Jane, mother of Kit's son William Davenant, dies, in Oxford.

1622 22 April Eng. John, Wm. Davenant's legal father, dies in Oxford. John's will provides college educations for the other boy children; William is to be apprenticed.

1622 April Eng. Bacon deals with Blount, who has 15 never-published plays sewed up with legal title, says he has access to three more (plays Mary Herbert owned? now in the hands of her sons?), plus another, and Blount will put them in folio if he can be in on the printing. (Charlton Hinman. Intro to The Norton Facsimile of the First Folio of Sh. p xxvi, *between the lines.*) The quarto of Troilus, it seemed, belonged to a Henry Walley who apparently balked. Hinman writes, ibid.: "whether an agreement was reached with Walley . . . or . . . the Folio publishers, having come into possession of a manuscript . . . felt safe to proceed . . . ." The publishers start to get legal about 17 others.

1622 early May Eng. Mary's boys, William & Philip Herbert, do donate plays; another, Troilus, is inserted in the Folio during printing—using Hen's presentation copy as copy? Or was that, too, really Mary's MS? Mary's sons get good press in Folio Dedication. (Ded. to First Folio of Sh.)

1622 early May Eng. Printing of the Folio begins. Ben Jonson writes that six "Mutes" work—with shades drawn—putting their eyes out "on an angle where the ants inhabit." (Ben Jonson. Antimasque, "The Prince's Masque or Time Vindicated." A good selection of bits of this antimasque is found in E. W. Smithson and G. Greenwood. Baconian Essays. Port Washinton, NY: Kennikat Press, 1970.) Who were the Mutes? Bacon as watcher, Jaggard as printer, Blount, Ben Jonson, George Carew (Baron Carew of Clopton), and—Robert Cotton? or George Herbert? No workers outside the clique were allowed. Looks like printing goes on till c. 31 Dec. 1623. Hinman writes, "the First Folio was 'in press' for almost two years." (Hinman. Intro. to the Norton Edition of The First Folio of Sh. op. cit., p x.) According to this Timeline, the process takes c. 20 months.

1623

1623 early Oct. Ven. Harry leaves Venice for the last time, crosses the Alps with all his possessions, goes down the Rhine from Basle. By 5 Nov. Eng. style, Harry's in Cologne, going home.

1623 7 Nov. Eng. Harry disembarks at Sandwich, with baggage. (L.P. Smith. vol 1, p 192.) Paintings, books, papers, skull? bones? death mask? Memories.

1623 8 Nov. Eng. "8th Novembris 1623. Mr. Blount Isaac Jaggard Entred for their Copie . . ." The Stationers' Register says, "16 Plays not before Printed." Two others never printed are not on the list but are in the Folio: King John and Taming of The Shrew. And Troilus and Cressida is a lonely outsider (though it had a quarto), rudely inserted in the book at the last minute. Still printing.

1623 December Eng. The Stratford Monument gets finishing touches. (Skull? Bones in the box?)

1623 end December Eng. The Folio printing is finished: binding begins.

1624

1624 January? Feb.? Eng. Ben Jonson's library burns. Where were Kit's scripts that had been used in the printing? As Ben was charged with expediting the print-job, almost surely they were piled on Ben's desk. *Bacon didn't want anyone to see Kit-Gregorio's well-known Italian handwriting on corrections in foul papers.)* All Ben's MSS and books were burned: no one knows the exact date, but the sooner after printing, the better for Bacon's plan to claim authorship. My guess is February at the latest—before the scripts could be passed around to friends. In the doubletalk of his masque, Ben rebukes Bacon for his deed and for his horrid, habitual arson. (Also see: Jonson's "Execration of Vulcan," published after Ben's death.)

1624 19 January Eng. Presentation of Ben Jonson's "The Prince's Masque, or Time Vindicated." At the end of the performance, the first copy of the Folio is brought to Prince Charles. Smithson guesses it was brought by a parade of characters from the plays, in costume. A good guess. (Smithson and Greenwood. Baconian Essays. op. cit.) The antimasque tells of the printing, makes wicked fun of Bacon as Chronomastix, the Time-Waster.

1623/'4 17 February Eng. old style. A bound copy of the Folio is placed in the Bodleian Library.

1624 31 May Eng. The Venetian ambassador writes: England and Scotland are sending troops to aid the Dutch against Spaniards. Southampton will probably be their leader. (C. C. Stopes. The Life of Henry . . . op. cit., p 452.) Hen is taking his son James, and Henry Vere is going, too. (There's a great picture of those Two Noble Kinsmen, riding side by side.)

1624 7 June Eng. The Venetian ambassador to the States writes; "The Spaniards comfort themselves that most of the men will die in the first few weeks . . . the Kingdom will get rid of three of the greatest enemies they have . . . Oxford [Henry Vere], Southampton, and Essex." [the *third* earl of Essex, Robin's son.]

1624 August Eng. Hen and his son James are leaving for Rotterdam; Hen is the leading colonel of English forces, Henry Vere the second of the four colonels. (ibid. p 457.)

1624 26 August Europe The Venetian ambassador to the States writes: "All the 6000 English of the new levies have arrived . . . the four Colonels are here at the Hague. The troops are in good order and very fine." (ibid.)

1624 Nov. The States There's a great pestilence among the soldiers. (ibid. p 461.)

1624 10 Nov. The States "Winter quarter at Rosendale was . . . fatal to the Earl of Southampton, and the Lord Wriothesley his son." Hen's son James dies on the 5th; Hen takes the body to Bergen op Zoom, meaning to sail with it to Southampton, but at Bergen he himself suddenly dies, "of a Lethargy." (ibid.)
One of the poems of Sir John Beaumont is about Hen, with these lines:

> "And thou, O Belgia, wert in hope to see
> The trophies of his conquests wrought in thee,
> But Death, who durst not meet him in the field,
> In private, by close treach'ry made him yield." (C. C. Stopes. The Life of Henry . . . op. cit.)

1625

1625 25, 26, 27 March Eng. James dies a painful 3-day death.
(G.P.V. Akrigg. op. cit., p 392-3.)

1625 late March Eng. Dr. George Eglisham, one of James' Scottish doctors, makes sweeping accusations: someone poisoned Southampton and the King. Eglisham blames Buckingham. Eglisham's Petitions, one sent to the new King Charles, one to Parliament, are [still?] preserved in Harleian Miscellany. ii. 69—80. (C. C. Stopes. op. cit., p 466.)

1625 summer Eng. New King Charles doesn't believe the murderer was Buckingham. Who could it have been? He asks Harry to use SSS skills. Harry steps away from his post as provost at Eton, investigates, deliberates, and that winter reveals to Charles some Bacon activities.

1626 2 April Eng. (Basil Montagu. The Works of Francis Bacon. op. cit., pp 446, 448.) Bacon is taken on a closed-carriage ride up through snowy Highgate with King Charles' Doctor Witherborne. Dr. Witherborne medicates Bacon, who vomits. Bacon stops the coach, gets out—wants to run away?—thinks better of it. He must preserve his dignity. He buys a plucked chicken from a nearby farmer's wife, stuffs it with snow, discoursing on refrigeration, gets back in the carriage. They drive to a Howard house. Admitted to an unused wing, Bacon goes to bed with more medication, sends for Julius Caesar to stay with him, dictates a polite note to his absent host, the earl of Arundel, Good Tom's cousin.

1626 early AM, 9 April, Easter Sunday, Eng. Francis Bacon dies. (Spedding. xiv, p 550.) Harry (and Kit?) had already made Bacon's epitaph: whimsical, touching—an anagram carved in stone.

1635

1635 April Eng. Delivered to the library at St. John's College, Cambridge: the remainder of Hen's books and MSS which he'd promised in his will. The thank-you note written by the Master and Seniors to Hen's executor Elizabeth Vernon is copied into the College Register. It begins: "*Madame, Having received your most noble gifts of Manuscripts which are already imprinted on our hearts,* wee desire now to testifie our due thankfulnes . . ." (C. C. Stopes. The Life of Henry, The Third Earl. op. cit., p 478.) The books Hen gave, Stopes writes, have been absorbed into the Common library, and most can be distinguished. Where are the MSS? (C. C. Stopes. ibid. p 479, quotes as ref. the Baker MSS among Harleian MSS.) Could these gifts have been presentation copies of Kit's plays, in his hand? Worth study.

1639

1639. 5 Dec. Eng. After years of academic life spent with time-off reading, smoking, fishing with Isaak Walton over the Black Pots at the bend of the Thames near Eton (and training youthful SSS and Resistance workers), Harry Wotton has burned papers, willed his old burglar tools to his lawyer, and on this day he dies, at Eton. (L.P. Smith. vol 1, p 223.)

(After this, several ancillary tales of Kit's children and descendants could be told.)

1643

1643 17 April Eng. Isabel-Elizabeth Cavendish dies, during the civil war. Shadows suggest she receives a serious bullet-wound trying to protect Henrietta-Maria from snipers at the time of the queen's landing at Bridlington in Feb. At Welbeck the queen seems to have visited Eliz, who says she's getting better, but the wound proves fatal.

f

G.B. Evans, editor of the *Riverside Shakespeare,* writes about research: "The real strength of a case rests not on any single piece or kind of evidence but on the quite remarkable manner in which several independent lines of approach support and reinforce one another in pointing to a single conclusion . . ."

A BIBLIOGRAPHY

for study of Christopher Marlowe's life and works,
compiled by Roberta Ballantine

A Concordance to the Plays, Poems, and Translations of Christopher Marlowe. Fehrenbach, Boone, Di Cesare, eds. Ithica: Cornell U. Press, 1982.

A Petition Directed to her most excellent Maiesty. Anonymous. B.M. English Books, 1475-1640. microfilm reel 376. Copy at Henry Huntington Library, San Marino, CA. [1st 50 pp and last p are Roger Manwood's, 1592]

Akrigg, G.P.V. *Jacobean Pageant, or The Court of King James I.* NY: Atheneum, 1974.

__________. *Shakespeare and the Earl of Southampton.* Cambridge, MA: Harvard U. Press, 1968.

All the Marprelate Tracts in Facsimile. Leeds, England: The Scolar Press, n. d.

Andrews, Kenneth R. *Elizabethan Privateering.* Cambridge: Cambridge U Press, 1964.

Anthony Bacon Papers at Lambeth Palace Library. vols. 3-9 (reels 1-5). Queen's Grove, London: World Microfilm Publications.

Anthony Bacon Papers Index, Lambeth Palace Library. Gateshead, London: Northumberland Press, 1974.

Anthony, Katherine. *Queen Elizabeth.* NY: The Literary Guild, 1929.

Arnold, Janet. *Queen Elizabeth's Wardrobe Unlock'd.* Leeds, England: W.S. Maney & Son, Ltd., 1988.

Asimov, Isaac. *Asimov's Guide to Shakespeare.* 2 vols. in one. NY: Avenel, 1978.

Aubrey's Brief Lives. Oliver Lawson Dick, ed. Ann Arbor: U of MI, 1962.

Bacco, Enrico. *Naples, an Early Guide (First Published between 1616 and 1671).* NY: Italica Press, 1991.

Bakeless, John. *Christopher Marlowe.* 1 vol. NY: Haskell House, 1976 (1938).

———. *The Tragicall History of Christopher Marlowe.* 2 vols. Westport, CT: Greenwood, 1970 (1942).

Balado, Hermida. *Vida del VII Conde de Lemos.* Monforte de Lemos: NOS Editorial, 1948.

Baldwin, T. W. *The Organization and Personnel of the Shakespearean Company.* NY: Russell and Russell, 1961 (Princeton U. Press, 1927).

Balloncí, Maria. *A Prince of Mantua.* NY: Harcourt Brace, 1956.

Bargrave, Cap't. John. *A Form of Polisie* (by Ignotus). Knole Park, Kent: Papers of Lord Sackville. [my copy from the print of Susan Myra Kingsbury. *Records of the Virginia Co. of London*, vol. IV.]

Barrera, D. Cayetano. *Nueva biografía de Lope de Vega.* The Spanish Academy, 1890 (MS 1850).

Beesly, Edward Spencer. *Queen Elizabeth.* London, NY: Macmillan, 1900.

Benstead, C.R. *Portrait of Cambridge.* London: Robert Hale Pub., 1968.

Bertarelli, L.V. *Muirhead's Northern Italy.* London: Macmillan, 1924 [detailed street maps].

Blackham, Robert. *The Story of the Temple, Gray's and Lincoln's Inn.* London: Sampson Low, Marston & Co., n. d.

Boas, Frederick S. *Marlowe and His Circle.* London: Humphrey Milford, 1931.

Bowen, Catherine Drinker. *Francis Bacon.* Boston: Little, Brown, 1963.

———. *The Lion and the Throne.* Boston, Toronto: Little, Brown, 1956, 1957 [Judge Manwood beloved by all].

Brooke, C.F. Tucker, ed. *The Shakespeare Apocrypha.* Oxford, London: Oxford U. Press, 1971 (1908).

Brulez, Wilfred. *Marchands Flamands á Venise.* vols. 1- and 2, with Greta Devos. (Études d' histoire économique et sociale, Tome VI, Tome IX). Bruxelles: L'institute historique Belge de Rome, 1965 and 1986.

Bullough, Geoffrey. *Narrative and Dramatic Sources of Shakespeare.* 8 vols. NY: Columbia U. Press, 1959-75.

Burgon, John William. *Life and Times of Sir Thomas Gresham.* 2 vols. NY: Burt Franklin, 1965 (1839).

Byron, William. *Cervantes, A Biography.* Garden City, NY: Doubleday, 1978.

Cable, Mary. *El Escorial.* NY: *Newsweek* Book Division, 1971.

Calendar of State Papers. Addenda. Elizabeth & James I. vol. 12 *passim.*

________. *Domestic Elizabeth.* vol. 3. A note from Essex, June 1593.

________. *Domestic Elizabeth.* vol. 6. 1601, p 140 [intelligencers employed abroad].

________. *Ireland Elizabeth.*

________. *Venetian.* vols. 9-17 passim, and in particular:

________. *Venetian.* vol. 9. August 1593, re Constantinople jail-break.

________. *Venetian.* vols. 10, 13, re Cavagion and Murano.

________. *Venetian.* vol. 13. Dudley Carlton letter, 15 July 1614 [re the two marciliane and the Tiger]. Allen B. Hinds, ed. footnote, p.155.

________. *Venetian.* vol. 14, 7 Oct. 1616. Gregorio de' Monti to Henry Wotton [Gregorio and wife.]

________. *Venetian.* vol. 15, Appendix 1. Berlingerio Gessi, Bishop of Rimini, to Cardinal Millino, re Gregorio de' Monti and Guarini.

Callimani, Ricardo. *The Ghetto of Venice.* Katherine Wolfthal, trans. NY: M. Evans, 1987.

Camden, William. *Remaines Concerning Britain.* London: Simon Waterson and Robert Clavell, 1657 [anagrams described].

Carleton, Dudley. *Dudley Carleton to John Chamberlain, 1603-1624, Jacobean Letters.* Maurice Lee, Jr., ed. New Brunswick, NJ: Rutgers U, 1972.

Carson, Edward. *The Ancient and Rightful Customs.* Hamdon, CT: Archon Books, n.d.

Carubel & Ravenstein. *Istanbul.* Munich: Wilhelm Andermann Verlag, 1961.

Castle, Edward James. *Shakespeare, Bacon, Jonson and Greene.* Port Washington, NY: Kennikat Press, 1970 reprint (n. d.).

Cavendish, Margaret Lucas. *The Life of William Cavendish, Duke of Newcastle.* NY: E.P. Dutton, Everyman's Library #722 (1677).

———. *Love's Adventures* and *CCXI Sociable Letters.*

Cervantes, Miguel. *Don Quixote I and II.* Shelton translation. 4 vols. Intros by James Fitzmaurice Kelly. NY: AMS reprint, 1967 (1896).

———. *El Ingenioso Hidalgo Don Quixote de la Mancha, I y II.* ed. Luis Andrés Murillo. Madrid: Editorial Castalia, 1973 and 1978.

———. *Novelas ejemplares.* Mexico City: Editorial Porrúa, 1981 (Madrid: 1613).

———. *Viaje del Parnaso.* Madrid: Editorial Castalia, 1973.

———. *The Interludes of Cervantes.* trans. by S. Griswold Morley. Princeton, NJ: Princeton U. Press, 1948.

Chamberlain, John. *Letters.* 2 vols. Norman Egbert McClure, ed. Westport, CT: Greenwood, 1979 (1939).

Chambers, Edmund Kirchener. *The Elizabethan Stage.* 4 vols. Oxford: Clarendon Press, 1923.

———. *William Shakespeare, A Study of Facts and Problems.* 2 vols. Oxford: Clarendon Press, 1930.

Cheney, Edward R. *A History of England from the Armada to the Death of Elizabeth.* London: Longmans, Green and Co., 1926.

Church, Richard. *Kent.* London: Robert Hale, 1979 (1948).

Chute, Marchette. *Ben Jonson of Westminster.* London: Robert Hale, 1954.

Clark, Eleanor Grace. *Ralegh and Marlowe.* NY: Russell and Russell, 1965.

Clubb, Louise George. *Giambattista Della Porta, Dramatist.* Princeton, NJ: Princeton U, 1965.

________. Italian Plays (1500-1700) in the Folger Library. Firenze: Leo S. Olschki Editore, 1968 [Gregorio here].

Collins' Peerage of England, augmented by Sir Egerton Brydges. vol. 3, pp 154-62. London: 1812.

Coniglio, Giuseppe. *I Viceré del Regno di Napoli.* Naples: 1730.

Connellan, Owen. *The Annals of Ireland.* Dublin: Brian Geraghty, 1846.

Crane, Thomas Frederick. *Italian Customs of the Sixteenth Century.* NY: Russell & Russell, 1971 (1920).

Craven, Wesley Frank. *Dissolution of the Virginia Co.* NY: Oxford Press, 1932.

Curtis, Edmund. *A History of Ireland.* London: Methuen, 1942.

Cygnus. prefatory poem for Ben Jonson's *Sejanus.* [Folger microfilm].

Davies, David W. *Elizabethans Errant.* Ithaca, NY: Cornell U, 1967.

Dawley, Powel M. *John Whitgift and the English Reformation.* NY: Charles Scribner's Sons, 1954.

Davenant, William. *The Dramatic Works of William Davenant.* Wm. Paterson, ed. 5 vols. Edinburgh, London: Sotheran & Co., 1872.

De Kalb, Eugenie. "Robert Poley's Movements as Court Messenger." *RES,* April 1931.

de' Monti, Gregorio. *L'Ippolito,* a comedy. First ed. 1611. [Folger owns copy of 3rd ed., 1620.]

Deacon, Richard. *John Dee.* London: Frederick Mulks, 1968.

Della Porta, Giambattista. *Gli Duoi Fratelli Rivali.* Louise George Clubb, ed. and transl. Berkeley: U. of CA, 1980.

Denniston, James. *Memoirs of the Dukes of Urbino.* London: John Lane, The Bodley Head, 1919.

Dictionary of National Biography. Leslie Stephen & Sidney Lee, ed's. Oxford: Oxford U. Press since 1917. [many pertinent monographs]

————. monograph on Sir John Borough.

————. Roger Manwood. by James McMullen Rigg.

Dixon, William Hepworth. *Personal History of Lord Bacon*. Boston: Ticknor and Fields, 1861.

Domenici, Domenico. Letter 1614 at the Frari, Venice: Senato, Dispacci Firenze. [de' Montis takes pirate ships]

Douay Diaries. *The First and Second Diaries of the English College, Douay, with Appendix of Unpublished Documents. (Intro by Thomas Francis Knox, D.D.)* London: David Nutt, 1878.

du Maurier, Daphne. *Golden Lads*. NY: Doubleday, 1975.

————. *The Winding Stair*. Garden City, NY: Doubleday, 1977.

Durning-Lawrence, Sir Edwin. *Bacon is Shakespeare*. NY: John McBride, 1910.

Eccles, Audrey. *Obstetrics and Gynaecology in Tudor and Stuart England*. Ohio: Kent State, 1982.

Eccles, Mark. "Brief Lives." *Studies in Philology*. vol. 79, #4. Chapel Hill, NC: U. of NC, 1982.

————. *Christopher Marlowe in London*. NY: Octagon Books, 1967.

————. monograph on George Buck in *Thomas Lodge and Other Elizabethans*. Sisson, ed. Cambridge, MA: Harvard U, 1933.

————. "Marlowe in Kentish Tradition." *Notes and Queries*. vol. 168. 13, 20, 27 July, 1935.

Ehrenberg, Richard. *Capital and Finance in the Age of the Renaissance*. NY: Harcourt, Brace, n.d.

El centro coordinador de bibliotecas, Cádiz, Spain.

Elizabethan and Jacobean Pamphlets. George Saintsbury, ed. NY: Books for Libraries Press, 1970.

Engelmann, Geo. J. *Labor Among Primitive Peoples.* St. Louis: J.H. Chambers, 1882.

English State Paper. "Ships and Home Ports in England. 1582."

Eslava, Antonio de. *Noches de Invierno.* Pamplona: Carlos de Labayen, 1609.

Evans, Alfred J. *Shakespeare's Magic Circle.* Freeport, NY: Books for Libraries Press, 1970 (1956).

Falconer, Alexander Frederick, Lieutenant Commander, Royal Naval Reserve. *Shakespeare and the Sea.* London: Constable, 1964.

Foss, Edward. *The Judges of England.* NY: AMS Press, 1966. 9 vols. Manwood, vol. 5.

Foster, Donald W. *Elegy By W.S.—A Study in Attribution.* Newark: U. of Delaware Press, 1989.

Fraser, Antonia. *Mary, Queen of Scots.* NY: Delacorte Press, 1969.

Galanté, Abraham. *Don Salomon Aben Yaeche, duc de Metelin* [Alvaro Mendes' bio]. Istanbul: U. of Istanbul, Societe Anonyme de Papeterie et d' Imprimerie (Fratelli Heim), 1936.

Gascoigne, George. "An Hundreth Sundrie Flowers." 1907 ed.

Gerhard, Sandra Forbes. *Don Quixote and the Shelton Translation, A Stylistic Analysis.* Studia Humanitatis, 1982.

Grant, J.M. Lewis. *Christopher Marlowe, the Ghost Writer.* Orillia, Ontario, Canada: Stubley Press. Part One 1967, Part Two, 1970.

Graves, Thornton Shirley. *The Court and the London Theatres During the Reign of Elizabeth.* NY: Russell and Russell, 1967.

Green, Edmund Wigfall. *Sir Francis Bacon.* NY: Twayne Publications, 1966.

Green, Otis H. "The Literary Court of the Conde de Lemos at Naples, 1610-1616." *Hispanic Review,* Oct. 1933.

Haile, Martin. *An Elizabethan Cardinal, William Allen.* NY and London: Sir Isaac Pitman and Sons, 1914.

Hall, Joseph. *Poems, 1597, 1598 (Toothless and Biting Satires).* NY: AMS Press, 1969.

Hapgood, Charles. *Maps of the Ancient Sea-Kings.* NY: E.P. Dutton, 1966-67.

Harrison, G.B. *An Elizabethan Journal.* NY: Cosmopolitan Book Corp., 1929.

__________. *Life and Death of Robert Devereux, Earl of Essex.* NY: Henry Holt, 1937.

Hasted, Edward. *History and Topographical Survey of the County of Kent.* 4 vols. Canterbury: Simmons and Kirkby, 1790-1799.

Hatchette Guide to Istanbul, The. Paris, 1961.

Hinman, Charlton, ed. *The Norton Facsimile of The First Folio of Shakespeare.* NY: Paul Hamlin for W.W. Norton, 1968.

Hinton, Edward M. *Ireland Through Tudor Eyes.* Philadelphia: U. of Penn., 1935.

Hoffman, Calvin. *The Murder of the Man who was Shakespeare.* NY: Julian Messner, 1955.

Hotson, J. Leslie. *The Death of Christopher Marlowe.* NY: Russell & Russell, 1967 (1925).

Howells, T.B. *A Complete Collection of State Trials* [the Overbury Case, James I, 1615, 1616]. London: Longmans, Hurst, Rees, Orme, Browne et al, 1816.

Hume, Martin. *Two English Queens and Philip.* London: Methuen & Co.; NY: G.P. Putnam's Sons, 1908.

Hurstfield, Joel. *The Queen's Wards.* Cambridge, MA: Harvard U, 1958.

Ingram, John H. *Christopher Marlowe and his Associates.* NY: Cooper Square, 1904, 1910.

Inner Temple Records, Calendar. vol. 1. F.A. Underwick, Q.C., ed., by order of Masters of the Bench. London: Henry Southeran & Co., 1896.

James I of England. Letter to Gregorio de' Monti. *English State Paper* 99-21-x/L09704. CSP, December, 1616.

Jenkins, Elizabeth. *Elizabeth the Great.* NY: G.P. Putnam's Sons, 1967.

_________. *Elizabeth and Leicester.* NY: Coward McCann, 1962.

Jensen, Hans Helmut. "Totenmasken," *Hessisches Arzteblatt.* Heft 11, Nov. 1975.

Jonson, Ben. *Execration Against Vulcan, with Divers Epigrams . . . Never Before Published.* London: J.O. for John Benson, 1640.

Kingsbury, Susan Myra. *Records of the Virginia Company of London, 1609-1626.* Washington, DC, USA: Government Print Office, 1906-1935.

Kortepeter, C. Max. *Ottoman Imperialism During the Reformation—Europe and the Caucasus.* NY: NYU, 1972.

Laing, Andrew. *Shakespeare, Bacon and the Great Unknown.* London: Longmans, Green, 1912.

Lane, Frederic C. *Venice, A Maritime Republic.* Baltimore: Johns Hopkins U. Press, 1987.

Lauritzen, Peter, and Alex Zielke. *Palaces of Venice.* NY: Viking, 1978.

Law, Ernest. *A Short History of Hampton Court in Tudor and Stuart Times.* London: G. Bell and Sons, 1929.

Lawrence, W.J. "Was Shakespeare Ever in Ireland?" *Shakespeare Jahrbuch,* XLIL, Autumn, 1906.

Le Comte, Edward. *The Notorious Lady Essex.* NY: Dial Press, 1969.

Le Froy, Sir John Henry. *Memorials of the Discovery and Early Settlement of the Bermudas, 1515-1685.* London: Longmans, Green, 1877-79.

Letters and Dispatches of Sir Henry Wotton in the Years 1617-1620 [&'21 Gregorian]. London: published by the Roxeburghe Club, printed by William Nichol, the Shakspeare [sic] Press, 1855.

Looney, J. Thomas. *Shakespeare Identified.* 2 vols. Ruth L. Miller, ed. Port Washington, NY: Kennikat Press for Minos Publishing, 1975 (1920). [re Edward de Vere]

Manfredi, Michele. *Gio. Battista Manso, nella vita e nelle opera.* Naples: Casa Tipografico Editrice, Nicola Jovene, 1919.

Manningham, John. The Diary of John Manningham, 1602-1603. Ed by J. Bruce. Camden Society Pub. 1868. entry Nov. 1602. (recalling 1592, Roger & sonne)

Marin, Luis Astrana. *La vida turbulenta de Quevedo.* Madrid: Gran Capitán, 1945.

Marloe, Christopher. *Lust's Dominion, or the Lascivious Queen.* J. Le Gay Brereton, ed. Louvain: Librarie Universitarie, Uystpruyst Publisher, 1931.

Marlowe, Christopher. *Complete Works of Christopher Marlowe.* 2 vols. 2nd ed. Fredson Bowers, ed. Cambridge: Cambridge U. Press, 1981.

Marlowe, Christopher. *Tamburlaine the Great, Part II.* London: Richard Jones, 1592. [two printings—one mislabelled 1590]. Proquest reprints, 2001.

Martin Spevack. *The Harvard Concordance of Shakespeare.* Cambridge, MA: Belknap Press of Harvard Press, 1969, 1970. [lines fit *The Riverside Shakespeare*]

Martin Marprelate Tracts. The Scolar Press Ltd. 93 Hunslet Rd. Leeds 10 England.

Marqués de Rafal, Alfonso Pardo Manuel de Villena. *Un Maecenas español del siglo XVII.* [Lemos]. Madrid: Imprenta de Jaime Ratés Martín, 1911.

Matthew, Arnold Harris. *The Life of Sir Tobie Mathew.* London: Elkin Mathews, 1907.

Mathew, David. "The Cornish and Welsh Pirates in the Reign of Elizabeth." *English Historical Review.* vol. 39. 1924.

Mattingly, Garrett. *The Armada.* Boston: Houghton Mifflin, 1959.

Mavrogordato, John. *The Erotokritos.* London: Oxford U. Press, Humphrey Milford, 1927.

Memorias de Valladolid. MS in British Library.

Mendenhall, Thomas Corwin, Dr. *A Mechanical Solution of a Literary Problem.* OCLC 397.09381, 1901. Copy at Ohio State U.

Montagu, Basil. *Works of Francis Bacon, Lord Chancellor of England.* London: William Pickering, 1834.

Morris, Jan. *The Venetian Empire.* Boston: Faber and Faber, 1980.

Mykill, Henry. *Portugal.* London: Faber and Faber, 1972.

Nashe, Thomas. *The Works of Thomas Nashe.* Ed. Ronald McKerrow, & ed. F. P. Wilson. 5 vols. Oxford: Basil Blackwell, 1958.

Nelson, Alan H. *Monstrous Adversary.* Liverpool: Liverpool U. Press, 2003 [Edward de Vere].

Nerval, Gerard de. *Journey to the Orient.* Norman Glass, transl. NY: NYU Press, 1972.

Nichols, John. *Progresses and Public Processions of Elizabeth.* vol. 1. London: J. Nichols & Son, 1823.

Norman, A.V.B., and Don Pottinger. *English Weapons and Warfare.* Englewood Cliffs, NJ: Prentice-Hall, 1979.

Norwood, Richard. (*Bermuda*) *Journal.* [censored in the original] NY: Scholars' Facsimiles and Reprints, 1945.

Ogburn, Dorothy and Charlton. *This Star of England.* Westport, CT: Greenwood Press, 1972. [Edward de Vere +]

Ordish, T. Fairman. *Shakespeare's London.* London: J.M. Dent & Co. and Aldine House, 1897.

Otway, Thomas. *The Complete Works,* including *The Orphan,* and appendix: *The Source of Venice Preserved.* Bloomsbury: The Nonesuch Press, 1926.

Oxford English Dictionary. passim, and item steganography, with Henry Wotton comment. Oxford: Oxford U. Press, 1972-1979.

Parker, Geoffrey. *Philip II.* Boston: Little, Brown, 1978.

Parrino, D.A. *Teatro eroico e politico de governi de' Viceré Spagnoli di Napoli.* Naples: Collana di cultura Napoletana, 1730.

Paulet, Amias. *The Letterbooks of Sir Amias Paulet.* London: Burns and Oates, 1874.

Phelps, Charles E. *Falstaff and Equity.* Boston: Houghton Mifflin, 1901.

Pierce, William. *An Historical Introduction to the Marprelate Tracts.* London: Archibald Constable, 1918.

Pike, Ruth. *Aristocrats and Traders: Sevillian Society in the Sixteenth Century.* Ithaca: Cornell U. Press, 1972.

Pitcher, Seymour. *The Case for Shakespeare's Authorship of the Famous Victories.* London: Alvin Redman, 1961.

Pohl, Frederick J. "The Death Mask." *The Shakespeare Quarterly*, 12, 1961.

Pollard, Alfred W. *Shakespeare Folios and Quartos, 1594-1685.* NY: Cooper Square, 1970.

Porter, H.Q. *Puritanism in Tudor England.* Columbia, SC: U. of SC Press, 1971.

Proper, Ida Sedgewick. Our Elusive Willy, Manchester, Maine: Dirigo Editions, 1953.

Quevedo y Villegas, Francisco. *Obras completas.* Madrid: Aguilar, 1981.

Read, Conyers. *Mr. Secretary Walsingham and the Policy of Queen Elizabeth.* Cambridge, MA: Harvard U. Press, and Oxford: Clarendon Press, 1925.

Registers of the Acts of Privy Council. vols. 22 & 23, 1591-92, new series.

Rennert, Hugo. *The Life of Lope de Vega.* NY: Benjamin Blom, 1968.

Richardson, Mrs. Aubrey. *The Doges of Venice.* London: Methuen, n.d.

Rogers, John C. *The Parish Church of St. Michael.* St. Albans: H.A. Richardson Publishers, 1973.

Rossi, Vittorio. *Battista Guarini ed il Pastor Fido, studio biograpfico critico.* Turin: Ermanno Loescher, 1886.

Rosten, Leo. The Joys of Yiddish. NY: Washington Square Press, 1968.

Rowe, Helen. *A Guide to the Records of Bermuda.* Hamilton, Bermuda: Archives.

Rowse, A.L. *The Poems of Shakespeare's Dark Lady.* NY: Clarkson Potter, 1978.

Saint-Real, Abbé. *La conjuration des Españols contre la Republique de Venise.* Geneva: Librarie Droz, 11 rue Massot, 1977 (1780).

Sams, Conway Whittle. *The Conquest of Virginia. The Third Attempt, 1610-1624.* Spartanburg, SC: The Reprint Co., 1973.

Savage, Richard. *Sir Thomas Overbury* [a play in British Library], 1775.

Schlegel, H. and J.A. Verster de Wulverhorst. *The World of Falconry.* NY, Paris, Lausanne: The Vendome Press, 1979.

Schoenbaum, S. *William Shakespeare, A Documentary Life.* NY: Oxford U. Press with the Scolar Press, 1975.

Selimas. Folger Shakespeare Library. Microfilm STC 5226. [a play]

Senior, C.M., David and Charles Newton Abbott. *A Nation of Pirates.* London: Crane, Russek, 1976.

Shakespeare, William. *Complete Works, from Text left by George Stevens.* Boston: Philips, Sampson, 1853.

_________. *Lucrece.* London: Richard Field for John Harrison. London: The Scolar Press, 1968 (facsimile of early impression of first printing 1594).

_________. *The Riverside Shakespeare.* Gwyne Blakemore Evans, ed. Boston: Houghton Mifflin, 1974.

_________. *Shakespeare's Plays in Quarto.* Michael J.B. Allen and Kenneth Muir, eds. Berkeley: U. of CA Press, 1981, facsimile edition.

_________. *Shake-speares Sonnets.* London: printed by G. Eld for T. T. Proquest reprint of the quarto, 1609.

Sidebothom, Rev. J.S. *Memorials of the King's School, Canterbury.* 1865.

Skilliter, S.A.S. *William Harborne and the Trade with Turkey.* London: pub. for the British Academy, Oxford U. Press, 1977.

Slater, Gilbert. *Seven Shakespeares.* London: Cecil Palmer, 1931.

Smith, John. *The General History of Virginia, New England, and the Summer Isles* [Bermuda]. Birmingham: Edward Arber, 1884 (1624).

Smith, Logan Pearsall. *Life and Letters of Sir Henry Wotton.* 2 vols. Oxford: Clarendon Press, 1907.

Smith, Michael Llewellyn. *The Great Island [Crete].* London: Longmans, Green, 1965.

Smithson, E.W. and G. Greenwood. *Baconian Essays.* Port Washington, NY: Kennikat Press reprint, 1970.

Spanish Cities of the Golden Age; The Views of Anton van den Wyngaerde. ed. Richard L. Kegen. Berkeley, CA: U. of C. Press, 1989.

Spedding, James, with Ellis and Heath. *Works of Francis Bacon.* vols. 8 through 14. (Life and Letters, vols. 1 through 7). NY: Garrett reprint, 1968. (London: Longmans, 1857-1874.)

Speed, John. *The Counties of Britain.* A modern edition, with intro Nigel Nicholson, comment Alasdair Hawkyard. NY: Thames and Hudson, 1989.

Spenser, Edmund. "A View of the Present State of Ireland . . ." in *Elizabethan Ireland.* James P. Myers, Jr., ed. Hamden, CT: Archon Books, 1983.

Stern, Virginia F. *Gabriel Harvey, A Study of his Life, Marginalia & Library.* Oxford: Clarendon Press, 1979.

Stokes, H.P. *Corpus Christi.* n.d.

Stopes, Charlotte Carmichael (Mrs. C.C. Stopes). *Burbage and Shakespeare's Stage.* NY: Haskell House Publishers, 1970 (1913).

————. *The Life of Henry, Third Earl of Southampton.* NY: AMS Press, 1969. (Cambridge: Cambridge U. Press, 1922).

Stow, John. *The Survey of London.* London: J.M. Dent & Sons, 1980 (1912) (1598).

Student Register, Padua U, 1594-'98. microfilm available from the university.

Swetz, Frank J. *Capitalism & Arithmetic, the New Math of the 15th Century.* David E. Smith transl. La Salle, IL: Open Court, 1987.

Taylor, John. *Sir Gregory Nonsence, His Newes from no place.* "Printed at London by N.O., 1622." Reprint in Charles Hindley's *Miscellanea Antiqua Anglicane,* 1873.

The Great Assizes Holden in Parnassus, 1664. A copy of this pamphlet [glances at an old SSS hierarchy] is held in the British Library.

The Norton Facsimile of The First Folio of Shakespeare. Prepared by Charlton Hinman. NY: W.W. Norton, 1968 [pages of thirty copies collated].

Thompson, James Westfall, and Saul K. Padover. *Secret Diplomacy.* NY: Frederick Ungar, 1965 (1937).

Thomson, George Malcolm. *Sir Francis Drake.* NY: Wm. Morrow, 1972.

Trease, Geoffrey. *Portrait of a Cavalier.* London: Macmillan, 1979 [William Cavendish].

Urry, William. "Marlowe and Canterbury." *London Times Literary Supplement,* 13 Feb. 1964, p 136.

_________. *Christopher Marlowe and Canterbury.* ed. Andrew Butcher. London: Faber & Faber, 1988.

Varie poesie di molti excellenti autori in morte del M. Illustre Sig. Cavalier Battista Guarini. ed. Gregorio de' Monti. Venetia: a presso Gio. Battista Ciotti, 1616. [some sonnets by Kit—copy in microfilm from Marciana Library, Venice.]

Walton, Izaak. *The Compleat Angler.* London: Dent, Everyman's Library, 1975.

Ward, Capt. E.M. *The Seventeeth Earl of Oxford.* London: 1928.

White and Black Books of the Cinq Ports. ed. Felix Hull. London: Her Majesty's Stationery Office & Historic MSS Com., ff. 254 & 260. 1966. [Judge Roger Manwood]

Wilkinson, Henry. *The Adventurers of Bermuda.* London: Oxford Press, 1958.

Willan, T.S. *The Early History of the Russia Company, 1553-1603.* NY: Augustus M. Kelley, 1968.

Williams, James A. *The Age of Drake.* London: Adam and Charles Black, n. d.

Williams, Ronald John. *Bermudiana.* NY: Rinehart, 1936.

Wilson, Charles. *Queen Elizabeth and the Revolt of the Netherlands.* Berkeley, CA: U. C. Press, 1970.

Wolf, Lucien. "Jews in Elizabethan England." *The Transactions of the Jewish Historical Society of England.* vol. XI, 1927.

Wotton, Sir Henry. *Reliquiae Wottanianae.* ed. Izaak Walton. Ann Arbor: University Microfilms, Proquest reprint-on-demand, 1982 (1685).

Wraight, A.D. & Virginia Stern. *In Search of Christopher Marlowe.* NY: Vanguard, 1965.

Wright, David and Patrick Swift. *A Lisbon Diary.* NY: Charles Scribner's Sons, n. d.

Yates, Frances. *The Art of Memory.* Chicago: U. of Chicago Press, 1966.

Young, Frances Berkeley. *Mary Sidney, Countess of Pembroke.* London: David Nutt, 1912.

Zuill, William. *Bermuda Journey.* NY: Coward, McCann, 1947.

f

NOTES ON THE BIBLIOGRAPHY

Arnold, Janet. *Queen Elizabeth's Wardrobe Unlock'd.* Leeds, England: W.S. Maney & Son, Ltd., 1988. Provides dates of alterations made in Elizabeth's clothes [matching times of pregnancy], lists scores of kirtles and loose gowns, along with lap-mantles and big furry muffs. We read of the complete discretion of the only tailor who served the queen from 1558 to 1582.

Bargrave, Cap't. John. *A Form of Polisie,* by Ignotus. Knole Park, Kent. Papers of Lord Sackville. My copy from the print of Susan Myra Kingsbury. *Records of the Virginia Co. of London,* vol. IV. Marlowe contracted to make a proto-constitution for a colony which Cap't. Bargrave wanted to start in Virginia. Marlowe had hoped to be pardoned and made governor of Bermuda. It was not to be, but he'd already made notes for a colonial constitution, necessarily acceptable to James but with some democratic thoughts. The work contains a magnificent narrative cipher, autobiographic.

Brooke, C.F. Tucker. *The Shakespeare Apocrypha.* Oxford, London: Oxford U. Press, 1971 (1908). This book contains valuable first reprints of earliest uncorrupted versions of 14 plays—all completely written by Marlowe except for *Sir Thomas More,* which Kit says he made "with others," and *The Two Noble Kinsmen,* which, according to his ciphers, he created with John Fletcher as a galloping farce, a play-party-vehicle for Henry Vere and Hen Wriothesley. Tucker Brooke's attributions are mistaken: some form of Marlowe's name is incorporated into meaningful anagrams in the first two lines of each of these works, linked to meaningful anagrams beyond. (Every playwright makes some pot-boilers, and though one of these works, *Mucedorus,* suitable for home-production, is laughed-at by literary critics, it's the most popular play Marlowe ever wrote—17 count'em 17 quartos.)

Calendars of State Papers. Venetian. Many cogent references vols. 9-17. References to de' Monti in the calendars are often *not* present in their indexes.

Davenant, William. *The Dramatic Works of William Davenant.* Wm Paterson, ed., 5 vols. Edinburgh, London: Sotheran, 1872. A bio of Davenant (Marlowe's son) by Henry Blount, detailed, touching and helpful.

Dictionary of National Biography. Oxford: Oxford U. Press since 1917. A useful but not infallible (what is?) tool.

Domenici, Domenico. His 1614 letter, kept at the Frari, Venice: Senato, Dispacci Firenze, about "de Montis" capturing pirate ships. Valuable.

Ehrenberg, Richard. *Capital and Finance in the Age of the Renaissance.* NY: Harcourt, Brace, n. d. The writer offers exuberant praise for Thomas Gresham.

El centro coordinador de bibliotécas, Cádiz, Spain. Holds material relevant to the 1596 English raid, an operation which Kit and Cervantes fixed before Essex arrived, so his English ships could win.

Eslava, Antonio. *Noches de Invierno.* Pamplona: Carlos de Labayen, 1609. Preserved in Library of the Hispanic Society, NYC. Kit used a friend's name as plaintext byline, put his own name inside. The work is dedicated in English cipher to his teen-age daughter Elizabeth [Isabel] Basset, whose first language was Spanish. Kit had taken her as an infant to Seville, where they'd lived with Cervantes from early 1595 to summer 1596. *Noches* is a series of entertaining winter nights' tales meant to advise a young lady about life.

Gascoigne, George. "An Hundreth Sundrie Flowers." A copy of a 1907 ed. in the Folger Shakespeare Library. Contains the first entertainment in which Kit may have acted.

Gerhard, Sandra Forbes. *Don Quixote and the Shelton Translation.* Studia Humanitatis, 1982. A deeply perceptive evaluation.

Grant, Lewis J.M. *Christopher Marlowe, the Ghost Writer.* Orillia, Ontario, Canada: Stubley Press. *Part One* 1967, *Part Two*, 1970. Lewis Grant, 90 years old when he wrote the last book, offers generous slices of Roger Manwood's will (unavailable to me through regular channels), including notice of his house at Shorne on Gad's Hill, above the Dover Road—the setting for a famous story about Ned de Vere.

Hasted, Edward. *History and Topographical Survey of the County of Kent.* 4 vols. Canterbury: Simmons and Kirkby, 1790-1799. These volumes contain valuable maps, mentions of neighbors at Shorne and Roger's purchase of the vicarage of Chalk Church on the Dover road near his Gad's Hill house [purchased in case Kit became a minister?—he was then a divinity student.]

James I of England's letter to Gregorio de' Monti, December 1616. *English State Paper* 99-21-x/L09704. This is a copy in Kit's Italian hand; the original is privately owned. William Davenant said he kept a letter written to his real dad by King James.

Jensen, Hans Helmut. "Totenmasken," *Hessisches Arzteblatt.* Heft 11, Nov. 1975. Pictures the "Shakespeare" deathmask, which today is preserved at the Universitäts-und Landesbibliothek, Darmstadt, Germany. Curator Brüning sent me three other views—well-lighted transparencies—and two letters.

Lane, Frederic C. *Venice, A Maritime Republic.* Baltimore: Johns Hopkins U. Press, 1987. Frederick Lane sent me a letter directing me to Wilfred Brulez's *Marchands Flamands a Venise,* vols. 1 & 2, collections of notarized documents, some of which contain crucial information about Jaques Coderin [Kit], and a view of Gregorio de' Monti moonlighting as legal aide to a sea captain.

Lauritzen, Peter and Alex Zielke. *Palaces of Venice.* NY: Viking, 1978. Peter Lauritzen sent me a handsome sketch of Henry Wotton's first English Embassy house in Venice, the Palazzo da Silva, Cannaregio, in which Lauritzen had an apartment.

Law, Ernest. *A Short History of Hampton Court in Tudor and Stuart Times.* London: G. Bell and Sons, 1929. Many useful illustrations, including a view of the great hall where Kit and Mary made their crucial error using Pembroke Players, Christmas 1592/'3.

Le Comte, Edward. *The Notorious Lady Essex.* NY: Dial Press, 1969. The Orphan Isabel, Kit and Marina's daughter (Isabel-Elizabeth Basset) is here. She was the "notorious" lady's sister in law—they lived in the same house, Audley End. The notorious lady was Frances Howard, and she was *not* evil: she was made a goat by Bacon as part of his convoluted, cruel damage-control plan to save King James from disgrace. It was because of Bacon's behavior that Kit left Bacon's service.

Letters and Dispatches of Sir Henry Wotton in the years 1617-1620 [and '21 Gregorian]. London: published by the Roxeburghe Club, printed by William Nichol, the Shakspeare [sic] Press, 1855. A copy at the Bodleian Library. Also at the Bodleian, a microfilm of the original MSS, preserved at Eton. Many of these letters were written and signed by Gregorio de' Monti as chargé d' affaires of the Eng. embassy in Venice. Last letter in the series is a startling communication from him.

Marloe, Christopher. *Lust's Dominion, or the Lascivious Queen* J. Le Gay Brereton, ed. Louvain: Librarie Universitarie, Uystpruyst Publisher, 1931. This work is a very early—childhood—play, later lightly revised keeping the style—probably inspired by Elizabeth's affairs with Philip of Spain and her Moor Walsingham.

Memorias de Valladolid. MS in British Library. In Spanish, in English secretary hand, it's a report on the Peace Party at Valladolid in spring 1605. Mention of Cervantes going around town "with a married woman." [Kit was there, too, with Jane Davenant. Oxford County Library offers information on the Davenants. A John Davenant letter is with Anthony Bacon Papers at Lambeth. The Davenants were a team of gov't. agents.]

Phelps, Charles E. *Falstaff and Equity.* Boston: Houghton Mifflin, The Riverside Press, 1901. Intrigued by Falstaff's remark in *I Henry IV,* Act II sc 2, "an the Prince and Poins be not two arrant cowards, there's no equity stirring," Phelps writes a book about conflict between the judges of England and the court of chancery. Roger Manwood stood for the right of the judges to uphold the law; Phelps supports the right of appeals to "equity" dispensed by the chancellor, with Chapter VI devoted to a case decided by Roger Manwood. Phelps, not seeing that Roger is Falstaff, characterizes Manwood as a as a nit-picking stickler for law. (The case was well-known: a man who didn't pay his rent had his property forfeited: he appealed to Chancery, where the case languished for 21 years. In 1597, Elizabeth brought together all the judges of England to examine the case, and they upheld Roger's decision. So Roger was vindicated, and late in 1597 Kit inserted Falstaff's glancing sentence in *I Henry IV.*) Though Phelps reaches wrong conclusions, his book is worth study. (On p.62, there's mention of the real author of the plays as "Jacques-Pierre.")

Rogers, John C. *The Parish Church of St. Michael.* St. Albans: H.A. Richardson Pub, 1973. Here's the carved-in-stone plaintext of Henry Wotton's humane ciphered epitaph for Francis Bacon.

Rossi, Vittorio. *Battista Guarini ed il Pastor Fido, studio biografico critico.* Turin: Ermanno Loescher, 1886. Told there was a single copy in USA, at Harvard, I read it in my local library under the eyes of the librarian. A chilling eyewitness report of how Anna Guarini was murdered by her husband in 1598. [A primary source for *Much Ado, Othello.*] Also a report of how in 1612 Guarini came to Venice and died in Gregorio's arms.

Savage, Richard. *Sir Thomas Overbury,* 1775. A copy of this play held in the British Library. The Orphan Isabel is the leading character in this *fantasy;* real people become very fictional characters.

Selimas. A very early play by Marlowe. Microfilm copy, STC 5226, kept in Folger Shakespeare Library. [Kit wrote this at age 14 after returning from a trip as ship boy to Constantinople. As in all his works, there are ciphers inside.]

Senior, C.M., David and Charles Newton Abbott. *A Nation of Pirates.* London: Crane, Russek & Co., 1976. Mentions Hen Wriothesley's [Southampton's] commission to fight pirates, 1614.

Shakespeare, William. *Complete Works, from Text left by George Stevens.* Boston: Philips, Sampson, 1853. In intro, a distorted shadow of a daughter mentioned as if she were *Will Shakespeare's* granddaughter, visited by Queen Henrietta Maria. It was Isabel-Eliz. Basset Howard Cavendish, Kit's daughter, who may have been visited by the queen.

Smith, John. *The General History of Virginia, New England, and the Summer Isles* [Bermuda]. 1624. reprint Birmingham: Edward Arber, 1884. Honest John Smith is the only writer I've found who shadows forth Kit's 1614 arrival at Bermuda with the two little ships for the colonists. All other accounts, even contemporary ones, have been brutally censored. Kit's own ciphers in his *Bargraves Polisie* make things clear. Cervantes, in *D.Q. II,* writes it as a story—Sancho on the Island.

Smith, Logan Pearsall. *Life and Letters of Sir Henry Wotton.* 2 vols. Oxford: Clarendon Press, 1907. An invaluable work. Harry was Kit's loyal friend, to his death and beyond. (These particular volumes offer seminal material for biographic study of Kit.)

Smithson, E.W. and G. Greenwood. *Baconian Essays.* Port Washington, NY: Kennikat Press reprint, 1970. This book contains excerpts from Jonson's anti-masque for "Time Vindicated." It's Jonson's tale of the laborious printing of the *First Folio.* Smithson and Greenwood make mistaken conclusions but carefully quote Ben Jonson, who reveals the truth.

Taylor, John. *Sir Gregory Nonsence, His Newes from no place.* "Printed at London by N.O., 1622." Reprint in Charles Hindley's *Miscellanea Antiqua Anglicane,* 1873. A saucy backhanded tribute to Kit by an SSS brother, with biographic ciphers, many of which seem to fade away, though the anagram printed beneath the title is clear. The work was written soon after Kit's real death.

The Great Assizes Holden in Parnassus, 1664. copy in the British Library. This pamphlet glances at an old SSS hierarchy, with Ben Jonson as keeper of the Trophonean Den and 'Shakespeere' as writer of weekly reports: While he served as *chargé d'affaires* at the English embassy at Venice, Kit as Gregorio was required to write reports to the secretary of state in London.

Index

A

Abbott, George 78, 79
Acuña, Diego Sarmiento de. *See* Conde de Gondomar
All is True. See *Henry VIII*
All's Well That Ends Well 12, 101, 104, 204, 220, 437, 566
Allen, William 9, 10, 22, 97, 98, 114, 286, 287, 363, 558, 560, 580
  death 40
  move to Rome 561
anagram 36, 80, 87, 92, 159, 307, 327, 336, 448, 465, 522, 549, 556, 600, 601, 602, 632, 636, 640
Andreini, Giambattista 54, 599
Andreini Players 36
Anglicanism 9, 301, 526
Antony and Cleopatra 44, 54, 56, 134, 277, 600
Arden of Feversham 13
Arthur, Julie (Mrs. Robert Hickes) 20, 113, 358, 570
Arthur, William 7, 92, 131, 553
Ashley, Cate 16
Asselinau (doctor) 72, 73, 152, 622, 623
As You Like It 40, 44, 45, 49, 125, 128, 130, 414, 415, 432, 582, 586, 587, 588, 589
Audley End 42, 44, 46, 61, 126, 143, 160, 229, 361, 432, 583, 587, 661
Avogadro, Count Paris 39, 125, 281
Azores 42, 584

B

Babington, Anthony 10, 100, 234, 562
Bacon, Anthony 109, 419, 582
Bacon, Francis 19, 49, 61, 85, 86, 98, 101, 109, 113, 119, 127, 133, 135, 137, 141, 149, 153, 155, 156, 159, 160, 161, 284, 287, 302, 320, 448, 474, 481, 552, 555, 569, 581, 584, 592, 608, 629
  badge 55
  Chronomastix 87, 639
  death 548, 640
  lord chancellor 76, 81, 158, 623, 633
  trial 153, 158, 159, 542, 611, 615, 633, 637
Bacon, Nicholas 18, 91, 108, 260
Bacon-Essex foreign service 19, 35, 38, 570, 579
Baines, Rick 22, 30, 113, 252, 557, 572
Bairam 38, 123, 273, 579
Banquet House 62, 63, 142, 495
  fire 77, 160
barcabudi 23, 115, 299
Barcelona 68, 617
Bargraves Polisie (Ignotus) 67, 69, 78, 80, 82, 136, 145, 148, 153, 156, 507, 508, 545, 553, 613, 614, 616, 617, 618, 626, 629, 632, 633
Barnes, Barnaby 27, 253

Barrowe, Henry 31, 97, 117, 118, 567, 574
Barton (ambassador) 38, 271, 578
Bassano, Emilia 23, 222, 250, 337, 576
as Emilia Lanier 57
shadows 29
Basset, Elizabeth. *See under* Isabel (Marlowe's daughter)
Basset, Judith 44, 461, 587, 591
Basset, William 44, 128, 129, 590
Baynard's Castle 21, 27, 28, 588
Bear Garden property 43, 350
Bedell, William 53, 55, 133, 601
Bedmar (Spanish ambassador) 621
Bembo, Doge Giovanni 71, 149, 620, 623
Bermuda 59, 63, 65, 76, 81, 137, 144, 146, 474, 484, 508, 513, 605, 613, 614
Bermuda Company 67, 144
Birnam Wood 55
Biron 20
Bishopsgate 8, 15, 26, 102, 554
Blackfriars Gatehouse 61, 141, 609
Black Pots 89, 641
Black Sea pirates 38, 579
Blount, Edward (also spelled Blunt) 70, 78, 85, 145, 446, 595, 601, 606, 618, 637, 638
Boleyn, Anne, Queen Consort of England 7, 16, 62, 212
Borough, John 85, 158, 333, 636, 637
Boyes, John 65, 66
Bradley, William 15, 568
Brenner Pass 68, 146, 531, 617, 633
Brenta River 635
Brewster, Will 97
Brochetta (fencing instructor) 55, 600
broken men 50, 132, 596
Brooke, William, Lord Cobham 13, 25, 42, 115, 287, 373, 374, 573, 583
Brown, Anthony, Viscount Montague 8, 128, 161, 554, 587, 634
Buck, Sir George 113, 159, 193, 265, 358, 576, 637
master of revels 86
work at Revels Office 29, 117
Bull, Elinor 31, 308, 577

C

Cádiz 159, 346, 349, 351, 360
Caesar, Juley 55, 600
Caius (doctor) 42
Candia 39, 124, 224, 280, 337
Cannaregio 49, 594, 629, 630
Canterbury 3, 7, 8, 12, 20, 26, 28, 42, 44, 52, 63, 88, 97, 104, 105, 112, 113, 116, 132, 155, 185, 209, 221, 236, 247, 260, 261, 363, 426, 555, 560, 567, 570, 574, 575, 577, 587, 597, 610, 628
Canterbury gang 7
Canterbury Town Serjeant 26
Cappadocia 35
Capriccio 61
Cardenio 41, 60, 87, 125, 608, 610
Carey, George 42
Carleill, Christopher 8, 10, 66, 94, 95, 98, 113, 256, 556, 559, 560, 571
Carleton, Sir Dudley 49, 58, 60, 61, 63, 66, 67, 69, 82, 144, 148, 157, 531, 593, 601, 605, 607, 612, 613, 614, 615, 616, 617, 619, 620, 621, 627, 630, 634, 636, 637
Carpan, Augustine 51, 55, 132, 597
Carr, Robert 61, 491, 616
Casaubon, Isaac 34, 269, 578
Castro, Pedro de, Count of Lemos 53, 56, 57, 65, 68, 71, 138, 465, 467, 469, 598, 602, 604, 605, 611, 615, 617
Catholic League 12, 197, 565, 630
Cattaro 38, 39, 124, 580
Cause of Uniformity 14
Cavagion, Mauritzio 50, 55, 131, 132, 596
Cavendish, William 78, 88, 154, 161, 607, 626, 631

Cecil, Robert 19, 38, 42, 44, 59, 129, 275, 320, 321, 322, 384, 405, 416, 448, 474, 476, 501, 552, 584, 591
master of wards 46
Cecil, William, Lord Burghley 19, 21, 22, 24, 29, 30, 95, 128, 133, 135, 295, 307, 384, 496, 565, 571, 572, 579, 606
Cervantes, Magdalena 51
Cervantes, Miguel de 7, 11, 40, 53, 56, 65, 70, 71, 101, 125, 126, 128, 130, 131, 139, 140, 145, 146, 226, 287, 346, 349, 360, 385, 423, 461, 464, 467, 502, 564, 567, 581, 582, 585, 591, 592, 594, 596, 598, 601, 608, 611
Don Quixote I 50, 55, 60, 86, 464, 594, 606
Don Quixote II 67, 86, 145
La Española Inglesa 46, 282
Novelas ejemplares 46
Viaje del Parnaso 41, 65, 140, 351, 608, 611
Chalk Church 12, 28, 104, 558, 575
Chamberlain, John 148, 154, 158
Chamberlain's Players 43, 60, 112, 583, 585
Chapman, George 61, 99, 141, 292, 355, 589, 609
Charterhouse 46, 591
Chartley 11, 100, 561
Chartres, Lord (governor of Malta) 21, 113
Cheshunt 16
Chiselhurst 18
Chronicon Angliae 76, 81, 633
Chronomastix. *See under* Francis Bacon
Churchyard, Thomas 8, 28, 93, 95, 109, 135, 556, 570
Cicogna, Duke Giandomenico 39, 124, 154, 280, 337, 406, 461, 580
Cicogna, Marina 39, 125, 154, 225, 337, 345, 422, 461, 580
Cicogna family vault 40, 45, 581, 590
Cinthio (author) 44
Hecatommithi 158
Ciotti, G. B. 54, 55, 56, 141, 611, 657
Ciotti Press 67, 68, 369, 513, 616, 617
Clement VIII (pope) 43, 127, 363
Coleraine 10, 98, 256, 559
Colerdin, Jaques 34, 561
Colombo, Prospero 38, 72, 74, 124, 579, 580, 623, 630
attack by Spanish employees 79
Colorno 35, 54, 60, 600, 607
Comedy of Errors 40, 115, 125, 297, 567, 569, 580, 581, 595
Commission for Ecclesiastical Causes 13
Constantinople 8, 22, 36, 79, 94, 96, 109, 110, 123, 155, 256, 269, 556, 559, 578, 579, 629
Contarini, Piero 73, 151, 153, 622
Dutch ships rented 73
Cooling Castle 28, 105, 357
Coriolanus 56, 159, 389, 392, 501
Corkine, William 26, 574
Corpus Christi College, Cambridge 9, 154
buttery book 9
Coryate, Tom 56, 134, 601
Cotton, Robert 70, 86, 158, 615, 637, 638
Council of Ten 55, 71, 72, 75, 132, 149
Court of Wards 46, 129
Crane, Ralph 70, 618, 636
Crown Tavern 62
Cuffe, Henry 42, 126, 419, 584, 588
Cynthia's Revels (Jonson) 44, 128, 406, 422, 588, 589

D

Dakin, Lawrence 28
Daniel, Samuel 19, 52, 99, 151, 154, 355, 563, 570, 623
Bristol Players 73, 77
Davenant, Jane 20, 51, 52, 54, 62, 597, 599, 637
Davenant, William 54, 62, 70, 88, 131, 135, 142, 160, 161, 603, 610, 619, 637
de Dominis, Marcantonio 78, 155, 526, 628, 629, 633, 635
de la Cueva, Alfonso, Marqués de Bedmar 72, 74, 150, 152, 625

de Vega, Lope 58, 131, 135, 136, 148, 465, 496, 513, 617
de Vere, Edward, 17th Earl of Oxford 16, 96, 206, 322, 346, 418
de' Monti, Cleo 82
de' Monti, Gregorio 82, 136, 333, 341, 343, 344, 369, 379, 383, 432, 457, 461, 477, 502, 506, 594, 601, 611, 617, 623, 632
  children 82
  death 83, 157, 524, 635
  knighting 80
  L'Ippolito 58, 115, 136, 604
  maritime legal work 38
  Marlowe's Italian name 3
  patent 71, 75, 149, 620
  purchase of pirate-chasers 65
de' Monti, Iseppo 82
death mask 83
Death of Christopher Marlowe, The (Hotson) 118, 577
Deering, Edward 82, 83, 158, 635, 637
Della Porta, Giambattista 35, 78, 121
Denball, Sampson 66, 95, 113, 319, 559, 563, 571, 599, 613, 627
Denmark House (Somerset House) 63, 73, 142, 481, 483, 610, 622, 627
Devereux, Lettice 18, 421
Devereux, Robert, 2nd Earl of Essex 18, 19, 20, 29, 31, 34, 35, 38, 41, 51, 54, 56, 109, 112, 118, 124, 126, 229, 266, 280, 301, 303, 308, 320, 334, 351, 366, 370, 371, 389, 390, 396, 397, 399, 403, 407, 412, 416, 418, 429, 437, 481, 501, 553, 569, 573, 574, 575, 577, 578, 579, 583, 584, 585, 586, 587, 588
  execution 127, 128, 589
Dickens, Charles 12, 31, 105, 109, 249, 303, 437
  Little Dorrit 19, 358
Dido, Queen of Carthage (Marlowe) 2, 17, 107, 117, 191, 265, 375, 549, 551, 558, 563
Don Quixote I (Cervantes) 50, 55, 60, 86, 464, 594, 606
Don Quixote II (Cervantes) 67, 86, 145
Donato, Doge Leonardo 53, 54, 60, 598, 599, 603, 607, 624, 627
Donne, John 27, 609
Dover 7, 12, 20, 63, 85, 92, 104, 112, 158, 190, 205, 284, 329, 334, 436, 552, 553, 555, 567, 570, 594, 597, 636
Dover Admiralty Court 7
Dover Road 12, 13, 104
Dowe, Ann 18
Drake, Francis 11, 40, 66, 72, 94, 95, 101, 139, 144, 256, 511, 562, 563, 564, 566, 627
  canal to Plymouth 60
Drayton, Michael 70
Dudley, Arthur 11, 40, 101, 121, 564, 580
Dudley, Robert, Earl of Leicester 11, 14, 17, 18, 54, 101, 107, 108, 552, 553, 557, 565, 567
Durres 39, 580

E

Edward II (Marlowe) 22,27,29,300,357,573,575
Edward III (play). *See Reign of King Edward III, The*
El buscón (Quevedo) 59
El Tigre. *See* ships:Tiger
Elizabeth I (queen) 7, 97, 100, 106, 107, 108, 109, 111, 112, 113, 118, 120, 129, 130, 131, 160, 209, 551, 552, 553, 554
  Progress 8, 21, 22, 46, 93, 95, 100, 152, 555, 556, 571, 572
  secret mother 15
Elvetham water show 21, 113, 571
Engelfield, Francis 11, 40, 556, 564, 565, 568, 569, 580
English Embassy (Paris) 11

Epitaph for Sir Roger Manwood (Marlowe) 28
Erotokritos (Kornaros) 9, 96, 125, 282, 360, 422, 556
Eslava, Antonio de 53, 55
Noches de inverno 55, 92, 124, 135, 137, 461, 553, 580, 602
Eslava, Ivan 55
Essex. *See* Robert Devereux, 2nd Earl of Essex
Exchequer, Lord Chief Baron of. *See* Sir Roger Manwood
Exeter 60, 151, 270, 279, 280, 606, 623

F

Falstaff, John 28, 42, 92, 105, 106, 116, 193, 346, 348, 354, 356, 357, 365, 373, 375, 377, 506, 584
Famous Victories, The (Marlowe) 20, 111, 193, 347, 556
Ferrobosco, Fonsie 23, 250
Fisher's Folly 11, 15, 20, 86, 102, 104, 568, 570
Fixer, John 11, 101, 563
Fletcher, John 153, 183, 504, 519, 534, 590
Fletcher, Nathaniel 50, 53, 76, 153, 625
Florio, John 20, 25, 223, 306, 573
Four de l'Evèque 12, 102, 104, 566, 568
Fox (SSS agent) 45, 128, 421
Frederick I, Duke of Württemberg 42
Frederick V, Elector Palatinate 61, 79, 141, 546, 547, 630, 634
Frizer, Ingram 31, 118, 577, 578
Funeral Elegy for Thomas Peter, A (Marlowe) 60

G

Gad's Hill 12, 28, 42, 104, 105, 357, 373, 5554
Gaitan, Juana 51
Galarato, Celso 79, 155, 526
Garter Inn 25, 573
horse theft. *See under* Count Mömpelgard
Geneva 34, 268, 269, 578
Genoa 36, 40, 269, 289, 423, 578, 582
Ghetto 49, 122, 594
Gifford, Gilbert 11, 22, 100, 101, 102, 114, 183, 197, 204, 414, 560, 561, 562, 563, 565, 568, 569, 572
Globe Theater 43, 62, 77, 154, 162, 481, 490, 492, 493, 497, 498, 500, 585, 605, 609, 610, 627
gold chain of offi ce. *See under* Sir Roger Manwood
Gondomar, Conde de 65, 72, 78, 81, 150, 156, 621, 626, 631, 632
Gonzaga, Duke Vicenzo 34, 35, 36, 60, 139, 578, 607
Great Wardrobe 62, 609
Greek playwrights' anagram 3
Greene, Robert 99, 100, 112, 563
Gresham, Sir Thomas 8, 10, 18, 93, 94, 95, 100, 110, 256, 554, 555
Gresshop, John 3, 118, 556
Grimani, Doge Marino 50, 51, 52, 53, 595, 596, 598
Guarini, Anna 43, 50, 362, 444, 585
Guarini, Battista 36, 42, 44, 50, 54, 55, 57, 60, 67, 68, 78, 83, 122, 158, 229, 231, 269, 327, 362, 365, 369, 444, 584, 594, 599, 616, 617
death 370, 608
Gunpowder Plot 52, 160, 598

H

Hackney 28
Hamlet 19, 45, 49, 50, 96, 133, 193, 353, 354, 359, 447, 563, 566, 595
proto-*Hamlet* 20, 571
Hampton Court 117, 262, 300, 321, 552, 575, 593, 627

Christmas festival 27, 29, 574
Hapsburg Alps 71, 471
Harvey, Gabriel 9, 98
Hawkins, Henry 18, 582
Hellespont 29, 292
Henri IV (king) 32, 34, 35, 54, 57, 78, 135, 266, 267, 308, 571
Henry IV 41, 96, 105, 422, 584
Henry IV, Part 1 42, 93, 346
Henry Stuart, Prince of Wales 61, 592
Henry V 20, 41, 93, 104, 111, 127, 206, 568
Henry VI 22, 27, 28, 29, 35, 38, 39, 115, 123, 125
Henry VI, Part 1 260
Henry VI, Part 2 117, 263
Henry VI, Part 3 39, 265
Henry VIII 63, 133, 497, 610
Herbert, Henry, Earl of Pembroke 18, 159, 637
Herbert, Mary Sidney, Countess of Pembroke 19, 49, 419, 434, 552, 570, 574, 583, 587, 588, 592, 593, 635
Herbert, Master 86
Hero and Leander (Marlowe) 29, 70, 86, 250, 292, 576
Hickes, Michael 50, 57, 113
Holland, John 73, 75, 151, 623
honest men 7, 14, 46, 62, 90, 160, 301, 492, 493, 552
House of Lords 156, 625, 633
court of impeachment 76, 81, 633
Howard, Good Tom, Earl of Suffolk 41, 44, 59, 70, 77, 81, 130, 141, 160, 350, 432, 461, 587, 591, 592, 605, 608, 613, 615, 624, 629, 634
knighted 566
Howard, Henry (Good Tom's uncle) 59, 61, 611
Howard, Thomas, 4th Duke of Norfolk 17
Humphrey (duke) 29, 576

I

Ignotus
Bargraves Polisie 67, 69, 78, 80, 82, 136, 145, 148, 153, 156, 507, 508, 545, 553, 613, 614, 616, 617, 618, 626, 629, 632, 633
Inquisition 36, 40, 56, 60, 85, 122, 286, 486, 580, 607
Ippolito (character) 10
Isabel (Marlowe's daughter) 40
as Elizabeth Basset 44, 92, 129, 461, 587, 590, 591
as Elizabeth Cavendish 78, 154, 291, 626
as Elizabeth Howard 47, 59, 61, 70, 480, 605
with Elizabeth I 46
Isle of Wight 49, 59, 63, 592
Ive, Paul 10, 98, 559

J

Jaggard, Isaac 86, 638
James VI and I (king) 49, 52, 55, 59, 61, 63, 67, 70, 71, 76, 77, 78, 89, 130, 134, 141, 146, 149, 150, 156, 452, 474, 481, 490, 491, 496, 498, 509, 590, 592, 593, 597, 599, 601, 602, 603, 604, 607, 609, 611, 613, 614, 616, 619, 620, 621, 622, 626, 627, 630, 633
Janissaries 37, 270, 579
Jaques-Pierre (captain) 71, 72, 74, 149, 621
Jew of Malta, The (Marlowe) 12, 22, 26, 104, 114, 116, 132, 235, 264, 566, 567, 572, 573, 594
Jonson, Ben 45, 53, 57, 70, 86, 125, 128, 160, 187, 348, 406, 421, 422, 446, 554, 581, 588, 589, 590, 591, 595, 598, 603, 638, 639
Cynthia's Revels 44, 128, 406, 422, 588, 589
Juliet's house 36
Julius Caesar 43, 55, 474, 600, 609

K

Kenilworth party 8, 94, 555
Kett, Francis 557, 567
King's School 3, 8, 59, 185, 556, 557
 headmaster's library 30
King James Bible 55, 593, 601
King John (play). *See* The Life and Death of King John
King Lear 2, 52, 54, 110, 141, 451, 598, 600
King Leir. *See* King Lear
Knole Park 67, 507, 508, 545
Kyd, Thomas 20, 30, 45, 355
 The Spanish Tragedy 46, 571, 591

L

L'Ippolito (de' Monti) 58, 115, 136, 604
La Española Inglesa (Cervantes) 46
La Guarina 42, 60, 82, 140, 584
La Loca. *See* Micaela Lujan
ladder (silk gut) 36, 37, 270, 273, 325, 329, 579
Lanier, Alfonso 23, 25, 26, 116, 223, 574
Lanier, Sidney 25
Laredo, Antonio de 57, 61, 139, 512, 604
Leander's Tower 37
Leete, Will 82, 153, 157, 625, 635
Lido 39, 71, 225, 284, 289, 458, 580, 582, 625
Life and Death of King John, The 21, 439, 568, 570, 573, 638
Liona. *See under* ships
Lister, Mathew 59, 605
Little Dorrit (Dickens) 19, 358
Locrine (Marlowe) 10, 189, 558
Lodge, Thomas 36, 43, 45, 99, 113, 122, 159, 204, 269, 355, 358, 377, 399, 414, 415, 418, 419, 561, 563, 566, 571, 578, 586, 589, 637
Longueville 20
Lopes, Ruy 19, 28, 109, 117, 122, 263, 300, 303, 304, 334, 569, 575
Love's Labour's Lost 30, 116, 360, 363, 491, 573
Lucchese, Marco 44, 127, 588
Lucrece. See The Rape of Lucrece
Lujan, Micaela 58, 61, 65, 68, 72, 73, 76, 79, 82, 89, 145, 146, 465, 467, 468, 470, 496, 502, 504, 512, 513, 518, 521, 528, 530, 531, 541, 542, 604, 605, 608, 612, 613, 614, 615, 616, 617, 618, 619, 622, 623, 625, 626, 628, 630, 632, 634, 635
Lujan Tower 68
Lylly (embassy secretary) 11, 102

M

Macaulay, Thomas 15
Macbeth 52, 450, 598, 599
MacDonnell, Sorley Boy 10, 95, 98, 256, 559
Madrid 11, 35, 40, 41, 58, 60, 67, 68, 70, 101, 136, 226, 464, 465, 502, 513, 518, 529, 531, 563, 564, 580, 581, 591, 594, 604, 611, 616, 617, 619
madrigals 56, 601
Mainwaring, Henry 72, 73, 623, 626, 627
Malta 21, 66, 73, 113, 144, 240, 244, 246, 247, 613, 622
Manso, Gianbattista 35, 41, 50, 78, 89, 121, 582
Mantua 34, 36, 54, 56, 330, 369, 414, 578, 599, 601
 murals 35
Manwood, Sir Peter 117, 143
Manwood, Sir Roger 3, 7, 8, 10, 12, 13, 14, 15, 19, 27, 28, 31, 34, 42, 45, 60, 61, 65, 70, 88, 91, 95, 97, 105, 106, 107, 112, 115, 116, 120, 122, 125, 126, 143, 144, 145, 160, 183, 185, 193, 211, 238, 251, 258, 261, 263, 291, 299, 303, 334, 336, 337, 346, 353, 357, 373, 379, 451, 506, 552, 554, 555, 556, 558, 563, 567, 568, 570, 571, 572, 607, 613
 gold chain of office 7, 20, 23, 29, 115, 251, 260, 297, 337, 451, 552, 572

Marino, G. B. 57, 72, 601
Marley, Christopher 3, 257, 553
Marley, John 26, 132, 553, 557, 596
death 52
Marley, Kate (née Arthur) 7, 8, 19, 26, 28, 32, 92, 97, 112, 118, 132, 185, 235, 240, 284, 303, 334, 426, 452, 520, 552, 553, 555, 567, 575, 578, 587, 596
death 52, 335
Marlow, Christopher 392
Marlowe, Christopher 1, 11, 15, 19, 26, 32, 38, 43, 45, 57, 67, 80, 86, 88, 91, 92, 96, 98, 100, 104, 107, 110, 116, 123, 132, 135, 137, 141, 145, 147, 148, 157, 160, 186, 189, 192, 197, 204, 208, 212, 214, 220, 223, 225, 233, 248, 258, 260, 266, 291, 307, 312, 320, 324, 326, 329, 333, 336, 337, 341, 346, 372, 374, 377, 379, 412, 429, 443, 447, 453, 461, 468, 474, 479, 501, 506, 508, 517, 540, 556, 564, 569, 574, 588, 596, 601, 605, 613, 635
A Funeral Elegy for Thomas Peter 60
aliases. *See* specifi c aliases
as mascot 7, 92, 553
as page 8
as ship boy 554
at Cambridge 9, 12, 76
at Coleraine 10, 256, 559
at King's School 3, 8, 59, 185, 186, 556, 557
at Ságres 11, 564
barber 37, 123, 269, 271, 578
breaks leg 67, 570, 617
children's drowning 67
death 26, 87, 95
Dido, Queen of Carthage 2, 17, 107, 117, 191, 265, 375, 549, 551, 558, 563
Edward II 22, 27, 29, 300, 357, 573, 575
factor for Essex 42, 584
Hero and Leander 29, 70, 86, 250, 292, 576
in Ireland 18, 43, 127, 412, 416, 558, 559
in Lisbon 11, 563, 564
in Rome 39, 327, 580, 585
Locrine 10, 189, 558
Marprelate aide 14, 221, 261, 336
reader in medicine 67, 509, 614
sailor and factor 8, 37, 93, 110, 282, 297, 579
Selimus 3, 8, 96, 110, 186, 556
Spanish plot eraser 72, 78, 149, 504, 519, 533, 628
Tamburlaine I 8, 19, 569
Tamburlaine II 8, 19, 248, 569
The Famous Victories 20, 111, 193, 347, 556
The Jew of Malta 12, 22, 26, 104, 114, 116, 132, 235, 264, 566, 567, 572, 573, 594
The Massacre at Paris 12
The Tragical History of Doctor Faustus 12, 92, 101, 103, 123, 195, 276, 565
trouble with law study 13
Marlowe, John. *See* John Marley
Marlowe, Kate (née Arthur). *See* Kate Marley (née Arthur)
Marlowe, Kit. *See* Christopher Marlowe
Marprelate, Martin 31
Marranos 7, 268, 299, 301, 337
Marston, John 3, 597
Mary Queen of Scots 100, 131, 141, 561
conspirators 10, 11
Massacre at Paris, The (Marlowe) 12
Mathew, Toby 57, 61, 73, 82, 85, 158, 592, 600, 603, 608, 612, 617, 620, 626, 630, 635, 636
Mauleon (patron) 55, 56
Mayerne, Theodore 71, 606, 608, 616, 621
Mayfield (East Rother) 10, 18, 100, 554, 556
Mayflower. *See under* ships
Measure for Measure 12, 49, 50, 70, 101, 103, 198, 199, 204, 565, 566, 594, 595, 618
Mendes, Alvaro 22, 37, 114, 238, 304, 555
Merchant of Venice, The 23, 42, 379, 583
Mercutio 15, 569
Merlin 36, 635
Merry Wives of Windsor, The 13, 16, 42, 70, 116, 372, 374, 573, 595, 618

Midsummer Night's Dream, A 40, 94, 422, 581
Milan 35, 54, 57, 580, 603, 604, 612, 625
Mildmay, Walter 15, 19, 107, 108, 299, 301, 337, 567, 570
Mill, William 30
Milton, John 89, 161
Mömpelgard, Count 25, 107
  horse theft 26, 42, 116, 573
Monte, Girolamo 55, 131, 132, 596
Montecasino, Gabriele 74, 624
Monteverdi, Claudio 36, 82, 134, 458, 601, 634
Moore, Richard 66, 144, 147, 238, 513, 613
Morley, Christopher 106, 119, 565
Moth 3
Much Ado about Nothing 43, 44, 63, 127, 386, 387, 444, 585
Mutes 87, 638
Mytilene 37

N

Naples 35, 50, 53, 56, 65, 71, 138, 465, 466, 467, 473, 492, 496, 499, 519, 531, 582, 593, 602, 604, 611, 617, 618, 620, 627
Nashe, Tom 10, 17, 20, 26, 43, 99, 107, 111, 355, 399, 419, 558, 560, 563, 569, 570, 586, 589
Naunton, Sir Robert 75, 78, 79, 153, 524, 536, 614, 626, 628, 629, 631, 632
Newman, Humphrey 14
Noches de inverno (Eslava) 55, 92, 124, 135, 137, 461, 553, 580, 602
Norris family 17
Novelas ejemplares (Cervantes) 46
Noventa 49, 82
Noyon 20, 34
nurses 51

O

O'Neal, Hugh, Earl of Tyrone 43, 394, 397, 398, 401, 402, 586
oath ex officio 13, 106
Octoberfest illness 82, 635
Oldcastle, Sir John (character) 194, 357
Oldcastle, Sir John (preacher) 12, 28, 105, 117, 337, 357, 575
Old Bailey 20, 21, 569, 597
Othello 43, 45, 46, 50, 87, 128, 129, 437, 443, 444, 585, 588, 591, 594, 595
Overbury, Sir Thomas 61, 65, 70, 490, 611, 615, 616, 621
Oziosos 67, 512

P

Padover, Saul 2
Padua 36, 40, 50, 55, 67, 80, 82, 122, 286, 337, 461, 511, 578, 581, 584, 588, 595, 600, 601, 605, 614, 626, 628, 631, 634, 635
Page, George 42, 373
Palazzo da Silva 49, 55, 594
Panza, Sancho 50, 67, 140, 144, 145, 146, 464, 502, 509, 592, 596
Paradin, Claude 10
Paris 11, 32, 34, 103, 201, 220, 237, 268, 282, 511, 554, 556, 561, 563, 566, 588
Parker, Matthew 9, 76, 97, 154, 557, 632
Parliament 42, 53, 56, 76, 79, 267, 270, 283, 584, 598, 613, 625, 631, 632, 633, 634, 640
Parma 22, 35, 370, 562, 572, 574
Parr, Catherine (queen) 16, 107
Paul V (pope) 53, 598, 631
Peace Party 51, 594, 596
Pembroke Players 27, 117, 574
Percy, Henry, 1st Earl of Northumberland 21
Pericles, Prince of Tyre 10, 40, 87, 125, 137, 344, 422, 581
Perrot, Sir John 10, 21, 24, 98, 113, 255, 256, 559
Phelippes, Thomas 34, 35, 82, 100, 131, 204, 267, 561, 568, 615, 635
Philip II (king) 58, 101, 108, 109, 121, 126, 187, 349
Pickering, William 14, 106, 155, 156, 356, 552, 598, 629

Pindar, Paul 79, 629
knighthood 155
Poley, Robert (Robin) 31, 316, 562, 575, 577
Pont de l'Arche 21
Prague 79, 631
Prior, Antonio 37
Prior, of Ocrato, Antonio 23
privy council 13, 14, 24, 27, 72, 73, 107, 113, 115, 143, 154, 252, 298, 564, 571, 572, 574, 622, 627
Progress. *See under* Elizabeth I (queen)
prostitutes of Venice 50
Protestant League 78
Puck (bas-relief) 12, 286, 558
Puddlewharf 62, 610
puritanism 9

Q

Queen's Players 73, 77, 504, 558, 568, 622
Queen Anne 62, 63, 72, 73, 77, 142, 151, 154, 496, 611, 620, 621, 622, 627
Quevedo, Francisco
El buscón 60
Quod me nutrit, me destruit 10

R

Ralegh, Walter 21, 30, 41, 46, 351, 590, 593, 626
Randolph, Thomas 15, 19, 20, 97, 107, 119, 299, 301, 337, 358, 570
Rape of Lucrece, The 35, 38, 74, 326, 564, 578, 579
Redman, William 28, 263, 575
Reggio 43, 127, 370
Reign of King Edward III, The 11, 234, 562, 563
Reims 9, 10, 11, 22, 98, 122, 286, 414, 557, 560, 563, 564, 566, 572
Resistance 35, 53, 57, 60, 63, 78, 89, 227, 564, 578, 582, 584, 598, 604, 607, 641
Richard III 34, 353, 573
Romeo and Juliet 15, 40, 281, 341, 343, 422, 569, 571, 581

S

Salamander. *See under* ships
San Felipe. *See under* ships
Sanseverino, Barbara, Countess of Sala 35, 54, 60, 78
Selimus (Marlowe) 3, 8, 96, 110, 186, 556
Seymour, Thomas 16, 107, 312, 354, 551
Shakespeare, William 1, 3, 137, 257, 260, 263, 265, 320, 321, 322, 333, 343, 344, 346, 372, 379, 386, 387, 389, 392, 414, 439, 443, 450, 451, 462, 474, 480, 497, 501, 578
death 70, 87, 156
ships
Liona 37, 38, 123, 271, 579
Mayflower 9, 97, 119, 267, 577
Rizzarda et Colombo 38, 124, 580
Salamander 119, 267, 577
San Felipe 11, 101, 564
Silvestra 37, 38, 122, 123, 271, 579
Tiger (El Tigre) 8, 65, 66, 94, 113, 144, 145, 256, 556, 559, 571, 599, 613, 614
Shorne 12, 25, 28, 42, 63, 105, 122, 373, 374, 555, 575
Sidney, Philip 17, 19, 20, 114, 434, 551, 563
Sidney, Sir Robert 22, 45, 46, 97, 120, 141, 552, 572, 589
Silvestra. *See under* ships
Sir John Oldcastle (play) 3, 115, 184, 299, 587
Spanish Tragedy, The 46, 128, 571, 591
Spenser, Edmund 10, 98, 557, 559
St. Stephen's 91, 552, 555
steganography 5, 109
Stuart, James 46

T

Tamburlaine I (Marlowe) 8, 19, 569
Tamburlaine II (Marlowe) 8, 19, 248, 569
Taming of the Shrew, The 28, 38, 117, 333, 553, 638
Taylor, John 80, 156, 524, 632
Tellez-Girón, Pedro, Duke of Osuna 58, 65,

71, 72, 75, 77, 149, 152, 518, 520, 533, 602, 612, 618, 620, 621, 622, 623, 627, 628, 629, 634
Tempest, The 59, 63, 70, 92, 137, 142, 474, 480, 497, 605, 609, 612, 618
Titus Andronicus 17, 110, 257, 568
Tragedy of Cymbeline, King of Britain, The 57, 70, 135, 137, 462, 604, 618
Tragical History of Doctor Faustus, The (Marlowe) 12, 92, 101, 103, 123, 195, 276, 565
Troilus and Cressida 44, 125, 127, 128, 159, 389, 392, 431, 586, 589, 638
Twelfth Night 49, 133, 138, 144, 262, 366, 576, 588

U

Ubaldini, Petruccio 12, 566
Underwood, Roger 24, 25, 115, 298, 572
University of Padua 67, 82, 509, 604
law school 580, 584
school of medicine 614
UΣ, 30

V

Venus and Adonis 34, 35, 74, 118, 121, 324, 429, 564, 578
Viaje del Parnaso (Cervantes) 41, 65, 140, 351, 608, 611
Vinci, Leonardo da 35

W

Walsingham, Sir Francis 8, 9, 10, 11, 15, 16, 18, 19, 20, 35, 61, 94, 95, 97, 98, 100, 102, 106, 107, 119, 120, 238, 256, 299, 301, 302, 303, 334, 337, 354, 414, 491, 551, 552, 554, 555, 556, 557, 558, 560, 561, 562, 563, 565, 567, 568, 569, 576, 609
Water Poet. *See* John Taylor
Watson, Thomas 15, 19, 21, 26, 99, 102, 265, 563, 569, 570, 573
Whitgift, John 9, 13, 19, 21, 24, 27, 47, 97, 106, 117, 120, 260, 261, 266, 268, 293, 299, 300, 305, 307, 308, 313, 314, 316, 317, 334, 359, 429, 555, 557, 558, 563, 567, 568, 570, 574, 576, 577, 592, 594
Wotton, Sir Henry 1, 35, 49, 50, 62, 72, 120, 153, 155, 419, 474, 506, 546, 548, 575, 578, 584, 586, 590, 593, 601, 621, 624, 625, 626, 628
Wriothesley, Henry, 3rd Earl of Southampton 1, 10, 19, 20, 46, 59, 71, 76, 78, 81, 89, 111, 113, 118, 128, 142, 151, 204, 239, 247, 251, 280, 295, 325, 327, 337, 353, 356, 418, 437, 441, 450, 463, 465, 474, 482, 499, 504, 519, 554, 560, 570, 571, 576, 628, 634, 640
Wriothesley, Hen. *See* Henry Wriothesley, 3rd Earl of Southampton

Y

Yat 3, 162, 406, 543, 635

Z

Zuccaro, Federigo 11, 35, 101, 121, 564

Printed in the United Kingdom
by Lightning Source UK Ltd.
127012UK00001BA/2/A